The OPERA.

A History of its Creation and Performance: 1600-1941

By WALLACE BROCKWAY, w.

& HERBERT WEINSTOCK

Simon and Schuster, New York

ML400
B78
c.2

MANUFACTURED IN THE UNITED STATES OF AMERICA
BY THE HADDON CRAFTSMEN, INC.

repl 6/06

For Mary Garden

Also by the same authors:

MEN OF MUSIC

Table of Contents

List of Illustrations

Acknowledgments

The authors' indebtedness to many authorities, living and dead, is obvious and is acknowledged wherever possible. However, the authors alone are responsible for all the opinions and, presumably, for most of the errors in this book.

The authors wish to express their thanks to the many friends who made valuable suggestions while the work was in progress. Because of their number, most of them must remain unnamed, though they are not thanked any the less. Among the few who must be specified, Robert A. Simon, who gave freely of his large store of operatic information, comes first. Grace Robert suggested many particular changes. The entire staff of the music division of the 58th Street Branch of the New York Public Library was unwearying in its courtesy and helpfulness. Benjamin Meiselman helped to prepare the index. Bart Keith Winer scrutinized manuscript and proofs with an expert editor's eye.

To George Clark Leslie, editor of *The Gramophone Shop Record Supplement*, the authors owe a debt that should not be dismissed in a brief note. His List of Recommended Recordings represents many hours of careful research and laborious collation, done out of love for opera and friendship for the authors.

The OPERA

Dull-Useful Information for Conscientious Readers

This is the story of the development of a form of entertainment that is neither pure music nor pure drama. Opera is a hybrid, but a hybrid with so much glamour that it annually draws millions to the box office and tens of millions to the radio. The authors have written in the belief that this glamour is not produced solely by the magic of the music or the holding power of the story: it depends on both—and on the impresarios, singers, conductors, costumers, stage designers, dancers, and mimers. Even the press agents work to produce this glamour—audiences, too, do their part. All of these have a place in the following narrative.

As this book is designed primarily for American readers, a considerable part of the performance data and lore is drawn from the history of New York's Metropolitan Opera House. Many of these data are as recent as the 1940-1 season, and the authors hope in future editions to extend them farther.

Titles of operas and separate numbers are given in their original language, unless that happens to be a not easily transliterated tongue (i.e., Russian) or unless, as in a few cases, usage has decreed a different nomenclature. Absurdities in nomenclature are passed by in silence.

Those who wish to read *The Opera* as a consecutive narrative should confine themselves to large-type matter, the small-type matter being devoted to performance data and lore. However, the authors hope that most readers will be ideal readers—that is, will begin at the beginning and, unutterably absorbed, read through to the end.

The List of Recommended Recordings, which is to be found on page 485, should not be read straight through, even by those who wish to increase their knowledge of various foreign languages. It is precisely what it was intended to be: an invaluable reference check list.

Chapter I

The Birth of Opera

ALL realistic discussions of opera begin at the Renaissance. It is possible to prolong its lineage back to the miracle and mystery plays of the Middle Ages, but only for the love of research. Opera, as we know it today, comes from the Florence of the dying sixteenth century, when the Renaissance mind was preparing for the carnival time of the baroque and the rococo. During the Renaissance, particularly at first, painting, sculpture, architecture, and letters had self-consciously advertised their intention of re-creating the antique. Fortunately, the intention was only partially carried out: those who abided by the letter of the contract were feeble apers of Cicero's periods and Apelles' line; the vital men, nursing a more dynamic conception of Greece and Rome, struck out for themselves. Music, meanwhile, had little traffic with ideas of the classic past: it was using almost all its energies in perfecting the difficult techniques of medieval church singing. Palestrina and Di Lasso, master masons of the piously erected cathedral of vocal polyphony, were recently dead, but Tomás de Victoria was adding the last jewel-like panes of stained glass to the edifice when a few obscure men, unaware that the Renaissance was dying, made music's first obeisance to the antique. Cold-bloodedly, they created operas.

These fathers of opera were a group of poets, singers, and composers who frequented the palace of Giovanni Bardi, a Florentine nobleman, about the year 1600. Of this *camerata*, as the Bardi circle was called, perhaps Vincenzo Galilei, father of the astronomer, deserves the most of posterity, for of the quality of his son's work there can be no doubt. Jacopo Peri, another of them, actually wrote the first opera, *Dafne;* but as the music is lost, it would be idle to waste reverence on it. The score of the second opera, *Euridice,* survives, though the details of its authorship are not wholly clear. Peri wrote most of it; Giulio Caccini, a singing member of the Bardi circle, made additions to it and also wrote a *Euridice* alone.

3

The fact that the Peri-Caccini mosaic was staged as part of the entertainment following a royal wedding at least calls into question a popular picture of the *camerata* as aloof idealists. It is probable that, as shrewd practicing musicians, Peri and Caccini had surveyed the possibilities of polyphonic music, had found them wanting in the allure desirable for a purely lay celebration, and had provided a novelty for it. The occasion was the marriage of Maria de' Medici to Henri IV of France, which was celebrated at Florence in October, 1600. As the reservations surrounding his kingly state did not permit Henri to go outside his own country to meet the bride, the princess' uncle, Ferdinand, Grand Duke of Tuscany, acted as his proxy.

The solemn stuff designed by Peri and Caccini for this pleasure-loving princess, whose preference for boisterous harlequinades was notorious, was thin and feeble, whether compared with the vocal polyphony of the age or with the full-bodied opera of later ages. An attempt to duplicate a stage production of the classical Athenians, it began by throwing overboard the musical methods of the polyphonists. Starting with the isolated fact that the ancient dramas had been accompanied with music, the musicians of the *camerata* read into the scanty texts at their disposal a theory that Greek music had consisted of single voices accompanied by instruments. Quite apart from this theory, there was an old popular tradition behind monodic music, but serious composers had barely begun to experiment with it when, about the beginning of the fifteenth century, it was swallowed up in the ground swell of polyphonic music at its golden maturity. Some attempt had been made in 1594, the very year of Palestrina's death, to graft his perfected instrument onto the inhospitable surfaces of popular comedy. This experiment was doomed to fail: a mere series of unaccompanied many-voiced pieces could not dramatically, or even logically, express the characters and situations of a play. So it was no wanton repudiation of usable dramatic material that made Caccini and Peri, who probably had witnessed some of these abortive polyphonic operas, decide

First Page of the Earliest Surviving Opera, Jacopo Peri's *Euridice*,
from a facsimile of the original edition in the
Library of Congress, Washington, D. C.

to make the single accompanied voice the basis of their innovation.

Both Caccini and Peri were men of talent, but apparently devoid of genius. Without commanding gifts to draw upon, without traditions to shore up their feeble inspiration, it is no wonder that, with nothing but the desire to unearth a novel antique, they produced operas of little value in themselves, serviceable only as rough models for future masters. In view of the sparseness of their operatic materials, it is just as well that Count Bardi's friends were less than geniuses. Stronger men might have forced the infant opera into a strait jacket of frozen forms from which it might have struggled vainly to escape. As it was, since their theory of the opera inevitably committed them to the subject matter of Greek and Roman mythology and history, they set a style in librettos that was to restrict even the greatest composers of tragic opera for more than a century and a half. During this period, the characters of the serious musical stage were the gods and goddesses of the classical pantheons, with a riot of nymphs and dryads, heroes and demigods, fates and furies, not to mention a select group of historical statuary, to bear them company.

Peri and Caccini, by their separate emphases and affinities, unconsciously marked the battle lines of opera's central dichotomy. Peri, primarily a composer, wrote simply and starkly, always keeping the musical interest subordinated to the dramatic. Caccini, not only a singer himself, but also father of the first prima donna, inverted the process: for him, the musical line was of the most passionate interest, and he decorated it with the earliest of those vocal adornments—roulades, cadenzas, and other *fioriture*—that have ever since characterized the singer's opera. Even today, some composers consider a play as merely a peg on which to hang music, and they are fiercely opposed by others who hold that music should but underline the action of the drama. The greatest of operatic composers, no matter which side they thought they were on, achieved, at their best, a balance between these two concepts of opera.

The infant art form was lucky that Claudio Monteverdi, its

first man of genius, was not theory-bound. Until his fortieth year almost exclusively a writer of madrigals, Monteverdi was already a master composer when the Florentine experiments attracted his interest. It is likely that he was in the small, invited audience that heard Peri and Caccini's *Euridice* on that epochal October 6 of the year 1600. Two years later, becoming master of the music to Vincenzo Gonzaga, the splendid tyrant who befriended Tasso, patronized Galileo, and murdered the "Admirable" Crichton, Monteverdi was encouraged to try his own hand at a *dramma per musica*. Nothing seems to have come of this until February 24, 1607, when his *Orfeo* was staged in Mantua. Because of the sheerly musical interest of the score, as well as because it contains, in embryonic form, several still universally used operatic procedures, the date of its production is a milestone in the history of music. Already, the gap between Caccini and Peri and this bold innovator, who seems miraculously to have known exactly where he was going, is tremendous. A polyphonist of genius, with an understanding of the techniques of many schools, he expanded the orchestra of the time where his own masters had been satisfied with a few not always happy combinations of instruments. Taking from polyphonic practice an acceptance of clashing melodies, he diversified the stream of his *Orfeo* with the drama and excitement of often shrieking harmonies.

There has been a heroic effort to insinuate *Orfeo* into the modern repertoire. In 1911, it was produced in Italy. A year later, on April 14, a condensed version of it was sung in English, in concert form, on a Sunday evening at the Metropolitan Opera House, New York. Unfortunately, it was preceded by a typical rag-bag recital by two of the Metropolitan's leading stars, Emmy Destinn and Pasquale Amato, so that by the time *Orfeo* was begun the audience had so tired itself by shouts and applause that it had no appetite left for the opera, and therefore Rita Fornia (Eurydice), Anna Case (a Nymph), Hermann Weil (Orpheus), and Herbert Witherspoon (Pluto) sang to little advantage. Cleofonte Campanini, musical director of the Chicago Grand Opera Company, was quite as unfortunate when, on January 4, 1913, he tried to force a concert performance of *Orfeo* on an Auditorium one third full. Mario Sammarco, as

Orpheus, gave a noble interpretation for the unenthusiastic Chicagoans. The first American stage performance of *Orfeo* took place at Northampton, Massachusetts, under the auspices of Smith College, on May 12, 1929, when a new edition, by the Italian modernist and Monteverdi scholar, G. Francesco Malipiero, was used. Charles Kullmann was the Orpheus, and Werner Josten conducted. In England, Professor Edward J. Dent revived *Orfeo* at Oxford, and with considerable success.

A year later than *Orfeo*, Duke Vincenzo asked Monteverdi to write an opera for the wedding of his son Francesco to Margaret of Savoy. Before *Arianna* was completed, the composer's wife died, and the very personal quality of the deserted Arianna's poignant lament may owe something to a direct transference of Monteverdi's grief. Six thousand invited guests are said to have heard the *première* of *Arianna*: apparently many of them went away with the tragic melody fixed in their minds—the lament was the first operatic hit song. It became familiar throughout Italy, and survives, though the rest of the score has been allowed to perish. It still has the power to move us, the key to its peculiarly modern quality being its audacious use of dissonance. But Arianna's lament, which at the *première* is said to have moved thousands to tears, is only an early, if most striking, example of Monteverdi's uncanny psychological verity—a flair for realistic exposition of character that his countrymen, three hundred years later, were to try to recapture.

Monteverdi, the mere enumeration of whose madrigals and church music fills several closely printed pages in a short-title catalogue, composed his few operas as a sort of fashionable side line. Although most of them have been lost, from those remaining we get more than a hint of the important revolution he undertook. His innovations were not the fumbling, graceless thinking aloud of a parched theorist, but the rapid, expressive strokes of a creative genius blocking out the architecture of a new medium, and hampered by only the flimsiest of precedents.

Under Monteverdi the orchestra expanded into an ensemble of diversified eloquence, specific instruments being used, singly, in choirs, or in combinations, to express every dramatic effect. Each character is differentiated from the others by his own instrumental accompaniment. In *Orfeo*, for example, Orpheus is supported by the bass viola, Eurydice by violas, and Pluto by the trombone. From a modern point of view, not all the instrumental assignments were so happy, and, as H. Sutherland Edwards pointed out in *The Lyrical Drama*, "Charon—a most unsentimental personage, one would think—sang to the accompaniment of that sentimental instrument, the guitar." Monteverdi was especially partial to claviers, organs, lutes, and harps, whose chord-making possibilities allowed the richest harmonic texture. Partly because of his influence, it was not until the eighteenth century that single-voiced instruments came to dominate the orchestra. He innocently used, but with discretion, the violin tremolo for pointing up moments of pathos, not realizing the bathetic ends to which less tasteful composers would take it.

In 1612, his health undermined by the dank air of the Mantuan marshes, Monteverdi left the scene of his first successes and within a year was installed in Venice as master of the music to the Most Serene Republic, a post he held until his death, some thirty years later. He blossomed in the luxurious capital of the doges. Successor at St. Mark's to a line of brilliant maestros, he did not in any way suffer by comparison, though his sacred works often wavered on the edge of the profane: into them there entered more and more the spirit of the pleasure-loving city Veronese had wooed with ripe color and spacious line. In 1637, when the Tron family inaugurated, at Venice, the Teatro San Cassiano, the first public opera house, a new phenomenon was born overnight—opera as a popular spectacle, so passionately delighted in that its subsequent fortunes are at least as much part of folk as of musical history.

For that mildly earth-shaking event in the story of European culture, a now unknown opera—*Andromeda,* by Francesco Manelli—had been chosen. Venice had to wait two years before hearing something from Monteverdi's long-dormant theatrical muse. Even Francesco Cavalli, his pupil, who specialized in robust melodies of easy tunefulness, established his works on the boards of the San Cassiano more quickly. The elder master's *Adone*, performed at a new and more sumptuous house, ran continuously from late 1639 until the Carnival of 1640; meanwhile, his revived *Arianna* drew crowds to still another theater. It is hard to believe, despite the later example of Verdi, that the septuagenarian composer could have written the, at times, almost vernal sequences of *Il Ritorno d'Ulisse* and the fresh and vivid *L'Incoronazione di Poppea*, possibly the first historical opera. However, they were first performed shortly before his death in 1643, soon enough, happily, to let him savor the pleasure of being a popular favorite.*

After Monteverdi's death, leadership among operatic composers was shared by his pupil, Francesco Cavalli, and Marcantonio Cesti, whose training had come from an early experimentalist in oratorio, Giacomo Carissimi. Both were important missionaries in carrying Italian opera beyond the Alps: Cavalli went to France at the invitation of Cardinal Mazarin, gained high position at court, and in 1662 wrote an opera for the wedding of Louis XIV to the Infanta Maria Theresa; Cesti, a Franciscan monk with a capable tenor voice, sought his fortune in Austria, where he was appointed vice-*Kapellmeister* to the Emperor Leopold, the ugliest prince in Europe. Cesti, whose sobriety and logic reduced to order certain chaotic elements of opera, replaced with *sinfonie*, brief instrumental pieces of atmospheric and descriptive character, the irrelevant little introductions previously used. How much this reform was needed may be deduced from the fact that even Monteverdi, with all his grasp of the dramatic, nevertheless had absurdly prefaced *Orfeo* with a nine-bar toccata, to be repeated three times. Cesti also tried, with less signal success, to reach a medium between bare recitative and the full-blown aria, evolving a kind of singing talk of monotonously Oriental effect. If Cesti's tendencies are extended in time, we can see

* The American *première* of *L'Incoronazione di Poppea*, at Smith College, on April 26, 1926, proved that this almost tercentenarian opera has more than antiquarian interest. Students of the Juilliard School of Music, in New York, performed it several years later, and in 1937-38 the Salzburg Opera Guild offered it in a new edition by Ernst Křenek.

their effects, remotely, in Gluck, Wagner, Debussy, and Alban Berg. Cavalli, less profound and not at all solemn, worked for his day: he truckled to the growing spirit of *fiesta* that was to take over Italy for more than a century, introducing comic relief into operas so starred with popular songs as to be little more than strings of arias.

Already, less than fifty years after the "invention" of opera, it had departed from the severe Greek ideals of Peri. The dominance of the singer, which Caccini, even as he pledged faith to classic austerity, helped to assure by the introduction of vocal ornamentation, had become absolute. Nothing of antiquity remained except the names of the characters, who were plunged into situations more fantastic than anything the fancy of Ovid could have invented. Operas began to become vehicles for popular singers, composers the slaves of the singers' whimsies. Thus, in its infancy, while it needed every ounce of strength to achieve reasonable form, opera frittered away its energies in pandering to the sensational and the ephemeral.

The sopranos came first—extravagantly feted creatures with voices of supernatural agility who ended up, if not ladies, duchesses. Some of them were more than mere machines: composers, poets, bluestockings, they commanded the worshipful attentions of the discriminating. One of them, Leonora Baroni, won a double immortality because John Milton happened to hear her at a fashionable gathering at Cardinal Barberini's, and indited three Latin poems to her; she was, moreover, a lifelong friend of the witty Cardinal Rospigliosi, the most popular librettist of the day, who became Pope Clement IX. There was Francesca Caccini, for whom her father wrote the first operatic roulades, and there was, most spectacular of all, Adriana Basile, mother of great daughters— among them Milton's Leonora. This amazing woman, whose services were bid for by crowned sovereigns, and whose enormous salary at the Mantuan court was supplemented by unparalleled *pourboires* of brocaded gowns and precious gems, became homesick for her native Naples. Returning thither, the ennobled singer was greeted by the entire city, while the local academy of highborn dilettantes laid their eulogies at her feet.

After the sopranos came the *castrati*, artificially preserved male sopranos and altos, though their heyday was reserved for the age of Handel. Out of the obscurity of a church singer's life (for the choir seems to have been their cradle), these emasculated warblers came to challenge the pre-eminence of natural sopranos. Intensively cultivated from early childhood, their voices were exotics we cannot well imagine—a woman's range produced with the power of a man's lungs. The effect was something pure and sexless, like a boy's voice in a mature throat. *Castrati* were introduced to circumvent the papal ban against women appearing on the stage, and at first played only female roles—the Venus of Manelli's *Andromeda* was a *castrato*. Soon, however, their vocal gymnastics in these parts made audiences clamor for their use in male roles as well. Thus, the ridiculous spectacle of a eunuch as Hercules was soon taken for granted, shrill voice and all. As the opera mania spread over Europe, the demand for *castrati* soon became almost too great for the supply. France alone did not take to the eunuchs, but even there, as late as 1660, Padre Francesco Melani, a male soprano belonging to the Servite order, sang the role of Queen Amestris, Xerxes' paramour, in Cavalli's opera *Serse*.

Long before the seventeenth century had run its course, opera, which in 1600 had begun as the expensive toy of the pampered few, was established as the most popular form of musical entertainment. Moreover, it was an important commercial enterprise. The *commedia dell' arte* was hard pressed to keep its audiences, notably in its very capital, Venice, where by 1699 no less than sixteen opera houses were flourishing, increasing the prestige of, and in some cases enriching, the great families who ran them—Tron, Grimani, Giustiniani, Vendremin, Venier, and Labia.

Yet, the theaters, except for a few luxuriously fitted-out loges, were anything but fine: they were dark and ill-smelling, and the seats were of rough wood. The managements concentrated their expenditures on popular singers and on fantastically elaborate staging. A seventeenth-century observer, quoted in Molmenti's *Venice*, speaks rhapsodically of the glories of the productions at the San Cassiano and other theaters, expatiating on their "marvelous transformation scenes, their crowded stage, their ingenious mechanism, their flying figures, their scenery representing the heavens, Olympus, the ocean, royal palaces, forests, groves, and innumerable other enchanting spectacles." In one case, a sumptuous ball-room, brightly illuminated, and with all its appurtenances, human and otherwise, was suspended over the permanent stage, and drawn up out of sight when not wanted. The over-emphasis on stage architecture reminds us that the seventeenth century was an age of engineering triumphs. Operatic architecture took the lead, theatrical architecture followed, and when the elaborate style finally evolved came to be used for the building of permanent edifices, the baroque came into being.

By 1700, regional schools of opera had arisen and died in Florence and Venice, and a third was being born in the south, with the Neapolitan Alessandro Scarlatti, who was simultaneously to emphasize the austere ideals of the Bardi *camerata* and to formulate certain rules without which further evolution could not have taken place. The first Florentine operas had suffered for two main reasons: first, they were mere workings out of a dubious theory; and second, like most self-conscious innovations, they were far less good than the best conventional work of the time, which happened to be the superb masterpieces of mature vocal polyphony. Peri and Caccini gave to their child little more than the gift of recitative, which in their uninspired view was only attaching a note to each syllable of metrical speech.

On the flickering flame of *le musiche nuove*—the monodic style of Peri and Caccini—Claudio Monteverdi had directed the bellows of his creative imagination. Himself an eminent polyphonist, he seems to have turned to opera because the old forms no longer gave scope to his expressiveness—the many strangenesses that make his madrigals far from orthodox show him desperate in the face of restrictions that are as much part

and parcel of the conventional madrigal as the fourteen-line
scheme is of the sonnet. Recitative, as starkly defined, could
not satisfy him: as dramatic situations demanded, he spon-
taneously expanded the frame of the musical picture. He had
no pedantic aversion to music itself, as the early Florentines,
lost in their visions of Greece and Rome, seem to have had:
he had, in short, no aversion to melody, and he had a positive
affection for harmony. Crises in the libretto drew from him
the most lyrical of phrases or the most savage harmonies. He
employed a nervous line capable of sudden departures, often
amazingly florid, from the contours of the speech—irruptions
of color which came to be called *colorature*. These Monteverdi
always conceived organically; some of his contemporaries and,
even more, his immediate successors, coming speedily under
the thumb of vain sopranos and altos of both sexes, subordinated their entire conception of opera to the manufacture of
these display passages. With this trend allowed to run wild,
opera was in danger of degenerating into a side show with
which no serious composer could concern himself.

Chapter II
Classical Austerity and Laughter

THE fame of Alessandro Scarlatti, the next vital force in operatic history, has survived outside of textbooks only because his son Domenico was one of the most delicious composers of keyboard music who ever lived. Yet, judged by pure musical standards, the now obscure father was incomparably the greater of the two. But whereas many of Domenico's sparkling harpsichord sonatas are as fresh and acceptable as on the day they were composed, Alessandro's more than one hundred operas are such obvious period pieces that, as operas, they could no longer draw an audience. Nor have his other compositions fared better. Still wonderful as music, they are today inadmissible as organisms. What has happened to Scarlatti is what would have happened to Handel if he had composed nothing but opera. Most people will probably go to their graves without hearing a single note of some of the best music composed in the seventeenth century, but for this state of affairs Scarlatti himself, as a canny child of his time, is to blame: he gave that baroque age exactly what it wanted, and no one has wanted him since.

Scarlatti was a learned, meticulous craftsman who was compelled, the greater portion of his life, to earn his living by hastily contrived operas. In them, except those composed late in life, it is difficult to find complete proof of his erudition. The key to that resides in his chamber cantatas, of which he wrote hundreds. Many of these cantatas are mere excuses for solving the most tortuous of technical problems, and it is fairer to describe them as puzzles than as operas for solo voice. We can imagine Scarlatti, after a racking day trying to devise a usable operatic score for some royal theater, turning to problems in pure music, and pouring into them that perfect understanding of technique and form which he could use only restrictedly in his workaday life. His chamber cantatas bear much the same relation to his operas as *Die Kunst der*

Fuge and *Das musikalisches Opfer* do to the *Cantor*'s labors of Bach. There, of course, the comparison ends, for the German did not have to worry overmuch about catering to the popular taste.

There is an apparently insoluble mystery about Scarlatti's origins and early life. Was he, as he occasionally described himself, a native of Palermo? Were his boyish studies guided by his father, or was his musical lore gained in two years with that same Carissimi who had taught Cesti, and whose only familiar work, today, is a strident love song, *Vittoria, vittoria,* that is all too familiar to recital audiences? Students have professed to find a strong trace of Alessandro Stradella in Scarlatti's early work, but where he could have heard an opera by that accomplished adventurer does not transpire.* If Stradella gave anything to young Scarlatti, it was a way with melody, but while the older man was given to maddening repetition of his tunes, his imitator knew when to stop. Also, Scarlatti's individual treatment of accompaniments may have been stimulated by a study of Stradella's music.

The first of Scarlatti's operas that can be dated was produced in Rome in 1679, when he was about twenty years old. Rome was already the seat of a flourishing if not very significant school of operatic composers, but though Scarlatti is the first considerable name in Roman opera, the fact that he lived in Naples for the greater part of his life has led to his being described erroneously as the founder of the Neapolitan school of opera. Thitherto, Rome had had to be content with the adequate journeyman's work of its operatic composers†: Scarlatti's *L'Errore innocente,* childish though it was in many ways, had hints of genius. It attracted the attention of Christina of

---

* Stradella was as unfortunate after death as he was in life: killed by a second set of assassins hired by an irate rival in love (after a first set had been charmed into harmlessness by his music), he became the subject of an opera by the composer of *Martha* and of a novel by F. Marion Crawford; moreover, his most famous composition, *Pietà, Signore,* may have been one of Rossini's hoaxes.

† Without being a great composer, one of Scarlatti's early Roman predecessors, Domenico Mazzocchi, was a clever innovator who advanced musical notation several steps. He was the first to use the signs $<$ and $>$ to indicate increasing and decreasing volume, as well as the abbreviations *p* (soft), *f* (loud), and *tr* (trill).

Sweden, most notorious of Roman converts, and she immediately extended her dangerous patronage to the young Sicilian. Although it is not wise to judge Christina by Greta Garbo's picturization of her character, Gustavus Adolphus' recreant daughter was a very strange woman; and those she befriended often lived to repent her generosity. Scarlatti, conductor in her private theater for over four years, came out unscathed. This was unusual, for Christina was as destructive in friendship as in wrath: she had her secretary killed, fought constantly with the almost sainted Innocent XI, and once, in an access of warmth, handshook Alexander VII so violently as to break bones in his fingers.

Although the first public opera house in Rome had been established during the pontificate of the most bitterly anti-operatic of pontiffs, Innocent XI, Scarlatti's earliest operas were performed in Christina's palace. The ex-Queen's interest in secular musical entertainment was long-standing and obstinate: she was an old friend of the charming, libretto-writing Clement IX, and even before his reign, during that of the irresponsible Alexander VII, cardinals thronged to her operas in such numbers that they were said to have been given "in consistory." In 1679, opera in Rome was still, because of papal ban, the toy of the high nobility, and there is no doubt that Scarlatti's development was retarded because his first efforts were made under such unfavorable conditions—had he gone early to Venice or Florence, where opera was already a people's art, his career might have been even more brilliant than it turned out to be. It is possible that in 1684, when he left Christina's service, he was weary of working under these straitened conditions. If so, he did little to improve them, for Naples, where he now went, had only the thinnest operatic tradition, and his post, as court conductor to the Spanish viceroy, though nominally a step upward, limited his activities quite as much as before. Yet, it would be a mistake to think of Scarlatti as very discontented with his official duties: of his more than forty years of active composing, twenty-eight were spent in Naples and eleven in Rome. This is not the record of a man driven to rebellion and flight.

Scarlatti, indeed, was anything but a rebel: he was a stand-
ardizer of already existing, but not completely realized, musical forms. He invented little, established much. To the
detriment of the dramatic unity of an entire work, he concentrated on perfecting a few elements. He was, with all his
great purely musical gifts, a baleful influence on the evolution
of opera as credible theater: not only did he wither whatever
improvisatory freedom opera had when he came upon the
scene, but he so congealed the patterns of various operatic
elements that even so resourceful a composer as Handel had
to turn to oratorio in order to free himself from the bondage
of Scarlattian precedents. A casuist might say that by freezing
its molds, Scarlatti made his most valuable contribution to
opera, as he thereby forced the reforms of Gluck. Only by
using the orchestra rather than the harpsichord alone to accompany recitative, thus softening the contrasts between it
and aria, did he look forward to the tendencies that still seem
to have the final word in the construction of opera.

Scarlatti's conception of the overture as a three-section, self-
contained suite, consisting of an allegro, a *grave*, and another
fast movement, is aesthetically above reproach; moreover, it
is probably one of the several ancestors of the sonata form.
But its very self-sufficiency cut it away, except in general mood,
from the body of the opera itself, and thus delayed the day
when, at the hands of Gluck and Mozart, it was to be persuaded
into the whole, either flowing effortlessly and without interruption into the action or anticipating it by suave quotation.

Likewise, Scarlatti's perfecting of the *da capo* aria (in which,
after a contrasting part, the third section merely repeats the
first), based on the sound aesthetic canon of statement, contrast,
and recognition, stultified his own output and fathered an
undramatic conception of opera that was to dominate the
musical stage for more than half a century. Nothing less likely
to carry forward the action of a libretto can be imagined than
a series of these rigorously devised, unassimilable *da capo*
arias: yet, beginning with *Teodora* in 1693, Scarlatti often used
fifty or sixty of them to an opera. This, more than any other
single element, was to deliver opera, a bound captive, into the

singer's hands. Whatever the beauty of its separate pieces, a Scarlatti opera has no more dramatic unity than a Broadway musical comedy. It has, indeed, even less carefully planned organization than a good revue, whose very flouting of rhyme and reason can be a very subtle thing. It is a concert of often impressively lovely songs connected precariously by recitative, and grafted, with slight relevance, onto a pseudo-classical libretto.

It is unreasonable to blame Scarlatti for concentrating on the purely musical aspect of opera and letting the dramatic go by the board. The Florentine fathers of opera had started at the other extreme. Nor can we assume that Monteverdi, whose few extant operas are superior to Scarlatti's as musical plays, had a conscious understanding of how to bring about a happy balance between the dramatic and musical elements. It is more probable that, with few traditions to follow, he was in that happy position of being able to indulge his own bent unhampered: fortunately for the longevity of his works, he had a native flair for drama as well as musical gifts of the highest order. Moreover, living when the Renaissance was dying and the baroque had not fully asserted its character, and before the age of the unrestrained sway of tyrant singers, Monteverdi had no persistent demands to meet: the age had not yet formulated them. Scarlatti, apparently accepting the standards of the high baroque without a question, discovered a popular formula which, until the end of his days, he was content to provide with ever-changing surface decoration.

Of Scarlatti's 115 operas, not half have been preserved, and of those extant many are incomplete. Most of them were designed for Rome or Naples, though a few were composed for Venice or Pratolino, the summer villa of Ferdinando de' Medici, outside Florence. To show to what lengths speculation on the flimsiest evidence can go, it is sometimes stated that the operas written for the Florentine prince were Scarlatti's finest, though scarcely a scrap of their music remains. To support this claim, Scarlatti's letters to Ferdinando, mentioning one of them— *Lucio Manlio*—as the best he had yet written, are brought forward. It is difficult to understand how these letters, which are typical high-flown fawnings on a patron, can be cited as proofs of anything except their author's eagerness to jolly the prince along. Artists have a way of talking a good picture, a good statue—or a good opera.

More convincing of the high quality of these lost Medicean operas is the score of *Il Mitridate Eupatore,* written for Venice during the period Scarlatti was working for Ferdinando. Fortunately, *Mitridate* survives in its entirety—a five-act tragedy with ballet. Written in a grand and elevated manner, the solemnity of which Scarlatti emphasized by the omission of the two comic characters whose presence had become a convention of serious opera, *Mitridate* registers a great advance over the hasty contrivances of his first Neapolitan period. Beautifully conceived, poetically felt, it exerts a pull on the feelings that the brilliant, hard, and showy *Tigrane,* a triumph of Scarlatti's second Neapolitan period, cannot. Possibly his most noted opera, but certainly not his best, *Tigrane* is nevertheless in some ways more interesting than the lovelier *Mitridate*: the comic scenes are frequent, diversified, and funny, affording a welcome contrast to the cardboard heroics of the ranting principals and foreshadowing the harebrained vivacities of *opera buffa*; also, this 105th of Scarlatti's operas, composed in 1715, shows that, only six years before abandoning a long, practical career, he was tentatively approaching the use of orchestra itself as a full-fledged dramatic element.

By the time of his death in 1725, Scarlatti was a figure from the past. Younger men, among them Handel, had already usurped his popularity in Italy and had coolly appropriated the few devices his musical genius had wheedled into life—the *da capo* aria, reiterative instrumental interludes (*ritornelli*) in arias, and, finally, the choice of the minor mode for expressing the elegiac or melancholy. The last seems an appropriate labor for the sad, appealing, and noble-looking man who watches us gravely from the cracked and faded portrait painted by Francesco Solimena, himself a dominating figure of the Neapolitan baroque.

Scarlatti's last years were not without moments of quickening. His son Domenico, his most eminent pupil, had already set Italy afire with his playing of the harpsichord; in London and Portugal his operas were preferred to his father's. Now, in 1724, only a year before Alessandro Scarlatti's death, a young German came to him and implored to be taken on as a pupil. This was Johann Adolf Hasse, destined to write more than a hundred operas and to be, in some respects, Scarlatti's most faithful and successful disciple. It was Hasse who persuaded Scarlatti to receive, against his will, another young German, Johann Joachim Quantz, already suffering from that lucky love of the flute which was to bring him high fame as the teacher of the most renowned of flautists, Frederick the Great. "Scarlatti," wrote Quantz, "let me hear him on the harpsichord, which he played in a learned manner, though he did not possess as much agility as his son." There, unwittingly, Quantz pronounced Alessandro Scarlatti's epitaph: he was a learned man, and he was the father of Domenico.

Italian opera, Scarlattian in its general lineaments, was to conquer the world and to hold it in fee for many a year, though it might present superficially different faces in different countries. In the process, the leadership was to pass sometimes to England, sometimes to France, even sometimes to Germany and Austria, occasionally in the hands of Italians, more often in those of Italianate foreigners. Italy continued to be a thriving song factory, as it does to this day, but few of its workers produced anything lasting until the first warblings of that quenchless songbird, Gioacchino Rossini, early in the nineteenth century. The Jomellis, Sacchinis, and Traettas, if not utterly forgotten, are commemorated only by special pleaders, notably that delicate eclectic of twilight yesterdays, Vernon Lee. Their music-making was not contemptible: some of their airs might pass as Scarlatti's. They had a correctness and elegance that are the ineluctible qualities of their age, and they were sweet, tender, and sometimes subtle melodists. A few isolated airs rise above this accomplished craftsmanship; but these minor musical poets of the eighteenth century in Italy, without the boldness needed for big issues, lacked, similarly, staying power. They are interim men, hangers-on of dying traditions.

More vigorous, because it did not rely on the stultified traditions of *opera seria* and, from the least promising beginnings, forced a respectable place for itself, was *opera buffa*. This variety of comic opera stemmed from the broadly farcical interludes with which, even before the days of opera itself, comic leavening had been inserted between the acts of an otherwise serious play. These *intermezzi*, as they were called at their first appearance in the sixteenth century,* had no connection whatever with the play in which they appeared and at first were merely comic songs or madrigals without dramatic content. Serious operatic composers, by retaining these *intermezzi*, weakened further the already feeble structural integrity of their tragedies—or comedies; but no doubt they wished to satisfy their audiences' persistent hankering after the rough-and-tumble of the *commedia dell' arte*. Even Alessandro Scarlatti did not disdain to compose *intermezzi*; by his time, however, they had developed certain conventions of their own, being, in many cases, musical Punch-and-Judy shows. As soon as plots began to be fitted to them, it was inevitable that the *intermezzi* would expand to self-sufficiency. In certain cases, indeed, they were lifted from the parent opera, and produced and published separately. At the moment when, having drawn to itself all the comic elements of the old opera, especially the two conventional farce characters, the *intermezzo* became the *opera buffa*, the distinction between it and *opera seria* was sharply defined.

Few composers of opera failed to try their hands at *buffa*, once it was established. The great Carlo Goldoni wrote librettos for the patrician Leonardo Leo and for the deft Baldassare Galuppi, whose present-day fame, however, depends on the rather accidental fact that Browning used one of his toccatas as a springboard for metaphysical acrobatics. The *buffe* developed along broad, simple lines, so much so, in fact, that in 1733, when the model *buffa—La Serva Padrona—*was produced, it depended for its effects on the general atmosphere of horseplay, the use of two strongly contrasted characters (there were three characters in all, one of them mute), and a time-honored plot that rang every conceivable change on the comic

---

* A more ancient lineage is claimed for them, carrying their genealogy back to the interludes in medieval mystery plays, and even to the Roman *saturae*.

aspects of jealousy. First used between the acts of one of its composer's serious operas, *La Serva Padrona* almost immediately received independent performance, and within a few years was a favorite throughout the peninsula. In 1752, it started a riot among the Parisian intellectuals, involving Rousseau and the Encyclopedists, as well as the aged Rameau—in his role, of course, of master theoretician. Its fame continued to spread and is not yet extirct: on February 23, 1935, the Metropolitan Opera Company revived it successfully, with Editha Fleischer, Louis d'Angelo, and Angelo Bada, the last as the mute. It was as the conspiring Serpina that, on August 12, 1861, Célestine Galli-Marié, the future creator of Mignon and Carmen, made her Paris debut.

Giovanni Battista Pergolesi, the contriver of this long-lived trifle (it runs little more than half an hour), had such an incredible and melodramatic life that he has ended up as the subject of two operas. Except for having died in his bed rather than by poison, and at the age of twenty-six instead of seventeen, Pergolesi might be termed the Chatterton of Italian music. He might better be compared to Mozart: legend has been busy blackening their names with exaggerated charges of profligacy and extravagance. Appealing figures both, they worked hard and earnestly against time, frequently on large and ambitious works, and died disregarded and penniless. Legend, furthermore, has said that Pergolesi completed his *Stabat Mater* on his deathbed: unfortunately for the parallel to Mozart's dying before he could finish the Requiem, Pergolesi wrote the *Stabat Mater* when he was only nineteen and in excellent health. This is the *Stabat Mater* Rossini regarded so highly that he hesitated—but in vain—to set the same text himself. His version, not inferior to Pergolesi's, is—to modern ears—even more theatrical. In our own times, Igor Stravinsky has done his bit to keep green the name of the composer of *La Serva Padrona*: in 1920, for the Ballet Russe, he pieced together a charming collection of Pergolesi's tunes and called the result *Pulcinella*. While it is possible to name Pergolesi, somewhat loosely, the father of comic opera, it must not be forgotten that *La Serva*

Padrona may have been, in its creator's mind, one of the least of his artistic children.

La Serva Padrona was the first important *buffa*, but the genre has flourished uninterruptedly ever since. Most of its practitioners, especially those who worked at it exclusively, have been obscure, but some of its occasional devotees have been geniuses. Cimarosa, its next great exponent in Italy, seems—though mostly for chronological reasons—to belong to another age: born only thirteen years after Pergolesi's death, he died in the nineteenth century, having composed his single masterpiece, *Il Matrimonio segreto,* in Vienna the year after the death of Mozart, himself a genius of *buffa*. That same year, 1792, was born Italy's greatest manufacturer of gaiety—Rossini. The line is not extinct: there lives in Italy Ermanno Wolf-Ferrari, whose *Il Segreto di Susanna* is in the most sparkling tradition.

Earthier and more robust, *opera buffa* steadfastly refused to employ the services of *castrati*, the pampered favorites of *opera seria*, sturdily insisting that full-grown men were either tenors, baritones, or basses, and women sopranos or contraltos. Thus it escaped in some measure the dictatorship of the singers, who thought of opera only as a testing ground for their agility. The star system, the imbecility of which even Hollywood could see through in a few years, had, by the beginning of the eighteenth century, so fastened itself on opera that librettists and composers were often the servants of the singers.

The librettists, if they had a shred of originality (which was not often the case), found themselves hedged in by restrictions at every point. The libretto was more rule-bound than the French classic drama: big parts had to be written for the principals, whether the logic of the story admitted such procedure or not; the order of the scenes in which the principals and secondary performers were to shine was based on a jealously preserved scheme of precedence that might tax the hair-splitting talents of the editors of *Burke's Peerage*. Not only was the

---

* Its revival by the Metropolitan, on February 25, 1937, was a failure, the whole affair proceeding with disconcerting listlessness. The English text used was not entirely successful, while Muriel Dickson, Irra Petina, Natalie Bodanya, George Rasely, Julius Huehn, and D'Angelo were pedestrian in their roles.

sequence and timing of solo and concerted numbers as inflexibly ordered as the laws of the Medes and the Persians, but the prerogatives of the principals had to be so nicely balanced that the writing of a libretto, even without these extra complications a difficult task, became as involved as a Chinese puzzle. Is it, then, strange that these librettos were seldom dramatic?

As for the poor composer who had to respect what pitiable fragments of drama were handed to him, he was not even allowed the luxury of fitting to the poetry the most appropriate music he could conceive. If a jealous singer felt himself slighted in the allotment of scenes, the wretched musician was often obliged to interpolate a number utterly irrelevant to the already twisted scheme of action. Finally, there was no guarantee that the singers would be satisfied with the music as written: many an operatic performance degenerated into a carnival of ad-libbing, with each entrant playing to the gallery with every vocal trick at his command.

A few strong composers tried to oppose the singer's despotism, but as long as they worked in the frame of the old opera, with its uninspired sequence of set scenes, orchestral *ritornelli*, and *da capo* arias, they were beaten before they started. Their audiences were not with them, but with the singers, as Handel was to discover more than once. Rebel librettists and rebel composers were needed who would house-clean opera from top to bottom. And a small rebellious minority in the audience was needed, too—a minority that would be interested in the dramatic unity of music and action.

Carlo Broschi, called Farinelli, after a contemporary portrait

Chapter III
Handel

A N EX-LAW student, the Saxon Heinrich Schütz, going to study music with one of the brilliant maestros of St. Mark's Chapel, arrived in Venice in 1609 while opera was still a novelty. Although pre-eminently interested in religious music, Schütz mastered both the contrapuntal style of the Venetian school and *le musiche nuove* come to light in Florence but a few years before. Returning to Germany, he served not only as a bridge between the great Italian contrapuntalists and the age of Bach and Handel, but also as the peaceful if not over-vociferous champion of opera. His fine musical education and abilities made him much sought after, and when he finally settled in Dresden, it was as *Kapellmeister* to the Elector Johann Georg I. A dozen years later, in 1627, when called upon by the Elector to provide something extra-special for the wedding of his daughter Sophie to the Landgrave of Hesse-Darmstadt, Schütz sent to Italy for a score of Peri's *Dafne*. It arrived safely, but in Italian. Although there was no more reason then than now for the audience to understand the words of a libretto, it was decided to have the honeyed Italian syllables translated into German by the philosopher-poet Martin Opitz. This precipitated one of those crises which so often confront opera impresarios: it was found that Opitz' lines did not fit Peri's music. So Schütz had to adapt some of the music and probably add some of his own.

Thus, almost three hundred years ago, there arose, for the first time, the problem of performing an opera with its libretto translated into a language other than that in which it was written, usually for the purpose of making the text understandable to a new group of listeners—the problem, in short, that Americans know as "opera in English." Obviously, to understand an opera fully, it is essential to know what is being said on the stage, and therefore efforts to secure this understanding by translation spring from a commendable intention.

However, the objections to performance in translation are manifold. Some important ones are phonetic: certain vowel sounds can be heard fully only if sung at certain pitches; some languages are practically stressless, and others—English, for example—are heavily stressed. The most sensitive composers have respected these considerations wherever possible. Other translation difficulties have to do with syntax: the order of the words often regulates the line of the melody and the ebb and flow of speed and volume. Still others have to do with the very essence of language: terseness, diffuseness, concentration, various imponderables. To translate a libretto from one language into another, keeping all these factors in mind, and producing a text that can be sung without altering the music, is impossible. To bring the problem to the United States again, it were better to provide oneself with a good literal translation of a foreign-language libretto, study the two texts side by side before a performance, and drop the meaningless cry of "opera in English." Needless to say, this last does not apply to opera originally composed to an English text.

Returning to Schütz, it was on April 13, 1627, at Schloss Hartenfels, near Torgau, in Saxony, that *Daphne*, not only the first opera heard in Germany, but also the first German opera, was performed. The fuss attending its production must have discouraged not only Schütz (who seems never to have written another opera), but also many of his successors who might have been tempted to set German texts. At any rate, serious opera in German did not establish itself for almost two centuries, though opera in Italian by both Germans and foreigners attained a great vogue before the end of the seventeenth century.

While it is impossible to gauge the full effects of the Thirty Years' War on the creative energy of Continental Europe, there is no doubt that it proved ruinous to any vigorous expression of German genius. The *Daphne* of Schütz and Opitz, produced in the full tide of the war, must be deemed a sport: besides, as the score was destroyed by fire in 1760, its quality is a matter of guesswork. Opera remained the occasional diversion of courtly life until shortly after the opening of the Hamburg opera house in 1678, when almost immediately an active school of musicodramatic writers sprang up in the old Hanse town. Of these early composers, the most interesting, if not the most gifted, was Johann Wolfgang Franck, who wrote fourteen operas for the Hamburg theater in half as many years. But, as in all probability we shall never hear a bar of them, Franck's fame is more likely to rest on the fact that he was one of the few murderers ever to achieve distinction as a composer: he stabbed his wife and killed a fellow musician in a jealous rage.

Franck's young contemporary, Reinhard Keiser, also led a violent and unkempt life, but is of more consequence in the history of music, if only because he influenced the career of Handel. This extraordinary man bestrode musical Hamburg, with a few intermissions, for forty years, reigning as dictator at the opera house and even insinuating himself as a canon into the cathedral revenues. Bounder, spendthrift, and prolific writer of stage pieces and quite as lively religious works, Keiser definitely lifted Hamburg to musical supremacy in northern Europe. He composed considerably more than one hundred operas, sometimes at the rate of eight a year. These works, which are estimated to contain no less than forty-five hundred separate airs, are often melodically attractive and even show an occasional feeling for dramatic verity. But most of them were written to German texts of such wretched workmanship and impoverished imagination that it is no wonder that by 1740, a year after Keiser's death, not a single one of his operas held the boards, which were thenceforth given over to various settings of more polished Italian texts.

Far more notable than Keiser's services to Hamburg or to the wives of its burghers was his hiring, in 1703, as second violinist in the opera orchestra, an eighteen-year-old youth from Halle, who, writing to Italian librettos and producing mostly in Italy and England, was destined to become the first great German musician to compose operas. George Frideric Handel (for such was the way Georg Friedrich Händel signed his name during the last forty years of his life) was, like so many of his musical confreres, a disgruntled law student.* He

* Like Schumann and Tchaikovsky, too. Handel was pushed into law by familial piety, Schumann by a nagging mother, and Tchaikovsky by lassitude.

happened to write his first stage work because the changeable Keiser tired of a libretto he had promised to set. Handel took it up, and quickly wrote *Almira*, the leading tenor part being sung by his friend Johann Mattheson, also an ex-law student, who wrote operas and was even more immersed in theory. Coming shortly after a duel between the two young men, *Almira* turned out to be not only an omen of Handel's flair for the stage, but also a compliment to Mattheson's vocal and histrionic ability. It had its *première* on January 8, 1705, and ran for seven weeks. Keiser, who endured no rival near the throne, was enraged, though he might have taken the success of Handel's maiden effort as a tribute to himself: stylistically, it was his own child. Happily for the general peace, Handel's second effort, *Nero,* was a failure and provided Keiser with an opportunity for revenge on his froward subordinate. He resolved himself to set the libretto of *Nero* to show how it should be done. But the Hamburgers would have none of his first fiddling Caesar, and a second try failed as miserably. What was meant to finish Handel ended by finishing Keiser—for the time being. A new director at the opera was friendly to Handel, but as Mattheson had jealously turned against him, the young Saxon decided to try his fortunes elsewhere.

Italy was his choice, a half-invitation from one of the minor Medici being decisive. For three years, until early in 1710, Handel posted up and down the peninsula, studying styles, playing the organ and harpsichord, and tossing off his earliest oratorios. At first he was famed rather as a performer than as a composer: he even outshone the scintillant Domenico Scarlatti, with whom he occasionally vied in friendly contest. A first opera, *Rodrigo,* brought him nothing more than a little money and a set of dishes from Alessandro Scarlatti's penurious patron, Ferdinando de' Medici. But *Agrippina*, mounted at a fine theater run by the Grimani family in Venice, on December 26, 1709, spread the news that Handel's name was to be reckoned with in the world of opera. *Agrippina* ran twenty-seven consecutive nights and remained in the theater's repertoire for almost a quarter of a century—at a period when operas were as frail as the virtue of their heroines. But it brought Handel more than fame: it brought him, in large measure, his future. For each night during that unprecedented run in 1709-10, an absorbed spectator from the dogal loge was Prince Ernst, whose brother, the Elector of Hanover, was heir presumptive to the throne of England. Once before, the Prince (the first of that very special group, the Handelians—as strange, in their way, as the Wagnerians) had invited Handel to become *Kapellmeister* at Hanover. Now he renewed his offer, and Handel, strangely, with Italy at his feet, accepted.

By 1711, tired in less than a year of the stodgy splendors of Herrenhausen, the Elector Georg's imitation Versailles, Handel was on leave in London and producing *Rinaldo*, his first opera there, to tremendous acclaim. What he saw evidently pleased him more than all the lush charms of Italy, for though expiration of his leave made him return to the Continent, he was back in London as soon as he could decently plead for another vacation. It was not the single fact that *Rinaldo* had been a great success in London that was the decisive factor in wedding Handel to England: in similar circumstances, when *Agrippina* was being sung night after night in Venice, he had unregretfully turned his back on Italy. Handel was more English than the English and knew his soil the moment he touched it. Thenceforth, for almost half a century, he was to remain in London, making only a few brief, hurried excursions abroad. Every year putting on a pound or two more of flesh, every year becoming more John Bullish, he eventually became one of the honored monuments of the town. Among all the great dead in the Abbey there is none less foreign than the man who was born Georg Friedrich Händel.

The paradox of Handel is that, despite his intense Englishness, he dealt the deathblow to indigenous English opera. Except for a rare sport, and that usually in some comic genre, no English operas have established themselves down to this day. And, indeed, English opera was always a halfhearted thing. Beginning during the latter days of the Commonwealth as a way of getting around the Puritan ban against stage plays, it took feeble wing from the hand of Sir William Davenant, poet laureate and playwright of parts, who amused himself by letting it be noised about that he was Shakespeare's bastard. Pleasant coxcomb that he was, Davenant had all the blatant confidence, if not the genius, to be expected of a love child of England's greatest poet; and when, in 1656, he advertised an experiment as *The Firste Dayes Entertainment at Rutland House by Declamation and Musick*; *after the manner of the Ancients,* he was not, as the last phrase might have indicated, aping Peri and Caccini. He was merely putting one over on the Protector. In cold fact, Davenant had no theories about opera at all—he merely wanted his dramatic poems set to music so that they could be presented legally.

Several months later, Davenant followed *The Firste Dayes Entertainment* with what is regarded as the earliest real English opera, *The Siege of Rhodes,* likewise staged at his private dwelling, Rutland House, *ca.* September 10, 1656. Given without dancing and without the scenic display characteristic of Continental presentations of opera, this miscellaneous effort enlisted the varying talents of five composers, chief among them Matthew Locke, who also sang in the first performances. The response encouraged Davenant to lease a theater for public performances of opera, though getting a license from the blue-nosed regime was a struggle. *The Cruelty of the Spaniards in Peru* and *The History of Sir Francis Drake* were thus produced at the Cockpit, and finally *The Siege of Rhodes* was revived for the same theater. It was doubtless of one of these, staged amid the troubles attending the disintegration of the timid rule of Richard Cromwell, that John Evelyn, under the date of May 5, 1659, entered in his diary: "I went to visit my brother in London and next day to see a new opera, after the Italian way in recitative music and sceanes much inferior to the Italian composure and magnificence: but it was prodigious that in a time of such public consternation such a vanity should be kept up or permitted. I being engaged with company could not decently resist the going to see it though my heart smote me for it."

The restoration of the Stuarts in 1660 reopened the theaters, and English opera ceased to breathe, but did not quite expire. Foreign musicians became the rage under the Francophile

Charles II, though but few operas—and those mostly French—
were heard. It was not until a few months after the resurrection of the national consciousness that accompanied the arrival of William of Orange on English shores that English opera
also revived and, in its lone hour of splendor, threw off its only
masterpiece. At Josias Priest's school for young ladies, in Chel-
sea, probably in September, 1689, was sung *Dido and Aeneas*,
the work of a thirty-year-old musician in the royal service,
Henry Purcell, "the greatest natural genius that the country
has produced, and one of the greatest of any country or period."

Nephew of a man who had sung a leading role in *The Siege
of Rhodes*, and son of another seasoned court musician, this
active, vigorous, worldly pluralist is a baffling figure. The simplest explanation of Purcell's failure to produce, during a life
as long as Mozart's—thirty-six years—the sovereign masterpieces
that might reasonably have been expected from so commanding
a genius is that he was born too early or too late. Possibly he
was a belated Elizabethan: his mastery extended to every phase
and form of the art of music as it had been developed up to
his own time in England, and had he lived in the time of the
great Queen, he might have so participated in its exuberance
and joyous life as to crown the achievements of the school of
Gibbons, Byrd, and Bull. Possibly he was a premature genius
of another sort, looking ahead into the eighteenth century, but
without the glass to see it. Living in an otherwise barren age of
English music, he had to vex himself finding the right garments
to clothe his ideas, and to fritter away his time in doing so.
In this process, he poured out a flood of works (the Purcell
Society edition already runs to twenty-seven folio volumes, and
the end is still far away), but had he been able to draw upon a
living tradition, as Bach and Handel were to do, he would now
be known not only as England's greatest composer, but also as
their peer.

It is more than too bad that this man, who in his profusion
of occasional odes, welcome hymns, and catches showed a lively
awareness of the contemporary scene, should have gone back,
in his single opera, to a classical subject instead of following
the lines of interest opened up in *The Siege of Rhodes* and

Davenant's other librettos. If Purcell had taken Davenant's hint, the reaction against the stultified and stultifying classical libretto might have come a half century before it did, and from a serious rather than a comic quarter. But Purcell took what was handed him. So, to a humdrum, fatuous text by Nahum Tate, noted along with Colley Cibber as the most egregious of the Shakespearean adapters, he composed a bona fide opera, *Dido and Aeneas*. Its three brief acts are crammed with all the complex machinery we are accustomed to find in opera today —dancing, recitative and arias, ensembles, instrumental interludes, and choral numbers. Each of the acts is held together in the framework of a very few persistently used key signatures: Act I, for instance, hovers between C and C minor. In a long act this might be unbearably monotonous, but Purcell's speed and concentration are always such that the effect is one of rightness and inevitability. If any criticism is to be leveled against *Dido and Aeneas* as music, it is that the motion is almost too rapid. In short, Purcell does not give his audience time to relax and savor the swift succession of delights. Fortunately, the finest thing in the opera—Dido's heartbreaking lament, "When I am laid in earth"—comes last: otherwise, the hearer, after this exhausting emotional purge, might resent the immediate irruption of another number, however fine.

Purcell went on to compose a wealth of incidental music for plays, many of them by Dryden, but never again did occasion or libretto come his way to spur him to compose another opera. Aside from being interpolated as a masque into a Grub Street adaptation of *Measure for Measure* in 1700, *Dido and Aeneas* vanished for two centuries and thus had no influence on the course of dramatic music in England. It was the cornerstone laid for a structure that was never reared, for though Purcell influenced Handel, contributing most markedly to that quality of the Saxon's music that we recognize immediately as "English," that influence did not exert itself on the atmosphere of Handel's operas. The peculiar intensity—that unique way of wringing pure music from the emotions—disappeared from England with its author.

Purcell's death in 1695 having removed the one English

genius who, had he desired, might have established indigenous opera on solid foundations, the way was open to an influx of foreigners. As early as Charles II, French and Italian singers had begun coming into the island, where their spectacular vocal prowess was much prized. In 1661, Davenant was already using a *castrato* in *The Siege of Rhodes*, but as he was a bad specimen, the populace did not take to him. The great male soprano, Giovanni Francesco Grossi, called Siface, seems to have introduced the vogue for *castrati*, which grew to such proportions that the English, simultaneously attracted and repelled, tried vainly to stem the current by forcing very high natural tenors to add falsetto notes at the top of their register. These countertenors were but a stopgap. Siface flourished under the Catholic Stuarts, but found England inhospitable after Dutch Protestant William came in. When he left, Purcell commemorated the event by a little harpsichord piece—*Sefauchi's Farewell.*

Other *castrati* were shortly to follow Siface, and meanwhile there appeared in London, in 1692, the first important Italian female singer to invade England, Margherita de l'Épine—she whom H. Sutherland Edwards, in his fascinating study of the phenomenon, was to call the first prima donna. As early as 1703, handbills announcing "positively the last time of her singing on the stage during her stay in England" were being passed out: this serves to date a familiar prima donna-ish frailty, for the signora continued to warble in London for fifteen years more and never left England at all. In 1703, in fact, the best part of her career was ahead of her: two years later, she sang songs before and after the performance of Thomas Clayton's *Arsinoë*, which had a libretto pieced together from an Italian source by Peter Motteux, famous for his pioneering translation, with Urquhart, of Rabelais. As *Arsinoë* was sung in English, De l'Épine had the humiliation of seeing her English-born rival, Mrs. Tofts, carry off honors in the opera itself. Poor stuff, *Arsinoë* succeeded. But Clayton's next opera, *Rosamond,* which boasted a libretto by Addison, failed miserably, dealing a body blow to the struggle to maintain English opera.

The Italians, singers and composers both, were not slow in

seizing the opportunity. While the wretched Clayton reputedly retired to Ireland, and there spread the blessings of opera as written in English, they slowly but surely began to take over the musical stage. Bilingual operas, sung partly in Italian and partly in English, marked an intermediate stage. Finally, in January, 1710, London heard its first uncompromisingly Italian opera—*Almahide*—which brought together a galaxy of brilliant Italian singers, including, besides De l'Épine, the *castrato* Valentini, who had been a contralto until his voice changed, whereupon he became a glorious soprano. Unhappily, the names of the composer and librettist of *Almahide* are not known: what is more important, perhaps, is that this historic opera required the services of two prima donnas and at least two *castrati*. The stage was set for Handel.

And Handel was ready. What might have been the effect on his future activities in England if the first opera with which he was to challenge the already securely entrenched Italian composers had been some trifle of the Clayton sort? Fortunately, the opera that he produced in two weeks under the loving eye of Aaron Hill, a prince of eighteenth-century impresarios, was *Rinaldo*. And *Rinaldo* was a masterpiece, and—furthermore— an Italian masterpiece. The cast that Handel and Hill had assembled for the *première* at the Queen's Theatre, on February 24, 1711, was superb: it included Giuseppe Boschi, leading basso of the age, and the *castrato* Nicolini, whose nightingale tones seemed to have been waiting for exactly the airs Handel had assigned to him. London, on which *Rinaldo* fell like a bombshell full of delights, carried the opera on its whistling lips for many a month, and years later, when Dr. Johann Christoph Pepusch was concocting that marvelous *pasticcio* known as *The Beggar's Opera*, he could not get his hated rival's airs out of his ears, and found them good enough to steal. *Rinaldo* played to sold-out houses fifteen times in five months, and on profits from printing the score John Walsh laid the foundations of his sizable fortune as a music publisher.

Handel led a crowded life as a manufacturer of stage music for so many years that it would be quite as monotonous to chronicle the composition and production of the forty operas he wrote in England as it would be to chronicle the separate transactions of a big businessman. For Handel was a big businessman—a speculator who made and lost fortunes, with a superb nose for what the public could be wheedled into buying. Nothing is more eloquent of his feeling of responsibility to himself as a shrewd dealer and man of substance than his half-amused, half-bitter remark, after the blazing success of Walsh's edition of *Rinaldo*, that Walsh should compose the next opera, and he would publish it. Until 1719, though engaged in a number of musical activities that were of the highest importance to his development, particularly as a writer of oratorios, Handel as an impresario and purveyor of popular operas was jockeying for a position he could not be sure of until he had regularized his relations with the new dynasty. For when Queen Anne died childless after a tragic round of painful childbearing, her successor was that Elector Georg of Hanover whom Handel had, in a sense, deserted for the attractions and fat profits of London. As George I, for all his objectionable qualities, loved music, he could not long remain piqued. So, after perfunctory pouting, he showed up at a Handel performance, and came again and again. All was forgiven.

In 1719, therefore, it was the most natural thing in the world for the King to suggest his good friend Handel when the parvenu but all-powerful Duke of Newcastle and some of his friends were seeking a general director for an opera company to be called, by George's permission, the Royal Academy of Music. Only a year before the bursting of the South Sea Bubble, selling £50,000 worth of shares in the Royal Academy was an easy matter, especially when the King led the list of subscribers with £1000. Lavishness keynoted the venture. Handel went to the Continent to secure singers, not only hiring the soprano Margherita Durastanti and the *castrato* Senesino, but also rehiring Boschi, who had shone so splendidly in *Rinaldo*.

In their desire to be magnificent, the directors of the Royal Academy sowed the seeds of future discord by engaging the services of what they called "associate composers," among them Giovanni Battista Buononcini. This gifted, but shady, haughty, and addlepated Italian, many years Handel's senior, and with notable successes in his past, willingly acceded to the wishes of a group of dissidents in the Academy itself to cast Handel from his pedestal, and foolishly set himself up as Handel's rival. When the storm finally broke, the King was supporting his compatriot, and the great Duke of Marlborough, who was all but tone-deaf, Buononcini.

Radamisto, the first Handel opera given under the auspices of the Royal Academy, opened without benefit of stellar cast* and without the scandal of an overt schism in the ranks of the shareholders. Yet, it was a sensation, running from April 27, 1720, until June 25. So persistent was its success that Continental musicians soon heard of it, and the very next year, Handel's old friend and enemy Mattheson staged it at Hamburg under the name of *Zenobia,* after its heroine. In England, Handel's star was never higher, and momentarily the opposition felt dashed. But in the fall of 1720, Buononcini's *Astarto,* already a favorite in Italy, was staged for Senesino's London debut, and all but equaled the success of *Radamisto.*

The battle lines were drawn: the shareholders divided into two camps. Even the most sanguine Handelians could not hope for easy victory. The dramatically inclined suggested a contest between the rival composers, decision to be awarded to him who wrote the finer act of a three-act opera, the opening act of which—doubtless to square things all around—was assigned to a complete nonentity. Handel's contribution to *Muzio Scevola* won him a bootless victory: the adherents of Buononcini, who were using Handel as a substitute target in their rage against the English-hating German monarch, would not acknowledge defeat in a fair fight.

The struggle between the alien lords of English opera seesawed back and forth for seven years, during which polite—and sometimes not so polite—factionalism raged. And for a time it actually seemed that Buononcini might win out: his light, sensuously tuneful operas proved irresistible to a large section of high society. In an attempt to strengthen his hand, Handel kept importing more and more vocal stars, until London became a vast cage of singing birds. First, there was Se-

* His stars, then under contract at Dresden, could not appear the first season.

nesino, with whom the future Empress Maria Theresa had deigned to sing duets: his incredible roulades, however, did not save the melodious *Floridante*, which Handel had picked as a winner in 1721. When Buononcini replied to *Floridante* with two hits, Handel was in despair. He had the further humiliation of seeing his rival, now at the top of his fame, asked to compose music for Marlborough's funeral. Bitterness made him rash: he had heard of Francesca Cuzzoni, a young Italian contralto who was then the wonder of Venice, and, sound unheard, sent her an offer of the unbelievable sum of £2000 a year. Cuzzoni came, ugly, intractable, every pound a prima donna. Handel tamed her so well that she re-established her master overnight by a magnificent performance at the *première* of *Ottone*, on January 12, 1723. Others in the cast were Boschi and Gaetan Berenstadt, both eminent bassos, Senesino, and the English favorite, Anastasia Robinson. So mortified was the last by the audience's marked preference for Cuzzoni that she retired forthwith and became a countess.*

For a time, Senesino and Cuzzoni were enough. Buononcini's strength was ebbing, and Handel fortified his position by composing two excellent scores, the first, *Giulio Cesare*, to an absurd rigmarole by Nicolo Francesco Haym. The second, *Tamerlano*, though provided with an equally harebrained pseudo-historical libretto by the same favorite collaborator, built up to a massive climax musically and an unusually intense one emotionally. Handel had begun to think out loud about his oratorio style. It was a good thing for him that he was doing so, for his audiences were beginning to tire of Italian opera, whether in Buononcini's light and lascivious manner or invigorated by Handel's buoyant masculinity and tolerance of dignified pathos. Also, the managing shareholders of the Royal Academy of Music, with their distinguished genius for spending the profits, were terrified at empty seats. Instead of cutting their budgets, these scatterbrained lords did precisely the opposite: they sent for Faustina Bordoni, called by her enchanted

* Although for a long time an unacknowledged one, as her husband, Charles Mordaunt, Earl of Peterborough, was a snob. He loved her, however, in his fashion, and once publicly flogged Senesino for hurling coarse words at Anastasia.

countrymen *la nuova sirena*. One of the most appealing and attractive figures of the entire musical stage, this lovely woman put a high price on her great abilities. Like Cuzzoni, she asked £2000 a year, and received it.

With superb showmanship, and as if daring the fire of the gods, Handel used both Bordoni and Cuzzoni in his next opera, *Alessandro,* carefully composing roles of equal importance and display for each. The divas were already rivals, having made their debuts together in Venice seven years before. Fireworks were expected (probably hoped for) at once, but for a time they contented themselves with singing gloriously to packed houses and acting toward one another with the cold decorum of Latins struggling to repress themselves. Then, suddenly, after the season had closed, hell broke loose. The ladies' followers began it, literally by wearing party emblems—possibly a Cuzzoni scarf, possibly a Bordoni riband. Soon a "Cuzzoni" and a "Faustina" were entered in the Newmarket races. By the middle of 1727, the battle had become so hot that the protagonists themselves joined in, spitting out rather than singing duets with each other. On the night of June 6, the opera (as though anyone cared) was a last feeble effort by Buononcini. A fight broke out in the pit and rapidly spread to the stage. It was climaxed, to everyone's joyful relief, when Faustina and Cuzzoni flew at each other and began pulling each other's hair out by the roots.

The Royal Academy of Music lasted but a year more. Handel, who had lately become a loyal subject of Great Britain, tried, in *Riccardo primo*, to woo his public with a patriotic theme. But even Faustina, Cuzzoni, and Senesino could not make it stomach an Italian-singing Richard the Lion-Hearted. And now "the rival queens," as Colley Cibber, the laureate, called them, departed. The Londoners, left with only music, did not like it. The ever-resourceful Handel then wrote to the young Roman poet Metastasio, already the acknowledged prince of librettists, and besought a lifesaver from him. Handel received a workmanlike accumulation of historical data about Cyrus the Great, which he incontinently turned over to Haym, who butchered it. The resulting collaboration, *Siroë,* was in rehearsal when, on January 29, 1728, London went to the first performance of *The Beggar's Opera*. The fate of the Royal Academy was sealed: it closed its useless doors in June.

The men who contrived *The Beggar's Opera* were cleverer than they knew. John Gay, its librettist, was a spoiled and witty party poet with a talent for broad, if not leering, salaciousness. Dr. Johann Christoph Pepusch, a transplanted Berlin theorist and authority on old music, had an equally lively talent for appropriating any melodies that happened to be lying about, whether folk tunes or scraps of Purcell and Handel. *The Beggar's Opera* both satirized the government of Sir Robert Walpole and parodied Italian opera, for the very excellent reasons that Gay had a grudge against the Whigs, while Pepusch, whom Handel had supplanted as private musician to the extravagant Duke of Chandos, wanted to get even with his fellow German. They offered their exhilarating novelty at the psychological moment: London was sick to death of assorted myths and historical snippets from Greece and Rome, not to mention more outlandish places; it was bored with the stiff attitudes and run-of-the-mill fustian of classical characters spouting their emotions in a foreign jargon. So Gay, taking a flimsy but not incredible tale, and peopling it with an unsavory crew of derelicts, footpads, and ladies and gentlemen of the highway who might have stepped from *The Rake's Progress*, contrived knowingly spiced dialogue interspersed with lyrics of a saucy and scurrilous nature. Pepusch adapted to these naughty trifles various ballad tunes, not only of English, but also of Irish, French, and Italian provenance: his sole original contribution was an overture.

Although only an analyst with a blind *parti pris* could find in *The Beggar's Opera* a unity much superior to that of a typical Handel stage piece, its sprightly tempo and easy comprehensibility, plus the obvious lilt of its tunes, made it an instant and conquering success. During the first season, it ran for sixty-two or -three nights, and Gay boasted, after its thirty-sixth performance, that he had already pocketed about £800 in profits (his manager made five times that in the same period). Polly, the heroine of the piece, made the fortune of Lavinia

Fenton, who created the role: while still on the stage, she became the mistress of Charles Paulet, Duke of Bolton; she retired from it to become his wife, and eventually to inherit his
vast estate. Soon *The Beggar's Opera* overran the British Isles.
Even the people of Minorca heard it—it seems unlikely that
they understood more of it than the Londoners did of Italian
opera. Within twenty-five years, it was sung in Paris and New
York: in the latter place, it preceded Italian opera by almost
half a century.

The Beggar's Opera has been revived often, notably in London
in 1920, when Sir Nigel Playfair produced it with the tunes orchestrated by Frederic Austin, and with *décor* and costumes by
Claud Lovat Fraser. This perfect rehabilitation made the names of
Gay and Pepusch even fresher in the twentieth century than they
had been in their own lifetime: before starting on a long tour,
The Beggar's Opera, in Playfair's version, ran at the Lyric, Ham-
mersmith, for two years and a half. A German adaptation by Bert
Brecht, rewritten to satirize (*à la* Karl Marx) modern Walpoles and
their dupes, was set to jazz music by Kurt Weill as *Die Dreigroschenoper*. Dr. Percy A. Scholes, the amusing and acidulous backbone of the Oxford University Press musical list, has called the
Brecht-Weill version "a gross travesty of the original," but it went
over in London nevertheless. Finally, G. W. Pabst, the eminent
German cinematographer, made from *Die Dreigroschenoper* one of
the first—and best—*avant-garde* movies. More than two hundred
years after its *première*, it is safe to predict a long and various
future for *The Beggar's Opera*, whether pure, adulterated, or entirely metamorphosed.

Handel, who after the failure of the Academy went into
partnership with John James Heidegger, an uncomely dwarf
known as "the Swiss Count," evidently interpreted the success
of *The Beggar's Opera* as a passing craze. True, women of
fashion carried its ballads on their fans, or obstructed their
living quarters with "Polly" or "Macheath" screens; but had
not they acted the same when his two rival canaries were dividing London? Was there not, for instance, the "Cuzzoni"
dress of brown and silver that had made the success of his
Rodelinda, and had given fashionable London dressmakers a

new color scheme? Yes, definitely, *The Beggar's Opera* was a fad. So, perhaps, did Handel rationalize as he doggedly set about concocting his twenty-fifth Italian opera. That he saw no *mene, mene,* is proved by the fact that he took no pains with music or libretto, though he introduced a singer of surpassing ugliness: Anna Maria Strada, known as "the Pig." During late 1730, by reimporting Senesino, and counting on the affection of London for some of his old scores, Handel managed once more to crowd the theater night after night. *Poro,* a new opera with a ripe Oriental book by Metastasio, was wildly acclaimed in 1731. Critics called it Handel's greatest work, and the presses of Walsh groaned to supply the demand for the airs Senesino had made fashionable.

Handel was again on top. Rather sentimentally, he revived his first London opera, *Rinaldo,* and then another blow fell. A heat wave wilted London and Handel's popularity. When it had subsided, his audiences were nowhere, and though he continued to compose Italian operas for ten years more— eighteen of them, in fact—he seems to have realized at last that he could never regain his pre-eminence unless he got another string to his bow. After 1731, Handel, magnificently revising an early effort as *Esther,* inaugurated his great series of oratorios. By these works in their native tongue he was to become the musical god of the English people.

Handel's last ten years as an operatic composer were full of drama and excitement. The opposition to him now crystallized in a group known unofficially as the "Opera of the Nobility." Semipolitical in character, it ranged itself under the banner of the rebellious Frederick, Prince of Wales, and the young Duke of Marlborough. It secured as its official composer the Neapolitan Niccolò Porpora, almost exactly Handel's contemporary, a man of talent and definite determination. Weaning away Cuzzoni and Senesino from Handel's company was congenial work for the sly Italian, but this *coup* merely divided the meager audiences between the two companies. It was not until he succeeded in hiring the greatest *castrato* of them all, Carlo Broschi, called Farinelli, that Porpora began to fill his theater. The golden-voiced soprano burst on London in December, 1734, in the *Artaserse* of Johann Adolf Hasse, which he had composed for Faustina Bordoni, who had become his wife in 1730. While that performance was notable for signing, once again, a death warrant for Handel's operatic career, it was even more notable for one of those too rare gestures of generous appreciation from one singer to another: after Farinelli had finished his first air, the veteran Senesino, who was also singing that night, strode over to his junior rival and impulsively embraced him.

Although the excellence of performers who lived before the days of gramophone records must be taken on trust, the fact that tradition is almost unanimous in calling Farinelli the first of singers is strong evidence of his surpassing merit. Reputedly of noble birth, he was, it is said, a *castrato* by accident and not by design; injured grievously while out riding, he had to submit to the effeminizing operation, or die. Equally, it happened that the induced voice became the most beautiful ever heard—after laborious training by Porpora and other singing masters. When Farinelli went to London in 1734, this handsome and intelligent man had already chalked up extraordinary triumphs in Italy and Austria, and for three years he had London in his pocket. When even his powers could no longer shore up Italian opera there, he left for France, where Louis XV presented him with a portrait framed in diamonds.

Traveling in royal style, Farinelli then proceeded into Spain, no doubt intending merely to get homage for his voice at the court before returning to the scenes of his earlier successes. He remained in Madrid a quarter of a century: Philip V, the melancholic Bourbon who dragged out a painful existence under the thumb of a domineering wife, was enchanted by his exotic guest and would not let him go. For ten years, at an annual stipend of fifty thousand francs, this strange David solaced the harmless Saul with a program of soporific monotony—a nightly program that never varied. Among the three (or perhaps four) songs Farinelli sang some thirty-five hundred times to the demented monarch were two from that very opera by Hasse with which he had first dazzled London.

When Philip died, and Ferdinand VI reigned in his stead,

Farinelli became more powerful through the magic of his voice and even took a hand in ruling the country. But when Ferdinand died, and his half-brother Charles came to the throne, Farinelli was hustled out of Spain.* The year was 1759, and the singer was fifty-four. He was too old to return to the stage, but he carried into retirement a vast fortune shrewdly amassed during his many years as popular and court favorite. Charles III was not vindictive: he not only allowed the erstwhile favorite to carry his gold pieces away with him, but also continued his salary, stipulating only that he was to reside beyond the Spanish dominions. Although Farinelli probably might have preferred to settle in his native Naples, he had, instead, to choose Bologna, where he passed the remaining twenty-three years of his life in luxurious ease. Dr. Charles Burney, the inquisitive and indefatigable father of the author of *Evelina*, visited him there in 1771, and brought away a glowing account of the man who, almost forty years earlier, had temporarily ruined Handel.

But only temporarily. The career of Handel shows a most amazing vigor and buoyancy—qualities that can be recognized again and again in his music—refusing to admit that disaster really mattered. It is true that after the catastrophe of 1737 (which, it must be remembered, was coincident with bodily ills of terrible severity) Handel wrote only six more operas, though he lived twenty-two years longer. But among those six was his sole essay in the comic—*Serse,* a work of great ingenuity, distinction, and charm, which with a little trouble could easily be revived today. And *Serse* contains unquestionably the most famous (though not necessarily the finest) of all Handel's operatic airs, the all too immortal *"Ombra mai fù,"* erroneously called the "Largo." The last of the six—*Deidamia*—was produced in 1741. But 1741 was more memorable in the history of music for another reason, for in that year, doubtless,

---

* Daniel-François-Esprit Auber wrote, in *Le Part du diable, ou Carlo Broschi* (1843), a rather charming semicomic opera about the happier part of Farinelli's Spanish adventure. There being no male soprano available in 1843, Auber gave the role of the great *castrato* to a woman. Wagner's friend Hermann Zumpe, and the popular Spanish composer of light operas, Tomás Bretón, composed operas on the same theme.

Handel was beginning to shape the vast fabric that has set his name alongside that of Bach—*Messiah*.

And it is as the creator of *Messiah, Israel in Egypt,* and a few other oratorios that Handel remains known as a composer for the stage. The best of the oratorios are definitely more dramatic than almost any of Handel's operas; some of them, and in particular *Semele,* have been performed as operas with great effect. Part of the superior dramatic impact of the oratorios lies not so much in the bar-by-bar excellence of the music itself as in the mighty surge of the great choruses, which are almost never used in the operas, which, moreover, neglect concerted numbers almost entirely. Writing for the lay stage, Handel was hampered by traditions of usage and construction which, by the beginning of the eighteenth century, had been so rigorously codified that only violent revolution could have freed the frozen dramatic element. Handel was no revolutionist; he took opera as he found it and left it in exactly the same state. Even the best Handel opera is but a concert of occasionally lovely airs and heroic or pathetic recitatives, interspersed with a much larger number of machine-made airs and recitatives. There is, in short, a kind of thoughtlessness, insouciance even, about the way this prodigal manufacturer of music strings his good, bad, and fair-to-middling numbers on the threads of a stilted, rambling, and altogether inconsequential libretto.*

Handel seems to have regarded an opera much as a modern tunesmith regards a musical comedy: something into which a number may be injected without much consideration of its environment, but with a great deal of consideration for the star who must have it there—and who will put it over. Handel was sure of his Senesinos and Cuzzonis and Broschis, even after they could no longer put his operas over merely by singing his

* The poor librettist was not wholly to blame. He might hit upon a powerful theme (like that of *Rinaldo*). He might have a poetic gift (like Metastasio). But the obligation to provide set arias for each of the principal singers at set points in each act, to end his story happily with all the living principals joining in a so-called "chorus" at the close of the last act, and to conform to any number of other laws was as stifling to him as to the composer. Add to these rules of operatic dramaturgy the general literary conventions of the times themselves—foppishness, extravagance, exalted diction, plumed heroics, strained classicism—and it is no wonder that even the best librettos Handel and the lesser composers of the day had to put up with strike us as spineless verbiage.

songs superbly. He asked himself no questions, even when whole audiences thinned away, deserting to Gay and Pepusch. He could not know that *The Beggar's Opera* was the precursor of his adopted land's only sound indigenous opera—that light, comic, broadly mocking strain which was to culminate in the delicious flummery of Gilbert and Sullivan.

Handel operas are occasionally revived today. Dr. Oskar Hagen, the distinguished historian of art, had produced nine of them at Göttingen when the First World War broke out and cut short his ambitious project of resurrecting them all. In the United States, the scholarly Werner Josten has staged several of them at Smith College with critical *réclame*. Yet, it seems unlikely that any of the Handel operas will be banishing Gluck's *Orfeo ed Euridice* from its honored place as the oldest opera in the standard repertoire. Quite apart from the objections already named, these operas, one and all, are too difficult for the modern vocalist: they require the lost supernal agility that seems to have died out with the last *castrato* along about the middle of the nineteenth century. It is a strange and tragic fact that a very large part of the total output of one of the very greatest of composers is likely to remain almost totally inaccessible.

Chapter IV

The French Way: Part One

THE sudden creation of a national opera that is instantly
recognizable as such is a phenomenon extraordinarily rare
in the history of music. National styles have usually evolved
slowly, but in France the Gallic flavor was at once evident.
One man, and he an Italian, seeming to disdain the models of
his native land, brought forth as if by impulse an intensely
French product that was substantially without ancestry. This
genius was Jean-Baptiste Lully, born in Florence in 1632.

Paris, which in the early seventeenth century was as much
the artistic capital of France as it is today, was exposed to
Italian opera almost as soon as was Florence itself. Powerful
propagandists for *le musiche nuove* presented themselves at the
court of Henri IV during the first decade of the century, evidently without lasting results. Although Caccini himself journeyed thither, it does not seem probable that a single opera
was produced. While a flourishing, quickly popular art was
spreading over Italy like a genial plague, France sang chansons
or cultivated ballet, which Catherine de' Medici had made
fashionable. Under the later Valois and Henri IV, ballets of
sumptuous magnificence crowded out almost all other court
entertainments. Under Louis XIII, the rage for dancing persisted. During the minority of Louis XIV, when the Italian
Mazarin was ruling France, the court heard its first opera,
doubtless because the chief minister, sincerely desirous of
championing amenities and luxuries from Italy, also wished,
for political reasons, to surround himself with Italians. With
a keen understanding of the role of entertainment in keeping
the masters of a people subdued, the wily cardinal imported an
opera company whole.

Orfeo, by the now utterly obscure Luigi Rossi (an unwearied
fashioner of cantatas), was produced in France in 1647. Possibly because of the superb performance of the Italian company under Rossi's direction, *Orfeo* has been called, with some

inexactness, the first opera given there. Actually, it had at least two, possibly three, predecessors. Despite Mazarin's anxiety to popularize the new art (he had a French analysis of the libretto of *Orfeo* distributed before the performance), the lords and ladies reacted coldly. Cavalli's *Serse*, produced at the Louvre in 1660 during the wedding fetes of Louis XIV and Maria Theresa of Spain, fared somewhat better, though the reception given to the Servite father who sang the role of Queen Amestris was far from flattering—he was a *castrato*, and the French did not like him. However, Cavalli was asked back, two years later, to help celebrate the Peace of the Pyrenees: this time he staged his masterpiece, *Ercole amante*. Even this admirable work did not establish opera in Italian, and at that date it would not have been unreasonable to predict that unless a French twist was given to it, the art would survive in France only as an occasional plaything of the court.

Less reasonable to predict would have been that the man to give opera a French twist was the pushing young Italian who had been commissioned to introduce into both *Serse* and *Ercole amante* some of his popular dance tunes. These commissions to a man who had been Louis' friend when he was still a crowned puppet under Mazarin's thumb were signs that the Sun King was rising and would shed his rays over a very French France. *Ercole amante* was a compatriot's epitaph on Mazarin, who had just died: Lully's dances in *Ercole* were the future. For a dozen years this brilliant, rough, and unscrupulous *compositeur du roi*, risen from an underscullion's greasy tasks to the domination of music in France, forged and tempered the instruments of his art. In 1664, the year of his perfectly attested marriage (the contract was witnessed by Louis XIV, Maria Theresa, and the Queen Mother, Anne of Austria), he began a happy collaboration with Molière, which just missed producing the first French opera, but which did father such masterpieces as *Le Mariage forcé*, *Le Bourgeois Gentilhomme*, and *Pourceaugnac*, with apt and sprightly incidental music. Racine also collaborated with Lully.

In 1671, the Molière-Lully team sired a work that was so close to full-fledged opera that only a miracle of omission kept

it in the category of *comédies-ballets*. So the honor of composing the first French opera went, through sheer accident, to a
team of well-known hacks, the poet Pierre Perrin and the
tunesmith Robert Cambert. Their pleasantly melodious five-
act pastoral—*Pomone*—was successfully produced in March,
1671. Cambert followed with another opera, equally well received, and the envious Lully intrigued to such effect that
within a year Cambert had to flee into England, where he was
eventually murdered by his valet.

Lully, like Louis, now reigned alone, and he celebrated his
coup d'état by joining forces with Philippe Quinault, a dramatic poet of considerable talent, if not actual genius. The
pair's first effort was a plotless pastoral, whose success augured
well for further collaboration. They therefore tried something
more ambitious and unified, and thus created the first of the
so-called *tragédies en musique*—*Cadmus et Hermione,* staged
on April 27, 1673. This tragic opera was the first of a series of
fifteen such (twelve of them with books by Quinault), all admirable in proportion, careful in workmanship, and nice in
declamation. While we are unlikely to hear the statement
proved by performance, the collaboration of Lully and Quinault may be compared in effectiveness with those of Gluck
and Calzabigi, Mozart and Da Ponte, Verdi and Boïto, and
Wagner and Wagner. Quinault received 4000 livres a year for
his share of the work. Lully apparently paid himself more
lavishly: dying in 1687, he left, in addition to four substantial
pieces of city property, a fortune estimated at 342,000 livres.

Lully was a voluminous workman: besides the fifteen operas
that he wrote in fourteen years, ballets, pastorals, dances, songs,
instrumental pieces of many kinds, and church music were
furnished to his avid patrons, at whose head stood the most
insatiable of them all—the generally unmusical Louis XIV,
who nevertheless composed pretty trifles, and who desperately
wanted to be amused and praised. The King, self-conscious,
vainglorious architect of a new France, applauded *Cadmus et
Hermione* with such obvious pleasure that Lully, an observant
courtier, realized that he had hit upon a workable formula. He
never found a reason for changing it, for it was already a very

French thing. Tailor-made, highly conventionalized, almost intemperately artificial, yet supremely correct, it naturally appealed to a monarch and a court who considered the grandly dull façades of Versailles the height of architectural perfection. When Lully's *Alceste* was staged in 1674, Louis asserted that he would hear it every day if he was in Paris.

Like every important institution that flourished in the France of the *grand siècle*, opera was a spectacle. Sumptuous costumes, elaborate *décors*, and incredibly ingenious and complex stage machines that were like vastly magnified clockwork toys made even the most severe *tragédie* essentially a visual delight. *Tableaux* and *divertissements*, for all the world like costly side shows, ministered to momentarily flagging appetites. But these attractions paled beside the incidental ballets, for which Lully often saved his finest effects. Ballet had acquired such popularity among the nobility during its first century of existence in France that it was a shrewd stroke of business on Lully's part to introduce it into his operas. Once there, be it noted, it stayed—not only in the native products, but also in imported operas whether or not their composers had provided for one in the original design (Wagner's dilemma over the Paris production of *Tannhäuser* is a most flagrant example of this French determinism). Lully, armed with a bottomless budget and a tradition of costliness,* was prepared to spend any amount of money and inject any innovation necessary to make his ballets the wonder of the times. He was the first to make use of trained male ballet dancers, though occasionally, as in days past, the King himself and some of the great lords eagerly deigned to impersonate Jupiter and Apollo and their separate trains.

Because Lully's operas were given at court, they were lavishly mounted, but this circumstance of production must not be confused with their essential structure and musical character. If submitted to analysis, these entities prove, under their costly swathe of superficialities, to be surprisingly close relatives of the early Florentine operas. They begin, to be sure, with a

---

* The *Ballet comique de la reyne*, staged at the wedding, in 1581, of Henri III's mignon, Anne de Joyeuse, to Mlle de Vaudémont, the Queen's sister, cost 3,500,000 francs.

so-called "French overture" invented by Lully himself; it was in two, sometimes three, sections—slow, quick and fugal, slow. Equally unfamiliar to Peri and Caccini would have been the accompanied recitatives which are among the strongest dramatic elements of a Lully score. Strangest of all, no doubt, would have been the vigorous and lofty choruses, sometimes as mighty as those of Handel. But the Florentines would quite have understood their descendant's approach to the central problem of reconciling the dramatic and the musical: Lully evidently viewed his task as the heightening and underscoring of a poetic text. He fitted the music to the words, and did not torture the words to fit the music. Nor was he a vocalist's pander. Italian-born though he was, Lully understood the subtlest problems of French prosody, treating its rich, tricky assonances with positive reverence, and evolving an admirable style of French declamation that is at once musical and dramatically eloquent. Yet he was no doctrinaire, and was bound by no philosophy of opera: his frequent interpolations of purely instrumental snatches, irrelevant except as sheer irruptions of beauty, prove that he let himself go whenever he felt like it.

Writing in *The Spectator*, in 1711, Addison, after praising Lully for fitting his music to the French language, continues:

> The Chorus in which that Opera abounds, gives the Parterre frequent Opportunities of joining in Consort with the Stage. This Inclination of the Audience to Sing along with the Actors, so prevails with them, that I have sometimes known the Performer on the Stage to do no more in a Celebrated Song, than the Clerk of a Parish Church, who serves only to raise the Psalm, and is afterwards drown'd in the Musick of the Congregation. Every Actor that comes on the Stage is a Beau. The Queens and Heroines are so Painted, that they appear as Ruddy and Cherry-cheek'd as Milk-maids. The Shepherds are all Embroider'd, and acquit themselves in a Ball better than our *English* Dancing-Masters. I have seen a couple of Rivers appear in red stockings; and *Alpheus*, instead of having his head covered with Sedge and Bull-Rushes, making Love in a fair full-bottomed Perriwig, and a Plume of Feathers; but with a Voice so full of Shakes and Quavers that I should have

thought the Murmurs of a Country Brook the much more agreeable Musick.

Lully's talent was protean, expressive of humor, heroism, and pathos. Yet, his instrumentation was not always the most inspired or even the most nearly correct—indeed, it was often labored and poor, partly because in this department of his art he was something of an experimentalist. Some of the products of his laboratory were deliciously absurd: once, to suggest the rocking of Charon's boat, he used the identical rhythm and counterpoint he had previously used in describing the hero's wrath in *Roland* (1685), which he considered his best opera. But Louis XIV, who listened suspiciously to sprightly melodies and brilliant passages (unless they happened to be the rollicking military marches in which Lully was surpassing), liked what his Italian favorite wrought for him. Which explains much concerning both Lully's good qualities and his defects. . . . Particularly does it explain the empty grandeur of some of his airs. Magniloquence is the blight on acres of Lully, but what is good is very, very good. It has style, elevation, character, sometimes real dramatic expressiveness. We do not demean the age of Boileau and Molière by calling it also the age of Lully.

Rameau, the next great composer of the French school of opera, was but four years old when Louis XIV's *maître de musique* died prematurely from the effects of striking his foot sharply with his long, wandlike baton while conducting a *Te Deum* to celebrate the King's recovery from an illness. As Rameau did not write his first important opera until he was fifty years old, there was a considerable interval during which the influence of Lully persisted, coloring the work of the lesser men of that transition. Although the names of these minor composers—Campra, Montéclair, Destouches—are almost unknown today, some of them were in themselves interesting, and produced music of mild charm. As the rage for ballet went on unabated, they saved some of their best melodies and dance tunes for that genre. An amusing incident, showing clearly that the art of deifying kings did not pass with the Grand Monarque, is connected with the public performance of Destouches' ingenious ballet, *Les Éléments*. When it was first given at Versailles, the young Louis XV danced in it, and was routinely complimented by various characters of the ensemble. When the ballet was staged in Paris, however, a bust of the King had to do service for his role: quite as fulsome compliments were addressed to this immobile dancer.

Mythology and the old romances still furnished these interim composers with most of their stories, but occasionally a Biblical theme was selected. Montéclair, whose music is not without wit, had great success with the lugubrious story of Jephtha, that rather foolhardy judge of Israel who, having promised to sacrifice to Jehovah, in return for victory over the Ammonites, "whatsoever cometh forth of the doors of my house to meet me," was greeted by his only child. Rameau, at the time of *Jephté's* success a middle-aged man still struggling for recognition, had once tried his own hand at a sacred subject. His choice was Samson, around whom Handel was to build one of the most impressive of his oratorios, but who was never the subject of a popular opera until Saint-Saëns thought of putting the emphasis on the enchantress Delilah.* Rameau's reading of the long-tressed Hebrew hero never reached the stage: its performance was interdicted at the last moment, apparently because it was feared that the libretto, by a rising publicist named Voltaire, might give offense to the religious.

It is perhaps typical of a professional organist like Rameau to try to storm the portals of the Académie Royale de Musique (predecessor of the Opéra), admission to which was essential for a profitable career as an operatic composer, with a Bible story. He soon saw that he was mistaken, and hired the Abbé Pellegrin, known as the *curé de l'opéra*, to sift the good old reliable subject matter of Racine's *théâtre* for a libretto likely to be acceptable to the authorities. Pellegrin chose the fairly threadbare story of Phaedra and Hippolytus, and extracted a promise from Rameau to pay him five hundred livres if *Hippolyte et Aricie* failed.† At rehearsal, however, he was so delighted

---

* Even *Samson et Dalila* was originally written as an oratorio.

† We do not know what the Abbé was to receive if the opera succeeded, but unless this was stipulated, the arrangement was one of the most quixotic in history, and struck at the very root of the law of contract.

with the music that he impulsively tore up the bond at the end
of the first act.

The first performance of *Hippolyte et Aricie*, at the Académie, on October 1, 1733, was a success, despite the fact that a
critical, almost savage opposition broke into full cry at once.
During the four years that elapsed between *Hippolyte* and the
première of Rameau's overwhelmingly popular masterpiece,
Castor et Pollux, in 1737, his colleagues and a very large
section of the public directed against him the most poisonous
shafts, usually in the name of tradition and Lully. This was an
ironical situation for the man who was to become the champion
of French music, but it is understandable. Before coming to
the operatic stage, Rameau had been an outsider—a mere
theoretician whose best jobs had been in the organ lofts of
provincial cathedrals. In short, he did not rate: his own transformation into the very symbol of *la musique française* was
far in the future, though Campra had perhaps shown in which
direction the wind would blow when, long before the days of
Rameau's canonization as the patron saint of French music, he
remarked that *Hippolyte et Aricie* had enough stuff in it for
ten operas and that its composer would someday outshine all
his contemporaries.

That peripatetic historian of music, Charles Burney, writing
an exact quarter century after the death of Rameau, gave a detailed description of *Castor et Pollux*, "long regarded in France
as the masterpiece of this composer":

> The overture is the best of this author, upon Lulli's plan.
> The opening symphony is beautiful; but why the same melody
> was not applied, in the same measure, to the poetry, I know
> not, unless the versification required a change of time; but, in
> that case, why write the symphony on a subject that would
> not suit the words? But those eternal changes in the measure,
> which teaze and disappoint the ear of all that are used to
> other Music, is general in serious French operas, and seem as
> much the fault of the poet as musician. It is, however, won-
> derful, that this defect was not sooner discovered. The over-
> charged tenderness of Rameau's Music appears in all his slow
> movements, which are in one style, and generally in triple time.

This master perpetually discovers himself to be a great harmonist; but inured to a bad taste and style of composition, as well as to bad singing, he has only augmented the defects of his predecessors, and rendered what was rude and clumsy in Lulli, still more offensive, by endeavours at sweetness or high seasoning. The appoggiaturas, or leaning notes, being so frequently incorporated in the harmony, renders it crude, and the hanging on every note, as if unwilling to relinquish it, checks and impedes the motion of the air, and gives it a slow and languid effect, however likely the theme on which it is composed. Every passage in such a melody resembles a French heroic verse:

"Each is an *Alexandrine*, through the song,
That like a wounded snake, drags its slow length along."

The opening of the second act: *Que tout gemisse,* is very fine, and the pathos well applied; but the subsequent air, which is cast in an admirable mould, is spoiled by frequent and unnecessary changes of measure; and yet in spite of these defects, and the vocal outrages of Mademoiselle Arnould,* I was more pleased and affected by this scene, than any other I ever heard at the French serious opera. The march, which has few appoggiaturas in it, is like other Christian Music.

The *prélude tendre,* at the opening of the third act, abounds with too many of these drags, which being equally harsh to the ear and injurious to the pulsation, seem to prevent the performer from ever falling on his feet; and bar eleventh, the chord of the superfluous fifth, which makes all nature shudder, except our Gallic neighbours, is here continued so long that it distorts the countenance of every other hearer, like *hiera picra.* The major minuet, page 121, after so long and tiresome a minority, is rich in harmony and graceful in melody. The voice is worse used by the composer than the most insignificant instrument. For after several symphonies that are extremely promising, and the ear has been made to expect a continuation of the prefatory strain, nothing is given to the vocal part but broken accents and dislocated measures. In the *chaconne,* which is admirable, the measure is well marked and well accented. . . . More genius and invention appear in the dances of Rameau than elsewhere, because in them, there is a necessity for motion, measure, and symmetry of phrase. And it may

* See page 73.

with truth be said, that nothing in Lulli's operas was imitated or adopted by the rest of Europe, but the style of his overtures, or in Rameau's, but the dances.

Not only is this an interesting bit of contemporary spectator criticism, but it is also an object lesson for music critics who are conscientious about their task. Those strictures that are Burney's prejudices against novelties or departures from his own rigorous ideas sound today merely irrelevant and old-fogyish. But when the fussy Doctor tested things by universal principles, his native sharpness led him to opinions that are as valid today as when he wrote them. The harmonic and rhythmic strangenesses that offended Burney are Rameau's chief claim to fame. From a purely musical point of view, he was a sorely needed innovator, both theoretically and in practice. As Burney declares, the instrumental sections are the best parts of Rameau's operas: he wrote awkwardly for the voice, but often inspiredly for instruments, introducing new ones and searching out new secrets of orchestral color. In his overtures he not only foreshadowed the romantic program overture of almost symphonic scope that Berlioz was to bring to maturity, but he also more clearly defined the sonata tendency that has characterized the symphony from that day to this. His operas, as such, are not very good, and he made no effort to change the form. In short, Rameau was not a great composer of operas, but a great composer who wrote operas.

This man, who completed his first successful opera when he was fifty, was still writing for the stage when he was nearly eighty. He had finally achieved a brilliant position, almost as favored by Louis *le bien-aimé* as Lully had been by Louis *le grand*, but without stilling vicious tongues. He had merely exchanged one set of enemies for another. Starting out as a reputed enemy of the national school as represented by the worshipers of Lully, he ended by being a French national school of his own, quite as venerated as Lully had ever been.

In 1752, a troupe of Italian comic singers arrived in Paris to help lighten a musical season that had got off to a bad start with a deadly fiasco by Destouches. These lively artists, known

A Performance of Lully's Alceste *at Versailles, 1674, after a contemporary print*

in France as *les bouffons*, staged Pergolesi's *La Serva Padrona*
with such thumping success that the old stand-bys of the
Académie Royale, who wrote almost nothing but *opera seria*
in French, found their position threatened. The situation became doubly serious when parties began to range themselves
under the *buffa* and *seria* banners: the supporters of French
opera found a protector in the King; the Italian party in the
Queen, who took their side mainly because Mme de Pompadour
had steered the King to the nationalists. Jean-Jacques Rousseau,
always spoiling for a good fight, led a motley band of Encyclopedists to the defense of *les bouffons*, remarking that all true
connoisseurs were with them, and that, anyhow, "There is
neither measure nor melody in French music, because the
language itself is not susceptible of either." It did not matter
that he himself had taken some pains to disprove the precise
truth of this statement by composing, in *Le Devin du village*,
a pastoral opera both in the French style and in the French
language that remained in the repertoire of the Opéra until
1829, and has since been revived. Jean-Jacques was not a slave
to logic, and was wont to gain most of his points by vehemence
rather than by fairness of argument.

Thus was precipitated, because of the enmity between Louis
XV's mistress and his Polish wife, the renowned *guerre des
bouffons*—an extraordinary war with but a single battle, and
that lost by the victors. The Queen's Corner (so called because
the Italianists took to sitting beneath her loge) had recruited,
besides Rousseau, Baron Grimm, Diderot, and D'Alembert,
and was threatening the King's Corner (musical, but chic),
when the single battle occurred. The director of the Opéra-
Comique, where *les bouffons* held forth, produced a comic
opera in French, announcing it as the work of a Viennese
Italian. When the Queen's Corner had applauded itself silly,
the director announced that his "Viennese Italian" was a fable
and that the composer of *Les Troqueurs* was a native-born
Frenchman, Antoine d'Auvergne, who had used a libretto by
a Parisian poet. Thus, by a scurvy Trojan-horse trick, were
Frenchmen made to swallow—and like—*opera buffa* in their
own tongue. While the wails of the victors mingled with those

of the defeated, few remembered that, almost ten years before, Rameau, chief of the nationalists, had himself unsuccessfully presented an *opera buffa* of the selfsame type as *Les Troqueurs*.

The point of the *guerre des bouffons* (if, indeed, it had one) was that comic opera with spoken dialogue was made respectable in France. And the stranglehold of the stiff, undramatic *opera seria* had been broken. Paris was ripe for the "reforms" of Gluck.

Chapter V.

The Age of Gluck

O NE of the oddest things about Christoph Willibald von Gluck was the length of time it took him to get ripe for himself. His biography is singularly edifying: it is almost as arresting as a case history in slow development. The dates are significant: Gluck was born in 1714; he wrote his first opera in 1741, and his first good opera in 1762. To be sure, the latter was *Orfeo ed Euridice*, still the oldest staple of the repertoire. But in 1762 Gluck was still five years away from the great reforms that were to make him one of the half-dozen surpassing figures in the story of opera. The history of Gluck's slow but at last gloriously fruitful development belongs quite as much to literature as to music.

The key to Gluck's superiority over his predecessors is the undoubted fact that, probably early in his career, he began to look at librettos, first with a critical, and finally with a jaundiced, eye. The superiority was sternly intellectual, not purely musical. Monteverdi is a master of intense emotional effect, archaic yet curiously romantic; Lully, ragged-edged and windily grand, can exhilarate and set one dancing; Scarlatti, as melodious as an antique Schubert, has a logic that the music of opera rarely achieves; Handel, fertile, resistless as the Nile flood, a force, lets loose an unmitigated song, and Rameau, scholarly, a little crabbed, yet resourceful beyond his time, sums up a musical nation's past with no small magnificence. In single departments of his art, Gluck cannot touch them. His achievement is less spectacular in detail, but wider in scope: it is the achievement, in short, of a man with a great idea. Stated simply, it is merely that an opera is not music plus book, but a thoroughly new entity—an amalgam, fused, compact. Gluck's predecessors, great and small, no matter what their intelligence (and certainly four out of the five named above were vigorously intellectual), either used music as a background for words or submerged words in the music.

In either of these approaches, the poor lyric poet failed to get his just due—even when he seemed to get more, as in the early Florentine operas. Like what must those pioneering works have been? Musically, extraordinarily thin. Dramatically, perhaps effective—but irrelevantly impeded by a trickle of musical sound. It is no wonder that the vaunted classical severity of the *camerata* had so brief a life, gave way so quickly to "abuses" and "corruptions"! Opera had to progress (if not grow up), and if it hobbled forward and jumped sporadically, that was mainly because its composers and librettists entertained such wild and widely varied conceptions of their separate roles, one of the wildest being that their roles were indeed separate. When the pendulum had swung completely away from Florence, the florid school came into its own, extraordinarily thin as to drama, its sometimes superb music impeded by a supernumerary line of words. Is it any wonder that the librettist, thwarted at every turn, pled with the world to judge his wares by the circumstances of their production?

"When I write for music, the last person I consider is myself. I think of the singers, I think very much of the composer, I think of the pleasure of the audience; and if my dramas were only represented and not read, I should dare to hope for more justice of Judgment." These are the words, not of a hack librettist writing for Handel or Buononcini, but of Carlo Goldoni, writing in 1756, only six years before Gluck's *Orfeo*, and at a time when Metastasio's pre-eminence had secured for his fellow craftsmen a sensible amelioration of their wretched status. It should be added that it was not by his librettos or in such a spirit of submissiveness that Goldoni reformed the Italian drama.

Rinuccini, the earliest librettist of them all, was a poet of real talent who stuck closely to his Greek models and so avoided the pitfalls of originality. Had it been possible to maintain his lofty conception of the libretto, Rinuccini's successors would not have lost their dignity so quickly. Unhappily for them, and for generations of operagoers ever since, the singer—by rights, servant of words and music—almost immediately gained the upper hand. Degeneration at the root (which speedily followed) resulted from overfloriation at the top: the librettist, in order to live, had to work for the composer, and the composer, also in order to live, had to work for the singer, whom audiences adored. Here, finally, we reach the crux of the situation—the principal reason reform was so long in coming to the opera was that the opera pleased just as it was. In England, when it ceased to please, it in effect died out, to be revived (an exotic toy, as it had begun) decades later. In countries where it was a popular native entertainment, opera was changed, almost by *force majeure*, before wide-voiced dissatisfaction began.

Italy, more through the stubborn conventionality of its audiences than through lack of imagination in its composers and librettists, was not to be the storm center of reform, though there were stirrings of revolt even there. The followers of Scarlatti—men like Niccolò Jommelli, Tommaso Traetta, and Antonio Sacchini, the leaders of the so-called second Neapolitan school—were more than intermittently aware that something was wrong with *opera seria*. Separately or together they anticipated practically every item on the Gluck program of reform, which, incidentally, was not given to the world in a single fulmination, but was disclosed progressively in both theory and practice. What defeated them, in addition to the invincible apathy of their audiences, was their slavish respect for the fashionable dramatists of the day, particularly the two Caesarean poets of the Vienna court, Apostolo Zeno and Metastasio.

Metastasio, born Pietro Trapassi, would have been an amazing figure in any age. The romantic reader can find enough interest in the story of this Roman's cometlike rise to fame and power, in his love affairs, in his Platonic attachment to the beautiful and virtuous Countess Althann, and, finally, at the end of his life, in his perfect achievement of domestic sobriety. He lived eighty-four years and wrote scores of librettos for opera and oratorio alike—wrote them, at least after a brief apprenticeship, with a felicity of versification and an understanding of clever detail that soon raised him to unquestioned primacy in his profession.

Such sureness did not go unrewarded: the foremost composers turned to Metastasio for their books as unerringly as we today go to the telephone company for telephone service. Hundreds of operas were composed to his librettos, sometimes each subject several times by the same composer. For example, of the forty known settings of Metastasio's *Artaserse*, three are by Hasse, who loyally set all but one of Metastasio's books. Besides Faustina's prolific husband, Handel, Jommelli, Traetta, Galuppi, Paisiello, Piccinni, and Porpora repaired constantly to his verse. Mozart and Haydn occasionally used Metastasio librettos, and as late as 1819 so shrewd a purveyor as Meyerbeer was setting a Metastasio book that was almost a century old. In fact, the *terminus ad quem* of the uncanny attractiveness of this stage poetry seems to have been 1838, when Giovanni Pacini turned to the sadly shopworn *Temistocle* as a vehicle for his pseudo-Rossinian cadences.

As soon as we leave the romance and statistics connected with Metastasio, we get into trouble. Aesthetically, he is a hard nut to crack. Although he himself wrote some music in addition to furnishing librettos to a century, he does not quite belong to the history of music; though he was an inspired master of prosody who is still studied by serious students of Italian belles-lettres, he does not quite belong to the history of literature. Of late years the target of almost unrelieved denigration, Metastasio deserves his present abased condition almost as little as the deification accorded to him by his own times. He improved immeasurably the general design of the libretto, shearing away many excrescences, and specifically reducing the number of acts from five to three. He wrote verse that was made for singing, the result of an infallible ear and the habit, which he shared with Lully's librettist, Quinault, of writing his books at the harpsichord. As a musical amateur of close to professional status, he was one of the prime movers in restoring the chorus to a useful place in the opera fabric. Similarly, he counseled the many composers who sat at his feet to use accompanied recitative more abundantly.

So far, all to the good. But Metastasio, poet though he was, customarily used an idiom so involved, twisted, and convolute as to drown in a sea of rhetoric the very dramatic effects at which he seemed to aim most carefully. Further, though his stage works were perfectly logical and sequential, they lacked dramatic intensity sufficient to animate their elaborate structure. Conflict and catharsis are lacking. The characters are mere sketches of men and women; the stories themselves are not of life: they are courtly charades or, worse, sermons.

Gluck, who eventually was to join hands with one of Metastasio's most violent critics and was thus to break the stranglehold of this one-man libretto trust, started out seemingly as an unquestioning admirer of the great Caesarean poet. He set almost twenty of Metastasio's librettos in all, three of them after the revolt had begun. Gluck's musical debut was almost as tame as Wagner's, and he developed far less quickly. A percipient critic, viewing the first ten years of Gluck's operatic career (during which he composed sixteen run-of-the-mill, and sometimes worse than run-of-the-mill, Italian operas), would have dismissed him as just another polite fabricator of court entertainments. His first opera, Metastasio's eternal *Artaserse*, was produced in Milan in 1741. Obvious and stereotyped as most of his early work was, it was liked. Gluck was long a popular mediocre composer before he was a reluctantly accepted great one. In London alone be failed: there, too, Handel told him off, and gave him good advice.

Gluck's operas of the early and middle fifties show flutters of originality. In 1755, provided with a simple and moving story by an anti-Metastasian, who occupied the strategic post of director of the imperial court opera, Gluck composed a significant score, *L'Innocenza giustificata,* where something of his future can be read, not in the whole work, but in single numbers. Its author, Count Giacomo Durazzo, would gladly have gone farther and might very possibly have been competent to handle the literary phase of a revolt. But in 1755 Gluck, at forty-one, was so little ready to take over the musical phase that he lapsed into his old imitative, timeserving ways and turned out four more examples of his neo-Milanese patchwork. Durazzo himself did not set Gluck on fire, but at least he served as catalyst in one of the most fruitful associations in the history of art: in 1761 he introduced his favorite composer to an exchequer official recently arrived from Paris—Raniero da Calzabigi.

The new librettist, the very spelling of whose name is as controversial as are the extent and originality of his part in the reforms, was probably born the same year as Gluck—1714. At first not only an admirer, but a line-by-line imitator of Metastasio, Calzabigi was obliged to give the Roman's texts finical scrutiny when preparing a critical edition of them—and his adoration did not survive. This edition, brought out in Paris in 1755, included a prefatory dissertation on Metastasio by the editor, in which, after analyzing the *tragédie lyrique* of Lully and Quinault, he let fall the following pregnant observations:

> If in the end the same ground plan could be reconciled with the exigencies of truth; if once purely human actions were to unfold themselves to the exclusion of pagan divinities and all that smacks of the devil and of magic; in short all that is beyond things within the control of human beings, there is no doubt that a delightful whole would result from the interplay of a large chorus, the dance, and a scenic action where poetry and music are united in a masterly manner.

Although the knowledgeable reader saw the names of Lully and Quinault attached plainly enough to these remarks, he must have realized that they were in part directed against Metastasio. But the aging poet, far from taking offense at the dissertation, retained it in his own edition of his works. It is a question, the answer to which must depend on an estimate of Metastasio's intelligence, whether he felt Calzabigi's barbs at all, or secretly agreed with his detractor.*

Calzabigi the reformer was anything but a bluenose. In fact, like many of the great librettists before the spotless Boïto, he was something of a scoundrel—and no less than Casanova, his very good friend and well-wisher, is authority for this statement.

* It would be a mistake to dismiss Metastasio as indifferent to certain problems of operatic reform. For example, he was vehement against the style of music that, he wrote, was "making the theater no longer resound with any other applause than that which is given to displays of execution, with the vain inundation of which she has hastened her own disgrace, after having first occasioned that of the mangled, disfigured, and ruined drama."

Calzabigi left Paris in 1761 rather too hurriedly for decency
and achieved an important government post in Vienna with
suspicious rapidity. Long after his association with Gluck,
Calzabigi, who seems eventually to have blossomed forth into a
species of international financier, is discovered managing—and
mismanaging—government lotteries and providing money (at
exorbitant rates) to impecunious princes. All this is incidental
to the essential qualities that he placed at the disposal of art:
intelligent, widely read, truly cultivated, the devotee of a
thousand intellectual passions, Calzabigi also had the boldness
that was needed to put into action ideas that other as gifted men
had been content to theorize about. The libretto which, at
Count Durazzo's bidding, he presented to Gluck in 1761
sounded a warning to the Metastasians that a new era was
coming.

But Metastasio himself needed no warning. As early as 1751,
he had written that Gluck "has surprising fire, but he is mad."
Five years later, writing from Vienna to Farinelli, he lamented:
"The opera which will be represented tonight in the public theater will certainly meet with applause. What is there that would
not please on such a day [the celebration of the birth of a
child to Maria Theresa]? The drama is my *Rè Pastore*, set by
Gluck, a Bohemian composer, whose spirit, noise, and extravagance have supplied the place of merit in many theaters
of Europe, among those whom I pity, and who do not form
the minority of the folks of this world. Thank God, we have no
want of such auditors here." Compare this with the words of
Alfred Einstein (1936), who had the advantage of looking back
on Gluck's entire career: "There is much beautiful and carefully fashioned music in the work, but not a single feature
that exceeds the most conventional of conventions. . . . It is
no more than the response to a command from the throne of
which Gluck acquitted himself with decency."

In 1761, Gluck was at last ready to do justice to a credible
vehicle. That same year, in composing a long and elaborate
dramatic ballet based remotely on Molière's *Don Juan*, he had
responded with constructive intelligence to another demand for
reform—the great dancer Noverre's insistence that the stereo-

typed, listless *ballet de cour* be revitalized into a more dramatic and lifelike form of entertainment. Naturalness, expressiveness, truth in depicting human manners and emotions: those were Noverre's demands. They were also Calzabigi's, and Gluck was as ripe for Calzabigi's ambitious program as he had been for Noverre's. Riper, perhaps, for in *Orfeo ed Euridice*, first produced at Vienna on October 5, 1762, with the famed male contralto, Gaetano Guadagni, as Orpheus, he composed one of the undeniable masterworks of the musical stage.

Orfeo is not perfect—far from it—either dramatically or musically. The Calzabigi of a few years later would have had more theatrical tact than to ruin a simple, moving story with a preposterous and uncalled-for happy ending. True, there was a strong tradition of happy endings—a tradition that appealed to opera audiences; but Calzabigi would never have won through if he had decided to cater at any point to such aesthetically infantile predilections. Nor would he err again in making an opera substantially a monologue for its hero. The fact that Eurydice, on her belated entrance, must act like a ravishing deaf-mute until the sudden outburst of galvanic excitement that causes her second demise is not calculated to intensify the drama. The role of Amor, whose thankless job it is to turn the whole tragedy into a farce, is the kind of supernumerary (actually hostile to the drama itself) that Calzabigi never again employed so blatantly. Gluck made fewer mistakes. Perhaps his worst was to compose an irrelevant overture of surpassing dullness. Almost as bad was a third act which even the presence of his most famous single aria cannot save after the double miracle of two perfect acts.

Yet *Orfeo*'s virtues so outweigh its faults that the most intelligent audiences have for almost two centuries rejoiced in opportunities to hear it. There is evidence that it was written in cold blood as the opening document of a revolt, and not the least of its triumphs is that in performance it shows not a trace of self-consciousness. Calzabigi's contributions were simplicity, ease of language, large understanding of situation and character, and all but complete disregard for the complex formulas of libretto construction.

Gluck contributed, besides the simple and unaccountable fact of his genius, a response to every subtle implication of Calzabigi's book. No more appropriate music has ever been composed, though later Gluck did achieve a more delicate balance between drama and music (the chief problem of opera, and solved flawlessly perhaps a spare five or six times in more than four hundred years). In no other score, however, did Gluck manage to stop the show as often as he does in *Orfeo*. The magnificent scene at the gates of Erebus, beginning with the hellish dance of the Furies (borrowed from his own *Don Juan*) and ending with Orpheus' pathetic plea to be allowed to seek his beloved among the shades, punctuated with explosive shouts of "No" from the Furies, is the sheer stuff of drama. The scene in the Elysian fields, with its serenely lovely "Dance of the Happy Shades," is Gluck's purest musical claim to stand, if only momentarily, with the very greatest of composers. Here the flute usurps the place of the human voice and produces an utterly unique magic. Finally—as hummability will be admitted by all good operagoers as at least a minor touchstone of the art—there is *"Che farò senza Euridice,"* a melody so beautiful and self-sufficient that only the most accomplished of singers can keep it within the frame of the opera's structure. Yet, this aria presents so many difficulties of interpretation that Gluck himself said of it: "Make the least change in it, either in the tempo or in the turn of expression, and it will become an air for a puppet show."

The revolutionary *Orfeo* was at first received coldly by a Vienna which was probably annoyed or bewildered by the bread and cold water of this strange and Doric score. For five years Gluck turned back to the mellifluous verbiage of Metastasio and his imitators: there were scant signs that things like *Orfeo* would increase his fortune—at least, so far as Vienna and Italy, his reliable markets, were concerned. Upsurges of high drama in *Telemaco* (1765) and the writing of his only full-length comic opera the year before show that Gluck was not too pleased with his potboiling. And yet, in *Alceste*, his next collaboration with Calzabigi, he himself made, and may have persuaded his librettist to make, concessions to the older styles, though *Alceste* is in general a work of even greater sobriety and sternness than *Orfeo*. For instance, the libretto brings forward, once again, the useless female friends of the heroine who cluttered up the scenery in many a Metastasian play. Quite as odd is Gluck's return to unaccompanied recitative after he had banished it summarily from *Orfeo*.

These evasions of uncompromising reform would attract less notice if *Alceste*, two years after its production in 1767, had not been published with a preface by Calzabigi (signed, and unquestionably concurred in, by Gluck), which minces no words about their avowed intentions. Except for the peroration—several lengths of soft soap for the ego of the dedicatee, the future Leopold II—this fiery yet unblushingly sensible manifesto deserves quotation in full:

YOUR ROYAL HIGHNESS,

When I undertook to write the music for *Alceste*, I resolved to divest it entirely of all those abuses, introduced into it either by the mistaken vanity of singers or by the too great complaisance of composers, which have so long disfigured Italian opera and made of the most splendid and most beautiful of spectacles the most ridiculous and wearisome. I have striven to restrict music to its true office of serving poetry by means of expression and by following the situations of the story, without interrupting the action or stifling it with a useless superfluity of ornaments; and I believed that it should do this in the same way as telling colors affect a correct and well-ordered drawing, by a well-assorted contrast of light and shade, which serves to animate the figures without altering their contours. Thus I did not wish to arrest an actor in the greatest heat of dialogue in order to wait for a tiresome *ritornello*, not to hold him up in the middle of a word on a vowel favorable to his voice, not to make display of the agility of his fine voice in some long-drawn passage, nor to wait while the orchestra gives him time to recover his breath for a cadenza. I did not think it my duty to pass quickly over the second section of an aria of which the words are perhaps the most impassioned and important, in order to repeat regularly four times over those of the first part, and to finish the aria where its sense may perhaps not end for the convenience of the singer who wishes to show that he can capriciously vary a passage in a number of guises; in short, I have sought to abolish all the abuses against which good sense and reason have long cried out in vain.

I have felt that the overture ought to apprise the spectators of the nature of the action that is to be represented and to form, so to speak, its argument; that the concerted instruments should be introduced in proportion to the interests and the intensity of the words, and not leave that sharp contrast between the aria and the recitative in the dialogue, so as not to break a period unreasonably nor wantonly disturb the force and heat of the action.

Furthermore, I believed that my greatest labor should be devoted to seeking a beautiful simplicity, and I have avoided making displays of difficulty at the expense of clearness; nor did I judge it desirable to discover novelties if it was not naturally suggested by the situation and the expression; and there is no rule which I have not thought it right to set aside willingly for the sake of an intended effect.

Such are my principles. By good fortune my designs were wonderfully furthered by the libretto, in which the celebrated author, devising a new dramatic scheme, had substituted for florid descriptions, unnatural paragons and sententious, cold morality, heartfelt language, strong passions, interesting situations and an endlessly varied spectacle.

Few will deny that the collaborators worked in the spirit, even if they violated the letter, of this epochal and cold-bloodedly intelligent document. A libretto even more simply worded and more dramatically focused than *Orfeo*'s gave Gluck his inspiration. A bodingly tragic overture, moving straight into the action* (of which, indeed, it is a part), magnificently lives up to one of the promises of the manifesto. The first act sets the forces of fate in action; the second sees them operating toward an inevitably violent end; the third provides, it is true, a happy ending, but a happy ending not unpalatable insofar as it is inherent in the whole impulsion of the drama. Furthermore, the joy of this *dénouement* is not degraded by a pagan

* So straight that if it were not for a special ending composed by Wagner this favorite concert number could not be heard apart from the opera.

neighborhood *fiesta* such as concludes the unhappy last act of *Orfeo.**

Alceste failed. "For nine days," complained one of the smart set at the *première,* "the theater has been closed, and on the tenth it opens with a Requiem." But this time Gluck waited only three years, and produced but one potboiler, before re- turning to the charge with *Paride ed Elena,* in some respects the most ambitious of his stage works. Calzabigi, working with Gluck for the last time, handed him what can only be called a study in ethnic contrasts (Sparta vs. Phrygia), made all the more interesting by the astonishing discovery that Helen of Troy was a prude. A silly business, without motion or climax, it is simply the story of Paris wooing Helen (who is merely affianced to Menelaus!). Not in the least stageworthy, *Paride* happens to contain much splendid music, as well as Gluck's most passionate love song, *"O del mio dolce ardor,"* whose appeal is more obvious than its beauty.

The Viennese did not like *Paride ed Elena,* and this time who shall blame them? But by 1770 their likes and dislikes meant little to Gluck: he was beginning to find the atmosphere of Austrian rigidity hostile to the highest ideals of his art. He was now stubbornly determined on exodus—otherwise he might have reconsidered if only to be near to, and to support, the youthful Antonio Salieri, his first and only full-fledged pupil, whose brilliant career was just starting. Almost at once, Gluck began to haunt the French embassy, hinting at prefer- ment in Paris, where his imperial pupil, the Archduchess Marie Antoinette, was established as the much-indulged wife of the Dauphin Louis. So well did he wangle that when he set out with his family for France, some four years later, he carried with him parts of the score of a French opera whose production at Paris was all but assured. And this time, Calzabigi having conveniently disappeared after a scandal, Gluck's librettist was his master wangler at the embassy—Marie-François-Louis Gand-Leblanc, Bailli du Rollet.

Paris, for so many years a proud beehive of reaction, had just

* Nevertheless, the Metropolitan Opera managed to turn this third act into just such a *fiesta* during its otherwise intelligent performances of *Alceste.*

laughed itself out of lethargy during the *guerre des bouffons*, and was probably the only city in the world where Gluck could carry his reforms to their logical conclusions. As far as the nationalists—the *rameauistes* and the King's Corner—were concerned, most of the logic consisted of the simple phenomenon of a French opera in his traveling bags. More important, finally, the Encyclopedists, though lingeringly Italianate, were sympathetic to Gluck's ideals, and he was assured of vigorous intellectual support. Marie Antoinette, too, was importantly in the picture. An impressive cast was assembled for the *première* of *Iphigénie en Aulide*: the great Sophie Arnould, at the full of her powers, created the name role, Joseph Legros was the Achilles, and the presence of Vestris, *le dieu de la danse*, lent the necessary aura of divinity; Du Rollet's libretto was based on Racine: everything looked propitious when the curtains of the Opéra parted on the night of April 9, 1774, with Marie Antoinette in the royal loge.

Before the *première* of *Iphigénie en Aulide*, Gluck had been merely one of a dozen celebrated composers for the stage: after it, he was without a peer. For the moment, France was delightfully stunned. The witty Abbé Arnaud, director of the influential *Gazette de France*, echoed the general enthusiasm: "With that air one might found a religion," he said of a certain melody in *Iphigénie*. Mme Du Deffand, who confessed to Horace Walpole that "M. Glou's" opera bored her to death, was almost a minority of one. There was reason for this magnificent ovation: *Iphigénie,* more than any other of Gluck's operas, puts its best foot forward at once—the overture, itself unsurpassed by any of his others, leads without pause into a strong situation, which it heightens immeasurably. The score, except in the last scene, sustains this tenseness: time and again, despite the librettist's sober presentation of a chain of psychological conflicts, the music threatens to boil over. Gluck followed his text with painstaking fidelity, but provided accents that were beyond the talents of Du Rollet. In the provision of such accents—in knowing surely what music could do better than words—Gluck showed his genius.

So powerful was the effect of some scenes in *Iphigénie* that people in the audience forgot that they were witnessing make-believe, and were with difficulty restrained from rushing onto the stage to deliver the hapless princess of Mycenae. The fact that none of Gluck's operas is likely to have this effect on a modern audience does not mean that they have lost vitality: our aural palate has become accustomed to the spices of verism and the rich wines of pure and neo-Wagnerism. By one of the familiar ironies of history, we who are used to the scarifying vocalism of Strauss' *Elektra* have come to consider as stylized and unexciting the opera of Gluck, which in its own day was condemned as the death of singing. To get at the drama in *Iphigénie*, we must borrow the ears of the eighteenth century—ears that had never heard Wagner* or Strauss, Verdi or Puccini.

During the two years following *Iphigénie en Aulide*, Gluck reworked *Orfeo* and *Alceste* to French translations of their original librettos. These adaptations are not wholly satisfactory, though *Orphée et Eurydice* was at least a success. Had local conditions allowed the use of *castrati*, it is probable that *Orfeo* would not have been so stringently handled. As it was, the role of Orpheus had to be transposed, and in part rewritten, for a tenor—for that Legros who had contributed so much to the initial success of *Iphigénie*. This upset the key relationships, and to remedy this, it has become the custom for a woman to sing the role in the original key. To compensate, however, Gluck added to the revised score a lot of superb new music.

Besides Legros, the principals at the first performance of *Orphée et Eurydice* included Arnould as Eurydice and Rosalie Levasseur as Amor. For the revival of November 18, 1859, at the Théâtre Lyrique, Berlioz, a worshiper of Gluck, crossed the versions of 1764 and 1774 in a way that allowed the in-

* Or, for that matter, Wagner's version of *Iphigénie*, parts of which are said to resemble *Lohengrin*. Not only did he substantially rewrite both words and music, but he interpolated stretches of his own contriving. As the crowning touch of this ambiguous devotion, he introduced the goddess Artemis into the cast of characters. When the Philadelphia Orchestra Association undertook the American *première* of *Iphigénie en Aulide*, on February 22, 1935, the original Paris version was used by Conductor Alexander Smallens. Rosa Tentoni (Iphigenia), Cyrena Van Gordon (Clytemnestra), Joseph Bentonelli (Achilles), and Georges Baklanoff (Agamemnon) were the principals. Despite critical acclaim, the opera has not since been revived in the United States.

comparable contralto, Pauline Viardot-García, to espouse the role of Orpheus. It turned out to be the greatest triumph of a great career, and Berlioz, who was, anyhow, in love with Viardot-García, poured out a rhapsodic tribute to her impersonation. Of her singing of *"J'ai perdu mon Eurydice"* (*"Che farò senza Euridice"*), he wrote:

> Mme Viardot treated it as it ought to be treated, that is to say, as what it is, one of those prodigies of expression which are well-nigh incomprehensible for vulgar singers, and which are, alas! so often desecrated. She delivered its theme in three different manners: at first in a slow movement, with suppressed grief; then, after the episodical Adagio:
>
> *Mortel silence!*
> *Vaine espérance!*
>
> *sotto voce, pianissimo,* with a trembling voice choked by a flood of tears; and, finally, after the second Adagio, she took up the theme in a more animated movement, withdrawing from the body of Eurydice, beside which she had been kneeling, and rushing away, mad with despair, toward the other side of the stage, the very picture of frenzy in her outcries and sobs. I shall not attempt to describe the excitement of the audience at this overwhelming scene. Certain maladroit auditors even so far forgot themselves as to cry *"Bis!"* before the sublime passage:
>
> *Entends ma voix qui t'appelle,*
>
> and great difficulty was experienced in imposing silence upon them. Some persons would cry *"Bis!"* for the scene of Priam in the tent of Achilles, or for the "To be or not to be" of Hamlet.

Superb as Viardot-García had been, her performance was equaled by that of Giulia Ravogli, who first sang Orpheus at Covent Garden, London, in 1890, her sister Sofia being the Eurydice. In 1892, between mid-October and mid-December, the Ravoglis appeared in *Orfeo ed Euridice* a dozen times. Among their idolaters was George Bernard Shaw, who wrote of Giulia's Orpheus: "In the singer, as in the composer, we saw a perfectly original artistic impulse naïvely finding its way to the heart of the most artificial and complex of art forms." The Ravoglis were also in the first Metropolitan *Orfeo*, on December 30, 1891—the opera had been heard in the United States in English, as early as 1863. On December 23, 1909, Arturo Toscanini conducted a still-remembered *Orfeo* at the Metropolitan, with Louise Homer (Orpheus), Johanna Gadski (Eurydice), Alma Gluck (the Happy Shade), and Bella Alten (Amor). Later Metropolitan Orpheuses under Toscanini's baton were Marie Delna, in her American debut, and Margaret Matzenauer. After 1913, *Orfeo* left the Metropolitan repertoire for twenty-two years, being revived during the resident company's first spring season (1936). The action was mimed by the American Ballet Ensemble in a wholly ludicrous manner, while the singers— not much better—were relegated to the orchestra pit. The singing Orpheus of this outrageous performance was Anna Kaskas. On November 26, 1939, the Metropolitan redeemed itself with the magnificently sung interpretation of Orpheus by Kerstin Thorborg, a majestic Swedish woman who, unfortunately, was given wretched support.

The operation Gluck perpetrated on *Alceste* for the Paris production was even more flagrant than that on *Orfeo*, especially as he was not the only surgeon in attendance. While Gluck was out of town, official busybodies at the Opéra allowed François-Joseph Gossec to insert into the score his rewriting of an old and forgettable aria from one of Gluck's earlier works and assign it to a character who had not appeared in the original Vienna version. Alfred Einstein has suggested that an ideal presentation of *Alceste*, like one of *Orfeo*, would consist of a combination of the best elements of the Vienna and Paris scores.

Following her triumph in *Orphée*, Viardot-García decided to try the role of Alcestis, and though it had to be transposed lower for her voice, several concerts of parts of *Alceste* indicated that she would excel in it. Accordingly, on October 21, 1861, it was staged at the Opéra, with the anticipated success. Not until January 24, 1941, did *Alceste* reach the United States, when the Metropolitan presented the young Australian soprano, Marjorie Lawrence, in the name role, René Maison (Admetus), and Leonard Warren (the High Priest), with Ettore Panizza conducting. Lawrence was a dramatic Alcestis, and improved to superbness in her third performance; Rose Bampton, much Lawrence's inferior in this role, sang it twice out of the five times the opera was performed during

MADAME VIARDOT, DANS L'ORPHÉE DE GLUCK

Pauline Viardot-García as Orpheus, in Gluck's *Orphée et Eurydice,*
after a contemporary print

its first Metropolitan season. Lawrence's majestic invocation of the underworld deities in the magnificent pages of *"Divinités du Styx"* will not soon be forgotten.

Soon after the Parisian *première* of *Alceste* there entered onto the scene a mild-mannered, big-hearted Italian composer of most respectable gifts, whose unwanted distinction it was to be carried aloft as the banner of the gathering opposition to Gluck. Left to himself, Niccola Piccinni might have continued his spectacularly successful career in Italy, and have occupied a less ambiguous position in the histories of music. In the first place, the reasons for his importation into France show a mystifying confusion in the minds of his patrons: it is all highly reminiscent of the time when the English decided to pit a little fribble of a man like Buononcini against a force of nature like Handel, apparently forgetting that a good fight requires opponents of almost equal weight. Piccinni, who was fourteen years Gluck's junior, had written many hits, most of them in the field of *opera buffa*. When he was thirty-two years old, he had composed *La Buona Figliuola*, which set Rome, then Italy, then all Europe, laughing. Only an Englishman could have appreciated its richest humor, for it was based on Richardson's solemn *Pamela*. The librettist, however, was Goldoni. Piccinni had also trafficked with *opera seria*, but usually with indifferent success. Two years before his French hegira of 1776, however, he had fished out an old Metastasio warhorse (titled sometimes *Alessandro nelle Indie*, sometimes *Poro*), set previously by himself, Handel, Gluck, and many others, and had reset it to quite unexpected *réclame*. This sealed his fate: he was imported not as a composer of *opera buffa*, in which he could easily have outdistanced Gluck, but as a master of *opera seria*, in which he was manifestly Gluck's inferior. Even before the innocent Piccinni had stirred out of Italy, he had received his credentials. Unfortunately for him, they were sealed orders.

The ultimate credit for staging the dogfight between the German and the Italian must go to that useless favorite of romantic history, Marie Antoinette. Assurance of her protection had brought Gluck to France; the same assurance was

extended to Piccinni. Like the serpent at Eve's ear, the crafty
and malicious historiographer royal of France—Jean-François
Marmontel—had whispered that it would be fun to have the
protagonists set the same libretto. The Dauphine agreed that
this would indeed be fun, and accordingly Marmontel sent
to each his own revamping of *Roland*, an ancient book by
Quinault. Gluck got wind of the plot and not only refused
indignantly to add another penstroke to the uncompleted score
of his *Roland*, but wrote to his old friend Du Rollet denounc-
ing the trickery and stating that he had thrown his share into
the fire. Du Rollet instantly published the letter, and overnight Paris divided into Gluckists and Piccinnists. Hundreds
went to pay court to Piccinni, who had just arrived accompanied by his large family and a complete ignorance of the
French language.

While some of Gluck's followers uneasily admitted that he
might have lost the first trick in refusing to compete, their
fears were somewhat quieted by the news that their idol was
hard at work on another of Quinault's tried-and-true librettos.
What he produced, with the quickly regained favor of the public was not, it is true, another step forward in his revolutionary
program, but a lumbering, old-fashioned five-acter, *Armide*,
notable only for the care he lavished on the dramatic exposition
of Armida herself, an unwholesome sorceress of profoundly
erotic tastes—an eighteenth-century foreshadowing of Wagner's Kundry. Ironically, five months later, when Piccinni's
Roland came out, it was found that he had written it to a neat
three-act package at which Calzabigi need not have blushed.
Both men had won, but it seemed that they had won each
other's battles.

Armide, which until that time had not been heard in the United
States, was chosen to open, on November 14, the 1910-11 season
of the Metropolitan. Manager Giulio Gatti-Casazza decided to
capitalize on the renewed interest in Gluck that had been created,
the season before, by the revival of *Orfeo*. A sumptuous performance was accorded *Armide*. Toscanini conducted, the galaxy of
stars was led by Olive Fremstad (Armida), Louise Homer (Hate),
and Enrico Caruso (Rinaldo), assisted by Alma Gluck, Marie Rap-

pold, Pasquale Amato, and many other competent artists. After
three performances that season, and four the next, *Armide,* with its
costly *décors* and elaborate dances, was dropped.

While the absurd and protracted conflict of the Gluckists
and Piccinnists, in which the points at issue were never clearly
defined, ended by embroiling almost every articulate Parisian,
the two figures around whom the battle raged stood above its
noise and turmoil. For Gluck and Piccinni really liked each
other. Gluck treated Piccinni with a scrupulous courtesy and
fairness that are pleasing to record of a man whose conduct
toward his colleagues was not infrequently marred by chicanery
and double-dealing. On his side, the Italian admired his unwanted rival, and had a full appreciation of Gluck's importance
to the evolution of opera. When Gluck died, Piccinni tried
in vain to get subscribers for an annual concert in memory
of the man to whom, in his own words, "the lyrical theater
owes as much as the French drama does to Corneille."

Piccinni's own career remained consistently checkered: after
Gluck went home for his last few stately and honored years in
Vienna, Piccinni was again cast for a seesaw role when Sacchini
arrived in Paris. When, in 1786, several years after his arrival,
this at first popular newcomer died of mortification at Parisian
fickleness, Piccinni came nobly forward to pronounce his compatriot's funeral oration. The Revolution drove Piccinni back
to Naples, where he lived in wretched poverty for nine years.
Then he decided to see France again. Bonaparte befriended
him and even created for him a tiny post at the Conservatoire.
But when Piccinni died in 1800, he was buried in the potter's
field, and no one pronounced an oration over his tomb.

The last set piece of fireworks in the Gluck-Piccinni war,
which turned out to be the dreariest squib, was a silly bit of
treachery that resulted in the chief actors' finally composing
music to the same libretto, *Iphigénie en Tauride.* Gluck's came
out first and settled the question, not of his principles, but of
his pre-eminence. The director of the Opéra had handed him—
and Piccinni—a faithful and straightforward adaptation of
Euripides. Gluck's purposeful intelligence recognized its possibilities and provided it with what is probably his best score

dramatically. Piccinni tampered with the text and, despite his once having boasted about his speed in composition, turned in his opera two years later than Gluck. That was exactly two years too late: when Piccinni's *Iphigénie* finally reached the boards, it suffered as much by comparison with Gluck's austerely classical masterpiece as it did from the unhappy circumstance that the leading lady was visibly drunk at the *première*, in 1781. "This is not *Iphigénie en Tauride*," decided Sophie Arnould, "it's *Iphigénie en Champagne*." Even the most loyal Piccinnists could not survive such a fateful combination of blows. Furthermore, by 1781, Paris was already beginning to forget Gluck, and the feud died of peaceful old age.

Gluck's Tauric *Iphigénie* was introduced to New York, at a Metropolitan matinee, on November 25, 1916. Oddly, it used neither the language of the original libretto nor the score as Gluck had made it. Both Richard Strauss and Artur Bodanzky, who conducted, had tampered with the music, the former adding a trio of his own devising, and the latter interpolating ballet music from *Orfeo*. Besides, *Iphigénie* was drastically cut, and sung in German. Outside of H. E. Krehbiel's extravagant praise of Rosina Galli's dancing, no one seems to have thought much of the production, and the chief singers—Melanie Kurt (Iphigenia), Rappold (Diana), Hermann Weil (Orestes), and Johannes Sembach (Pylades) —were rather too Germanic in tradition to be adequate in an opera which was, except for the language in which it was sung, French.

Gluck's reform of opera did not permanently reform it: opera is an incorrigible. Any "reform" is merely a set of specific circumstances, unlikely to endure, and certainly not susceptible to effective imitation. Gluck himself had no magic formula that could be copied even by himself. He had the creative intelligence to see how the various dramatic and musical elements could best be balanced. He had, moreover, to face new problems in every libretto he undertook to fuse with his music into a single new entity. His actual musical idiom was not noticeably different from that of his most gifted contemporaries: he did more with it only when the drama carried him to heights normally beyond him. He taught what few have learned:

that a musicodramatic unity can be achieved and its continuity maintained. In 1782, just after the slothful old reformer had commanded a special performance of Mozart's *Die Entführung aus dem Serail,* he delightedly asked the youthful composer to his fine mansion in the suburbs of Vienna. He wined and dined him—and no doubt there was plenty of talk about music. What Gluck did not know, could not know, was that much of the future of opera lay not with himself—the already forgotten reformer—but with this belated disciple of Hasse and Piccinni.

Chapter VI

Mozart

IN THE slightly more than two hundred and fifty years of operatic history before the appearance of Gluck's series of masterpieces, perhaps only one composer succeeded in producing that fusion of music and drama which obliterates every trace of opera's hybrid ancestry. Purcell worked the miracle in *Dido and Aeneas.* Then followed a long hiatus until *Orfeo ed Euridice,* after which the continuity of occasional perfection was established almost without a break. Creatively, Gluck died in 1782, just when Mozart was beginning to write his more astonishing series of masterpieces: the reformer died in 1787, the year of *Don Giovanni.* Only three months intervened between Mozart's death and the birth of Rossini, whose *Il Barbiere di Siviglia* was the next miracle. As Rossini survived until 1868, he lived to witness not only the births of all the composers of the greatest operatic masterpieces since his own, but also the creation of several of those masterpieces. Wagner, for instance, had composed *Tristan und Isolde, Die Meistersinger,* and most of *Der Ring des Nibelungen* before Rossini died. Verdi, it is true, was a quarter century away from his best operas, but he was already world-famous and the composer of several works of near-genius. Mussorgsky was engaged on the first version of *Boris Godunov,* though Bizet had done little that was not mediocre. Except as problems to their parents, Debussy and Richard Strauss were not to be reckoned with, for they were respectively six and four years old when the Swan of Pesaro passed to his dubious reward.

With the exception of Purcell, whose one opera is a curiously isolated phenomenon coming from nowhere and leading to nothing, Mozart is the most baffling member of this royal line. Gluck was a theorist whose best operas perfectly ground his axes. Rossini, whose *Barbiere* is Mozart with a difference, deliberately founded French grand opera. Wagner, another theorist, made opera the vehicle of philosophy, vastly extended the orchestra's role, and discovered the musical equivalent of the loins. Verdi, assuming in old age, and with equal grace, the masks of high comedy and high tragedy, achieved in pithy, gnomic saying and tragic soliloquy the perfect foil to Bayreuth's dark suggestiveness and eloquent, sensual narrative. Bizet and Mussorgsky, atacking problems of color, style, and dramatic accent, solved them in varying, yet oddly related, ways, and immeasurably enriched the whole musical palette. Debussy, a Wagner in reverse, returning to the ideals of Peri and Caccini, made a single dream opera of whispers and asides and further broke down the musical spectrum into shades, tints, and tonalities. Finally, there was Strauss, the Saint Paul of Wagnerism and the Mahomet of the libido, who nevertheless poured out the most effervescent champagne in an opera of waltzes.

To capture Mozart's quality in a phrase, or even a series of phrases, is impossible. No composer, not excepting Bach, deals so exclusively with the pure stuff of music, working always in seeming abandon and utter unself-consciousness with self-sufficient patterns of sound. While the metaphysics of Mozart's music can be discussed to the point of verbosity, attempts to program it do well if they produce one germane phrase in twenty pages of exegesis. Music that has literary, philosophical, or pictorial overtones and intentions can, of course, be described: faced with Mozart, literature admits itself defeated, and recourse must be had to the grammar of formal analysis. The problem becomes more complicated when it is realized with what versatility he uses the several styles at his command. Despite the Mozartian flavor of each, would we not be inclined to divide his widely varying masterpieces among several powerful geniuses, if we did not feel that only Mozart could have written any of them?

Furthermore, Mozart did a number of apparently contradictory things. In opera, for example, he brought Italian *opera buffa* to its perfection, and also launched the Singspiel on a career of respectability. His achievement in the former was, if anything, the more remarkable of the two. Taking that *buffa* tradition much as he found it, and doing almost nothing to change it, he composed operas that are living today, while

his models have survived only as museum pieces. Apparently
working without definite dramatic theories, and taking any
libretto that happened to be lying about, he created a gallery of
characters comparable to the creations of a great novelist—
characters whose being is built solidly out of situation, music,
and words. In this respect, in the creation of operatic characters
in the round, Mozart has never been excelled: compared to
his, Gluck's are but embodied emotions, Wagner's embodied
philosophical and nationalistic concepts.* The final miracle—
paradox, if you will—of *Le Nozze di Figaro, Don Giovanni,* and
Die Zauberflöte is that the creations of the wonder child of the
most crystalline reaches of the eighteenth century should have
become recognized touchstones of universal art.

Until 1781, when he wrote *Idomeneo,* Mozart's career as an
operatic composer is of interest only to close students of pre-
cocity and of influences and tendencies. His early efforts, while
marvels of mimicry and technical ease, are otherwise immature
and tentative. One of the earliest, *Bastien und Bastienne,*†
dating from his twelfth year, has been revived: it is a curiosity
—and nothing more. Metastasio furnished two of his librettos;
a third has been attributed to Calzabigi. From *Il Rè Pastore,*
written when Mozart was nineteen, comes an exquisite aria that
is still often heard in the recital hall, *"L'amerò, sarò costante."*
In all these early operas there are pages that for modern ears
diffuse the antique charm characteristic of most eighteenth-
century music that is not actually bad. It is significant that when
Mozart showed the first sure signs that he had grown up as an
operatic composer, he should have celebrated his coming of
age with an opera conforming more to Gluck's ideals than any
he ever composed later. It is significant, too, that Mozart was
closer personally to Gluck the year of *Idomeneo* than at any
other time.

Idomeneo, Rè di Creta, is an old-fashioned *opera seria* cut to
the Gluck pattern, but with innumerable musical touches of an
independent artist. It is in no sense an epochal work, nor is it,

* It does not need charity to except Hans Sachs.
† Its libretto, by Andreas Schachtner, is a parody of Rousseau's *Le Devin du
village.*

with its mixture of styles, a perfectly integrated one. There is a special grandeur in *Idomeneo*, traceable alike to its Gluckian ancestry and to its theme (but not to its plot, which is as silly as any parody libretto Robert Benchley ever evolved). But with all its grandeur, *Idomeneo* is a synthetic creation. Mozart's genius, which might have delighted in setting one of the more lively Platonic dialogues, was simply not interested in the starker machinations of Greek fate. No one can question the elevation of Mozart's style when he chooses to be elevated, but it stops short of the marmoreal: his forms are too plastic to assume the static magnificence of Gluck. There is just enough willfulness, just enough spirit of play, in *Idomeneo* to mar its Greek-tragedy pretensions; and those who can read the signs, even in the first five bars of the fine and basically serious overture, must see that this is the work of a potential master of comedy, not quite happy in the company of Agamemnon's daughter, which role was created, as far as modern audiences are concerned, by Elisabeth Schumann—in Richard Strauss' revision of the score. Mozart probably sensed his native genre, for he only once again attempted *opera seria*. This time he failed. *La Clemenza di Tito,* composed in the heyday of his maturity, is as poor stuff as he could write.

After *Idomeneo*, Mozart turned to a relatively unexplored phase of the musical stage. This was the Singspiel, of rather obscure, and far from respectable, history. The Singspiel, very simply, is an opera in German containing spoken dialogue: it is the German counterpart of *opéra-comique* and the English ballad opera. Depending on one's ability to trace ancestry to unpromising origins, the Singspiel, in 1781, could have been regarded as an antique or a parvenu. It was very remotely descended from medieval religious plays. Looking at it more realistically, it seems to date back to a German translation of *The Devil to Pay,* one of the most successful imitations of *The Beggar's Opera.* After being the rage in England for some seasons, this was taken up in Germany, where it eventually, in a version composed by J. A. Hiller, rivaled its popularity in England. Hiller, who rather inappropriately filled Bach's shoes as Thomascantor, has been called the father of the Singspiel.

Deservedly so, for he took the hint given by the excellent box office of *Der Teufel ist los* and wrote countless more. He bought his trumpery puff paste in Paris, and seems to have saved what truly musical gifts he had for the art lied and the giving of concerts. He filled his Singspiels with snatches of song as trivial as the words that went with them. Like the ballad operas whence they derived, these early Singspiels were as broad as the popular taste—by strict definition, merely farces with music.

Despite Mozart's flair for the light comic, his connection with the Singspiel came about accidentally. Josef II, that not quite great son of Maria Theresa, had a sincere and quite un-Hapsburgian passion for culture. Having been instrumental in putting German spoken drama on a firm footing in Vienna, he decided in 1778 to lend his imperial favor to opera in German. The repertoire at the Burgtheater, where the German operas were given, has, with a single exception, no place in the history of art. In fact, the entire story of this short-lived project would have only academic interest had not Gottlieb Stephanie, an official in the theater, happened to rewrite someone else's libretto and then hand it to Mozart. That it was not quite his to hand made no difference to this knavish actor-manager-quasi-playwright, who was famous for his complicated schemings and a version of *Macbeth* even more melodramatic than Shakespeare's. In August, 1781, Mozart began to set *Die Entführung aus dem Serail* in a great hurry, having been told that it would be used to entertain the Grand Duke Paul of Russia, who was arriving in six weeks. But that personage delayed his coming, and when he finally appeared, Gluck's *Alceste* was sung instead. The reasons for this substitution are not clear, but one possibility may have been that *Die Entführung* was considered too frivolous for the gloomy heir apparent of all the Russias. Not until July 16, 1782, was this delicate peepshow into seraglio life presented at the Burgtheater. It had a very considerable success.

Die Entführung suffers from a variety of faults, any one of which might have been fatal to the work of a less gifted composer. To recount them is to make one amazed that it has survived at all. In the first place, the Pasha Selim, one of the four principal characters, is musically mute, which means that, in an opera, he is dramatically forceless. It does not seem that Mozart's failure to make Selim sing arose from a well-considered intention to produce a specific effect: it is more likely that either he did not have peculiarly Selimlike music on tap or he could not find a singer for the music he thought suitable for a Turkish pasha. If, however, he (or his librettist) purposely limited the noble Turk to conversation, the result was no more dramatically effective than when, fifty years later, Auber tried it again in *Masaniello*, in which the *première danseuse* mimes the role of the dumb girl. In Auber, the effect is at least fey; in Mozart, it is merely inept.

The nonvocalizing Selim is surrounded, but scarcely supported, by a group of characters who, with one exception, are, for Mozart, wooden without parallel. The heroine is simply not characterized at all: she is as much a vocalist as Selim is not—a singing-school star. Finally, *Die Entführung* cannot be viewed as a musical unity. It is, instead, a medley of styles, some used with nice appreciation of their character, others haphazardly. The opera, in short, has no central unmistakable manner from which diversions are excusable as legitimate sources of contrast or underlinings of character. In this exaggerated eclecticism, true contrast is lost.

Reputation, chiefly, has kept *Die Entführung* on a few stages. Good things it has in some abundance. It boasts one superb character—the major-domo Osmin, first of the great line of Mozart's *buffa* varlets, ancestor of Leporello and Monostatos. Time and again, it breaks into gay and delicious song. Occasionally, there is something even finer: Constanze's aria in Act II—*"Martern aller Arten"*—is rather too magnificent for its surroundings. *Die Entführung* is a comic opera verging on farce; *"Martern aller Arten"* is noble and sublime, belonging in spirit to *Die Zauberflöte* and technically to the very highest phase of Mozart's art. In it we can detect the beginning of a new symphonic conception of opera, German in practice but not obviously national. Yet it is only a beginning, for there is a certain naïveté, by no means artless, in treating the voice as but one of several concertizing instruments. But it is not this aria, any more than it is Osmin's comic interludes, the vivacious drinking song, or the absurdly anachronistic, utterly amusing Chorus of Janissaries, that has kept *Die Entführung* alive. It is, rather, the belief that, being the earliest full-length opera in German by an undisputed master, it must necessarily be the first great German opera, and therefore worth performing. What performability it has depends upon how high a value is to be placed upon reproducing in costume an eighteenth-century concert of vocal music, some of it extremely beautiful.*

While working on *Die Entführung*, Mozart kept his demanding father informed by letter of the vicissitudes of its creation, and nowhere did he suggest that the libretto was the mediocre thing it most certainly is. True, details displeased him, and he imperiously changed them. But neither here nor in any of his earlier correspondence are there signs that Mozart ever seriously analyzed the qualities a good libretto should have. He once wrote: "In an opera, the poetry must be the obedient daughter of the music," and he was perfectly willing to bend the verse to his will without the slightest scruple, the more particularly as he had a talent for adroit jingles. Unlike Gluck, he seems to have been totally indifferent to any speculations about the wholeness of opera. In this negligent attitude, he was true to himself: all his life he worked miracles with material that happened to come his way and which he accepted without question. A flagrant example of his noncritical attitude where all except the pure stuff of music was concerned is in his song writing. Like Schubert, he set any stray verse that came his way—and as a catchpenny hauler he was less lucky than Schubert, who often found Goethe or Heine in his net. There is reason to believe that if a good libretto or two had not all but been thrown at him, Mozart would have gone on pouring out glorious music into unworthy vessels.

* The first American performance of *Die Entführung* occurred in Brooklyn, in February, 1860, disguised as *Belmonte e Constanze*. Reverting to the German text, the German Opera House, New York, offered it on October 10, 1862. The Russian tenor Vladimir Rosing, as director of the Rochester (later, American) Opera Company, staged an English version in New York and other American cities.

This dark picture of Mozart's incuriousness about one of the central problems of opera needs some slight qualification. If it was indeed he, and not the librettist, who suggested that Beaumarchais' *Le Mariage de Figaro* would make a good opera, he must be credited with having hit upon one of the most inspired ideas in the history of art. That the quality of the inspiration was on a par with that of the person who happens to be first in dramatizing the season's runaway novel is no more valid criticism than the fact that Paisiello's *Il Barbiere di Siviglia*, a setting of the first half of the same story, had all Europe talking. *Figaro*, Beaumarchais' sequel to *Le Barbier de Séville*, had created a scandal in Paris, which made it tremendously popular. Mozart read the play, and point-blank asked Lorenzo da Ponte, Josef II's Latin secretary and theater poet, to make a libretto from it. He had met his Calzabigi.

Da Ponte was just the man to take on a tough job of this sort. *Le Mariage de Figaro* was not only ribald: it was political dynamite, and a less intrepid and practiced wangler would not have touched it. But Da Ponte was an altogether odd sort: an unfrocked priest, a converted Jew, an ex-university professor, and a boon companion of Casanova, he was an eel in wiggling into and out of domestic and political scandals. Mozart was but an incident in his life: after presenting him with three excellent librettos, Da Ponte resumed a wandering life that took him by way of London, where he taught Italian, wrote more librettos, and failed as a bookdealer, to New York, where he established a series of spasmodic and rapidly crumbling business enterprises. There, after failing to support himself and his wife by the sale of tobacco, groceries, or strong waters, he turned again to opera, and made musical history by helping Manuel del Popolo Vicente García to establish the first Italian opera company in New York. The year was 1825, and as García was the mighty sire of three great children—Maria Malibran, Pauline Viardot-García, and Manuel Patricio García—the last of whom died as recently as 1906—the influence of that amiable reprobate Da Ponte seems to span the centuries. Born in 1749, and thus Mozart's senior by seven years, he learned his craft from Metastasio, whom he knew intimately. In the United

Lorenzo da Ponte, after a painting by Samuel F. B. Morse

States, where he died in 1838, he sat for his portrait to Samuel
F. B. Morse, and was patronized by Clement C. Moore, who
wrote "The Night Before Christmas." Da Ponte ended his
days as a teacher of Italian at what is now Columbia University,
where there exists the Da Ponte professorship of Italian.

Even in 1786, Da Ponte was not a man to quail before the
prospect of Josef II's wrath. In six weeks, he was presenting
the libretto to the Emperor in person. Whereupon, according
to his more or less truthful *Memoirs*, the following remarkable
dialogue ensued:

> "What?" he [the Emperor] said. "Don't you know that Mo-
> zart, though a wonder at instrumental music, has written only
> one opera, and nothing remarkable at that?"
>
> "Yes, Sire," I replied quietly, "but without Your Majesty's
> clemency I would have written but one drama in Vienna!"
>
> "That may be true," he answered, "but this *Mariage de
> Figaro*—I have just forbidden the German troupe to use it!"
>
> "Yes, Sire," I rejoined, "but I was writing an opera, and not
> a comedy. I had to omit many scenes and to cut others quite
> considerably. I have omitted or cut anything that might offend
> good taste or public decency at a performance over which the
> Sovereign Majesty might preside. The music, I may add, as far
> as I may judge of it, seems to me marvelously beautiful."
>
> "Good! If that be the case, I will rely on your good taste as
> to the music and on your wisdom as to the morality. Send the
> score to the copyist."

Had all of Josef II's decisions been as wise as this, history
would have passed a more favorable verdict on him than that
he meant well. *Le Nozze di Figaro* evoked, on its first performance (May 1, 1786), an ovation of such proportions that
Mozart must have felt that he had found a formula of success.
Every number was encored, and the Austrian counterparts of
that very *ancien régime* at which Beaumarchais had directed
his shafts howled their delight, apparently not realizing that
in the insolent Almaviva, with his brutal indifference to the
feelings of social underlings, they were seeing themselves. In
a very short time, Prague, which thenceforth became a center of
hysterical Mozartolatry, discovered *Le Nozze*. Mozart went there

to conduct it, and was deified. Not only did golden kronen flow into his pockets, but a fat contract for a new opera was signed. The Viennese stupidly shelved *Le Nozze* that same season in favor of *Una Cosa rara*, a trifle by a young Spaniard, Vicente Martín y Solar, which happened to contain a number that began the Viennese waltz craze. But the Praguers, who never tired of *Le Nozze*, were on the side of history: it is still one of the unfailing joys of Western civilization wherever that civilization is intact, and occasionally where it is not. Oddly, Italy has not responded to this most characteristic creation of the greatest of *buffa* composers. Its own plethora of operas, good, bad, and indifferent, spewed forth by living favorites, has been partly accountable for this situation, but there is no doubt that a rather different concept of *buffa* has militated against *Le Nozze's* complete acceptance there.*

It has often been said that *Le Nozze di Figaro* is the easiest of Mozart's great operas to stage under modern conditions. Almost the opposite of this statement is true. Certainly, it needs no such elaborate paraphernalia as does *Don Giovanni* (which are of such a challenging nature that when the Residenz Theater, Munich, which possessed the first revolving stage in Europe wanted to show it off, for the first time, they chose [1896] *Don Giovanni*). Nor does it ask for miracles of vocal agility such as are required to sing Ottavio in the *Don* or the Queen of the Night in *Die Zauberflöte*. True, furthermore, the audience is not required to suspend disbelief in barefaced nonsense as it is in *Die Zauberflöte*. But these are feathers if weighed against the difficulty a modern audience has in trying to sense unity in what is, through constant hearing via radio, concert, transcription, and home music-making, a succession of gems.

This unhappy situation is not, of course, Mozart's fault: he perfectly fitted music to book, perfectly sustained characterization, perfectly established the wholeness of the opera. Equally, it is not the audience's fault: Mozart worked on each section with such inspiration coupled with such flawless craftsmanship that each section stands, if possible, too obviously on its own

* Types of *buffa* are more fully discussed in later sections of this book that deal with Rossini, Verdi, and Wolf-Ferrari.

merits. One would like, finally, to say that the singers are not
to blame, but unfortunately they are usually only too willing
to regard their part as done if they only do a good singing job
in a recital that happens to be divided into acts. Only in a performance in which the listener is resolved to hear an opera and
not a collection of songs sung by a galaxy of stars,* and in which
impresario, stage director, and each member of the cast are
equally resolved to give due emphasis to the development of
the drama—a great one, be it remembered—can *Le Nozze* be
the complete experience it should be. These optimum conditions place upon the lover of Mozart and of opera at its best a
strenuous if not onerous obligation: he must go hopefully to
every performance of *Le Nozze*, for only about once in a generation does a perfect creation emerge.

Le Nozze is not the overture, *"Se vuol ballare," "Non più
andrai," "Voi che sapete," "Deh vieni, non tardar,"* and a dozen
or more other airs or concerted numbers, including the splendidly contrived group finales, revolutionary in conception and
far-reaching in influence. It is not the unrivaled series of living,
rounded characters—Figaro, Susanna, Cherubino, Count Almaviva, the Countess, Dr. Bartolo, and the rest. It is a peerless
jeu d'esprit which knows where it is going from the first note
of the lightsome and exactly right, perfectly proportioned overture to the joyous finale, when the reconciled principals announce that they are about to turn night into day. Complex as
the plot is, the opera proceeds to its destination as swiftly and
unerringly as a homing pigeon making its way back through
the trackless mazes of the sky. Frivolous, impudent, and witty
in every scene and situation, *Le Nozze* carries the profound
internal reality of its own made world and has the razor-sharp
edge of seriousness that the mature satire of Beaumarchais
deserves. Opera could justify its existence on the basis of *Le
Nozze di Figaro* alone. A few operas as great were composed by
Mozart himself and by perhaps half a dozen others: they are
different in kind, not better.

As *The Follies of a Day*, *Le Nozze* may have been sung in New
York as early as 1799. Its authenticated *première* in England dates

* Although now (1941) galaxies of stars are getting rarer and rarer.

from June 18, 1812, when Angelica Catalani, one of the first women ever to manage an opera house, was the Susanna. For that performance, the baritone role of Almaviva was offered to a noted tenor, who answered that he considered it beneath his dignity to sing in a comic opera. The first authenticated American performance took place at the Park Theater, New York, on May 10, 1824. When Joseph Wood and his more famous wife, Mary Anne Paton, gave the opera in Boston, on April 8, 1835, Charlotte Cushman, later a queen of American tragedy, was the Countess—it was her operatic debut. In the same role, at Venice in 1847, Sophie Cruvelli (nee Crüwell) first appeared in opera. Sir Charles Santley was the most admired of English Figaros, and Pauline Lucca, as Cherubino, was equally applauded.

Le Nozze entered the repertoire of the Academy of Music, New York, on November 23, 1858. On January 31, 1894, it was first heard at the Metropolitan Opera House, with the following resplendent cast: Lillian Nordica (Susanna), Emma Eames (the Countess), Sigrid Arnoldson (Cherubino), Mario Ancona (Figaro), and Édouard de Reszke (Count Almaviva). The following have been outstanding interpreters of Le Nozze at the Metropolitan: as Susanna, Marcella Sembrich and Frieda Hempel; as the Countess, Johanna Gadski and Margaret Matzenauer; as Cherubino, Zélie de Lussan, Suzanne Adams, Fritzi Scheff, and Geraldine Farrar; as Figaro, Victor Maurel, Giuseppe Campanari, and Giuseppe de Luca, and as Count Almaviva, Antonio Scotti and Adamo Didur. After 1918, Le Nozze was dropped from the Metropolitan repertoire for twenty-one reasons: it was revived on February 20, 1940, with Bidu Sayao (Susanna), Elisabeth Rethberg (the Countess), Risë Stevens (Cherubino), Ezio Pinza (Figaro), and John Brownlee (Count Almaviva). In some recent performances, Jarmila Novotna has been the Cherubino. In the season of 1940-41, Le Nozze was given six times, and it is establishing itself as a popular favorite.

Da Ponte's eminent role in the collaboration that created Le Nozze must not be underestimated, particularly as it can be proved by the next book he gave to Mozart. Undoubtedly he saw exactly where his composer's strength lay: it was ability to create drama by means of vigorously painted portraits, and Da Ponte realized, therefore, that his own duty was to provide the types into which Mozart could breathe life. A significant passage from his Memoirs shows how he served Mozart in comparison with another composer: "For Mozart I chose *Don Giovanni,* a subject that pleased him mightily; and for Martini [Da Ponte's name for Martín y Solar] the *Arbore di Diana.* For him I wanted an attractive theme adaptable to those sweet melodies of his. . . ." Paraphrased, Da Ponte says that Diana's tree is good enough for the ordinary composer of pretty tunes, but for Mozart nothing less than one of the great primal figures of European literature will do. At the same time, he was also helping Salieri to turn a French opera into an Italian one. When Josef II remarked that he would never succeed in doing all three jobs at once, Da Ponte replied: "Perhaps not, but I am going to try. I shall write evenings for Mozart, imagining that I am reading the *Inferno;* mornings I shall work for Martini, and pretend I am studying Petrarch; my afternoons will be for Salieri—he is my Tasso." The Emperor was pleased to say that Da Ponte's parallels were well chosen.

Don Giovanni is not the flawless thing *Le Nozze di Figaro* is. Although, like all of Mozart's operas, it was designed as a musical unit (for instance, it begins and ends in the same key, and the big moments of the action are either in that key or closely related keys), it does not produce an effect of coherent structure. The reasons for this are twofold: first, it is never given in the original version—Mozart himself began the orgy of revision that managers and singers have been indulging in ever since; second, the libretto is a patchwork of Da Ponte and conventional scenes and stock characters borrowed from other writers. The circumstances under which the poet worked suggest that he did not give full attention to his task:

> I returned home and went to work. I sat down at my table and did not leave it for twelve hours continuous—a bottle of Tokay to my right, a box of Seville to my left, in the middle an inkwell. A beautiful girl of sixteen—I should have preferred to love her only as a daughter, but alas . . . !—was living in the house with her mother, who took care of the family, and came to my room at the sound of the bell. To tell the truth the bell rang rather frequently, especially at moments when I felt my inspiration waning.

In some ways, this sounds like the ideal recipe for writing about Don Juan, but even Byron did not combine reality and fiction in such a reckless manner when he was working on his interpretation of the great philanderer.

Don Giovanni suffers mainly from Da Ponte's failure to surround the magnificently built-up character of the Don with strong independent personalities. Just as Leonora dwarfs the rest of the *Fidelio* cast, so, with one or two exceptions, the Don dwarfs all the other personages of the action. The juvenile lead (and, from a Hollywood's-eye-view, the hero), Ottavio, is a ninny, and Donna Anna, leader of the betrayed ladies, is a female ninny. The chief exception, significantly, is the Don's familiar and servant—the comic, cowardly toad at his ear, Leporello. The Commendatore, the instrument of justice, is never more than an animated statue. Masetto and Zerlina, on whom much of the delicately silly byplay of the opera depends, have been given such delicious music that we are almost induced to believe that they are more than conventionalized rustics. Neither the functions nor the portrayal of these characters are as definite as those in *Le Nozze*. The Don (or Leporello—which comes to the same thing) is so strongly realized that even when he is off the stage, his personality towers over the action. This is, of course, a triumph of characterization, but it tends to weaken conflict and, by overheightening contrast, reduce it to ineffectiveness. Thus, *Don Giovanni* is a superb projection of character, but a feeble drama.

There is a story that Mozart, who arrived in Prague with the score of *Don Giovanni* only partially complete, did not get around to composing the overture until the night before the final rehearsal, and that his wife had to keep him awake with a jug of punch and the reading of fairy tales. This may account for the fact that *Don Giovanni* has the least auspicious opening of any of Mozart's great operas. Thereafter, however, the magic works throughout. Soon we hear Leporello's *"Madamina, il catalogo"* (that brazen list of the Don's conquests with which Feodor Chaliapin invariably disrupted the performance). Shortly after that comes *"Là ci darem la mano,"* loveliest of all duets. Straight to the end follows a wealth of wonderful airs and ensembles, rising in the second act to its florid peak in "*Il mio tesoro*," a tenor showpiece of excessive difficulty and great melodic beauty. But of course the most popular excerpt from *Don Giovanni* is the minuet at the end of the first act. It is used as music for a party in the Don's palace and at its first appearance is played by a small orchestra on the stage.

All these elements add up to an opera that is neither comic nor tragic, but an artful mingling of the two that comes—if correctly performed—close to life. The Don, alternately comic, pathetic, and villainous, and a blend of all these when music and action are most intense, becomes—in the last scene—a fully realized hero of nineteenth-century romanticism. His engulfment by the flames of Hell is far indeed from Orpheus at the gates of Erebus, but only next door to Weber and Marschner. There is a symphonic power, not of a classical kind, and certainly found in no one before Beethoven, in this tremendous finale. Mozart himself did not explore this precise vein further in his operas, but its presence was enough to suggest to others its vast possibilities.

Not quite thirty years after its *première* at Prague, *Don Giovanni* was introduced to England. On April 12, 1817, William Ayrton staged it at the King's Theater, London, and it was repeated more than twenty times the first season. The first American performance occurred the very next year, on December 26, when Philadelphia heard it, but in English. The Garcías brought *Don Giovanni* to New York on May 23, 1826, at the Park Theater, with the elder Manuel—a tenor—as the Don, and the younger Manuel as Leporello; the elder Manuel's wife was Donna Elvira, and his daughter Maria (later, the famous Malibran) was Zerlina. Notable productions of *Don Giovanni* were frequent during the century, one of the most outstanding being that of July 6, 1861, at Covent Garden, with Giulia Grisi (Donna Anna), Adelina Patti (Zerlina), Jean-Baptiste Faure (Don Giovanni), Enrico Tamberlik (Don Ottavio), Karl Formès (Leporello), and Giorgio Ronconi (Masetto). Had Luigi Lablache lived to sing Leporello with this cast, it would have been next to perfect.

Early in its first season, the Metropolitan Opera House welcomed *Don Giovanni*, on November 29, 1883, with Emmy Fursch-Madi (Donna Anna), Christine Nilsson (Donna Elvira), Marcella Sem-

brich (Zerlina), Giuseppe Kaschmann (Don Giovanni), Italo Campanini (Don Ottavio), and Mirabella (Leporello). On December 27,
1899, Antonio Scotti, as the Don, made his Metropolitan debut,
supported by Lillian Nordica (Donna Anna—she had made her
world debut, at Milan, as Donna Elvira), Suzanne Adams (Donna
Elvira), Sembrich (Zerlina), Thomas Salignac (Don Ottavio), and
Édouard de Reszke (Leporello).* Victor Maurel and Maurice
Renaud divided honors as the finest of New York Dons, the latter
at the Manhattan Opera House. On January 23, 1908, the Metropolitan revived *Don Giovanni* with superb casting, Eames, Gadski,
Sembrich, Scotti, Alessandro Bonci, Chaliapin, and Robert Blass
(the Commendatore) being the principals and Gustav Mahler the
conductor. The four performances that season were the last there
until November 29, 1929, when the chief roles were taken by Leonora Corona, Rethberg, Editha Fleischer, Pinza, Beniamino Gigli,
Pavel Ludikar, and Léon Rothier. In the most recent performances,
Zinka Milanov, Novotna, Sayao, Pinza, Tito Schipa, and Salvatore
Baccaloni were the principals, with Bruno Walter a vociferously
acclaimed conductor.

Don Giovanni, which evoked lusty bravos from Prague at its
first performance, on October 29, 1787, had favorable repercus-
sions in Vienna. Little more than a month later, Gluck having
died, Mozart was appointed to succeed him as *Kammerkompo-
nist* to Josef II. Although the Emperor seemed, in cutting the
annual stipend of the post from 2000 to 800 gulden, to be passing judgment on the respective merits of Gluck and Mozart,
it was fortunate for the latter that he received the preferment
when he did. For Vienna, when it heard *Don Giovanni* in
May, 1788, cold-shouldered it. Entrenched at court, however
insignificantly, Mozart was certain of a few crumbs, even though
Salieri for personal reasons as well as because of his position
as Gluck's spiritual heir, opposed everything he did. And as
Salieri had just become court conductor and was himself a
darling of the Viennese opera lovers, his opposition was almost
blighting. As it was, Mozart's ever being employed again for the
Vienna stage may have rested on the happy accident of *Figaro*'s
being revived there in August, 1789, with record-breaking suc-

* Édouard's brother Jean sang the role of Don Giovanni while still officially
a baritone.

cess. On its heels followed an order from the Emperor for a comic opera, which was to be rushed through to completion.

Mozart and Da Ponte, once more his collaborator, obeyed: the manuscript score of *Così fan tutte*, with its countless abbreviations, testifies to the composer's anxiety to finish in time. The reason for Josef II's hurry is not known, but certain it is that he survived the *première*, on January 26, 1790, by less than a month. With his death, Mozart lost his most understanding collaborator, for Da Ponte had relied solely on the Emperor for his position at court: now he had to flee for his life, whether from debtors, politicians, or vengeful husbands is not clear.

With misfortune stalking him and almost ready to pounce, Da Ponte gave to Mozart one of the most sparkling products of his wit, and that despite the fact that neither he nor the composer had anything to say about the plot itself. It was based on certain recent happenings in Vienna that had so delighted the Emperor (discouraged about everything else in the world) that he ordered them to be immortalized. Few librettos have been so denigrated, largely for moral reasons, and indeed the virtuous Josef seems a strange sponsor for it. Briefly, two gentlemen, goaded by a cynical oldster, test their sweethearts' fidelity by returning to them in disguise. The ladies succumb to the rich-seeming cavaliers, and just as a double wedding is about to be celebrated, the young men make their identities known. All ends happily to the moralizing refrain: *"Così fan tutte"*— Women Are Like That! This plot will probably impress most modern readers as vapid rather than immoral, though it would be interesting to know what Beethoven, whose puritanical morals were outraged by *Figaro* and *Don Giovanni*, thought of this. It is significant that when Barbier and Carré, the shrewd librettists of Gounod's *Faust*, tried to find a more palatable story for a French version of *Così fan tutte*, the best they could think up was a translation of one of Shakespeare's most insipid efforts, *Love's Labour's Lost*.

While *Così fan tutte* has not won as many admirers as Mozart's three other great operas, it nevertheless has interests of its own to which they cannot pretend. Possibly because of the circumstances of its creation, it has a period quality that approaches realism. We find Mozart the analyst of types rather than the creator of individuals.* The characters have no motor force of their own, but must respond to the touch of that merciless, teasing, galvanic wire. Don Alfonso, the one initiator of all the opera's imbroglios, is, in one respect, nothing but our old friend, the *deus ex machina*. But this is a superficial evaluation, and though his role in the opera is confined, with a single short exception, to recitative, Don Alfonso is, in another respect, one more in that immortal gallery of dramatic middlemen that begins with Osmin and ends with Papageno. Of this gallery, Don Alfonso is in one way the most interesting: he is more cerebral than his compeers—he represents a point of view, a philosophy of a sort, not perhaps of the highest order, but nevertheless consistent and unmistakable. Through him speak those worldly-wise teammates, Mozart and Da Ponte. Don Alfonso's complement is the ladies' maid Despina, who never quite achieves his solidity, but who is an unforgettable figure of fun. A creature of disguises, she seems, in her notary's gown, like a parody Portia; and the enormous, somehow shocking spectacles she wears as the doctor have some of the powerful conventionality of a Greek mask.

All of Mozart's operas have their special problems for the listener. That of *Così fan tutte* comes from the importance of the recitative, which, instead of being used secondarily to connect the dramatic rises, is the very *élan vital* of the action. Reading the text through is a requisite to listening, nor will the task be a bore: it is Da Ponte at his wittiest and most sarcastic best, as deft and sure as Beaumarchais himself. Only by doing so can we fully recognize how Mozart has made music the distillation of this satire: until then, we must be prepared to find *Così fan tutte* amorphous and, at best, a harebrained projection of nitwittery. But when the argument is known in full, then everything in the musical scheme falls into its ordained place, and what emerges is one of Mozart's most aerial

---

* In other operas, Mozart occasionally did not take the trouble, or have the energy, to create individuals, and so was satisfied with mere types—quite another matter.

and imaginative structures. That we must not expect a succession of delicious and magical airs such as we find in *Figaro* may disappoint many and explain *Così fan tutte*'s comparative lack of popularity. This is not a flaw: it is a different, perhaps a more difficult, technique. Seduction does not come at once, as it does in *Figaro*: but when it does come, it is likely to be more complete if less intense.

Although *Così fan tutte* was heard in London as early as 1811, it has never been truly popular there. In America, it has fared even worse, for the *première* did not take place until March 24, 1922, when the Metropolitan offered Florence Easton as Fiordiligi, Lucrezia Bori as Despina, Frances Peralta as Dorabella, George Meader (Ferrando), De Luca (Guglielmo), and Didur (Don Alfonso). Artur Bodanzky led the orchestra. Twelve performances in four seasons were called for before *Così fan tutte* was dropped. More recently, it has been revived with some success in England, at Glyndebourne.

Between *Die Entführung* and *Figaro* Mozart had written a trifling but pretty one-acter called *Der Schauspieldirektor* that is still occasionally heard, sometimes with a different libretto. Now, between *Così fan tutte* and the completion of *Die Zauberflöte*, he wrote another trifle, but one of huge proportions and dull lineaments. This was *La Clemenza di Tito*, whose Metastasio libretto had already been set by such old-time masters as Gluck, Hasse, Leonardo Leo, and a minor stripling of the Scarlatti family. As archaic in style as if it had been composed by any of these men, Mozart's version, provided with a libretto liberally but not successfully recast for the occasion, is the poorest dramatic work of his maturity. Possibly the circumstances of its composition have much to do with this—it was written to order in eighteen days, the consignees being the loyal burghers of Prague, the occasion the crowning of Leopold II as King of Bohemia. It shows evidence of haste throughout, and haste and Mozart's mounting illness may have been his excuse for allowing his pupil, Franz Xaver Süssmayr, to compose portions of the recitative. Apart from showing again that Mozart was not happy trying to cope with the creaking machinery of *opera seria* (he was able to accept and transcend the almost as creaking machinery of *opera buffa*), *La Clemenza di Tito,* as a potboiler, contains the music it deserves. Oddly enough, it gained a considerable popularity that did not languish until the nineteenth century was well advanced.*

But *La Clemenza di Tito,* to its extenuation, had the ill fortune to be composed while both *Die Zauberflöte* and the Requiem, works on which Mozart was lavishing his most sublime inspirations, were in progress. On them he had staked his hopes, respectively, of final triumph as a composer for the stage and of immortality. He died before finishing the Requiem, but lived to conduct the opening performance of *Die Zauberflöte,* on September 30, 1791. That *première* was far from a triumph, and unfortunately the composer was too ill to be present to see the gradual turning of the tide. News of it did, however, trickle into the death chamber, cheering him when he could get his mind off the unfinished Requiem. But even the cheer had a quality of the macabre in it, for it consisted of his taking his watch in hand and timing the performance as, every evening at curtain time, it began to unroll in his imagination. Sixty-six days after that first frigid performance at the Theater auf der Wieden, Mozart was dead.

Some of *Die Zauberflöte's* early history, outside its native Vienna, was decidedly curious. In 1801, there was heard at Paris a pastiche called *Les Mystères d'Isis,* which consisted largely of sections of *Die Zauberflöte,* plus bits of *Don Giovanni, Le Nozze di Figaro, La Clemenza di Tito,* and Haydn symphonies. This sort of potpourri was in no way unusual for the period, and this one was enthusiastically received. The untainted version of *Die Zauberflöte* did not reach Paris for many years. Meanwhile, it was faring better in London, being introduced by Giuseppe Naldi, who, impressed by the welcome accorded to *Così fan tutte* in 1811, chose *Die Zauberflöte,* almost certainly as *Il Flauto magico,* for his benefit at the end

* For instance, *La Clemenza di Tito* was the first Mozart opera to be heard in London, the Prince Regent lending the full score from his own library. Elizabeth Billington and John Braham were the distinguished leaders of an otherwise inadequate cast that sang it at the King's Theater, Haymarket, on March 27, 1806. Catalani succeeded Mrs. Billington as a surpassing Vitellia. The American *première* was via the radio: dividing it between two night sessions, Alfred Wallenstein presented it over the Mutual Broadcasting System, on June 22 and 29, 1940.

of the same season. In 1821, Wilhelmine Schröder-Devrient sang the role of Pamina in her world debut at Vienna.

A dozen years later, on April 17, 1833, New York heard an English version at the Park Theater, the original text and uncut score having to wait for a hearing there until November 10, 1862, when it was sung at the German Opera House. Covent Garden presented an important revival in 1851, when Anna Zerr was imported from Vienna to sing the role of the Queen of the Night. She did not satisfy, but the rest of the cast did—Giulia Grisi (Pamina), Viardot-García (Papagena), Mario (Tamino), Ronconi (Papageno), and Formes (Sarastro). Ilma di Murska was, according to Herman Klein, the most nearly perfect Queen of the Night ever heard in London. The first Metropolitan *Zauberflöte* was heard in Italian, on March 30, 1900, with Sembrich, Eames, Zélie de Lussan, Andreas Dippel, Giuseppe Campanari, and Pol Plançon; in minor roles were such celebrated artists as Milka Ternina, Eugenia Mantelli, Suzanne Adams, Rosa Olitzka, and Antonio Pini-Corsi. For the Metropolitan revival of November 6, 1926, in the original German, the principals were Marion Talley, Rethberg, Louise Hunter, Rudolf Laubenthal, Gustav Schützendorf, Paul Bender, and Meader (Monostatos). While Rethberg and Meader were models of what Mozartian style should be, Talley was utterly unfitted for the difficult role the Metropolitan management had carelessly assigned to her. Editha Fleischer, playing a small part, made her Metropolitan debut in this performance.

Fully to appreciate *Die Zauberflöte* as one of the great flawed works of art, one must wrestle with the task of trying to understand its libretto in terms of the period that produced it and of its meaning to Mozart. Read with these considerations in mind, what seems on the surface the veriest jumble of complicated nonsense takes on a certain mad logic. Emmanuel Schikaneder, its fabricator and one of Mozart's childhood friends, tried to cram into this strange mélange of parable, fairy tale, and blatant, gallery-wooing extravaganza all the esoteric symbolism and grandiose revelations of the Grand Oriental Lodge of Freemasons, of which both he and Mozart were members. As if this were not enough, Schikaneder is alleged to have woven into this crazyquilt a rather belated attack on the *Realpolitik* of Maria Theresa. Those who believe this last pretend to read

in the vicious, quite incredibly malignant Queen of the Night
the housewifely features of that Queen Victoria of the eighteenth century who had once dandled Mozart on her knee.
Similarly, they identify the wily Monostatos with the Jesuits,
and Prince Tamino with the virtuous Josef II.

Mozart set the whole shooting match with intense seriousness. After all, he was as good a Mason as Schikaneder, and
besides, the libretto offered opportunities for every kind of
musical treatment, ranging from a more solemnly religious
style than he ever achieved (if, indeed, he had ever wished to
achieve it) in his Masses to the most unqualified slapstick. If
one were to hear a recital that contained the high priest Sarastro's exalted utterances—"*O Isis und Osiris*" and "*In diesen
heil'gen Hallen,*" the Queen of the Night's icy pyrotechnics,
and the ripely tender duet—"*Bei Männern, welche Liebe
fühlen*"—between Pamina and the birdman Papageno, he
would be justified in not believing them to be parts of the
same work. (That they are all Mozart he could never doubt.) A
good performance of *Die Zauberflöte* does, if with difficulty and
not without a sense of strain triumphantly overcome, establish
the unity Mozart saw in the book. Even the usual performance
is not a thankless experience, for never is the music less than
Mozart at his most apt. Each number, if exposed to careful
scrutiny, is found to be flawless of its kind and uncannily right
in its place. And its greatest moments, whether of sublimity,
buffoonery, amorousness, playfulness, or villainy, are not surpassed, if they are equaled, in any of Mozart's other masterpieces. If the characterization in *Die Zauberflöte* is less eloquent than that in *Figaro*, it is because the characters are
frankly symbols, and, as such, faithfully exemplified.

It is difficult to classify *Die Zauberflöte*. Technically a Singspiel, it seems like a farce oratorio in costume. Its comic interludes, however, are incidental: they perform, and perfectly,
the same function as Shakespeare's dubious comic relief. *Die
Zauberflöte*, as one is fairly admonished by the solemn strains
of the magnificent overture, is primarily a religious work.
The scene of purification, in the second act, is fit music for an
Eleusinian initiation, while Sarastro's has been called by Ber-

nard Shaw the only music that would not sound out of place in the mouth of God. Nor, similarly, are the arias of the Queen of the Night out of place in the mouth of that female devil. Certainly, they are ideal protagonists in this quasi-mystical struggle between the forces of good and evil. Musically and spiritually, *Die Zauberflöte* is a more convincing paean to life transcendental than the sick fervors of the Requiem.

While Mozart's other great stage pieces, though operating in frameworks from the past and cheerfully accepting equally hoary conventions, pullulate with ideas for the future, *Die Zauberflöte,* not less great, was too much the product of a special need and of a unique personality's obligations to his most intimate being, to be easily imitable. Thus, in general, it has had no easily recognizable descendants. The mold died with the maker.

Chapter VII

The Beethoven Heresy

IN CONSIDERING Ludwig van Beethoven as an operatic composer, facts and figures are significant. He composed nine symphonies, eleven overtures, sixteen string quartets, thirty-two piano sonatas—and one opera, *Fidelio*. Beethoven appeared just when Mozart, one of the most skillful and understanding of musical dramatists, and Haydn, who thought in sonatas and had only the most parochial idea of the nature of opera, had managed between them to give the *coup de grâce* to the previously all but unchallenged supremacy of the human voice in music. Haydn was the first composer to achieve greatness almost exclusively by instrumental means, unless the term "greatness" be construed to include such restricted masters, working always in small, as Couperin *le grand* and Domenico Scarlatti. Yet, in 1795, when Haydn had dried the ink on his last great symphony, and Mozart was already four years dead, it was still a question whether the orchestra was to assume first place in the world of music. It needed a titanic resolver of queries to answer this question one way or another. Beethoven answered it for the orchestra, and since his time the voice has never regained its sovereignty. Translated geographically, this meant that the center of musical gravity had shifted from Italy to Germany. Italy became the voice's last stronghold and has remained so. And, to show how the emphasis was changing in opera itself, Germany also became the center of operatic gravity.

The problem of *Fidelio* is but one of innumerable problems in the artistic life of a man who would not be a whit less famous if he had never composed a line of operatic music. It must be seen in perspective, without excessive claims and without excessive faultfinding. Its importance stretches into infinity not because of its intrinsic qualities, but because of its rather disproportionate influence on later men. It is well to remember that, in the mammoth corpus of Beethoven's work, *Fidelio* is merely Opus 72. Critics and biographers, noticing that Beethoven was always on the verge of composing another opera, have claimed that the reason he did not follow through was his inability to find another suitable libretto. Many, certainly, came to his attention, but for one reason or another, he either refused or forgot them. He carried on long and laborious correspondences with several leading writers of the day, only to give up in despair. He was, of course, a very difficult man to please: his ethical bent was strong—he preferred, therefore, simple situations in which evil was punished or good triumphant. Plot, as such, scarcely interested him at all. As for characters, he saw them less as human beings than as symbols of right or wrong. With such desiderata for his book, it is not surprising that his one opera is not very good. What is surprising is that Beethoven wrote an opera at all. And that he never wrote another is susceptible to the common-sense interpretation that he was a good enough artist to realize—at least subconsciously—that his aims were better achieved in the more abstract forms of instrumental music.

In avoiding the task of another opera, one of Beethoven's favorite excuses was to point out that a proffered libretto had already been set by someone else or resembled another libretto. Obviously, as by the early nineteenth century every situation under the sun had already been used by stage poets, Beethoven could be easy in his mind that he would never have to write another opera. That he had not at first demanded originality is proved by the ancestry of *Fidelio, oder Die eheliche Liebe,* the libretto of which was a translation and adaptation by his friend, Josef Ferdinand von Sonnleithner, of a French original, *Léonore, ou L'Amour conjugal,* which had already been set to music by Pierre Gaveaux for the Opéra-Comique. Its first begetter, Jean-Nicolas Bouilly, had taken the incidents from an episode of which he had had direct knowledge while serving as a government administrator in the province of Tours during the Terror. Before Beethoven's *Leonora* (as *Fidelio* was called until 1814) saw the light, the prolific Ferdinando Paër, a fashionable Parmesan who eventually became court director to Napoleon, had staged at Dresden *Eleanora,* his own setting of an Italian version. Yet, nothing could chill Beethoven's almost adolescent infatuation for this altogether usual tale, once he had set his heart on it. Perhaps it would be more accurate to say that his heart was set on the heroine and on the heroic role she plays in saving her husband's life at the risk of her own.

Beethoven's connection with the stage had begun as early as 1791, when he was twenty-one years old, with some dance tunes he composed for a ballet. This music, which was foisted on the public of Bonn as the work of his patron, Count von Waldstein, was adequate, but nothing to advance its real composer's reputation. Ten years later, he tried again, this time in Vienna, with an overture and dance numbers for an allegorical ballet on the legend of Prometheus. This is certainly bright, attractive music, but definitely not Beethoven in a very dramatic mood. Yet, on the basis of hearing it, Emmanuel Schikaneder, Mozart's old librettist, and still grimly holding on as impresario of the Theater an der Wien, invited Beethoven to compose an opera for his house. The solicitation came at the height of a war between Schikaneder and Baron Braun, chief at the Hoftheater, each of whom had for years fought to beat the other in getting the Vienna *première* of every new opera by Cherubini, the reigning favorite, whom, incidentally, Beethoven much admired. Braun had just outwitted his rival by going to Paris with a black-and-white proposition for Cherubini, and in desperation Schikaneder approached both Beethoven and the facile, half-charlatan, and entirely suave Georg Josef Vogler, immortalized in Browning's *Abt Vogler*, and notable in the history of opera as the teacher of Weber and Meyerbeer. Schikaneder produced the *abbé*'s opera, but before Beethoven could get his offering ready, the veteran was forced to the wall, and his theater bought out by Baron Braun. Schikaneder, whose managerial troubles were as grievous though not as various as Handel's, tried several schemes for recouping his losses, but as they either failed or were stillborn, he went insane en route to Budapest. After much suffering, he died poverty-stricken, in Vienna, in 1812.

Baron Braun at once renewed the contract with Beethoven, who had by this time become so noteworthy a figure in Vien-

nese society that he could dare to dictate to the management
of the Hoftheater just the kind of libretto he would deign
to set.* Sonnleithner's book called for an opera in three acts,
and accordingly, disregarding the fact that the type of plot
doomed the first two acts to triviality or inaction or both, that
is what Beethoven wrote. Working passionately through the
summer of 1805, trying, testing, expanding, contracting, trying
again, and for many reasons repeating the process over and
over, Beethoven completed the opera by the fall.

Leonora was produced at Schikaneder's old house, on November 20, 1805, played three consecutive nights, and was a
dismal failure, partly because of intrinsic faults in the opera
itself, but also because, Napoleon having just occupied Vienna,
the audience consisted mostly of his soldiers. Despite this miti-
gating circumstance, Beethoven reacted violently, almost
despairingly, and began to revise the opera, though only after
threatening to put the score in the ash heap. Friends, with
no great difficulty, made him change his mind, and one of them,
Stephan von Breuning, agreed to overhaul the libretto. Thus
was the first revision of *Leonora* engineered. Breuning condensed the first two acts into one, and shortened the former
third act. These changes were good, but they were not enough.
Again, early in 1806, *Leonora* was tried out, and this time was
beginning to show signs of some small popularity when Beethoven up and quarreled with his impresario. He demanded—
and got—the score back, chucked it into a trunk, and left it
there for eight years.

It is the second revision (shorter than most standard-repertoire
operas), undertaken by the competent dramatist and play doctor, Georg Friedrich Treitschke (a kind of early-nineteenth-
century George S. Kaufman), that is largely responsible for the
version presented today. Treitschke expanded the finales of
both acts, making them dignified and impressive—that of the
second has been so built up, indeed, that it requires a change
of scene. Furthermore, he painstakingly went through the

---

* It seems that Beethoven had done nothing for Schikaneder, and had even
been negotiating with Baron Braun before disaster overtook the Theater an der
Wien.

text and made good German of it. Altogether, it was a credita-ble job, though the material was so refractory that even Treitschke's most conscientious work could not strike a balance between the first and second acts. Beethoven's revisions of the music followed and outdid his librettist's revisions of the text. Those who have devoted painstaking study to the various texts of the opera say that this final overhauling, while clearly the most stageworthy, lacks, being a patchwork of Beethoven's early and middle periods, the spontaneity and stylistic unity of Ver-sions I and II. Reputedly undertaken at the request of some singers from the Kärntnerthortheater, this finally revised ver-sion was produced there in May, 1814, under the name of *Fidelio*. Beethoven had fought to the last against changing the name, but it was probably pointed out to him that the name Leonora used when disguised as a boy only temporarily con-ceals Leonora the woman. And, no doubt, the great and im-mediate success of *Fidelio* did much to console the sulking hero.

One of the chief problems of *Fidelio* is to uncover the reason behind Beethoven's complicated shuffling and reworking of the overtures that accompanied each revision. First, let us straighten out their chronology. "Leonora" No. 1 may conceivably have been written first, and discarded by its composer in the mis-taken belief that it was too slight. But as there was talk of using it for a Prague performance in 1807, it may just as con-ceivably have been composed then. The performance in Prague fell through, and there is no record of "Leonora" No. 1's having been performed publicly during Beethoven's life. With No. 2, we are on firmer ground: it was used at the *première* of the first version. (An alternative version of this has lately been dis-covered.) A revised and much enlarged form, now known as "Leonora" No. 3, preluded the Breuning revision of 1806. This, too, was scrapped in the 1814 version, for which Beethoven composed what is still called the "Fidelio" Overture.

Briefly, "Leonora" No. 1 is a light overture, and would serve well enough to introduce the trivialities of the first act of this ill-balanced score. If it was written first, it signifies that Beethoven, in the beginning, felt called upon not to sum up

the entire drama, but merely to provide an adequate curtain
raiser. With "Leonora" No. 2, his mind was obviously beginning to focus upon the heroic proclivities of his heroine: this
overture, germane enough to Act II, already begins to lower
over Act I. Its expansion—the truly magnificent symphonic
poem known as "Leonora" No. 3—is utterly intolerable in
an opera, and the custom* at the Metropolitan Opera House
of playing it between the first and second scenes of Act II can
be excused only as an understandable desire to get in, willy-
nilly, the best music inspired in Beethoven by the Leonora
theme. The effect is much as if the "Jupiter" Symphony were
played between the acts of *Le Nozze di Figaro* or *Don Giovanni*.
Between 1806 and 1814, Beethoven would seem to have returned to his original feeling about the type of overture required by his opera. The "Fidelio" only suggests the depths
of Leonora's soul and busies itself with the more human drama
of the first act. That Beethoven had set his face against the
heroic Nos. 2 and 3 is proved by the fact that, as the "Fidelio"
was not ready for the 1814 *première*, he used the shallow
"Ruins of Athens" Overture for that event.†

As operatic history continues to be made and unmade, and as
tastes change for better or for worse, it seems likely that the only
parts of *Fidelio* to hold the boards will be the two magnificent
overtures that Beethoven, in a belated understanding of
dramatic effectiveness, discarded. In the past, *Fidelio* has secured revivals for two reasons. First, an opera by Beethoven—
merely because it was by Beethoven—would be bound to secure
a hearing every now and then. Second, the role of Leonora has

* Could Gustav Mahler, who introduced it at the Metropolitan, have thought
that this orchestral interlude produced a Wagnerian effect? Just as ingenious,
but more excusable, was Artur Bodanzky's metamorphosis of *Fidelio* from the
Singspiel Beethoven composed into a grand opera. He did this by changing the
spoken dialogue into recitative and adding accompaniments of his own. As the
Singspielness of *Fidelio* is wholly irrelevant, nothing has been lost. At all events,
the *Fidelio* New York audiences heard until the 1940-41 season, when Bruno
Walter restored the spoken dialogue, was not Beethoven all the way, either in
material or in arrangement.

† While "Leonora" Nos. 2 and 3 are both great music, they are, for two reasons, outside the scope of this chapter: (1) they do not figure in Beethoven's
final reworking of *Fidelio*, and (2) they had almost no influence on later operatic
composers, being, rather, sublime notebook schemes in their composer's thinking
about symphonies.

proportions and possibilities that must inevitably attract an ambitious dramatic soprano who can manage the German tongue and has the lungs for the prison scene.

Anna Milder-Hauptmann, an unrivaled interpreter of Gluck's monumental female roles, first sang Leonora. Malibran, Viardot-García, Therese Tietjens, Lilli Lehmann, Margaret Matzenauer, and Lotte Lehmann have been among the best of her successors. But the most famous of all Leonoras was Wagner's tempestuous friend and one-time idol, Wilhelmine Schröder-Devrient. Henry Fothergill Chorley, dean of mid-nineteenth-century English music critics, said of Malibran and Schröder-Devrient respectively: "The Spaniard threw more horror into the scene in the vault than her predecessor; but the German is before me when, in the introduction to the Chorus of Prisoners, as they creep out of their cells, she questioned one ghastly face after another with the heart-piercing wistfulness of hope long deferred."

The first Metropolitan Leonora was Marianne Brandt, who made it her New York debut role on November 19, 1884. The most recent Leonora at the Metropolitan has been Kirsten Flagstad, who first sang the role there on March 7, 1936, with René Maison as an appealing Florestan. Her almost unrivaled popularity has undoubtedly been the decisive factor in securing a revival for *Fidelio* in recent years. Even though Beethoven is more than ever the most idolized of composers, his one opera needs a great drawing card for its Leonora. Otherwise, its revival can prove financially direful.

For *Fidelio* has neither catchy tunes nor pervasive dramatic strength, at least one of which is essential to operatic popularity. While Beethoven was thoroughly captivated by his noble-acting heroine, there is evidence throughout the score that the libretto itself rather bored him. And no wonder. *Fidelio* has the most conventional of patterns. Beginning as a comic opera, opening, indeed, into a scene of broad farce involving minor characters, it works up to a situation of crisis from which the protagonists are rescued in the nick of time. Despite the several revisions, only two characters emerge with sufficient sharpness to engage Beethoven's deepest interest. And one of these, the scoundrel Pizarro, is, it must be admitted, something of a stock villain. So Leonora, the beloved heroine after whom he had insisted upon naming the opera until the final revision, remains the only full-bodied human being in the book. And even here, as Beethoven treated her, Leonora, built up far beyond the stature of those around her, becomes a superwoman, very essence of very *Frau*, and finally discards human lineaments. As if to provide this epical creature with a comfortable arena in what is, after all, a comic opera, he prolongs and magnifies the resolution of the crisis with a ceremonial paean of unearthly joy that is in a startlingly different key from the genial good humor and slapstick of the early portions. Mozart could, and did, combine farce, comedy, and tragedy; Beethoven did, and could not. It is significant that of all Mozart's operas, Beethoven preferred *Die Zauberflöte*—a very dangerous model from which to borrow even scraps.

The worst that can be said about Beethoven's working out of *Fidelio* is that he seems to have been in collusion with the playwrights and play doctors in getting as little theatrical material as possible out of the plot. More simply and more fairly, Beethoven lacked a sense of the theater. He was utterly ignorant of what constitutes a stageworthy play or opera, and was not interested in working out those minutiae of characterization and incident that give motion and life to a stage spectacle. Not a scene of *Die Zauberflöte* but bears the unmistakable stamp of its composer: in *Fidelio* there are long stretches that might have come from the pen of any workmanlike German of the time who revered Mozart, Cherubini, and Beethoven. There are long stretches, too, that could be moved around without loss or gain, so little are they related to the action.

But when these manifest defects have been admitted, there is much in *Fidelio* that we would not willingly sacrifice. Exclusive of the overtures, there are those moments, rare indeed, but exceedingly powerful when they come, when the action demands a special expenditure of creative energy, in the expression of a single dominating emotion—hatred, love, joy. It was in such concentration that Beethoven excelled: for that reason, Pizarro's *"Ha, welch' ein Augenblick"* is a distillation of fiendish rage; Leonora's *"Abscheulicher, wo eilst du hin?"* a hymn of faith in the power of love, and the duet of Leonora and Florestan, *"O namenlose Freude!"* another ode to joy. It

Wilhelmine Schröder-Devrient as Leonora, in Beethoven's *Fidelio*, after a contemporary print

is in *"Abscheulicher"* that Leonora doffs her more human traits, and becomes, like a German Beatrice, an abstract ethical force. This aria, too, like a *"Martern aller Arten"* of more magnificent proportions, looks forward to the great scenas of Beethoven's disciples, Weber and Wagner, and to a new conception of the dramatic role of the human voice. Yet, perfect though it is, flawlessly though it lights up a noble conception of womankind, it just as relentlessly shows up Beethoven's basic misunderstanding of opera: *"Abscheulicher"* freezes the action in a heroic attitude, and substitutes a generality for an individual. Taking this mightiest moment of *Fidelio* as a test case, we see why an unsurpassed creator of dramatic music was unable to evolve a successful music drama.

Chapter VIII

The German Way

THE Congress of Vienna, which finished the hopes of Napoleon, also shriveled the hopes of that classicism which the Emperor had made part of the panoply of his glory. Throughout Europe, the folk was awakening—by the proxy of artistic middlemen—to a lively sense of itself, of its background, traditions, and strength. Romanticism (for such is the name aestheticians have elected to call this phenomenon) first appeared in different countries at different times, and in each country it wore a special face. There is, for instance, little relation between English romanticism, which, though responding to Continental radiations, went to the facts of nature for its primary source and material, and German romanticism, in which a wondering, childlike, and sometimes childish interest in folklore, particularly of the supernatural and grisly order, was from the first most evident. Also evident from the first was the intense nationalism of the German variety. Germany, with its score of large and small states, had been crushed by the French: naturally, its arts now became German through and through. England, which had not been touched physically by Napoleon, had no spiritual need to assert its national individuality in its arts.

Just as Stein, architect of the modern Prussian state, discovered in the soul of his people, at a crucial moment, the iron that was ultimately, with England's help, to defeat Napoleon, so it was the critics and aestheticians and philosophers who discovered in the folk the base metals from which German romanticism was forged. The movement was engineered and stage-managed from the top: the concepts came before the creations. Such a man as Ludwig Tieck pointed out the path of German romantic literature before many feet had trodden it. The truth is that he and his confreres were working passionately for a German expression, and secondarily for art. Many of the creations of their disciples are strangely dual—made-to-

117

order, and yet wild and undisciplined. For romanticism, despite its authoritarian, semipolitical activations, was partly a rebellion against the rules. The result was that the average romantic artist—writer, musician, painter, sculptor—was merely wild and undisciplined, without being anything else. The pride of the stock, the golden fruit of the tree, was, of course, Goethe. It is possible to call him the greatest of the German romantics; he was equally the greatest of the classicists: in short, he was an eclectic who took what he wanted wherever he happened to find it.

There are portents of romanticism in Mozart, most particularly in *Don Giovanni*, and there are hints of it even in the young classicist Beethoven. But the immediate inspiration of full-cry German musical romanticism was literary. While every shudder and excess cannot be laid at their doors, two men of letters, Johann Paul Friedrich Richter and Ernst Theodor Amadeus Hoffmann, famous in their own days but unread now, concentrated in their work tendencies that proved most attractive to composers. The first of these, familiarly known as Jean-Paul, was a voluminous novelist, critic, and general essayist, abounding in playful humor, unbridled imagination, and patches of the exotic and grotesque. The second was a kind of German Poe, less careful as an artist, but as fanciful, horrific, and macabre. He delighted in projecting himself, as a character, into his writings—in fact, Offenbach's *Les Contes d'Hoffmann* is based on three fantastic adventures that he pretended had befallen him. A composer of tendentious operas, Hoffmann yearned, as did Weber, Schumann, Berlioz, and Wagner (like him, writers as well as musicians) after the synthesis of music and literature. By no means a first-rate writer, Hoffmann exercised an influence far beyond his merits, the reason being that he summed up all the more obvious aspects of the German romantic movement.

The year 1817 was epochal in the career of German romanticism, for it was then that Friedrich Kind presented Carl Maria von Weber with the libretto of *Der Freischütz*. In certain fields, the movement was already in lush maturity, but it was awaiting a salient musical expression of sufficient propor-

tions and popularity to challenge the efforts of classical and
pseudo-classical musicians, native or foreign, plying their trade
in the German states. Weber was marked from birth to sweep
German music into the romantic camp: he was qualified by
heredity, experience, and special talents. There were, of course,
huge chunks of romanticism in Schubert and the later Beethoven, not to mention lesser men, but the work of the former
was, except in his own small circle, unknown, while Beethoven's, except in *Fidelio*, was in classical forms. Schubert's
songs were too delicately wrought and intimate to be effective
rallying points. *Fidelio* might have served had it been more
popular, more theatrical, more stageworthy. In effect, it was
merely a huge straw in the wind.

Weber's training for his mission included a childhood in
traveling theatrical companies and a young manhood in operatic work, ranging from prompting to directing (at the age of
twenty-six) the Prague opera house. Further, his personal life,
disordered by the unpredictable behavior of a rogue father
who dabbled in music, playwriting, acting, politics, and
lithography, was itself a timid romantic extravaganza. Weber
felt the strong call of the new, still heterogeneous Germany,
and in 1814 had composed a group of patriotic songs and
choruses that had touched the hearts of millions of his countrymen. The next year came his fervidly nationalistic cantata,
Kampf und Sieg, about which an old Prussian fire-eater of high
rank had been pleased to remark, "With you I hear nations
speaking." It was only natural, then, that Friedrich Augustus,
King of Saxony, seized upon this redoubtable patriot when, in
1816, he was looking around for a *Kapellmeister* for the German opera at Dresden. But this was a political appointment,
pure and simple, and the King, who doted on Italian opera,
may have thought that his new employee would not take his
job too seriously. If so, Friedrich Augustus had mistaken his
man.

From the first, Weber fought tenaciously for the prerogative
of the German opera. Actually, the native fare was scanty, and
the *Kapellmeister* had to content himself with staging Meyerbeer, then at his most Rossinian, and Méhul's *Joseph* (in Ger-

man, of course), a cantatalike opera in a dignifiedly lyrical
vein. Oddly enough, he waited six years to give a Dresden performance of *Fidelio*, which he had staged in Prague as early
as 1814. In moments he could snatch from onerous official
duties, petty squabbles, literary efforts, composition of ceremonial folderol, touring as a piano virtuoso, getting married,
and begetting his first child, Weber was himself preparing to
swell the German repertoire. He was not utterly without experience as an operatic composer: two, possibly three, of his
efforts, including the delightful little Singspiel *Abu Hassan*
(Munich, 1811), had reached the boards. Most characteristic of
these (in a Weberian sense) was *Silvana*, a rewriting of a Singspiel he had composed and produced at the age of thirteen.
Silvana was tried out at Frankfort on the Main in September,
1810, but as a female balloonist was making an ascent outside
the town, not only was the house practically empty, but some
of the singers, in their frenzy to get a glance at the spectacle,
skipped whole arias. The *première* was therefore far from propitious, but Weber always had a tenderness for *Silvana* and in
his palmier days revived it. The libretto was outrageously,
absurdly romantic—and the heroine was a mute. The score
abounds in effects instantly recognizable as Weber's.

   After *Abu Hassan*, no new opera by Weber was mounted for
ten years, and then it was one based on a story that he was
actually thinking of setting when the idea for *Abu Hassan*
struck him. *Der Freischütz*, the cornerstone of German romantic
opera, was achieved in the most haphazard and vacillating
manner. Far from seeming to be pursued by a Teutonic demon
that would not let him rest from his task of destiny, Weber
acted just the opposite of a man about to make history. He
discovered the story in 1810, but it was not until seven years
later that he began talking it over with Friedrich Kind. He
then wrote excitedly to his wife: "Friedrich Kind is going to
begin an opera book for me this very day. The subject is admirable, interesting, and horribly exciting. . . . This *is* super-
extra, for there's the very Devil in it. He appears as the Black
Huntsman; the bullets are made in a ravine at midnight, with
spectral apparitions around. Haven't I made your flesh creep

upon your bones?" This was February, 1817. Kind, doubtless fired by Weber's enthusiasm, produced a libretto in ten days. Immediately, the composer's interest seemed to flag. During the remainder of that year, he squeezed out only one aria and a few rough sketches. Three days were all of 1818 that he devoted to the score. In March, 1819, he sketched the first-act finale in one day, and then abandoned work for six months. Suddenly, he apparently regained his old enthusiasm, and completed *Der Freischütz* between September, 1819, and May, 1820, writing the overture last.

Piqued by Dresden's seeming indifference to the prospects of German opera, and infuriated by its officials' scurvy treatment of himself as an operatic composer, Weber promised *Der Freischütz* to Berlin, then the seat of a vast if undiscriminating expansion in all the arts. There he was evidently appreciated, for Count Brühl, intendant of the court theaters, pledged his word that the new opera would be the first to be sung at the Schauspielhaus. Weber stuck to his part of the bargain: when the opening of the Schauspielhaus was delayed for a year, he simply laid *Der Freischütz* aside, and went about his other business. Copenhagen heard a sample of the opera when Weber went there on tour: the ever-popular overture received its first acclamation. In 1821, when the Schauspielhaus was finally ready, *Der Freischütz* was billed for June 18.

Meanwhile, however, something had happened to depress Weber's friends: Gasparo Luigi Pacifico Spontini, a composer of vast operatic canvases, and extraordinarily honored in France, had secured the lucrative post of royal music director in Berlin in 1819. He had already tested, with flattering success, Prussian response to his music, and the Berlin *première* of his lavish *Olympie*, with a libretto translated by Hoffmann, was scheduled for May 14, little more than a month before *Der Freischütz*. *Olympie* was so magnificent as a spectacle that the Berliners were hypnotized into believing that the music was better than it really was. Weber alone kept his head, certain that his own opera was a masterpiece. So calm, indeed, was he that between rehearsals he composed the still-famous *Concertstück*. When the Prussian capital heard *Der Freischütz* on that sixth anniversary of Waterloo, it was found that Spontini had met his Wellington.

Various operas have established the reputations of their composers overnight, but the wild acclamation that greeted *Der Freischütz* was something special. The excited temper of the audience was evident from the moment the overture was encored, the ardor being heightened by the fiery applause of the many members of the *Landswehr*, all of whom had, during the fateful years of the Napoleonic crisis, thrilled to Weber's patriotic songs and choruses. Representatives of the arts were there in force, including Hoffmann, Felix Mendelssohn, and Heine, nor was society less brilliantly shown off at this historic performance. From his peers Weber received the accolade he seems to have anticipated—after the opera was over, Hoffmann crowned him with a laurel wreath. But his final triumph came from a wider quarter. Before six months had elapsed, *Der Freischütz* had been presented to clamorous audiences throughout Germany and had become a loved favorite of the people, which it remains. In Vienna, even a truncated version caused by an imperial ban on the Devil himself, as well as on the guns and bullets that are essential to the salient scene, could not stem this wildfire. Finally, on January 26, 1822, Dresden was converted. And, on March 2, 1825, less than four years after its world *première*, New York heard *Der Freischütz*, in English, the first true opera to be heard there.

Although it is never presented as one, *Der Freischütz* was originally a Singspiel, with a great deal of the plot carried forward by spoken dialogue. While Tieck, the great spokesman of romanticism, sneeringly remarked that it was just another Singspiel, he could not deny that it was brimming over with true-blue romantic feeling. It was (and this was an aspect of *Der Freischütz'* success that Weber came to resent) the sort of thing that ordinary people, especially those without artistic sophistication, took to their hearts and kept there. It is tremulous with emotion (not excluding sentimentality), full of shudders, full of plot, and extremely proper—Agatha, the heroine, is more nicey-nice than Parsifal; not unnaturally, this role was chosen for the operatic debut of Jenny Lind, on

March 7, 1838, at Stockholm. It is drenched with that quality for which only German has a word—*Gemüthlichkeit*—and the very fact that the peculiarly heart-warming and folksy Hunting Chorus, from Act III, was, and in its native land still is, the most popular number from the opera shows that it was this quality that first captivated Germany.

The overture sums up all these qualities, being an enormously clever patchwork not only of musical segments, but also of theatrical effects and moods. It is played constantly by both symphony orchestras and bands. Outside Germany, very little more of the opera survives in popular musical memory. Occasionally, a soprano with a big enough voice will revive the dramatically tender *"Leise, leise,"* and even more rarely a tenor may be heard in the still fresh *"Durch die Wälder,"* an ingenuous evocation of woodland spirit. New York has not heard *Der Freischütz* for over a decade, and in the entire history of the Metropolitan, only seventeen performances are recorded.

Of the historical importance of *Der Freischütz* there can be no doubt. Meyerbeer and Wagner owed much to it, and so did lesser men, including Marschner and, in his own despite, Spohr. It is difficult not to hear echoes of it in Rossini's *Guillaume Tell*. What Weber passed on to those men was not only such specific things as new orchestral effects, both in general color and in the handling of separate instruments, but also a broad understanding of music definitely for the stage. He gave them a new atmosphere to play with, to draw out into subtleties, and, finally, to spiritualize. This new atmosphere was, of course, musical romanticism—the something that throbs through *Der fliegende Holländer, Tannhäuser, Lohengrin,* and *Die Meistersinger,* through Schumann's overture to *Manfred* and the *Symphonie fantastique* of Berlioz. Unfortunately, it also pulses blatantly through the overtures of Suppé and whole cohorts of imitators of that king of imitators. It is a currency that has become so debased that we thoughtlessly extend to the model the stigma of the counterfeit. Too much din of this variety has assailed our ears—too many challenging horns, too many slow, moon-bathed introductions and galloping finales—for us to be able to "hear" *Der Freischütz* as Weber conceived it (with its unquestionable originality) and as those first audiences heard it (with its unquestionable impact of novelty).

Der Freischütz had made Weber the operatic man of the hour in Germany. Yet, after the first savor of the laurels, he began to feel vaguely annoyed over his new-found fame. Tieck's sneer rankled, and the belittling of the merely jealous Spohr riled. In a sense, it was the very popularity of *Der Freischütz* that Weber came to regard as an aspersion on his professional honor. He yearned to be, not a popular composer, but the creator of works that would meet Tieck's exacting standards. This state of mind led him to the most serious mistake of his career—the decision to compose, at all costs, a grand opera.

At this juncture, Domenico Barbaia, who had already squeezed several excellent operas out of Rossini, sent Weber a commission to compose, for the Kärntnerthortheater in Vienna, an opera *à la Freischütz*. Weber accepted the commission, but not the specification. In his headlong flight toward ill luck, he wheedled from Helmine von Chézy, a loony if aristocratic *littérateuse*, one of the wildest and most unsettable librettos in the history of opera. Eleven times did the book suffer revision without becoming half as stageworthy as would have been a translation of *Cymbeline*, basically the same story. Compared to his snail's pace on *Der Freischütz*, Weber worked on the new opera at fever speed. Begun on December 15, 1821, *Euryanthe* was completed in less than a year, despite the fact that, as a grand opera, it had to have much more music than *Der Freischütz*, not being allowed to use the spoken dialogue that is a feature of the Singspiel.

Barbaia did not get around to scheduling *Euryanthe* until 1823, and when Weber set out for Vienna, in September of that year, he was a tired, ailing man. In his job, in the face of enmity from his coworkers, royal negligence, and ceaseless petty annoyances, he had been burning up his energies, already sadly wasted by tuberculosis. Yet, he threw himself into the rehearsing of *Euryanthe* with his accustomed abandon and was not daunted by singers' complaints—requests for the insertion of special arias, star billing, and so on—and the adverse criticism of his friends, professional and nonprofessional. Except for certain reservations about the libretto, Weber seems to have been as complacent about the high quality of *Euryanthe* as he had been about that of *Der Freischütz*—he was certain that it was a good opera. True, young Franz Schubert, who had succumbed completely to the folk magic of the earlier opera, was cool about the new, which he heard in rehearsal and pronounced lacking in melody. This must have annoyed Weber, for when Schubert showed him the score of one of his own ill-fated operas, he said that first operas, like first puppies, should be drowned. This remark, in turn, must have incensed Schubert, for later he spoke even more acidly of *Euryanthe*: "This is no music. There is no finale, no concerted piece according to the rules of art. It is all striving after effect. And he finds fault with Rossini! It is utterly dry and dismal."

So too thought Vienna, which had just risen from a feast of its beloved Rossini. By comparison, *Euryanthe* was funeral meats. Although the three hours consumed by the *première* of the opera, on October 25, 1823, would not seem long by modern standards, they bored the local wits, who cruelly said that Weber was evidently writing for eternity. The critics were more forthright, but quite as harsh. Strangely enough, *Euryanthe* persisted for twenty performances that season before being retired for many years. It has never been a lasting success anywhere. The Metropolitan has given it only nine times in all, the last performance being in 1915. For, with reservations, Schubert and the Viennese were right: as a stage work, *Euryanthe* is an unmitigated failure. The reservations, then, are musical, not theatrical. It is impossible now to discover why Weber, who had smelled grease paint from his infancy, and who knew what was theatrically effective and what was not (his mountings of other composers' operas were notable for their point and taste), had not summarily tossed the libretto aside. Beside it, the rigmarole of *Die Zauberflöte* is Euclidean logic. Admitting that the libretto would throw any man, it is nonetheless odd that Weber, once having accepted it and perspired over its revisions, did not compose more apposite and telling music for the few dramatic high spots it has.

Actually, *Euryanthe* lives more dimly than *Der Freischütz*.

Weber pieced together, in one of his précis overtures, the best of his purely musical inspirations, and that is still often heard. As for the rest, even the several pleasantly lyrical airs are never resurrected. Weber had failed in his chief purpose of writing a grand opera that would prove his position as a serious composer, and was left with the chill comfort of a studied encomium from Ludwig Tieck. Yet, again, *Euryanthe*, like *Der Freischütz*, exerted considerable influence on the course of opera, for from its elaborate first scene—a full-dress ceremonial at the court of Louis VI of France—stem those similar scenes of pomp and circumstance that Meyerbeer used in *Les Huguenots*, Wagner in *Tannhäuser, Lohengrin,* and *Die Meistersinger,* and Verdi in several operas, notably *Aïda*.

As early as the rehearsals of *Euryanthe*, Weber was in agonizing ill health. Now he began to die. Nothing could save him except complete inactivity, but the harrying duties of his position, as well as his neurotic financial fears, would not permit him to rest. For a time, public coldness to *Euryanthe* suspended his operatic activities, despite the fact that *Der Freischütz* was going on from success to success, abroad as well as in Germany. For fifteen months, Weber composed nothing. Then, when his anxiety for the future welfare of his increasing family had reached an acute stage, a commission for a new opera came from the actor-manager Charles Kemble, then lessee of Covent Garden. The offer specified an English libretto and a world *première* conducted by the composer. Weber, fully realizing that the exertions of learning a new language, composing a full-length opera, and daring the rigors of an English journey in winter would be fatal to him, very properly acted like a shrewd barterer and jacked up his price—to £1000, said his pupil and friend, Sir Julius Benedict. Agreement was reached, and Weber set to work on his last opera, *Oberon, or The Elf King's Oath.* He was given the option of setting *Faust,* but refused this much more fruitful subject because it had already been made into an opera by his critical friend, Ludwig Spohr.

Oberon was composed under even more difficult circumstances than Weber may have anticipated. He had been punctilious in learning English, but his librettist in London was not equally so in sending him the libretto. It arrived act by act at intervals of a month, and the composer was thus forced to begin work before seeing the complete book or knowing in detail the exact development of the plot. When its development did become manifest, it was found to be quite the most fantastic concoction of the English antiquarian, herald, playwright, and novelist, James Robinson Planché—as convoluted and absurd as *Euryanthe*, which it resembled in being the story of true love tested. While Weber kept in the back of his mind a plan to turn *Oberon*, translated for performance in Germany, into a true grand opera, for the London version he contented himself with alternating music and lengthy expository bits of spoken dialogue. In his frantic eagerness to finish the opera before death finished him, Weber adapted sections from his own earlier operas—the finale of *Oberon*, for example, is lifted chiefly from *Peter Schmoll und seine Nachbarn*, a probably unperformed opera he had composed twenty-five years earlier.

Weber broke his trip to London by stopping in Paris, where he visited his idol Cherubini and his chief detestation Rossini. The meeting with the former was the consummation of a tiny mutual-admiration society, but it was Rossini who gave the dying man the excellent advice to turn back. Weber, however, was determined to stand by his contract and see his family better provided for. He manfully went through his agony, conducting the *première* of *Oberon*, on April 12, 1826, and several succeeding performances, but at the dreadful price he and his friends had foreseen—three months to a day after his arrival in London, he died there in his sleep.

The trip to England had at least been lucrative for Weber's heirs: his average daily earnings during his ninety days there were the equivalent of sixty dollars. His artistic success was less unqualified. What *Oberon* would have been like had Weber lived to revise it, it is difficult to guess, but certainly in its present form it leaves much to be desired. Nor have its inadequacies been effectively masked by the fumbling remedies of the patchwork artists of varying degrees of grandeur, from Benedict to Bodanzky, who have sweated over the score. Unhappily, *Oberon* has a central organic disease—chronic rather than acute—that defies the blue pencilings and additions of learned musical doctors.

As Weber left it, *Oberon* is a bad play, preceded by his best overture, and interrupted by fine outbursts of song. There is a sort of mutual courtesy between the action and the music that does not allow them to get in each other's way—they alternate, but do not co-operate. The result is emulsion, not solution. The musical reflection of the drama's play and contrast is all in the overture, which, in addition to its sheer loveliness, is an adroitly calculated piece of stage music. The *scena* "Ocean, thou mighty monster," which already has been quoted copiously in the overture, is Weber's most brilliant writing for voice: symphonic in scope, epic in style, and too taxing for any but the strongest and most gifted of dramatic sopranos, it is of the lineage of *"Abscheulicher, wo eilst du hin?"* and the *Liebestod*. The rest of the opera is tuneful, with the separate numbers eloquent enough in illustrating the rather painful *tableaux vivants* that turn up.

Thus, the most famous German operatic composer of the early nineteenth century left three immortal operas that are almost never performed, even after—in two cases—most auspicious beginnings. *Oberon,* for instance, boasted an ideal cast for its *première*: Mary Anne Paton, its Rezia, and John Braham, its Sir Huon, were the idols of the English public, and almost as well liked was the Fatima, Lucia Elizabeth Vestris. Weber pronounced the orchestra the best he had ever heard. Yet, despite Weber's popularity in England both personally and as a composer—*Der Freischütz* had been a notable attraction there for some years—*Oberon* scarcely outlived the furore attending the performances the composer himself conducted. Similarly, although it reached New York two years after its London performance, it disappeared from the American stage for ninety years. Then, in 1918, Artur Bodanzky collected the excellent cast of Rosa Ponselle, Alice Gentle, Giovanni Martinelli, Paul Althouse, and Marie Sundelius for his own reworking of the score, and in three seasons the opera achieved thirteen performances. In the twenty years since, the Metropolitan has not revived *Oberon.*

Euryanthe has always been unfortunate, though Weber secured the seventeen-year-old Henriette Sontag for the title role,
thus helping to launch one of the most brilliant operatic careers
of the century—a career that brought this poor girl a countess'
coronet and unstinted professional and domestic happiness.*
On December 23, 1887, with its first American performance,
Anton Seidl began a vain campaign to establish *Euryanthe*
here, his cast including Lilli Lehmann, Marianne Brandt, Max
Alvary (a true matinee idol), and Emil Fischer. Toscanini tried
it again in 1914, with a cast headed by Frieda Hempel, but five
performances ended the experiment. New York has not heard it
since that date. A Salzburg performance in 1937, under Bruno
Walter, was notable for the singing of Kerstin Thorborg as
the wicked Eglantine.

Der Freischütz has been most widely retained of all the
Weber operas. New York has heard it in German, French,
Italian, and English. After a single performance at the Metropolitan in the season of 1884-85, a quarter of a century intervened; then sixteen repetitions were bunched into twenty
years, the last in 1929, when Elisabeth Rethberg appeared
triumphantly as Agatha. In France, the opera, though in an
abominable distorted version that aroused the bitter maledic-
tions of Berlioz, attained a success that at first rivaled its vogue
in Germany. The perpetrator of this scandal was François-
Henri-Joseph Blaze, better known as Castil-Blaze, a respectable
enough musicologist but a fiendish Procrustes to what he considered intractable operas, who in the course of his nefarious activities operated similarly on stage works by Mozart, Rossini,
and Donizetti.

In 1824, Castil-Blaze prepared a translation and adaptation
of both the book and music of *Der Freischütz*, called it *Robin
des bois*, and had it presented at the Odéon. The performance
was so sloppy that it was hissed off the stage, and Castil-Blaze
wisely withdrew it for revision, particularly of the casting.
But when it was staged again, many of those who had hissed the
first performance of *Robin* returned to vent their spite on the

* After triumphs in the United States, she had just begun a season in Mexico
City, when she was attacked by cholera, and died within a few days, on June
17, 1854. She was forty-eight years old.

refurbishment. When Castil-Blaze saw how the wind was blowing, he papered the house night after night for more than a week. At that point, popular curiosity was strained to such a point that demand broke through his all-sold-out artifice, and legitimate ticket sales forced 327 consecutive performances.* Not realizing what they were seeing and hearing was a caricature, the French romantics—Victor Hugo among them—went into ecstasies over *Robin des bois*. Before the craze evaporated, articles of dress and other objects were named after *Robin*. Only Berlioz, the purist, continued to object, though it is worth noting that, years later, when he himself was in a position of authority at the Opéra, he felt called upon to adapt Weber's score to certain realistic exigencies of production.

In Germany, at Weber's death, only five years after the *première* of *Der Freischütz*, there was already the beginning of a flourishing school of romantic opera, the strongest member of which was, without question, the young man who for two years had served as joint-*Kapellmeister* (with Weber and his hated Italian colleague Francesco Morlacchi) at Dresden. This was Heinrich Marschner, who had industriously studied Weber's operas to give added atmosphere and stage effects to his own already romantic style. Marschner was a pleasing melodist, besides being musically clever and a humorist of the broadest sort. His first great success, *Der Vampyr*, almost sensually indulged a leaning toward the macabre, the supernatural, and the grotesque. He followed this with *Der Templer und die Jüdin*, a version of *Ivanhoe*. His most famous opera, however, was *Hans Heiling* (1833), which is still popular in Germany. The libretto, by Mendelssohn's friend Éduard Devrient, deals with gnomes and human beings, being the sort of mixture that we are already familiar with through the librettos of Weber. Wagner was strongly influenced by Devrient's book and Marschner's music, particularly in *Der fliegende Holländer*. Marschner, indeed, through his longer span of years, was the bridge between Weber and Wagner.

* Castil-Blaze's treatment of *Euryanthe* was even more highhanded. Taking large slices of it, mixing them with slices of Beethoven, Meyerbeer, Rossini, and others, and using a comic book, he achieved the pastiche known as *Le Forêt de Sénart*. This, however, did not have the success of *Robin des bois*.

Beside Marschner, other German romantic opera composers —excepting that strange composite, Meyerbeer—fade into insignificance. Mention must be made of the peculiarly stiff-necked violin virtuoso, Ludwig Spohr, whose *Faust* (not after Goethe) and *Jessonda*, whose heroine is the ancestress of such disparate figures as Lakmé and Lohengrin's Elsa, had a fleeting success. Chorley accurately dismissed him as ". . . Spohr, who had a strange desire for being—that which he could not be— fantastic and supernatural (and who showed a choice in his opera books as curiously courageous as his music was timidly orderly) . . ." For instance, *Jessonda* included a daring scene of suttee, an institution of which the Europe of that day had not heard.

Also, there was Otto Nicolai, whose prankish, good-humored overture to *Die lustigen Weiber von Windsor** is practically the only survivor of a mass of half-romantic, half-Rossinian operas. Rather more individualized was Gustav Lortzing, a broad painter of genre pictures built on vigorous *Volkslieder* themes. He wrote an opera about Hans Sachs that antedated Wagner's portrayal of him in *Die Meistersinger* by more than twenty years, as well as a sentimental comedy of contrasts, *Czar und Zimmermann*, which has retained its hold on the German public.

Finally, there was the oversweet Friedrich, Freiherr von Flotow, whose *Martha, oder Der Markt zu Richmond* (usually sung in Italian, as *Marta*) is absolutely indestructible. It is, perhaps, as well contrived an operetta as *Blossom Time*, though inferior in tunes simply because Flotow had only his own inspirations to work on, while Sigmund Romberg had Schubert's. Even so, the best-known number in *Martha* is "The Last Rose of Summer," an Irish folk melody interpolated by Flotow himself. Only slightly less famous (now that it has been a swing best seller) is the lachrymose tenor air *"M'appari,"* which sounds as if it had escaped from the pen of Donizetti, but instead had been interpolated from one of Flotow's earlier operas.

---

* It was produced at the Academy of Music, New York, on February 5, 1886, in an English translation by H. E. Krehbiel. In 1905, at the Berlin Hofoper, it was the vehicle of Frieda Hempel's operatic debut.

Martha's career has been more honorable than its music. The original Vienna production, on November 25, 1847, brought forward Anna Zerr (Lady Harriet), Alois Ander (Lionel), and Formes (Plunkett). In the first American performance, at Niblo's Garden, New York, on November 1, 1852, Ann, the estranged wife of Sir Henry Rowley Bishop, composer of *Home, Sweet Home* (but, see page 167), *Lo! Here the Gentle Lark,* other heart songs, and numerous operas, was the Lady Harriet. Almost every famed coloratura of the second half of the nineteenth century sang the role of Harriet, while not a few eminent tenors were attracted by that of Lionel. At the Metropolitan, *Martha* has been a favorite in spurts, not a perennial, and the death of the bass, Armand Castelmary, during a performance of the Italian version on February 10, 1897, was not calculated to increase the popularity of the opera either among singers or audience. Castelmary's death had been the final touch on a memorable bit of energetic stage business between him and Jean de Reszke, the Lionel of the evening; it was too much for his heart, and he collapsed, dying in Jean's arms while an unsuspecting audience applauded. The cluster of Metropolitan performances that occurred from 1906 to the season of 1907-08 was due largely to the magnificent quartet of Sembrich (Lady Harriet), Edyth Walker (Nancy), Caruso (Lionel), and Plançon (Plunkett). In the last revival, on December 14, 1923, Alda, Kathleen Howard, Gigli, and De Luca established a record of six performances the first season. After 1928-29, *Martha* was again dropped from the Metropolitan repertoire.

A man like Flotow would not have been recognizable to Weber as one of his legitimate progeny, so pervasive had become the softening, relaxing influence of the melodymongers of the South. The more effete descendants of Weber ended by surrendering to this influence with almost indecent abandon: Wagner, more solidly protected by the buckler of Teuton *Kultur,* did not.

Chapter IX

The Divine Opera-Grinder

THE precocious Rossini, who achieved masterpieces quite as early in life as did his artistic ancestor, Mozart, lived more than twice as long. At thirty-seven he all but abandoned music to devote his lively talents to the full-time job of becoming an international wit. While we are accustomed to think of Rossini as a comic-looking, portentous old gentleman with an all-too-obvious wig perched on his head, his actual creative life in opera—his true métier—was as brief as Mozart's. But whereas the Austrian was brutally cut off by death, Rossini cold-bloodedly turned off the faucet of his inspiration when there was no indication that it would run dry, in doing so serving only the professional musicologist who, as it is, finds difficulty in differentiating sharply between the almost forty products of his nineteen years of diabolic fecundity.

Fortunately, only a dozen or so operas from this shoal need concern us, and of those, only a few as wholes. Rossini himself was a most dismal prophet of his prospects for survival, fore-seeing a future only for the third act of *Otello*, the second of *Guillaume Tell*, and all of *Il Barbiere di Siviglia*. Time has proved him wrong in detail and, in general, far too modest. Only *Il Barbiere* survives, a vigorous perennial still, but along with it are a number of overtures and arias from various other operas the composer failed to name. But his sad self-evaluation was made when Rossini was old and, despite his sense of humor, embittered, when the fame of Meyerbeer was at flood, and Rossini saw the works of his very slightly older contemporary crowding him off the stage,* apparently leading to his own comparative oblivion. With a sheerly musical endowment that has seldom been surpassed, Rossini yet does not seem to have realized that by its very nature the best of his work had, in the long run, to be preserved. The long run was, in his case, long indeed, and there was a perilous moment, toward the end

---

* Except, of course, *Il Barbiere*, whose longevity was never in question.

of the last century, when musical criticism was dominated by German nationalists of an extraordinarily self-assertive stripe, when Rossini's cause seemed lost—along with that of everyone except Wagner. Our own century has rediscovered him as a musical genius, if not, primarily, as a composer of operas, and were Rossini alive today, he would no doubt chuckle over the comparative fates of Meyerbeer and himself: while *Il Barbiere* still makes the rounds, and symphony orchestras delight in the overtures to a half-dozen or more of his operas, Meyerbeer rates only an occasional dusting off.

Rossini started out as a composer of eighteenth-century *opera buffa*, and it will save time to admit that his greatest triumph was scored in this field. It was *Il Barbiere di Siviglia* that, one hundred and twenty-five years ago, established his fame without qualification, and it is *Il Barbiere* that today keeps that fame well burnished in the opera house. Yet, when Francis Toye wrote, ". . . it may be doubted whether any previous opera, Mozart's *Entführung* and Cimarosa's *Matrimonio segreto* not excepted, had ever before been characterized by such sparkle, such a wholly irresponsible sense of fun," he was referring, not to *Il Barbiere*, but to its fifteenth predecessor, *La Cambiale di matrimonio* (1810), Rossini's first try, which that cherubic country bumpkin had dashed off at the age of eighteen. Now, Mr. Toye, whose *Rossini: A Study in Tragi-Comedy* is an enchanting book, is perhaps oversold on his hero, but his rippling delight in *La Cambiale* was anticipated by those early audiences whose demands for more and ever more Rossini led to his composing five operas in 1812 and four in 1813. Of the first group, the overture to *La Scala di seta*, in which the crescendo *à la Rossini* (of which more later) made its debut, has been called "a brightly colored puppy chasing its tail": it is a favorite of Toscanini's. Of the 1813 group, one—*Il Signor Bruschino*—was a pleasant curtain raiser to Strauss' *Elektra* some seasons ago at the Metropolitan; a second—*Tancredi*—includes that charming and eternal *"Di tanti palpiti"* which flows from the tongue with such effortless ease, while a third—*L'Italiana in Algeri*—starts with an overture of brisk color and good-natured raillery: it,

Maria Malibran as Desdemona, in Rossini's *Otello,* after a
contemporary portrait

too, is a constant orchestral stand-by. It is significant that of
these early operas which have survived at least in excerpt, only
one—*Tancredi*—is not an *opera buffa*.

By 1816, the year of *Il Barbiere*, Rossini had perfected the
buffa aspect of his art, while the *seria*, which must be stigmatized as synthetic, was still in the groping stage. Every detail
of the former came to him easily. He had a guileless love of
fun, nonsense, triviality even, and a spontaneous genius for
expressing them in music—a genius that bubbled up irrepressi-
bly even when he was writing his admirable and influential
exercises in *opera seria*. His earliest *opere buffe* were mainly in
the tradition of Pergolesi, Cimarosa, and Paisiello, and were
couched in a brilliant eclectic style that selected their best effects,
as well as those of several other men, without sacrificing the
unquestioned originality that appeared as early as *La Cambiale*.
That originality, briefly, was an effervescence, a stanchless un-
corking of melodic and rhythmic champagne, an intoxicating
brio that even the near-genius Pergolesi did not match. Other
telling touches may have been borrowed, but so cleverly that
Rossini made them his own. For instance, he was familiar with
Mozart's operas and with Haydn—he had conducted *The Creation* in Bologna in his nineteenth year. From them, very possibly, he learned the lesson of painstaking craftsmanship, all the
more remarkable because rare among his Italian contemporaries: almost from the beginning, he refused to accommo-
date his vocal line to any old accompaniment, and produced
beautifully contrived scores. Even before the gorgeously fashioned *Semiramide*, in which the orchestra blazed forth with
a, for Italy, previously unheard exuberance and volume, his
hankering after big orchestral effects had earned him the nick-
name of the "Little German."

But all of Rossini's innovations were not confined to the
orchestra. In *Elisabetta, regina d'Inghilterra,* one of two operas
written in 1815 and now completely forgotten, he applied himself to the problem of the singer. The opera was tailor-made
to suit the vocal gifts, histrionic abilities, personality, and appearance of Isabella Colbran, then the mistress of the impresario
Barbaia, Rossini's chief at the Teatro San Carlo, Naples, but

later his own mistress, and finally his wife.* Because of her amiability toward him, the young composer—Colbran was seven years his senior—was emboldened to take the unprecedented liberty of writing out in full the vocal ornaments in the score. Previously, these had been left to the ingenuity and whims of the individual singer: nowadays, it is taken for granted that the singer performs exactly what the composer wrote, adding nothing, subtracting nothing.† But it took no small courage on Rossini's part to pioneer in emancipating the composer from the tyrant singer. It was also in *Elisabetta*—which by some chance startlingly parallels the plot of Scott's *Kenilworth*, published five years later—that Rossini drew completely away from unaccompanied recitative and first wrote an *opera seria* in which

The situation that developed at the San Carlo was laughably similar to certain aspects of Stendhal's description of a typical opera company in an Italian town many times smaller than Naples: "The mechanism of an Italian theater is as follows. The manager is frequently one of the most wealthy and considerable persons of the little town he inhabits. He forms a company, consisting of a *prima donna, tenore, basso cantante, basso buffo,* a second female singer, and a third *basso.* He engages a *maestro,* or composer, to write a new opera, who has to adapt his own airs to the voices and capacities of the company. The *libretto,* or poem, is purchased at the rate of from sixty to eighty francs from some unlucky son of the Muses, who is generally a half-starved *abbé,* the hanger-on of some rich family in the neighborhood. The character of the parasite, so admirably painted in Terence, is still to be found in all its glory in Lombardy, where the smallest town can boast of five or six families with incomes of three or four hundred a year. The manager, who, as has been already said, is generally the head of one of these families, entrusts the care of the financial department to a *registrario,* who is generally some pettifogging attorney who holds the situation of his steward. The next thing that generally happens is that the manager falls in love with the *prima donna*; and the progress of this important *amour* gives ample employment to the curiosity of the gossips. The company, thus organized, at length gives its first representation, after a month of cabals and intrigues, which furnish conversation for the whole period. This is an event in the simple annals of the little town, of the importance of which the people of large places can form no idea. During months together, a population of eight or ten thousand persons do nothing but discuss the merits of the forthcoming music and singers, with the eager impetuosity which belongs to the Italian clime. The first representation, if successful, is generally followed by twenty or thirty more of the same piece; after which the company breaks up. This is what is called *stagione* or season; the last and best of which is that of the carnival. The singers who are not engaged in any of these companies are usually to be found at Milan or Bologna, where they have agents, whose business it is to find them engagements, or to manoeuvre them into situations when opportunity offers."

† In theory, of course. The singer still adds and subtracts, particularly the latter, if the score is too difficult. Opera singers are no longer the gymnasts their predecessors were.

all the recitative was accompanied by the orchestral strings. And in *Tancredi* he had already upset the moldy tradition that the bass voice was essentially comic and could not be used in serious opera.

Thus, it was no novice who, in the space of a fortnight, in the winter of 1816, cast a double defi to the operatic world by setting the first part of Beaumarchais' Figaro trilogy. Mozart had already spun a golden web from the second part in *Le Nozze di Figaro*, while the doddering but revered Paisiello, whom the Neapolitans worshiped only less than San Gennaro, had set the first part under the title of *Il Barbiere di Siviglia*. Not that Rossini was an upstart: he had several tremendous hits to his credit and had earned the right to dare the lightning. Under the circumstances, however, he was rashly brave, for his *Barbiere* was the second of two operas he had composed for Rome, and the first had been a dismal failure.

Rossini sought to evade the indignation of Paisiello and his cohorts by calling the new opera *Almaviva*. Vainly. 'At the *première*, on February 20, 1816, they had posted a strong-lunged claque, which found an easy pretext for abuse when the great Spanish tenor, Manuel García, proceeded to tune his guitar on the stage before accompanying himself to its plunk-ings—a piece of stage business that a modern audience, edu-cated by the antics of Chaliapin and other realistic singing actors, would certainly love. Rossini, inclined (like many wits) to pessimism, felt certain that the opera was a fiasco and rushed home to sleep it off. He stayed there the second night and was shamming sickness in bed when friends burst in on him to announce that Rome rather liked his second offering, after all. It ran out the week, which closed the season. Elsewhere, it gathered popularity slowly, then with acceleration, and when Rome heard it again, five years later, it was the rage of Europe and had been heard, though in an abbreviated English edi-tion, in New York. All in all, it ended by being probably the most popular opera of the nineteenth century, praised by such a motley collection of fellow musicians as Beethoven, Schubert, Berlioz, Wagner, and Brahms. While not precisely fashionable today, *Il Barbiere* has survived every change of fashion and seems likely to continue to do so. At the Metropolitan, whose repertoire it entered on November 23, 1883, with Sembrich (Rosina), Roberto Stagno (Almaviva), and Giuseppe del Puente (Figaro), it has been performed, during the twentieth century alone, ninety-four times.

Il Barbiere di Siviglia is audaciously arranged. Rossini sets the pace with one of his most dashing overtures, and then, fairly early in the first act, as if to hint that the vocal delights are to be as fine, brings forth the *"Largo al factotum,"* Figaro's whirlwind lament of an overworked Jack-of-all-trades. There is no letdown: in fact, *Il Barbiere* is one of those rare stage works we leave with a sense of having been cheated—we actually wish there had been more.* The rapid-fire action never lags; the witty and copious inventiveness never lapses. Now, as that inventiveness is not of the same order, and certainly not of the same kind, as Mozart's, we do not, as we ransack the score, find so many memorable separate numbers as make *Le Nozze,* though a unity, one of the most richly varied vocal concerts. Rossini is always apt, but he is not uniformly a supreme melodist.

In composing *Il Barbiere,* Rossini was always the vessel of the *buffa* spirit, and his first services were to it rather than to music. Mozart's first services were always to music. Take the high spots of *Il Barbiere* and analyze them: *"Una voce poco fa,"* aside from being cleverly located in the action, is more a florid display piece for generations of footlight-craving Rosinas than pure music; the "Calumny Song" almost entirely loses its significance when separated from the context—musically, it is negligible, as characterization flawless. Here, again, the contrast between Mozart and Rossini is instructive: the latter set the broad, mocking, and thoroughly irreverent Beaumarchais play to a tee; Mozart, while respecting his libretto, used it as a taking-off place for a display of his own unique magic.†

Il Barbiere, as now presented, has several curious features

* But this refers to the shrewdly cut version we always hear.
† That the mistake of confounding the comic genius of Rossini with that of Mozart is of some antiquity is suggested by the fact that, on November 16, 1837, at the National Theater, New York, a mixture of *Il Barbiere* and *Le Nozze* was presented, in English, as *The Two Figaros.*

about it. The overture is not the one Rossini wrote for the *première*, which was unfortunately lost early in the opera's career. It must have been an interesting piece of music, for it was based on authentic Spanish themes given to him by Manuel García. The present one, though it seems made especially for *Il Barbiere*, had actually served as the overture to two of Rossini's *opere serie*—*Aureliano in Palmira* and *Elisabetta*—before being moved, a further proof of the essentially *buffa* quality of his genius. Rosina, the heroine, who for ages has been a giddy coloratura of the most incorrigible variety, began life as a humble contralto. Sopranos, who have always been more popular than contraltos, could not bear to see so juicy a role outside their own hunting grounds and simply ordered it transposed. Unfortunately, we do not know either the time or the first perpetrator of this role-snatching, though it is possible that the June, 1826, debut of Henriette Sontag is the answer. A third curiosity of *Il Barbiere* is Bartolo's famous aria in Act II, which is not by Rossini at all—though the fine one he composed for this scene exists—but by a nonentity named Romani. Item: Romani's *"Manca un foglio"* is much easier to sing than Rossini's *"A un dottor',"* which, however, was restored recently in both Metropolitan and Juilliard School performances.

Finally, there is the "Lesson Scene," about whose absurdities oceans of ink have been spilled. Rossini wrote some delightful music for Rosina's singing lesson, but when her voice changed, that was discarded, and interpolations of almost any sort were substituted. In flagrant cases of egocentricity, Rosina has been known to exercise her voice for more than half an hour, choices ranging from such simple heart songs as *Home, Sweet Home* (the astute preference of Adelina Patti, who thereby gave her voice a rest) and *Annie Laurie* to the "Mad Scene" from *Lucia di Lammermoor* and inane vocal variations that are little more than agility contests with the flute.

Rosina has been the favorite role of countless sopranos and of at least one recent mezzo, the fascinating Spanish artist Conchita Supervia, who frequently sang it in Paris. Many of them chose it for their debuts. Among the great Rosinas of the past have been Malibran, Fanny Persiani, Maria Caradori-Allan,* Luisa Tetrazzini, Nellie Melba, and Sembrich; among the living, Hempel, María Barrientos, Mabel Garrison, Amelita Galli-Curci, Lily Pons, Bidu Sayao and Josephine Tumminia. To name the leading Figaros would be to call the roll of many of the most eminent baritones of the past and present: it suffices to name Manuel García, Jr., Michael William Balfe,† Campanari, Ancona, Riccardo Stracciari, Pasquale Amato, Titta Ruffo, De Luca, John Charles Thomas, and John Brownlee. Almavivas have included Alessandro Bonci, Charles Hackett, Schipa, and Bruno Landi, while among notable Don Basilios have been Édouard de Reszke, Chaliapin, and Ezio Pinza. Before his tenor days, Jean de Reszke was frequently heard in Europe as Figaro. At recent Metropolitan performances, Baccaloni has excelled as Bartolo.

Il Barbiere di Siviglia was the first opera to be sung in Italian in New York: the epochal performance, which took place at the Park Theater, Park Row near Ann Street, on November 29, 1825, brought forward a cast of distinction, consisting mostly of Garcías, including the great Manuel del Popolo Vicente himself, who sang the role he had created in Rome, and the future Malibran as Rosina. Manuel, Jr., sang Almaviva. Even Señora García had a minor role. Lorenzo da Ponte was a doubly interested spectator at this *première*, for not only was he a Rossini enthusiast, but he also was financially interested in the García company, which, on this occasion, was making its first bid for American patronage.

The period from December, 1816, to May, 1817, was the most efflorescent in Rossini's life, for in those six months were bunched the *premières* of three of his best operas. *Otello*, heard at Naples on December 4, was the first of them and, in some respects, the most beautiful. It is deeply interesting, both historically and psychologically. First, it was laid at the feet of Colbran, whose acting ability Rossini sincerely admired, and

* More notable in oratorio than in opera, Caradori-Allan was the first real foreign star to sing opera in the United States, when she appeared in *Il Barbiere*, at Niblo's Garden, New York, in 1837.

† The future composer of *The Bohemian Girl* made his operatic debut in this role, at Rossini's special behest, at the Théâtre Italien, Paris, in 1827. For many years, Balfe was better known as a singer than as a composer.

with whom he was now in love. This circumstance, added to the fact that the story itself, despite the crimes perpetrated upon it by a highborn librettist, really affected him, stimulated Rossini to a serious and almost passionate style quite in keeping with it. *Otello* is surprisingly free from that undertone of banter which previously had given a note of levity to even his gravest efforts—nineteenth-century critics exhausted their superlatives while swooning over the tragic beauties of the third act. The compromise with the old unaccompanied recitative was finally abandoned: in *Tancredi*, Rossini had accompanied it with strings; now, using the full orchestra, he was able to treat scenes as musical wholes. Audiences accepted this innovation without a murmur, but the librettist's bold retention of the tragic ending alienated many spectators, some of whom spoiled the calculated dramatic effect by audibly warning Desdemona that the Moor was approaching.

Yet these circumstances were not enough to stop the spontaneous enthusiasm for Rossini's reading of the pathetic story. Indeed, so much was it appreciated that within a few years *Otello*, like a tragic pendant to *Il Barbiere di Siviglia*, became one of the standard operas of the world. The fame of Verdi's opera of the same name has driven from the boards this old-time favorite, in which such artists as Giuditta Pasta, Sontag, Malibran, Viardot-García, and Christine Nilsson scored some of their brightest triumphs. Annoyed by the pallidness of the character of Desdemona, Pasta secured for herself a *succès de scandale* by attempting the part of the Moor. She was unforgettable—but a dubious success. Almost without question, the greatest Othello of them all was Enrico Tamberlik, the vainglorious tenor whom Rossini confessed himself happy to welcome "if he'll only leave his high C outside with the wraps."

The other two operas of this period were as frivolous as *Otello* was serious. Of these, the first was a setting of the Cinderella story, with all the magic element taken out by the composer's order, possibly because he had a native dislike for such stuff, possibly because stage machinery was so clumsily managed in Italy as to make any illusionist tricks too risky. This left it with a libretto that is far from unamusing—almost realistic in its acerbity. *La Cenerentola* paralleled *Il Barbiere* by failing on its opening night, and then going on to become a smash hit of long duration. It was very popular in the United States during the first half of the last century,* and in it Marietta Alboni made her American debut. The score is, in spots, as fresh and witty as *Il Barbiere*, but it is more of a patchwork, the self-borrowings (in which Rossini almost always indulged in his operas) being sometimes quite inept. But that fact in itself would not have caused *La Cenerentola* to disappear. The real cause of its vanishing was the decline of florid singing. It contains the most difficult vocal music Rossini ever composed, particularly that for the name part, which requires that practically extinct phenomenon—a mezzo with coloratura agility. Conchita Supervia was the last singing artist who was akin to that remarkable succession of women who seemed to have a nest of nightingales in their throats, and she, who died in 1936, was the last to portray this Italian Cinderella.

La Cenerentola was first given at the Teatro Valle in Rome, on January 25, 1817. Little more than four months later, on May 31, Milan heard what Stendhal, in his *Vie de Rossini*, called the most successful first night he ever attended, that of *La Gazza ladra*. Rossini took special pains with this absurd mixture of frivol and melodrama, for he was not in the good graces of the Milanese, and they were showing a perverse liking for German opera. To scotch this, Rossini determined to outsmart the Germans on their own terms: he gave the orchestra a much more important role, he went to unusual lengths to find suitable music for each character, and he stole from the monstrously prolific—and now quite forgotten—Peter von Winter the idea of inserting a prayer to bolster dramatic lag. So effective was this theft that Rossini thereafter used the device *ad nauseam*. The overture to *La Gazza ladra* is really dramatic, and so, too, is much of the vocal score. There is no good reason why this opera, with its engrossing and highly flavored

* *La Cenerentola* was the latest, in point of composition, of the Rossini operas given in the United States by the García troupe. Their repertoire included, besides *Il Barbiere*, *Tancredi*, *Otello*, and *Il Turco in Italia*, all by Rossini, two of the elder García's mediocre fabrications, Niccolo Antonio Zingarelli's *Romeo e Giulietta*, and Mozart's *Don Giovanni*.

tale of aborted tragedy brought about by the thieving pranks of a magpie, should not be revived. Until it is, however, we must be content with the appetite-whetting overture, certainly one of the most adroit adventures in musical suspense ever devised.

It was *La Gazza ladra* with which Lorenzo da Ponte and his partner, the Chevalier Riva-Finoli, inaugurated the first theater in New York built solely for the production of opera. The Italian Opera House, located at Church and Leonard Streets, in a then fashionable, but now completely commercial, district, opened on November 18, 1833. Philip Hone, a former mayor of New York, was present, and wrote in his diary a lively account of the evening:

> The opera, they say, went off well for a first performance; but to me it was tiresome, and the audience was not excited to any degree of applause. The performance occupied four hours—much too long, according to my notion, to listen to a language which one does not understand; but the house is superb, and the decorations of the proprietors' boxes (which occupy the whole of the second tier) are in a style of magnificence which even the extravagance of Europe has not yet equaled. I have one-third of box No. 8; Peter Schermerhorn one-third; James J. Jones one-sixth; William Moore one-sixth. Our box is fitted up with great taste with light blue hangings, gilded panels and cornice, armchairs, and a sofa. Some of the others have rich silk ornaments, some are painted in fresco, and each proprietor seems to have tried to outdo the rest in comfort and magnificence. The scenery is beautiful. The dome and the fronts of the boxes are painted in the most superb classical designs, and the sofa seats are exceedingly commodious. Will this splendid and refined amusement be supported in New York? I am doubtful.*

For five years following *La Gazza ladra*, Rossini manufactured a series of stereotyped operas, most of them successes. Only two of them have a flicker of interest: *Mosè in Egitto,*

---

* What Hone apparently wished to have supported was not opera itself, but the lavish interior decorations of the opera house and the social whirl that went with them. In any event, his doubts were justified: the Italian Opera House lasted two years, after which a decade passed before Italian opera made another stand in New York.

with its once universally popular "Prayer" for chorus, and its bold use of the bass voice—both Moses and Pharaoh rumble in the lowest register; and *La Donna del lago*, a fantastic setting of *The Lady of the Lake* that does as much justice to Scott as does Donizetti's version of *The Bride of Lammermoor*. Although forgotten, these and Rossini's other operas of the period were important in showing how indomitable he could be when convinced of the worth of certain innovations. In them, against constant and often violent criticism—a music lover once confessed that he had seriously entertained the idea of murdering the composer because of the two drum rolls in the overture to *La Gazza ladra*—he continued to play up the orchestra, to assign important roles to the bass, and to write out the vocal ornaments. As most of these operas were written for Colbran, whom Rossini married in 1822, he was unopposed in this last. And, because the novelties of treatment were Rossini's, they were eventually adopted by other Italian composers. The final result was that, except for its peculiar Latinness and melodic turn, Italian opera tended to become more like German. But there was give-and-take between the two schools, and Wagner himself was not uninfluenced by Rossini.

In 1823, Rossini composed the last, and heaviest, of his serious Italian operas. Ironically, this long, ponderous, almost Meyerbeerian work was composed right after a triumphal visit to Vienna, where Beethoven gave Rossini that famous advice which he was to ignore almost entirely: "Give us more *Barber*s." Incest is the theme, Babylon the locale, of *Semiramide*, which the more earnest operagoers of the mid-nineteenth century persisted in considering the masterpiece of this essentially *buffa* spirit. It is a three-ring circus of ingenious tricks—a collection of shudders and shams brought together with a ruthless eye to effect that its composer never surpassed.

Aside from several affecting numbers, *Semiramide* is a museum of the horrors of nineteenth-century Italian opera. The overture survives, still popular with fourth-rate orchestras and brass bands: it is abominable, shameless claptrap, in which a few innocuous ideas are blown up and stretched out in a chain of those patented crescendos which were among the most obvious signatures of Rossini's style. The overture fairly represents the poorer parts of the opera, but even it can give no idea of the vocal extravagance of this amazing score. The text, based on Voltaire, makes sense most of the time; the music frequently does not. Rossini called it a "tragic melodrama," and so it is— in more ways than one. And yet, Bernard Shaw no doubt was only telling the exact truth when he wrote: "The general opinion, especially among literary men who affected music, used to be that there was an Egyptian grandeur about *Semira-mide*, a massiveness as of the Great Pyramids, a Ninevesque power and terror far beyond anything that Beethoven had ever achieved."

Venice heard the world *première* of *Semiramide* on February 2, 1823, and gave it a rousing send-off. There is some mystery about its arrival in America: there is a now discredited legend that the Garcías produced it on April 25, 1826, in New York; actually, New Orleans may have been the first American city to hear it, on May 1, 1837. If this latter is so, the first New York performance may not have been until January 3, 1845, at Palmo's Opera House, on Chambers Street, west of Broadway. Melba, Sofia Scalchi, and Édouard de Reszke were the principals in the only Metropolitan performances of *Semiramide*, which occurred during the seasons of 1893-94 and 1894-95. From the very beginning, the opera attracted brilliant casts, starting with Pasta, Malibran, and Antonio Tamburini as Semiramis, Arsaces, and Assur respectively, though the great Spanish mezzo occasionally attempted the name role. The delightful Angiolina Bosio, called by Chorley "next to Mme Sontag . . . the most ladylike person whom I have seen on the stage of the Italian opera," and who died prematurely, was a widely acclaimed Semiramis. Giulia Grisi and Marietta Alboni, Therese Tietjens and Zelia Trebelli, and Patti and Scalchi made singing history in the duets between the imperious Babylonian queen and her son Arsaces. Sontag was Rossini's favorite Semiramis. In 1868, when at his suggestion Patti first considered playing the part, Rossini composed special cadenzas for her, though before she could use them she was singing at his funeral in Père-Lachaise.

Semiramide closed Rossini's Italian career. A circuitous tour took him finally to Paris, and there he rounded out his operatic life, within five years of his arrival, with a tally of one official opera-cantata in Italian and four operas in French. The ceremonial piece celebrated the crowning of Charles X, who provided Rossini with a well-paid government post. Of the four operas, two were rewrites of earlier works in Italian, and two were originals. All of them, significantly, were produced after Rossini helped launch Meyerbeer in France by an almost piously careful production of *Il Crociato in Egitto,* thereby, though unwittingly, paving the way for his own exile from the Parisian stage. But Meyerbeer's first great success—*Robert le diable*—did not occur until after Rossini had stopped composing operas and had borrowed enough from him to enable him to found French grand opera. He lived on almost forty years after writing his last opera, *Guillaume Tell,* and grew to resent Meyerbeer's usurpation of his place. Meyerbeer, however, never spoke of Rossini except in terms of the warmest gratitude and admiration.

Before attempting anything of importance for the French stage—his opera-cantata, *Il Viaggio a Reims,* is a patchwork of old Rossiniana and national airs, and so does not enter into the argument—Rossini, from a strategic outlook as director of the Théâtre Italien, studied the technique of French singing, the tastes of his potential public, and, finally, the French language. He secured as his personal coach the eminent tenor Adolphe Nourrit, who created many a role in famous operas. Never did this precocious, bouncing boy of thirty-odd work harder or more conscientiously. He was stimulated by new and better conditions: a larger and more highly trained orchestra, superior and more reliable stage machinery, and more time in which to do things.

Le Siège de Corinthe was Rossini's first French opera, and did much to still the criticism, bolstered by *Il Viaggio,* that he was an unrepentant confectioner of pastiches. Produced at the Opéra on October 9, 1826, *Le Siège,* in addition to its solid musical qualities, was helped decisively by its libretto. Dealing with a high-minded Greek girl who refuses to marry her childhood sweetheart, now Sultan of Turkey, because of his ill treatment of her people, it inflamed the audience, all fashionably pro-Greek, to riotous acclamation. Rossini had so slaved over the score, a rewrite of *Maometto II*, one of his Italian failures, as practically to make a new opera of it. Already he saw that his florid Italian ornaments would not get by with his French hearers, partly because French singers could not deal with them adequately. Therefore, *Le Siège* is a step toward a simpler melodic line and, though as big as *Semiramide*, is less elaborate.

In *Le Siège de Corinthe*, Rossini had capitalized, doubtless deliberately, on a vogue: in *Moïse*, a rewrite of the Italian *Mosè in Egitto*, he dealt with subject matter that was dramatic enough, but forbidding in character. The original *Mosè* had been well received in Paris: *Moïse* was Rossini's most signal French success. Nourrit and Laure Cinti-Damoreau, the tenor and soprano who had been cheered at the *première* of *Le Siège*, and Nicholas Levasseur, a much-admired bass, were in the cast of *Moïse* when it was first presented at the Opéra, on March 26, 1827. The scenery used in the passage of the Red Sea (which was made of real water) behaved unworthily, but the sneers and titters that ran through the crowd were soon drowned out by deafening applause.

Moïse established Rossini as a respected French composer. As if to prove its Frenchness, it even had a ballet, the music of which was drawn in part from one of his less important Italian operas, *Armida,* which alone of them boasted a ballet. But in the French version, as in the Italian, the mighty choruses, particularly the "Prayer," became for the public the opera's chief attractions. Their almost Handelian strength and largeness, and the Biblical theme, were responsible for the opera's strange fortune in England and the United States, where for many years it reigned as a favorite oratorio.* Balzac judged *Moïse* "a tremendous poem in music," and from the Conservatoire the usually frosty Cherubini sent down word that he was pleasantly surprised.

Moïse was nothing if not austere, but Rossini himself was

* To meet the requirements of the censor's ban against Biblical personages in the theater, *Moïse's* Italian ancestor had already had comic adventures in England, emerging first as an opera about Peter the Hermit and later, with injections of Handel, as an oratorio, *The Israelites in Egypt.* Perhaps this helps to explain why, after visiting England, Rossini decided to become a Frenchman.

not fatally changed. At heart still the comedian, he followed his Biblical opera with a delicate shaft of wit, *Le Comte Ory,* written around a featherbrained legend only half whipped into shape by Eugène Scribe, the most quenchless librettist of the nineteenth century. *Le Comte Ory* is not another *Barbiere*: where the earlier opera is brilliant and brisk, *Le Comte* is elegant and graceful. In *Il Barbiere* there is much holding of the sides, much shaking with laughter: the French comedy, without being lighter, more often contents itself with knowing smiles and leers, sly archness, and sheer musical cleverness. It has not the pace of *Il Barbiere,* but it has attractions that cry out for revival.

Le Comte Ory was an enthusiasm of that leading anti-Rossinian, Hector Berlioz. Rightly so. No opera of Rossini's contains more delightful music, though one would never know it nowadays, mainly because the Italians, who have been allowed the all but exclusive purveyorship of Rossini, never have taken to it. There is not a single recording of any number from it, despite the fact that Toye has this to say of the second-act trio, *"A la faveure de cette nuit obscure"*: "For loveliness of melody, originality of harmony, charm of part-writing, it is beyond praise, worthy of Mozart at his best."

French comic-opera composers, notably Offenbach, Lecocq, and Auber, have done homage to *Le Comte Ory* by borrowing its very atmosphere, just as Rossini had taken hints for it from their predecessors, Grétry, Hérold, and, particularly, Boïeldieu, whose influential *La Dame blanche* had been produced only three years before *Le Comte*. If any American opera house ever succeeds again in gathering together the kind of French company that made Oscar Hammerstein's Manhattan one of the brightest musical memories of this continent, it should remember that a whole untouched repertoire is at its disposal, among the first items of which might well be *Le Comte Ory*.

For his next opera, which turned out to be his last, Rossini mustered all his forces to create a masterpiece—a grand opera on the heroic scale. Until this time, he had proved himself beyond question a master of music: he now aspired to be a doctor of music. To get his degree, he composed a thesis called

Guillaume Tell. His reward was that the critics applauded rapturously, and the people listened with respect. He produced a five-act compendium of grand-operatic resourcefulness which became as famous as *Il Barbiere*—and about one fiftieth as popular. *Guillaume Tell* has exerted a tremendous influence, but itself is regarded as a white elephant—a magnificent embarrassment. It unquestionably excites admiration—it is so obviously serious and sincere; its proportions have a certain grandeur, and its characters have a painstakingly achieved psychological truth. It marks another big step in the symphonization of opera. It even foreshadows closely Wagner's use of the leitmotiv. And, with Auber's *La Muette de Portici,** it marks the true birth, after some pretentious false alarms, of French grand opera—which Wagner interpreted as the last development of opera before the advent of his own product, the music drama. Yes, *Guillaume Tell* excites admiration; it also excites profound boredom.

One of *Guillaume Tell's* handicaps is its excessive length: in 1856, when the directors of the Opéra took the bit in their teeth and staged an uncut performance, the experiment cost each listener six hours. Yet, critical acclaim had kept it alive and intact through fifty-six performances during the season of its *première* (August 3, 1829). A fine cast, with whose principals—Cinti-Damoreau (Mathilde), Nourrit (Arnold), Levasseur (Walter), and Dabadie (Tell)—he had already worked, had also helped to get the opera off to a good start. After the first

* Historically, *La Muette de Portici,* which is as well known under the title of the Italian version, *Masaniello,* can claim a more important role than *Guillaume Tell,* which it preceded by a year and a half. By a curious coincidence, Daniel-François Auber was, like Rossini, chiefly a composer of comic opera. Also, like *Tell, La Muette* is a huge five-acter based on the political struggles of an oppressed people—this time, Neapolitans. Musically, it is far inferior to *Tell;* scenically, it looks forward to the impressive ceremonial operas of Meyerbeer. Besides having a leading lady who does not sing, it is a tissue of improbabilities, ending, as Professor Edward J. Dent has observed, with the heroine's leap "from the balcony of the royal palace at Naples into the crater of Vesuvius, a distance of some eight or nine miles." A performance of *La Muette* at Brussels, in 1830, served as the tocsin of the Belgian rebellion against the suzerainty of Holland. One of the few modern performances of the opera in America was that of October 25, 1915, at the Lexington Theater, New York, when Anna Pavlova was the dumb girl—a role which she later portrayed in a spectacular cinema version.

season, however, drastic cuts were made—one by one, the acts
were telescoped or dropped, until the result was truncated beyond recognition. Finally, nothing but the overture and Act II
remained, and these were used as a curtain-raiser to other less
lengthy works. In 1837, new life was injected into *Tell's* veins
when Gilbert-Louis Duprez selected the role of Arnold for his
triumphant debut at the Opéra, on April 17. But this revival
was of short duration, and since then, both in France and
abroad, *Tell's* fortunes have been mediocre. It has been sung
in French, Italian, German, and English, but nothing seems to
win a public for it.

Despite its ill fortunes, not a few great singers have found congenial roles in *Guillaume Tell*. Francesco Tamagno's Arnold,
Ancona's Tell, and Édouard de Reszke's Walter were famed, while
the Metropolitan *première*, on November 28, 1884, brought forward
the incomparable Marianne Brandt in the insignificant role of
Hedvig, Tell's wife. Ten years later, almost to a day, *Tell* was the
occasion of a catastrophe on the second night of a Metropolitan
season, when Libia Drog, a well-equipped young Italian soprano,
substituting at the last moment, forgot the words of Mathilde's
famous and florid aria in Act II, "*Selva opaca*," better known under
its French words, "*Sombre forêt*." It took all the efforts of Tamagno,
De Reszke, and Ancona to save the evening. Yet, the very next
night, Signorina Drog sang the name role of *Aïda* with perfect
composure.

There is enough good music in the five acts of *Guillaume
Tell* to make a very listenable three-acter. Unfortunately, it is
married to an adaptation of Schiller that is cast iron in its
intractability and talky in its undramatic listlessness. If Rossini
hoped to stir up enthusiasm by depicting the heroism of a suffering people, and so repeat the success of *Le Siège de Corinthe*,
his librettists failed him. Wherever they squeezed an ounce of
drama from a situation, the shrewd Italian blew it up into a
generous pound. There is something epic about his handling of
the gathering of the cantons in Act II, something about these
choruses that calls to mind the bigger and differently styled,
but scarcely more impressive, ceremonials in Meyerbeer and
Wagner. "*Sombre forêt*" has real atmosphere, almost as deli-

cately sensed as if Weber had composed it, while the trio sung
by Arnold, Tell, and Walter is strenuous and convincing. Tell's
prayer in Act III and Arnold's lyric *"Asile héréditaire"* in Act
IV are other high spots. Most famous of all, of course, is the
still tremendously popular symphonic overture, which has no
thematic relation to the much-cut version of *Tell* that we now
hear. It has suffered so much from ill treatment by brass bands
and *n*th-rate orchestras that it has come in for wholly undeserved sneers. As performed by a great orchestra, it can be a
thrilling and dramatic experience. As a piece of program music,
it stands midway between the "Pastoral" Symphony of Beethoven and the "Scotch" Symphony of Mendelssohn, the overtures of Berlioz, and countless pages of Wagner.

Guillaume Tell ended Rossini's career as an operatic composer. While the reasons for his forty years' aloofness from the
stage are still guesswork, certain it is that he is unique in the
realm of music in giving up while still unchallenged ruler of
a rich kingdom. Rossini's knowledge of this kingdom was
complete: he had devoted nineteen years of exceedingly active
life to making it so. The instruments of his success were palpa-
ble—an unsurpassed sense of the theater, based on native flair
and experience in the leading opera houses of Europe; a comprehensive musicianship as much at ease with the orchestra as
with the voice; a detective's genius for picking out new talent,
and, finally, managerial astuteness and tact. To these he added
a sort of tempered audacity in innovation; an unceasing melodic
inventiveness; taste and elegance, not so infallible as his greatest admirers might wish, but of combined strength and delicacy
when in play, and, to leave the best to the last, a wit broader
and more robust than Mozart's, but quite as resilient and
accessible.

Considering the road Rossini traversed between *La Cambiale
di matrimonio* and *Guillaume Tell*, and the milestones he set
up along it, his nineteen active years seem not brief, but extraordinarily long. This progress, if not predictable on the
basis of *La Cambiale* and those other works of his minority, is
at least not miraculous if we remember that Rossini was a considerable genius who traveled widely and reacted, despite his

pretended laziness, to all the aesthetic forces operative in the Europe of his time. In *opera buffa* he found his own idiom almost at once, and in this field, which was indeed his own, he changed least, though *Le Comte Ory*, possibly because *opéra-comique* is not precisely *opera buffa*, has a new tang.

It is in his *opere serie* that the change is marked. His early examples are static historical charades, mere eighteenth-century carry-overs that would have found him, like the pre-*Orfeo* Gluck, a place in only the most detailed music dictionaries. But just as his childish ears had been exposed to Pergolesi, Jommelli, and Paisiello, he later heard Mozart, Haydn, Beethoven, Weber. The results were that his last Italian operas were within hailing distance of Verdi, his French operas a school for Meyerbeer. In atmosphere and texture, they are romantic through and through; only the melodic line at times betrays their classical origins. In the end, as this Italian reacted more and more to German influences, he came to regard himself as a French composer: as a matter of fact, Rossini, much like the German Meyerbeer (who cherished a similar illusion of successfully achieved Gallicization), was a cosmopolitan.

Chapter X

Mad Scenes

Uⁿᵗⁱˡ Rossini, Italian composers had borrowed little from the operatic art of neighboring nations. If they traveled, they tended not only jealously to preserve their national traits, but also to Italianize music in the countries they visited. With the exception of Lully, who went into France at an early and impressionable age, they remained Italians, abroad or on their native soil. Foreign musicians visited Italy at a risk of becoming as Italian as their hosts. Handel, Hasse, Gluck, Mozart—all succumbed to the lure of that disorderly and poverty-stricken land, rich only in song and color. Beethoven and Weber did not take the Italian tour, and so hit upon a new, German style of operatic writing.

Rossini was the first Italian to be influenced by other than native styles, or at least the first since the contrapuntalists borrowed polyphonic gambits, tricks, and end games from the Flemings. His last development was toward further symphonization of opera, toward Beethoven, that is; and this Parisian Italian lived to regret not having had an academic start in Germany. "For," as he said disarmingly to Wagner, "I had some talent and a certain intuition." Although he had effected wide changes in the operatic pattern, it might not have seemed so to this bewigged, gently acidulous old man, so quickly had Meyerbeer stepped in to take the reins in France, and so completely had Rossini's own countrymen gone on being unregenerate Italians. They accepted him as papa, but not as *père*. It might have been humiliating to a less realistic man than Rossini that his Italian disciples, from Bellini through Donizetti to Verdi, owed little or nothing to the thoughtful works of his maturity and far too much to those stereotyped *opere serie* and heedless *buffa* pieces of his nonage. All they wanted from him, it seemed, were his melodic stintlessness, understanding of the voice, and elegancy of ornamentation—and more than these went to the making of an opera.

When Rossini was a great man in the French capital, wielding an influence comparable to Cherubini's at the Conservatoire, he did everything in his power to help along the chances there of his most talented compatriots. He paved the way so effectually for Giuseppe Mercadante that that prolific composer of almost sixty operas (more than Rossini himself) died a member of the French Academy. More important was his sponsoring of Bellini and Donizetti, and the way he chivvied the former about the weakness of his orchestration (in 1834, however, when it was all but too late, with the culprit dying of an incurable disease) shows that he was not content merely with bringing his protégés to the capital. He wanted them to see things his way, but his method of persuading—with Bellini, anyhow—was of the gentlest. Rossini's wonted public manner, compounded of wit, sarcasm, and brusqueness, might have paralyzed the delicate, oversensitive young Sicilian.

The problem of giving Bellini advice was a difficult one for several reasons. He had heard that Rossini was cynical and grasping, and was therefore inclined to suspect his motives. Rossini, on his part, thought that Bellini had regressed since *Il Pirata* (1827) in the direction of untoward simplicity. That Bellini came not only to trust, but eventually to worship, Rossini, even doctoring his last opera, *I Puritani,* according to Rossini's prescriptions, is a tribute to the elder man's diplomacy and a gauge of what the young musical talents lost when, in 1836, their generous mentor fled from the artistic capital of the world to seek retirement in an Italian provincial town.

In viewing the history of opera, as in viewing the history of music in general, we are too used to allow certain imposing figures, some great, others not, to usurp the stage. In the opera of the first half of the nineteenth century, Weber, Rossini, and Meyerbeer bulk so large that other composers seem to huddle in the background like so many shadowy supernumeraries. No view can be more false. In those five decades, these eminent shapers of operatic destiny had as their associates such men, each of real significance in the unfolding story of the art, as Marschner, Cherubini, Spontini, Boïeldieu, Bellini, Donizetti, and Auber. But they only seem to huddle: in their own days,

Marion Telva (Adalgisa) and Rosa Ponselle (Norma), in Bellini's
Norma

they were great men, worthy and feared rivals of the giants who have made the most noise in the history books. Further, two of them, Cherubini and Spontini, were veritably worshiped, and Rossini, even at the height of his power, never equaled the dictatorial license Spontini was encouraged to indulge. If active survival of several operas by Weber, Rossini, and Meyerbeer could be contrasted with the complete disappearance of the other men from the repertoire, then the curious perspective of history might be explained rationally. But the fact is that only one opera by Rossini and one by Donizetti belong among the perennial favorites. The key to the puzzle lies in the historian's habit of giving space to men in proportion to their influence on the future of their art.

Bellini, who had little influence on the history of opera in the most limited sense, and so is dismissed with a few lines in most modern textbooks, bulked very large indeed a century ago. His influence was exerted on singing and on the history of music in general. He, more than any other composer, summed up, and displayed extravagantly, a style of singing that became at first impossible, and then unfashionable—or vice versa. *Bel canto* is a phrase susceptible to several interpretations, but it is above all, and always, Bellinian. *Bel canto* relies primarily on purity of tone and ease of production and only secondarily (sometimes never) on dramatic projection. *Bel canto* is partial to long passages of simple melody alternating with outbursts of vocal scrollwork, the latter usually for no better reason than that they illustrate the essence of *bel canto* itself. *Bel canto* really makes the voice a wind instrument. Its perfect practitioners make sounds of quite unearthly beauty and move the listener quite as a miracle would, so well do they do something it seems superhuman, or inhuman, to do at all. Whether true *bel canto* disappeared because people grew tired of it, or because its practitioners fell off in everything but weight, is a question—and a very unimportant one. What is certain is that it did disappear, and with it a formidable part of Bellini's reputation.

But Bellini has had his revenge. A melodist of great originality, on not quite the highest level of inspiration, he introduced into music a note that was quickly taken up by his contemporaries, became an easy adjunct with the next generation, and is still echoing, sometimes in the most unlikely places, throughout the world. What was that note? It is a kind of hushed, neurotic ecstasy, a kind of gently languorous orgasm in moonlit, bloom-pervaded gardens. Long before Verlaine, it was always crying in Bellini's heart. Chopin heard it, and it is the very stuff of his sulphurous, elegant nocturnes. Thereafter, almost immediately, began the degradation and cheapening. Liszt sobbed out his player's heart to the tune of these long, singing melodies, these throaty cantilenas with their heartbreaks stabbed out in maddening repetitions of the same torturing note. After Liszt, the Bellinian melody proliferated like a cancer, and found its way into the creative language of even the most austere composers. It was not only the Rubinsteins and Alabievs and Massenets and Kerns who succumbed to it: you can hear it in Brahms, Wagner, Tchaikovsky, and Debussy, glinting out like fool's gold from its less showy surroundings. One whiff of this Sicilian perfume, and—

My heart aches, and a drowsy numbness pains
My sense, as though of hemlock I had drunk,
Or emptied some dull opiate to the drains
One minute past, and Lethe-wards had sunk. . . .

Thus Keats, after listening to a nightingale. It would not be kind to quote what Alabiev did, after listening to Bellini. Anyhow, with the debasing of his most characteristic note into the "linkèd sweetness long drawn out" of dinner music, another formidable part of Bellini's reputation has gone. Which proves that reputation has nothing to do with influence.

The frail Bellini was lucky in always having powerful backers. Born of poor parents in a remote Sicilian town, he found a wealthy nobleman to send him through music school in Naples. There the noted Zingarelli, whose pert and lightsome songs are still occasionally heard, guided his talent for easy melody and sentimental phrase. In 1826, when Bellini was twenty-three years old, the same Barbaia who had furthered Rossini's career and had given *Euryanthe* to an ungrateful

Vienna heard the young man's first opera (a school exercise), which was produced privately. It was made possible for his first professional opera to be given at the Teatro San Carlo in 1826, and this was sufficiently successful both to stimulate Barbaia into ordering a second work, *Il Pirata,* and to cure at once any feeling of unprofessionalism Bellini might have had. His luck held: the librettist Barbaia found for him was Felice Romani, the best in Italy; the cast for the *première* at La Scala included the golden-voiced Rubini and Henriette-Clémentine Méric-Lalande, a popular French soprano. This was a hit: Bellini's fame spread beyond Italy, and Rossini tendered his compliments. The opera repeated its Milanese success in Vienna three months later, and it went on to become something of a favorite because of the tenor Rubini's partiality for the sentimental *"Tu vedrai,"* in which his much-admired vibrato had full play. But as *Il Pirata* was a weak and poorly constructed score, it disappeared before the middle of the century.

As Bellini's last three operas are the only ones we are ever likely to hear, there is no point wasting time on the preceding ones. Remarkably selected casts gained for most of them a measure of success quite beyond their intrinsic deserts. For instance, when *La Straniera* was first performed at La Scala in 1829, with Caroline Unger, Méric-Lalande, and Tamburini, the composer was called to the stage thirty times—an ovation he never equaled; on the other hand, when *Zaïra* was sung at Parma with a dim galaxy of local stars, it lasted for just one night and was never heard again. This taught Bellini that a man's career cannot be entrusted to incompetent throats: thereafter he stipulated in his contracts the singers to be assigned to various roles—and he never failed again.

This partial usurpation of the manager's prerogatives marks an important development in the production end of opera: the composer has now become so important that the opera house which wants the prestige of a *première* must accede to his demands that full justice be done to his work. And the singer's tyranny has become a legitimate one: he no longer dictates to the composer, but has been moved to his proper place on the auction block—a precious something on whose best efforts the success of an opera is largely dependent.

Late in 1830, it happened that the Teatro Carcano in Milan had a fine troupe of singers at its disposal, and, unwilling to waste their good fortune, the managers commissioned an opera apiece from Bellini and Donizetti. Fatefully for the future of a seventeen-year-old peasant boy by the name of Giuseppe Verdi, the censor stepped in and prevented Bellini from finishing his setting of a Romani libretto based on Hugo's *Hernani.* The subject was too hot for a Europe having one of its periodic spasms of revolution. So Romani, who was supplying Donizetti with a safe biography of Anne Boleyn, gave Bellini an even safer one about the tragicomic vicissitudes of a female sleepwalker. Henry VIII's addlepated queen reached the stage, as *Anna Bolena,* three months before *La Sonnambula:* it was Donizetti's thirty-third opera, but the first to give him a Continental reputation. Yet, Bellini scored heavily over his more practiced rival. When Pasta and Rubini got through their performance of *La Sonnambula* on March 6, 1831, they had launched one of the most nearly indestructible masterpieces of the florid school and had been first to sign a register that was to contain the names of the greatest sopranos and tenors of many decades.

As Pasta was not a light soprano, but a dramatic type who excelled in emotion, and never entirely mastered *bel canto,* it is not surprising that a few definitely heavy sopranos have found the role of Amina attractive. Yet, it is primarily a role for coloraturas. Patti like it so well that she used it for her Paris and London debuts, as well as for her second appearance at the Academy of Music, New York. The great Canadian soprano, Emma Albani, played Amina at her world (Messina, 1870), London, and New York debuts. The famous García sisters, Malibran and Viardot-García, both sang it, though the former was a contralto who had added an effective upper register to her voice by sheer obstinacy. Malibran was also the first to sing *La Sonnambula* in English—a custom that did much to popularize the opera in an England that had hesitated to accept its composer. Jenny Lind was one of the greatest of Aminas, and of her singing of the aria *"Ah! non credea"* Queen Victoria rhapsodized in her diary: "It was all *piano,* and clear and sweet, and like the sighing of a zephyr; yet all heard. Who could describe those long notes, drawn out till they quite melt away; that shake which becomes softer and softer; those very piano- and flute-like notes, and those round, fresh tones that are so youthful." Minnie Hauk, an Amina of fourteen, first appeared in public at the old Brooklyn Academy of Music. Ilma di Murska and Fanny Persiani were amazingly agile, if less subtle than Lind or Patti, while Etelka Gerster, who made her American bow in *La Sonnambula*, was in some ways the most admired Amina ever to sing in America. More modern interpreters of the role have been Sembrich, Tetrazzini, Galli-Curci, and Pons, the first in a historic performance at the Metropolitan in 1905, when she was supported by Caruso and Pol Plançon. Malibran and Lind had no doubt considered themselves realists in the part, but Elvira de Hidalgo, a Spanish singer of somewhat less than first magnitude, distanced all comers by playing Amina barefooted.

The really tremendous vogue once enjoyed by *La Sonnambula*—it was, for example, the first grand opera to be heard in Chicago (1850)—is easily understandable. A brief musical tale, notable for its straightforwardness and unwillingness to spin itself out to irrelevant lengths, this little opera is primarily pleasant entertainment. The well-constructed, uninvolved, if (to the skeptic modern mind) rather silly libretto was exactly right for the effusions of Bellini's fundamentally unpretentious muse: it presented simple situations, obvious emotions, strong but not violent contrasts. Of them Bellini made the most, unless realism be considered a *sine qua non* of "the most." *La Sonnambula* is as romantic as *Der Freischütz*, but its romanticism is Italian, delicately tinted by what was doubtless a superficial acquaintance with the current fashions in European literature. There is an idyllic, a positively sentimental, note here, traceable to that faded chronicler of French Darbys and Joans, Bernardin de Saint-Pierre.

This idyllic note, miscalled "elegiac," was Bellini's peculiar forte, and he illustrated it in *La Sonnambula* with melodies such as had never been heard before—melodies that seem at their most characteristic here, because here in purest form. The line of Amina's song in *"Ah! non credea"* is impeccable in draftsmanship and is traced in silverpoint. It is utterly irresistible even when sketched out in the piano's faulty legato, and something inexpressibly better when sung by a great soprano. The ending of this aria illustrates one of Bellini's strengths, for when Amina begins to warble whole cascades of sixteenth notes to a syllable, these *fioriture* seem to rise inevitably as the only possible resolution of the built-up emotion. Compare it with the more showy, almost Rossinian air that follows on its heels—the famous *"Ah! non giunge,"* and see what was Bellini's real métier. The second aria is exciting fireworks, but little more.

The *réclame* Bellini reaped because of *La Sonnambula* brought him another commission from La Scala. This time the fecund Romani turned to the Druids of Gaul, and spun a libretto that Schopenhauer, otherwise a man of common sense, exaggeratedly called the best libretto in existence. *Norma* was certainly constructed with loving care and provided with richly pathetic scenes to set Bellini's pen to weeping. Late in 1831, the score was ready, and, on December 26 of that year, it was staged with the kind of cast Bellini demanded. Pasta was the tragic priestess Norma, Giulia Grisi the Adalgisa, and Domenico Donzelli the Roman proconsul and deceiver, Pollione. At the *première*, *Norma* failed utterly and without qualification. But not Bellini's luck, for his expensive cast and the Scala management rallied to him, confident that the opera had the stuff of which successes are made. They played it until it succeeded, and succeeded so well that it has outstripped, in fame and staying power, any other of Bellini's operas.

At first *Norma*'s fame stopped short of England, and though Bellini went there in 1833, and Pasta sang in its London *première* at that time, all was far from smooth going. Only when Pasta retired temporarily from the stage, and Giulia Grisi was promoted from chief confidante to heroine, did *Norma* really catch on there. And Grisi went on to become the greatest of Normas. Jenny Lind also was graduated from the role of Adalgisa to that of Norma, which became one of her favorites. It is not vocally a remarkable transformation, as both roles are for soprano. Before long, Grisi had as her Pollione her own husband Mario, and together, on October 2, 1854, this incomparable Norma and Pollione sang at the opening of the New York Academy of Music. A more recent Norma was Lilli Lehmann, who made the amazing statement that it was easier to sing all three Brünnhildes than one Norma. In Wagner, she explained, "You are so carried away by the dramatic emotion, the action, and the scene that you do not have to think how to sing the words. That comes of itself. But in Bellini you must always have a care for beauty of tone and correct emission."

Norma is as dramatic as *La Sonnambula* is undramatic. Further, Romani's libretto is far more dramatic than Bellini's music. Despite the many beauties of his score, it seems that the story would have better suited Verdi's vigorous and theatrical genius—the cold precision of the musical line is not at all times germane to the romantic violence of the book, but is, rather, a holdover from the frigid classicizing of the first Napoleonic empire. It has been said that Bellini was weakest when not composing arias. The overture to *Norma* is a vicious example of his moments of utter noninspiration: melodramatic and banal claptrap, it is quite unsuited to the dignified tragedy it preludes. Nor can the construction of the opera, even after the curtain is raised, be called craftsmanlike: the scenery along the roads between arias and concerted numbers is remarkable chiefly for its intemperate listlessness. Although not boiled down to a formula (possibly because Bellini would not even take that trouble), these dull musical turnpikes are as boring as the most formula-ridden passagework. If *Norma* did not have its few great arias and affecting duets, it would yield even its stubborn fragments of popularity to *La Sonnambula*, which is, on the whole, far more tolerable to listen to today.

But *Norma* has "*Casta diva,*" that miraculous exercise in the balance between *bel canto* suavity and florid vocal tracery. Absurdly, "*Casta diva*" alone keeps it breathing, and it requires some thought to realize that after this (which comes early in the opera), a few other luscious numbers hold us in our seats until the end. It would be a mistake to pretend that these ripe melodies are cleverly spaced: even in his shrewdest score, Bellini never gives us the feeling of conscious competence— more, he seems to have lacked, in almost criminal measure, intention and foresight as those qualities are translated by a master of drama. No. Bellini was, in his way, a force of nature, however minor. *"Casta diva"* is a lyrical impulse. But lyrical impulses unaided do not make an opera—if they could, Schubert's operas, to take a flagrant case, would not have been stillborn. No one has thought of reviving the operas of that matchless song writer. Perhaps the writing of songs was Bellini's real métier too, and had he written hundreds of them, we might not have to revive his operas in order to remember his genius. But, for that matter, were not the recent Metropolitan revivals of *Norma*, after a lapse of thirty-five years, rather to display the magical art of Rosa Ponselle at the height of her powers than to honor Bellini?

For all practical purposes, *Norma* was Bellini's last opera but one. True, he composed three more works for the stage, but of them one was never produced except privately, and another suffered from a libretto so execrable and uninspiring that Bellini angrily broke off relations with its author, his old stand-by Romani. The third, however, though it reached the stage, and went on to equal *Norma* in renown, was even more a curiosity than the other two. This was *I Puritani di Scozia*, whose librettist, Count Carlo Pepoli, justified its title by boldly locating Plymouth in Scotland—something that the at least accurate Romani would never have done. *I Puritani* was, in another respect, a departure for Bellini: it was not for Italy, but for Paris. Rossini had persuaded the Théâtre Italien to commission it and had lured Bellini to France.

While the score of *I Puritani* was being composed, Rossini was clucking around his protégé like a stout hen around a scrawny chick. Not only did he make suggestions in general, but he criticized the music page by page, line by line. At first, Bellini was suspicious of this mothering: he had always heard that the Swan of Pesaro was notoriously devoid of the softer parental feelings. But he was already under the spell of Rossini the composer of *Guillaume Tell*, which, after twelve hearings, he was comparing to *La Divina Commedia*. Then Rossini the social genius got him. In short, Bellini capitulated, and for the remaining months of his brief life loved his new friend without qualification. Finally, he fell so much under his spell that when *I Puritani* was first produced, on January 25, 1835, it turned out to be almost as much Rossini's last opera as Bellini's. The master's touch is evident mainly in the strong and earnestly worked out orchestration, and the *longueurs* between arias and concerted numbers are not so tiresome. Finally, *I Puritani* contains two bass roles, one of them the weightiest Bellini ever composed.

Nothing, literally, was so important about *I Puritani* as its original cast, particularly the four principals for whom Bellini had designed it. First of these was Giulia Grisi, the Elvira. Next was Rubini, the Arturo, who was responsible both for the pristine fame of the opera and for the almost complete desuetude into which it fell when he retired from the stage. For, besides his famous shake, Rubini boasted a voice of phenomenal range, from bass E to treble B—three octaves and a half with ease, and more on occasion. Arturo's tessitura therefore lies very high, and the role—and the opera—practically died with Rubini. To sing Arturo, the average tenor would have to do a lot of falsetto squeaking. Third in this cast was Tamburini, the Riccardo. Luigi Lablache, the greatest bass of the age, who had been chosen for the honor of singing in the Mozart Requiem at both Haydn's and Beethoven's funerals,* was the Giorgio, rounding out what came to be known as the *"Puritani"* Quartet. For years, they toured Europe, and it was the dream of every operatic composer to write for them. Even after Rubini was replaced by Mario, the Quartet survived, just as famous as ever, and for it Donizetti, in 1843, composed *Don Pasquale*.

So, finally, the chief function of *I Puritani* became helping other composers to make operatic history. Not that the opera itself died completely. Both Bosio and Gerster were excellent Elviras.† When, at Athens, on June 7, 1877, Sembrich made her first appearance on

* But not, in both cases, singing bass. On the earlier occasion (1809) he was a boy contralto.

† Gustav Kobbé, in his *The Complete Opera Book*, says of a Gerster revival: "It was in the duet at the end of Act II . . . that I heard break and go to pieces the voice of Antonio Galassi, the great baritone of the heyday of Italian opera at the Academy of Music. '*Suoni la tromba!*'—he could sound it no more. The career of a great artist was at an end."

an operatic stage,* she chose Elvira as her debut role. It was Sembrich, too, who brought *I Puritani* to the Metropolitan in its first
season (1883-84). While New York has heard the opera rarely in
this century, it was chosen in 1844 to open Palmo's Opera House,
on Broadway, above Duane Street. Sixty-two years later, Hammerstein selected this far from popular work to launch his Manhattan Opera House—and supply a vehicle for the American debut
of Alessandro Bonci, as Arturo—on December 3, 1906. Tetrazzini
and the Spanish tenor Florencio Constantino also sang *I Puritani*
under the Hammerstein aegis. For the Metropolitan's revival of
1917, three of the principals were Spanish—María Barrientos,
Hipólito Lazaro, and José Mardones; De Luca completed the
quartet.

There is good reason to regret the complete disappearance
of *I Puritani*. It has an abominable book, and parts of it have
to be transposed into odd keys in order to be sung at all. But
it is, if not Bellini's most characteristic music, at least his most
mature and dramatic. It has a vigor lacking in the earlier
operas, besides some attempt at musical characterization. Elvira's "Mad Scene" in Act II (it was the year for mad scenes—
Lucia di Lammermoor came only nine months later) does not
quite achieve plausibility, though it is not quite so silly as
Lucia's. Certainly, *"Qui la voce"* is musically on a higher level
than the languorous waltz to which Donizetti's heroine loses
her mind, while Elvira herself is more tolerable in the gay
"Son vergin vezzosa," another Rossinian inspiration. The concerted finale, with principals and chorus (for *I Puritani* is
melodramma serio, not *tragedia lirica*, and the hero and heroine
are therefore alive at the end), is a strong and vivacious essay
at part writing, indicating that the dying composer had untouched reserves of creative strength.

Definitely, Bellini had not yet had his complete say when he
died at less than thirty-four. Had he lived, he might have de-
flected the stream of the development of opera in France. Were
there not rumors that he was already too apt in stealing Ros-

* The daughter of a famous violinist, Praxede Marcelline Kochanska (as she
was called in her preoperatic days) studied violin and piano until she was
eighteen. Liszt granted her an audience, at which she performed as violinist,
pianist, and vocalist. The *abbé* advised her to sing.

sini's thunders? When he died, the rumors changed to slander-ous whispers. Rossini was accused of playing Salieri to Bellini's Mozart—but quite as unjustly: the autopsy on which he in-sisted proved that his compatriot had died naturally. Autopsy aside, Bellini was still more spectacular dead than alive. His funeral was stage-managed by four composers, Rossini and Cherubini at their head. A special musical department, pre-sided over by that audacious orchestral conductor of generous impulse and uncertain tempo, François-Antoine Habeneck, ar-ranged a funeral service that was at least unique—part of the Requiem was sung to a melody from *I Puritani*, the executants being Rubini, Tamburini, Lablache, and the Russian tenor, Nicholas Ivanoff.

Bellini's death, as well as Rossini's continuing abstention from the stage, left the field of Italian opera to the facile and copious Donizetti, their most considerable rival. Far and away the least interesting of the three, he was, both temporally and stylistically, a link between them and the young but rapidly maturing Verdi of *Ernani* and *Luisa Miller*. With touches of Rossini's verve and pace, Bellini's *bel canto* languid smooth-ness, and even, at rare moments, Verdi's realism, Donizetti lacks a strong musical personality. As a composer, he was something of a virtuoso, with all the accompanying defects. In the space of twenty-six years he composed sixty-five operas (some of them, it must be admitted, mere one-act operettas). Many of these are but improvised banquets of song, with not a few of the viands warmed over from previous feasts. He com-posed a one-acter* in nine days, and the last act of *La Favorite*, one of his most popular scores, was spun off in a few hours.

The results of this slapdash haste in composition are what we would expect (Donizetti was not Mozart, and only occa-sionally was he Rossini): poor construction, feeble passagework, drearily manufactured accompaniments, acceptance of anything

* It was called *Il Campanello di notte*, and by a mere chance it has sur-vived. In 1917, The Society of American Singers, having made a hit with two Mozart one-acters, *Bastien und Bastienne* and *Der Schauspieldirektor*, revived it in an English adaptation at the Lyceum Theater, New York. The leading role in this obscene work was sung by David Bispham, the eminent Quaker baritone.

that came along. He had a good-natured contempt for anyone who worked more slowly than he did. Once, when told that Rossini had composed *Il Barbiere di Siviglia* in thirteen days, he replied, "Why not? He's so lazy." In short, Donizetti was the exact opposite of Bellini, who once wrote to Giovanni Ricordi, his publisher, firmly but politely demanding four times the usual fee for an opera, on the grounds that he composed only one opera while other men did four.

Donizetti exaggerated the tendency inaugurated by Rossini to look in almost any direction for a libretto. In Rossini, this freedom of choice had an element of creativeness; Donizetti, inheriting it, construed it as a license to accept any story. Glancing over the titles of his operas, one visualizes him poring over a terrestrial globe, suddenly darting down to fix a pin in some, to him, exotic spot, and thinking triumphantly, "Here I shall erect another opera." In *La Regina di Golconda* he reached India's coral strand, though his nearest approach to Greenland's icy mountains was Liverpool, which he celebrated in a score about some evidently not very fussy girl who dwelt in a hermitage there. From his titles alone comes evidence of an interest in such ill-assorted places as Calais, Chamonix, Saardam, Rome, Granada, and Kenilworth. Was the oddly captioned *Otto mese in due ore** laid in the United States, then, as now, the home of speed? Did *Il Diluvio universale*† end on Mount Ararat? There is no way of knowing: these, like the scores of most of Donizetti's operas, will not be available—if, indeed, they survive at all—until travel in Italy is resumed. At any rate, they are a very far cry from the Greek and Roman myths that constituted the subject matter of the earliest operas, and almost as far from the heroic exploits, historic and pseudo-historic, that had for so long been the whole business of *opera seria*. Rossini had indeed opened a Pandora's box when he turned to Shakespeare and Scott, to actual modern history, for the materials of his musical invention. The last ill lies doubtless in that box, and no man can prophesy what it will be.

* *Eight Months in Two Hours.*
† *The Universal Deluge.*

Since Paul Hindemith dramatized a daily news report in his audacious *Neues vom Tage,* all bets are off.

Donizetti's first thirty-two operas can be dismissed completely without loss to history, and certainly without loss to music. Then, with his thirty-third, exactly at the halfway mark of his output, he rang the bell with *Anna Bolena.* It was a bell that was destined to clang and clamor, tinkle and knell, through thirty-two more operas, and to echo and re-echo through every opera house in the world, dimly and ever more dimly, up to the present time. It was a bell of base alloy, often flat, often murderously shrill, often soporific, yet occasionally emitting a silvery tone, all the more surprising because so rare. Of his second thirty-two, *Lucia di Lammermoor* is still a fixture wherever opera is given, and another, *Don Pasquale,* should be. A scant five rounds out the roster of those Donizetti operas which, for one reason or another, are still presentable. *Anna Bolena* itself is not among the presentable. Its glory departed with the great trio who sang it in its youth—Pasta as Anne Boleyn, Rubini as Percy, and Lablache as Henry VIII.

Yet, a presentation of this faded score would certainly astonish English-speaking audiences, for in Act III occurs a melody they know as *Home, Sweet Home.* Will not every loyal Englishman swear that Sir Henry R. Bishop, perpetrator of *Lo, Here the Gentle Lark,* was the only fabricator of this most epidemic of heart songs? Where, then, did Donizetti get the tune he used in *Anna Bolena?* Did he borrow it from Bishop himself, who years before applying it to John Howard Payne's verses in his opera *Clari, or The Maid of Milan,* had published it as a Sicilian folk melody? Possibly it was just what Bishop had at first said it was—a Sicilian folk melody—and not his own brain child, as he established in a court of law . . . after it became famous.

Not so exemplary in its sentiments as *Home, Sweet Home,* but more attractive musically, was the aria *"Una furtiva lagrima"* that made the fortune of the sparkling *buffa* score Donizetti wrote two years after *Anna Bolena.* This was *L'Elisir d'amore,* to words by Felice Romani, an opera much inferior to *Don Pasquale,* and scarcely the equal of *La Fille du régi-*

ment, yet witty enough to show the strength of Donizetti's comic talent. Incidentally, it has seemed to be more popular in this century than any opera of Donizetti's except *Lucia*, a fact which at the Metropolitan was due to the role of Elvino's being one of Caruso's favorites. Naturally, as the tenor is given *"Una furtiva lagrima."* Yet, the role proved ultimately thankless to its superb interpreter, for he was singing it at the Brooklyn Academy of Music, on December 11, 1920, when he was stricken with the pleurisy of which he died eight months later. At his first Metropolitan performance of it, he had been supported by Sembrich and Scotti; at the fatal Brooklyn repetition, Evelyn Scotney was the Adina, Scotti the Belcore, and Adamo Didur, the great Polish bass, the Dulcamara.

Practically all the great lyric tenors of the past and present have sung Elvino, among them, recently, Bonci, Schipa, and Gigli, while famous Adinas would constitute an equally impressive roster of female talent, including Lind, Gerster, and Gadski.

Within a few months of *L'Elisir*, Donizetti composed five operas, not one note of which has been heard across non-Italian footlights for over fifty years. Then Romani supplied him with a violent and grotesque, if at that time conventional, twisting of the story of that now thoroughly whitewashed Renaissance heroine, Lucrezia Borgia. Even as operatic melodramas go, this absurd version of an absurd play by Victor Hugo was absurd. It is simply too full of corpses. Yet, to it Donizetti set a whole series of charming, shallow, lightheaded melodies that might better have gone into the making of a musical keepsake. There is one still-famed exception—a drinking song, or *brindisi*, sung by a contralto roughneck: it is even more charming, shallow, and lightheaded than the rest. It sounds just like something from a Savoy opera.

While on its opening night at La Scala, with Méric-Lalande as the poisoner, *Lucrezia Borgia* failed (as it should have), it rose from its ashes with amazing celerity to become a trustworthy warhorse for the dramatic sopranos of the era. Grisi and Sontag's last role, Lucrezia was most memorably associated with the powerful Hungarian soprano, Therese Tietjens, who made her debut in it at

Hamburg in 1849, and sang it as long as she had breath to do so, being carried, dying, from the stage after singing it for the last time. Marietta Piccolomini, a capable actress with a voice more suited to lighter roles, also chose it for her debut. In its early days, *Lucrezia Borgia* was given with the classic constellation of Giulia Grisi (Lucrezia), Mario (Gennaro), and Alboni (Orsini), the last having made her operatic debut in this male-impersonation role in 1842, at Bologna, through Rossini's personal intervention. The principals of the only Metropolitan performance, on December 4, 1904, included Edyth Walker, Caruso, and Scotti.

Five operas later, Donizetti created his most famous and enduring work, *Lucia di Lammermoor*. Almost as if anticipating its destined success, he wrote it specifically for two of the most notable stars of the time, Fanny Persiani and Gilbert Duprez. For its libretto, a vulgarization of Scott's *The Bride of Lammermoor*, he forsook Romani, the hero of a hundred texts, for Salvatore Cammarano, who, eighteen years later, was to provide Verdi with the book of *Il Trovatore*. First produced at the Teatro San Carlo, on September 26, 1835, *Lucia* was an immediate triumph. The exhilaration of the stormy *première* sent the composer to bed with a fever. The opera leaped through Europe like wildfire, and reached England as early as April, 1838, with Persiani and Rubini as the luckless lovers.

In 1843, New York heard *Lucia* at Niblo's Garden. Adelina Patti chose Lucia for her debut, which took place at the New York Academy of Music, on November 24, 1859. Also in this role, on October 24, 1883, an equally beautiful voice, that of Sembrich, was first heard in America. Latest of famous Lucias to be heard here is Lily Pons, who made her sensational Metropolitan debut in that part on January 3, 1931. In the interim, every soprano who could compete with what Pitts Sanborn called "an agile and obedient flute" has attempted Lucia; among the successful ones have been Lind, Gerster, Melba (who made her London and Metropolitan debuts in the role), Tetrazzini, and Galli-Curci.

Since 1900, *Lucia* has been given almost one hundred times at the Metropolitan, which puts it, as a popular fixture, in the same class with *Aïda, Carmen,* the Wagnerian favorites, *Faust, Pagliacci,* and half a dozen others. This phenomenon is curious, and not easily explicable. The book is flat, dull, and unrelievedly gloomy: it is as inferior to the novel from which it is taken as that is to the best of Scott. The music is not very much better than that of most Donizetti scores, and has faded perceptibly, without acquiring patina or antique grace. Present-day singers capable of executing its really prodigious vocal difficulties have not been numerous.

If there is any explanation of its popularity, it must be that *Lucia* has been saved for perennial revival by two numbers, the Sextet and the "Mad Scene." The first is still in every whistler's repertoire; the second, however, is a mystery within a mystery: for all its fame, it would probably stump nine out of ten in a musical-memory contest. There are many other effective numbers, mostly negligible as music, that in every performance are listened for by the hardened operagoer. Lucia's cavatina, *"Regnava nel silenzio,"* is a melancholy, pensive melody of Bellinian cast, quickening into the ecstatic *"Quando rapita in estasi."* Edgardo's final aria, *"Fra poco a me ricovero,"* has been a favorite showpiece of tenors from Duprez and Sims Reeves to John McCormack, Schipa, and Giacomo Lauri-Volpi. But it is by the Sextet and the "Mad Scene" that any performance of *Lucia* is judged. Without them, it would not last.

The Sextet, *"Chi mi frena,"* has been called the greatest concerted number in Italian opera, but those who have called it that have listened inattentively to the Quartet from *Rigoletto* and the Octet from *Falstaff*, to mention only two. Its principal quality is its catchiness, and it has a way of going wild at the climax in a sort of unrestrained florid grandeur that gives an air of spontaneity to the whole thing. As characterization, it is buncombe, and yet such is its sweep that it seems as though the six personages involved had to get it out of their systems or burst. Cheap and banal the Sextet is, but it has the something that lasts.

Quite different is the "Mad Scene," that maddeningly long piece of silly music. It is not catchy; it is all but prim in its decorous, calculated pace; it has no spontaneity at all. The Sextet is, in its way, an inspiration: there is nothing inspired about the "Mad Scene": from beginning to end, it is a cold-blooded vocal lesson, and through most of its length an arduous but inane contest between voice and flute. In the "Mad Scene," the florid soprano, who had threatened to unbalance opera from its very birth, achieved her purpose. Here, for fourteen solid minutes the already enfeebled action is halted for an exhibition of virtuosity that has no dramatic relevance, and almost as little musical. As Paul England has expressed it, in his witty *précis* of *Lucia*: "The heroine now wanders on to the scene to show us that, whatever the state of her mind may be, she has her voice under perfect control."

Whatever one may think of overprolonging the "Lesson Scene" in *Il Barbiere di Siviglia*, at least Rossini provided against the chief absurdity by motivating the interruption. Various composers of the nineteenth century, faced with the problem of making a star soprano happy, artificially used a "mad scene"* as an excuse for allowing her to warble acres of *fioriture* that only an insane woman would think of singing, but that no insane woman would have the control to sing. Commenting on this absurd convention, H. Sutherland Edwards, a juicy nineteenth-century writer on matters musical, wrote: "The exceptional personage in serious opera is the light soprano who does *not* go mad—as, for instance, Gilda in *Rigoletto*. Martha, in the opera of that name, only abstains from becoming insane because Lionel, the tenor, saves her the trouble by becoming insane in her place. Catherine, in *L'Étoile du nord*, is crazy from the beginning almost to the end of the third act; Dinorah is, throughout the opera to which she gives her name, as mad as the proverbial March hare, and she becomes madder still after the climax at the end of the second act—that critical juncture at which the reason of nine heroines, of the 'light' order, out of ten gives way. The ordinary operatic heroine trusts in the first act, is deceived in the second, and goes mad in the third. She is without character, and is remembered not as an individual, but as a member of a large and uninteresting class of melodious lunatics."

In the four years following *Lucia*, Donizetti composed nine operas, only one of which, *Poliuto*, retains a glimmer of in-

---

* The first mad girl in opera seems to have been the heroine of Nicolas Dalayrac's *Nina, ou La Folle par amour* (1786).

terest, and that only because a king of Naples (not of a witty race) made a *mot* about it. Nourrit, who was to sing it, had the reputation of being a radical, and Ferdinand II was tempted to forbid the performance. Nourrit expostulated, explaining that "Poliuto" (despite his depraved-sounding name) was a saint. "Keep," thundered indignant majesty, "the saints in the calendar, and do not bring them on the stage."

The tenth opera after *Lucia, La Fille du régiment,* produced in Paris, at the Comique, early in 1840,* had better luck. It was Donizetti's first try at a French libretto, and it was coldly received. With Italian words, and called *La Figlia del reggimento,* it fared better. In fact, when Lind took it up, it went on to become a favorite with the nice-thinking subjects of Queen Victoria, who were pleased to overlook the heroine's uncouthness in view of her moral rectitude. For *La Fille* is a miracle play: the *vivandière* Marie, though she swears like the troopers she has lived among, is, in her heart of hearts, pure Windsor Castle.

Although Marie has not warbled in New York in French or Italian since 1918, it is not safe to pronounce her dead. For instance, a war fever is apt to resurrect her.† Singing the role during the early days of the Civil War, with real Union zouaves on the stage, Clara Louise Kellogg (who learned to play the drum for the occasion) aroused a patriotic storm. Her reminiscences exult in the possibility that several young men may have joined up as a result. Fifty-seven years later, three days after the signing of the Armistice, Frieda Hempel stepped out of her role to sing, rather *en retard,* Ivor Novello's great patriotic lied, *Keep the Home Fires Burning.* The revival of *La Fille,* outside

* The Marie of this *première* was Sophie Anne Thillon, an English importation. It was this lady, singing in America in 1850-54, who is said to have introduced opera to the San Franciscans.

† This is precisely what happened after this chapter was written. *La Fille du régiment* was announced for revival during the season of 1940-41, as a vehicle for Pons. Immediately, pictures of the vivacious diva in military costume graced the Sunday supplements; she learned to play the drum; she was inducted as an honorary member into a regiment of the United States Army. While all this was going on, things in Europe were getting very grim, and the United States was swinging resolutely into the Allied orbit. *La Fille* was revived on December 28, 1940, again at the Metropolitan. Pons was overshadowed by Salvatore Baccaloni's broad farcical interpretation of Sergeant Sulpice.

of a war mania, depends largely on a florid light soprano who is also a capable comedienne.

Finally, *La Fille* is almost too thin musically for modern ears, almost too silly dramatically for modern minds—in short, it is operetta, and not to be mentioned with *Don Pasquale*, the composer's comic masterpiece. What Mendelssohn might have produced if he had turned his undramatic pen to opera may be surmised from his once having snubbed a group of musicians who were making fun of *La Fille* with a pontifical "I should like to have written that myself."

Eleven months after the cold reception Paris had accorded *La Fille*, Donizetti was represented at the Opéra, on December 2, 1840, with a full-fledged grand opera, complete with ceremonial scenes, ballet, and the other trappings of the *Guillaume Tell*-Meyerbeer school of stage crowding. *La Favorite*, the new work, was as woefully heavy as *La Fille* was inanely light. Naturally, it was pseudo historical, being based on a long and nasty skit, by two Frenchmen, about the mother of Pedro the Cruel of Castile, a woman who had done much to corrupt the morals of fourteenth-century Spain. It reads like a scissors-and-paste adaptation of *The Garden of Allah* and *Tess of the d'Urbervilles*. The presence in the cast of Rosine Stoltz, the reigning star at the Opéra, and in her own quiet way as remarkable as Pedro's mother,* could not bring popularity to this finest of Donizetti's tragic operas. Again translation and rechristening were needed, and as *La Favorita* the opera had a long and sanguinary career.

La Favorite's success in the English-speaking world dates from the furore created by Grisi and Mario when they first sang it in London in the late forties. For many years it was a staple at the New York Academy of Music, where Annie Louise Cary was a favorite Leonora. The Metropolitan failed to produce it during its first dozen years; the taste was beginning to run against anything but high sopranos as heroines, and Leonora is a mezzo or contralto role. But when the Metropolitan finally got around to producing

---

* After marrying a commoner (but a powerful one—he was manager of the Théâtre de la Monnaie, at Brussels), she successively espoused a baron, a count, and a duke, accomplishing these social strides after her forty-fifth year. She died Duchesse de Bassano, at Paris, in 1903, at the age of eighty-eight.

it* on November 29, 1895, Manager Grau compensated for past neglect by providing the truly magnificent cast of Eugenia Man-

* Something of the difficulty of producing opera is suggested by the following excerpt from *The Mapleson Memoirs*, referring to Colonel Mapleson's vicissitudes at the New York Academy of Music:

"Early in December I was within a very close shave of closing the theatre. The opera announced for the evening in question was *William Tell*. At about four o'clock I received a doctor's certificate from Mdlle. Dotti, who performed the principal female character, notifying me that she had been attacked with diphtheria. I therefore had to set about to find a substitute, having decided to give the opera anyhow. Shortly after a notification came from Mierzwinski, the tenor, who was also indisposed, though after a deal of trouble he promised to go on and do his best.

"I was, however, compelled to change the opera to *Lucia di Lammermoor*, as the lady who had undertaken to replace the prima donna in *William Tell* was in such a nervous state. There was no time for a rehearsal; I therefore decided to give *Lucia* instead. On the notice being sent to Mdlle. Laura Zagury, the soprano, she informed me that although *Lucia* was in the *répertoire* she furnished me on her engagement she had never sung that *rôle*. The opera therefore had to be changed to *Aïda*. Orders had just been given to the various departments as to the scenery, dresses, music, etc., when the news came that Mdlle. Rossini, whom I had counted upon for the principal part, was lying ill at her house on Fifth Avenue.

"I now changed the opera to *Rigoletto*; but Mdme. Zagury was not ready with the part of 'Gilda,' and absolutely refused to appear. *Les Huguenots* was next announced, it being now half-past five. Everything was set in motion for the production of that opera, when Mdme. Fursch-Madi declared her inability to assume the part of the heroine, as she had taken some medicine, believing that her services would not be required until the early part of the following week. Thereupon an attack was made on Mdme. Savio, who however, regretted that she was unable to appear as 'Valentine.'

"Nothing was left but to try *La Favorita*; but Signor Ravelli, who had just finished a *Carmen* rehearsal, declared it would be utterly impossible for him to sing the *rôle* of 'Fernando.' Then Minnie Hauk was sought for; but she was saving herself for her appearance in Brooklyn on the morrow, and distinctly declined.

"I now took a decision either to perform *La Favorita*, or to close up, as it was already 6:30 P.M. I at length persuaded Signor Clodio, one of the tenors, to assume the part of 'Fernando.' But a new difficulty arose, as, being a very portly gentleman, there were no costumes in the house to fit him. The tailors were then set to work, who promised to have the dress ready in time. At this juncture word came from Mdme. Galassi, who was to have taken the part of 'Leonora,' that she was in bed suffering, and that it would be impossible for her to appear. I immediately went off to Mdme. Galassi myself. She assured me of her willingness to do her best; but she had two large boils under her right arm which caused her acute agony. At that moment she nearly swooned from the pain. To fetch Dr. Mott, our talented theatrical surgeon, was the work of a moment. We raised her up and the boils were lanced, which at once gave her relief, and I got her down to the theatre just at five minutes to eight. She had time to dress, as 'Leonora' does not appear until the second act. The performance went off successfully; I had got out of another serious difficulty after changing the opera seven times.

"In the midst of my trouble a deputation arrived from Kalakaua I., King of the Sandwich Islands, informing me that they were comanded by his Majesty

telli (Leonora), Giuseppe Cremonini (Fernando), Ancona (Alfonso XI), and Plançon (Balthazar). Plançon retained his role in the revival of 1905, with Edyth Walker, Caruso, and Scotti as the other principals. But the main item in the stage history of *La Favorite* came from Venice: there, at the Fenice, in January, 1874, Giovanni di Reschi made his operatic debut as the King. Thus, as a baritone, was Jean de Reszke introduced to the singing stage. Five years later, in Madrid, he essayed, with brilliant success, the tenor role of Fernando. Louise Homer sang Leonora when, in May, 1898, she made her operatic debut at Vichy.

For an opera with so many beautiful and expressive pages, *La Favorite* opens suspiciously with an ambiguous overture, its first section Bach *à l'italienne* moving unreasonably into the jumpiest, cheapest kind of motion-picture music. There are a couple of good numbers in the first two acts, but also ballet music so infernally tum-tummy as almost to send one home discouraged at that point. In Act III, things begin to happen in the music as well as in the action. First there comes a baritone aria, *"A tanto amor,"* nervous and sensitive in line, its eloquence heightened by the interjections and asides of the infatuated tenor and mezzo—its pointedness is almost Verdian at times. Only a few moments later, Leonora pours forth her love in *"O mio Fernando,"* a torrentially passionate musical declaration, one of the sultriest outbursts in pre-Verdian opera. It is long and too taxing for any except the surest type of voice. The finale of the third act, too, has found admirers in the most alien camps: it is a large, amply conceived, and altogether impressive concerted number for the principals and full chorus. Something of its proportions may be deduced from the fact that it runs to thirty-nine pages in piano score. Act IV, though no longer than the finale of Act III, constitutes Donizetti's most ponderable claim as a serious composer. It lends weight to the most lurid idea of inspiration, having been scribbled out in a few hours. The music is truly expressive of the demands of the plot, and, as an artistic statement of a harrowing situation

the King of Hawaii to confer on Mdme. Patti the Royal Order of Kapirlani. They had the diploma and jewels with them, and they were accompanied by the King's Chamberlain. I had to entreat them to wait 'a moment' while I got through my troubles. That moment must have been nearly two hours."

brought to violent climax, it is without flaw. In fact, it is so good that one wonders why Donizetti did not do it more often. The tenor aria, *"Spirto gentil,"** is only less famous than *"Una furtiva lagrima"*: a few years ago, no less than twenty separate recordings of it were available. It is lyrically persuasive without being tantalizing.

Between *La Favorite* and Donizetti's most brilliant contribution to comedy, *Don Pasquale,* three operas and three years intervened. The third of these—a light and imbecilic melodrama about the mortgage on the old homestead, the farmer's pure daughter, the rich villain, and the faithful lover—was *Linda di Chamounix,* a work that is in process of vanishing completely from the repertoire. Its original success, on May 19, 1842, at the Kärntnerthortheater in Vienna, is easily explained by the cast, possibly the most star-studded ever assembled for a *première*: Persiani, Marietta Brambilla, Mario, Tamburini, and Lablache. But if it had not been for a mad scene and a hysterical first-act coloratura aria, *"O luce di quest' anima,"* it might not have survived the year of its birth. Because of them, every notable coloratura of the nineteenth century and even some of this have taken a fling at the role of Linda.

Clara Louise Kellogg,† Patti, Galli-Curci, and Pons have been among favorite American Lindas. The last, singing in its first production by the regular Metropolitan company, on March 1, 1934, was supported by Gladys Swarthout, Richard Crooks, De Luca, and Pinza. After seven performances in two successive seasons, *Linda* has not been heard in New York.

Brilliant as was the first cast of *Linda di Chamounix*, Donizetti composed—and wrote the libretto of—*Don Pasquale* for a cast of unsurpassed glamour—nothing less than the original *"Puritani"* Quartet, with Mario replacing Rubini, but with Grisi, Tamburini, and Lablache as of old. The opportunity evidently quickened his senses and warmed his imagination,

* As this number was drawn from a score—*Il Duca d'Alba*—which was not performed until thirty-four years after Donizetti's death, his spectacular speed in writing Act IV is partly explained.

† Miss Kellogg's considered judgment on *Linda*: "It is a dear little story. . . ."

for this *opera buffa*, first heard at the Théâtre Italien, on January 4, 1843, suggested that Rossini's comic muse might have to vacate the throne on which she had been sleeping for so many years. Not that *Don Pasquale* is the equal of *Il Barbiere*. Slighter, less mordant, and less incredibly abounding, it has its own unfailing brand of deliciousness. Fortunately, this swiftly written score, composed in between eight days and three weeks (there is no agreement on this point), had no time for the lachrymosity that mars the larger part of Donizetti's comic work. *Don Pasquale* is primarily, inflexibly, a great comedy of central situation: stemming from Pergolesi and Cimarosa, it is of the line that seems to have ended with the acidulous humor of Puccini's *Gianni Schicchi* and the more polite and suave, but as crisp, social comment of Wolf-Ferrari's *Il Segreto di Susanna*.

One of the most remarkable things about *Don Pasquale* is its unspoiled freshness, remarkable because it was the sixty-fifth opera of a man who, for twenty-five years, had been purveying all kinds of vehicles for all kinds of singers and all kinds of audiences, and who was, at the time of its creation, on the verge of a nervous collapse that was to end in imbecility and death within five years. It shares with the best comic works of the Italian school (with the notable exception of Puccini's) a singular youthful quality on which the passing years have no effect. There is springtime in *Don Pasquale*, and though the music is undeniably thin, it is not so familiar as to be worn threadbare. In short, the charm persists. The chattery, saucy overture, a potpourri of good things from the opera, is Donizetti's most tolerable, and might almost pass for good second-rate Rossini. The barefaced nonsense of the plot is matched by the high-spirited, often farcical numbers, reaching their most delicious absurd in the prolonged quartet at the end of Act II. Of the solo numbers, it is difficult to choose between Norina's entrance song, *"So anch' io la virtù,"* a pert, madcap melody, wonderfully hummable and shrewdly underlining the situation, and Ernesto's serenade, *"Com' è gentil,"* a suave love song of unmistakably Latin origin, with mandolinlike effects from the chorus.

During the rehearsals before the *première* of *Don Pasquale*, both the composer and the principals felt that the extra something that every opera needs to get across was lacking. Rummaging around in a pile of his manuscripts, Donizetti found an aria that he sent to Mario with the words: "Sing this to Norina in the garden scene." This was *"Com' è gentil,"* with which, with Lablache strumming a lute accompaniment behind scenes, the great tenor brought the fashionable Parisian audience to its feet on the opening night.

While some revivals of *Don Pasquale* have been chiefly to give a popular tenor the chance to sing the serenade in an appropriate setting (even though most of it is sung offstage), and others to infuse variety into the coloratura repertoire, the true glory of the opera, conceived as Donizetti conceived it, belongs to Don Pasquale himself. At the Metropolitan, where it has received twenty-five performances in all, it was the gusty acting of Baccaloni, the Don Pasquale, that secured the record-breaking number of performances —four—in the 1940-41 season. With him, in the *première* of this revival, on December 21, were Sayao, Nino Martini, and Francesco Valentino.

It happened that the best interpreter of the name role in *Don Pasquale* was its creator, Lablache. Of his interpretation, the usually cautious and generally faultfinding Chorley let himself go with abandon:

> It used to be said in Paris that the bouquet which the dear, silly hero of the farce-opera wore in the coat which stuck to him with as terrible a closeness as the outside garment of a sausage does to the contents within, was offered, night after night, by anonymous admirers. But throughout the entire farce of Lablache's performances nothing was more admirable than his entire avoidance of grossness or coarse imitaton. There was, with him, that security which only belongs to persons of rare and admirable tact; and, with that security, the highest power of expressing comedy, tragedy, or grotesque,—because it belongs to one who will risk nothing hazardous, but who is not afraid of daring anything extraordinary. When I hear of this person's style, and that person's high note, and when I think of Lablache, I am tempted to feel as if I had parted company with real comic genius on the musical stage for ever!

Donizetti's best comic opera was also his last success: *Don Pasquale* was followed by three failures, written successively for Paris, Vienna, and Naples. It was public coolness to the first of these that is said to have hastened his mental disintegration. The second, *Maria di Rohan*, is now remembered, if at all, because the mighty Giorgio Ronconi, during a performance at St. Petersburg, indulged in a flight of facial acrobatics which, as an illustration of operatic acting of the period, is at least worth a footnote.* The third, Donizetti's last opera, was heard in 1844. He died four years later.

Donizetti is a man whose career and works will, unless operatic taste changes completely, continue to take up a disproportionate number of pages in histories of opera for many a year to come. He provided roles for the leading singers of singing's golden age, and as long as there are singers willing to match their voices with memories of that age, *Lucia* and a few others of his operas will be in the repertoire, some of them more often heard, unfortunately, than *Don Pasquale*, the one opera in which he surpassed himself by consistently striking higher than his own average. It is this gay comedy that gives his otherwise transparent figure the little question mark that stands beside the names of those prolific second-raters who only once have snatched at genius, cramming the highest power of all their potentialities into one burst of creation. Yet, even *Don Pasquale* is no exception to the truth that had Donizetti never lived, the subsequent history of opera would have been exactly the same.

* Ronconi had boasted to Nicholas I that while singing, he could express tragedy with one side of his face, and comedy with the other. As Clara Louise Kellogg told it, in her *Memoirs of an American Prima Donna*, the night of *Maria di Rohan*, Ronconi "managed to turn one side of his face, grim as the Tragic Mask, to the audience, while the other, which could be seen from only the Imperial Box, was excessively humorous and cheerful. The Czar was greatly amused and delighted with the exhibition." Doubtless because it was the only gay spot in a gory evening.

Chapter XI

The French Comic Spirit

IN PARIS, the impudent incursion of the *bouffons* in 1752 had had other consequences besides the well-intentioned reforming efforts of Gluck. One, and perhaps the more natural, result was the rise of a considerable school of French composers who, though they wrote in other styles, directed their major efforts to illustrating the comic spirit. Their origins are obscure, and as remote as one wishes to make them. It is possible that, late in the thirteenth century, the *trouvère* Adam de la Halle composed, in his pastorals with music and dialogue, the first essays in *opéra-comique*. The solemn tone of one of these calls to mind at once the curiousness of certain French musical terms: thus, *opéra-comique* may be, but is not necessarily, comic—the main thing is that it must contain spoken dialogue. To illustrate further, all *opéra bouffe* (almost but not quite equivalent to *opera buffa*, for whose unaccompanied recitative it substitutes spoken dialogue) is *opéra-comique*, but all *opéra-comique* is not *opéra bouffe*, as a moment's thought about *Carmen*, the most famous of all *opéras-comiques*, shows.

Whether Adam de la Halle's pieces were true *opéras-comiques* or not, French comic opera took a Rip van Winkle's slumber until roused by the noise of the *bouffons*. Roused completely, that is, for even the classically minded Rameau had composed an *opéra bouffe* of moderately hilarious temper. But the year of the *bouffons*—1752—Jean-Jacques Rousseau composed, in *Le Devin du village*, a comic piece that had a popular currency far beyond that of Rameau's. So it was the busy philosopher of Geneva who thus offhandedly set the stage for a persistent school of French operatic composers, sometimes flourishing, sometimes languishing, but finally the most characteristic product of the French musical stage.

As is so frequently the case in the checkered, illogical story of French music, the first recognizable figure of this industrious race of frippery sellers was an Italian migrant, one Egidio

Romualdo Duni. Further to complicate the matter, he wrote his first French comic opera in Parma at the suggestion of Duke Philip, who was enough of a Bourbon to give the whole transaction a French twist from the start. This opera, *Ninette à la cour* (1755), was so well received in Paris that Duni removed thither and worked there for the remaining twenty years of his life. He soon found imitators of, if not his style, his way of tickling the public palate.

The precarious state of infant French *opéra-comique* may be deduced from the character of Duni's early colleagues: the first, François-André Danican, better known under his father's assumed name of Philidor, was primarily a chess player of international celebrity; another, Pierre-Alexandre Monsigny, was maître d'hôtel to the Duc d'Orléans when seized by an ambition to become a light-opera composer. Therefore, when Philidor and Monsigny composed their first operas, they no doubt thought of composition as a side line. And, though Philidor remained true to chess, Monsigny gave up household economics for the more satisfactory business of bidding for fashionable adulation and, finally, the glory of membership in both the Institute and the Legion of Honor. At the same time that Marie Antoinette was playing at rusticity by turning over in her mind plans for the Petit Trianon, Monsigny was delighting the Parisian exquisites of both sexes with his naïve scores, with their simple melodies, transparent accompaniments, and unquestioned charm. But neither Duni nor his two confreres were sufficiently vital to give real sap to a comic-opera tradition.

André-Erneste-Modeste Grétry, born, in 1741, a few leagues outside France itself, but ultimately more Parisian than Jean de Paris, was a timid Belgian who was pushed to eminence by the right people, and pushed onto the scene just when the resourcefulness he so abundantly had was most needed to shore up the uncertain fortunes of French comic opera. A rich Belgian prelate had sent him to Rome, and after eight years of study in the riotous capital of Clement XIII, he set out vaguely for Paris. He stopped in Geneva en route, where Voltaire refused to write a libretto especially for him, but assured him that

Paris was indeed the place for a young artist. Success came to him with absurd ease. He had been in the capital for less than a year, as a petted protégé of the Swedish ambassador, when his *Le Huron* was produced with great éclat. Based on Voltaire's silly conception of an American Indian's innocence, and of a girl who dies of shame after sacrificing her honor to save her lover's life, *Le Huron* made a powerful appeal to audiences inoculated with the fashionable Rousseauism of the day.

With *Lucile*, another piece in sentimental vein, and which, like *Le Huron*, boasted a libretto by the eminent and shallow Marmontel, Grétry found himself established. *Lucile* contains a didactic, smugly virtuous quartet—*"Où peut-on être mieux qu'au sein de la famille?"*—that swept France for fifty years and was used on the least likely occasions. Its homey sentiment rose like incense to the bourgeois Louis XVI during the short-lived reaction in his favor just before the period of inflexible hatred set in. And—final irony—to the poor dupes of the Grande Armée the decent, humdrum burgher celebrated in the quartet became identified with the figure of the Little Corporal surrounded by his guards.

When Grétry was twenty-eight years old, he produced his first true *opéra bouffe, Le Tableau parlant*. Apotheosis followed: he was compared to Pergolesi, and his admirers began to call him "the Molière of French music." Adulation could go no further. Vigée le Brun was to paint him, Dr. Burney to pronounce him the idol of the Parisians, and Napoleon to pay him court—nothing could exceed the excessive greenness of this earliest laurel. Diderot and the Encyclopedists, still fighting the already decided *guerre des bouffons*, took up this new Pergolesi, and the cautious, opportunistic young man was soon the lion of the *salons*. Social success was his, and after he composed two short operas for Marie Antoinette's wedding festivities, he became a court favorite. One of these was *Les Deux Avares*, a really amusing score full of delicious program effects—just the sort of thing to captivate the not too spoiled young girl the Dauphine still was.

In 1770, the year of *Les Deux Avares*, though Grétry's career was but five years old, it was already apparent that he was not to be a reformer. His was a static talent, more or less dependent on momentary inspiration, though he had a respectable enough academic background. Grétry was not a thinker, and though he associated with the wits and savants of the capital, from D'Alembert to Mme de Staël, from Grimm to Mlle de Lespinasse, he was not really one of them. As a musician, he had the strength and weaknesses of a dilettante, and he never mastered anything beyond the rudiments of musical architecture. He seems to have escaped the influence of the theory-loving Rameau, who had died only the year before Grétry reached Paris. Also, though he worshiped Rousseau, he was never infected with a passion for big general ideas or a feeling that he had to revolutionize the world. He wrote melodies because they came to him, but his harmony was barren and his orchestration wan, again in contrast to Rameau, who had evolved a lavish orchestra and who used varied and meaty harmony. Only twenty-six instruments are called for in a typical Grétry score, and it was sneeringly said of his harmony that one might drive a coach and four between the bass and the first violin.

What charmed Grétry's public was the spontaneity of his melodies,* the aptness of his pictorial effects, and the happy way he joined words and music. Few French composers have surpassed Grétry in the perfection of a declamatory style. Characteristically, he admired Haydn's charming but insignificant operas, but was put off by Mozart, whose stage works he dismissed impatiently: "Mozart puts the pedestal on the stage, and the statue in the orchestra." Unfortunately, Grétry himself was never tempted to make the same error. To compensate for his lack of adventurousness, he was ingenuously self-analytical: "I received from Nature the gift of appropriate melody, but she denied me that of strict and complicated harmony."

Grétry, child of nature and discreet courtier, had a magnificent career as long as the *ancien régime* lasted, and then a tolerable one under the Terror, for—still a courtier, and basi-

* Speaking of Grétry in 1817, Weber said, "It would be impossible to equal the really exquisite purity of his melodies, which are always inspired to suit the exigencies of the moment and not according to stereotyped forms."

cally without political convictions—he knew how to bend with the storm. Mme du Barry shed precious tears over his *Zémire et Azor*, and granted him a pension. Marie Antoinette stood godmother to one of his three pretty daughters. When the whimsical Austrian found opera that pleased her better than his, he retired from the scene so gracefully as to seem to be conferring a compliment on her taste. Pensions and sinecures were showered on him. A street in Paris bore his name. Amiable and well balanced, he received these honors without losing his head. His one meeting with his hero Rousseau passed off badly, but he bore no grudge, and in 1796, long after the philosopher's death, purchased the Hermitage, the house Rousseau had occupied at Montmorency.

The Revolution interrupted, but did not halt, Grétry's career: true, it confiscated his property, but after some hesitation did not prohibit the performance of his works. By the time Napoleon appeared on the scene, *le citoyen* Grétry had become one of the venerated musicians of the French Republic. The Emperor restored and augmented his honors. Grétry died at the Hermitage in 1813: had he lived on into the reign of Louis XVIII, he might have acquired even greater rewards, for had he not flattered that prince, then Comte de Provence, by setting, thirty years before, his libretto of *La Caravane du Caire*? This collaboration, be it said, worked out most happily for both parties—*La Caravane* became a great hit at the Opéra, and before Louis' death in 1824, was approaching its five-hundredth performance at that institution.

Yet, despite his almost invariable good luck, Grétry did not go through life uncriticized. *Céphale et Procris,* sung at Versailles in 1773 for the marriage of the future Charles X to Maria Theresa of Sardinia, boasted Sophie Arnould and, in its Paris production somewhat later, that temperamental singing star's successor at the Opéra, Rosalie Levasseur: this did not keep La Harpe from calling *Céphale* feeble, or Mlle de Lespinasse from finding it "rather anemic." This dissatisfaction, even among his friends, with Grétry's far from searching music was heightened by the production, the very next year, of Gluck's first Paris operas. But when the local demand for Grétry dwindled to performances on Sunday—the unfashionable day—the composer could console himself with the knowledge that his operas were being performed simultaneously in half a dozen European countries.

By refusing to greet Piccinni when he arrived in Paris, Grétry unwittingly seemed to take sides in the great Gluck-Piccinni strife. The Piccinnists took revenge by creating disturbances during performances of his operas. Fortunately, in 1784, when his masterpiece, *Richard Coeur de Lion,* was produced at the Opéra-Comique, most of this animus against him was a thing of the past, and, after a mildly successful *première,* in which exception was taken to the ending, this work, slightly altered to disarm future criticism, soon became epidemic. Its fame spread almost immediately to England, where two versions, one by "Gentleman John" Burgoyne, the absent-minded blunderer of Saratoga, strove with each other to hold the town.

Today, when the rest of *Richard* (and most of Grétry) is completely forgotten, Blondel's air—*"Ô Richard! ô mon roi!"*— gets a rare hearing. Its popularity during the last fifteen years of the eighteenth century, and well into the nineteenth, can scarcely be imagined. During the Terror, citizens were guillotined for no more heinous crime than singing its royalist strophes, and the fact that he had composed it placed Grétry in momentary peril. The air became, in fact, the Bourbon anthem, though all manner of men sang or hummed its deliberately archaic measures. That dour republican, John Quincy Adams, went around singing to himself the doleful lines, *"Ô Richard! L'univers t'abandonne"*: he had failed of re-election, and no doubt liked to fancy himself as abandoned by the universe. Although most of Grétry's previous success had been made in lighter works, his most enduring reputation came from *Richard,* a serious opera.

Richard was in every sense the summit of Grétry's achievement: although he lived almost thirty years longer, and through 1792 wrote at least one opera every year, and did not cease writing operas until 1804, he gradually declined as a composer. The honors Grétry received under Napoleon were paid to

A Metropolitan Performance of Offenbach's *Les Contes d'Hoffmann*, with Stella Andreva (Olympia), Sydney Rayner (Hoffmann), Angelo Bada, and Louis d'Angelo

the shade of greatness. In 1790, his mediocre *Pierre le grand* was almost the last opera to depict royalty in a favorable light; the following year, his *Guillaume Tell* was a successful effort in coat-turning. Much like the present-day officials of totalitarian states, the revolutionary committees were soon ordering French artists of every stripe to produce works of propaganda —it was not enough, ruled the bureaucrats, for a work to be neutral: it must be violently pro-Revolution.

Among those who responded without scruple to the government's demands was the former archcourtier Grétry. In December, 1793, posters appeared announcing his one-act opera, *La Fête de la Raison,* evidently intended as a placatory offering to the ideally coolheaded deity who was to usurp the place of *le bon dieu* on the lips, if not in the hearts, of all prudent revolutionaries, and whose installation at Notre Dame was soon to take place. But the authorities, after reading the libretto, were themselves revolted, and Grétry had to apply his tunes to new subject matter. As *La Rosière républicaine,* celebrating the planting of the tree of liberty, it was given at the Opéra on September 2, 1794. Some idea of the tone of these made-to-order revolutionary operas may be gathered from the fact that one scene of *La Rosière,* depicting nuns seduced into dancing lasciviously, was described by *Le Journal de Paris* as "very gay." A ballet suite from this opera, more sweetly staid than gay, is one of the few compositions by Grétry still occasionally heard.

One of the most extraordinary performances of this time was a ribald, antiroyalist business called *Le Congrès des rois,* composed communally by a dozen more or less distinguished men, bringing together such disparate spirits as Grétry, the sober Cherubini, the fashionable Kreutzer (to whom Beethoven dedicated the too-famous sonata), Dalayrac, and the young, still-struggling Étienne-Nicolas Méhul. It was topical without being accurate: kings, betrayed by their mistresses (a shaft directed ineffectually at the faithful Du Barry, who had just been guillotined), are forced to disguise themselves as sans-culottes to escape vengeful justice. The skit might have had point through one short act, but in three long acts it was merely tiresome. It lasted one performance, and was lucky for only one of its collaborators: Méhul received an appointment at the Comédie Italienne and an annual stipend of one thousand livres.

Méhul's reward was at least poetically just, for of the entire group, not to mention the dyed-in-the-wool conservatives who were apathetically obeying the dictates of the rabble, no one was more enthusiastically for the basic principles of the French Revolution—*liberté, égalité, fraternité*—than he. In fact, Méhul became unofficial composer extraordinary to the French Revolution and, until its energies had dribbled away into muddle, composed countless hymns, chants, and cantatas celebrating its transient deities and shibboleths. His *Chant du départ*, first sung in July, 1794, for a time vied in popularity with the *Marseillaise*: it was the marching song of the conscript armies of the Republic, and to the ragged legions who went impudently to match themselves with the tried, well-accoutered armies of Austria it was distributed by the tens of thousands. Its words flowed from the pen of Marie-Joseph Chénier, whose brother André was, at the moment of its writing, awaiting execution for those imprudent deeds which Umberto Giordano (or his librettist) has construed as heroism in the modern veristic opera *Andrea Chénier*. It was when this same Marie-Joseph proposed a *conservatoire de musique* (which still exists) that the authorities gave Méhul the most important sign of their satisfaction by creating him its first inspector of instruction.

During their lifetimes, Grétry and Méhul were known respectively as the Molière and Corneille of French music. It is an illuminating generalization if not interpreted too particularly, for it points up the essential antithesis between the lighthearted *liégeois* and the more earnest peasant lad from the foothills of the Meuse. Like Grétry, Méhul had come to Paris as a green boy, but he had not conquered the city as easily. He did not know the ropes—in fact, never got to know them as well as the suaver Grétry. Nor did a letter of introduction to Gluck, who was busy staging *Iphigénie en Tauride*, bring him anything tangible. Good advice he got: the Austrian

composer strongly urged his sixteen-year-old caller to give up
the idea of composing church music, and take to the stage.
Méhul acted immediately on this advice, choosing a poem that
had won a government prize. *Cora* was the first of a lifetime
of bad, absurdly chosen librettos, which were instrumental in
shaping his ambiguous career. With few exceptions, Méhul's
operas enjoyed an opening spurt of popularity, followed by a
languishing box office and final dissolution. For, despite the
usually charming music the composer lavished on them, their
librettos were too much for even an undiscriminating public
to swallow. The amiable Méhul, almost stupidly humble,
blamed the ultimate failures of his operas not on his flawlessly
inept taste in librettos, but on his delightful music. Time and
time again he begged the pardon of his hack librettists for
spoiling their precious handiwork.

And yet, Méhul got along and had his successes. His public
understood, even if he did not. Within thirteen years of his
arrival in Paris, two of his operas had been received warmly
enough to give him an enviable position among the musicians
of the capital. In his small way, he got caught up in a social
whirl. Even in the days before Mme Récamier began wearing
Directoire gowns, he was welcome at her *salon*, and among
his other friends he numbered the actor Talma, Rouget de
Lisle, and many of his fellow composers, including Gossec,
Grétry, and Boïeldieu. In 1794, Méhul was definitely on the
way up, and perhaps for that very reason was momentarily in
peril—in those days, success (no matter whose) was enough
to make the nervous authorities listen to any tale brought them
by a jealous ill-wisher.

Méhul's opera, *Mélidore et Phrosine,* a tale of incest, was
forbidden because the book "was not sufficiently Republican
in spirit. . . . The word 'liberty' does not appear once." The
sacred word was obediently inserted at frequent intervals, the
censors (callous to incest) were appeased, the opera was produced, and Méhul's head was safe for the time being. The
opera was denounced again, this time for "unseemly extravagance in the costumes": as this detail was outside his province,
Méhul very sensibly ignored the new charge. Considering his

hairbreadth escapes as he peacefully pursued his artistic career in Revolutionary France, it is no wonder that Méhul changed easily from sincere republicanism to no less sincere Bonapartism, and served enthusiastically as an official of the Empire.

The Terror was almost spent when Méhul, already on intimate terms with the man who, beginning his career as a soldier of the Revolution, was to end as Emperor of a vaster France than ever before, heralded the changing times by composing an opera with a king as hero. Perhaps, however, this is crediting Méhul with too much consciousness in the matter: he may merely have taken the first story that came his way, and the bold one may have been his librettist Bouilly, the hack who, despite his shortcomings, and in addition to writing the book on which *Fidelio* was based, managed for many years to provide the first composers of France with librettos. *Le Jeune Henri,* based on an incident from the youth of Henri IV, was thin in plot—too silly, in fact, to be resented for more than a night or two. At the third performance (May, 1797), the composer was called out for an ovation: the offending white plume of Navarre was forgotten in the loveliness of the music.

The overture to *Le Jeune Henri* got a hold on Parisian hearts: it had been encored from the first, and for thirty years was used as a kind of instrumental entr'acte. Called *La Chasse du jeune Henri,* it is a sparkling bit of program music, frankly delighting in realistic tricks and touches—a swift, courtly hunt carried on amidst vicissitudes of weather, the whole mildly presaging the most famous of program overtures, that to Rossini's *Guillaume Tell.* It is no accident that the rest of *Le Jeune Henri* has been silent for a century or more, while *La Chasse* can be heard even on records. Méhul, who later turned to writing symphonies patterned on Haydn's, was almost invariably most successful as an instrumental composer. In an otherwise sloppy transitional period, when melodies were allowed to speak all too barrenly for themselves, Méhul was notable for the exquisite joinery of his musical craftsmanship.

Méhul is often catalogued as a founder of the French light-opera school that culminated in Auber and Offenbach. Actually, his forte was not only serious opera but, beyond that, a form of such intense sobriety and devout elevation that it can only be called opera-oratorio. In 1799, he presented, in *Ariodant*, a score of grave beauty and fastidious workmanship, with a book one step removed from Ariosto. Eight years later, when his usually dim star was burning with unwonted splendor, he wrote his masterpiece, *Joseph*, a work of lyrical fecundity without a trace of the deft and the gay so often associated with his name. It is this movingly noble work which shows that Méhul's real master was not his elder colleague Grétry, but in truth the great Austrian whom he had sought, as a faltering novice, almost thirty years before. The loftiness and austere grandeur with which Gluck had mantled his pagan themes Méhul claimed for the Biblical story of Joseph and his evil brethren. Unfortunately, *Joseph* has the usual poor Méhul libretto. Cohesive enough, it is completely devoid of love interest, a lack that has not endeared it to the French people. In Germany, however, it came to be regarded almost as a native work, probably because the rising masters of the New German School saw in it some faint prevision, and that not wholly accidental, of their ideals.

Classic in declamation, classic, too, in harmonic mood, *Joseph* turned its face to the rising sun of romanticism in its free-singing melodic line. A study of the score is amply rewarding, and not only in pure aural delight: it reveals throughout a musical scholar of ranging curiosity, taste, and liberal refinement. The overture and the prelude to Act II carry us persistently to the best traditions of Haydn and Mozart, while Joseph's still-famous recitative and air in Act I—*"Vainement, Pharaon"* and *"Champs paternels!"*—are, at least in considerable stretches, new territory. No wonder that Weber, who staged *Joseph* lovingly at Dresden in 1817, after a judicious qualification as to its "drab tone," went on in an all but rapturous strain about this work "imbued with a sentiment, a pathos, a purity of line and composition beyond compare." No wonder that Wagner called it "a magnificent work, which transported me to a higher world."

Méhul lived until 1817, but the last decade of his life was an anticlimax spent pleasantly enough in a rose garden, where, with the same scholarly and loving solicitude that he lavished on his music, he produced some rare blossoms. At his funeral, the oration was quite fittingly pronounced by another, and greater, musical scholar, Cherubini, and among the mourners were Méhul's friend Boïeldieu and his pupil Hérold, both of whom mimicked the cleverest effects of his comic style.

Grétry and Méhul, like Garrick in Reynolds' famous picture, were torn between the Tragic and the Comic Muse. François-Adrien Boïeldieu had slight conflict of that sort. He chose early in life to be a composer of comic operas, and rarely deviated. While he had composed ten mediocre operas before his twenty-fifth birthday, his eleventh, just squeezed in before that date, showed a new shrewdness in supplying what his Parisian audience wanted. *Le Calife de Bagdad* (1800) would be rated a smash hit even today: it ran for seven hundred consecutive performances. Despite its Oriental theme, the opera makes no attempt to sound Oriental—Boïeldieu was nothing if not unadventurous. Oriental stories were the rage in those dawn days of French romanticism, but Boïeldieu, knowing the simple, easy melodies his Frenchmen knew they liked, was not risking even a Turkish march. Cherubini was scandalized at the adulation being paid to *Le Calife*: "Wretch!" he is said to have exclaimed to Boïeldieu with heavy playfulness as he accosted the younger man in the lobby of the theater where the opera was running: "Are you not ashamed of such undeserved success?" Instead of answering no (like everyone else, Boïeldieu was a little afraid of Cherubini), he enrolled with the formidable Italian for a stiff course in counterpoint.

His head swimming with glory, Boïeldieu quickly married— a shrew. As quickly repenting, he fled to Russia, where he remained for eight years, there exposed to the dazzling barbaric edges of its folk music and completely failing to be touched by them. He came, he saw, he stopped his ears, and, like the gentle lamb he was, served as *maître de chapelle* to the inventor of the Holy Alliance. During this comparative suspension of life, he penned several harmless Parisian operas. They gave him practice, steadied his hand, and in the eyes of the Autocrat of All the Russias took nothing from his stature. But the St.

Petersburg winters were inclement, and when Russia and France went to war in 1810, Boïeldieu seized this as a pretext, and returned home, loaded—as was the custom in those polite, hypocritical days—with imperial largess. Two years later, he was fully re-established as one of Paris' musical darlings. In that fateful year 1812, when Napoleon was losing his all in the east, Boïeldieu treated his admirers to a romantic flummery called *Jean de Paris*. Based on one of the half-dozen fundamental plots, it deals with a prince who wants to be loved for himself, and so woos his lady as a rich bourgeois.*

By 1817, Boïeldieu's position was such that, on Méhul's death, he succeeded to the vacant seat in the Institute, thereby literally humiliating to death his rival, Nicolo Isouard, a sulky Maltese who seems to have proceeded on the theory that, by smothering the musical stage in a rain of hastily concocted operas, he could bully his way into fame. Meanwhile, for another eight years, the Institute's new ornament also went on grinding out fragrant trivialities which proved that Cherubini had lectured him on counterpoint in vain. Then, fifty years old, Boïeldieu begat a masterpiece. The Scott cult was at its height, and Scribe, at the opening of a career that was to leave in its wake more than five hundred librettos of varying quality, had patched together *La Dame blanche* from parts of *The Monastery* and *Guy Mannering*. The resulting story has, for some reason, found admirers, though its spectral trappings, fake horrifications, and tortuous mazes would do for nothing better than a Grade B cinema mystery. The best that can be said for Scribe's book is that it contains every sort of situation except a tragic one.

Unfortunately, Boïeldieu was not a profound musician. Nor was he gifted with imagination in its highest reaches. For these he substituted, in *La Dame blanche*, pleasing surfaces, a fancy buoyant and carefree, and a finely tempered and tireless wit. Moreover, *La Dame blanche* is, without being windy or diffuse, borne forward through its three long acts by a gusto— a musical ebullience—that never flags. In this single opera,

* It was in a Graz production of *Jean de Paris* that Emil Fischer, the renowned Wagnerian bass, made his operatic debut.

Boïeldieu carved out a small but not unprincely territory of his own. When *La Dame blanche* became the most popular comedy of its day, its creator modestly disclaimed his right to the more fantastic tributes by saying that maybe the Parisians were merely fed up with Rossini, who, incidentally, was a devotee of the melodious White Lady.

La Dame blanche has been called the French counterpart of *Der Freischütz*, and it has been pointed out that it is an expansion of the *chanson*, just as the musical feel of Weber's masterpiece descends from the old *Volkslied*. All this is quite true, but in *La Dame* there are also musical quotations from Scotland and not a few touches of pure 1825 Paris—moments of vaudeville, even. Something of the brimming-over quality of Weber's melody is in *La Dame blanche*, and evidently the Germans have discovered it, for the opera has long been a favorite east of the Rhine.

It was in a German translation that patrons of the Metropolitan heard *La Dame blanche* in a single performance, on February 13, 1904, with a cast that included Johanna Gadski and Louise Homer, with Felix Mottl conducting.* New York had first heard it in French only two years after its *première*, and then, in 1832, in an English translation by John Howard Payne, with the score impiously fattened with slabs of Rossini, Weber, Auber, and others. When a local troupe did it in 1887, Victor Herbert's wife took the female lead. In Paris, after its wildly applauded *première*, on December 10, 1825, it retained, with few interruptions, its hold on French affections, and has passed its fifteen hundredth performance at the Opéra-Comique.

Although he was only in the middle fifties, Boïeldieu was doing little more than spend the liberal and much-needed pension Thiers had bestowed upon him when, in 1831, Louis-Joseph-Ferdinand Hérold, the most brilliant of Méhul's pupils, produced his still-famous *Zampa*. For nineteen years this prodigiously active composer, one of the first Prix de Rome winners,

---

* As a side light on operatic strategy of the time, it is worth noting that Heinrich Conried, then in his first season as manager of the Metropolitan, chose this (to New Yorkers) unfamiliar opera as the vehicle with which to introduce a much-heralded new tenor, Fran Naval, who, incidentally, did not return to the Metropolitan for a second season.

had been turning out, sometimes anything but shoddily, shoals
of symphonies, ballets, sonatas, operas, and musical miscellany.
Wonderful things had been predicted of the boy Hérold, who
in the course of the years turned into a feverishly productive
near-genius running a losing race with consumption. In the
whole history of music no man has wasted away so energetically.
Had he turned his talents entirely to the symphony, he might
have done great things there, but he was attracted by the more
spectacular rewards of opera. He died just short of forty-two,
lamenting with almost his last breath that he had just begun
to understand the musical stage. Yet he had learned a great
deal, and two operas, produced in consecutive years, bear witness to great gifts.

Zampa, an opéra-comique though not a bouffe, was the first
of Hérold's masterpieces. Like La Dame blanche, it has the sort
of grisly plot that Weber loved, and is, furthermore, not much
inferior in color and dramatic intensity to the German. Although nothing is done to prove it today, Hérold is quite
Weber's peer, if not his master, in stageworthiness: not unnaturally, for his connection with the leading Parisian opera
houses was long and intimate. Nor does the analogy end there:
Zampa's overture, once so dazzling and even startling, and now
so hackneyed and sleazy, is reminiscent of a Weber potpourri.

In reading the score of Zampa, it is well to give your prejudices a rest by skipping the overture and examining the action
at once. There is something finely efficient in the way that
Hérold proceeds through the musical exposition of a difficult
and implausible book without sacrificing romance or verve.
Invention never falters, tempo is ever right. The romantic note
is effectively sounded throughout, but without Weber's over-
insistence. Hérold, too, is less sentimental—he has a feeling for
measure that saves him. In some respects, he is perhaps closer
to Marschner than to Weber, not least of all in the fact that his
brilliance occasionally razors off into shrillness. But to con-
descend to Zampa because it is a French opéra-comique is to
give oneself away and, in these days of German and Italian
domination of the opera houses, to confess oneself afraid of
adventure. Chorley has amusingly described London's attempt

to stage *Zampa* in 1844, when Persiani, usually so resourceful, was reduced to confusion when placed vis-à-vis a tenor who was none too good to start with and was incapable of singing Zampa's low notes. For it must be admitted that *Zampa* is difficult to produce: the name role, probably written for the eminent tenor-baritone, Jean-Baptiste-Marie Chollet, requires that type of wonderfully useful freak voice.

The Germans have taken *Zampa* to their hearts, though when they give it, the vocal extremities of Zampa himself are often excised. The French prefer Hérold's more lighthearted master-piece, *Le Pré aux clercs* (1832). The scene is Paris, the story is from a Mérimée novel—in short, the whole thing is unqualifiedly French. More dashing than *Zampa*, it has chalked up more than a thousand performances at the Comique—the great Marie-Caroline Miolan-Carvalho sang in the thousandth. Maurice Cauchie, a specialist in the field, has called *Le Pré aux clercs* "the culminating point of *opéra-comique*, French and foreign." It is the work of a man who has mastered his medium completely and therefore has leisure to devote his talents to those details which give finish and point. It is notable that the bold innovator Berlioz complained of Hérold's chromatic heterodoxies, and it is equally notable that even today Hérold's late scores retain a faint but recognizable exoticism. The overture to *Le Pré aux clercs*, which is not played as often as it deserves, gives us that experience of refreshing novelty of which we are deprived in the overture to *Zampa*, which is played ten times more than it deserves. Nor is the complete score of *Le Pré* less good than that of *Zampa*—it is, if anything, more scintillant, with moments of wit and epigram and a total impression of unified style.

One month after the *première* of *Le Pré aux clercs*, Hérold, with the imperishable Cherubini hovering over him to pronounce the *éloge*, gave in to phthisis. Less than two years later, on October 8, 1834, Boïeldieu died, and with him an epoch in French comic opera.

Boïeldieu's place was taken by Auber, who by this time had already shown himself in a dual role—the composer of the generally serious *La Muette de Portici* and of a large number of *opéras-comiques* so frivolous, as to both text and music, as to be little more than operettas. Auber was a musical lightweight, but what he did was fastidiously clean in detail and had real dash to it. Rossini said that Auber "may have produced light music, but he produced it like a great musician." There was a large and unceasing demand for his entertainments, which he lavishly supplied, in good times and bad, until nearly the end of the Second Empire. A great wit and man of the world, he put much of his own dandified personality into his sophisticated scores. Some of them, such as *Le Cheval de bronze* (later made into a grand opera), *Le Domino noir,* and *Les Diamants de la couronne*, became staple revivals of light-opera companies, and excerpts from them are still occasionally heard. However, the only one of Auber's comic operas that we are likely to hear is *Fra Diavolo*, a romantic tale, by Scribe, of brigandage in the Papal States. For many years it was a favorite staple in America, where it has been produced, in chronological order, in English, French, German, and Italian versions. The Metropolitan has mounted it only once, for three performances at the New Theater—the first on February 4, 1910, with Bella Alten as Zerlina and Edmond Clément as the Fra.

Auber's trending toward operetta exerted an influence even on the sober Halévy, who wrote the sparkling *L'Éclair* (1835), the scenes of which are laid in colonial Boston, a few months after completing his grim tragedy of *La Juive*. The next year, Adolphe Adam, a deeply religious man who poured comic operas, ballets (including the eternal *Giselle*), and Masses out of the same shallow phial, brought out *Le Postillon de Longjumeau*, a naïve business that became a constantly revived stand-by in the United States, where, during the sixties and seventies, New York audiences were delighting in the broad interpretation of Theodor Wachtel, Senior, a one-time hack driver, as the coachman in a German version.*

The retreat from *opéra-comique* to operetta became a rout with the advent of the German-born Jacques Offenbach, who may be said to have crystallized the latter form. During the

* Another ex-coachman, Heinrich Bötel, was a favorite in this role, also in a German version, at New York's Thalia Theater, in the late eighties.

Second Empire, this son of a cantor in a Cologne synagogue fought his way to the top in theatrical Paris, supplying the incorrigibly superficial subjects of Napoleon and Eugénie with more than ninety operettas in twenty-five years. All are mere names today, though overtures to several of them, as well as the ballet *Gaité parisienne*, keep a number of their best tunes alive.

But Offenbach has to place his chance of survival on a work that started in an operetta version, and ended as almost a grand opera. This is *Les Contes d'Hoffmann*, which Jules Barbier and Michel Carré based on three fantastic tales from E. T. A. Hoffmann's fanciful autobiography. Produced in its first version as early as 1851, it was then shelved until Offenbach, almost at the end of his career, took it up for refashioning. He died before completing the revision, and the New Orleans-born Ernest Guiraud arranged it, with an expert's hand, for performance. It opened at the Comique, on February 10, 1881, and was repeated there a hundred times before the year was up. In December, it was presented at the Ringtheater, in Vienna, but on the second night of what promised to be a long run, a great fire broke out in the building, causing much loss of life and temporarily putting the opera on the black list of superstitious singers.

Les Contes d'Hoffmann reached New York, at the Fifth Avenue Theater, on October 16, 1882, but it was not until Hammerstein sponsored it at his Manhattan Opera House that its American popularity began. This *première*, on November 14, 1907, brought together Alice Zepilli, Eleanora de Cisneros, Charles Dalmorès, Maurice Renaud, and Charles Gilibert. The cast of the Metropolitan *première*, on January 11, 1913, included Hempel, Fremstad, Bori, Jeanne Maubourg, Umberto Macnez, Didur, Dinh Gilly, Rothier, and De Segurola. Since then, it has been given thirty-nine times in eleven seasons, not always happily. A particularly deft interpreter of the doll Olympia was Mabel Garrison.

Reminiscent in some ways of the episodic construction of many Russian operas—*Les Contes* consists of three separate episodes in the hero's life united only by the tenuous thread of disillusionment—it is, as music, far less interesting. It preserves a kind of musical unity by the clever sentimentality of its idiom and its unflawed superficiality. The banal Barcarole, originally a duet for soprano and mezzo, with choral background, was banal to begin with—now it is hackneyed besides. It not unfairly represents the entire score, in which the merely stunt "Doll's Song" is something of a relief. As the culmination of a career, *Les Contes d'Hoffmann* suggests that Offenbach should have stuck to operetta. But he had many followers who imitated, or rang the changes on, his formula for comic opera. Some of them have been worthy of their master in providing an evening's entertainment, and some of them have made large fortunes doing so. None, however, has contributed anything lasting to the story of opera.

Chapter XII

Damaged Demigods

E VERYWHERE except in its native home, French opera has been
under a cloud for so long that there is slim hope that an
Oscar Hammerstein or a Mary Garden will come along to revive it. Yet, the slim hope will be realized: operatic cycles do
change, and someday the managers of the big opera houses will
have to look around for new staples. Even lovers of *Aïda* must
reach satiety, even worshipers of *Der Ring des Nibelungen*.
There will be a moment when even the most loyal will hear
with languid ear that Floria Tosca, for the ten thousandth
time, is slated to kill Baron Scarpia and cast herself from the
battlements. Opera will not always mean Verdi, Wagner, and
Puccini. Looking over a roster of the Metropolitan's entire
repertoire, we shall not find *La Dame blanche* represented by
one performance, and *Richard Coeur de Lion, Joseph, Zampa,*
and *Le Pré aux clercs* by none at all.

This prediction belongs at present all too definitely to the
Forlorn Hope Department. Yet, a century or more ago, these
operas delighted audiences quite as sophisticated as any our
own age can muster. Now they are considered too old-fashioned
for remounting. By the same token, should we not wonder at
the thousands who still delight in the pictures of David and
Ingres, in the *Confessions* of Jean-Jacques, in the early outpourings of Victor Hugo? The analogy must not be pressed
too far: obviously, anyone can look at pictures or read books—
he has only to have access to a gallery or a library. But in
hearing music, he requires a whole series of middlemen who
are not always to be found. Prominent in such a series is the
manager willing to take his chance with adventure and—in the
case of the particular works under consideration—an adventure
not underwritten by that tradition-bound artistic Lloyd's, the
confraternity of music critics and musicologists.

Critical contempt for French opera, excepting the archaic
Lully and Rameau, the all but unperformable Trojan epic of

Berlioz, and the isolated phenomena of *Carmen* and *Pelléas et Mélisande,* may be taken for granted. It is even possible that this contempt has helped to poison the official managerial attitude. By some curious quirk of criticism, three great Italians, working importantly in Paris during the period covered by Grétry, Méhul, Boïeldieu, and Hérold, have been saved from the blight criticism has managed to cast over the French masters of the period. The case of Rossini has already been examined: it is worth mentioning that he did not escape denigration and is, in fact, only now in process of critical resuscitation. Of the other two, Cherubini and Spontini, the first has ever been a sacred cow, hung with wreaths from the hands of the musical mighty, from Beethoven to Brahms. Not a musical theorist or historian but speaks of him with verbal genuflections. Yet, had Cherubini's descendants to live on the royalties from performances of his twenty-five operas, they would not have, for whole decades, a crust of bread among them. In New York, at least, he who could recognize a dramatic fragment of Cherubini other than the overture to *Anacreon* would be rare indeed. In its entire course of fifty-eight variegated years, the Metropolitan, which has got around to producing *Diana von Solange,* the masterpiece of Prince Albert's brother, Ernest II of Saxe-Coburg-Gotha, has never staged a work by Cherubini. All the critical pother has, in his case, been to no avail. If this fact means anything, it means that the critic pulls no weight in the manager's sanctum on the other side of the box office.

Of course, the neglect of Cherubini is a kind of poetic justice. He spent his extremely long life terrifying people: not only was he a formidable man personally, but he knew everything. He was a kind of perpetual mailed fist of Parisian musical life, and he had the lore and laws of all ages at his finger tips. Even Beethoven, whom he visited in Vienna something in the style of the Angel of the Lord descending upon Jacob, seems to have stood in awe of him. Haydn, with admirable simplicity, merely called him the greatest of living composers. Of all his contemporaries—he lived from 1760 to 1842—Berlioz alone had the originality to send in a minority report. Liszt, it is true, disliked him—but for a very Lisztian reason: the

Tuscan-born Cherubini refused him admission to the Conservatoire on the grounds that he was not French. In short, the man who gazes at us with such somber oppressiveness, with such chill melancholy, from out the depths of Ingres' great portrait was an ogre, and the opera manager is justly frightened by his ghost.

Cherubini was a great theorist: even today, his *traités* on this, that, and the other thing are standard. He was a great religious composer: his Mass in F is one hundred measures longer than the *Missa solennis*. Upon his shoulders, no doubt, Palestrina's mantle eventually fell. He composed, besides, a single symphony and much chamber music, each piece of which is a formal model of what chamber music is supposed to be by those who do not like it. Examining these pieces without further data, one would not be tempted to say that their composer also wrote operas. Actually, he wrote more than two dozen, though the first twelve, written in Italian, scarcely count—they were nothing more than clever imitations of the musical patter of Paisiello and the other pretty Neapolitans. From these frivolities we no more predict the mature Cherubini of *Médée* and *Les Deux Journées* than we predict the mature Gluck of the *Iphigénie*s and *Armide* from the fluff of the Italian and early Viennese periods. Lifeless and faithfully imitative works, these typical Metastasian illustrations brought their composer his portion of success and failure, and left the path of opera cluttered but undeflected. Momentarily, it seemed that Cherubini might emulate the career of Handel: an invitation to England ended, finally, with his appointment as court composer. Fortunately for his future greatness, perhaps, this lasted but one year, and he migrated to France. With this change of locale, his creative life, as in the case of many artists, may be said to have begun.

The germs of a new style were evident, even to the critics, in Cherubini's first French opera, *Démophon,* produced on October 5, 1788. This coldly styled music, mated to an awkward book by the tireless Marmontel, was received coldly. As Cherubini did not produce another opera of his own for three years, and contented himself with inserting extra attractions into the popular scores of Cimarosa and Paisiello, it might have been suspected that he was abandoning his neo-Gluckism. Nothing could have been farther from the facts. All this time he was maturing plans for a more rigorous interpretation of dramatic verity in terms of music, and he hurled his new defi at the ominously bloodthirsty Parisian populace on July 18, 1791, just two months before Mozart's last great opera was staged in Vienna.

Cherubini's daring and intellectual integrity were unlikely to make friends for him with audiences who, because of the rising temper of the times, were fast losing the ability or desire to criticize fairly. Yet *Lodoïska* won out: two hundred performances marked its first-year triumphs, and as many more were soon called for by Cherubini's infatuated public.* It was an odd object of adulation: the spectacular story of a wild, impossible Poland is flagrant romantic gush: the music is severe, restrained, classical—a music for statues. The enthusiasm aroused by its marmoreal strophes reminds one now that the dawn of the magnificent inertness of French classicism was already at hand. *Lodoïska* was elaborately worked out, richly and, by comparison to the French operas of the time, heavily orchestrated—a theorist's masterpiece. Melody there is, some of it beautiful, but all of it dry and somewhat solemn in character.

Cherubini, to whom circumstances were kind only in his crabbed old age, was not allowed to proceed logically with his operatic career. The Revolution in its full frightfulness intervened, and Cherubini, a suspected royalist, fled to Normandy, where he hid out in a well-stocked monastery converted to secular uses. There he did little but putter: it was only when the Terror was practically over (Robespierre was six months dead) that he ventured to produce another work in a purged Paris. The unwonted tenderness of many pages in *Elisa, ou Le Voyage aux glaciers du mont Saint-Bernard,* has caused Cherubini's loyal biographers to indulge in an orgy of face-saving explanations: his father had died, and he wrote

* After a performance in English, at the Lafayette Theater, on December 4, 1826, *Lodoïska* became a favorite in New York for about two decades. The use of many horses on the stage—the heroine is rescued by Tatars—was apparently the chief reason for its local popularity.

the new opera before he had a chance to get his usual grip on his emotions. What had happened was that some of his natural Italian fluency for melody was allowed to creep into an otherwise well-mannered score. This did not prevent the critics from finding *Elisa* "too learned, too German." One word suffices to describe the libretto: inane; and the libretto cut *Elisa's* career short.

There is something touching about Cherubini's persistence as an operatic composer. Things were always coming up to delay his progress or deflect his course. After *Elisa*, it was the founding of the Conservatoire, to whose board of study inspectors he, as France's leading musical pundit, was promptly appointed, along with Gossec, Méhul, Grétry, and Jean-François Lesueur. Routine absorbed him, and as an official of the Directoire government, he was called upon to compose sundry republican hymns and ceremonial pieces, a chore to which he was, it must be admitted, eminently suited. As he poured out these windy evocations, his creative mind became a crystal-clear, superhumanly unruffled repository of pure theory, all of which, unfortunately, was to be used whether occasion demanded it or not, down to the last demisemiquaver. What, one wonders, was actually blowing down the corridors of that mighty mind as he manufactured *Le Salpêtre républicain*, a chorus to be sung at the opening of a saltpeter works? What, as he poured out his musical odes on the 18th Fructidor, the 1st Vendémiaire, and all those other holidays of the curiously named Revolutionary months?* The precise answers are lacking, but certainly it was nothing revolutionary, unless revolution be construed narrowly as going against the currents of musical fashion.

The kind of revolutionary Cherubini was became absolutely clear when his next opera, *Médée,* was produced at the Théâtre Feydeau, on March 13, 1797. In it, his mold for seri-

---

* This brings up the not uninteresting question of what any composer thinks while grinding out the official pieces demanded by the government for which he labors. In the case of an Elgar, it is perhaps only too obvious, but the problem is more difficult when a Shostakovich is involved in a *Symphonic Dedication to the October Revolution* or a Strauss in a hymn for the opening of the Olympic Games at Garmisch-Partenkirchen.

ous opera was finally set. Cherubini's true role was established by this intensely drafted and yet decorous music: he was to be the Justinian of opera, recodifying the laws of his master Gluck, making them more stringent, applying them without pity, and proceeding everywhere with unresilient justice. Measure was his god, and he came to regard innovation as the devil. His whole program is implicit in *Médée*, which is of all his operas the one most worthy of resuscitation. A possibly accidental evidence of Cherubini's pitilessness is the fact that the title role is one of the most taxing ever assigned to the soprano voice. It is this circumstance that is most often advanced as the chief reason for not staging *Médée*. Quite apart from this, there are other reasons—among them the very beauties the opera undoubtedly has. Cherubini breathes such rarefied air that we doubt his mortality: certainly, we doubt the humanity of his creations, and are reminded in time that Jason was a demigod and Medea scarcely less. In short, even more than Gluck, Cherubini took Greek mythology at its word.

The overture to *Médée* is the Gluckian type, and the sort Beethoven hoped to use for *Fidelio*: that is, it is a microcosm of the whole, not in the sense of a potpourri, but in a more imaginative, more evocative way. It is all done on a scale vaster than opera had previously used, and it is done irreproachably. It is a strange truth that *Médée* is noble, lofty, beautiful, even at moments starkly dramatic, and yet in its totality curiously removed from the humanly approachable. Like Pygmalion, Cherubini created beauty, but unlike him, could not bring it to life.

Medea is a role that, for more than half a century, challenged the indomitable will of every possessor of a stentorian and untiring soprano voice. Mme Scio created the role and is said to have injured her lungs fatally while singing it—her death was, in turn, attributed to the lung complaint. More famous artists succeeded her, including Margarete Schick, whom Mozart so admired, and who created the role in Berlin in 1800. Clara Stöckl-Heinefetter, one of six singing sisters (the others were Sabina, Mathinka, Eva, Nanette, and Fatima), assailed the part and had even worse luck than Scio: she died insane. Pauline Anna Milder-Hauptmann, for whom Beethoven had written the part of Leonora, sang Medea in Vienna. The undisciplined Schröder-Devrient tried it. Unfortunately, Pasta wasted her Medean talents on a tame version of the story by Simon Mayr, Donizetti's teacher, instead of trying Cherubini's "grand fiendish part." So there was none to touch Tietjens when, on June 6, 1865, that favorite English household institution revived the role under Colonel Mapleson's regime at Drury Lane. Sir Charles Santley was the Creon, but the heroine dominated the performance: evidently it was an unforgettable experience to hear her. Her last presentation of this *tour de force* was in 1870: although she continued to appear in opera almost up to the day of her death in 1877, she apparently dropped this role because it was too much for her. Since then, *Médée* has not been sung in England; no American performance is recorded anywhere. No doubt, part of this neglect is due to the extreme difficulty of the title role: not only is Medea's music most strenuous, but she is almost always on the stage—the opera is definitely top-heavy.

Despite its many beauties, *Médée* was never truly popular. The acid Auber, asked his opinion of it, answered dryly, *"C'est la musique bien faite,"* and this probably echoed the consensus, though Schubert admired it immensely. In 1800, however, Cherubini produced, at the Théâtre Feydeau, a considerably lighter opera, still definitely on the grand side, that had an immediate and lasting vogue. This was *Les Deux Journées*, known equally well under its German title of *Der Wasserträger* and its English one of *The Water Carrier*. At last the dramatically obtuse Italian had found a libretto of such excellence that Goethe, who knew good melodrama when he saw it, spoke of it as a model. This superior book came from the unequally inspired fancy of Jean-Nicolas Bouilly, often no better than a scribbler. It was Beethoven's admiration for the libretto of *Les Deux Journées* that resulted in Bouilly's unhappy collaboration with Sonnleithner, and Beethoven's acceptance of their monstrous *Leonora*.

Mme Scio was the first Constance, and the *première*, on January 16, 1800, developed into a tumultuous ovation. Number after number was encored, and when it was all over, Cherubini might have been excused for believing that he had won the people. Almost two hundred performances followed in the same year, and then Paris began to cool. The enthusiasm passed to Germany, and that country has remained loyal to it. About *Les Deux Journées* do not cling those stories of famous casts that cluster about other, less successful operas. The roles are evenly distributed, and so do not appeal to jealous stars. Perhaps the most brilliant cast was assembled for a Drury Lane production in 1872. Sir Michael Costa conducted, the Constance was Tietjens, Luigi Agnesi the Mikeli; Mathilde Bauermeister and Marie Roze (Mrs. Henry Mapleson) sang smaller roles. Santley later distinguished himself as the water carrier.

Beethoven, besides begrudging Cherubini the libretto of *Les Deux Journées*, positively venerated the music: the score of the opera lay constantly on his worktable. The two composers had many traits in common, but this is not enough to explain the fact that so much of *Les Deux Journées* sounds to us like Beethoven. But Cherubini did not copy Beethoven: rather, Beethoven studied Cherubini with such love that some of Cherubini's turns of phrase passed unceremoniously into his admirer's musical language. The overture sounds only less Beethovian than the more famous, more frequently played overture to *Anacreon*. For instance, it abounds in those reflective pauses which Beethoven was to use with such dramatic force, and there are two or three melodies that might easily have occurred to him, though he would have developed them more boldly. These resemblances, had Cherubini noted them, would have annoyed him immeasurably: he had little use for Beethoven's music, of which he once said plaintively: "It makes me sneeze." A disciplinarian rather than a truly searching master of theory, he sneered at the "Leonora" No. 3: "I can't tell the key it's in," thus unconsciously disavowing his own patent influence.

Les Deux Journées is, in truth, the excelling achievement of a second-rate Beethoven. It seemed much larger than that to many composers of reputation, among them Weber, Mendelssohn, and Spohr. The last threw away caution (for him a tremendous job), and professed himself "intoxicated with delight by its music." But these transports had their reason: *Les Deux*

Journées is the most appealing of Cherubini's operas, the most melodious, the most human, the least statuesque. Cherubini gets through its three acts without freezing his hearers and without making it too obvious that he has let them in on something surpassingly noble and learned. In short, the unpleasant edges of the man's character show here less than in any other of his operas. For him, *Les Deux Journées* comes close to being simple, unaffected entertainment, and several of its melodies are unusually beguiling. The opera is more than interesting historically, and its complete neglect is inexcusable. A Hammerstein would have got around to it eventually, and we can at least hope that the Metropolitan will someday discover it. It would pay artistically; it might even do so commercially.

Cherubini dedicated *Les Deux Journées* to Gossec—a fine example of his tactlessness, for he had rather pompously refused to allow himself the privilege of dedicating it to Haydn: "No, as yet I have written nothing worthy of such a master." Nor did he, if we judge him by his own high standards. The history of Cherubini's later career as a composer for the stage is, with the single exception of one opera, unedifying. *Anacreon,* his twentieth opera, has the delightfully fresh overture that is still deservedly popular, but nothing else to hold the modern listener. *Faniska,* with a libretto by Sonnleithner, is the exception.

Produced in Vienna in 1806, in the presence of a crowd of notables that included Beethoven and Haydn, *Faniska* was, for its composer, an unusually lively score, and did much to establish his fame in central Europe. It seemed for the moment that it would do even more for him, for as he tarried in Vienna, no doubt basking in the approbation of his colleagues, Napoleon, flushed with the victory of Austerlitz, took up his residence there. Although the Emperor and Cherubini had never hit it off, the latter, to his surprise, was appointed director of music at Schönbrunn. But this led to nothing back in Paris, and after three more operas designed to force Napoleon to give him some court position commensurate with his unquestioned eminence as a composer, Cherubini gave up the struggle and retired bitterly from the field. After *Les Aben-cérages* (1813), he held aloof from the stage for twenty years.

At first, Cherubini in his retirement hardly drew a staff: he ostentatiously gardened, and affixed little landscape pictures to the walls of his hide-out. During the Hundred Days, the Legion of Honor, denied him when it was given to Gossec, Grétry, and Méhul, became his. Louis XVIII appointed him to the Institute and finally made him superintendent of the king's chapel. But by that time these great appointments were being showered on him because of another career, on which he had embarked almost accidentally when, in 1809, during one of his periodic sulks, he had been wheedled into composing a Mass in F whose large proportions and splendor of conception showed that his early Palestrinian studies and imitations were still viable, and in a most magnificent way. When, in 1822, Cherubini was made director of the reconstituted Conservatoire, it was to the greatest of living religious composers that the honor went.

Yet, eleven years later, he ill-advisedly once again tried the stage: *Ali Baba,* the last fruit of a withered bough, and largely a rewriting of an unproduced early opera, was a failure, despite a cast got together to do homage to the master, and including Nourrit, Levasseur, Cinti-Damoreau, and Cornélie Falcon. The sole interest of what Berlioz called an "operatic fossil" is as an example of misapplied tenaciousness: it came out fifty-three years later than his first opera—only Verdi was to beat this record with his *Falstaff,* which had its *première* fifty-four years after his stage debut. After *Ali Baba,* though without relaxing his rigorous rule at the Conservatoire, Cherubini began, as a composer, to run down like a clock. In 1838, Paris heard the first performance of his last important work, the Requiem in D minor. In 1841, mindful of the greatness of his position, Cherubini sat for Ingres, and as the picture turned out very well, he graciously sent the painter a token of appreciation in the form of a little canon to words he had written himself. This was his last composition. Two months later, on March 15, 1842, he died.

Thus ended the long life—or reign—of a most accomplished musician. This Italian who spent much of his life in a capital

Cherubini and the Muse, after a portrait by Ingres

synonymous with tolerance was a puritan who regarded music as a high calling and practiced it conscientiously. For devotion to his task, for painstaking workmanship, he is not surpassed in the whole history of the art. Yet it may be questioned whether he should ever have composed an opera: as a religious composer, using formulas whose very rigidity made them capable of perfection, and in a field where his whole personality responded, Cherubini was of the first rank. His best Masses, especially those written for the crownings of Louis XVIII and Charles X, have an emotional richness truly amazing to those who have judged him by his operas alone. For even *Médée* and *Les Deux Journées* are a little parched; the flesh that clothes these masterpieces of theory is always thinly drawn. Of this thwarted genius of the stage, Sir Donald Tovey wrote: "If his melodic invention had been as warm as Gluck's, his immensely superior technique in every branch of the art would have made him one of the greatest composers that ever lived. But his personal character shows in quaint exaggeration the same asceticism that in less sour and more negative form deprives even his finest music of the glow of that lofty inspiration that fears nothing."

In 1807, after Cherubini's return from Vienna, and just when his star had seemed to be favorably in conjunction with Napoleon's, he, along with most of the leading French operatic composers, had failed to win a newly inaugurated decennial opera prize offered by the Emperor. This desirable plum—10,000 francs—went most unexpectedly to a man who had shown few signs of being a strong contender. The opera, *La Vestale,* was written to a libretto Cherubini had himself rejected. The composer, Gasparo Luigi Pacifico Spontini, was a pushing young Italian from a little hill town. Immediately, the lucky contender found a powerful faction leagued against him, and so strong was it that the promised prize was never awarded. But this was a secondary matter to Spontini: in the Empress Josephine he found a champion who could dissipate all opposition merely by commanding the performance of *La Vestale* at the Opéra. Its success was so great that Cherubini was discouraged: this, as much as anything, was responsible for his self-imposed exile,

shortly after, from the boards. Like Rossini faced with Meyerbeer, he had no taste for the struggle, and his rivalry was at
best desultory. His withdrawal saved the balance of power in
musical Paris: it is doubtful whether the capital could have
supported two composers whose classicizing was so stringent.

Spontini had first tried to win Paris with much the same
sort of Neapolitan trivialities Cherubini had begun with, and
had got just as little response. He struck, if not a more serious,
at least a more somber note in an opera based on episodes from
the life of John Milton—surely an unusual subject for dramatic
comment. *Milton* was produced in 1804, and *La Vestale* was
composed the very next year. Such a grand and gloomy subject
Gluck would have loved, and he would not have been in a
position to criticize severely the happy ending brought about
by the kind offices of Vesta. For this rather highfalutin libretto,
Spontini provided a carefully worked-out score, which—during
the two years that elapsed before its *première*—he turned over
and over again on the lathe of his imagination, revising, adding,
subtracting, pruning, polishing, and then beginning the process
all over again. For Spontini had a passion for perfection which,
beginning with *La Vestale*, rode him mercilessly for the rest
of his life. The final result of this wrestling was a score of considerable magnificence, elaborate, heavily orchestrated, and conscientiously varied with the rise and fall of the action and the
comings and goings of the characters, whose personalities are
always mirrored in the music.

La Vestale is a score of classical texture, and has been called
Gluckian—certainly, Julia's magnificent aria, *"Tu che invoco,"*
is precisely that, though Spontini probably learned much of
what is in it from Gluck's rival, Piccinni, who had been one of
his teachers. Allowing for slight idiosyncrasies of manner, *La
Vestale* might have come from the workshop of Cherubini.
Close investigation reveals larger differences: Spontini seems
less crabbed, less static, than the other Italian, has more eye
for theatrical effect, and, though his personal history gives the
lie to such an allegation, more warmth. Otherwise, Spontini
might, except in the actual turn of musical phrase, be a continuation of the composer of *Médée*. As far as technical innova-

tion is concerned, the pompous and self-glorifying composer
told Wagner, forty years later, that in *La Vestale* he had ushered
the suspension of the sixth into orthodox harmony and had
first used the big drum in the orchestra!

La Vestale established Spontini in Paris, and in Germany,
whither it soon found its way, it long remained verdant. In the
mid-forties, when Wagner was on the way up in the course
of one of his many rises and falls, he staged it at Dresden,
inviting the old composer to rehearse and conduct it. This
invitation grew out of Wagner's sincere admiration for Spontini's music, and it is to his credit that this admiration survived
a visitation from the ancient martinet. Even at seventy, Spontini ruled orchestra and singers with an iron hand—and an
ebony baton, with an ivory ball at each end, which he wielded
like a field marshal. By the time of the performance, Spontini's
were the only intact nerves in operatic Dresden, and Schröder-
Devrient, who had been the erring Vestal, feigned illness in the
hope of speeding Spontini's departure. Naturally, perhaps,
Schröder-Devrient did not precisely shine in the part, but Cruvelli became much admired in it. Chorley preferred Lind's
Julia, though at times he found it a bit too prissy.

La Vestale reached New Orleans and Philadelphia within twenty-
five years, but a whole century more went by before New York
heard it. The production that Gatti-Casazza assembled seemed, in
its magnificence, to expiate this neglect. Joseph Urban designed the
scenery, Tullio Serafin conducted, and Ponselle headed a superb
cast, including Matzenauer, Johnson, De Luca, José Mardones, and
Paolo Ananian. It was given eight times in the 1925-26 season,
and was chosen to open the next, with Giacomo Lauri-Volpi substituting for Johnson, and Ezio Pinza, in his American debut, for
Mardones. After three performances the work was shelved, and has
not since been revived. In 1933, *La Vestale* had a handsome production in Florence: the Vestal, as signifying selfless devotion to the will
of the State, was approved subject matter in Fascist Italy.

It is odd that New York had to wait until 1925 to hear *La
Vestale,* for as early as early as January 6, 1888, the Metropolitan was the scene of a most spectacular production of Spontini's
next opera, *Fernand Cortez.* This setting by an Italian of a

French libretto about the Spanish conquest of Mexico was sung in an English-speaking country in German, by Germans, among them such luminaries as Emil Fischer, Albert Niemann, and the Teuton Adonis, Max Alvary. "The people employed in the representation," Krehbiel wrote, "rivaled in numbers those who constituted the veritable Cortez's army, while the horses came within three of the number that the Spaniard took into Mexico." This would have delighted Spontini, who, by the time of *Fernand Cortez* (1809), had gone far on his career of vast spectacles, in which he preceded both Rossini and Meyerbeer.

When *Fernand Cortez* first came out, it was immensely popular, among its most enthusiastic supporters being Napoleon, who hoped that the villainous portrayal of the conquistadors would intensify the people's dislike of the Spaniards (it was the eve of the Peninsular War)—by no means the first time politics looked to music for aid. In 1817, after interest in the opera had somewhat abated, Spontini revised it throughout, shuffling the three acts with a thoroughness only he could have devised. It was this version that was heard at the Metropolitan. More theatrical than *La Vestale*, this misreading of Mexican history is certainly more noisy—from it Wagner drew inspiration for the thunderous *Rienzi*.

Having said the last word, musically, on a Roman and a Spanish-Mexican theme, Spontini, after a decade devoted to the raising of musical taste in Paris and to tortuous intrigues and conduct of a domineering sort, turned his attention to Graeco-Macedonian culture. Olympias, the mother of Alexander the Great, was the heroine of his third great opera. Voltaire's tragedy was the basis of the book that was presented to Spontini for his musical commentary. The last act alone engaged him for four years. Finally, on December 15, 1819, *Olympie* was produced, and for the first time since his transformation into a despot, Spontini failed. He was not daunted, but set heroically to work, revising the music to a revised libretto. Version No. 2 had a happy ending and was altogether more "operatic" in its book than the first. In a German translation by E. T. A. Hoffmann, it was given at Berlin on May

14, 1821. But though this version was received with acclamation, Spontini set his face against so easy a success and prepared still another version, and with that, which was received warmly in Paris in 1826, he was content. It was *Olympie*, which some authorities consider the best of his operas, and on which he bestowed the most work, that brought him the sharpest disappointment.

In 1819, Friedrich Wilhelm III of Prussia, who had long admired Spontini, made him chief *Kapellmeister* and general music director at Berlin. Rather like an Indian maharaja who receives a salute of nineteen guns at home and seventeen abroad, Spontini was also provided by the considerate monarch with the title of superintendent general of the royal music, to be used while traveling outside the kingdom. The title was fine; even better was the salary—the fattest in Germany. After a year or so of insignificant official efforts, Spontini chose the second version of *Olympie* to introduce his real self to the Berlin public. Nothing approaching the elaborateness and vastness of this production had ever been seen there, and before the curtain went up on the *première* there had already been a royal reprimand because of the cost of the forty-two rehearsals, the fabulously expensive scenery and costumes, and the general lavishness of the whole thing. But the King forgave all when he saw how Spontini had spent the money. Berlin gasped. Spontini triumphed, and for forty-four days was the most talked-about composer in Europe.

Then came *Der Freischütz*, and Weber tumbled Spontini from the skies. It was a popular catastrophe, for almost from the beginning Spontini had, by his arrogance and grasping self-assertiveness, alienated his colleagues and subordinates. Faced with a new spirit in music—a spirit completely outside his comprehension—he grew more and more unbending, choleric, overweening. He was only forty-seven when the triumph of romanticism lost him the substance of power: he retained the shadow for twenty years—in short, as long as his royal protector lived—and one of his last official acts was to try to thwart the advancement of young Felix Mendelssohn.

But even if the old warhorse was incapable of understanding

the nature of the artistic forces arrayed against him, and most expressively crystallized in Weber and Marschner, he was by no means a fool, and he attempted to regain his prestige by meeting the enemy on what he supposed to be their own grounds. In the mind of this sublime egocentric, the idea that Weber had nothing more to offer the Germans than a national libretto led immediately to the decision to vanquish the Saxon whippersnapper with a German opera of his own. The theme was lofty, the heroine no other than an unfortunate lady of the House of Hohenstaufen. As far as the book was concerned, the opera was German through and through, but the music was in Spontini's own style—a strange composite most aptly called Roman imperial. The scale was grander than ever, the first act alone being long enough for an evening's entertainment.

By an arrangement possibly unique in the annals of opera, the vast first act of *Agnes von Hohenstaufen* was given separately, as a kind of trial balloon, in 1827. Two years later, on June 12, 1829, the entire three acts of this finically contrived medieval tapestry were gradually unrolled. The circumstances attending this solemn *première* made the opera very German indeed, though the music was not: it was staged as part of the celebrations connected with the wedding of Prince Wilhelm of Prussia, later the first ruler of a united Germany. Eight years afterwards, a revised version of this noisy historical pageant appeared, but Germany remained indifferent. *Agnes von Hohenstaufen* was Spontini's last completed opera, though he lived until 1851.

Spontini's last years were not notably happy. In the first place, before losing his position in Berlin, he committed various indiscretions, culminating in an insult to the new king, Friedrich Wilhelm IV, who was a friend to everything in the arts (grandeur excepted) that Spontini detested. Indictment for *lèse-majesté* followed, along with a threat of imprisonment. On April 2, 1841, Spontini appeared to conduct *Don Giovanni*, which, with Gluck's *Armide*, was the only opera not of his own composition that he deigned to produce in Berlin. This time he was hissed from the podium, and the long tenure of office was at an end. The King forgave him his misdeeds, generously provided him with a pension not one groschen less than his salary, and sent him out of the country. He now became a wanderer, honored everywhere, if not welcomed. He was decorated by the King of Denmark, and the Pope made him a count. Already he was a member of the Institut de France. It gradually became apparent even to him that he was a relic from the past, and though he never once doubted the superiority of that past, neglect by the present hurt. Attacks of melancholia were frequent. He became deaf. In 1851 he died, leaving his very large fortune to the poor of his native village. So, after all his quarrels and storms, his ill humors and pontifications, the end was edifying.

Spontini's life may be read as tragedy or comedy, depending on the emphases. The temptation is to see him too unrelievedly as a figure of fun. There is even something a little comic in his music—so often it is pompously empty, merely noisy, unreasonably orotund. But a composer whom the ungracious Wagner praised, and whom the churlish Berlioz worshiped just next to Gluck, was not all mediocrity. Not all of his effects are pompous: some have the authentic classical ring and speak with a rare and individual nobility; in the orchestral din, the piled-on brasses, not all is sound and fury: at times, there is real eloquence in these volumes. Technically, Spontini was scarcely less accomplished than Cherubini, and if he lacked his fellow classicist's taste and measure, he went beyond him in achieving a unity that Cherubini never attempted. Spontini's acts are not only unities in themselves, but they flow into each other and thus give each of his four major operas satisfying formal design. Wagner realized this and studied Spontini's scores to great effect. Nor was Spontini's brilliant handling of choruses lost on him, and there is much in the theory that the composer of *Die Meistersinger* was at least as much in debt to Spontini as to Meyerbeer.

Chapter XIII

Berlioz

HECTOR BERLIOZ was one of those people—and there is at least one in each of the major arts—whose idiom is so personal that they are likely to be left out of a general survey. Into that part of criticism which consists of finding ancestors and descendants, he fits badly, or scarcely at all. In a survey of opera, therefore, he is included not as a step in the evolution of the art, but because he composed several operas interesting in themselves. He was not a traditionalist: he did not sum up any of the previously accepted styles of operatic composition; he was not a radical: he did not overturn the fabric of opera as he found it and put something totally new in its place. Nor did he write his operas according to a theory of his own devising. His style of operatic writing has something of the accidental about it: it happened once and may never happen again. The final challenge of this tortured, difficult man, who was so conscious of his originality, might have been the defi: imitate me if you can.

In discussing any segment of Berlioz' career, the natural temptation is to go off on a tangent about his melodramatic life, to weigh the fact and fiction in his own fascinating writings about himself, and to take sides prematurely for or against his merits as a composer—to talk about everything except the point at issue, the music itself. There is some reason for these evasions. Of the large body of his works, only one major composition, the *Symphonie fantastique* (and that not typical of his more mature styles), an overture or two, and about as many fragments are familiar to contemporary American audiences. More, no composer loses as much as Berlioz does in piano score, as practically the sum total of his radicalism is, aside from certain harmonic and melodic personalisms, a way of thinking constantly in terms of orchestral sound. It is no wonder, then, that the baffled critic, unable to hear Berlioz' major compositions or to appreciate their effects on his own

219

piano or by silent score reading, falls back on the padding of biographical detail.

Berlioz was a little over thirty years old when he began to work, not on his first opera, but on the first one that reached the stage. Barely more than a decade before, in 1823, when he was the most callow of music students, he had dared to write, out of his voluminous ignorance of the essentials of composition, a something which at the time he very much wished to see produced, though in later years he was grateful that it had remained on paper. As so much of even the later Berlioz is variable in quality, we need not regret the loss of *Estelle et Némorin*. Three years later, in 1826, a student of Lesueur, for whom he felt an affectionate but patronizing respect, he tried again. This time he dropped the project before completing it. The pleasant overture—superior prentice music—to *Les Francs-Juges* survives, and whole chunks of the rest of the opera, which has vanished as such, later cropped out in various works, particularly the *Symphonie fantastique*.

Although all the music Berlioz composed for the next few years was highly dramatic, even theatrical, in quality, it was not until 1834 that he got around to beginning another opera. To show, however, that his thoughts were never far away from the stage, he was experimenting with overtures and cantatas— *Le Roi Lear* (1831) is the most attractive of the former and is an occasional concert number. Tovey has pointed out that though this is a tragic work, it is written in a bright major key—an interesting example of Berlioz' very personal way of interpreting a situation.

After 1833, when Berlioz married the heroine of his *idée fixe*—the impossible Henrietta Smithson, an Irish actress of disputed merit—he gave up the most salient extravagances in his music, though he did not renounce melodrama in his life. Artistically, he settled down, and since, in Berlioz, everything goes by contraries, began to do his best work. He chose what, in view of his recent marriage, could scarcely be called a tactful libretto—the story of Benvenuto Cellini. Those who have not called *Die Zauberflöte* the worst libretto have reserved that description for this, which was promptly rejected by the

Opéra-Comique. This did not discourage Berlioz, who had started to set it as soon as it was delivered to him, and pecked at it sporadically for the next four years. By the time it was completed, it had been accepted by the Opéra, and Berlioz had taken time off to compose, besides smaller pieces, one of the most impressive of his achievements—*Grande Messe des morts*, a Requiem for those who had been killed when Fieschi's bomb failed to assassinate Louis-Philippe.

Berlioz' first staged opera was not a success: in four months *Benvenuto Cellini* reached only four performances, and was then dropped. A number of causes were alleged for its failure: a coterie of musicians was ranged against it; Duprez, generally a favorite, and certainly a competent artist, muffed the title role; Habeneck, the conductor at the Opéra, and one of Berlioz' bêtes noires, is said to have connived against it. At any rate, at the *première*, on September 10, 1838, the overture alone was encored, and most of the rest was hissed. Much of this animosity may have been directed at a composer who had a talent for putting people's backs up, but quite as much was undoubtedly directed at the music itself. It was not cacophonous, it was not extravagant as was so much of Berlioz' early music—but definitely it was strange. Some of it would still seem strange—most of it, however, is like Auber or fledgling Wagner—for reasons that were as valid a hundred years ago as today: Berlioz' whole concept of musical idea is outside the main lines of development, and from the hearer's point of view, the great length of his single melodic phrases makes them seem, to all but the most tutored ears, not melodies at all. Today, the commonest adverse criticism of Berlioz is that he has no tunes and, doubtless, that was the commonest criticism in 1838. Testimony to the contrary by all those who have qualified themselves to listen expertly cannot change public insistence that melody resemble either the repetitive patterns of Italian song or the packed germinal phrases of Wagner.

After having been rejected by Berlioz' compatriots, *Benvenuto Cellini* lay untouched for fourteen years, except that, in 1844, Berlioz took certain sections, mainly vocal sections from the finale of the second act, and recast them in purely instrumental form. The result was the most brilliant and popular of his overtures, the *Carnaval romain*. In 1851, at the request of Liszt, who admired Berlioz and had an unselfish interest in furthering the spread of his music, he began rewriting the entire opera, for Liszt had promised to produce it at Weimar. The next year, after further revisions suggested during rehearsals, it was produced there most successfully on March 20. Unfortunately, Berlioz was in England conducting the concerts of the New Philharmonic Society, and was not present either to taste success or to witness the beautifully disciplined performance Liszt had somehow managed to draw from his small forces. However, in November of that year, Liszt twice repeated *Cellini* to honor Berlioz on his visit to Weimar. As the Germans were by way of taking him up because he had been repudiated by the barbarous French, the warmth that greeted these repetitions did Berlioz' ego a lot of good, but also gave him the unhappy idea of having the opera staged in London. Of that miserable performance at Covent Garden, on June 25, 1853, Chorley wrote: "*Benvenuto Cellini* failed more decidedly than any foreign opera I recollect to have seen performed in London," and that despite the fact that the composer himself, one of the best conductors of the age, directed.

Berlioz' next opera had a fantastic history: it began, five years before *Benvenuto Cellini* was started, as a suite of songs, then developed into a cantata, and was finally made into an opera— twenty-four years after the composer's death. *La Damnation de Faust* grew out of his youthful enthusiasm for Goethe's poem, which, however, he knew only in a prose translation by the exotic Gérard de Nerval. Berlioz became so infatuated with it that he could not tear himself away. The first fruits of this mad obsession was a song cycle—*Huit Scènes de Faust*—of cantata-like aspect: this he published at his own expense in 1829. As Berlioz never had any too much money, this meant consuming passion, and the Faust idea continued to smolder in him until 1846. That year, in the midst of a tour through central Europe, he got quite excited by the idea of Hungarian independence, and for a concert in Budapest made a shattering orchestration of the piously revered patriotic *Rakóczy March*. This created such a sensation that, though it had no relation to either Goethe's poem or Nerval's translation (or his own emendations of both), he incorporated it into the first part of the "dramatic legend"—really a cantata—he was concocting out of fragments of the *Huit Scènes* and some new material.

Krehbiel, who, with some justification, called *La Damnation de Faust* "a thing of shreds and patches," amusingly described how the work was strung together:

> Traveling from town to town, conducting rehearsals and concerts, he wrote whenever and wherever he could—one number in an inn at Passau, the Elbe scene and the Dance of the Sylphs at Vienna, the peasants' song by gaslight in a shop one night when he had lost his way in Pesth, the angels' chorus in Marguerite's apotheosis at Prague (getting up in the middle of the night to write it down), the song of the students, *"Jam nox stellata velamina pandit,"* (of which the words are also Berlioz'), at Breslau. He finished the work in Rouen and Paris, at home, at his café, in the gardens of the Tuileries, even on a stone in the Boulevard du Temple.

Finally it reached completion and was summarily presented to the public on December 6, 1846. As if anticipating its operatic destiny, *La Damnation de Faust* was given, not in a concert hall, but at the Opéra-Comique. Again the French would have nothing of Berlioz—they did not like cantatas, however lively, and the work fell flatter than *Benvenuto Cellini.* The next year, Berlin heard it, and the Germans, being consistent too, liked it better. But it was in England that *La Damnation* was most appreciated: the English took it as a very pious work, and after 1880, when Sir Charles Hallé gave it at Manchester, it soon became a festival feature. What these performances had become by 1893 is best suggested by Shaw, in a critique in his best and rowdiest manner, ending with the sad reflection that "the damnation has been lifted from the work. It has been 'saved,' so to speak."

The next operation on the helpless carcass of *La Damnation de Faust* was performed, appropriately, at Monte Carlo, the very year that Shaw was scoffing at the tameness of the Albert Hall rendition. The surgeon was the Rumanian composer

Raoul Gunsbourg, who at that time was impresario of the local opera house. Whatever the flaws of Gunsbourg's adaptation (which continues to flurry the purists), he had the right idea: *La Damnation de Faust* is more opera than oratorio, and in this way, if in no other, resembles a composition that set out to seek its fortunes in much the same way—Saint-Saëns' *Samson et Dalila*. Jean de Reszke ensured the success of the Gunsbourg *première*, and when Monte Carlo heard it again, nine years later, he joined Melba and Maurice Renaud to make a truly stellar cast. The next year, the centennial of Berlioz' birth, Paris heard Gunsbourg's Berlioz, with Emma Calvé, Albert Alvarez, and Renaud, as Marguerite, Faust, and Mephistopheles respectively.

In 1906, New York, which in 1880 had become acquainted with the cantata form of *La Damnation* as interpreted by Leopold Damrosch, was afforded a view of the opera on the evening of December 7. On that notable occasion, Geraldine Farrar, only two weeks old as a Metropolitan debutante, was Marguerite; she was supported by Charles Rousselière, who had begun life as a blacksmith in Algeria, as Faust, while Plançon was the greatly admired Mephistopheles. Five performances that season constitute its Metropolitan career to date, but scarcely had the last note of the fifth performance died away when Hammerstein gave New York another opportunity to compare Berlioz' with Gounod's *Faust*, which was then (as always) popular. The Manhattan cast included Charles Dalmorès and Renaud. Finally, if the sparse and apparently garbled newspaper dispatch can be trusted, the Paris Opéra opened its 1940 season with *La Damnation de Faust*. The audience was composed largely of German officers and Spanish Falangists: there was no gaiety.

After *La Damnation de Faust* (which, we must remember, was not an opera), Berlioz was extremely busy for almost ten years giving concerts, conducting operas, writing criticisms, and waging war with his musical contemporaries. He was a driven man, finding it hard to earn enough to live on. It is impossible to tick off the endless number of projects that entered into his whirling brain, but the idea of composing a new opera was not apparently foremost in his thoughts, even in a period that was by no means barren of big works. In 1854, he completed a tremendous triptych, the oratorio *L'Enfance du Christ*, just about the time when he suffered the disappointment of not being appointed to the post of director of the Hofoper at Dresden, from which Wagner had been ousted a half-dozen years before. As this had happened despite the efforts of Liszt and Hans von Bülow, both most influential men, to get the post for him, Berlioz had ample reason to feel dispirited and outraged.

The next year brought compensations: Liszt had never relaxed his good soldiering to gain for Berlioz a sympathetic and, if possible, large following, and in 1854 had put on a miniature Berlioz festival in Weimar. While there, the revived composer was seized upon by Liszt's mistress, the earnest but gaga Princess Carolyne Sayn-Wittgenstein. They had long, serious talks, during which Berlioz doubtless mentioned his old passion for Virgil. Naturally, the Polish-born Princess had had the same passion, and she immediately suggested that Berlioz compose an opera about the Trojans at Troy and their vicissitudes after the fall of the city. He was so interested that she took up one of the most tireless pens in the history of literature and produced a scenario for his guidance.

In 1856, by the time he was ready to begin work on *Les Troyens*, the availability of a government sinecure, as well as a small inheritance from his father, secured Berlioz comparative leisure and some financial ease. Semipublic readings of the libretto of *Les Troyens*—his own fabrication of whole sections of the *Aeneid*, original lines, and expansions of Princess Sayn-Wittgenstein's script—aroused anticipatory enthusiasm about the opera, and Berlioz went plowing ahead hopefully. Although much of this very long composition was written at top speed, it was not finished until March, 1858. Then began the lengthy, pride-draining business of trying to sell the idea of producing this seven-act epic to an opera house, and Berlioz was as unwearying as his weakened physical condition would allow (he had what was then called "neuralgia of the intestines") in hawking it from one manager to another.

It seemed that Berlioz' round of humiliation was to be endless. It was especially scarifying when a gleam of hope bright-

ened for a moment, then waned the next. For instance, as early
as 1858 Napoleon III was showing interest in this superopera
by one of his subjects, and in 1861, when he summoned Berlioz
to dine with him, the composer must have gone hopefully into
the presence. But Napoleon was not a real music lover: he did
nothing for the wretched man who thought that he was going
to die, and could not bear to die without once having heard
what he believed to be his masterpiece. The worst case of hope
frustrated came the same year, when it looked as if the Opéra
might accept *Les Troyens*. However, in 1863, Léon Carvalho,
impresario of the Théâtre Lyrique, and one of the original
enthusiasts for the work, promised to produce it late that year.
But even this did not mean victory: Carvalho could not run
the risk of mounting the excessively long opera complete.
Therefore, Berlioz reluctantly divided it into two unequal
parts, and the second, longer part—*Les Troyens à Carthage*—
was sung twenty-two times that season, beginning on November 4.

Berlioz' press was mainly laudatory, and if there were a few
dissenting comments, he could explain them by the fact that
he had never given quarter in his own critiques. His accusa-
tions, in his *Mémoires*, against Carvalho, whom he declares responsible for the opera's disappearance after the first season,
can be dismissed as the ravings of a sick man. Generally, the
people who meant something artistically were impressed, Meyerbeer being in the van of those who did not hesitate to call the
opera a masterpiece. The simple truth is that the public did
not like *Les Troyens à Carthage* enough to warrant either its
restaging or, more, the production of the opera as a unit. Indeed, Berlioz died without ever having heard the first part—
La Prise de Troie.

At last, twenty-one years after his death, Felix Mottl, famous
for his Wagnerism, consummated, on the nights of December 6
and 7, 1890, a long devotion to an unpopular cause by giving
the world *première* of *Les Troyens*—in German. It was not
Paris, it was Carlsruhe, a provincial but progressive little town
in the Rhineland, that was vouchsafed to be the scene of this
epical event. Both parts have since been given at the Opéra,

Hector Berlioz, after a portrait by Daumier

but when Paris hears the "complete" opera, it is in a grotesquely telescoped perversion that is forced into a single evening. Dr. Erik Chisholm staged *Les Troyens* intact in Glasgow in 1935, apparently the only reverent treatment it has received since 1890, except for a solitary staging in French, at Brussels, in 1906. Neither part of the work seems to have been mounted in the United States, though concert versions have been heard.

Les Troyens was Berlioz' last opera but one. His swan song was, in size, a mere two-acter, in spirit a bit of fooling, in genesis a commission from the Baden-Baden theater. It was written around *As You Like It*, a subject Berlioz had toyed with as early as thirty years before. With a curious inattention to Shakespearean nomenclature, he called his little comic opera *Béatrice et Bénédict*. Conducting its *première* at the opening of the Baden-Baden theater, on August 9, 1862, Berlioz was in such agonizing pain that he could not savor the warmth with which he and his comedy were received. It would be a pleasant task to recount how he ended his tortured, misunderstood career on a note of comedy because, like Verdi penning *Falstaff* in his eightieth year, he had finally won through to some kind of inner serenity. Unfortunately, the truth is that this feckless piece had no relation at all to Berlioz' state of mind: Baden-Baden had ordered a comic opera, and he had filled the order. *Béatrice et Bénédict* was not only his last opera, it was also his last considerable composition of any sort. Berlioz was a ruin— a man wilting away of a spiritual *malaise*—the physical decay was secondary. A few more years, a few footling trifles, and then the end, on March 8, 1869.

No one in the whole range of musical history, no one, that is, with comparable gifts, tried so hard during his lifetime for the recognition he deserved, and failed so disastrously. Posthumous reward has been similarly delayed, and even now it cannot be said that the battle of Berlioz has been won. He has not even the fame conferred by imitation: except for his discoveries in scoring, it is almost as if he had never lived. However, in this refusal to give Berlioz his due (which can be done only by performing him to the verge of complete recognizability), there is no malice. New ideas in any art, and particularly

those that do not fall easily into accepted categories, meet
naturally with the sheer dead weight of the time lag, represented
by men working with the old, accustomed formulas or their
implicit extensions. Berlioz suffered, quite literally, from being
too original: he took next to nothing from the past (except the
very ABC's of musical speech), and gave nothing to the future
except the inimitable heritage of his own works.

To compare Berlioz with a man who struggled as hard and
almost as long as himself, but with quite different results: Wagner gained his comparatively quick victory firstly by the tangible seductiveness of the mere externals of his music; Berlioz
has no such physical allure, no such easy sensuality. It was
possible, once one was accustomed to the novelties of the Wagnerian vocabulary, to lie back and bathe in the drugging clouds
of sound. Berlioz invites to no such physical languors: to appreciate his long-breathed melodies requires a constantly attentive ear; to hear him at all, in fact, means listening every minute.
It means foregoing most of the sensuous appeal that his
contemporaries exuded with romantic fervor, and collaborat-
ing, as a listener, imaginatively and intellectually with the
music. Not that Berlioz' music has no appeal to the emotions:
it has, but by way of the head rather than the loins.

On the face of it, Berlioz chose a hard path for a would-be
popular composer of opera: he has been called, with exact
justice, a creator of great melodies, but he wrote few tunes—the
Danse des sylphes and *Menuet des feux-follets* from *La Damnation de Faust* are early and exceptional; he wrote vocal passages
that are nightmares to singers, not only because they are difficult
to sing, but because conquering them brings no startled applause from the audience, and finally, this most theatrical of
men was without that sense of the theater which knows instinctively how to prepare for, and underline, dramatic effects.
He made the tactical error of absorbing the drama into the
music instead of keeping music and drama wedded to each other
in a fair marriage. Wagner frequently made the same error,
but was saved from popular neglect by his rich sensory attractiveness; Berlioz had no such palliative to offer, and thus, in
his case, the error was almost fatal. It has reduced his first
surviving opera to two overtures, one a successful afterthought.

It has maimed his greatest opera and all but kept it from the stage.

Berlioz is usually brought forth as the typical rebel romantic, particularly by those whose knowledge of his work is limited to two or three concert warhorses. The most considerable of these, the *Symphonie fantastique*, was a youthful, not wholly successful extravagance.* It is disappointing to those who judge Berlioz by the *Fantastique* not to find the Byronic hero of that orgy in his later works. It is particularly disappointing to those who read the libretto of *Benvenuto Cellini* before hearing its music. The truth is that after 1833, those early porings over the scores of Gluck in the library of the Conservatoire began to have their sequel: the pull of classicism became so intense that Berlioz gave way. By the time of *Les Troyens*, he was very possibly the least romantic composer in Europe, and the only vestige of his rebelliousness was his umbrellalike thatch of untamed hair. By that time, too, he was really elect to set Virgil's great story. How well he succeeded, and what position he may yet attain among his peers, is powerfully suggested by two quotations from great English critics of opposing schools.

First, Cecil Gray: ". . . here in *Les Troyens* he is a classical master in the pure Latin tradition; the volcanic, tempestuous energy of the early works gives place to a majestic dignity and restraint worthy of Sophocles himself, and to a serenity and sweetness that can only be called Virgilian. In sheer grandeur and vastness of conception there is nothing in the whole range of opera to be compared to it with the exception of the very different *Ring*."

The second quotation is from Sir Donald Tovey. After saying flatly that Berlioz "has no patience with the more serious problems of the musical setting of words," he changes his mind in the following footnote: "We must be careful! You never know where you are with Berlioz. Towards the end of March 1935 Dr. Erik Chisholm produced the whole of both parts of *Les Troyens* in Glasgow, and revealed it as one of the most gigantic and convincing masterpieces of music-drama."

* In fairness to Berlioz' detractors, it must be admitted that few, if any, of his large works are wholly successful. But this argument should be advanced only by those who know his entire output extremely well.

Chapter XIV
Grand-Opera Fanfare

O NE year after the death of Giacomo Meyerbeer, *L'Africaine,* the opera he considered his masterpiece, was given a spectacular *première* at the Paris Opéra, and so universal was his fame that before the year was over the opera had traveled to London and New York. From 1831, he had been the most famous of active operatic composers—a man so powerful in his field that the neurotic Rossini had retired from the lists partly because he would not struggle against so dangerous a rival. For thirty-three years the living Meyerbeer ruled, and for a decade after his death he exercised a ghostly sovereignty. Then came Bayreuth, and the operatic world recognized a new master. During the bloody Wagnerian revolution, many a musical princeling was guillotined and yet managed to survive.

In the case of Meyerbeer, the procedure was not so peremptory (because more difficult), but when it was finally finished, it was thorough. Thus, though Meyerbeer's hold on the stage lasted into the nineties, the public had long ceased to worship him, and the great all-star revivals of *Les Huguenots* and *Le Prophète* were for the purpose of animating what the more advanced critics loudly proclaimed to be corpses. In time, these proclamations had their effect, and fewer and fewer operatic nights were given over to this supreme master of theatrical magic. For instance, *Robert le diable,* the opera that first enthroned Meyerbeer, has not been heard at the Metropolitan since that theater's first season, almost sixty years ago. *Les Huguenots,* the most popular of his scores, has not been sung there since 1914. At the present writing (1941), Meyerbeer has not been represented at the Metropolitan for eight years.

The reasons for Meyerbeer's demise, after a promise of almost endless longevity, are to be found as much in the facts of his life as in the intrinsic qualities of his operas. Meyerbeer was tireless in offering a helping hand to deserving fellow artists, and it was this attractive quality that worked for his posthumous ruin. He made the central mistake of being kind to Wagner, and at the same time of being a success while Wagner was a failure. Furthermore, he was born about ten or fifteen years too early to share in the blessings of the Wagnerian dispensation. Finally, though a German, Meyerbeer—and this was a fact that caused his tried and true friend Weber untold agony of spirit—was anything but a German composer: his first successful operas were written in Italian to a Rossinian pattern, his last ones in French in a cosmopolitan polyglot musical lingo all his own. Wagner never forgave him. Besides, while any musical ignoramus could point to Wagner's pilferings from the opulent Meyerbeerian hoard, who ever heard of Meyerbeer taking anything of Wagner's?

From decent gratitude—a period of very short life—Wagner's feeling toward Meyerbeer changed to hatred, manifesting itself chiefly in the form of repeated denunciation. Meyerbeer was made to figure as the Antichrist of Wagnerism, and as the pious Wagnerians, who came to dominate music and music criticism, joyously inherited the feuds of the *Meister*, his enemy's reputation became blacker and blacker.* Their task was ridiculously easy: Meyerbeer worked largely during one of those periods when opera is dominated not by purely musical or dramatic considerations but by absorption in theatrical effect—and in nothing do the fashions shift so rapidly. One of the few long recent articles in English on Meyerbeer is in a volume entitled *Down Among the Dead Men*.

Meyerbeer was one of the spoiled children of music. He was born rich and remained so. He was prodigiously gifted, so gifted, in fact, that he could pick and choose from a number of careers. He could, it is said, have become the foremost piano virtuoso of the period: instead, he turned to opera, and by the age of twenty-one had produced a score so learned and solemn that it sounded like an oratorio. This was written in German, as was his second opera. These were so indifferently received

---

* At this point, it may well be asked whether Wagner did not hate Meyerbeer primarily because he was a Jew. It is the other way around. A chronological analysis of Wagner's anti-Semitic sayings and writings shows that he hated Jews primarily because Meyerbeer was one.

by his countrymen that when Salieri, no doubt previsaging a parallel between Meyerbeer's and Gluck's career, advised him to visit Italy and learn how to write for the voice, he leaped at the idea.

Meyerbeer arrived in Venice in 1815 during the *Tancredi* madness, and at once was converted to Rossini. Three years later came the first of six unadulteratedly Rossinian operas, one of them a setting of Metastasio's *Semiramide*. Several of these were successful and were performed in various parts of Europe, but by the time the last of them was composed (1822), Meyerbeer was becoming dissatisfied with himself. His plumes were borrowed, and the fascination of Italy, if not worn thin, had at least become easier to exorcise. Weber, who had been a fellow student at the curious academy of the arts conducted by that learned charlatan, the Abbé Vogler, staged one of Meyerbeer's Italian operas at Dresden and also, in the hope of calling the expatriate back to his German senses, restaged his second German opera. As Meyerbeer had a high regard for Weber, he tried to write another German opera and failed so miserably that it never reached the stage. This catapulted him back into the arms of the Circe Venice, where, in 1824, his last and most successful Italian opera was performed.

Il Crociato in Egitto is, in many respects, a fascinating score. In this big spectacle opera based on the Crusades, and with a libretto by that same Gaetano Rossi who fabricated the book of Rossini's *Semiramide*, Meyerbeer stands at the parting of the ways. Gone is the obsession with pure lyric melody, gone the easy, undramatic flow of his first Italian efforts. It is the work of a restive Rossinian. In it, a seer might have found signs of Meyerbeer's future: those few but affectionately contrived *coups de théâtre*, those rumblings of a still-muffled orchestra, those moments of eloquent declamation, that all-over pomp and glitter—were not these the very elemental devices of that eclectic style which Meyerbeer was finally to choose as his own?

At the Venice *première* of *Il Crociato*, at the Fenice, Giovanni Battista Velluti, the last of the great *castrati*, took the soprano part of Armando, the Christian knight, and when the

opera was given in London in 1825—the first by Meyerbeer*
to be heard there—with Malibran and Caradori-Allan, he again
sang Armando. The Earl of Mount Edgcumbe, a dilettante
critic and composer, said of Velluti: "At the moment when he
was expected to appear, the most profound silence reigned in
one of the most crowded audiences I ever saw, broken on his
entering by loud applauses of encouragement. The first note
he uttered gave a shock of surprise, almost of disgust, to inex-
perienced ears; but his performance was listened to with attention and great applause throughout, with but few audible
expressions of disapprobation speedily suppressed. . . . To the
old he brought back some pleasing recollections; others, to
whom his voice was new, became reconciled to it, and sensible
of its merits, while many declared that to the last his tones
gave them more pain than pleasure. However, either from
curiosity or real admiration, he drew crowded audiences, and
no opera but the *Crociato* was performed to the end of the
season."

In *Il Crociato*, Meyerbeer knows with fair certainty which
way he is going, and when it was produced successfully in
Paris, he did not hesitate to take the next obvious step. Being
a man with leisure to command, he spent the next five years
forging the instruments of his craft, and by 1831 he was ready to
show the world of Paris, which had become his home, what he
could really do. He labored on *Robert le diable* for four years,
constantly changing details. It was a huge five-act opera to an
inordinately complicated libretto by Scribe and Germain Delavigne. So costly were the stage properties demanded by the
score that they probably explain why Louis Véron, the new
director at the Opéra, demanded a financial guarantee from
Meyerbeer, though he was already a composer of standing.

The guarantee could well have been dispensed with, for
when *Robert* came to the stage, on November 21, 1831, its
success was so overwhelming as to ensure the stability of the
Véron regime. True, this little bourgeois of genius—impresario,

* A performance of the overture to *Il Crociato*, at the Bowery Theater, New
York, on May 9, 1833, was advertised as the first music by Meyerbeer to reach
America.

doctor, journalist, and politician—had collected a resplendent foursome for the chief singers, while the mimed role of the Abbess was given to Maria Taglioni, the leading dancer of the period: Julie Dorus-Gras was the Alice, Cinti-Damoreau the Isabelle, Nourrit the Robert, and Levasseur the Bertram. But for once it scarcely mattered what these excellent artists did: they were engaged, all unwittingly, in an inevitable revolution, for if *La Muette di Portici* (1828) and *Guillaume Tell* (1829) had not set the pattern of French grand opera, it was set, and for the rest of the century, that night in 1831. Cinti-Damoreau had played a truly leading part in this revolution, having appeared in the *premières* of all three operas.

Meyerbeer really cast the deciding vote for the new order, inasmuch as Rossini had abandoned the operatic stage immediately after his ambiguous triumph with *Tell*, while Auber, having laid one of the foundation stones of French grand opera, soon renounced this solemn role for one closer to his twinkling, genial nature. It was Meyerbeer, the serious student not only of musical styles but also of all cultural history, the conscientious eclectic, who established the spectacle opera—the opera of constant effects and ever-changing picture and pageantry. He found, as a coadjutor, a scenic designer of such genius that it has been said that *Robert* could not have come off without his realistic and sumptuous settings and his ingenious mechanical effects: this was P. L. C. Cicéri, whom an ungrateful Paris was calling old-fashioned as early as 1836. The music was suited to both the frenziedly romantic libretto by Scribe and Delavigne and Cicéri's settings. That is, it was grandiose, searchingly characteristic, highfalutin, and grotesque—on the edge of the Gothic. Even so, for all its high orchestral coloring, often produced by then recondite combinations of instruments (one of its melodies is scored for four kettledrums), and for all its reiterated rhythmic patterns, *Robert* was not yet pure Meyerbeer—in other words, he had not found the right proportions for the preternaturally clever mosaic he was to make his own

The spirit of Rossini is by no means dispelled: *Robert* teems with those easy melodies Meyerbeer had learned to write in Venice—graceful, fluent, singable, and, yet, somehow slipping from the mind while Rossini's remain. *Robert* is still a pastiche: the elements are there, but not the integrating hand of the master *confiseur*. In it, there is the absurdly macabre yet curiously effective scene of Bertram's invocation, when the Fiend summons the ghosts of a company of immoral nuns to take part in a bacchanale—a tableau of high self-sufficiency that could only be Meyerbeer's. But the most famous aria in the opera—Alice's *"Robert, toi que j'aime"*—could be from any of Meyerbeer's scores—or from those of several other composers.

While Paris raved indiscriminately about *Robert*, London received it with chill respect until, in 1847, Jenny Lind chose Alice as her debut role there.* In it, she became so popular that the opera was cut to reduce the role of the rival soprano—the Isabelle. A great London cast of the fifties brought together Grisi, Tamburini, and Mario, but it was spoiled by the fact that Grisi had attempted an unsuitable role, and the Bertram—Karl Johann Formes—overacted to the point of impeding the performance. Alice was one of Nilsson's most powerful impersonations, and in London she was once supported by Di Murska as Isabelle, the stentorian Mongini as the accursed Duke, and "Signor Foli" (*né* Allan Foley, of Tipperary) as Bertram. In 1869, a popular baritone by the name of Jean de Reszke raised his voice to sing the tenor role of Robert, and never sang low again: his sister Josephine was the Alice, and Madrid the scene, of this historic event. In only three years, *Robert* reached the United States, where it was given in English at the Park Theater, New York, on April 7, 1834, with Mary Anne Paton as Isabelle. Bosio sang the same role in New York in the fifties. On November 19, 1883, less than a month after opening, the Metropolitan staged *Robert* in an Italian version, with Emmy Fursch-Madi, an eccentric but distinguished soprano, as Alice, supported by Alwina Valleria and Roberto Stagno. After two repetitions that season, the opera was retired permanently from the company's repertoire.

It took Meyerbeer five years after the *première* of *Robert* to get his next opera ready. It was about a fictitious episode from the massacre of St. Bartholomew's, and to prepare himself for

* Apparently, though not ill supported, Lind was the one ray of light in an otherwise wretched performance. It was so bad that Mendelssohn, who was almost idolatrous in his devotion to Lind, left the theater at the end of the third act.

composing suitable music for it, he saturated himself in the history, memoirs, diaries, and other documents of that dramatic period. Nor did he neglect the painting and sculpture of the time. Scribe again supplied the libretto, this time with the help of Émile Deschamps. They gave Meyerbeer for *Les Huguenots* a very long, five-act libretto, the fifth act of which is ludicrously anticlimactic. As originally "typed," the book called for five sopranos, five tenors, and six basses of various kinds, from bass-baritone to *basso profondo*. The mob scenes need choruses of unexampled size. The settings required include a banquet hall in a château, a garden with bathing pools, the Pré aux Clercs (a field on the banks of the Seine), a salon in a sumptuous Paris mansion, and a barricaded street during the massacre—the giant tocsin bell especially cast for this scene still takes up a large space in the storehouse of the Opéra. At the end of the third act, a gaily decorated nuptial barge must move down the river.

The Meyerbeerian orchestra, already almost as large as Wagner's, has, in *Les Huguenots*, to be augmented by several archaic period instruments. Dancing is called for in three separate acts, though in the truncated version used in later years, the very elaborate ballet in Act V vanished when that act was sheared off. What all this adds up to, of course, is a vast historical extravaganza—a series of amazingly detailed canvases reminiscent of the boldly figured tapestries of the later Valois. It was treated musically with the gusto, incisiveness, and psychological aptitude to which a historical theme that appealed to him always roused Meyerbeer.

The opening night of *Les Huguenots* fell, inappropriately enough, on one of Rossini's rare birthdays—February 29, 1836, at the Opéra. While the leading female role of Valentine was assigned to the great dramatic soprano Cornélie Falcon, who had made her debut four years previously as Alice in a repetition of *Robert*, three of the other stellar roles went to veterans of *Robert*'s first night: Dorus-Gras was the Marguerite de Valois, Nourrit the Raoul, and Levasseur the Marcel. The opera was well received, but was by no means the instantaneous hit *Robert* had been. On the basis of the first few performances, Meyerbeer could not know that *Les Huguenots* was to become the favorite of all his operas.

There were two salient reasons for the reticence of the popular reaction: the first was that *Les Huguenots* was far from being a duplication of *Robert*—in it, there was nothing but Meyerbeer; the second was that while presenting a succession of tableaus, each treated with a nice feeling for its content, Meyerbeer had yet managed to give a feeling of unity to each act by robbing, at least partly, the set numbers of their autonomy, previously—particularly in France and Italy—unchallenged. Although *Les Huguenots*, despite being a tissue of foreign styles, was unquestionably French, it was not France that finally appreciated its endless possibilities of exploitation. Had the French managers but realized it, here was an opera that could make fortunes for them even bigger than the very sizable ones it did make: it took the wily impresarios of London and New York to grasp the fact that if a star could be secured for each of the seven definitely stellar roles, unheard-of prices could be charged. In their hands, *Les Huguenots,* becoming a seven-ring circus, became again and again that superb show Meyerbeer must have wanted it to be.

It is possible to give only a sampling from the numerous splendid casts that were assembled in England and America for *Les Huguenots*. Perhaps it was the tepid reactions to *Robert* that kept its successor from getting an adequate production in London until July 20, 1848, when Viardot-García, by her flashing intelligence and grand voice, alone saved a performance that, despite the fact that her Valentine was supported by Mario as Raoul, Tamburini as Saint-Bris, and Jeanne Castellan as Marguerite, was well headed toward ruin. Furthermore, for this Italian version—a command performance, with hosts of royalty scattered about in the loges— Meyerbeer, besides other overhauling, had rewritten the soprano part of the page Urbain for Alboni, a contralto. But it was Viardot-García who, by making a success of *Gli Ugonotti*, laid the foundations of Meyerbeer's truly enormous vogue in England. Tietjens, Lucca, Patti, and Materna were much-admired Valentines, and Trebelli and Scalchi divided adoration as Urbain. A wonderful London constellation of the nineties included Albani, Giulia Ravogli, the two De Reszkes, Maurel, and Ernest Van Dyck, the last chiefly famed for his Wagnerian interpretations. After twenty-four years' service at Covent Garden, Albani made her farewell operatic appearance there, in July, 1896, as Valentine, with Melba as the Marguerite.*

The first American performance of *Les Huguenots* occurred in New Orleans in 1839, and it was there, in 1860, that Patti first sang Valentine. New York heard the opera in French, Italian, German, and English, but it was not until the Academy of Music casts of the seventies and eighties that the city had a chance to savor the real quality of the opera when performed by better than competent artists. The first noteworthy one was assembled in 1872 by Carl Rosa, and included his wife, Euphrosyne Parepa-Rosa, the elder Theodor Wachtel, and Santley. The next year came Nilsson, Cary Del Puente, and Italo Campanini. Beginning in 1891, and continuing for fifteen years, Nordica was the established Valentine of the Metropolitan forces, though during the same period Lilli Lehmann occasionally sang the role. With the performance of December 26, 1894, Abbey and Grau began the experiment of raising the top prices to $7 a seat for seven-star casts of *Les Huguenots*: that night the seven were Nordica, Melba, Scalchi, the De Reszkes, Maurel, and Plançon. Sembrich sometimes replaced Melba as Marguerite, while Mantelli or Louise Homer sometimes played Urbain. Jean Lassalle was a notable Saint-Bris. In 1905, Caruso became the Raoul. *Les Huguenots* bade farewell to the Metropolitan during the season of 1914-15, the cast of December 30 including Destinn as Valentine, Hempel as Marguerite (she had made her Metropolitan debut in the role two years earlier), Mabel Garrison as Urbain, Caruso as Raoul, Scotti as De Nevers, and Rothier as Saint-Bris. When it is possible to get casts of equal luster, we may again have *Les Huguenots* and "nights of seven stars."

Les Huguenots is rich in characteristic concerted numbers and arias, and not one of the stars is neglected in Meyerbeer's conscientious effort to let his characters portray themselves. Marcel, the bigoted Huguenot whom Édouard de Reszke and Adamo Didur excelled in representing, has the first stop-the-show air, *"Piff, paff,"* a bragging soldier's hymn of vindictiveness. Urbain has a florid, mock-formal cavatina, *"Nobles sei-*

---

* Early in her career, when the many-gifted Venezuelan, Teresa Carreño, was uncertain about her ultimate career, the future piano virtuosa once memorized the role of Marguerite in four days.

gneurs, salut!" whose very lack of dramatic impact is in itself a comment on the functions of this character. Act II begins with Marguerite's extraordinary coloratura paean of love for her native land, *"O beau pays de la Touraine,"* which modulates into a second air, both combining to make one of the most difficult *scenas* in vocal literature. Valentine has nothing as important alone, but figures dramatically in several concerted numbers, culminating in the great duet with Raoul, *"O ciel! où courez-vous?"* in Act IV, the most sheerly passionate love music Meyerbeer ever created. But the theatrical climax of the opera occurs earlier in Act IV, in the tremendous double scene of the oath-taking and benediction of the swords, and the fact that Meyerbeer could follow this gigantic, full-blooded scene of furore, fanaticism, and conspiracy with a love duet that keeps us breathless is a proof of undisputable mastery. In fact, Act IV, in its entirety, is one of those unities of action, words, and music to which all opera should ideally aspire. Meyerbeer may never have been a truly first-rate composer, but here, at least, he was a first-rate composer of opera.

Edgar Istel, the eminent German musicologist, has justly called Act IV of *Les Huguenots* "a play within a play." Wagner, archenemy of Meyerbeerism, could never deny its power. In 1840, before he turned on his benefactor, Wagner wrote of it in prose strophes of wild rhapsody, and even as late as 1851, after excoriating Meyerbeer in *Oper und Drama*, he tempered his words with an admission that beside the love scene "none but the most finished works of musical art are worthy to be set." Even after his own apotheosis at Bayreuth, Wagner was honest enough to admit the strange power of this act. One evening, during a sojourn in Italy, he mentioned having been moved by an opera he had heard the day before. When asked what it was, he answered, after some hesitation: "I will let you know, if you promise me not to speak about it. Now then— yesterday evening I was at *Les Huguenots*, and was positively wrought up by that fourth act. I implore you not to let a soul know about it—otherwise the Wagnerites will flay me alive!" Fortunately, the Princess von Bülow, who was present at this confession, told the story to a recording angel.

It was said by his enemies that the Jew Meyerbeer made capital out of the wickedness and dissension of Christians: in *Robert le diable* he introduced a chorus of lascivious nuns; in *Les Huguenots* he aired the bloody feuds of the French Catholics and Protestants, and in his next important opera, *Le Prophète*, he chose a page from the heretical disputes of the Anabaptists. In 1842, Friedrich Wilhelm IV appointed Meyerbeer his general music director at Berlin, and about the same time Scribe handed him the book based on some unpleasant happenings from the life of John of Leyden, the Dutch heresiarch. They were much to Meyerbeer's liking—in fact, years before, he had considered setting such a book for his favorite tenor, the unfortunate Nourrit, who had, however, neurotically abandoned the Opéra in 1837 and committed suicide two years later. Once more he immersed himself in the lore of the period and within a year had completed *Le Prophète*. But his duties in the Prussian capital, including the composition of a German opera, *Der Feldlager in Schlesien*, in which Lind scored one of her early successes (he rewrote it for Paris, as *L'Étoile du nord*, in 1854), and the staging of *Euryanthe* and *Rienzi*, retarded its production, which he would not allow without his supervision.

Unfortunately, by the time Meyerbeer was able to oversee the production, Duprez, Nourrit's successor at the Opéra, had retired to become a singing teacher, and the best of the available tenors in the company were not competent to sing the role of Jean as originally composed. Meyerbeer, therefore, tried a bold experiment. Viardot-García, the greatest contralto of the age, was available: by reducing the roles of Jean and his betrothed, Berthe, and by building up the contralto role of Fidès, Jean's mother, he created the first great mother role in opera. This involved wholesale reconstruction of the score, and so it was not until April 16, 1849, that Paris had its first opportunity to hear and see another of its idol's grand historical spectacles. On that night, the role of Jean was assigned to Hippolyte Roger, a useful but not spectacular tenor. Viardot-García scored one of her remarkable triumphs, but Meyerbeer himself did not receive an ovation. Had he set *Le Prophète* in the style of *Les Huguenots*, he might have conquered at once, but he was too conscientious to copy himself. However, the sequence of *Robert* and *Les Huguenots* was paralleled, and soon Paris was wildly applauding *Le Prophète*.

The fact that *Le Prophète* caught on at all was a victory in itself, for the experiment of making an older woman the real heroine of an opera was revolutionary, and Meyerbeer did anything but soften the blow by making the hero an execrable creature. The success in the beginning, both on the Continent and in England, was largely a personal one for Viardot-García, who was reputed to have suggested many detailed changes to Meyerbeer, and its continuing life depended on finding other singing actresses with the right voice. Fidès is the biggest thing in the opera.

At the time of its composition, it is unfortunate that Meyerbeer, who had by then achieved an indisputable supremacy on the musical stage, did not compose *Le Prophète* on the bold, simple lines of a mother-and-son drama; instead, he crowded his canvas with a multitude of tableaus, some of them theatrically effective if dramatically irrelevant, others mere period scenes smelling of research and uninspired historic conscientiousness. As a result, *Le Prophète* has a hysteric and disheveled quality that is less pertinent to the riot of the times Meyerbeer tried to portray than to the chaos Scribe gave him, and to which the whole musical score is party. The best that can be said of Scribe's book is that it gave Meyerbeer an opportunity to provide for a spoiled public a sample of practically every device in his huge bag of musical tricks. For taking advantage of this opportunity, instead of seizing on the essentials of Scribe's book to make the magnificent drama that was there for the taking, Meyerbeer has been accused of being consciously untrue to himself. But, as Cecil Gray has wisely said, "Meyerbeer has often been wrongly reproached with insincerity; he simply lacked entirely any very strong or definite convictions. He was an artistic opportunist from want of a clear sense of direction rather than from a lack of moral integrity or conscience."

Le Prophète contains many musical numbers of great distinction, several of considerable fame. Most popular of all is the pompous and very circumstantial Coronation March in

Act IV, in which Meyerbeer struck the perfect generic note—perhaps it is carping to say that it would serve as well for the enthronement of King Arthur or George V as for that of a false prophet. Meyerbeer never invented a more universally known tune. Not quite in the same category is the Skaters' Quadrille in Act III, an engagingly rhythmic number that Liszt twisted into a satanically clever and difficult encore piece. The same master arranger put his claws into the dour, turbulent chant of the Anabaptists, *"Ad nos, ad salutarem undam,"* which recurs as a sort of musical basting throughout the score, and concocted a muzzy and magniloquent fantasie and fugue for organ. But there are better things in *Le Prophète* than these sops. Two of Fidès' solos stand out: *"Ah! mon fils"* is a great voicing of consoling motherhood, while *"Donnez, donnez"* is a tremulously and affectingly scored expression of sorrow. Few airs in contralto literature are finer than these. Quite different is Fides' scornful and passionate *"O prêtres de Baal."* Jean's music is, on the whole, much less interesting, while Berthe's is almost always frankly perfunctory.

The preponderance of emphasis on Fidès has naturally made *Le Prophète* a desired vehicle for those successors of Viardot-García who have the requisites. It happened that in London the same great contralto who had established the role in Paris sang it with Mario as Jean, thus creating a memory for opera-loving Londoners that they were loath to see blemished. They refused to tolerate the otherwise idolized Grisi when she foolishly attempted to sing Fidès a few years later. New Orleans had the American *première,* in 1850. Three years later, *Le Prophète* had reached Niblo's Garden, New York. The Metropolitan *première* occurred during the first season, on March 21, 1884. Nine months later, on December 17, Leopold Damrosch conducted a German version of the opera, with Marianne Brandt as Fidès, Anton Schott as Jean, and Marie Schröder-Hanfstängel as Berthe, and the opera became so popular that season as to equal *Tannhäuser* and *Lohengrin.* A particularly brilliant cast of the late nineties found Jean de Reszke, Marie Brema, and Lilli Lehmann in the three star parts, supported by Édouard de Reszke and Plançon. Schumann-Heink numbered Fidès among her richest characterizations. On February 7, 1917, Caruso, Matzenauer, Muzio, Didur, and Mardones sang *Le Pro-*

phète, and for three seasons the opera came close to becoming a favorite at the Metropolitan. The last revival took place during the season of 1927-28, with Matzenauer again as Fidès. The Jean of Martinelli was not one of his most admired performances.

Between *Le Prophète* and Meyerbeer's last and, in some ways, most magnificent opera intervened two scores, both composed for the Opéra-Comique and both designed (even if Meyerbeer did not so intend them) for a featherbrained type of coloratura display. The first of these was the rewritten *Der Feldlager in Schlesien,* given a new libretto by Scribe and christened *L'Étoile du nord.* The impossible hero of this impossibility was Peter the Great, the heroine the peasant girl he was to seat beside him on the throne. *L'Étoile* all but died with Meyerbeer—a brief career for an opera that had its *première* in 1854. In its youth, it was kept alive by the miraculous agility with which Lind coped with two flutes in the mad scene from the last act, and by the intelligence that Lablache, the Chaliapin of the mid-nineteenth century, brought to the role of Peter's boon companion. Today, outside of Germany, *L'Étoile* no longer shines even momentarily on the concert stage, for few contemporary coloraturas can safely try the cruel tessitura of Catherine's mimetic bouts with the flutes in *"Là, là, là, air chéri."*

The second of these comic operas was *Le Pardon de Ploërmel,* better known under the name of the Italian version, *Dinorah.* For the book of this nonsensical Breton tale, Meyerbeer deserted Scribe for Barbier and Carré, the librettists of Gounod's *Faust,* the *première* of which preceded *Le Pardon's,* on April 4, 1859, by only a month. The music is of the slightest and lightest, and quite apt for the idiotic girl who idiotically wanders through the three acts. Except for the gracious baritone air *"Ah! mon remords te venge,"* the opera is a shameless coloratura vehicle. It contains the most famous single air that Meyerbeer ever composed, the giddy, tripping, trifling waltz song, *"Ombre légère,"* and this alone has kept for the opera its now precarious hold on the boards.

Most coloraturas of the last eight decades have at least tried

"Ombre légère." In some cases, it made their fortunes, most notably that of Amelita Galli-Curci, who finally became so attached to the role of Dinorah that she is said to have left the Chicago Opera Company because the managers insisted that she sing it less often. During her North American debut in this role, at the Auditorium, Chicago, on November 16, 1917, someone threw a stench bomb and all but caused a panic. Cleofonte Campanini, who was conducting, immediately changed from Meyerbeer to *The Star-Spangled Banner*; Galli-Curci, who did not know the words, vocalized the melody, a brave fireman carried the hissing bomb to the street, and the evening was saved. No bombs went off when Galli-Curci, still with the Chicago group, made her New York debut in the same opera, on January 28, 1918, but the curtain calls were so numerous that wiseacres in the packed Lexington Theater knew that the Metropolitan would soon have a new major star. And so it happened, though even Galli-Curci was unable to establish *Dinorah* at the Metropolitan, where, despite the showy and costly production Gatti-Casazza gave it, she sang it but twice, during the season of 1924-25, when she was supported by De Luca as Hoël and Tokatyan as Corentin. All the Metropolitan performances—there was a single earlier one, in 1892, when Marie Van Zandt sang Dinorah to Lassalle's Hoël—have been in Italian.

Dinorah was the last of his operas that Meyerbeer was destined to hear. Way back in 1838, Scribe had given him a fantastic libretto about an African slave girl. By 1849, the score was finished, but Meyerbeer was satisfied neither with Scribe's work nor with his own. Therefore he asked for a new libretto, and finally, after endless bickering, Scribe, who at one time had angrily withdrawn the libretto altogether, gave him the revision in 1852. This for the first time included the figure of the opera's present hero, Vasco da Gama, after whom it was temporarily named, and who had been suggested to Scribe by the fact that Jessonda, in Spohr's opera of that name, falls in love with another Portuguese navigator, Tristan da Cunha. There was nothing in the life of Vasco da Gama remotely resembling this foolish sequence of events, and the "African slave girl" Selika is obviously an East Indian, but these facts did not deter Meyerbeer from doing his usual research job and worrying the score to completion in eight years. It was ready in 1860, but production was delayed for four years while the finically conscientious composer changed details, even after the opera was in rehearsal. But Meyerbeer was seventy-two years old, and this time procrastination was fatal. On May 1, 1864, the copying of the last corrections was completed at his house in the Rue Montaigne, and the next day he died. Less than a year later, *L'Africaine*—after three friends* of Meyerbeer had shifted many scenes around to produce harmony between the score and the libretto (as they conceived its requirements)—was sung for the first time.

Much of the delay between the finishing of the score in 1860 and the production at the Opéra on April 28, 1865, was caused by casting difficulties, and even the first Selika—Marie Sax, an ex-*variétés* artist—was not of Meyerbeer's choosing. In the same cast, and far outshining his fellows, was the almost mythically famous Jean-Baptiste Faure, who sang the baritone role of Nelusko. Emilio Naudin followed the dictates of Meyerbeer's will by creating the role of Vasco, while Louis-Henri Obin, Levasseur's successor as professor of singing at the Conservatoire, was the High Priest of Brahma.

On July 22, Pauline Lucca, the great singing actress whom Meyerbeer himself had coached in the part of Selika, sang it at Covent Garden, in Italian. Four years later, as *Die Afrikanerin*, at the Imperial Opera House, Vienna, it served to introduce a popular operetta singer to grand opera. Her name was Amalie Materna, and she eventually won her greatest fame as Brünnhilde at Bayreuth in 1876. Hermann Klein called Lucca's impersonation of the passionate slave "a supreme achievement to be mentioned in the same breath with the Rosina of Adelina Patti and the Marguerite [*Faust*] of Christine Nilsson." In more recent times, Selika has been the debut role of such disparate types as the statuesque and thrilling French dramatic soprano, Lucienne Bréval, and the Spanish coloratura, María Barrientos.

L'Africaine, in the Italian form of *L'Africana,* reached American shores on December 1, 1865, at the New York Academy of

* One of them, the formidable music critic, François-Joseph Fétis, in some places cruelly maltreated Meyerbeer's ingenious orchestration, ineptly substituting a saxophone for the bass clarinet—out of friendship for Adolphe Sax, a fellow Belgian, who had invented the instrument.

Music, and there Lucca sang it seven years later. The first Metropolitan performances began in the season of 1888-89. On January 15, 1892, Lassalle made his New York debut as Nelusko in a repetition also remarkable for the first American appearance together of the already famous trio of Lassalle and the two De Reszkes. On February 13, 1895, there was a moment of unexpected drama for a Metropolitan audience that had come chiefly to hear Nordica as Selika, Tamagno as Vasco, Ancona as Nelusko, and Édouard de Reszke as Don Pedro. Lucille Hill, singing the role of Vasco's sweetheart Inès, fainted, and Mathilde Bauermeister, stepping out of her menial role as Inès' attendant Anna, assumed Miss Hill's for the rest of the performance. Lilli Lehmann and Félia Litvinne were other Selikas of the nineties. On January 11, 1907, Olive Fremstad sang Selika to Caruso's Vasco, with Marie Rappold as Inès and Riccardo Stracciari as Nelusko, and with Plançon and Journet in lesser roles. After sixteen years, on March 21, 1923, *L'Africaine* was revived for Rosa Ponselle, a magnificent Selika. With her were Queena Mario, Gigli, Giuseppe Danise, Didur, and Rothier. Later, Elisabeth Rethberg sang the slave girl, but for the last performances, during the 1933-34 season, Ponselle resumed the role, with Martinelli as her Vasco. With the third of these, Meyerbeer ceased to be heard in New York.

L'Africaine is an ambiguous score: though the most disciplined of all Meyerbeer's operas in its separate numbers, it is a throwback to the hysterical days of *Robert le diable*, when the composer was just beginning to understand the importance of integrating his several idioms. Plainly a work pieced together over a long period, and written from a number of unreconciled points of view, it is not a successful opera. It is, generally, a gorgeous and somber score, with *longueurs* of spotless academic writing. While it is scenically as spectacular as *Les Huguenots*, the music is less theatrical. The false touches that blemish the score of *Le Prophète*, but which can be excused there as results of a misreading of history, are much more egregious in *L'Africaine*, whose fake Orientalism came from a faulty reading of an alien culture. (Meyerbeer does not seem to have been sure as to which alien culture he was trying to evoke.)

Yet, when Meyerbeer succeeds in *L'Africaine*, it is, perhaps, on the highest musical level he ever attained. *"O Paradis,"* the great tenor air in Act IV, with its continuation, "*Conduisez-moi vers ce navire*," is so surpassingly lovely and so just as to seem an act of pure serendipity. Quite as dramatic is Nelusko's primitive evocation of Adamastor, deity of sea and storm, in Act III— "*Adamastor, roi des vagues.*" Most effective of the pseudo-Oriental numbers is Selika's lullaby in Act II, "*Sur mes genoux, fils du soleil*," an air of entrancing tenderness, while in the final duet between Vasco and Selika—"*Ô transports, ô douce extase*" —Meyerbeer almost reopened the vein of passion he had found in the last duet between Valentine and Raoul in *Les Huguenots*. As in two or three others of his scores, there are enough fine things in *L'Africaine* to make it tragic that Meyerbeer never managed to produce an opera in which he was consistently at his best from beginning to end. Such an opera would unquestionably have been among the finest ever composed.

"*Aïda* is musically little more than a grandiose pendant or sequel to *L'Africaine.*" Thus Cecil Gray. This is a careless exaggeration: *Aïda* grew, not out of the hints Verdi took from Meyerbeer, but from Verdi's searching study of past opera and of his own abilities as they had developed. Meyerbeer, in truth, founded no school, even though his best tricks can be found in the scores of the most unlikely people. He was like a teacher whose influence persists in detail long after his teachings, in the broader aspects, have been repudiated. There are Meyerbeerian elements, it would be fair to say, in *Aïda* and other Verdi scores, in *Rienzi*, in much French opera of the nineteenth century, but the only opera that might have come from Meyerbeer's own pen is the passionately written *La Juive*, by Jacques-François-Fromental-Élie Halévy, seven years his junior. And even *La Juive*, composed when only *Il Crociato* and *Robert* existed to show how Meyerbeer was maturing, was less a slavish imitation than a natural expression of a man whose character was much like Meyerbeer's—scholarly, devoted to craftsmanship, eclectic. Halévy, in his best opera, is almost as much Cherubini's pupil as Meyerbeer's friend.

In one respect, *La Juive* is superior to any score of Meyerbeer's: it is more truly felt, establishes an integrity, preserves a unity, with a persistence that would have carried Meyerbeer to the heights of musical greatness. Halévy, unlike Meyerbeer, never allows his flair for experimentation to run away with him: it is almost always religiously controlled. The tragedy of the perfectly schooled Halévy was that he was facile and prolix, and set without enthusiasm almost thirty operas, most often to any catchpenny book that came along. In Scribe's *La Juive*, for all its rant and fustian, he found a dramatic story that set his devoutly Jewish imagination on fire.

The intellectual Nourrit, who had an advisory voice in the shaping of several Meyerbeer scores, played an even more important role in *La Juive*. He was tired of portraying amorous young men and so persuaded Halévy to make Eléazar, the heroine's father, a tenor rather than a baritone or bass, which would have been traditional procedure. He is even said to have written the words to Eléazar's thrilling air in Act IV—*"Rachel! quand du Seigneur."* He was, naturally, the Eléazar of the opening performance, at the Opéra, on February 23, 1835. The Rachel was Cornélie Falcon, the Eudoxie was Dorus-Gras, and the Cardinal was Levasseur. Viardot-García, a little later, was unexcelled as Rachel. Among the tenors of the time who sang Eléazar, Duprez was superb, and Mario was insufferable—possibly because the role gave him no opportunity to look handsome. Marianne Brandt, the future Wagnerian mezzo, made her operatic debut, in Graz, as Rachel.

La Juive, like so many French operas of the period, was first heard in the United States at New Orleans (1844), and the next year reached New York, where it has been sung in French, German, Italian, Russian, and Yiddish. Materna was the Rachel of the first Metropolitan performance, of the season of 1884-85, given in German under Leopold Damrosch. The revival of December 7, 1887, brought together the largely Wagnerian cast of Lilli Lehmann, Schröder-Hanfstängel, Niemann, Fischer, and Alvary. The next season, Paul Kalisch, Lehmann's husband, took Niemann's role. After two more performances in German during the 1889-90 season, *La Juive* was dropped from the Metropolitan repertoire for thirty years. Then, on November 22, 1919, it was revived in French. Caruso, as the Eléazar, was singing his thirty-sixth and last Metropolitan role, with

Ponselle and Rothier, besides Orville Harrold, who was making his Metropolitan debut.

Of Caruso's performance, Irving Kolodin, in his informative *The Metropolitan Opera: 1883-1939*, wrote: "It was without doubt the most striking artistic triumph of his career. Some quality in the character had inflamed Caruso's imagination; and the impersonation he finally presented was the product of more care and study, especially dramatically, than any of the thirty-five other roles he sang during his career in New York. It was particularly impressive as the accomplishment of a singer whose position in the esteem of the public was inviolate; and spoke more highly for his development as an artist than any verbal tribute could."

A year later, on November 15, *La Juive,* with the same principals, was used to inaugurate the Metropolitan season of 1920-21. It was Caruso's last opening night. On December 24, with Florence Easton replacing Ponselle, he sang *La Juive* once more. It was his farewell to the Metropolitan—and to opera. He was a sick man, and eight months later, after apparent recovery, he died at his native Naples.* *La Juive* did not drop from the repertoire with his death: it has been given more than two dozen times since, with Martinelli as Eléazar and Ponselle, Rethberg, and Lawrence as his erring daughter.

* Comedy as well as tragedy is connected with the history of *La Juive.* In a Chicago performance, in the early twenties, Rosa Raisa, until then a passionately doleful Rachel, was the innocent victim of a ludicrous anticlimax in the final scene. Thrown into what purported to be a huge caldron of boiling oil, she bounced practically back onto the stage. A too-coddling stage director had over-cushioned her landing by flooring the caldron with some elastic material. In this instance, even those in the pit, who seldom have any fun, could see Raisa's death gymnastics.

Ernestine Schumann-Heink as Fidès and Enrico Caruso as John of Leyden, in Meyerbeer's *Le Prophète*

Chapter XV
Valhalla

SOME time after the Easter of 1842, Wilhelm Fischer, stage manager of the Dresden Hofoper, had to worry about scenery for a new five-act opera of unprecedented size by a man whose only past performance was a fiasco so thorough that it completed the ruin of the company that produced it. Fischer was required, substantially, to put medieval Rome upon the stage, not forgetting its principal ruins, and to provide, as a denouement, for the destruction of the Capitol, without setting the theater on fire and without breaking the heads of his singers. Ferdinand Heine was faced with an equally harrowing task: as costume designer, he had to get 537 period costumes ready for the dress rehearsal. But, though Fischer and Heine did not realize it when they first received their orders, their most onerous duty was to work with the little dynamo who had composed the opera to his own libretto, and who was, at twenty-nine, already the leading fussbudget in central Germany.

No detail of costuming, scene painting, choral work, or dancing was too minute for the personal intervention of Richard Wagner. He had set out, with *Rienzi*, to surpass Meyerbeer at his own game, and he was not to be balked by mere material limitations. Novice though he was, he had secured the services of several noted singers for the leading roles, among them Schröder-Devrient and Joseph Aloys Tichatschek, a Bohemian tenor. Miraculously, though after numerous delays, *Rienzi* reached its opening night on October 20, 1842, and Wagner had his first taste of popular favor. Oddly, though self-confident to the point of arrogance, he was afraid that *Rienzi* had failed the first night, despite the fact that the audience remained from six to eleven-fifteen, and was still applauding loudly at the end of the fifth act. The next day he rushed to the theater at eight in the morning, bent on slashing the opera to a more tolerable length. Tichatschek, who was enraptured with the music of the name role, forbade the major cuts and gradually convinced the agitated composer that *Rienzi* had been a success.

There was no reason *Rienzi* should not have succeeded: there was very little new about it. The libretto, based on the Bulwer-Lytton novel, was a historical pageant of familiar type—Meyerbeer called it the best he had ever seen; the music was vigorous, noisy, harmonically conventional, and, in one or two numbers, notably the Prayer, catchy; there was nothing experimental about the style—nothing that would rile the most sensitive devotee of Meyerbeer's complicated eclecticism. In fact, anyone who examined Wagner at this point in his history, and knew nothing of the quite different score tucked away in his traveling bags, could be forgiven for having dismissed him as an imitation Meyerbeer, not without talent, but certainly without the versatility of the older man. Nor would he have been likely to change his mind if he had examined the scores of the unperformed *Die Feen** or the self-consciously licentious *Das Liebesverbot*, that unfortunate comic opera, chiefly Auberian in style, to which the Magdeburgers, in 1836, had said, "Once is enough." There was nothing in Wagner's first three operas to show that the disciple was at hand for whom Weber, passionate after a real German composer who would go on from where he himself had left off, had prayed. In 1842, Wagner seemed to be going the international way.

Only by reason of its position as Wagner's first operatic success (it came within a fraction of being his last) and by a certain rude gusto does *Rienzi* stand out from the general run of second-rate operas of its period. Even were it to vanish from the boards (which it seems in danger of doing in the United States), *Rienzi* would be remembered through its still-popular, slapdash, patchwork overture, whose unctiousness triumphant is the first faint (though noisy) premonition of that aspect of Wagner's artistic nature which would ultimately be fulfilled in the least attractive pages of *Parsifal*. In the body of the opera itself, Wagner's willingness to borrow styles wherever he chose

---

* Wagner had been dead five years when *Die Feen* was first produced, its *première* having taken place at Munich in 1888, under Hermann Levi, the *Meister*'s favorite conductor.

is nowhere better evidenced than in the tumultuous finale to Act I, which Eduard Hanslick, the eminent Viennese critic, later described well, to Wagner's fury, as a mixture of Donizetti and Meyerbeer and an anticipation of Verdi.

Rienzi has always, except for its initial spurt, been the least popular of Wagner's major operas. In the United States, it was preceded by *Tannhäuser, Lohengrin,* and *Der fliegende Holländer.* Max Maretzek conducted its first American performance, at the New York Academy of Music, on March 4, 1878, with Charles R. Adams, a Boston tenor who was one of the first American singers to win laurels in Europe, as Rienzi, and Eugenia Pappenheim in the male-impersonation role of Adriano. *Rienzi* reached the Metropolitan in its third season, when Anton Seidl conducted a distinguished cast, including Marianne Brandt, Lilli Lehmann, and Emil Fischer. The last of the total of thirteen performances given at the Metropolitan occurred on February 26, 1890, when the singers, except for Sophie Traubman, the Irene, were second-raters. The German Opera Company, on December 26, 1923, revived *Rienzi* at the Manhattan Opera House, with Heinrich Knote as the Roman tribune. At that performance, Editha Fleischer, later one of the most serviceable all-round sopranos of the Metropolitan, appeared in a minor role. Since then, *Rienzi* has not been heard in New York.

Those who think of Wagner primarily in terms of *Der Ring des Nibelungen,* and come unprepared to *Rienzi* without a knowledge of its antecedents, are in for a rude shock. At first sight, it is just an old-fashioned opera, in some of its elements not unlike certain operas produced in Paris from the French Revolution on. It is, in fact, just the sort of thing a clever borrower (which, in one way or another, Wagner remained all his life), with a complete knowledge of fashionable styles in opera picked up in eight years of conducting and stage-managing in the provinces, would be likely to contrive.

But close examination of the score shows that there is more to *Rienzi* than first meets the ear. The music is integrated with the action in a wonderfully ingenious way: certain of the characters and salient situations have musical themes that reappear with them. In short, here was the most extensive use, thus far, of the leading-motive idea, which was as old as the

invention of opera itself and which had been used by the
Florentine *camerata*, by Monteverdi, and—notably in *Don Giovanni* and *Die Zauberflöte*—by Mozart. However, in *Rienzi*
Wagner was not using the leitmotiv as an occasional device, as
earlier men had done, and as he himself had done in *Das
Liebesverbot*: here it was a cohesive element, not merely a trick
for sharpening dramatic stab. There are more than thirty leitmotivs in *Rienzi*, all clearly defined for those who take the
trouble to seek them. But not only are they not the same sort
of leitmotivs used in the *Ring*, they are not even conceived for
the same purpose or used in the same way. They are not the
brief, gnomic, vibrating phrases that—developed, altered, combined, and reshuffled—make up the close, shimmering web the
later Wagner magically wove. They are long-lined, static labels,
by their very nature not susceptible to symphonic treatment in
the Beethovian style Wagner adopted as his last manner.

Rienzi grew out of nothing more personal to Wagner than
his passion for the romantic novel and his determination to
succeed as an operatic composer. *Der fliegende Holländer,* however, was the first chapter in a musical autobiography that was
finished only when he blotted the last notes of *Parsifal*. It is a
tremendous picture of storm and sea: Wagner, fleeing from
Riga in 1839, had endured a four weeks' crossing from Pillau
to Gravesend that, according to his description, was rather more
scarifying than the first voyage of Columbus. The *Holländer*
is an epic tale of a sinful man redeemed by the self-sacrificing
love of a woman: Wagner embarked on it partly as a love gift
to his first wife, Minna Planer, whom, at least during the composition of Acts I and II, he still considered the angel of his
own redemption—before completing the last act he had begun
to discover that so mentally limited an angel could not redeem
Richard Wagner. Added to these elements, even if not specifically identifiable in the libretto and score, were the grinding
destitution and months of failure in Paris, where he finished
the opera in 1841.

Wagner sent the score to Berlin, along with a personal plea to
Meyerbeer, then general music director. Accepted provision-
ally, the *Holländer* was still unproduced, despite Meyerbeer's

efforts in its behalf, when *Rienzi*, also helped to the stage by Meyerbeer's influence in Dresden, scored its success in 1842. Wagner then impatiently withdrew it from Berlin, and it was accepted for production in Dresden. Its *première* was January 2, 1843, with Schröder-Devrient as the faithful Senta (originally christened Minna) and Johann Michael Wächter, the original Orsini of *Rienzi*, in the baritone role of Vanderdecken, the Flying Dutchman. There was no tenor role important enough for Tichatschek: he was consoled by the knowledge that Wagner was composing an opera in which he would again have the name part.

Der fliegende Holländer, in the city of its *première*, started out by being as much a debacle as *Rienzi* had been a hit. It was given four times and then dropped for more than twenty-two years. There were various reasons for its failure, not least of them being *Rienzi* itself, whose qualities were such as to make the Dresdeners want the same thing with the label changed. Instead of dazzling historical pageantry, gaudy scenery, polychromatic costumes, they were offered three acts of unmitigatedly somber story, dark scenery, and dreary costumes. Instead of bright, blaring, brassy music, much of it to jolly rhythms, they received gloomy, thunderously whispered surges of man and elements—music that might give one a headache, but which was hard to remember. It was a mistake to produce this untuneful stuff in the pleasant social capital of Saxony, where Weber's untiring efforts to stir up an interest in German opera—words and music both—had apparently been in vain. For the *Holländer* was as obviously a Weberian opera as *Rienzi* had been a Meyerbeerian one: in it, Weber would have recognized—for the first and perhaps the last time—his true disciple. In some respects, it was a direct descendant of *Der Freischütz*; in others, it was as wholly new as *Der Freischütz* itself had been when it dethroned Spontini at Berlin.

Der fliegende Holländer is the first symphonic opera, the first opera in which the music grows out of a few germinal themes, and grows continuously without being divided up into a series of autonomous entities. It was not the first opera to possess unity, but it was the first to possess the sort of musical

unity that had been achieved in the most mature development
of the symphony. True, in the *Holländer*, the music drama—
that superb side show to the main edifice, that side show Wagner was to make his own—had not yet arrived. For instance,
he had not yet thrown overboard completely all the separate-
number machinery and other conventions of the older opera.
Vanderdecken's carefully prepared-for *scena*—*"Die Frist ist
um"*—in Act I clearly evidences this, while Senta's ballad—
"Traft ihr das Schiff im Meere an"—is, for all its Valkyrielike
ho-hos, only an old-fashioned set number of the French *romance* type, equipped with exciting music of unmistakable
Wagnerian cast. It is possible, after allowing for the few magnificent things in the *Holländer*, to commiserate with the Dresden art lovers: the opera is ingenious, and undeniably
represents a gigantic step forward in the evolution of the most
significant operatic composer of the nineteenth century, but
those who heard it for the first time could not guess from it its
composer's destiny as the musical *Übermensch*. Most of *Der fliegende Holländer* is just plain dull, and the Dresdeners had a
reasonable preference for entertainment.

Der fliegende Holländer was the first of Wagner's operas to reach
England, where it was given in Italian on July 23, 1870, with Santley
as the Dutchman and Di Murska as Senta. In America, the *première*,
also in Italian, occurred at the Philadelphia Academy of Music,
on November 8, 1876, with Pappenheim as Senta. The next year,
on January 26, Clara Louise Kellogg, ill-supported by a cast of
nonentities, presented it in English at the New York Academy of
Music. George A. Conly, a former printer, sang the bass role of
Daland, Senta's sea-captain father—Miss Kellogg records, apparently
without seeing the sardonic humor of the fact, that Conly died by
drowning. The *Holländer* was finally presented in the United States
in German when the Metropolitan undertook it on November 27,
1889, with Theodor Reichmann, the original Amfortas of the
Bayreuth *Parsifal*, as Vanderdecken, Kalisch as Erik, Fischer as
Daland, and Sophie Wiesner as Senta. On March 31, 1892, an Italian version brought forward Albani, making her last operatic appearance in the United States, Lassalle singing Vanderdecken for
the first time anywhere, and Édouard de Reszke. Ternina or Gadski
was the Senta of some later performances, while Schumann-Heink

sometimes sang the secondary role of Mary. After dropping the *Holländer* for twenty-three seasons, the Metropolitan revived it on November 1, 1930, with Friedrich Schorr a superb Vanderdecken and Maria Jeritza hopelessly miscast as Senta. Kirsten Flagstad has been the most recent Metropolitan Senta, and Kerstin Thorborg has sung Mary.

Tannhäuser, the opera in which Tichatschek had been promised the name role, was produced at Dresden on October 19, 1845. Schröder-Devrient was Venus, Wagner's niece Johanna was Elisabeth. The shrewd Venus had warned Wagner against this casting, protesting with humorous candor that she herself was too stout to make a credible goddess of love (a protest her biography belies), that the nineteen-year-old Fräulein Wagner was too immature to grasp the role of Elisabeth, and that the bluff Bohemian tenor would misread Tannhäuser. She was right in every way. At the first, the principals were little more than figures of fun, and the opera suffered accordingly. The shoddy, secondhand scenery added to the audience's annoyance, and Wagner, who by then had become assistant conductor at the Hofoper, was in despair, particularly as his bellowing tenor had strained his voice so badly as to make repetition impossible for more than a week. But the new sets for the big singing-contest scene arrived, and the interim, moreover, had given Wagner a chance to drill his singers in the interpretive niceties of their parts. Thus the second performance, though poorly attended, was so much better received that *Tannhäuser* was started on the road to a popularity that has never waned. At the Metropolitan, for instance, it runs practically neck and neck with *Die Walküre* as the second most performed of Wagner's operas, though far behind *Lohengrin.*

Tannhäuser has all the elements of popular appeal that *Der fliegende Holländer* lacks, but without the blatant self-advertisement of *Rienzi.* As played today, with the expanded Venusberg music composed for the Paris production of 1861, it has the further lure of a tone poem of singular blandishments, couched in the mature style of the composer of *Tristan und Isolde.* It has an overture starting at once with Wagner's best-known tune—that later used for the Pilgrims' Chorus—and working itself up into a triumphal frenzy. The opera is, indeed, a succession of high spots, beginning with the Bacchanale and Tannhäuser's Hymn to Venus in Act I; from Elisabeth's nobly joyful *"Dich, teure Halle,"* through the pompous ceremonial march, to the songs of the contending singers, including Wolfram's serene *"Blick' ich Umher,"* in Act II, and from the Pilgrims' Chorus through Elisabeth's Prayer to Wolfram's third-act apostrophe to the evening star, *"O du mein holder Abendstern,"* which has become almost as hackneyed as the Pilgrims' Chorus.

Tannhäuser, even as a product of the year 1845, is an ambiguous work. Its libretto does not represent Wagner's most advanced convictions about the functions of a libretto; moreover, it shows a mingling of story elements—myth and history —that he would not have admitted even a very few years later. On the other hand, the music—not to speak of the Paris additions—is, besides being more attractive than that of *Der fliegende Holländer,* of greater interest technically. The texture of the score is more characteristically Wagnerian than anything preceding it: the rich complexity of *Tristan* and the later bonafide music dramas is here plainly previsaged in harmony, orchestration, and use of leitmotivs. Here, too, are moments of that overripe sensuousness deepening into sexuality—that indulgence in torrid musical color for its own sake—which was to mark the *Meister's* strangely un-Germanic hand right up to, and even in, *Parsifal.*

Herein lies the ambiguity: a largely old-fashioned libretto is fitted to music that is speeding ahead to a new condition of, despite its composer's pet theories, symphonic self-sufficiency. The music of *Tannhäuser* is new, advanced, but a final element is lacking: it has not yet cohered ideally, has not shaped its own inevitable form. It is the stuff of the future music drama just before the last moment of illumination. For that reason, no doubt, it seems almost a retrogression from the *Holländer,* whose all but uninterrupted unity of musicodramatic mood gives it a superficially closer resemblance to the *Ring.* In the *Holländer,* Wagner was working with simpler, more easily malleable elements, and so success was easier. In *Tannhäuser,* he boldly enlarged his scope, and began to try to achieve something far more difficult than a mere unity of mood. He did not wholly succeed, but by and large he took a step forward.

Tannhäuser, historically, is bound up with Wagner's personal vicissitudes. When, in 1849, as a political refugee, Wagner was scurrying over the frontier into Switzerland, Liszt, his future father-in-law, was preparing to stage it in Weimar. It was the first opera that Wagner managed, a dozen years later, to peddle in Paris, and it was with *Tannhäuser,* despite the inspiredly clever music he composed especially to win over the ballet-mad habitués of the Opéra, that he suffered the most wounding setback of his middle career. That performance, on March 13, 1861, with Marie Sax as Elisabeth and Albert Niemann as Tannhäuser (the first Wagnerian role of one of the most eminent of Wagnerian tenors), was the occasion of the notorious riot when members of the Jockey Club, having come too late to see the choreographic splendors of Lucien Petipa, brutally expressed their disapproval of the ballet's being in the first act. After three nights, during which the opposition raged, Wagner himself insisted upon withdrawing the opera, though there were definite signs of a popular reaction in its favor.

Tannhäuser was not thereafter heard in Paris for over a quarter of a century, when Charles Lamoureux' courageous production of *Lohengrin,* in 1887, opened the French market to a Wagnerian invasion. A famous revival of *Tannhäuser* occurred at the Opéra on May 13, 1895, when Ernest Van Dyck, a French tenor who had actually been greeted with plaudits when he essayed the role of Parsifal at Bayreuth, took the lead, his Elisabeth being Rose Caron, and his Venus the powerful Swiss dramatic soprano, Lucienne Bréval; Maurice Renaud was the Wolfram, Jean-François Delmas the Landgrave.

London heard its first *Tannhäuser,* in Italian, on May 6, 1876, with Maurel and Albani as Tannhäuser and Elisabeth. This was seventeen years later than the American *première,* which, moreover, was in the language in which the opera was written. In fact, this performance at the Stadt Theater, New York, on April 4, 1859, was the first opera by Wagner ever to be given in the Americas. "Some objections," wrote Henry Lahee, "were made . . . to the thoroughly German atmosphere pervading the whole affair. Boys went through the aisles with beer in stone mugs for the thirsty, and huge chunks of *Schweizerkäs* for the hungry." That, of course, was the Dresden version, which was also used when to *Tannhäuser* fell the honor of opening the second Metropolitan season, on November 17, 1884. It marked, also, the beginning of a heavy wave of operatic Teutonism, when, in addition to naturally German operas, French and Italian works were given in German. Leopold Damrosch conducted a performance that might not be considered notable today, but was then a revelation because of the *chef d'orchestre*'s fine command of his ensemble. Auguste Kraus, Anton Seidl's wife, was Elisabeth, Anton Schott was an explosive Tannhäuser (Krehbiel called his singing "monstrous"), and Anna Slach was Venus.

During its almost six decades of Metropolitan existence, *Tannhäuser* has been in the repertoire of that house almost uninterruptedly. Oddly enough, it had been given over thirty times before the much more attractive and spectacular Paris version was first used there, on January 30, 1889, with Lilli Lehmann as Venus and Kalisch as Tannhäuser. In the late nineties, Emma Eames was a favorite Elisabeth, though some of the performances in which she sang were a little less than artistic, with French and Italian mingled indiscriminately. After the World War interim of eight seasons, *Tannhäuser* was revived on February 1, 1923, for Jeritza, with Matzenauer as the ample but golden-voiced Venus; Curt Taucher was the Tannhäuser, Clarence Whitehill the Wolfram. It was as Wolfram that, on February 14, 1924, Friedrich Schorr, the Hungarian baritone, began a distinguished Metropolitan career. A list of the Metropolitan Tannhäusers, Elisabeths, Venuses, and Wolframs would include most of its greatest non-Italian alumni; Florence Easton, a superb Elisabeth, had made her world debut at Newcastle-on-Tyne, in 1903, in the minor role of the Shepherd. Oscar Hammerstein, during the brilliant seasons when his Manhattan Opera House rivaled the Metropolitan, brought forward some notable casts, one of them presenting Mariette Mazarin, a fine singing actress, as Elisabeth, with Renaud as Wolfram, and Giovanni Zenatello an unfortunate choice as the Tännhauser. Among active singers today, Lotte Lehmann, Rethberg, Flagstad, and Helen Traubel have sung Elisabeth. Thorborg is a magnificent Venus, Lauritz Melchior, vocally at least, an accomplished Tannhäuser.

Lilli Lehmann as Brünnhilde, in Wagner's
Der Ring des Nibelungen

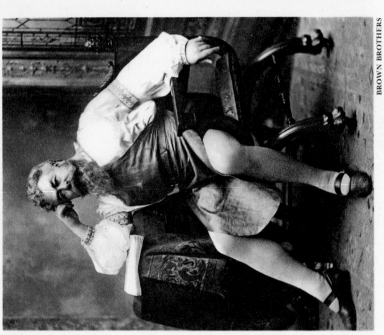

Emil Fischer as Hans Sachs, in Wagner's
Die Meistersinger von Nürnberg

Wagner had supervised and conducted the *première* of *Tann-häuser*. When *Lohengrin*, his next opera, was first staged, he was a fugitive from Saxon justice, living in exile in Switzer-land. It was Liszt, not entirely convinced of the practicability of producing this "superideal" opera, and with skimpy forces in the pit and on the stage, who took upon his resigned shoul-ders the task of introducing yet another revolutionary work by his unreasonable friend. The scene was the tiny Hoftheater at Weimar, already one of the magnets of artistic life on the Con-tinent; the date was August 28, 1850. Wagner had completed *Tannhäuser* in April, 1845, and in the summer of that year, after toying with ideas that he eventually shaped into the libret-tos of *Die Meistersinger* and *Parsifal*, wrote the poem of *Lohen-grin*. The music was composed in odd sequence: Act III came first, then Acts I and II, followed by the Prelude—a mode of procedure familiar to students of the *Ring*. The scoring was completed in 1848. Now, two years later, Wagner was fretting for word from Weimar.

The first news was bad: the lengthy work had not worn well with the first-night audience, and Liszt, clever though he was in making ends meet where others could not, was unable to do first-class things with second-rate singers and an orchestra of only thirty-eight men. Some of the singers were almost paralyzed with fear because of the difficulty of their roles. Liszt, having done what he could, told the bad news to Wagner, who, be-sides being an exile, was recuperating from a badly managed love affair with another man's wife. The failure of *Lohengrin* completed, temporarily, his prostration.

Yet, after a slow, listless beginning, *Lohengrin*, seemingly gathering strength from within itself, leaped over Germany in nine years: by 1859, it had been presented in fourteen Ger-man towns, besides Riga and Prague. As we have seen, Lam-oureux used *Lohengrin* in 1887 to test French readiness to listen to Wagner with unprejudiced ears. A dozen years before that, the Wagner craze had seized upon London with such intensity that two competing houses presented *Lohengrin* only a few days apart. As is so often the case in these rivalries, the one that managed to be first on the scene did the inferior job, though both suffered in appropriateness by being given in Italian.

The English *première*, such as it was, took place at Covent Garden, on May 8, 1875, with Albani as Elsa, supported—unreliably—by one of Patti's husbands, a French tenor who called himself Nicolini. Maurel was the Telramund of a production marred by many un-Bayreuthian cuts. Several days later, Colonel Mapleson staged his version at Her Majesty's. Sir Michael Costa, whose wry sense of humor was provoked by a badly mismanaged swan, to which he referred as "dat goose," held his superior orchestra, cast, and chorus in a firm rein.* Nilsson was perhaps not ponderably better than Albani, but Tietjens, the Ortrud, was so far superior to her rival in the Covent Garden cast as to make comparisons irrelevant. Italo Campanini sang Lohengrin superbly, while Antonio Galassi "appeared," wrote Herman Klein, "to step naturally into the part of a Telramund only too ready to hearken to his wicked spouse." When London finally heard *Lohengrin* in German, Rosa Sucher, a future heroine of many Bayreuth festivals, quickly established herself as a thoroughly admirable Elsa, while Hermann Winkelmann, whose English debut was as the Knight of the Swan, was her peer.

As in the case of *Tannhäuser*, America was ahead of England in getting *Lohengrin*. Four years before the London productions, on April 3, 1871, Adolf Neuendorff conducted the New York *première* at the Stadt Theater. Three years later, at the Academy of Music, an Italian version was given by the Strakosch company —in every way superior to the Stadt Theater attempt. With Nilsson and Campanini were associated Annie Louise Cary as Ortrud and Giuseppe del Puente as Telramund. Nilsson and Campanini again headed the cast when, as the seventh offering of its first season, the Metropolitan staged *Lohengrin* on November 7, 1883. The Ortrud of that occasion was the eminent French dramatic mezzo, Emmy Fursch-Madi, the Telramund the Italian baritone Giuseppe Kaschmann.

Almost at once, *Lohengrin* became, in New York, the favorite it has remained, but to all early Wagnerians the announcement that it was at last to be sung adequately in German came as a relief. On November 23, 1885, the occasion being Anton Seidl's debut

---

* Nevertheless, Costa used a score and parts that Hans Richter, a few years later, found to contain over four hundred mistakes.

as a conductor in the United States, *Lohengrin* was given as the opening opera of the season. Seidl's wife was Elsa, while the Ortrud was Marianne Brandt, the Viennese contralto who introduced many late Wagnerian roles in America, and who was unquestionably among the first half dozen of magnificently voiced, intelligent Wagnerian interpreters. Until Brandt left the company, Ortrud was as clearly her property as it became that of Schumann-Heink, who, after using it as her American debut role, in Chicago, on November 7, 1898, likewise chose it for her first Metropolitan appearance, on the following January 9, when her associates were Jean de Reszke (Lohengrin), Nordica (Elsa), David Bispham (Telramund), and Édouard de Reszke (the King).

The De Reszkes sang Wagner in both German and Italian. *Lohengrin* had been the De Reszkes' first Wagnerian opera, when, on June 22, 1888, at Covent Garden, Jean sang Lohengrin, and Édouard the King. It was in these roles that they made their American debut, at the Chicago Auditorium, on November 9, 1891. Both of these performances were sung in Italian, as was that of December 5, 1894, when Jean headed a cast that included Nordica, Mantelli (Ortrud), Ancona (Telramund), and Plançon (the King). On January 2, 1896, however, the brothers sang in the German version of *Lohengrin*, assisted by Nordica, Brema, and Kaschmann. It was not unnatural, therefore, that Jean, who had made his New York debut as Lohengrin, chose that role for his farewell to the Metropolitan, on March 29, 1901, with Ternina, Schumann-Heink, Bispham, and Édouard.

As *Lohengrin*, up through the season of 1940-41, had been presented at the Metropolitan 269 times in fifty-two separate seasons —yielding only to *Aïda*, which has achieved 301 performances— it is impossible to mention even one twentieth of the famous artists who have sung it there.

Lohengrin is the best romantic opera ever written, and in many respects it is Wagner's finest—certainly his most nearly perfectly achieved—stage work. Here Wagner arrived at a rare equilibrium of his intensely demanding, often reciprocally nonco-operative talents as dramatist and composer. The book of *Lohengrin* is passable poetry and better drama; the music is perfectly expressive of the book, and chooses, moreover, a lofty but ingratiating lyricism—as distinct from mere easy melody—as its formula of expression. The story is not just breathless, episodical plot, neither is it distended by those soggy chunks of undigested philosophizing that slow up the action of Wagner's later stage pieces. In it, the crudities of *Rienzi* and the *Holländer* have been largely exorcised; so, too, the Latin echoes of *Tannhäuser* are no more. *Lohengrin* is a German work, and on that alone depends much of its exemplary unity. In it, Wagner finally quiets the restless shade of Weber: in it, German opera, as the composer of *Der Freischütz* conceived it, comes of age, and though Wagner, after *Lohengrin*, does not cease to consider himself the prophet of German music, his experiments become, nevertheless, the highly individual outpourings of an egocentric psyche. In *Lohengrin*, most of the drama is still taken up by the voice, though the powerful and brilliantly used orchestra, not yet smothering the singers' prerogatives, takes part in it to a degree unprecedented in the works of earlier composers.

After an impartial survey of Wagner's heroic achievement, it is impossible not to understand, and sympathize with, Ernest Newman's wistful summing up of his reactions to *Lohengrin*: "The Wagner of this period reaches the supreme height of his powers in *Lohengrin*; and as one watches that diaphanous and finely-spun melodic web unfold itself, one is almost tempted for the moment to regret that the daemon within him drove him on so relentlessly to another style."

Those who are not fully acquainted with the cranky theorist in Wagner, which is another name for the "daemon" that drove him on to the *reductio ad absurdum* of the *Ring*, find it hard to understand why he did not consider *Lohengrin* the sufficient earnest of his ideas. *Oper und Drama*, written just after the first performance of *Lohengrin*, helps to explain this apparently perverse flight from his own perfection. There he ventilated the oddly arbitrary ideas that the musician should be the servant of the poet, and that the poet should use only myth. *Lohengrin* still contains a tiny core of history, and in it the balance between music and drama is so subtly maintained, so ideally even, that the relentless application of theories could only destroy it. Musically, Wagner has by this time created a new instrument—a continuously unfolding web of sound evolved from a collection of brief leitmotivs susceptible to symphonic treatment. In *Lohengrin*, too, the orchestra in itself has become a wonderful medium of its own magic—a thing of varied hues and lights, predominantly shimmering in effect, brought about by using the separate timbres and colorations of the instrumental families in a way new to music. In *Lohengrin*, this sensuous agent is held justly in check, but the potentialities of its unleashing were so obvious that Wagner became intoxicated with them, though he surely never recognized this central fact in his later aesthetic.

A final proof of the real maturity of Wagner's operatic style in *Lohengrin* is that the opera as a totality is more attractive, has more Impact, than any one of its parts. The only flaw in its continuity is exactly when Wagner lapses into a careless, loose idiom from his past—this halt, as old-fashioned as anything in *Rienzi*, and far more wounding in an otherwise seasoned score like *Lohengrin*, is the humdrum, mock-joyous Bridal Chorus. The Prelude to Act III is less a lapse to an earlier idiom than a lapse in musical taste. Its appalling bumptiousness and rudeness of statement are all the more glaring because the opera opens with another Prelude that is beautifully proportioned and exquisitely expressed—an utterly perfect thing.

Lohengrin was, except for an inspired recession in *Die Meistersinger*, the last of Wagner's operas. *Tristan und Isolde* was the first of the music dramas to be produced, but as its *première* occurred fifteen years after that of *Lohengrin*, many important things had happened to Wagner in the intervening time. First among these was the conception of the *Ring*—a moment which, in the history of the arts, can be compared to Gibbon's decision to write *The Decline and Fall of the Roman Empire*. But whereas Gibbon, as he heard the monks singing the Roman service at the Ara Coeli, saw his idea whole, Wagner had been working on his a long time before he realized quite what he was doing. In 1848, two years before the Weimar production of *Lohengrin*, he wrote the poem of *Siegfrieds Tod*. Three years later, he realized, tardily, that an epic about Siegfried's

death and the twilight of the gods would not have the necessary impact unless it followed an earlier poem of the hero's
first exploits: *Der junge Siegfried* was the result.

The next year—1852—was big in eventfulness: Wagner met
Otto Wesendonck and his wife Mathilde, who for five years
were to be among the chief pawns in his dramatic quest of
love; he also, partly because of Mathilde's warm sympathy,
completed the poems of the *Ring*. He had begun to feel the
cyclic nature of his Siegfried story, and so to put himself somewhat in the position of his future audiences. Thus, he began to
ask himself questions about the parentage of the young Siegfried,* and realized that he had to tell the story of that incestu-
ous generation. And when he had told it, in *Die Walküre*, he
had a hunch that a basic motivation was needed to propel his
three poems on their proper path. The theft of the Rhinegold,
which started all the mischief, was therefore made the subject
of a further prefatory poem, *Das Rheingold*. Finally, after *Die
Walküre* and *Das Rheingold* had been written, in that order,
Wagner went back, and rewrote *Der junge Siegfried*, eventually
called *Siegfried*, and *Siegfrieds Tod*, eventually called *Die Götterdämmerung*. The entire epic, entitled *Der Ring des Nibelungen*, was printed in 1853 in a most luxurious format.

The poems of the *Ring* were written in reverse chronological order over a period of five years. The music, composed in
proper sequence, took twenty-one years to complete, and was,
moreover, interrupted by, among other things, the composition of two other stage works. Wagner began *Das Rheingold* in
1853, and finished scoring it in 1854. At once he set to work on
Die Walküre, and this he completed in 1856. The same year,
Siegfried was undertaken, and was well under way when, in
July, 1857, Wagner dropped it for eight years: his love for
Frau Wesendonck had burst the dike, and he became obsessed
by a desire to symbolize their yearnings in a music drama about
a, to him, similar pair of lovers—the legendary Tristan and
Isolde.

* In regard to Lohengrin, Wagner not only answers part of this same question
in *Lohengrin* itself, but answers it, rather more amply than necessary, in *Parsifal*,
his definitive life of Lohengrin's father. Who Lohengrin's mother was, however,
Wagner never made clear.

Under the love-filled glances of Mathilde (the Wagners had moved to the Asyl, a small house in the grounds of the Wesendonck estate in suburban Zurich), he was hectically active, though Mathilde was far from occupying his every waking thought. He labored on the poem of *Tristan und Isolde,* thought sporadically of Parsifal and the Grail legend, and wondered how he might rid himself of his wife. Some of the music to *Tristan* was composed before the inevitable explosion occurred. During the ensuing coolness, he completed the score, partly at Venice, partly at Lucerne. The last notes were scored on August 8, 1859. The next five years saw Wagner constantly on the move, struggling for place, harassed by debt, failing miserably in Paris again, and at last, unprecedentedly, beginning to question his unquestionable vocation. Yet, in the midst of this almost unalleviated anguish, he conceived the idea of *Die Meistersinger von Nürnberg* as a comic pendant to *Tannhäuser,* and even wrote the poem and composed the prelude and part of the first act before wearily laying the idea aside.

Suddenly, overnight, Wagner's situation changed. Called to Munich by the impulsive young Ludwig II of Bavaria, the fifty-year-old composer found himself the indulged and powerful male sultana of this strange monarch. Neither personally nor as an artist did he waste time. Having parted from his wife in 1862, he was soon having a love affair with a young woman who was the illegitimate daughter of one of his best friends and the legitimate wife of another—Cosima Liszt, who was married to a promising Saxon musician, Hans von Bülow. In 1865, Frau von Bülow bore Wagner a daughter, who was christened Isolde. Exactly two months later, with Von Bülow conducting, Munich was the scene of the earliest official triumph of Wagnerism, when *Tristan und Isolde,* almost six years old, was first performed. Had the reaction of the audience been decisive in determining Wagner's position or the future of *Tristan,* one might have been untenable, the other black. For that audience, faced with music that was really new, could only listen with polite, cold attention. It was Ludwig, again, who saved Wagner by his candidly shown effusiveness, accompanied by a command for three repetitions. With them, *Tristan* ended for several years: Ludwig Schnorr von Carolsfeld, the "heroic tenor" who had sung Tristan, died, and Wagner could find no one to replace him, even if Malwine Schnorr von Carolsfeld, the first Isolde, had consented to resume her role immediately with someone else in her husband's place.

In *Tristan und Isolde*, we are permitted to examine the most nearly perfect carrying out of Wagner's theories about music drama. The score has uninterrupted continuity: the old set numbers have now vanished completely, and even the division into acts is, for the first time, rather a method of giving musicians and audience chances to relax than a way of showing that one musicodramatic unit is over and another about to begin.* The ceaseless musical flow is apparently natural and spontaneous: in the Prelude, Wagner plants the seeds out of which the whole opera grows. In a drama whose central situation inevitably involves tremendous intensity of expressiveness, this technique of continual exfoliation is uncannily apt. So, too, is the chromatic harmony that produces constant, painfully gradual motion, a psychological inching along that is the musical artist's only *perpetuum mobile*, because it does not demand periodical resolutions that give the effect of full stops.

In *Tristan*, that story of incorrigible, forbidden passion, the pressure grows, the tension mounts, until human nature can no longer bear it. But Tristan and Isolde, though flesh, are also creatures of myth, and, more importantly, are the tempest-battered fantasms of Wagner's relentless imagination. Happily, the line of passion ebbs as well as surges, and thus the needed contrast that every work of art must have is supplied. Those parts of the score that have been excerpted widely—for instance, the *Liebesnacht* and the *Liebestod*—are simply those long moments when intensity multiplies itself for the consummate thrust. When so excerpted, they suffer from being torn from their context: they are the climaxes alone, without the reason and the result.

Tristan und Isolde overflows with beauty, and that beauty is of a very special and rarely created sort. It is a beauty set richly amid connotations of sexual craving and fulfillment, and

* Though Wagner's "curtains" are most often brilliantly timed.

so the reactions to it are bound to be more belligerently personal, more conditioned by experience, than those to most works of art. The most intelligent child in the world would find *Tristan* a mystery, and not at all the sort Wagner intended. Among those capable of understanding it fully, there will always be some who find it a salutary and healing purge; others will find it vaguely, yet agreeably, disturbing; still others will be disgusted. To these last, *Tristan und Isolde* is pornography. The average operagoer, equable in state of mind and point of view, is unlikely to be reduced to delirium or driven to moral outburst: to him, *Tristan* is tremulously beautiful, often exciting, but not without boring calms.

For it is on the purely musical level alone that *Tristan* is a nearly perfect carrying out of Wagner's theories. When the musician subordinates himself to the poet (doubtless in the belief that he is co-operating with him), the drama is in most peril. In short, the obligation of getting along with the story, of producing the central situations, involved Wagner in narrative doldrums that can be compared to the most mechanical passagework in a classical sonata. When the lovers are together on the stage, and the story tells itself, Wagner's theories collapse like a sand castle. Here the musician reigns, and Tristan and Isolde might as well be exchanging numbo-jumbo as the words they do exchange. The text is there, but only the music matters. Far from being poetry's handmaiden, the music of *Tristan* is gloriously self-sufficient, and ends by making us forget everything except itself. This is often doubly fortunate, for the lines Wagner gave to the protagonists even in the climaxes are, on occasion, drivel.

Announcement of the first London performance of *Tristan und Isolde*, for June 20, 1882, raised high expectations among critics, musicians, and operagoers. Hans Richter, who had been associated personally with Wagner, and who had taken upon himself the heavy burden of converting a skeptical England to the *Meister*'s gospel, conducted. Sucher was the Isolde, Winkelmann the Tristan, while Brandt, whom Wagner had pronounced ideal in the role, sang Brangäne. Both Sucher and Winkelmann were singing the lovers for the first time. The event produced a great, if mixed, impression. Herman Klein, then music critic of *The Sunday Times*, later wrote of his reactions: "My first action on regaining my mental equilibrium was to solemnly vow that I would never write another word in disparagement of Richard Wagner or his music so long as I lived." The performance left London an armed camp of critics spitting at each other, but nevertheless *Tristan*, rather than the previously produced *Meistersinger*, established the later Wagner as a staple of the English stage.

The American *première* of *Tristan*, on December 1, 1886, was, if anything, more of a sensation. Another Wagnerian apostle, Anton Seidl, conducted. Niemann and Lilli Lehmann were the guilty pair; Brandt was the Brangäne, Fischer the King Mark, and Adolf Robinson the Kurwenal. The relatively unimportant role of a sailor was assigned to Alvary. The opera was in every way a huge success: it was repeated seven times that season and was used to open the following one. Krehbiel led the chorus of excited Wagnerians who acted as if a new dispensation had arrived. Yet, exciting though these first performances were, *Tristan und Isolde* attained its greatest vogue in 1895, when Nordica and the De Reszkes, a trio as famous as the *"Puritani"* Quartet, began to sing in it. To their Isolde, Tristan, and King Mark, on November 27 of that year, Brema was the Brangäne, Kaschmann the Kurwenal. The honor of being the greatest of Tristans lies between Niemann and Jean de Reszke. On January 1, 1908, Olive Fremstad first sang Isolde, at Gustav Mahler's debut as a Metropolitan conductor, and went on to become one of the most admired interpreters of the role. (This versatile Swedish woman also tried to sing Brangäne, a role usually left to such deeper voices as Matzenauer's, Sigrid Onegin's, or Thorborg's, but never repeated the attempt.) In recent years, with the adored team of Flagstad and Melchior, *Tristan* has become such a favorite with New York audiences that it has often been the most frequently performed opera of a Metropolitan season.

Die Meistersinger von Nürnberg, Wagner's next produced opera, bears as curious a relation to his biography as *Tristan*. The latter is an opera of self-projection, Wagner confessing his passion across the footlights. *Die Meistersinger*, apparently the most detached, most objective, of all his later works, can be construed quite as autobiographically as *Tristan*. During the composition of most of it, Wagner was carrying on, and un-

questionably consummating, the most fervid love relationship
of his whole career. *Tristan* was the expression of desires either
not at all, or only clandestinely, fulfilled, while *Die Meistersinger* was completed after he had settled down, at Triebschen,
in Switzerland, with the woman who was to become his second
wife. There were as many legal barriers to a happy affair with
Cosima von Bülow as there had been to one with Mathilde
Wesendonck. But whereas Mathilde was adoring and timid,
Cosima was adoring and eager: the first was hedged in by bourgeois convention; the other, natural daughter of Franz Liszt,
was a willing accomplice. She and Wagner understood each
other perfectly at once and entered freely and without scruple
into the life they wanted—a life which, from their point of
view, turned out to be entirely satisfactory. With Mathilde, he
had had to cry out his passion unspent; no such need colored
his life with Cosima: in *Die Meistersinger*, there is, from his
new relationship, love bounteous and harvested.

As early as 1845, Wagner had dallied with the idea of a stage
work about Hans Sachs, the poet-cobbler of Nuremberg, but
it remained in seminal condition for sixteen years. By 1861,
when he began writing the poem of *Die Meistersinger*, the
original conception of a comic treatment of the same sort of
Sängerfest that had yielded such dramatic effects in *Tannhäuser*
was augmented by several other ideas connected intimately
with his artistic theories and the vicissitudes of his fortunes.
First, it was to glorify German art; second, it was to lampoon,
in the twisted figure of the maladroit Sixtus Beckmesser, those
critics, particularly Eduard Hanslick, a power of the Vienna
press, who were luckless enough to be anti-Wagnerian.

With unceasing gusto and great good spirits, Wagner rapidly wrote his best dramatic poem: it is humanly credible, is
truly funny, and is poetic throughout. The energy that served
him in this task carried him through the overture* and some
of Act I, at which point the combined drive of his trouble and
his ambitions carried him off on a tangent. When, after many

---

* Ernest Newman has pointed out, in Volume III of his masterly life of Wagner, that as the melody common to the overture and the *Preislied* was composed
before the present words of the *Preislied* were written, Wagner was here going
counter to his sacred rule that the music must in all cases grow from the poem.

wanderings and the episode with King Ludwig, he took up *Die Meistersinger* again, at Triebschen, in 1866, he finished it in little more than a year. Under a royal patronage manifestly less effulgent than that which had dictated the first performance of *Tristan, Die Meistersinger* had its *première* at Munich on June 21, 1868, with Von Bülow (still Cosima's husband) conducting, and with Richter in charge of the chorus. The cast, though all but unknown to compilers of musical dictionaries, was excellent—in fact, Edward Dannreuther, writing in 1889, said that it was the best Wagnerian performance that had ever been given.

Immediately, *Die Meistersinger* took the town, then Germany. And why should it not have? This lusty, heartily created big comedy of manners evoked the soul of sixteenth-century Germany. Everything about it was right, beginning with the locale: Nuremberg is the most flavorsome of towns, where a seen past lingers on every stone, and where even the least imaginative can call up the late-medieval atmosphere of guilds, journeymen, and apprentices. Again, the libretto was right, though to be so it had to break with some of Wagner's pet theories: there is no element of myth in *Die Meistersinger*, which is all human and credibly everyday historical. To a poem that carried conviction and radiated charm, Wagner added music of varied but always surpassing beauty and life. It was music that he could not have used to body forth the doings of gods and goddesses or even of superlovers like Tristan and Isolde. In order to create such music at all, he had to recede some distance from the ironclad theorizing that had produced *Tristan* and, constricted into dogma, was to challenge dissent in the *Ring* and *Parsifal*.

Die Meistersinger opens with an overture constructed, rather like that to *Tannhäuser*, on a few telling themes from the body of the opera, though treated with wonderful contrapuntal ingenuity. It is the old-fashioned potpourri overture, but so cannily contrived as to seem new. It is utterly appropriate to the largely good-natured entertainment that follows: curiously, in glorifying German art Wagner had returned to the old idea of opera as mere entertainment, but on a plane so lofty that no invidious comparisons could ever be made. For his purpose, a potent germ like the Prelude to *Tristan* would have been inappropriate. Too, he had chosen for much of the melodic idiom the type of song theme that the actual Meistersinger had sung, and had even introduced surviving historical melodies. Thus, while he continued the use of leitmotivs, he could not entwine these longer-phrased melodies into the sort of shifting, turning, ceaseless musical mesh that had been so logical for expressing the fatally indestructible passion of Tristan and Isolde. Also, the condition of his melodies called for predominantly diatonic harmony: periodical resolutions were inevitable, and a partial return to the old set-number scheme was concomitant. Finally, the primary plot requisite of a singing contest is a series of recognizable set numbers: thus, the young, lyrical *Preislied* quite correctly stands out from the rest of the music. However, unity is not sacrificed: the whole is simply not of one piece.

Each of Wagner's operas has, in addition to its essential Wagnerian something, a special quality that distinguishes it from the others. Thus, *Rienzi* is brash and gaudy, the *Holländer* somber and menacing, *Tannhäuser* exultant, festive, and contrite, *Lohengrin* lyric, light-shot, and noble, *Tristan* passionate and jungle-rich. *Die Meistersinger* is warm and earthily human: its joys, its high-singing raptures, its lighthearted wit, its lovingly mingled humor and wisdom, and even its satire, sometimes cruelly barbed, are human. Hans Sachs is one of the towering figures of the operatic stage, and in him Wagner most nearly approaches the German conception of the poet—the *Dichter* who speaks wisely for the race. His greatest moments, as in the magnificent monologue on the world's madness— *"Wahn! Wahn!"*—have the eloquence of speech and the power of music. Yet Sachs, though his amplitude of understanding can encompass the world, never alone reaches the plane that Wagner reserved, with wonderful dramatic sense and sympathy, for the quintet in the last act, one of the supreme concerted numbers of all opera. Here, with the *Volk* standing symbolically on the side lines, Sachs and the two pairs of lovers he has befriended hymn their mutual joys in rhapsodic cantillation.

It is the most impressive outpouring of that communal spirit which is diffused throughout the entire opera, and which Wagner expresses in such different ways as the purposely clumsy, peasantlike Dance of the Apprentices, with its comical stumbling rhythms, and the pompous ceremonial March of the Meistersinger, perfect music for self-sufficient men of good will engaged in civic festival.

It was in German, on May 30, 1882, that *Die Meistersinger* was first given in London. That night, the Drury Laners heard Sucher as Eva, Winkelmann as Walther, and Eugen Gura, a famous *Ring* baritone at Bayreuth, in the leading role of Sachs. Richter conducted, and magnificently. Seven years later, to mark Jean de Reszke's growing interest in Wagnerian roles, Covent Garden staged an Italian version in which, according to Bernard Shaw, Jean's singing was far better than his understanding of the part of Walther. The top honors of this performance of *I Maestri cantori* went to Lassalle, the Sachs, and to Albani, the Eva. Meanwhile, three years earlier, on January 4, 1886, the ambitious Seidl had trotted out an uneven cast for the Metropolitan *première* of the German version, which, because of its excessive length, was much cut—to this day a complete *Meistersinger* has never been heard at the Metropolitan. In the cast were Fischer (Sachs), Seidl-Kraus (Eva), and Brandt (Magdalena), with most of the other roles taken by relatively second-flight artists. The work was repeated seven times that season. Given twenty-eight times in German in the course of six seasons, it was kept in the repertoire when the Italian regime took over in the fall of 1891. Then New York heard almost precisely the same stars who had sung *I Maestri cantori* at Covent Garden in 1889. On March 25, 1901, the De Reszkes having for some time increased their fame by singing Wagner in German, the Metropolitan presented their first German *Meistersinger*, with Jean a more understanding Walther, and Édouard a lusty Sachs; Gadski was the Eva, Schumann-Heink the Magdalena, and Bispham the Beckmesser. This performance was just four days before Jean's Metropolitan farewell. In recent years, Schorr's interpretation of Sachs has outdistanced all rivals.

Except for a brief spell right after the first performance of *Tristan*, Wagner did not take up the *Ring* seriously again until after the first hearing of *Die Meistersinger* in 1868. Here, de-

spite a growing coolness on Ludwig's part, the fact that the
monarch had shared his box with the composer, besides the
patent enthusiasm of the people for his music, doubtless gave
Wagner some hope that his vast four-part music drama, if composed, would have a chance to be produced. By September,
1869, he had completed the preliminary score of *Siegfried*, and
the next month had begun *Die Götterdämmerung*, which, after
some interruptions, was finished in full score by November,
1874. As Wagner had in the meantime completed the full
score of *Siegfried*, that date meant the achievement of a project
on which he had been engaged, in one way or another, for
twenty-six years.

It was Wagner's desire, nay, his determination, to give the
Ring only in cyclic form, and in a theater built especially for its
production, but the Bavarian king was equally determined to
hear the separate parts, on which he justifiably felt he had a
lien. Thus, it was by royal command that *Das Rheingold* was
sung at Munich, on September 22, 1869, and that *Die Walküre*
was sung there on the following June 26. But that was as far
as Ludwig got: by the time the next two scores were ready, the
specifically designed Festspielhaus was well in process of erec-
tion at the little Bavarian town of Bayreuth. After heroic
struggles by Wagner, his friends, and his well-wishers all over
the world, the money for the completion of the theater and
Wagner's adjacent home—Wahnfried—was finally got together.* When the first Bayreuth festival was announced for
1876, the theater was far from ready, and for a time there was
some doubt that the necessary funds would be forthcoming.
But by the fanatically determined Wagner, obstacles were cut
down as they arose. (His natural choler stopped short of apo-
plexy even when he found that the dragon ordered for *Siegfried* had been sent to Beyrouth, in Syria, by mistake.) Finally,
the invitations were released with a feeling of certainty that
the invited notables stood an excellent chance of hearing the

* A fraction—$5000—of the more than $250,000 needed for the theater alone
came from the *American Centennial March* Wagner wrote in 1876 for the world's
fair at Philadelphia.

four scheduled performances. The composer's luck held, and the Festspielhaus opened on August 13, 1876.

As a less conspicuously stellar cast had been assembled for *Das Rheingold*, the "fore-evening" of the *Ring* trilogy, than for each of the following music dramas, which are peopled by the more important characters of the epic cycle, the audience had its best chance not only to listen to the strange sounds issuing from singers and orchestra and to watch the odd antics of the players, but also to survey the house itself, and to realize that half the brilliance and high society of Europe was there. Richter conducted (as he did throughout the festival), and in addition to Heinrich Vogl, a famous early Tristan, as Loge, Franz Betz, who had created Sachs, as Wotan, and Gura as Donner, Lilli Lehmann, swimming next to her sister Marie, sang the relatively unimportant role of Woglinda, a Rhinemaiden. To her fell the dangerous honor of warbling the doggerel lines with which the great machinery of the *Ring* begins to move: *"Weia! Wage! Woge, du Welle, walle zur Wiege! wagala weia! wallala, weiala weia!"*

In *Die Walküre*, given on August 14, the Brünnhilde was Materna, the Siegmund was Niemann, and the Lehmann sisters again sang minor roles; Wagner's niece Johanna, now turned fifty, and with her great days well behind her, had a bit part. The guests were then given a day's breathing spell, and, on August 16, the festival was resumed with *Siegfried*. This, unlike the first two, was a world *première*, and Georg Unger, hand-picked by Wagner, had the title role, with Materna and Betz in their parts as before. Finally, on August 17, the last of the cycle, *Die Götterdämmerung*, brought forward, besides Materna and Unger, Gura in the new role of Gunther, Johanna Wagner as a Norn, and the Lehmanns again as Rhinemaidens.

After *Die Götterdämmerung*,* that unparalleled audience dispersed to talk and write about the most controversial event in the whole history of opera. They left Wagner, at the age of sixty-three, the most discussed artist alive, and with a deficit of $30,000.

It is not recorded how many of the fifteen hundred guests

* The entire *Ring* was repeated twice during the balance of the festival.

left the first *Ring* in dazzled but puzzled rumination, but as that is the effect the *Ring* still has on its novices, probably a large percentage departed from Bayreuth in that state. The *Ring*, if played continuously, would last something over twelve hours, and understanding it depends upon a fund of complex special knowledge that is imparted as the dramas unfold. Listening intelligently to the *Ring* can be no idle pastime: the mind must ever be alert, the ear sharply attuned. Nor can the dreamily closed eye, that favorite device of passionate music lovers, be indulged: details of costume, scene shifting, and gesture are freighted with meanings whose comprehension is essential to the understanding of the action. As the *Ring* is Wagner's most audaciously thoroughgoing experiment in the use of leitmotivs, naturally every one of them must be understood not only when it first appears alone, but also when it reoccurs changed, twisted, and contrapuntally joined with one or more other leitmotivs. This would be difficult enough if there were ten or a dozen to keep in the head, but thirty appear in *Das Rheingold* alone, and there are sixty more to be struggled with before the curtains close on *Die Götterdämmerung*. In addition to the musical and dramatic meanings conveyed by the sights and sounds, Wagner intended them to have philosophical and symbolical ones.

Listening to the *Ring*, therefore, is at first a task. Assuming, however, that we have familiarized ourselves, by constant, attentive listening and watching, supplemented by many hours of collateral reading in the compendious *Ring* literature, and by playing over and over again the special disks devoted exclusively to drumming the leitmotivs into eager heads, with the entire machinery of the cycle, what do we have when it is all over? Not, all too clearly, that one supersynthesis of all the arts which Wagner intended. There was a time when our not having that supersynthesis was blamed upon the always faulty, frequently ridiculous way of staging the *Ring*, particularly outside Bayreuth. But even Wagnerians have now largely discarded that excuse.

No performance of the *Ring* could so hypnotize the informed listener as to hide the gross crudities of the four-part poem that serves as its libretto: it is repetitious, often gaseous, often silly. The fact that it was written backwards compelled Wagner to synopsize the earlier action of the dramas he had still to write. He composed the music itself in correct sequence, but did not excise the synopses in the poems as he fitted them to music. The result is that the audience has often to listen to long monologues in which one of the characters retells what has already taken place on the stage. Other monologues, as well as an occasional dialogue, expound none too original chunks of philosophy, during which the action goes completely to sleep: it was no wit, but a hardheaded thinker, who remarked that Wagner mistook the epic for the dramatic. A logical outcome of this odd error is Wagner's emphasis on certain elemental figures— Wotan, Erda, the dragon Fafner, and the dwarf Alberich, for example—who have no means of communicating humanly with the audience.* In the *Ring* poem there is enough truly dramatic material for two good librettos, which as it stands is distributed through hours and hours of quite undramatic verbiage.

As Wagner was an inspired musical translator, and as he earnestly set every word, phrase, and nuance of his poem, the music of the *Ring*, as an entity, suffers from the selfsame faults that vitiate the libretto. Where the poems are dull, the music is dull; where they flash into life, or where they lead naturally into a lyric interlude, Wagner does not miss his chance, and becomes, as necessity dictates, a supreme musical dramatist, a protean tone poet—in short, a program symphonist without equal. The *Ring* is necessarily a most spotty performance, rather like a transcontinental journey from New York to California, with all the variability of landscape, unfortunately so much of it poor. But there are canyons and torrents, grand mountains, mighty rivers—and these keep us going to the *Ring* long past the first time we say that the whole damn thing should be condensed into concert performance. Even four evenings of the *Ring* are not too much if measured in terms of the high spots

---

* Wagner's insistence on working exclusively with myth thus served to hoist him on his own petard. The epic figures whose tragedy is their humanness bear the focus of audience interest throughout the entire *Ring*, even when Wagner planned his specific situations otherwise.

it would otherwise take five to ten years of steady concertgoing
to hear.

Between the Prelude to *Das Rheingold* and the last stupendous half-hour of *Die Götterdämmerung* occur some of
the most magnificent passages in not only opera, but all music.
They are orchestral passages pure and simple, whether the
voice takes part in them or not: by the time Wagner was composing the *Ring*, he had come to treat the voice as but one of
the most important instruments of a tremendously expanded
orchestra. In practice, he had unconsciously completed a right-
about-face: far from making music (and the other arts) hand-
maidens of poetry, he had stifled them all under a passion for
symphonic sound. As thinker, stage revolutionary, poet, Wagner is already a tarnished figure: as musician, he is secure among
the great. Fashion may tend to diminish his vogue, but never
in the degree that it has diminished the vogue of a Bellini or
a Meyerbeer: they were occasionally composers of great opera,
but Wagner was, and more than occasionally, the composer of
great music. In *Lohengrin, Tristan, Die Meistersinger,* and
parts of the *Ring*, he added enduringly to the artistic heritage
of the ages.

The first cyclic performance of *Der Ring des Nibelungen* outside Bayreuth occurred, both in England and in the United States,
after separate performances of some of its component parts had
been given. Angelo Neumann, in 1882, convinced the reluctant
Meister of the practicability of touring Europe with a *Ring* stock
company. Wagner, though shocked by the sacrilege, succumbed
to the dazzle of possible profit. It was the Neumann troupe that
carried the cycle to Austria, Italy, Paris, and London, where, on
May 5, 1882, the English first heard the *Ring* entire. Except for
Hedwig Reicher-Kindermann, who had sung only a minor part
at the 1876 Bayreuth performances, and was now promoted to be
the Brünnhilde, most of the leading artists from that epochal
world *première*—Niemann, Unger, Vogl, and Lilli Lehmann—sustained their original roles.

Die Walküre was the first section of the *Ring* to reach America.
In that sadly truncated, badly given performance at the New York
Academy of Music, on April 2, 1877, Pappenheim was the Brünn-
hilde. Bad as it was, it was doubly historic, being the first time

any part of the *Ring* was given outside Germany. The real American "first" took place at the Metropolitan, on January 30, 1885, under Leopold Damrosch, with the Bayreuth Brünnhilde in the person of Materna, whose principal colleagues were Seidl-Kraus, Brandt, Anton Schott, and Josef Staudigl. Two years later, on November 9, 1887, *Siegfried* had its Metropolitan *première*. Seidl conducted, the chief roles being taken by Lilli Lehmann (Brünnhilde), Seidl-Kraus (the Forest Bird), Brandt (Erda), Alvary (Siegfried), and Fischer (Wotan). Ten weeks later, on January 25, *Die Götterdämmerung*, also under Seidl's baton, followed, with Lehmann again as Brünnhilde, Seidl-Kraus (Gutrune), Brandt, Traubmann, and Louise Meisslinger (Rhinemaidens), Niemann (Siegfried), Robinson (Gunther), and Fischer (Hagen). Then, on January 30, 1888, the Metropolitan did an extraordinary thing: it began a cyclic production of the *Ring* without *Das Rheingold*, which had to wait until January 4, 1889, for its *première*, with Alvary and Fischer, respectively Loge and Wotan, heading the cast. Finally, on the following March 4, began the first complete cyclic performance of the *Ring* in America, with Seidl on the podium, and Lehmann, Alvary, and Fischer taking the leading roles.*

Among recent performers at the Metropolitan, Flagstad is notable for her Sieglinde and Brünnhilde, and it was in the former role that the phenomenally popular Norwegian made her American debut on February 2, 1935. On the afternoon of January 11, 1936, Marjorie Lawrence, an excellent Brünnhilde, astounded the audience by mounting her steed and riding from the stage—a custom that she has continued. Melchior has been equally famous as Siegmund and Siegfried. Schorr's Wotan is as much part of Metropolitan tradition as his Hans Sachs. These are, of course, only the current (1941) interpreters of these roles, for the honor of singing which the greatest artists of the German wing have competed. Some outside it, like the De Reszkes, whose early successes were made in Italian and French opera, lived to become as applauded

---

* Seidl had a reasonable prejudice against uncut versions of the *Ring*, and none was given under his regime. After he left, Franz Schalk, a Viennese conductor, in the season of 1898-99, initiated the pious but ill-advised course of giving the *Ring* in its pristine entirety. The Schalk idea was revived on February 21, 1930, by Artur Bodanzky, who held the first-day audience in their seats for two hours and a half without an intermission. As *Das Rheingold* is the shortest of the *Ring*, what followed tried the patience even more. Yet, such is the popularity of Wagner in New York that this barbarous custom has been adhered to ever since.

in Wagnerian roles: for example, Jean for years was the favorite Siegfried, Édouard the favorite Wotan or Hagen.

Their debuts in *Siegfried,* on December 30, 1896, brought laurels to the De Reszkes, but disgrace to their Brünnhilde, and serious trouble to the Grau management. Lillian Nordica, who had once cowed the formidable Cosima Wagner into letting her future husband, an indifferent Hungarian tenor named Zoltán Doeme, sing Parsifal at Bayreuth, failed to convince Grau that he should not give Melba exclusive rights, for a whole year, to the role of Brünnhilde, and angrily left the company for two years. She had her revenge. Melba sang Brünnhilde, and very badly, so hurting her voice in the attempt that she had to retire from the stage for a long rest. The final irony of the situation lies in the story that her singing Brünnhilde at all came about through a misconception of Jean de Reszke's recommendation that she sing in *Siegfried:* it seems that he had intended to advise her selection as the Voice of the Forest Bird—a warbling part that would have suited her admirably—and not as Wotan's lusty-throated daughter. Melba's teacher, the great Marchesi, had warned her against attempting Brünnhilde, but she had persisted. About the resulting disaster, she wrote candidly in her memoirs: "The music was too much for me. I felt as though I were struggling with something beyond my strength. I had a sensation almost of suffocation, of battling with some immense monster. . . ."*

An artist rarely concludes his life with his biggest work, much less with his most nearly perfect. After the mighty *Ring,* after the comparative flawlessness of *Lohengrin, Tristan,* and *Die Meistersinger,* Wagner, though ill and weary, was not content to rest until he had added a religious music drama to the already imposing list of his works. The theme of salvation had haunted him all his life, appearing in one form or another in every one of his operas from *Rienzi* on, sometimes, as in *Tannhäuser,* supplying the mainspring of the drama, sometimes, as in *Die Meistersinger,* developed as only one of many motives. Now, when his life was petering out, and he had achieved per-

---

* *Siegfried* was the setting of another Metropolitan casualty of a quite different nature. On March 19, 1925, Curt Taucher, singing the name role, stepped into an open trap door, and disappeared from view. He fell twenty feet, and was so bruised that, though he finished his performance, he sang little during the rest of the season.

sonal beatification,* he was in the mood to turn again to this idea, and give it a more pious twist. His mind was crowded with the religious lore of the ages, from Buddhism to Christianity. It was crowded, too, with fragments of various philosophies, including many dubious ideas of his own.

As far back as 1845, Wagner had considered a poem about the Holy Grail and the perfect, spotless knight who found it— Parsifal, the father of Lohengrin. Twenty years later, as a favor to Ludwig of Bavaria, who was entranced by the idea, he sketched the story, though not in poetic form. The apotheosis at Bayreuth was the impetus needed to produce the actual libretto. This was completed in April, 1877, and published the same year. Composition progressed slowly: Wagner was constantly ailing, and, besides, was engaged in a struggle to pay off the Bayreuth deficit and raise money for another festival. But by January, 1882, the second festival was assured, and *Parsifal*, which was to be its only attraction, was finished. By late spring, rehearsals were in progress, and on July 26, at a private performance that ranked high among the social events of that year, *Parsifal* had its world *première*. Winkelmann created the title role, Materna that of the sorceress Kundry,† while Emil Scaria, Karl Hill, and Theodor Reichmann were Gurnemanz, Klingsor, and Amfortas respectively. Conducting was Hermann Levi, a Jew whom the intermittently anti-Semitic Wagner had inconsistently chosen to usher in this holy Christian mystery.

Because of its quasi-religious character, Wagner did not wish to have *Parsifal* performed outside Bayreuth: there the special facilities for its production had been brought into being under his own supervision, and there, too, a tradition of reverence had, from its first performance, clung to this last of the *Meister*'s music dramas. Yet, there is evidence that, toward the end of 1882, he had so

* Did not Wahnfried, Wagner's home, stand in relation to the Festspielhaus much as the bishop's house does to a cathedral?

† Adelina Patti made the incredible statement that Wagner had composed the role of Kundry for her. According to the diva, she declined the honor because the sorceress has "too much screeching" to do. Almost as incredible is the story that Mary Garden, with her frail, subtle voice, once had designs on the role—doubtless a singing actress', not a singer's, yearning.

relaxed his point of view that he was willing to give Angelo Neumann a contract to take *Parsifal* on tour. He died, however, on February 13, 1883, without giving Neumann the precious document. Frau Cosima, *plus royaliste que le roi,* was fanatical in her efforts to restrict stage performances to Bayreuth. Oratorio versions and concert excerpts were another matter, and almost at once advantage was taken of this concession. During the Edmond C. Stanton regime at the Metropolitan occurred, on March 4, 1886, under Walter Damrosch, the first oratorio presentation of *Parsifal* in America, the principals, including Brandt and Fischer, singing in German; the Oratorio Society chorus sang in English.

Late in 1886, Stanton played with the idea of giving *Parsifal* as an opera, but was dissuaded by, among others, Lilli Lehmann, who considered the scheme a sacrilege. It was therefore shelved for fifteen years, when Conried, desiring something unusual for his first season at the Metropolitan, determined to brook all protest, and scheduled *Parsifal*, as a music drama, for Christmas Eve, 1903. It was a publicity move of genius: ministers thundered at him from their pulpits, Mayor Seth Low was asked to intervene, and the Wagner family, through their American representative, brought suit against Conried. But he was unmoved, confident in his knowledge that Wagner's operas were not protected by copyright in the United States. He won the suit, and produced the opera in an atmosphere of excitement comparable to that attending the election of a president. Fannie Bloomfield Zeisler, the pianist, chartered a special "Parsifal" Limited from Chicago, and the New York *Evening Telegram* brought out a "Parsifal" extra. At the *première*, Alfred Hertz conducted, with Ternina (Kundry) and Aloys Burgstaller (Parsifal) heading a fine cast, including Anton Van Rooy, Marcel Journet, Robert Blass, Otto Goritz, and Louise Homer. The performance went off magnificently, and ten repetitions were called for that season. Only the new Italian tenor, Enrico Caruso, measured up to the furore created by *Parsifal*. Since then, despite its great length and difficulties of staging, *Parsifal* has been out of the Metropolitan only those two years when German art was being excoriated along with the Kaiser. It has become a fixture of the Lenten season.* In recent years, Flag-

* During Gatti-Casazza's first season at the Metropolitan, *Parsifal* was apparently an integral outgrowth of American history, for of the five performances during 1908-09, three took place on Thanksgiving, Lincoln's Birthday, and Washington's Birthday.

stad and Melchior have been the Kundry and Parsifal, Schorr the Amfortas.

In *Parsifal*, most of Wagner's great qualities have ripened beyond palatability. He had set himself a task of integration too much for the solving genius of mortal man. The poem is a rope of shoddy, with the luminosity of *Tristan* and much of the *Ring* turned to the phosphorescence of decay. In it, "You see," according to James Gibbons Huneker, "a lot of women-hating men, deceiving themselves with spears, drugs, old goblets, all manners of juggling formulas, and yet being waited upon by a woman—a poor, miserable witch. . . . In Act II, you are transported to the familiar land of Christmas pantomime. There a bad magician seems to destroy the castle of the noble knights, and evokes a beautiful phantom to serve his purpose. There are spells, incantations, blue lights, screaming that makes the blood run cold. . . ."

In short, *Parsifal* is sillier—and far more pretentious—than *Die Zauberflöte*. Through episodes fit only for one of those interminable Italian marionette shows which depict Boiardo or Ariosto down to the last comma, the guileless Parsifal wanders in sickly innocence, while the voice of that ancient man Gurnemanz endlessly explains. How could anyone, how could even Wagner, make a credible music drama out of this sanctimonious, neurotic, and completely undigested twaddle?

Thus, *Parsifal*, even more than the *Ring*, has to be judged on the merits of its music alone. And as music it suffers from defects as grave as, and not very different from, those of the libretto. All the portentous machinery that oftentimes worked miracles with the unpromising episodes of the *Ring* is here set in motion with singularly stale and flat results. It is set in motion, but nothing moves. The wheels go around—the leitmotivs appear, develop, and intermingle; the huge orchestra is made drunk with color and winey harmony; the scenery itself has an unholy life of its own: for five hours the gyroscopic action continues. The musical miracle fails to take place. Either these legends, rituals, philosophies, did not really move Wagner or, as some critics have hinted, his creative power had so failed

with his health that little was left him except the dry bones
of his theories and his amazing technique. His sensuous evocations have become shrill and strident, as if the creator himself
had sickened of passion. And the contrasting purity—the themes
given to Parsifal himself—is of a pale and negative hue that
has as little relation to childlike innocence as to masculine
self-denial. The lapses into straight narrative exposition—always a weakness with Wagner—in *Parsifal* stultify the action
completely. Hours of the music drama are plain dreary. Nor
can much of the whole be salvaged, for even the recognized high
spots tend to flounder in this slough of musical despond. The
Good Friday Spell, for instance, has, for all its beauty of statement, so low a vitality that the result, after several dozen measures, is so much maunder. Compare the Prelude, the best music
in *Parsifal*, with that to *Lohengrin*: the latter is a flood of light,
the former a memory of that light. One is the sun, the other a
glimmer of candles, well out of the open air. That, finally, is
Parsifal, the creation of a weary sorcerer poring wearily over
musty books.

Parsifal supplied Wagner with the final opportunity of forcing upon the public, without the slightest qualification, a conception of opera so radical that Bayreuth had had to be built to
demonstrate it. Not only was the subject matter calculated to
inspire a reverential attitude, but all the circumstances of its
production were focused in the same direction. To Wagner,
the audience was as much a participant in a perfect presentation
of a music drama as the rest of his forces: it was to provide the
appropriate ambience, the atmosphere, without which the
music drama could not, in fact, be performed successfully.
Moving away from the conception of opera as entertainment,
he substituted one of lofty, ritualistic seriousness. Since he
thought of the works of his maturity as syntheses of all the arts,
and therefore wholly enriching, he did not think it too much
to ask special conduct and complete concentration from his
audience.

At Bayreuth, every small detail was prearranged with an eye
toward unity of effect, even the musical themes to be played for
reassembling the audience after intermissions being stipulated

by Wagner. He supervised everything about productions, with the exception of drilling orchestra and chorus—that function was, however, safely in the hands of men who had dedicated their very existence to the service of Wagner's ideals. Not content with being the first composer of operas to set only librettos of his own writing, and with having designed, down to the smallest acoustical detail, a great hall especially adapted to his music, Wagner ordered the scenery, designed the costumes, chose the singers, and made mandatory minutiae of voice and gesture. Applause and encores would have marred the continuity of the Wagnerian drama: they were banished. For the same reason, latecomers were not admitted until intermission. This was a long way, indeed, from the days when people had license to cook spaghetti in their loges, play chess, or indulge in chatter that drowned out whatever was coming from the orchestra pit and the stage. Unpermitted in Wagner's operas were the irrelevancies of virtuoso singers—even the spoiled Alvary could not sing an encore, add a special passage of vocal flourish, or interpolate some music he and the audience happened to like. The most practical commandments of Wagner in respect to conduct of both performers and audience still hold good in the best-run opera houses and concert halls, and thus guarantee to the modern music lover a chance to listen undisturbed.

Ironically, Wagner founded so short-lived a school of opera that it can scarcely be said to have an existence at all. *Hänsel und Gretel* (1893), the best opera of Engelbert Humperdinck, most notable of his unquestioning disciples, is not recognizably Wagnerian to the average listener, so cleverly is the idiom watered down for the child consumer. It is, of course, a masterpiece of its kind.* Curiously, the only other even partially successful operas modeled earnestly on the Wagnerian *Aesthetik* were by Frenchmen—Ernest Reyer's *Sigurd* (1884) and *Salammbô*

---

* *Hänsel und Gretel* was, on Christmas, 1931, the first opera to be broadcast from the stage of the Metropolitan. This performance was notorious for the excessive bad taste of NBC in having the commentator speak while the music was in progress. The radio career of Humperdinck's delicious fairy tale has been unfortunate. Its charmingly fresh Prayer has been rendered nauseating by its constant repetition as the opening theme of the Ford Sunday Evening Hour.

(1890) and Vincent d'Indy's *Fervaal* (1897), none of them musically of the first order. Richard Strauss was undilutedly Wagner in his first try at opera, *Guntram* (1894), but after that his derivations became more indiscriminate. What Wagner gave most effectively to opera *per se* were liberty and scope, not, primarily, modes of expression or, fortunately, subject matter.* Music in general was his real heir. Full discussion of his estate and of the way it has been used is outside the province of this book: suffice it to say that no composer since Wagner has been uninfluenced either in harmony or orchestration by his revolutionary practice.

* One full-fledged Wagnerian disciple, August Bungert, did try an epic cycle of four music dramas, the books of which were adaptations of episodes from Homer. One of them, *Odysseus Heimkehr*, was mildly successful, and Bungert suggested that he, too, should have his Festspielhaus, but in vain.

Chapter XVI

A Perfect Opera

BORN a quarter of a century later that Wagner, and living little more than half as long, the unpretentious and bourgeois Bizet left, besides heaps of journeyman's work in many forms, one perfect opera. Wagner entertained the most exaggeratedly romantic conception of the artist and his sacred calling that the world has ever seen. R. G. Collingwood might have been thinking of him when, in his amusingly perspicacious *The Principles of Art*, he wrote: "In the later nineteenth century the artist walked among us as a superior being, marked off even by his dress from common mortals; too high and ethereal to be questioned by others, too sure of his superiority to question himself, and resenting the suggestion that the mysteries of his craft should be analyzed and theorized about by philosophers and other profane persons." Bizet was as old-fashioned, and as prosaic, as the Greeks and Romans about his art, which to him, as to them, meant, "a craft or specialized form of skill, like carpentry or smithying or surgery." He wrote no tracts, expounded no theories. He did not ventilate philosophical or religious profundities in his music. In his cool and clearheaded understanding of what constitutes a musician's role, he did his jobs as they came along as well as he knew how. He adhered quite frankly to the old pre-Beethovian attitude toward secular music as something that should be essentially entertaining. In that hardheaded, unsentimental point of view, Bizet was rather like a latterday Haydn.

Had Bizet been innately a romantic, the circumstances of his early career might have turned his head. A child prodigy, he was admitted to the Conservatoire at the age of nine, reaping a considerable harvest of medals. When not yet twenty, he won in rapid succession Offenbach's prize for a one-act operetta for the Bouffes Parisiens* and the Prix de Rome, among the judges

---

* Bizet divided the prize money with Alexandre Lecocq (1832-1918), who later scored huge sucesses with *La Fille de Mme Angot* and *Giroflé Girofla*. The winning compositions ran alternately at the Bouffes for a brief time.

in the former contest being Scribe and Bizet's future father-in-law, the composer Halévy. His three years in Rome resulted in an uninspired batch of student work, though *Don Procopio*, a two-acter of that period, was given as a curiosity during the Monte Carlo season of 1906. Another trial flight was accepted by the Comique, but not by its composer, who destroyed the score. It was not until 1863 that he produced an opera of any importance, that being *Les Pêcheurs de perles*.

Staged at the Théâtre Lyrique on September 29, 1863, *Les Pêcheurs* caused average comment, and was forgotten after a polite interval, to be revived after Bizet's name had become known throughout the world. Philadelphia was, in 1893, the first American city to hear it. On January 11, 1896, it reached the Metropolitan in a truncated two-act version, with Calvé (Leila), Cremonini (Nadir), Ancona (Zurga), and Édouard de Reszke (Nourabad). As it signally failed to please, the Metropolitan withdrew it after a single performance, and did not try it again for twenty years, when, on November 13, 1916, it was used in its entirety to open the season. But even the four-star cast of Hempel, Caruso, De Luca, and Rothier could not establish it, and after three performances it disappeared permanently.

Les Pêcheurs de perles is a hodge-podge of commonplaces, time-tried orientalisms, Italianisms that include an echo of a Verdi who had reached all but his most mature utterances, and the honeyed phrases of an assiduous Gounod pupil. The libretto is feeble, and the characters are sticks. Even so, the score is not worthless. In the midst of much that is perfunctory and derivative, there are evidences of a composer of vigor, imagination, and dramatic power. Further, there are moments of lyric beauty, points of color and song, and a way with themes that point to the future composer of *L'Arlésienne* and *Carmen*.

In almost every way, *Les Pêcheurs* is superior to Bizet's next opera,* *La Jolie Fille de Perth*, which has been described nastily as "a long way after Scott." It was written to order for the Théâtre Lyrique, which had made a fair profit out of *Les*

* Next, that is, of his surviving operas: something called *Ivan le terrible* was composed for the Lyrique in 1865, but withdrawn and destroyed by the composer in a fit of healthy self-criticism. An extant fragment reads like a pastiche of Verdi.

Pêcheurs. The new score, produced in 1867, was much less successful, and silenced Bizet's operatic muse for several years. The failure of *La Jolie Fille* was not entirely Bizet's fault, though he cannot be absolved from setting the impossible libretto drawn from one of Scott's poorest novels. Bizet's Scotsmen are as Italian as Donizetti's, and that he managed to obtain a flickering half-life for some of them was a small triumph. Musically, *La Jolie Fille* is of so little distinction, is such a mosaic of the derived, that it is dead beyond power of revival. It lies, moreover, outside Bizet's line of development: a flash of vigorous characterization, a growing facility in the handling of choral masses—and that is all that is needed for the record.

As of the close of the year 1869, Bizet's prospects were not much above those of a talented hack. He had just married the daughter of his old friend and teacher Halévy, who had died seven years before, and in an access of filial piety, he had undertaken to complete the score of his father-in-law's last opera, *Noë.* This Biblical extravaganza wanted orchestration and a last act, both of which Bizet supplied with flaccid adequacy. His creative energies were being frittered away on arranging other men's work for a living and on salon pieces of the utmost triviality. The big career open to him seemed to be that of a pianist, though even at this dark period the ailing Berlioz was sufficiently perspicacious to note that Bizet had to be taken into account primarily as a composer: others dismissed him as a brilliant runner-up to Saint-Saëns, another acclaimed piano virtuoso whose operatic triumphs were in the future.

Yet, two years were to change Bizet, the chief influences being his very happy marriage and the horrors of the Franco-Prussian War and the Commune. The first brought him not only a sympathetic and intelligent wife, but also her considerable inheritance, which freed him from the sordid and petty tasks of Paris' frightfully underpaid Grub Street. The second made him think not only of life and art in general, but also of his own life and art. He had served some time as a fusilier, and had witnessed many bloody scenes. When the Commune had slaughtered its last victims, and he was able to move to a pleasant country house, a new Bizet, more serious, and with an increased

understanding of the realities of life, entered upon a thoughtful phase of a career that had previously been lived in scatterbrained half-consciousness. Fortunately, his experiences did not
turn him into a solemn, nondoing theorist, for he retained
intact his native balance and *esprit*, and never allowed his seriousness, particularly about himself, to weigh him—or his creations—down.

The change was quickly evident. Early in 1871, a commission
from the Comique resulted in a neatly executed little masterpiece of pointed humor. *Djamileh*, based on a poem by De
Musset, did not enjoy a dramatic libretto, but at least it was
easy to follow and had some sparkle in its language. Bizet
worked tirelessly at it for several months, and on May 22, 1872,
the first real sample of his rapidly maturing style was offered
to the Parisians. They stood *Djamileh* for only four performances, despite a kind and encouraging press. The indifference
of the public enraged Saint-Saëns, who wrote: "The ruminating
bourgeois, pot-bellied and ugly, sits in his narrow stall, regret-
ting separation from his kind; he half opens a glassy eye,
munches a bon-bon, then sleeps again, thinking that the
orchestra is a-tuning." The discreet boldness of the score, some
of which was stigmatized as Wagnerism by the critics (who used
the term to cover every deviation from textbook rule), was
doubtless responsible for some of the public apathy and annoyance. Also, the libretto, frankly immoral, may have shocked
some of the good bourgeois whom Saint-Saëns derided. A decade later, when Parisian manners and morals had once again
assumed their wonted liberality, the little one-acter would have
had a better fate.

A faintly perfumed exotic, *Djamileh* shows with what success Bizet had sloughed off his derivations in little more than
two years. Without the almost fatal facility that came perilously
close to turning the composer of *Les Pêcheurs de perles* into a
clever but inert imitator, *Djamileh* has the moments of unsure-
ness that betray an experimenting hand. But, as Ernest Reyer,
Wagner's chief disciple in France, pointedly said: "The musician who falters as he makes a step forward is more interesting
than the musician who shows us the ease with which he steps

backward." *Djamileh,* with its apt, insinuating music, its happy strokes of characterization, and its witty contrasts of broad *bouffe* and sensuous, melancholy lyricism, cries out for resurrection. It vies easily with other such excellent curtain raisers as *Il Segreto di Susanna, Gianni Schicchi,* and *Il Signor Bruschino,* and would be a decided relief from *Cavalleria rusticana* or *Pagliacci.* Gustav Mahler's gallant effort to revive *Djamileh* in Vienna, though successful, was unfortunately not imitated elsewhere.

Bizet's next work for the theater was not an opera, but twenty-seven pieces of incidental music to Alphonse Daudet's *L'Arlésienne.* These are important because they show what Bizet was capable of when given subject matter that aroused his talents for dramatic portraiture. Previously, except for the passable *Djamileh* (whose merits, moreover, were literary rather than theatrical), he had accepted without question the librettos that came his way. *L'Arlésienne,* a brilliantly nervous play about the fierce, passionate types of the Midi, gave him a whole gallery of vividly differentiated individuals, presented in the contrasted situations of melodrama. Bizet not only draws the characters with harsh, telling strokes, but also surrounds them with the native colors of sun-intoxicated Provence. Yet, it is all done with singular delicacy: with all his sureness of definition, Bizet underlines Daudet's situations, but does not usurp the dramatist's function.

The step forward from *L'Arlésienne* to *Carmen* is no such long stretch as that from *La Jolie Fille de Perth* to *L'Arlésienne.* In this incidental music Bizet has already arrived at a mastery of the orchestra that he never excelled. He is no innovator— no one will speak of "Bizet's orchestra" as one speaks of Wagner's or Strauss'—and, if anything, he created his best effects with even slighter means than those used by his quite conventional colleagues. His one act of daring in *L'Arlésienne* was to include a saxophone (for which he wrote beautifully), an instrument at that time still connotationally innocuous. The whole orchestra called for only twenty-six players.

L'Arlésienne was produced at the Théâtre du Vaudeville, Paris, on October 1, 1872, with considerable acclaim for both the play and the music. And now, though the former is dead,* the music is more popular than ever, as presented in suites arranged for symphony orchestra by Bizet himself, his friend Guiraud, or Sir Landon Ronald. Even before the fate of Bizet's incidental music to *L'Arlésienne* was known, he had been approached by the Comique to do a full-length opera to a libretto by his wife's cousin, Ludovic Halévy, and Henri Meilhac. With a daring amazing for those stuffy times, the subject chosen was Prosper Mérimée's *succès de scandale* of the year 1845, *Carmen*.

The choice was daring, the treatment was not. For in order to make *Carmen* at all acceptable to the management of the Comique, then presided over by the strait-laced Camille du Locle (one of the literary middlemen of *Aïda*), the sordid, consistently vicious tale of an unreclaimed Gypsy tart had to be denatured and translated into the realm of polite, delicious license. For bourgeois consumption, the librettists robbed Carmen of her spouse, made the *espada* Escamillo (in the story a mere *picador* named Lucas) her sole infidelity to Don José, instead of merely an unimportant one of many, and, finally, created, in the simple-hearted Micaëla, a symbol of pure womanhood as a foil to the hard-boiled cigarette girl. In this delousing process, the librettists did a truly wondrous job on Carmen herself, washing her, clothing her in decent, finally splendid raiment, and cleaning up her language. In short, the heroine whom Halévy and Meilhac gave to Bizet was, comparatively speaking, a lady, though with enough brass, vigor, and viciousness left to make her a happy contrast to the spineless, lachrymose, and inanely sentimental heroines of most operas of that time.

Literary purists as well as psychologists have railed at Meilhac and Halévy for distorting the careful verity of Mérimée's always credible tale, but they must be exonerated of blame. As realistic practitioners of their craft, they had to bow to audience scruples as well as produce that rare kind of drama to which music fits naturally. They did their job surpassingly well, so well, in fact, that it has been said of the libretto that, slightly

* As dead, in fact, as *L'Arlesiana,* the opera that Francesco Cilèa, an Italian verist, made from Daudet's drama in 1896.

adapted, it would be quite tolerable as an unaccompanied stage play. It cannot be pretended that dramatic autonomy is the only criterion of a good libretto, but as that of *Carmen* supplies throughout the necessary points for musical exposition, the answer is sufficiently made. In *Djamileh*, and even more in *L'Arlésienne*, Bizet had shown what he could do if the inflammatory material happened to come his way. And when he saw the libretto of *Carmen*, he knew at once that with it he could create a masterpiece. His self-confidence in this instance is a completely clear example of his realistic understanding of what he was doing. When twelve hundred pages of sketch lay on his worktable, he could see the earnests of his conscientiousness. From that point the project took wings: he arranged, polished, and orchestrated this difficult material in two months.

Bizet was utterly confident of success as the curtain rose on the first performance of *Carmen*, at the Opéra-Comique, on March 3, 1875. He had spared no pains, and the management, though dubious about the morals of the plot, had co-operated nobly. The cast was excellent, at its head being Célestine Galli-Marié, who had created the role of Mignon eight years before. The audience was large and widely representative. The opera was well but not enthusiastically received, and the press was well mannered without being cordial. Bizet left the Comique the first night in a mood of mild disappointment. Shortly afterward, his always fragile health failed more visibly, and, on June 3, he unexpectedly died.

Immediately the legend sprang up that a broken heart, brought on by the failure of *Carmen*, had killed Bizet. But *Carmen* had not been a failure. The night Bizet died, it was being performed for the twenty-third time at the Comique, and it was repeated fourteen times more that season. This run was far in excess of the average enjoyed by new operas, and the box-office receipts were considerable. Far from giving up in despair (an action quite foreign to his volatile and resilient nature), Bizet was, at the time of his death, revolving several new projects in his mind. The legend was not easily scotched, however. It was a favorite of a whole generation of sentimental historians of music, and still possesses a breath of life.

It is only in view of its later—and present—position as one of the most popular of all operas that *Carmen* can be said to have failed at first. What prevented it from catching on in a big way from the very start? First, the shocking libretto. Second, the tragic nature of the story and its tragic end: audiences at the Comique were used to operas that would answer roughly to the English phrase "comic opera," rather than to tragic works that were *opéras-comiques* merely because they contained spoken dialogue. Finally, there was some prejudice against *Carmen*, mainly from the critical press, because it contained harmonic vagaries that could easily be mislabeled Wagnerian. These were all reasons that may have caused the tepid Du Locle to leave *Carmen* on the shelf after the first season. Before Paris heard it again, it had established itself elsewhere, notably at Vienna, where the spoken dialogue was discarded in favor of the accompanied recitatives by Guiraud that are now accepted as integral parts of the opera except in France. As this occurred in 1875, the tradition for the use of the recitatives is almost as old as the opera itself. Brussels followed with an extraordinarily successful production, and by the end of 1878 *Carmen* had been given in the United States, England, Russia, Italy, and Germany, besides several towns in the French provinces. In 1880 Tchaikovsky was prophesying that within a decade it would become the most popular of all operas.

Finally, eight years after the *première*, Carvalho, Du Locle's breezy successor at the Comique, was bulldozed by Ludovic Halévy into restaging it. The revival took place on April 21, 1883, and though the performance was bad—so bad that the audience yowled its complaints of the whole sad affair—press and public joined in hailing *Carmen* as a masterpiece. When, in October of the same year, Galli-Marié was brought back to re-create her role, the result was a triumph. By 1887, *Carmen* had reached its three hundredth performance at the Comique,* and on December 23, 1904, its one thousandth was duly solemnized. In 1911, a Paris newspaper took a poll of opera pop-

---

* In 1890, Galli-Marié, then fifty years of age, headed a special Comique cast got together to raise funds for a Bizet monument. Her principal associates were Melba, Jean de Reszke, and Lassalle.

Enrico Caruso as Nadir and Giuseppe de Luca as Zurga, in Bizet's *Les Pêcheurs de perles*, after a photograph taken in Genoa, 1899

Emma Calvé as Carmen, in Bizet's *Carmen*

ularity among its readers: *Carmen* was first with 26,116 votes; *Manon*, its nearest competitor, was more than five thousand votes behind. Elsewhere, though not the prime favorite at the biggest houses (at the Metropolitan, for instance, it ranks ninth), in the provinces it is a staple with every tiny company that boasts operatic ambitions.

In the sixty-six years that have elapsed since the original production of *Carmen*, the reasons that militated against immediate acclaim have utterly lost their force. The libretto is effective, but far from shocking a generation that now considers *Salome* tame. The tragic ending is so seasoned a convention that we accept it without thought, the corollary to that being that most operas are produced so shoddily that it is rare to hear an effectively comic comic opera or an effectively tragic tragic one. Finally, Bizet's harmonic vagaries have become as friendly to the ear as the most limpid passage from Mendelssohn, and even to mislabel them Wagnerian would not scare us. Half of the best numbers in the score are today popular—in the exact sense of the word: the Habanera, the Seguidilla, and the Toreador Song are as familiar as anything in music. Crowding on them are such numbers as the Gypsy Song, Don José's *air de fleur*, Micaëla's song, and several instrumental entr'actes.

Much of *Carmen* is assumed to have the quality of Spanish folk melody, though Spaniards have never thought so. The myth has thrived on the fact that most pseudo-Spanish music imitates one or another part of *Carmen*. The most truly authentic Spanish music in the opera, in both sound and source, is probably the entr'acte before Act IV, which Bizet may have borrowed from a totally forgotten stage work by the elder Manuel García. What really happened was that Bizet, who knew a lot of Spanish music, and had assimilated its essential characteristics—rhythms, harmonies, colors, melodic piquancies—used this fund of technical resource toward the creation of a theatrical and convincing Spain of his own. That he never tried to fortify his conception of Spain by visiting the actuality shows how little interest he had in trying to re-create anything except an imaginary reality.

Within that reality (and it is an easy one to accept), Bizet

has worked miracles. The most striking of these is his evocation
of an all-pervasive atmosphere. The music of *Carmen* is itself
a landscape, an ambience, a Mediterranean atmosphere in
which, until the last curtain falls, we exist with the protagonists. The characters are aptly, inevitably, placed in this landscape, but placed without losing their individualities—if anything, they gather strength from it. Carmen, even when she is
not on the stage, dominates the action: the opera is tilted
toward her, and yet preserves an exquisite balance. She is unforgettable—a symbol, yet a complete personality. She is one of the
few living characters in opera, and those who are pawns in her
dangerous game are less vital only because to have given them
equal stature with her would have ruined the effect for which
Bizet was striving.

Don José, a tragic weakling, is presented as the precise sort
of awkward but charming bumpkin who might easily attract
the wayward Gypsy, but would be unable to cope with her.
Escamillo is a popinjay, a braggart, a great man of the world on
a small scale, who, in his unmoved self-assurance, gives just the
right contrast to José's helplessness. Bizet presents the logic of
Carmen's preference for the dashing *espada* with devastating
clarity. Finally, there is Micaëla, good, wholesome, simple of
heart—but not of mind, as she is usually played. Have ever the
lines of battle been more clearly drawn? That much, perhaps,
is obvious from the libretto. But Bizet did not lazily permit the
libretto to do his work for him. The protagonists and their conflict are all in the music—in its bite and acerbity, its dry wit
and acid elegance, its spleen and banter, its sun and somberness,
set off by interludes of unabashed sentimental lyricism. Here is
as nice a balance of musical and dramatic elements as can be
found in opera: they add up to a perfect work of art. In neat-
ness of statement, variety of exposition, and poignancy of conclusion, *Carmen* is unsurpassed.

The lore about *Carmen* productions is so vast that it is possible
to give only a sliver of it. The name role was first associated, outside of Paris, with the great American singing actress, Minnie
Hauk, who created it in both England and the United States. A
difficult young woman, she would not undertake to sing Carmen

for Mapleson's company at Her Majesty's unless she was allowed to choose the cast. Thus, for the *première*, in Italian, on June 22, 1878, her chief companions were Italo Campanini (Don José), Del Puente (Escamillo), and Valleria (Micaëla), all of whom had started out by objecting to their roles as too slender for their talents and position. Campanini pointed out that his only love duet was with the *seconda donna*, as his conventional Italian tenor's mind labeled Micaëla. Del Puente suavely suggested that Mapleson had accidentally sent him a chorus man's part, and Valleria's objections were much the same. These temperamental squabbles vitiated the first few performances in London, though before the season was over the chief delinquents were learning from the applause how good their assignments were, and the performances gained tone amazingly. More, they learned to love the roles so much that Campanini became a famed Don José, and Del Puente was never surpassed as the bullfighter.

Hauk, Campanini, and Del Puente took part in the first American *Carmen*, likewise in Italian, on October 23 of the same year, at the New York Academy of Music. During its first season, the Metropolitan, on January 9, 1884, gave the Italian version, again enlisting Campanini and Del Puente, but substituting Trebelli for Hauk. On November 25, 1885, with both Lilli Lehmann (Carmen) and Alvary (Don José) making their American debuts, with Seidl conducting and his wife as Micaëla, the Metropolitan staged a German version which discarded the Guiraud recitatives for the spoken dialogue.

Meanwhile, other prima donnas were interpreting their Carmens on European and American stages. The role, however, in a proprietary sense, passed from Hauk to Calvé, who first sang it in America in the Metropolitan's bold return to the original language, on December 29, 1893, when she was assisted by Jean de Reszke (Don José), Lassalle (Escamillo), and Eames (Micaëla), with Eugène Dufriche, the Zuniga of the 1875 Paris performances, returning to his role. This production established Calvé, in American minds at least, as a peerless Carmen, Eames as a not-to-be-bettered Micaëla. As Krehbiel peevishly remarked, Calvé's Carmen became a fad, and for years the public would hear no other. Many professional critics agreed that her impersonation was the most satisfactory. Herman Klein, for instance, called her the greatest, adding, "Albeit I find it hard to differentiate between her and Lucca, whose conception had in it more originality but less of the pure Spanish type.* To what extent, if any, Calvé had had an opportunity of studying the Carmens who preceded her, I cannot say. Nor do I believe for a moment that she consciously imitated any of them. The fact remains, nevertheless, that her delineation seemed to combine the most fascinating characteristics of each in turn. It had the calm, easy assurance, the calculated, dominating power of Galli-Marié's; it had the strong sensual suggestion and defiant resolution of Minnie Hauk's; it had the panther-like quality, the grace, the fatalism, the dangerous, impudent coquetry of Pauline Lucca's; it had the sparkle, the vim, the Spanish insouciance and piquancy of Zélie de Lussan's."

Again other singers tried vainly to wrest the title from the reigning Carmen, the most successful among them being the Italo-Swiss mezzo Clotilde Bressler-Gianoli, whose coarse, strident interpretation was based more on Mérimée than on Meilhac and Halévy. This ill-fated singer—she died at the age of thirty-six—made her bid when Calvé's voice was declining, and yet so persistent was the Calvé tradition that it was not until Geraldine Farrar, a former Micaëla, tried the role that its ghost was laid. Farrar was New York's favorite Carmen for eight years, from her debut as the *gitana*, on November 19, 1914, with Toscanini conducting, and with a spectacular supporting cast, including Caruso (Don José), Amato (Escamillo), Alda (Micaëla), Sophie Braslau (Mercédès), Rothier (Zuniga), and Désiré Defrère† (Morales), down to her last interpretation of the role, on April 17, 1922, with Orville Harrold as her Don José.

Farrar's tenure of the role of Carmen was marked by various amusing incidents, among them a scuffle with Caruso that Carl Van Vechten has reported in his entertaining *Music and Bad Manners*: "Mme Geraldine Farrar, just returned from a fling at three five-reel cinema dramas, elected to instil a bit of moving picture realism into *Carmen*. Fresh with the memory of her prolonged and brutal scuffle in the factory scene as it was depicted on the screen, Mme Farrar attempted something like it in the opera, the first act of which was enlivened with sundry blows and kicks. More serious still were her alleged assaults on the tenor (Mr. Caruso) in the third act which, it is said, resulted in his clutching her like a struggling eel, to prevent her interference with his next note.

* But is this a desideratum for a gypsy?

† This was the Metropolitan debut of the present (1941) stage manager of that house.

There was even a suggestion of disagreement in the curtain calls which ensued."

Since Farrar's retirement, no singer has come forward with a conception of the role so original as to make it her own. In the United States, recent Carmens have included Florence Easton, Jeritza, Ponselle, Bruna Castagna, Rose Pauly, Marjorie Lawrence, and Gladys Swarthout. On January 16, 1936, Gertrud Wettergren, a Scandinavian contralto, called upon in an emergency, sang the title role in Swedish while her Metropolitan confreres stuck to French. Even the sketchiest résumé cannot omit to note that Schumann-Heink included Carmen in her enormous repertoire of more than one hundred and fifty roles, and that in Chicago Mary Garden, though not truly a superb interpreter of it,* made Carmen her own for many years.

* Garden was perhaps not primarily a great interpreter: her unique art consisted in creating whole a gallery of characters whose definitions had, for some reason or other, been left shadowy by the composer.

Chapter XVII

The French Way: Part Two

I T TOOK Bizet twelve years after the production of his first
professionally performed opera to achieve the masterpiece
that ended his career at the age of thirty-six. Gounod, his senior
by exactly twenty years, did not write his first opera until he
was thirty-three. An ex-theology student, and interested primarily in religious music, he turned to opera only because it
offered, at the moment, the one field in which a serious French
musician could gain renown. Even so, only eight years elapsed
between *Sapho* (1851), his first essay, and *Faust,* the best of his
operas. And though Gounod lived on for thirty-four years, he
never bettered that fourth opera in quality, and never faintly
approached it in popularity. Bizet never doubted that the stage
was his real métier. Gounod came to it with doubt, almost
with a sense of sin, and that he succeeded more quickly than
his younger colleague was due to his voluptuous, insinuating
melodies, not to any special flair for drama, which, indeed, he
all but completely lacked. Into opera he projected a new type
of melody, less technical than spiritual in its novelty: this was
a note of yearning, a kind of cloying upsurge that partook both
of ecstasy and of prurience, and which has done its part in
vitiating the quality of French music ever since, being evident
in the work of composers of such divergent aims as Franck and
Massenet, as well as in the early, still popular effusions of
Debussy.

That commanding woman of affairs and great artist, Pauline
Viardot-García, did much to shape the early resolve of Gounod
to attempt an opera. *Sapho,* about the unhappy poetess of ancient Lesbos, and not about the magnanimous heroine of
Daudet's romance (which inspired Massenet's *Sapho*), was
therefore written for a mezzo-soprano. Viardot-García had it
produced at the Opéra, and though commercially a failure, it
was reviewed with enough kindness to give Gounod hope that
his efforts would ultimately succeed. Berlioz praised the last

act, which contains the only number that still survives, *"O ma lyre immortelle."* Three years later, Gounod tried again at the Opéra, with a very long five-acter based on Matthew Gregory Lewis' fantastic novel, *The Monk*. The libretto, poor thing that it was, had been refused by Meyerbeer, Halévy, and Berlioz before Gounod accepted it. The career of *La Nonne sanglante* repeated that of *Sapho*: produced on October 18, 1854, it received pleasant notices and no public support.

Gounod was somewhat dashed, but did not despair, and his many famous friends—was he not, after all, a Prix de Rome?—urged him to go on. His third attempt, to a libretto based on Molière, was *Le Médecin malgré lui*, which Carvalho staged at the Lyrique on January 15, 1858. In this comic genre, Gounod failed as disastrously as before. But for the book he had found collaborators with whom he could work harmoniously: these were Jules Barbier and Michel Carré, and it was to them, accordingly, that he turned when he wanted another libretto to set for Carvalho.

Gounod had traveled in Germany after his sojourn in Rome, and he had fallen somewhat under the spell of the German romanticists, particularly Goethe. For years he had been thinking of *Faust* as a possible source of operatic material, and it is possible that before he asked Barbier and Carré to adapt the poem for him, he had already written some of the music. It is conceivable that a great dramatist or even a shrewd librettist—someone of the stature of Strauss' private man of letters, Hugo von Hofmannsthal, for instance—could condense the most stageworthy elements of *Faust* into an evening-long libretto that would possess elements of credibility and yet retain that poetical force which made the original the central work of German romantic literature. Barbier and Carré did not do so. Their operation, apart from the selection of scenes (which phase of their work was not in itself bad), was fundamentally emasculating. They turned *Faust* into a boudoir comedy acted outside the gate of heaven.

The hero of Barbier and Carré's morality play is a spineless ninny whose character is without those possibilities of growth which Goethe developed in the second part of his great drama.

In short, Faust is not Faustian. Marguerite is as weakly conceived, even if more comparable to the original Gretchen of Part I.* But with Mephistopheles the librettists missed the point completely. Goethe made him an experimenter with human passions, and a lineal descendant of the skeptical Satan of the Book of Job. Gounod's literary team vulgarized him, turning him into nothing more than a flashily dressed pimp, and there is no good dramatic reason why, as far as their libretto was concerned, he should ever have been anything more. Characters of low caliber and small interest, Faust, Marguerite, and Mephistopheles are aptly placed in a commonplace plot that can be summarized as the evil results of paying too high a price for the pleasures of seduction.

The measure of Gounod's genius may be gauged by the fact that his musical treatment of Barbier and Carré's libretto acquiesces completely in their commonplace. Nowhere in the score does the music penetrate beneath the surfaces that satisfied his collaborators. Gounod was a brilliant academic musician, and in some respects went even beyond textbook facility. His command of orchestration was in advance of his time, characterized by a freedom and spaciousness that allowed him to progress from banality to banality with spurious audacity. His harmonies, while never in advance of his time, were seasoned with archaic modal passages that reflect his painstaking study of the old Church composers. His writing for the voice is often brutally insensitive, lying generally either too high or too low for the type of voice specified. As a dramatist in tone, as an interpreter of situations, he was quite without imagination, and his developments of crises are invariably pedestrian.

Gounod, in fact, might have gone on composing one unsuccessful opera after another if it had not been for his unique gift of pathetic melody shallowing off into bathos. With that gift at flood, he succeeded, in *Faust*, in riding roughshod over his otherwise fatal deficiencies, and creating one of the most popu-

---

* Goethe, as the dramatist of man's fate, is throughout *Faust* most interested in the problems of his hero. Woman, whether Gretchen in Part I or the many legendary creatures of Part II, is as much an abstraction as woman in the poetry of Donne.

lar of operas. With few exceptions, the familiar numbers in
Faust (and there are many) have the crushing sweetness of
salon music. That they have a kind of perfumed charm is
unquestionable, but their almost total lack of dramatic sinew
makes their use in an opera at first incredible and then enrag-
ing. With *Faust* as a precedent, fortune awaits the *pasticheur*
with the temerity to string together the *Caprice viennois*, the
Simple aveu, the *Liebestraum*, No. 3, and other favorites of
dining-room ensembles, provide them with a libretto, and call
the result an opera.

Much of the popularity of *Faust* has always depended upon
the ease with which many of its tunes touch emotions that are
universal. These are sentimentality, religiosity, vague aspira-
tion—those directionless gropings of adolescence never wholly
sloughed off by even the most sophisticated and mature. They
pervade the score, but there are places where one or another
of them can be isolated in pure state: Siebel's song in Act II is
tremulous with jellylike passion, and is not improved by being
sung by a soprano in boy's clothes. The final trio—*"Anges purs,
anges radieux!"*—has a catchy, jolly, but nonetheless unctious
tune that is quite devoid of deep religious feeling, so much so
that, despite the assurance of the libretto that Marguerite is
about to soar toward heaven, her feet remain comfortably an-
chored to the opera-house stage. Where Gounod has failed to
turn on his strangely limited battery of emotional effects we
get, in *Faust*, simply straight salon music, sometimes excellent,
sometimes mediocre, always meaningless. Its very use of a restricted emotional palette, coupled with its sugary charm, sufficed to make *Faust* a favorite with Victorians throughout the
civilized world. As Victorianism is a state of being rather than
a temporal aberration, *Faust* still enjoys a marked if declining
popularity. Helpless juniors who inherited from parents and
grandparents the necessity of hearing *Faust* are now the elders
who hand on the same obligation to their children. Its tunes
naturally have taken on the aspect of a group of friends so old
and so familiar as not to be questioned, much less listened to
with critical attention.

The history of *Faust* in France can be summed up by saying

that on December 31, 1934, it received its two thousandth performance at the Opéra. It began humbly enough, more than eighty years ago, when, on March 19, 1859, it was staged at the Lyrique, with Marie Miolan-Carvalho, the manager's wife, as Marguerite, and with, except for Constance Betsy Rosabella Nantier-Didiée, the Siebel, a strictly secondary supporting cast. Its greatest popularity in France dates from ten years later, when the Opéra, which had cold-shouldered Gounod after his second failure, but which had recanted as early as 1862 to stage *La Reine de Saba*, another failure of the by then world-famous composer, undertook to put on a grandiose production of *Faust*, with its most brilliant luminary, Christine Nilsson, as Marguerite, supported by Faure as Mephistopheles. Twenty-five years later, in 1894, the Opéra had given it one thousand times —an average of once every nine days. Its popularity then began to slacken, and it can be seen that it took forty years for its second thousand to be completed, which meant only one performance a fortnight.

Faust migrated to London in 1863, where it had two separate *premières* within three weeks. In the first, on June 11, Mapleson brought forward Tietjens (Marguerite), Trebelli (Siebel), and Santley (Valentine) as the chief singing attractions. Luigi Arditi, the sprightly composer of *Il Bacio*, conducted. On July 2, Gye's rival company produced *Faust* at Covent Garden, with Miolan-Carvalho in her old role, Tamberlik as Faust, and Faure as Mephistopheles. Arditi records in *My Reminiscences*, that *Faust* "did not immediately force its way into the hearts of the people," and that for Mapleson, at least, twenty performances the first season resulted in a financial loss. On January 23, 1864, an English text by Chorley was first used, as was an interpolated song, *"Avant de quitter ces lieux,"* which Gounod, who had been much impressed by Santley's pure intonation the previous year, had consented to write for the great baritone as a way of making the secondary role of Valentine more worthy of his talents.

As *Faust* began to settle into its place in English life, it became a favorite of Victoria herself. As late as 1900, when the Queen had but several more months of life, she wanted the De Reszkes to sing certain scenes from it at Windsor. Édouard, a famed Mephistopheles, could meet her command, but Jean could not, and in his place

Albert Saléza, a fine French tenor, sang Faust. Klein, who was present, testifies that his ailing sovereign's "face lighted up and her lips parted with a transient smile of recognition whenever some well-known phrase occurred."

The first New York Marguerite (the first American, except for whoever sang the role, in German, in Philadelphia exactly one week before) had a realistic—that is to say, low—opinion of the role. "Stupidity is the real keynote of Marguerite's character," she wrote fifty years after that New York *première*, adding, "She was a well-brought-up but uneducated young person of an ignorant age and of a stupid class, and innocent to the verge of idiocy." Thus Clara Louise Kellogg, who, nevertheless, was much admired in the part, "dear Longfellow" (as she calls him), who was present at the Academy of Music on that November 25 in 1863, summoning lines from Dryden to describe the quality of her performance:

> So pois'd, so gently she descends from high,
> It seems a soft dismission from the sky.

By 1883, *Faust* had become so popular in the United States that it was chosen to open the first season of the Metropolitan Opera House, on October 22, 1883. Naturally, for this great occasion, an impressive cast was assembled by Manager Abbey. The Marguerite was Nilsson, no longer in her best voice, singing opposite Campanini, one of the most satisfactory of Fausts. Others in the cast were Scalchi (Siebel), Del Puente (Valentine), and, as Mephistopheles, Franco Novara (*né* Nash), a much valued bass during the early years of the Metropolitan. As all these artists had been heard in precisely the same roles at the Academy of Music, this was not an epochal performance, except as it initiated a better-equipped house. Patrons of the Academy were enjoying, the same evening, a performance of *La Sonnambula*, with Gerster as Amina: New Yorkers must have felt that there was to be healthy competition between the two houses. When fashion finally decreed the extinction of the Mapleson company, that sane hope was, for all practical purposes, thwarted until the challenge of Oscar Hammerstein.*

Faust became epidemic in New York with the arrival of the De Reszkes at the Metropolitan. Jean, with his chivalrous bearing and silvery voice, suffused the title role with unequaled romance.

* The Academy of Music lingered on, occasionally housing frail operatic ventures, then spoken drama, and, finally, motion pictures. In 1925, it was torn down, and the northeast corner of Fourteenth Street and Irving Place is now occupied by the tower of the Consolidated Edison Company of New York.

Édouard, whose interpretation of Mephistopheles impressed Bernard Shaw as a caricature, was nevertheless hardly less admired. In the season of 1896-97, they pulled the repetitions of *Faust* up to ten, provoking W. J. Henderson to dub the Metropolitan *"Das Faustspielhaus."* Édouard, who remained in the company two years after his brother's retirement, used Mephistopheles as his Metropolitan farewell role, on March 21, 1903, when the other principals were Nordica (Marguerite), Alvarez (Faust), and Scotti (Valentine). Also, this was the afternoon performance on the last day of the Grau regime.* The *Faust* furore waned with the departure of the De Reszkes, though it was still important enough to be chosen to inaugurate, on November 14, 1908, at the Brooklyn Academy of Music, the Dippel-Gatti-Casazza joint management of the Metropolitan company, the cast being headed by Farrar and Caruso, both of whom had made their world debuts in these roles, the former at Berlin (October 15, 1901), the latter at the Teatro Bellini, Naples (1894). Today, though it ranks immediately after *Aïda* and *Lohengrin* in total performances, it has averaged only three a year in the past decade, and the much more popular *La Bohème* and *Pagliacci*, its nearest competitors, will soon doubtless outstrip it.

Among the most intelligent of Mephistopheles have been Plançon, Chaliapin, and Whitehill, the last of whom, on April 19, 1920, sang in an admired all-American aggregation of principals, including Farrar (Marguerite), Mary Ellis (Siebel), Kathleen Howard (Marthe), Harrold (Faust), and Thomas Chalmers (Valentine). Chaliapin, on November 30, 1923, returning to the role after sixteen years, caused some scandal among lovers of tradition by encoring his first-act aria. The Valentine of that performance was Tibbett, in his first important role. Calvé was an excellent Marguerite—it was the role in which she had made her debut, at the Théâtre de la Monnaie, at Brussels, on September 29, 1882—but could not persuade New Yorkers to accept from her anything but her literally adored Carmen.

Faust's most recent fortunes in the Soviet Union would have infuriated the clerical Gounod. Frederick H. Martens, in his *A Thousand and One Nights of Opera*, has summarized the transformed libretto fitted to *Faust*, by order of the Commissar of Public Art, when it was revived in Moscow in 1925:

* Édouard actually appeared once more at the Metropolitan, again as Mephistopheles, when the fifth act of *Faust* was presented as part of a gala farewell for Grau. Eames was the Marguerite, Alvarez again the Faust.

Faust becomes "Harry," an American millionaire who, in his luxurious Berlin apartment, tells "Mr. Mephistopheles" life is vain unless he wins Margaret, a Hungarian moving picture actress, poor but pretty. Margaret, Siebel her lover, and Valentine, her brother, all communistically inclined, are tracked by the malefactor of great wealth to a Bavarian village (Act II) where the girl's noble ideals succumbing to the lure of an enormous package of thousand-dollar bills laid temptingly on her window sill, she breaks out into a "Money Waltz" ("Jewel Song") and allows Faust to lead her from the straight and narrow Marxian path while Mephistopheles, evil spirit of capitalism, laughs hideously. She is deserted by "Harry" (Act III) and condemned to death for the murder of her babe. When the millionaire, stung by remorse, comes to prison to rescue her, she kills him and is saved by the timely arrival of revolutionary troops. Gounod's music has been "pepped up" by the interpolation of jazz tunes (Acts II, III) to lend it "modern color."

After *Faust*, Gounod wrote eight operas (nine, if his complete revision of *Sapho*, in 1884, is counted), only two of which— *Mireille* and *Roméo et Juliette*—succeeded. The first of these can scarcely be said to endure, and it is possible that at its *première*, on March 19, 1864, only Miolan-Carvalho's talents saved it from an indifferent reception. It contains some charming lyrical passages, and Mireille's graceful waltz song, *"Hirondelle légère,"* is only less well known than Juliette's.

Two acts of *Mireille* were produced in Philadelphia, in German, only eight months after its Paris *première*, and in the eighties the entire opera was heard, in English or Italian, in Chicago, Brooklyn, and New York. It did not secure a Metropolitan mounting until February 28, 1919, when Pierre Monteux conducted the French version in shortened form. The principals then were Barrientos (Mireille), Charles Hackett (Vincent), Whitehill (Ourrias), and Rothier (Ramon). Victor Maurel, who had settled in New York after his great career on the operatic stage, was a Provençal by birth and upbringing, as well as a former art student. He was therefore chosen to design the Metropolitan settings for Gounod and Carré's version of *Mireïo*, Frédéric Mistral's charming poem of Provençal life. After four performances, *Mireille* was dropped from the Metropolitan repertoire. The opera is unusual in that it possesses an alternate happy ending, and it was doubtless in that version that Edmond Clément inaugurated, on November 29, 1889, his twenty-one-year reign as chief tenor of the Opéra-Comique.

Roméo et Juliette, like *Faust,* is in the standard repertoire of almost all major opera houses. At its world *première* in Paris, on April 27, 1867, with Miolan-Carvalho as the heroine, it was instantly acclaimed, and ran one hundred consecutive perform-ances at the Lyrique, easily asserting itself as the most popular opera ever written on this Shakespearean theme.* It then moved triumphantly to the Comique, and finally ended at the Opéra, where it remained a beloved fixture.

With its New York history dating back to November 15, 1867, when Hauk sang Juliette in Italian at the Academy of Music, *Roméo* was chosen to open the Metropolitan season of 1891-92. This was in some respects a more significant performance than the *Faust* of 1883, for whereas in the earlier performance familiar artists had merely moved uptown, this first Metropolitan *Roméo,* on December 14, 1891, introduced three artists who were to be-come mainstays of many succeeding seasons—Eames and Jean and Édouard de Reszke in the respective roles of Juliette, Roméo, and Frère Laurent. As the De Reszkes had created these roles at the Opéra *première* of *Roméo,* on November 28, 1888, and as Eames had made her world debut as Juliette at the same institution on March 13, 1889, replacing Patti, they had a thorough understand-ing of their roles, besides a sense of teamwork that had come from singing them often together. This performance was also the be-ginning of a—at that time—bold experiment of turning away from giving little but German opera, and most of that little in German. *Roméo* was excellently enough produced to make the Metropolitan patrons breathe more easily. The same trio sang *Roméo* for the opening of the 1894-95 season, and would have done so for that of 1899-1900 but for the absence of Jean: in his place was Alvarez, who had made his world debut at the Opéra as Roméo, and on this occasion made his Metropolitan debut.

* The most admirable of its predecessors had been Bellini's *I Montecchi ed i Capuletti,* thirty-seven years before. Composers have been attracted to the sub-ject for almost two centuries, the most recent interpreter being the lyrical Riccardo Zandonai, whose *Giulietta e Romeo* was first heard at Rome in 1922. This, however, was based less on Shakespeare than on the sources from which he took the materials for his poetical drama—principally Bandello.

On November 23, 1906, Geraldine Farrar made her Metropolitan debut as Juliette, opening that season. But she was not happy in the part, and during the reign of this gifted lyric soprano *Roméo et Juliette* was all but allowed to lapse. On November 25, 1922, with new settings designed by Josef Urban, it was revived for Bori, supported by Gigli (Roméo), De Luca (Mercutio), and Rothier (Frère Laurent). Thereafter it was heard at least once a year until the season of 1935-36, with Grace Moore or Eidé Noréna (*née* Kaja Hansen Eidé), the Norwegian soprano, as Juliette. More recently, the role has been sung by the Brazilian Bidu Sayao, the Flemish Vina Bovy, and the American Helen Jepson.

In Chicago, too, *Roméo* has had an exciting history. Not only did it open the Auditorium, on December 10, 1889, with Patti, but it was also the last opera to be given there—January 26, 1929—before the resident company moved to the luxurious Insull-sponsored skyscraper on the Chicago River. There it was that, with Roméo's sword, Jean de Reszke held at bay a lunatic who had leaped upon the stage, pinning him to a wall until members of the behind-the-scenes crew could come to his assistance, thus permitting the opera to continue. On January 26, 1918, at the Lexington Theater, the Chicago Opera Association gave New Yorkers an excellent *Roméo* with singers almost unknown to the Atlantic seaboard. Lucien Muratore, a second Jean de Reszke in the elegant suavity of his acting and in his glamorous stage presence, sang Roméo. His Juliette was not his songstress wife, the widely advertised "most beautiful woman in the world," the Roman Lina Cavalieri, but the lovely Breton soprano, Geneviève Vix. Others in that interesting cast were Hector Dufranne, Gustave Huberdeau, and Alfred Maguenat.

Barbier and Carré's libretto concentrates on the central love interest more than Shakespeare did and therefore is a lyrical effusion rather than a true drama. It has no Mephistopheles, who, absurd as he is, provides *Faust* with a sort of crude contrast. The invented Stephano, a mezzo-soprano page boy, is as obvious a parallel to Siebel in *Faust* as the music in general is a faint reminder of that of the earlier opera. One of Gounod's admirers calls *Roméo* "a series of love duets," and does not mean it as a compliment. The sensuous lyricism of *Faust* reappears in *Roméo*, and, washed out though it is, is carried to extremes. As a fusion of music and drama, the opera fails. As sentimental entertainment, it succeeds rather better—if the lovers happen to be an attractive pair with enough intelligence to keep their interpretation of both action and music from melting away into sticky amorphousness. Unlike *Faust*, which first brought into unseemly prominence a type of melody that was to haunt French music for fifty years, *Roméo et Juliette,* which was more of the same thing, had absolutely no influence on the progress or degradation of opera.

Faust, Mireille, and *Roméo* are the only effective survivors of Gounod's persistent wooing of the boards. In all, he composed a round dozen of operas, not all of the remaining nine being utterly worthless. *Philémon et Baucis* (1860), for instance, a little one-acter written for the gaming rooms at Baden-Baden, but later stretched to three acts for the Lyrique, has some piquancy, charm, altogether polished surfaces—and a static libretto. It was a failure, and not even Gounod's position as the Grand Old Man of French opera could save his last stage works from humiliating fiasco. The recluse of the spendid house on the Boulevard Malesherbes, half priest, half voluptuary, remained* until the end the composer of *Faust*. When that end came, in 1893, Gounod was regarded throughout much of the world as solidly seated among the titans of music—a place to which his beautifully kept patriarch's beard seemed to give him title. Even ten years before his death, when those wise men responsible for beautifying the auditorium of the Metropolitan Opera House decided to grave upon the proscenium arch the six greatest names in operatic history, on the left side they set Gluck, Mozart, and Verdi, and on the right, beneath Wagner, it is true, but above Beethoven, they set Gounod.

In the Master's operatic heyday, his most dangerous French competitor was the formidable academician and nightmare of budding original talents, Charles-Louis-Ambroise Thomas, seven years his senior. Like Berlioz and Gounod a pupil of Lesueur and a Grand Prix de Rome, Thomas came from behind to win. After thirty years of middling success as a com-

* Except in England, and fleetingly in the oratorio societies of the United States, where his large religious works made him temporarily seem a second Mendelssohn. These are musically much like *Faust*—perhaps a shade more sensual, certainly as saccharine.

poser of *opéras-comiques*, ballets, and grand operas, at the age of fifty-five he brought forth *Mignon*, an equally conventional stage piece that overnight made Gounod realize that a rival had appeared on the native heath. Two years later, Thomas all but repeated this success with *Hamlet*. After that, though he lived nearly thirty years, and did not entirely abandon composition, he figured chiefly as Auber's much-feared successor at the Conservatoire. Official honors smothered his unoriginal talents, and at the Opéra his *Mignon* vied with Gounod's *Faust* in keeping Goethe's fame green. During the fete attendant on the one thousandth *Mignon*, Thomas received the grand cross of the Legion of Honor. Less that two years later, in 1896, he died in his eighty-fifth year.

Those ghoulish tamperers with masterpieces, Barbier and Carré, supplied the books for both of Thomas' principal operas. Having watered down *Faust* into small beer, they did much the same with *Wilhelm Meister*, and in selecting episodes from that philosophical novel, they conscientiously removed most of the philosophy and all of the literary quality. The result is something exuberantly skittish and totally incredible, ending with a happy tying together of loose ends in a hysterical jollification unusual even on the operatic stage. Miraculously, Barbier and Carré took a segment from a predominantly tragic story, carried it within shouting distance of its natural denouement, and then sidestepped it with a slick device of mistaken identities. It is this libretto which Thomas conscientiously followed, not Goethe's thoughtful and poetic narrative.

At sporadic intervals, as in their translation of the charming lyric, *"Kennst du das Land,"* when the librettists allow Goethe the poet to have his say, Thomas rises to the occasion. In that lovely air, *"Connais-tu le pays,"* Gounodlike in contour, but somehow more convincing than most of Gounod as a fragment of dramatic expression, Thomas is at his best, and there are two or three other spots in the opera that match it. When the libretto is stale, flat, and unprofitable, Thomas is stale, flat, and unprofitable with it, and is not averse to adding a bit of silliness of his own. A ponderable part of *Mignon*'s popularity depends upon the polonaise, *"Je suis Titania,"* which is put into the

Geraldine Farrar's New York Debut, as Juliet, in Gounod's
Roméo et Juliette, Metropolitan Opera House, 1906

mouth of a middle-aging coquette, and which is one of the most sheerly idiotic display pieces ever composed. It is the Marguerite's Jewel Song and the Juliette's Waltz Song of *Mignon*, but in this kind of fluff Thomas showed himself much inferior to Gounod. Altogether, *Mignon* is a thing of shreds and patches.

Galli-Marié, a mezzo-soprano, was the first Mignon, and did much to make the *première*, at the Opéra, on November 17, 1866, an unmistakable success. When it became obvious that *Mignon* was to become a staple, Thomas decided to make over the title role for Nilsson, who first sang it in England and the United States. It was a wise move, for in her day the Swedish soprano was surpassed by none in the role and equaled only by the vivid Lucca. For the original London production, at Drury Lane, on July 5, 1870, not only did Thomas compose a special number for Nilsson, but he also devised for Trebelli, the Frédérick (*sic*), a charming gavotte based on the entr'acte between Acts I and II. Maurice Strakosch staged *Mignon* at the New York Academy of Music, on November 22, 1871. Victor Capoul, a glamorous-voiced tenor who had come up from the ranks of *opéra bouffe*, was Nilsson's Wilhelm Meister, and this pair resumed their roles at the first Metropolitan *Mignon*, on October 31, 1883, when Valleria was Philine, Scalchi was Frédérick, and Del Puente was Lothario. The opera did not succeed, despite Capoul's convincing transports of love, and it had been given only eight times during the four scattered Metropolitan seasons when it was revived, on March 6, 1908, for Farrar, supported by Bessie Abott, whose light voice showed to advantage in Philine's music, Bonci (Wilhelm Meister), and Plançon (Lothario). Even then, New York heard *Mignon* coldly.

It was not until 1927 that *Mignon* established itself so solidly in New York that a season without it has become a rarity. On March 10 of that year, Bori was the Mignon, and a superb one, the usually maladroit Marion Talley the Philine (her best role); Gigli sang Wilhelm Meister, Whitehill Lothario. Later, Pons became a favorite Philine, and when Bori dropped from the company, Swarthout or Risë Stevens revived the mezzo version of the name role, the latter making her Metropolitan debut in it, on December 17, 1938, with Crooks and Pinza. Oddly enough, during a season when its popularity was by no means striking, *Mignon* was used for the first commercially sponsored Metropolitan broadcast, the sponsor being Lucky Strikes, the singers Bori, Pons,

Swarthout (on this occasion Frédérick), and Schipa, the date December 30, 1933. An interesting interim performance of *Mignon* occurred at the Park Theater in 1918, when the ex-Metropolitan bass, William Wade Hinshaw, presented the fascinating English soprano Maggie Teyte in the name role.

Thomas' other masterpiece, *Hamlet,* followed the pattern of *Mignon,* with Barbier and Carré once more mutilating a great work of art, and Thomas once more carefully setting the letter of their libretto. The reckless trio had impudently selected a subject that had already balked, besides Domenico Scarlatti, a score or more of lesser men. The tortured melancholia of the Danish prince is not material for the action operas of the age of Thomas, and could not well have been used until operatic music had profited by the psychological suggestions of a Debussy or a Strauss. *Hamlet* was not half so successful as its predecessor. However, its *première*, at the Opéra, on March 9, 1868, was brilliant, Nilsson warbling exuberantly as Ophélie under the convincingly dour eye of Faure, as Hamlet.

While France took to the opera at once, beyond its frontiers *Hamlet* has been far from lucky. In the first place, the hero's role is given to a baritone—an audacity that audiences, spoiled by mellifluous tenors, did not easily tolerate. Then, too, the libretto, which did not worry Frenchmen generally unfamiliar with the Shakespeare play, puzzled or infuriated English-speaking hearers, who could not condone making Polonius an accomplice at the old king's murder, and thus giving Hamlet a legitimate excuse for not marrying Ophelia. Finally, it was difficult for them to accept the interpolated Drinking Song on its own merits. Yet, when *Hamlet* did occasionally succeed, it was because a stirring baritone stopped the show with that very interpolation. Such was Lassalle, who included Hamlet among his staple impersonations during the last three decades of the nineteenth century. Such, too, was the great Italian baritone Titta Ruffo, who, making his New York debut on November 19, 1912, at the Metropolitan (with, however, the Philadelphia-Chicago Opera Company), broke a long-standing house rule by encoring this elegantly Parisian prayer to Bacchus.

Also, Ophélie goes mad and distributes her withered flowers to a flossy waltz tune, which is little more than an obstacle race for a coloratura. Naturally, this florid creation, if sung by an accomplished technician like Sembrich, the first Metropolitan Ophélie (*Hamlet*, with Kaschmann as the hero, was, like *Mignon*, presented the first season), produces an astonishing effect. Ophélie was Melba's second role at the Metropolitan, but added little to her fame. After reaching seven performances by 1897, *Hamlet* was dropped permanently from the Metropolitan repertoire, though it has been given in New York by the visiting Chicago Opera Company as recently as 1920, with Ruffo and Florence Macbeth.

Gounod and Thomas were the typical grand-opera composers of the gilt-and-white splendors of Napoleon and Eugénie's Paris, just as Auber and Offenbach were its entertainers in a lighter vein. Their suave, polished surfaces, their decorative details, their voluptuousness, their long, complicated, and expensive ballets—all this reflects the heavy, sense-drugging luxury of the Second Empire as clearly as it is reflected by the deft brushwork of Winterhalter. Gounod and Thomas were heirs to the grandiosity of Meyerbeer, to his tricks—but not to his dramatic genius. They faded, literally, after Sédan, and when the curtain rose again on the operatic scene, a new group of men was making the stage works of a chastened and embittered people. Wagnerism, so long fought against, entered French music almost at the moment when Germany humiliated France to the extreme. Yet, the French Wagnerians, as an official school, never enjoyed popularity: they cast themselves as opponents of native taste, and to the end there was much of the ivory tower about their productions. Even so gifted a man as Ernest Reyer half stultified his talents by pious imitations of the *Ring*.

The post-1871 men who first gained the applause of Paris were totally uninfluenced by Wagner, whose circle was definitely among the musical intellectuals. Léo Délibes was not of that esoteric group. A practical man of the theater to his fingertips, before attempting an opera he had had a long and glittering career as a fabricator of sparkling operettas and ballets.

Several of the former obtained large box-office success in the years just before the Franco-Prussian War, while excerpts from two of his ballets—*Coppélia* (1870) and *Sylvia* (1876)—are immortal dining-hour fixtures. *Coppélia* equaled the popularity of *Giselle*, by Délibes' master Adam, himself a disciple of Boïeldieu. From Adam, and even more from Auber and Offenbach, Délibes picked up his brisk and sophisticated style. In 1873, he began to compose operas for the Comique. The first two failed, but the third lifted him overnight to equal fame with his elder operatic contemporaries—those entrenched academicians whose chief business, according to Saint-Saëns, was plotting against his own, Délibes', and Bizet's stage careers. The lucky inspiration was *Lakmé*, produced at the Comique on April 14, 1883.

Marie Van Zandt, the beautiful Brooklyn soprano for whom Délibes had composed the title role of *Lakmé*, and whom he himself coached, was the hapless Hindu maid. With many rival singers spitefully arrayed against her, she nevertheless secured a clear triumph for herself and immediate success for the opera. Van Zandt, whose Paris career was virtually ended by a never-proved accusation of having appeared drunk on the stage, was not, however, the first New York Lakmé. Pauline l'Allemand, a native of Syracuse, headed the Academy of Music cast which, singing in English, introduced the opera to the United States on March 1, 1886. With her were William Candidus (Gerald), Jessie Bartlett Davis (Mallika), and others Americans of chiefly local eminence. Theodore Thomas conducted. *Lakmé* was not particularly liked, and efforts to restage it were attended by discouraging vicissitudes.

On April 2, 1890, Patti sang the role of Lakmé once at the Metropolitan, but not with the resident company. Van Zandt tried to endear it to New Yorkers in 1892, but without success, and after two attempts the Metropolitan dropped the item until 1907, when Sembrich carried it through three performances. Three years later, Hammerstein made a gallant effort to convince skeptics that *Lakmé* was indeed worth their time, and put the responsibility of proving it onto the shoulders of Tetrazzini and John McCormack. This also failed, as did Gatti-Casazza's effort in 1917, with Barrientos and Martinelli. Galli-Curci, who had won Chicago for *Lakmé*, was an interesting interim interpreter, but it was not until the advent of Lily Pons that Délibes' masterpiece finally was established in New York. She first sang it at the Metropolitan on February 19, 1932, in a performance notable for the advanced dishabille of the ballet. Since then, the opera has become a stand-by of the Metropolitan repertoire.

The libretto of *Lakmé* is quite as silly as anything Gounod or Thomas ever set, but it takes place in a fictional India that allows the composer to invent a number of seductive, fake-Oriental melodies, as well as to introduce a nautch ballet. Délibes treated the melodramatic and tragic plot with a discretion calculated to spare the emotions of his hearers: at its most intense, *Lakmé* is pleasantly sad, charmingly wistful. It is lyric, not dramatic. The Oriental coloring, depending on reiterated harmonic and rhythmic tricks, palls sharply after Act I, which, moreover, contains most of the best music—the famous Bell Song occurs in Act II. Altogether, its history shows that *Lakmé* is a vehicle for an attractive coloratura. It has no power otherwise to hold listeners, and even as superficial entertainment it is far less satisfactory than *Coppélia*. Yet, flimsy though the score is, it is easily the best of Délibes' four operas, the last of which, *Kassya*, though based on a tale by the shocking Sacher-Masoch, and completed, after Délibes' death, by the urbane pen of Massenet, was a profound failure.

A more interesting composer than Délibes, but less successful in his stage efforts, was Édouard Lalo, now known chiefly for his *Symphonie espagnole*. A man of superior intellect, widely informed in the means of his art, Lalo might have written great music if his creative imagination had equaled his knowledge. He was primarily a composer of symphonic outlook, and his operas were by no means the most personal of his works. Of the three, only *Le Roi d'Ys* has had any career. It had its *première* at the Comique in 1888, and was slow in getting to London and New York, though it had a New Orleans hearing as early as 1890. Elsewhere, the overture, a subtly orchestrated symphonic movement, was popular long before the opera itself was performed; indeed, this had been true in Paris ten years before the Comique *première*, for Lalo had played it separately. During the season of 1921-22, the Metropolitan finally staged *Le Roi d'Ys,* thus fulfilling a promise first held out in the prospectus of the German season of 1889-90. Gigli, as Mylio, had the star number, the lovely *aubade, "Vainement, ma bien-aimée,"* based on a haunting Breton folk song. Alda (Rozenn), Ponselle (Margared), Danise (Karnac), and Rothier (the King) completed the cast that failed to carry *Le Roi d'Ys* beyond the five performances of that season. Its signal lack of success is in glaring contrast to the almost baneful popularity of the piano piece Debussy based on the same Breton legend of a city inundated by the waves of an avenging sea—*La Cathédrale engloutie.*

One of the characteristics of these French composers is their seeming inability to chalk up more than a single permanent addition to the operatic repertoire. Gounod is only apparently an exception, his *Roméo et Juliette* now hovering precariously on the edge of oblivion. Thomas' *Hamlet* is in even worse straits. Délibes never had an effective second-string opera, while it is doubtful whether today Lalo can be said to be in the repertoire at all. And Bizet remains the composer of *Carmen.* Saint-Saëns suffered from the same inability, in his case all the more striking because in several varieties of instrumental music he left compositions that are still often performed. He tried long and sincerely to gain an equal repute in the opera house, but of his twelve attempts, composed between 1864 and 1911, only one—*Samson et Dalila*—lasted, in any practical sense of the word. Some of the others were sumptuously produced, but almost all were failures. *Henri VIII* had a certain vogue in France, but beyond its graceful ballet music, based on true English themes, it is unknown elsewhere.

Saint-Saëns was one of the foremost piano virtuosos of the century. His playing was concise, perfectly finished, and exquisitely ordered, but lacked warmth and fervor. This deficiency he largely overcame in the carefully worked-out *Samson,* begun in 1868 and finished in 1872. He was so proficient technically that his creative ease was often the same as automatic writing: in *Samson,* this fatal facility never gets full sway— throughout, the composer models his work. In it, too, his melodic gift was not only abnormally consistent, but also attained unusually high levels. Always a frighteningly competent second-rater of utmost respectability, in *Samson* he came close to greatness in setting a story of tremendous inherent vitality.

The heroic mold of the temptress Delilah would suggest that Saint-Saëns was himself enthralled by her: the rich sensualism of the music with which her character is built up is far from typical of him. Delilah engages him so strongly that the other figureas, including Samson, are secondary, and it is significant that the erring Hebrew hero has few solo moments of arresting interest, while two of Delilah's arias—*"Printemps qui commence"* and *"Amour, viens aider ma faiblesse"*—always stop the show. Even the tremendously famous duet, *"Mon coeur s'ouvre à ta voix,"* is arranged to give the impression of being primarily a mezzo-soprano solo with tenor chimings-in. Only the ballet music can compete with Delilah. Altogether, the score is vastly entertaining, even, at times, thrilling. Throughout, *Samson* is the work of an admirable musician—colorful but not to excess, cleverly orchestrated, dramatic. The choral writing is solid and telling, and even the seeming lack of balance caused by Saint-Saëns' passion for his enchantress is evened up by the tenseness of the struggling Samson, who does not, appropriately, gain heroic stature until, at the very end, he pulls down the temple on the heads of the Philistines.

Samson et Dalila has had a curious history. When Saint-Saëns had completed it, no French theater would stage it, despite the fact that its composer was already very distinguished. Its alleged seriousness and gloom were held against it. Fragments were publicly performed, and Viardot-García gave the second act at her summer place, herself singing Delilah. Liszt, from whom Saint-Saëns had already borrowed copiously in forging his instrumental style, now came forward with his usual generosity and offered to stage the opera at Weimar. There, accordingly, a German version was brought out on December 2, 1877. The next year, Brussels heard *Samson*, and Hamburg followed in 1882, with the composer conducting, and Rosa Sucher as the heroine. (Sucher was a dramatic soprano, but the role is most often sung by mezzos or contraltos.) In 1890, *Samson et Dalila* finally arrived in France, though not in Paris, when it was performed at Rouen. Seven months later, on October 31, it reached the capital, but still not the Opéra, which did not capitulate until November 23, 1892, when the cast included Lassalle as the High Priest. Since then, in France, *Samson* has joined the company as such overplayed favorites as *Faust, Mignon, Carmen,* and *Manon.*

The Anglo-Saxon prejudice against representing Biblical characters on the stage led to oratorio performances of *Samson et Dalila*, in English, in both England and the United States. In the former country, it was not heard as an opera until 1909. New Orleans, a predominantly Catholic city of liberal cosmopolitan cast, secured the first American *Samson* at the French Opera House (January 4, 1893). Little more than two years later, on February 8, 1895, the Metropolitan gathered a magnificent cast for a polyglot *première*. Tamagno was the Samson, Mantelli the Delilah, Campanari the High Priest, and Plançon both Abimelech and an Old Hebrew. Possibly the confusion of tongues was too much for the staid patrons of Grau, and the opera was immediately retired.

Hammerstein is credited by Pitts Sanborn with having established *Samson* in New York by his superb revival of November 13, 1908, when Jeanne Gerville-Réache sang Delilah to Dalmorès' Samson, Dufranne's High Priest, and Félix Vieuille's Old Hebrew. Cleofonte Campanini conducted, and in the bacchanale Odette Valéry, later a music-hall queen, writhed voluptuously with a pet snake. *Samson et Dalila* did not crop up again at the Metropolitan until it was used to open the season of 1915-16. On that November 15, Giorgio Polacco conducted, Caruso and Matzenauer were the lovers, and other principals were Amato and Rothier. For eleven seasons, *Samson* remained in the Metropolitan repertoire, and was used, moreover, to open another season—that of 1918-19, when Caruso and Homer were supported by the High Priest of Robert Couzinou.* After Caruso's death, Martinelli succeeded, and admirably, to the role of Samson, playing opposite a series of Delilahs, including Matzenauer and Karin Branzell. After ten years' inexplicable absence, *Samson* again returned to the Metropolitan on December 26, 1936, with a new hero and heroine—the Belgian René Maison and the Swedish Wettergren. The most recent performances

* The date—November 11, 1918—was epochal. To meet the emotions of a resplendent first-night audience throbbing with the excitement of the signing of the Armistice, the management staged a tableau that was more effective than artistic. After Act I of *Samson*, the curtains parted to reveal the Allied flags held aloft by singers of more or less appropriate nationalities. Homer, Caruso, and Rothier accounted for three of the chief victors. As there was no English singer in the cast, the British flag was carried by Paolo Ananian.

have continued Maison's excellent Samson, while both Bruna Castagna and Risë Stevens have sung Delilah.*

Gounod, Thomas, Délibes, Lalo, Saint-Saëns—what an uninteresting group for the student of the musical development of opera! It would not be fair to say that had they never lived music would be exactly the same, for some of them exerted a powerful influence on salon music both sacred and profane, and at least two of them—Lalo and Saint-Saëns—wrote instrumental music of importance. They had imitators, chiefly attenuaters and diluters of whatever originality they could discern in their models. The eclectic Massenet is linked strongly to this group, but stands apart by reason of his superior excellence, his sensitivity to other influences, from Wagnerism to *verismo*, and the fact that his operatic activity extended well into the twentieth century. The importance of Gounod, Thomas, and the rest depends only upon the physical additions they made to the repertoire, and on that basis Lalo, in some respects the best of them all, can scarcely be included. They added largely to operatic lore, gave a whole new gallery of roles to aspiring singers, and found, at least with one opera each, the secret of lasting box-office success. And the secret? In their cases, it seems to have been an ability to write charming and easily remembered melodies, relevant or irrelevant to the situation, it scarcely mattered.

* One of the most dramatic, almost terrifying incidents in the voluminous *Samson* lore occurred at the Chicago Auditorium during a performance starring the ample Marguerite d'Alvarez, Muratore, and Dufranne. Edward Moore tells the story in his *Forty Years of Opera in Chicago*: "Mme D'Alvarez on her first entrance, standing at the top of the steps of the temple, slipped and fell all the way to the bottom. In fact she slid into the middle of the stage. It was one of the most striking instances of the self-discipline of artists on record, for while the audience gasped, thinking she might have cracked her spine, she, with practically a continuation of the same motion, rolled to her feet and came up with the note between her teeth and on pitch. She finished the opera with no delay and no complaint, though she was rather lame the next day. But the next time she appeared in this work she took the precaution to apply rosin to her sandals until you could have heard their squeak to the back of the house."

Chapter XVIII

The Russians

THERE is a persistent belief that the history of Russian opera began on December 9, 1836, with the first performance, in St. Petersburg, of Mikhail Ivanovich Glinka's *A Life for the Tsar*. This is false. Russian opera was over a century old when the first of Glinka's two masterpieces was performed. Nor was *A Life for the Tsar* a revolutionary work: its difference from numerous Russian operas that had preceded it lay almost exclusively in its superior quality. But Glinka came to be recognized as the father of the self-conscious, highly assertive Russian nationalist school, and it was his followers who decided to begin the history of native opera with this patriotic piece cast chiefly in the conventional Italian style.

The truth is that a kind of Russian opera was flourishing as early as the reign of the Empress Anne, who imported a whole Italian opera company in 1734. Francesco Araja, its head, is credited with having composed the first opera ever sung in Russian—*Procris and Cephalus*. By the middle of the reign of Catherine the Great, importation of Italian musicians was in full swing: among the facile melody makers she brought in were Galuppi, Traetta, Paisiello, and Cimarosa. To another, Giuseppe Sarti, the great Tsarina once acted as librettist. And finally, Catterino Cavos (1776-1840), another Italian, set up an *entente cordiale* with *Ivan Sussanin* and other operas on Russian subjects.

These Italians had their Russian imitators, feeble fellows all. One of them, however, took the important step of using librettos in Russian about Russian subjects, though his melodies were Neapolitan. This was the short-lived Evstignei Fomin (1761-1800), who might possibly have taken the next step had he had a longer life. The somewhat younger Alexei Titov (1769-1827) wrote many operas in dilute Mozart, while Alexei Verstovsky* (1799-1862), like Glinka a pupil of that Chopinist

---

* His most popular opera, *Askold's Tomb*, was sung, in Russian, at the Théâtre Français, New York, on December 15, 1869.

before Chopin, John Field, was so successful with his Italian imitations that he ended up as manager of the Imperial Opera at Moscow. A third composer of this period was Alexander Alabiev (1787-1851), who, though he turned out a profusion of completely forgotten operas, is occasionally heard in the opera house for the curious reason that coloratura sopranos, following precedents set by Viardot-García and Patti, sometimes sing his show song, *The Nightingale*, in the "Lesson Scene" of *Il Barbiere di Siviglia*. Liszt transcribed this song for piano solo, and Glinka's last completed composition was an arrangement of it for small orchestra to accompany a singer.

Titov and Alabiev were army officers, and Verstovsky was a civil engineer: it almost seems as if they set a pattern of amateurism or dilettantism for Russian composers. Nearly without exception, the Russian masters of the nineteenth century did their composing as a side line or came to it late, after another career. Even Glinka, the child of rich landholding gentry, worked in a government office for some years before his laziness rather than a passion for music made him resign. He remained a dilettante all his life. The great Five all led extramusical lives, at least for a while: Balakirev was a railway employee; Cui was a lieutenant general of engineers; Borodin was a chemistry professor; Mussorgsky was a small-time civil servant, and Rimsky-Korsakov was a naval officer. Tchaikovsky was a government attorney. Only Rubinstein, the child prodigy, was a musician from the very beginning. It was this lack of technical grounding and continuous practice that flawed many inherently interesting Russian compositions, and in some cases delayed their acceptance, particularly by critics. But these very lacks were, in the case of the nationalist composers, frequently twisted into strengths, and to them the Five owed a good portion of their spontaneity, audacity of experiment, and strangeness—in the best sense of the word.

Glinka is more interesting than most fathers of schools, and for the unreasonable reason that he was personally quite insignificant. The mere mention of his name aroused Tolstoi to a tempest of moral indignation—Mikhail Ivanovich was such a worthless, sensual fellow! Tchaikovsky expressed astonishment that so commonplace a man could be so good an artist. That Glinka was worthless and a libertine cannot be deduced from his music: that he was commonplace is, on occasion, all too obvious. Most of his work is banal, and even the best of the remainder is spotted with banalities. In most respects, *A Life for the Tsar* is a continuation of the stuff turned out by the Titovs and Verstovskys, and it even uses the same story Cavos had used in *Ivan Sussanin*. But it is, in one sense, a revolutionary work, the product of an impatient mind. In its acres of imitation Bellini we meet with strange formal devices Bellini would have considered quite unnatural: the same year as *Das Liebesverbot*, not one note of which Glinka could possibly have heard, he used a system of theme repetition more extensive and more effective than Wagner was to achieve for many a year. These themes are not the pulsating nodes that Wagner favored eventually, but longer, more lyric phrases, quoted unchanged. Otherwise, except for lavish use of Slavic color in places, *A Life for the Tsar* is a deftly orchestrated, harmonically unadventurous, and dramatically feeble piece.

A Life for the Tsar was popular: it was patriotic, easy to understand, elegantly old-fashioned. Other Russian gentlemen had produced operas of this kind, though not such good ones. The Tsar gave the happy little composer a ring valued at four thousand rubles and appointed him master of the Imperial Chapel. For a few years he was referred to as a genius. Then he made a mistake: he wrote a second opera in a quite different style, and had it produced on December 9, 1842, the sixth anniversary of *A Life for the Tsar*. His friends could not make head or tail of it; its complexities shocked society, and the critics, many of whom considered themselves artistic radicals, were not quite prepared for *Ruslan and Lyudmila*. The Grand Duke Mikhail Pavlovich told Liszt that instead of arresting refractory officers, he punished them by ordering them to a performance of *Ruslan*, and thought Liszt was making a bad joke when he referred to Glinka as a genius.

In some respects, Glinka's erstwhile admirers had reason to be annoyed at him: *Ruslan*'s verse libretto, a silly wandering fairy tale, though based on Pushkin (who, however, was killed in a duel before finishing it), had been filtered through the foggy minds of numerous collaborators, and finally tampered with by the good-natured composer himself.. It is utterly lacking in dramatic interest—a fact of which Glinka seems to have been happily unaware. Dostoyevsky alone not only tolerated but adored the libretto, and constantly dragged his family to performances of the opera. In it he saw an elaborate political allegory—a kind of Slavic *Zauberflöte*.

But in a world where bad librettos were the rule, another bad one was not enough to alienate critics and public. The music itself was the offender. Formally, the opera was harmless, even the leitmotivs that had been used so effectively in *A Life for the Tsar* being absent. But the harmonic, rhythmic, and melodic audacities spoke a new musical language of which, to a large extent, Glinka was the inventor. Partly from hints taken from Russian and Oriental folk music, partly from his own knack for exotic combination, Glinka had evolved that unmistakable, highly colored idiom that obviously differentiates Russian from other types of music. *Ruslan and Lyudmila* is an opera of examples, and from it almost every Russian composer since Glinka's day has borrowed freely whenever he wishes to be Russian. What Tchaikovsky said of Glinka's orchestral fantasia *Kamarinskaya* (1848) could have been said with modifications about *Ruslan*: "The present Russian symphonic school is all in *Kamarinskaya*, just as the whole oak is in the acorn." When *Ruslan* was first given, it sounded just as foreign to Russian critical ears as the first Russian music sounded to the ears of foreigners. It sounded, that is, discordant, barbaric, and just a trifle improper.

Glinka's neglect at home was compensated for by the adulation of later Russian composers, both nationalist and cosmopolitan. To the former he was an idol, and the latter regarded him as a god who was not absolutely to be trusted. When he died in 1857, he was, except to a few enthusiasts of advanced views, like Liszt and Berlioz (both of whom had visited Russia), unknown beyond the borders of his native land. However, for all his dilettantism and casualness, Glinka had a sense of his mission and a feeling that the future was with him. Only the year before his death, in deciding upon who was to supervise the musical education of a favorite niece, he hit upon Mili Alexeivich Balakirev, the future tsar of the Five, then but nineteen years old. "No one else has ideas so like my own," he told his sister. "One of these days he will be a second Glinka." This prediction was not precisely carried out, but Balakirev did indeed live to become the most powerful preacher of Glinka's ideas. It was Balakirev who conducted a Prague performance of *Ruslan and Lyudmila* in 1867, but that was as far west as he carried his master's music.

When Russian music spread to western Europe, and then to the United States, and particularly when books had been written about it, Glinka's fame became international. But as far as his two operas are concerned, he is like one of those great unread classics of literature everyone reveres and no one knows. Neither opera has been given in the United States, and performances any place outside Russia have been few.* Of the operatic music of Glinka, only the high-spirited little overture to *Ruslan* is widely familiar, and that, except for the use of the whole-tone scale, fifty years before Debussy, is notoriously uncharacteristic of the original material in *Ruslan*.

Alexander Sergeivich Dargomizhsky, the eldest of the younger men, began as a passionate disciple of Glinka, and ended, after borrowing from him what he pleased, by going off in another direction. Glinka's strength was lyrical, Dargomizhsky's dramatic. The former produced his best and most attractive effects with the long, singing line; Dargomizhsky, by comparison, is gnomic and short-winded. His sole training in musical theory consisted in copying out the five notebooks Glinka had taken down during studies in Berlin—in contrast to the earnest, ambitious Dargomizhsky, Glinka was musically erudite. Furthermore, whereas Glinka always had native flair to rely on in cases of theoretical uncertainty, Dargomizhsky needed much more technique than he ever commanded. His deficiencies were always bringing him up sharp against problems he could not solve.

* A French version of *A Life for the Tsar* was sung at Covent Garden in 1887, with Julián Gayarré, the Basque tenor, as Sussanin.

Dargomizhsky's *Russalka*, based on a Pushkin fairy tale, and produced at the Maryinsky Theater, St. Petersburg, on May 4, 1856, immediately showed that Russian opera had enlisted a master of characterization, especially in the extremes of tragedy and comedy. In general color deriving strongly from Glinka, it struck out boldly with a powerful type of declamation, halfway between aria and recitative, and particularly telling when a realistic effect was intended. *Russalka*, because of a skimpy production, was only a moderate success, though before Dargomizhsky died in 1869 he had the satisfaction of seeing it well established in the Russian repertoire. In its early career, the opera gave fine opportunities for the singing and acting of the phenomenal Ossip Afanassievich Petrov, who created the role of the Miller with the same sensitive intelligence he brought to that of Sussanin in *A Life for the Tsar*, and of Ruslan in *Ruslan and Lyudmila*. In later years, Fyodor Ivanovich Chaliapin, Petrov's renowned successor, made the Miller, especially in the scenes of his insanity, one of his supreme interpretations.

Russalka brought Dargomizhsky the flattering attention of Balakirev and his two acolytes, César Antonovich Cui and Modest Petrovich Mussorgsky. But his demanding and vainglorious nature left him only Cui, the most trivial of the Five, and a man who wanted to have his finger in every musical pie. Not until the spring of 1866, when work was well under way on another opera, *The Stone Guest*, which was to express without compromise or dilution all Dargomizhsky's musical ideals, did the younger talents again cluster around him. Then the jealous and fame-loving man, who in 1862 had petulantly asked a friend, "In what respect am I inferior to Glinka?"* found himself the center of an idolatrous group, among it at least two geniuses. It was for some years like a not ignoble page from the Renaissance. Then the master died, his work unfinished, the orchestration not even begun.

In any other country, this might have meant the end of *The Stone Guest*, but as the Russian composers had already formed

---

* The answer of his friend—it was Yuri Arnold, the critic—is worth recording: "My dear Alexander, you are endowed with sufficient sagacity to be able to find the answer for yourself."

the habit of writing each other's works, and as Nikolai An-
dreievich Rimsky-Korsakov was already on hand, its career had
only just began. Cui finished the first scene (or tableau, as it
was called), and Rimsky orchestrated the whole. It was his first
major midwife's job, and though the opera failed when it was
finally produced at the Maryinsky, on February 16, 1872, Rimsky wrote complacently: "I was content with my orchestration
and quite delighted with the opera." Thirty years later, his
professorial conscience began to bother him, and he did the
job over, "softening here and there the extreme harshness and
harmonic follies of the original."

The Stone Guest, an exact setting of Pushkin's version of the
Don Juan legend, has three well-differentiated characters—Don
Juan, Donna Anna, and Leporello. As early as 1857, Dargomizhsky had written his artistic credo in a letter to a friend.
It ended with this significant sentence: "I wish the notes to
express exactly what the words express: I want truth." His
method of arriving at this truth was that of using an unmitigated "melodic recitative" (his own words), its rise and fall
dictated by the accent, meaning, and inflection of the words.
The voice was more important than the orchestra. In the hands
of a first-class composer, equally impatient of Italian models
and inspired by certain developments in Western music, notably Gluck's and Wagner's, these intentions would have served
admirably in helping to emphasize the heroic stature of the
three principal characters. At certain moments, they served
Dargomizhsky as well as he could have wished. But he was too
sketchily endowed to carry his own theories to ends other than
those provided by dry-as-dust logic—for page after page of
The Stone Guest, we wonder what has happened to the creative
artist. And so, today, the chief interest in that much-labored-
over score is that it contains harmonies more advanced than
anything else done that side of the twentieth century. It even
dispenses with key signatures. It is, in very truth, a musicologist's playground. It had a visible influence on greater men than
Dargomizhsky, and Mussorgsky, particularly, was much in its
debt in his finest work. Unlike Glinka's *Ruslan* and Dargomizhsky's own *Russalka,* it would probably be thankless in revival.

Standing aside from the disciples of either Glinka or Dargomizhsky, Alexander Nikolaievich Serov, quite apart from the
fascination of his mercurial personality, demands attention because he happened to compose the most popular Russian operas
of the nineteenth century. Primarily a practicing critic, Serov
found himself at loggerheads not only with the nationalists,
but also, at one time or another, with almost every musician in
Russia. During a trip to Germany in 1858, this irrepressible hero
worshiper (who was always changing heroes) became enslaved
to Wagnerism. The next year, meeting Wagner himself in
Switzerland, he clinched the one musical loyalty that lasted
until his death. But when he came to compose an opera himself, Serov was not unimpeachably a Wagnerian. He had heard
both *Tannhäuser* and *Lohengrin*, and his first opera, *Judith*,
based on a familiar Biblical story, is full of echoes of them. But
as there are many strong dashes of Meyerbeer in *Judith*, the
total effect resembles early Wagner—*Rienzi*, for example. Produced at the Maryinsky Theater on May 28, 1863, *Judith* was a
big success, somewhat to Serov's surprise (his career, up to that
time, had been anything but a series of triumphs), and altogether to the chagrin of his many enemies in every conceivable
camp.

Serov, the critical analyst, dissected the reasons for the popularity of *Judith*, and designed his next operatic venture on the
basis of his findings. He realized that his strength lay in playing
the Meyerbeerian gambit all the way. He had a story in mind,
but no definite libretto. Almost in parody of Meyerbeer's
method of working in tableaus, Serov conceived his story as a
series of sensational situations, each to be a sensational stage
picture. He adapted words to the music for these situations as
he went along. *Rognyeda,* the outcome of this peculiar method
of work, was crowned with the tumultuous success at which
Serov, an unrelenting critic of false ideals in other men's work,
had aimed. Within five years of its *première* at the Maryinsky,
on November 6, 1865, *Rognyeda* had been given seventy times
at that theater alone, besides many performances elsewhere in
Russia. It is a work of small musical value, but so much is hap-
pening on the stage all the time that it has much the appeal of

a circus. There was point in Dargomizhsky's remark: "Why shouldn't Serov's operas succeed? He has camels in one and real dogs in the other."

The effect of this double success of Serov was to rid him of his feeling of insecurity as a composer and also to soften his temper. He became almost friendly to the nationalists, lectured admiringly on Glinka and Dargomizhsky, and even got on easy terms with the Rubinstein group of conservative cosmopolitans. Having assured himself of their respect, he then tried to give musical expression to his Wagnerism, choosing a sordid drama by the gloomy Ostrovsky. He made the experiment of fusing Glinka and Wagner, but did not get far. An Italian operatic company, starring Patti, Lucca, and Mario, came to St. Petersburg, and Serov forgot Wagner for Patti and the kind of music she liked to sing. Laying aside the almost completed *Hostile Power*, he started a thoroughly Italianate vehicle for her, based on George Sand's *Consuelo*. This rash inconsistency was too much for the just gods: he died on February 1, 1871, without having completed either opera. *Consuelo,* indeed, was never finished, and *Hostile Power,* completed by a hand even more mediocre than Serov's own, did not add to his fame.

Of the Five, the core of that nationalist group with which Serov was at war most of his life, four—all except Balakirev—wrote operas. Cui, a busybody who aspired to the leadership of the Five whenever Balakirev was absent, had more theoretical grounding than most of his colleagues, having once studied with the great Polish nationalist composer, Stanislaw Moniuszko, and so found his claims respected. Vocally a vigorous and caustic asserter of Balakirev's most cherished ideals, Cui had the same difficulty as Serov in carrying over his critical opinions into musical creation. A Russian nationalist without a drop of Russian blood (he was half French, half Lithuanian), Cui wrote purportedly nationalist operas that, on analysis, show themselves to be based solidly on Auberian models with strong transfusions of Schumann. Passionately desirous of feeling every throb of the nationalist pulse, Cui had been in the van of those who had seen Dargomizhsky's importance, and it is obvious that he considered his own lackluster scores as inspired by Dargomizhsky rather than by Glinka. The best of his ten operas, all mediocre, is *William Ratcliffe*, based on a Scots blood bath coagulated by Heinrich Heine.* Cui's chief contribution to the cause of Russian opera was his unresting championing of it—he lived until 1918—in French and Belgian periodicals. He never realized that his own operas, only two of which, significantly, have Russian stories, were not contributions to nationalist music.

The eldest of the Five, and next to Mussorgsky its commanding genius, was Alexander Porfirievich Borodin, a bastard descendant of the ancient kings of Imeretia, a part of the Caucasus. One of the most attractive figures in the history of Russian art, Borodin was devoid of that morbid introspection which makes the biographies of many of his confreres, when read in succession, seem repetitive: he was sunny in disposition, optimistic, easygoing, unassuming, and brilliantly gifted in several fields. Unfortunately for music, he had some of the defects that frequently accompany those virtues. A creative chemist of all except the highest genius, a pioneer in the field of education for women, and a composer of rare originality, he lacked that personal ambition which might have driven him to the very top in any one of his interests, instead of next to the top. What Bernard Shaw said of Haydn—that he "would have been among the greatest had he been driven to that terrible eminence"— might as fittingly have been said of Borodin. As it is, his two greatest works—the Third Symphony and *Prince Igor*—remain unfinished: in the first case death overtook him as he dawdled, and in the second the fructifying self-confidence was not there to make him complete it. One of the most tragic situations in the history of music as an evolving art is that in his last years, Borodin expressed delight instead of annoyance when Rimsky-Korsakov offered to complete *Igor*.

When Borodin died in 1887, it was eighteen years since he had begun to work on *Prince Igor*, but only a small fraction of that time had gone into the opera. Vladimir Vassilievich Stas-

* This little matter of three murders, a suicide, and one case of insanity also inspired operas by Xavier Leroux and two Italian verists, Pietro Mascagni and Emilio Pizzi. Like the characters, none of these survives.

sov, the great nationalist critic who, though not a composer himself, directed, quite as much as Balakirev, the thinking of the Five, had suggested the subject to Borodin, who was attracted to it because of its Caucasian subject. Basing it on two ancient chronicles, Stassov wrote out a ten-page scenario Borodin followed, gradually and constantly altering it and writing the actual libretto as he composed separate numbers. Everyone who heard these fragments was enthusiastic, as Borodin himself testified: "It is curious to see how all the members of our set agree in praise of my work. While controversy rages among us on every other subject, all, so far, are pleased with *Igor*—Mussorgsky, the ultra-realist, the innovating lyricodramatist; Cui, our master; Balakirev, so severe as regards form and tradition, and Vladimir Stassov himself, our valiant champion of everything that bears the stamp of novelty or greatness." But Borodin progressed slowly: among his multifarious activities music came after chemistry, and had to be pieced in when time allowed. "In winter," Borodin explained, "I can only compose when I am too unwell to give my lectures. So my friends, reversing the usual custom, never say to me, 'I hope you are well,' but 'I do hope you are ill.' "

When Rimsky-Korsakov and young Alexander Glazunov, Borodin's musical executors, began searching through his effects, they found, of *Prince Igor*, only a few scenes, individual songs, and sketches and memoranda for the rest. None of the opera was orchestrated, and no complete libretto was at hand. Rimsky at once saw his duty and communicated his feeling about the situation so successfully to his collaborator that Glazunov wrote a full-dress overture based on a few themes from the fragments of the score. All of Act III, except the opening march, is from Glazunov's pen. Rimsky arranged and orchestrated the rest. The result is therefore something of a hodge-podge: to Borodin's male vitality and Oriental primes were added the flaccid touches of Glazunov's classicizing mind and the tempered, oversweet exoticism of Professor Rimsky-Korsakov. These conscientious musical executors strove to denature a product that might have proved too barbaric, too heady, if taken raw. They fussed at *Igor* until it was respectable enough for the stage, and accordingly, on November 4, 1890, it was produced at the Maryinsky Theater, Rimsky afterwards observing, "Both Glazunov and I were pleased with our orchestration and additions."

Prince Igor was a success, but the management of the Maryinsky soon took the precaution of cutting Act III, and finally of dropping it altogether. This left of Glazunov's handiwork only the overture, and even that was omitted when the opera at last reached New York, in Italian, on December 30, 1915. The Metropolitan's decision to produce *Prince Igor* came as a result of the interest in Russian opera aroused by the first American performance of *Boris Godunov* two years earlier. Toscanini had enthusiastically taken it under his wing, intending to conduct it, but left the company in the spring of 1915, when a natural desire to offer his services to Italy, which had just entered the First World War, offered the temperamental conductor an excellent excuse for putting into effect his oft-expressed intention of withdrawing from the annoyances to which, he alleged, he was subjected at the Metropolitan. So it was Giorgio Polacco who conducted this important *première*. The principal roles were taken by Alda, Amato, and Didur. New York was not as responsive as the management had hoped, and after eight repetitions spread over three successive seasons, *Prince Igor* was dropped permanently from the Metropolitan repertoire.

In France, where it had the benefit of a Diaghilev production, with Chaliapin as Prince Galitzky, *Igor* fared better. In London, Sir Thomas Beecham added it to the Covent Garden repertoire in 1912, with Chaliapin again as Galitzky, and there it drew large and warmly appreciative audiences. Its survival, in the United States at least, is limited to the ballet music— the Polovtsian Dances from Act II—that Fokine used for one of his most vivid and popular choreographic creations. This is not opera's loss, but music's: full of attractive pages, some of them transcending its surface color and dynamism, *Prince Igor* is structurally invertebrate, of no significance in the morphology of operatic forms. Its influence has not been as a totality, but its tradition-unencumbered harmonies, its Orien-

talisms that sprang from the Georgian Borodin's native convictions, and its brutal, free rhythmic patterns sank deeply
into the imaginations of such disparate men as Debussy and
Stravinsky.

But more important than Borodin in influencing later composers was Modest Petrovich Mussorgsky, the youngest but one
of the Five. The legend of this singularly gifted man as a
naïve, untutored, and bungling worker of accidental miracles,
all of them marred by a child's technique, is one of the most
serious blunders of the muse of history. Mussorgsky was actually more cultivated than Borodin: he was a man of good education and sound musical training, and his whole life, with the
exception of the last few tragic years, was a continuous process
of further self-education. Curiosity was his passion, and he pursued it relentlessly after hours spent first as a subaltern in the
Preobazhensky Guards and later in a routine government job.
It has been fashionable, as an extension of the legend, to call
Mussorgsky a dilettante, but he had a sharp critic's knowledge
of the art movements of his day, and the creative imagination
to draw from them materials to be used in his own work. Without being politically minded, he knew the significance of what
was going on about him and had a sane appreciation of what
the liberation of the serfs meant to Russia. The realistic trend
in literature and painting, with their fresh and vigorous interest in the folk, interested him mightily. Such a work as *Pictures
from an Exhibition* suggests that his sharp eye for visual detail
and personal idiosyncrasy would have enabled him to become
a painter or novelist of power if his métier had not been music.
It was natural for such a man to find his model in Dargomizhsky, that indomitable searcher for truth.

Mussorgsky's first protracted attempt to write an opera occurred before he was twenty years old. The subject—Flaubert's
Salammbô, a novel with a wealth of realistic surface detail, but
with no reality at the core—defeated him. He was much happier with Gogol's *Marriage*, a genre comedy of *petit-bourgeois*
life. Like Dargomizhsky with *The Stone Guest*, what Mussorgsky started to set, in June, 1868, was the play itself, not a
libretto based on it. One act was finished in piano score—

twenty-seven day's work—and then it was laid aside while he began to think ahead. When the one act was performed privately early in October, everyone except Stassov, while admitting the eloquence of Mussorgsky's declamation and the vividness of his character drawing, thought that he had, at one point or another, gone too far in the rawness of his harmonies. Even Dargomizhsky, who sang one of the roles (Mussorgsky himself and Rimsky-Korsakov's future wife also took parts), had reservations. Stassov, fifteen years the composer's senior, alone was enraptured by what he heard and at once assumed toward Mussorgsky the double role of father and prophet of his greatness. By his very enthusiasm, Stassov prevented Mussorgsky from completing *Marriage**: he told him excitedly about Pushkin's Russo-Elizabethan drama, *Boris Godunov,* and from then on Gogol was forgotten.

Working rapidly, Mussorgsky finished *Boris* between the fall of 1868 and December 27, 1869. It was rejected overwhelmingly by the acceptance committee of the Maryinsky, six votes being cast against it, and only one—probably that of the Czech composer-conductor, Eduard Franzevich Napravnik—for it. Aside from scandalous harmonies and the lack of a big female role, *Boris* sinned in treating an episode in Russian history far from popular with the authorities—and the committeemen were nothing if not politicians. Mussorgsky began reworking *Boris* at once, paying no attention to any strictures except those about the necessity of enlarging Marina's part. Before the revision was completed in 1872, he resubmitted the opera, which was again rejected.

This time, however, there was a strong bloc not only of Mussorgsky's friends, but also of the curious of all parties, that was infuriated by the arrogant stand of the Maryinsky committee. In February, 1873, the stage manager of the theater had several excerpts from *Boris* performed at his benefit, and later in the same year Y. F. Platonova, an admired staff soprano, is said to have refused to renew her contract unless the opera

* In 1931, Mikhail Mikhailovich Ippolitov-Ivanov, an elderly heir of the Five, and one of the official composers of the Soviet Union presented a version of *Marriage;* the first act was Mussorgsky's, and the other three were his own.

was staged. Whatever the cause of their change of heart, the committeemen finally agreed to produce *Boris Godunov*. The *première* took place on February 8, 1874, with Platonova as Marina and Petrov as Varlaam. Before the season was over, nine repetitions had been called for, and, according to Rimsky, Mussorgsky's character sharply changed for the worse. Despite the organized opposition of those whom Stassov called "the old men, the indifferentists, the routinists, and the worshipers of banal operatic music," *Boris'* popularity persisted through 1876, at which point the barbarous cuts and unrepaired decay of the production began to tell against it.

Mussorgsky's unmitigated *Boris* (even at the *première* it had been slightly cut) was first heard only after publication of the two original versions in 1928, under the auspices of the State Music Publishers, Moscow. At Sadler's Wells, in 1935, English audiences clamorously expressed their complete satisfaction with it. Ordinarily, we are not permitted to hear either of Mussorgsky's versions, but a wholesale reworking by Rimsky, and only sections of that. The great orchestrator was impelled by friendly piety and a sincere belief that, though a great genius, Mussorgsky did not quite know what he was doing. In reality, this meant only that Rimsky did not agree with what Mussorgsky had done.

In the middle nineties, Rimsky began his revision, but facile though he was, he found *Boris* a soul-racking experience. As late as 1906, he was working, in an agony of conscientiousness, on parts he had been criticized for omitting in his first edition. When he died in 1908, there were still sections that lacked the suave touch of the master polisher. The ideas of the *Boris* usually heard are Mussorgsky's; the surfaces, the trappings, are Rimsky's. It is all very splendid, very glittering, very Muscovite even, if you will—but it is not Mussorgsky. His jolting abruptness, his harsh, cruel harmonies, have been restored away. Naturally, a modernist critic would be expected to prefer the original—did not Edwin Evans, Jr., once suggest that if editing had indeed to be done, someone like Stravinsky undertake the job?—but it was the temperately conservative Olin Downes who, after hearing one of the composer's own drafts in Russia, wrote, "The music of *Boris* as a whole is far superior, far more dramatically truthful and modern in texture in Mussorgsky's original version than in the Rimsky-Korsakov editing."

In order to appreciate *Boris*, it is essential not to approach it with a *parti pris*, particularly a Wagnerian one. Mussorgsky was not trying to compose a constantly unfolding Wagnerian music drama. Wagner in his maturity conceived of opera symphonically, while Mussorgsky built *Boris* block by block, conceiving it as a series of tone episodes. Wagner's musical means were complex, elaborate: Mussorgsky's were simple, bare. The unity of *Boris* is obtained by the establishment of mood and by the fierceness of the psychological concentration. Mussorgsky's separate characterizations are unforgettably credible and in the round, inviting comparison with Mozart's. His characterization of crowds is even more remarkable, for he painstakingly thought of them not as mobs, but as groups of individuals occasionally forced into mob action. He was allowed the luxury of writing this way because in Russia the most insignificant member of the chorus thought of himself as an individual artist and created his part with the same care as a principal. *Boris* re-creates life: its foremost virtue is vitality, not conventional beauty. The score is packed with the results of close observation of people in every walk of life and doing every conceivable thing: the miracle of Mussorgsky's achievement is in no way diminished by the circumstance that many of the elements of sixteenth-century Russian life survived almost unchanged in his own day.

Boris requires for its interpretation artists of a very special sort. It is no accident that though other singers of justly acquired repute have sung the name part, it has been all but inextricably connected with Chaliapin. Critics have accused him of using *Boris* as a vehicle for one of his stunt performances, but it is a fact that in it he created a never-to-be-forgotten personality—one which, incidentally, Mussorgsky would probably have approved. Not playing—at the Metropolitan and other American houses—with actors of ability equal to his own, Chaliapin tended to throw *Boris* off balance. The result was that unity seemed better preserved when a less robustly in-

tellectual singer was the Tsar. But to twist this illusion into
a criticism of Chaliapin is to make a tacit plea for mediocrity.

The first American *Boris* had the advantage of a production
brought as near perfection as the circumstances allowed: Toscanini rehearsed it for two months, and so the Metropolitan
orchestra and chorus never more gloriously fulfilled themselves
than on March 19, 1913, when the opera had its American
première. But this impeccable conductor could not find sixteen principals, not to speak of an enormous chorus, who sang
Russian or could even be imbued with an understanding of
Russian ideas of declamation. So this performance, so flawless
in many purely musical respects, began with the handicap of
slighting many equally important dramatic values. The Polish
Adamo Didur was as admirable as any non-Russian-singing
Boris can be, but as he and all his colleagues sang in Italian, the
force and dramatic stress of Pushkin's Russian words that
Mussorgsky had converted into musical sound syllable by syllable were necessarily lost. The *décor*, brought wholesale from
Paris, was as atmospherically correct as the presence, in major
roles, of such otherwise excellent, but incurably Occidental,
artists as Homer, Anna Case, Andrés de Segurola, Rothier, and
Althouse (making his debut) was jarring. Yet, despite these dis-
advantages, *Boris* had a terrific impact, and box-office receipts
heartened Gatti-Casazza (ordinarily no friend to innovation),
who had said, in a rather *ex cathedra* strain immediately after
the *première*: "I consider *Boris* the most important performance artistically that I have given at the Metropolitan."

After Toscanini left the Metropolitan, *Boris* continued in the
repertoire, but indifferent performances were reflected in cooling
public interest. Chaliapin changed all that: he first sang the role
in New York on December 9, 1921, and kept the opera a going
concern until he, too, left the Metropolitan, eight seasons later.
Singing in Russian, he gave Manhattan its first opportunity to
get the full force and flavor of Mussorgsky's projection of the Tsar,
but the management provided him with Italian-singing confreres
even less satisfactory than those who had supported Didur. After
ten years, *Boris,* enlarged by certain scenes not before given at the
Metropolitan, was restored to the repertoire, on March 7, 1939, in

the all-Italian tradition. Thorborg, the Marina, was alone superb. Pinza was a capable but not inspired Boris, and the production, in general, had degenerated to the point where only a complete overhauling in every department could make it satisfactory. Oddly, though the popular Bruna Castagna had made her operatic debut as Marina, in Mantua, she has never sung the role at the Metropolitan.*

Mussorgsky began two other operas, but never finished either. During the last years of his life, when excessive alcoholism had undermined his physical and moral being, one group of his well-wishers was giving him one hundred rubles a month to finish the tragic *Khovantchina*, while another was giving him eighty to finish the comic *Fair at Sorochintzy*. The result was that when he died, on March 28, 1881, nothing of either was in final form. Fortunately for friends eager to construct wholes out of the unconnected parts, large sections of both were amply sketched out. The facts in the later history of both are quickly told. Rimsky-Korsakov orchestrated and completed *Khovant-china*, publishing it in 1883. *The Fair at Sorochintzy* found four separate architects, each of whom carried it to completion in his own way: the first (1913) was by I. Saknovsky, and was a hopeless hybrid; the octogenarian Cui produced his version in 1917; Nikolai Tcherepnin, evidently adding as little as possible from his own pen, tried out a third version, in French, at Monte Carlo in 1923; finally, Vissarion Shebalin, a young artist of the Soviets, gave Moscow his reading of Mussorgsky's ideas in 1930. The Rimsky *Khovantchina*, in Russian, and the Tcherepnin *Fair*, in Italian, have been heard in New York.

Strange to say, *The Fair at Sorochintzy*, the weaker of the two scores whether considered as Mussorgsky left them or as worked over by others, has received production, with a not undistinguished cast, at the Metropolitan. *Khovantchina* has not. *The Fair*, begun as a relaxation from what Mussorgsky called his "two heavyweights," *Boris* and *Khovantchina*, was always a stepchild—and shows it. Parts of it are said to be extremely funny, but unhappily only to Russians, for the humor is too

---

* Odder still, the original Mussorgsky score has not been staged at the Metropolitan, though Gatti-Casazza considered this radical step just after its publication.

regionally topical for foreigners. For those who understand the point of the situations, the music is forceful, and there are not lacking, even for non-Russians, bursts of Mussorgsky's bold and vivid characterization. Yet, the music as a whole is disappointing, and uncharitable critics who heard the Metropolitan performance, on November 29, 1930, frankly said that the best thing in the score was the already familiar, interpolated *Night on Bald Mountain*, which is more Rimsky than Mussorgsky. The broadest lines went to Pinza, who was supported by Maria Müller, Ina Bourskaya, Frederick Jagel, and Danise, with Serafin conducting. *The Fair* achieved five performances that season, and has not been heard since.

Khovantchina, which would well repay Metropolitan staging, has been heard in New York only at the Mecca Temple, where, however, it had the advantage of a Russian-singing cast. At that American *première*, on March 7, 1931, though the singers were less renowned than the Metropolitan aggregation for *The Fair*, *Khovantchina* came through as not unworthy of the composer of *Boris Godunov*. Musically, and in particular orchestrally, it has long sections quite as impressive, as beautiful, as anything in *Boris*. The libretto of *Khovantchina*, which is based on a fugitive idea of Stassov's, and which Mussorgsky developed by cribbing the needed historical information from a multitude of books, evidently stirred him far more than the excellent Gogol story around which he wrote *The Fair*. Its theme—the conflict between the old and the new in seventeenth-century Russia—was exactly the sort of thing to inflame a typical man of the liberating sixties.

The central flaw of *Khovantchina*, as we know it, is its diffuseness, its lack of dominating characters around whom conflict should inevitably rage. It seems as if Mussorgsky tried to show as many different types as he possibly could, and the result is that the stage is too often filled with an unindividualized confusion—a confusion which may be very much like life itself, but which lacks sufficient dramatic concentration to focus our attention. Our sympathies have to shift so often that eventually we have none at all. Rosa Newmarch hit off a fine comparison when she said: "*Khovantchina* reminds us of those early ikons belonging to the period when the transport of pictures through the forests, bogs, and wilderness of Russia so restricted their distribution that the religious painter resorted to the expedient of representing on one canvas as many saints as could be packed into it."

Nikolai Andreivich Rimsky-Korsakov, the youngest of the Five, and, next to Tchaikovsky, the most popular of all Russian composers, would never have made the mistake of crowding too many saints into one ikon. The story of his fifty years as an active composer, from his fumbling musical ABC's to that last period when he was the most revered master of techniques outside Germany, is one of constant self-discipline, husbanding of forces, polishing, filing, tempering, and revising. Had Rimsky confined this self-discipline to himself and not extended it to the works of others—some of them original geniuses—he would have left a fairer name.

Unfortunately, rather like the pest who has some inner drive always to touch fresh paint, this unrelenting *magister musicae* felt it his duty to Rimsky-Korsakovise the "flawed" scores of Dargomizhsky, Borodin, and Mussorgsky, to correct their excessive audacities, to give them an alien suavity, and, in short, to provide them with a shimmering outer garment not precisely their own. A sample of Rimsky's noble self-dedication follows: "Only when I have revised the whole of Mussorgsky's works shall I begin to be at peace and feel that my conscience is clear; for then I shall have done all that can and ought to be done for his compositions and his memory." Thus, as Mrs. Newmarch acidly observed, "When it came to a question of what he believed to be an offense against art, he saved his friend's musical soul at the expense of his originality." We must agree that Rimsky's highminded smugness is infuriating. But it is irrelevant to a fair judgment of his own compositions, which are among the most delicious fruits of the Russian musical efflorescence.

Yet, any evaluation of Rimsky's fifteen operas (and the same stricture can be applied to his songs and instrumental pieces) must begin with the admission that these fruits come all too obviously from a single tree. Gerald Abraham, the most reliable guide through the labyrinth of Russian music, has pointed out that Rimsky "practically sums up the aesthetic contribution to music of the entire group." At one point or another in his operas, the influence of each of his great Russian contemporaries, as well as Glinka, is patent. Nevertheless, so pervasive is Rimsky's own musical personality that though it is possible to mistake one of his operas for another, it is quite impossible to mistake any one of them for the work of anyone else.

Rimsky's first opera, *Pskovityanka*, dates from the years of his closest intimacy with Mussorgsky: begun in 1868, it was finished in 1872. This was a crude affair—an imitation of his friend's mingling of Dargomizhsky and folk music—but was produced with ponderable success in 1873, partly because of the political connotations of some of the music (Rimsky, at twenty-nine, was already an old-fashioned liberal, and had had censor trouble). In the following three years, during which he was working hard at harmony and counterpoint, he must have fretted about the crudities of *Pskovityanka*, for even before beginning a second opera, he spent two years completely polishing this first one and adding a prologue. The second version, notable chiefly for casting out whatever attractive roughness he had achieved in the first, introduced much extraneous matter by way of displaying his newly found technical knowledge. No one liked it, and it was never produced, its sole virtue even to its perpetrator being its solid respectability. Eleven years later, Rimsky started on a second revision, during which the prologue was detached and made into a one-act opera, *Boyarina Vera Sheloga*.

The third *Pskovityanka* was finished in 1893, and five years later provided, in the role of Ivan the Terrible, one of the earliest of Chaliapin's triumphs. For years, Rimsky had been revising his works, and he was able, after* the completion of the third *Pskovityanka*, to make this curious pronouncement of virtuous self-examination: "I closed my account with my past. Not one of my major works of the period before *May*

---

* Or possibly in 1891, when the second revision was half done. Rimsky's own statement is somewhat obscure on this point, but either interpretation is admissible.

Night [his second opera, composed in 1878] remained in its original form." It is this final version of *Pskovityanka* that has become known, particularly in France, as *Ivan le terrible*.

Never again did Rimsky-Korsakov labor so hard and drearily on an opera as he did on *Pskovityanka*. *May Night*, his next opera, was a facile essay in the Glinka style, and overflows with bright folk color of an agreeable if not very memorable sort. Still in the Glinka mode, he composed *Snegurochka* on a text by the popular dramatist Ostrovsky. It was composed under very happy circumstances, and Rimsky threw himself into the work with gusto. The subject—a fantastic fairy tale of pagan Russia—appealed to him, and he wrote much of the vocal score at a country paradise outside Moscow, where every sight and sound awoke in him the pantheistic feelings that seem to have inspired heathen tales of the type of *Snegurochka*. Although it was first produced under trying circumstances (its great length necessitated cuts that he resented, and, moreover, his wife was recovering slowly from her first childbirth), Rimsky, years later, when a feeling that his powers were permanently on the wane had induced in him a mood of sad reminiscence, spoke of *Snegurochka*, which the critics had treated harshly, with loving pride. He felt then, in 1893, that "*Snegurochka* is not only my best opera, but, on the whole, perhaps the best of all contemporary operas."* One naturally wonders exactly what he meant by "contemporary," but there is no doubt that it is a charming score.

In 1881, when *Snegurochka* was finished, Rimsky was not the supreme orchestral wizard that he was to become within a few years, but even so, the relatively simple score is already charged with that magic, that sense of fantasy, peculiar to him. The delicately gamboling song of Lehl, in Act III, is one of his loveliest inspirations, while the Dance of the Buffoons, from the same act, is as broadly bumbling as its name implies. It would seem that these and several other numbers would endear *Snegurochka* to any audience with a shred of childlike

* The man who could offer himself such consolation was obviously on the way to recovery. Ten more operas were to come from him before death alone stopped his composing, fifteen years later.

Fyodor Chaliapin as Boris, in Mussorgsky's *Boris Godunov*

wonder left, but when the opera was produced, in French, at the Metropolitan, on January 23, 1922, almost forty years to a day after its Moscow *première*, it was received without apparent interest. The much-loved Bori was the Snow Maiden, and the almost idolized Bodanzky led the orchestra—but a few performances each in two seasons sufficed to sate New York's appetite.

During the fifteen years that elapsed between the completion of *Snegurochka* and that of *Sadko* in 1896, Rimsky-Korsakov composed two other operas, the first of which, *Mlada,* had a curious history. About 1870, S. A. Gedenov, director of the imperial theaters, invited Cui, Borodin, Mussorgsky, and Rimsky to compose a collaborative pageant opera with ballet. The first of them faithfully completed his mediocre share, but the others abandoned the project after halfhearted attempts. In 1888, years after the Five had broken up, and Borodin and Mussorgsky had died, Anatol Liadov suggested that Rimsky revive the idea for himself alone. But there was a curse on it from the very beginning, and Rimsky's own *Mlada* was manufactured rather than created. He himself came to dislike it so much that he actually forgot its name, and the public, to which it was presented in 1892, wearied of it quickly.

Even worse was the fate of Rimsky's attempt to reset that legend of Vakula the Smith which had fascinated Tchaikovsky so much that he had tried twice to make a successful opera out of it. No sooner had Tchaikovsky been buried than Rimsky set his own version of the legend, calling it *Christmas Eve.* Like *Mlada*, this suffered from being a synthetic thing, and so, when it was put into production in 1895, Napravnik not unjustly insisted on stringent cutting. Rimsky, the Procrustes of other men's creations, could not bear to have the length of his own altered, and his nerves were cruelly exacerbated. Even worse were last-minute cuts and changes in the libretto demanded, after the dress rehearsal, by outraged members of the imperial family, who could not endure seeing their ancestors— or even their ancestors' tombs—on the stage. So both the Romanovs and the Rimskys were conspicuously absent from the *premiére*, and altogether circumstances helped the opera into early desuetude.

Christmas Eve was the first extended work Rimsky attempted after a serious nervous breakdown. Shortly after beginning it, he started another opera, likewise of mixed antecedents, legendary and historical. This seven-acter, produced in 1898, was *Sadko*, after *Le Coq d'or* the most popular of his stage works. The libretto was his own, its story of an itinerate guzla player who falls in love with the Ocean King's daughter supplying him with the fantastic background he could illustrate so aptly with his gorgeous pictures. In it, he carefully steered clear of tragedy, though there is enough suspense in the action to make the story worth following. In the libretto he set himself no task that his musical powers could not execute. He provided it with dazzling ballet music and sinuous chromatic melodies, particularly, in Act IV, the Song of the Hindu Guest, known the world over as the "Song of India," overwhelmingly his most popular fragment.

No other composer could have competed with Rimsky in creating the submarine never-never land of *Sadko*. The effects are all his own, but he accepted tools from others in creating them: from Balakirev and Borodin, he extracted a way of achieving national color, from Liszt a pungent chromaticism, from Wagner a fuller use of leitmotivs than he had ever before attempted in an opera, and from Liszt's tone poems, via Wagner, a dramatic organization of whole scenes on a symphonic basis. That Rimsky was perfectly conscious of these borrowings is obvious, and he once rebuked a too idolatrous friend with the caustic admonition: "Study Liszt and Balakirev more closely, and you'll see that a great deal in me is—*not* me."

Like many of Rimsky's later operas produced after *Christmas Eve* had put him out of favor with the authorities and the imperial family, *Sadko* was produced at a nongovernment theater. It took thirty-one years to reach its American *première* (parts of it had already been given in New York in concert form, under Kurt Schindler). On January 25, 1930, the Metropolitan sponsored a magnificent production, with Edward Johnson in the title role, supported by Fleischer, Bourskaya, Swarthout, and Rafaelo Diaz, who, playing the role of the Hindu Guest, had the big moment of the performance. The opera was popular, attaining sixteen performances in three seasons, after which it was dropped. It is hard to understand why it has never been revived.

Between *Sadko* and Rimsky's last operative masterpiece, *Le Coq d'or,* the completion of which was practically coincidental with his death in 1908, he composed, besides four Russian operas, three with foreign subject matter. The third of the non-Russian group, *Mozart and Salieri* (1897), is altogether the most curious of Rimsky's operas. Based on Pushkin's reading of the now discredited idea that Mozart was poisoned by the jealous Salieri, it superimposes Dargomizhsky's idea of musical "truth" on a deliberate imitation of Mozart's musical style. In the original production, Chaliapin was a convincingly fiendish Salieri, and for some years this was one of his favorite impersonations.

The four Russian operas of the same period are of varying interest. The least attractive of them, *The Tsar's Bride* (1898)— Russian folk tunes with a dash of Bizet—is among the four Rimsky operas heard in New York (New Amsterdam Theater, May 9, 1922, in Russian). Rimsky followed it with *The Legend of Tsar Saltan* (1899-1900), one of the most glowing of his scores, again with Wagnerian machinery and symphonically built-up scenes. Act III contains the brilliantly contrived "Flight of the Bumblebee," a faithful evocation of that insect's erratic flight and droning noise. The *première* of this opera, at Moscow in October, 1900, was conducted by Ippolitov-Ivanov, himself one of Rimsky's pupils and a composer of numerous operas flatteringly imitative of his master.* In November, 1940, a cut, English version of *Tsar Saltan,* called *The Bumble Bee Prince,* was presented in New York, to an audience of children, through the efforts of Junior Programs, Inc., a nonprofit organization headed by Mrs. Dorothy McFadden, a New Jersey music lover who had herself made the translation.

The Legend of Kashchey the Deathless (1901-02) is an ad-

* It does not seem likely that Ippolitov-Ivanov's *The Last Barricade,* a Soviet opera written in the composer's seventy-fifth year, conforms to the old fantastic model.

vanced score, pitting diatonic harmonies against chromatic in an attempt to point up the differentiation between human and supernatural elements. The last of the four Russian operas was *The Tale of the Invisible City of Kitezh* (1903-04). Except for the fact that Rimsky went on to write one more opera, this might be called his *Parsifal*. Strongly influenced, like *Kashchey*, by Wagner's lengthy essay on the sacred and the profane, this opera is almost its Slav counterpart in sumptuous religious ceremonial, pervasive mysticism, moments of heated fleshliness. Yet, this glittering score lacks drama, has something of the stasis of a Byzantine mosaic.

In 1905, at a time when Russian blunders in her war with Japan were reflected in local disorders of a revolutionary nature, Rimsky, by his defense of the rights of student dissenters, broke with the authorities and unexpectedly found himself the hero of the liberal groups. When a temporary ban on his music had been lifted, it became tremendously popular. Meanwhile, these events contributed strongly to Rimsky's feeling of disillusionment and spiritual malaise. On September 4, 1906, while summering at the Lake of Garda, he wrote finis to his autobiography, thinking that his career as a composer was at an end. He had seriously underestimated his powers: before 1906 was over, he had entered the cockcrow theme of *Le Coq d'or* in his notebook and thus was on the eve of his finest achievement in the operatic field. His rage over governmental stupidity in the war with Japan was bearing fruit, and for once in his life he felt a violent personal drive to make music.

Rimsky found precisely the arsenal of his own scorn in Pushkin's fairy-tale satire on the officialdom of an earlier day. The libretto of *Le Coq d'or* is as preposterous, as hard to follow, as that of *Die Zauberflöte*, and for the same reason: we do not possess the entire key to either. We are told that the bumbling King Dodon represents Nicholas II, that the council of war in Act I mirrors the bureaucracy that bungled things for Russia, but we do not know the functions of most of the other characters and situations. Yet, Rimsky, like Mozart, holds us with his music, whether the libretto adds up to something or not. In *Le Coq d'or*, he is altogether at his best, even though the score has not the drugging richness of some of the others, *Kitezh,* for instance. To compensate, Rimsky's flair for the typical, the onomatopoetic, and the illustrative was never more sure. His piquant harmonies, flowing melodies, prismatic colors, and shifting rhythms create with their own magical touch the fairy-story world. Throughout, his deft, transparent orchestration answers each vibration of the lissome fantasy.

It is not strange that *Le Coq d'or* is Rimsky's best-known opera: from the first triumphant performance at Moscow in May, 1910, almost two years after the composer's death, down to the present, it has held its place as, next to *Boris Godunov,* the most popular of Russian operas. At the Metropolitan, where it was introduced on March 6, 1918, in a French translation by the noted Greek musicologist, M. D. Calvocoressi, with a double cast in the Fokine version of dancers on the stage and singers in the pit, *Le Coq d'or* has been given more than fifty times. Barrientos, Braslau, Sundelius, Didur, and Diaz were the principal singers, while Rosina Galli, the future wife of Gatti-Casazza, and Adolf Bolm led the miming dancers. This version aroused the wrath of several local commentators, among them the powerful critic of the *New York Tribune,* H. E. Krehbiel, but it was not until 1936 that a straight singing version was substituted. Among sopranos who followed Barrientos as the Queen of Shemakha, and so had the privilege of singing the second most famous of Rimsky's operatic airs—the Hymn to the Sun—have been Garrison, Galli-Curci, Thalia Sabanieeva, Talley, and Pons. In recent years, Pinza justly scored a real hit as King Dodon.

Rimsky just escaped being a genius—a situation that he himself recognized, but the escape was sufficient to make his music, cleverly contrived, beautifully put together though it is, finally unsatisfactory to dwell with. With him, it is the first impression that counts, and it is fair to say that the first impression is often magnificent, as is indeed natural in the works of an artist who founded so many of his effects on pageantry and ceremonial. It is not only that these effects have a certain easily recognizable family resemblance, but also that repeated hearings of any one Rimsky composition, even such dazzling masterworks as *Le Coq d'or* and *Scheherazade*, bring no new experiences. There is simply nothing beneath those perfect surfaces. The truth is that aridity derives logically from Rimsky's lack of conviction in what he was doing. This is no theorizing after the fact—he condemned himself out of his own mouth: "I doubt if you would find anyone in the whole world more incredulous of everything supernatural, fantastic, phantasmal, or lying beyond the grave, and yet as an artist it is just *these* things that I love above all. And *ceremonial*—what could be more intolerable than ceremonial? . . . Yet with what delight I have depicted 'ceremonial' in music! No—I'm definitely of the opinion that art is essentially the most enchanting and intoxicating of lies!"

Standing considerably apart from his Russian nationalist contemporaries, but not quite so far as certain of his critics have asserted, is Piotr Ilyich Tchaikovsky. The composer of almost a dozen operas, the first written when he was still a prentice at his craft, and the last after all of his major works except the Sixth Symphony, he was generally unsuccessful in this genre. This intensely subjective man could convincingly set only librettos that contained characters with whom he could sympathetically identify himself, and it is precisely in *Eugen Oniegin* (1878) and *Pique-Dame* (1890), his most popular operas, that he found protagonists who reflected his own spiritual struggles. The chief appeal of these scores is the deeply felt lyricism that ebbs and rises with his own collaboration with the stage characters, and it is through this lyricism that the audience is reached.

For *Eugen Oniegin* and *Pique-Dame* are fundamentally little more than projections of Tchaikovskyan mood. Formally, their composer did nothing to enrich opera: content to fall back on the easily learned structure of Meyerbeer, he filled it out with melodies that, at their convincing and beautiful best, are quite beyond the German's short-winded muse. Meyerbeer's genius for the theatrically apt Tchaikovsky totally lacked, and the moments of dramatic power in his operas are accidentally wrought by the lyric passages themselves. The glib use of Italian and French musical phraseology is the irrelevant mimicry of a master assimilator, as is his occasional, and almost invariably un-dramatic, use of leitmotivs. Tchaikovsky was an eclectic less by conviction than by the circumstances of self-education, and he as willingly took for his purposes a Russian folk tune as a phrase or two from the Occidental past. Thus, to deny Slavic influence in Tchaikovsky's work is to deny his whole *modus operandi*.

Tchaikovsky was thirty-nine years old when the Pushkin-inspired *Eugen Oniegin* was produced for the first time in 1879. It failed, but what hurt him more than public indifference was the hostile silence of Anton Rubinstein, who had traveled from St. Petersburg to Moscow to hear it. As the creator of numerous colossal stage works,* the great pianist was regarded by the then far less renowned Tchaikovsky as an oracle. After five years of neglect, *Oniegin* was restaged at St. Petersburg by im-perial command, and the acclaim was so vociferous that after that night Tchaikovsky's fame snowballed.

As early as 1908, Walter Damrosch conducted a concert version of *Oniegin*, in English, at Carnegie Hall, New York, with Emilio de Gogorza singing the title role. On March 24, 1920, the Metro-politan mounted an Italian version of *Oniegin*, with De Luca as the Byronic baritone hero, Muzio as the badly abused Tatiana, and Martinelli and Didur in supporting roles. The opera lasted two seasons—seven performances in all. On October 28, 1940, the Philadelphia Opera Company revived *Oniegin* for a single per-formance in Philadelphia, using a new English translation, but failing utterly to win either audience or critics. *Oniegin* seems fated to be remembered as the source of the soprano's "Letter Scene," a familiar waltz from Act II, and the polonaise from Act III.

Yet, even more melancholy has been the history of *Pique-Dame*, almost the first nineteenth-century Russian opera to be staged in the United States. Despite Gustav Mahler as conductor and a fine German-singing cast headed by the gigantic Bohemian tenor, Leo Slezak, and his compatriot Emmy Destinn, Alma Gluck, and Didur, New York asked for only three repetitions after the Metropolitan *première* of March 5, 1910. In 1922, *Pique-Dame* (which has a libretto by Tchaikovsky's brother Modest, based on a Pushkin story)

* Not one of which has succeeded in deflecting the course of opera one milli-meter.

was sung by a Russian company at the New Amsterdam Theater. At present, it can scarcely be said to survive even in excerpts outside the Soviet Union, where both it and *Eugen Oniegin* have won astounding popularity in recent years, one of the reasons being, perhaps, that Stalin has declared them his favorite operas.

Russian opera as such produced little effect on the formal development of opera, chiefly because it never emancipated itself from the episodic. On the purely musical side, the story is different. First in driblets, then in a widening stream, Russian music—its harmonies, rhythms, color, sheer vitality, and fresh feeling for instrumental timbres and combinations—flowed into the receptive artistic imagination of Western European musicians. When Debussy first cupped his ear to its pungent sounds, it was an exotic outlander from the East. When Stravinsky, Rimsky-Korsakov's most famed pupil, had become the admitted leader of modern music (outside of a Germany that, even in its most arid period of devitalized theorizing, refused to surrender leadership), it seemed for a time that the tributary stream would altogether absorb the indulgent parent. Quickly, that crisis passed, and today Russian music has lost its preeminence and become but one of the many sources of whatever richness modern music may possess.

Chapter XIX

Verdi

THE year 1813 was a great one, particularly for the Germans. At the battle of Leipzig, Napoleon suffered the defeat that broke the backbone of his power, and in the town of Leipzig itself was born Richard Wagner, who was to assert the greatness of German music and to become its symbol. The same year, at Munich, young Meyerbeer managed to have his first opera—a German one—produced, and so raised delusory hopes among his admirers, particularly Weber, that he was to be a prophet of musical Teutonism. In 1813, German opera was not much, and an impartial observer could have been forgiven for believing that it had begun with *Die Entführung aus dem Serail* and *Die Zauberflöte* and ended with *Fidelio*. Everywhere the Italians, pure and adulterated, had their few feeble rivals on the run. In Paris, Cherubini reigned, and Spontini, though momentarily under a cloud, had great things still ahead of him. Even in remote Muscovy, Italian composers and their imitators amused the court and the great nobles. In Italy, too, 1813 was an *annus mirabilis*. Rossini, only three years a practicing maker of operas, found his fecundity almost unequal to the task of satisfying his enraptured admirers—he gave them *Tancredi* and three others, and still they clamored for more. Finally, the same year, far from the great world of Paris, the decaying splendors of Venice, and the solid bourgeois comforts of Leipzig, there was born, in an insignificant village of a paltry Italian state, Giuseppe Verdi.

During the twenty-six years that elapsed between Verdi's birth and the staging of his first opera, *Oberto, conte di Bonifacio,* the face of opera in Italy changed completely. Rossini had turned himself into a composer of French operas, and then retired from active composition. Bellini had already gone his brief and limpid way. But Donizetti, with four good years ahead of him, was at the peak of his career. Not having been much exposed to Rossini's late French operas, with their heavier orchestration and richer harmonies, Italy, in 1839, was still producing composers content with diatonic harmonies, flowing tunes, the barest of guitarlike accompaniments, and a nicely assorted selection of pretty vocal effects. Verdi, to judge by the mildly successful *Oberto*, was to be one of them: the score was at once labeled Bellinian—and looks that way. *Oberto* was an old-fashioned *opera seria*, its comic successor—*Un Giorno di regno*—an old-fashioned *opera buffa*.

Without accepting as dogma the idea that only suffering can produce a work of art, it must be said that Verdi's very next opera, *Nabucodonosor* (irreverently nicknamed *Nabucco* by the composer), which shows an astonishing advance over his first two efforts, was composed after the death of his wife and infant daughter and a serious illness of his own. *Nabucco* is an individual's work and already shows traits that can definitely be pointed to as Verdian. It has drive and rude vigor that well compensate for an appalling libretto, frequent *gaucheries*, and stretches of pure banality. In the words of Toye, the characters "live separate and genuine musical lives of their own." *Nabucco* is, indeed, so full of promise that it is surprising that nine years —and twelve operas—passed before Verdi created a thoroughly satisfactory opera.

Why did Verdi develop so slowly? The chief reason is that, not being a man of contemplative intellect, he worked things out through experience—by the trial-and-error system. By comparison, Wagner, once his serious career as an operatic composer had begun, advanced on seven-league boots, mainly because he thought things out before trying them. He thought out the whole libretto problem long and earnestly, for example, and even wrote his own librettos because he felt that he knew exactly what they ought to contain. Verdi, on the other hand, shows no signs of ever having thought about the libretto as an aesthetic problem and was generally quite willing to accept any book that came to his hand so long as it contained a few dramatic situations, the more violent the better. His letters show him haggling with his librettists over details, but rarely piercing to the essential weaknesses of their work. Once he had accepted a libretto, he attacked its detail with shrewdness and acumen, but he might have composed fewer operas and developed faster if he had earlier learned to question the worth-whileness of his subject matter.

Far from trying to foist upon an unwilling public a new conception of opera, Verdi considered himself a devoted servant of the public. What changes he ultimately effected in the fabric of opera were due to an honest workman's determination to give that public the best he had in him, and not to a conscious revolutionary's determination to reform either opera or opera-goers. In his early days, before his public was international, and when it was confined to an Italy in the throes of a long-drawn-out struggle for liberty and unity, Verdi was so much its servant that he gave it good rousing patriotic tunes more often than the music most properly demanded by the situations of the libretto.

I Lombardi alla prima crociata (1843), which followed *Nabucco*, shows at their worst the faults of a Verdi groping his way toward maturity. On the credit side, it has his flair for dramatic emphasis, apt underlining of character, and dynamic melody. Also partly on the credit side, but partly not, is its full, vigorous, and sometimes noisy scoring, certainly a relief after Donizetti's feeble accompaniments, but at its worst too reminiscent of the town band. It was this sort of scoring that was demanded by the rabble-rousing tunes his admirers could turn into marching songs and battle cries. Deep on the debit side are the libretto—a thoroughly incredible hodgepodge of high-flown historical romanticism—and those places where Verdi's nervous energy shrills into strident vulgarity or his easy tune-making degenerates into banality.

It cannot be said that *Ernani* (1844), which was the first of Verdi's operas to carry his name beyond the Alps, was much of an improvement: in it, the bad simply does not outweigh the good, as it definitely does in *I Lombardi*. The libretto, an adaptation of Victor Hugo's *Hernani* (it was one of Verdi's quaintly naïve ideas that any good play would necessarily make a good libretto), was the first furnished him by Francesco Maria Piave, a hard-working mediocrity whom the composer un-critically favored for eighteen years, until, that is, Piave was incapacitated by paralysis.

In a very short time, *Ernani* was given in Vienna, where Donizetti supervised it, in Paris, in London, and in New York, where, after being first heard at the Park Theater, on April 15, 1847,* it was used, on the following November 22, to open the first season of the Astor Place Opera House (whose orchestra was notoriously unruly and unwilling to co-operate), the principal lessee of which was Salvatore Patti, father of the famous Adelina. *Ernani*, too, reached San Francisco in 1853, the first grand opera to be sung there. It was not produced at the Metropolitan until January 28, 1903, when Marcella Sembrich headed a cast that included Scotti and Édouard de Reszke. After three performances, it was dropped until December 8, 1921, being revived then for Rosa Ponselle, with Martinelli, Danise, and Mardones. It has now been out of the repertoire a dozen years, and survives only on the concert platform through *"Ernani, involami,"* which, though a plea for elopement, is strangely unurgent. The much finer *"O sommo Carlo"* can be heard only on records, for it requires a chorus to support the baritone. It was as the heroine Elvira that the eighteen-year-old Pauline Lucca, one of the most individual singing talents of the mid-nineteenth century, made her debut, at Olmütz, on September 14, 1859.

The four operas that followed *Ernani* advanced Verdi's development not an inch, but, in view of the way he worked, the mere experience of composing them no doubt helped. Then came *Macbeth*, which caused him more heartburnings, over many years, than any other of his numerous works. He was passionately attached to it,† as he wished, through it, to offer fitting homage to Shakespeare, his lifelong idol. Unfortunately, it turned out to be, not a total failure (for that, at least, might have closed that chapter peremptorily), but one of those odd changelings that contain, amid many excellences, some fatal

* *I Lombardi* was the first Verdi score heard in the United States—at Palmo's Opera House, New York, on March 3, 1847.

† Verdi was only one of a number of composers who have been fascinated by *Macbeth*, beginning with Milton's friend Matthew Locke, whose incidental music on the theme dates from 1672, and has been described as "a pure emanation of genius." Beethoven's notebooks contain sketches for the overture and opening chorus of a projected opera on the subject. Completed *Macbeth*s exist by the French violinist Hippolyte Chélard, whose libretto was furnished by the composer of the *Marseillaise*, and by Ernest Bloch, whose version was produced in Paris in 1910. Shostakovich's *Lady Macbeth of Mzensk* has nothing to do with Shakespeare.

flaw. Because he loved its excellences, Verdi accepted the flaw as a challenge, and toyed—and sometimes toiled—at reconstruction off and on for eighteen years. It was his evil fortune that his own and Piave's original libretto was bad, more of the same that his friend Andrea Maffei's retouchings were worse, and finally, that the French translation for the 1865 Paris production was the worst of all.*

But Verdi had only himself to blame for not realizing, after his first disappointment with *Macbeth* in 1847, that it required, not revision, but complete rewriting. Yet, as the revising he did for Paris belonged to his maturity, he very much improved his first ideas, and added others. It was this later score that was enthusiastically applauded when *Macbeth* was revived in Germany some years ago. That score is chiefly in Verdi's advanced idiom, but even in the first draft he had been laboring toward a new conception of opera. In 1848, writing to Salvatore Cammarano, one of his librettists, about a projected performance of *Macbeth* at Naples, he aired some then radical ideas about the importance of unified musicodramatic effect:

> I understand that you are rehearsing *Macbeth*, and as this opera interests me more than any other, I ask you to allow me to say a few words about it. Mme Tadolini is, I believe, to sing Lady Macbeth, and I am astonished that she should have undertaken the part. You know how highly I think of Mme Tadolini, and she knows it too; but in all our interests I think it necessary to remark that she has too great qualities for this part! This may seem an absurdity! Mme Tadolini has a beautiful face and looks good, and I would have Lady Macbeth ugly and wicked. Mme Tadolini sings to perfection, and I would not have Lady Macbeth sing at all. Mme Tadolini has a wonderful voice, clear, liquid, and powerful, and Lady Macbeth's voice should be hard, stifled, and dark. Mme Tadolini's voice is the voice of an angel, and Lady Macbeth's should be the voice of a devil. Please bring these comments to the notice of the directors, of Maestro Mercadante, who will understand my

---

* That production was a failure. Saint-Saëns, who had been attracted to *Macbeth*, commented bitterly, in his memoirs: "I suggested to Carvalho that I write a *Macbeth* for Madame Viardot. Naturally enough he preferred to put on Verdi's *Macbeth*. It was an utter failure and cost him thirty thousand francs."

ideas better than any one, and of Mme Tadolini herself, and do what you think for the best.

It was along these lines, rather than by means of leitmotivs and other Wagnerian techniques, that Verdi approached a sort of music drama that was certainly not Wagnerian, but was quite as valid. He never labeled his most advanced scores "music dramas," or advertised his innovations, and Wagner was therefore credited automatically with all the reforms. Verdi's reticence in this direction was quite natural, for though there is evidence that he knew where he was, however slowly, going, he never wrote theory music as such. Until the publication of his correspondence many years after his death, the public had no way of knowing that Verdi had conscious aims of any sort. Only if audiences listened analytically to his best operas seriatim, from *Macbeth* on, could they deduce the fact that Verdi was as much a creative revolutionist as Wagner.

Of the six operas (one of them a French version of *I Lombardi*) between *Macbeth* and *Rigoletto*, only two are of interest, one for historical reasons, the other for musical. *I Masnadieri*, based on Schiller's *Die Räuber*, was the first opera Verdi wrote expressly for foreign production. Its reception at its London *première*, on July 22, 1847, was none too happy, despite Lind's appearance as its heroine. Chorley, whose antipathy to Verdi's music was to be almost lifelong, pontificated: "Her Amalia . . . could not have pleased had it been given by Saint Cecilia and Melpomene in one, so utterly worthless was the music."

Chorley was quite as stringent about the also Schiller-inspired *Luisa Miller* (1849) when it was first given in London about a decade later: "There are staccato screams in it enough to content any lover of shocking excitement; but the entire texture of the music implies (I can but fancy) either a feeble mistake or else a want of power on the part of an artificer who, obviously (as Signor Verdi does) demanding situation and passion and agony to kindle the fire under his cauldron, has also only one alphabet, one grammar, one dictionary, whatsoever the scene, whatsoever the country—one cantabile, one spasmodic bravura, one feverish crescendo, as the average tools by pressure of which the stress on the public is to be strained out."

But *Luisa Miller* is better than that. It starts with the advantage of a superior book, which must not be judged by the fact that its three acts are entitled "Love," "Intrigue," and "Poison." It is put together with great care and cunning (it is an unusually erudite score for this period of Verdi's development), and shows Verdi treating new types of situation and character. The way in which simple, effective touches are produced by learned musical means adumbrates *Falstaff*, while the intimacy of the situations and the homeliness of the characters look forward to *La Traviata*. Far from being anything like the monstrosity Chorley makes it out to be, *Luisa Miller* is comparatively restrained in tone, and is altogether a work of considerable charm. The overture is one of the best Verdi composed.

Chorley ended his denunciation with an arrogant guess: "I cannot conceive any English audience returning to *Luisa Miller*, and fancy that already the opera may be dead in Italy." Almost seventy-five years later, *Luisa Miller* was revived by the Sadler's Wells company. In America, its career dates from a production at Castle Garden, New York, on July 20, 1854. In the Academy of Music, it was sung on October 20, 1886, with Giulia Valda (a Boston soprano, whose real name was Julia Wheelock, and who had made her debut at Pavia, seven years earlier, as Leonora in *Il Trovatore*) in the name role. The Metropolitan did not stage it until December 21, 1929, when Rosa Ponselle was the Luisa, assisted by Marion Telva, Lauri-Volpi, De Luca, and Pavel Ludikar, with Serafin conducting. The opera was received tepidly and reached only a handful of performances. It is by no means improbable, however, that *Luisa Miller*—and *Macbeth*—may soon be revived successfully.

With *Rigoletto*, his seventeenth opera, Verdi wrote a masterpiece. Unquestionably—everything about the score proclaims it to be so. As staged, it is anything but a masterpiece—through no fault or omission of Verdi's. In it, he began breaking down the barriers between the individual numbers and the encompassing action, tending toward a continuous musical flow; he arrived at a mastery, just this side of supreme, of character creation, and he reached a new high in the projection of atmosphere. He was merely stating the truth when, on being urged to transfer to a much altered libretto music he had already completed, he retorted: "My music—good or bad as it may be—is written in no casual manner": in much of *Rigoletto*, music fuses indissolubly with action. Only when he fails to examine the dramatic requirements of a situation, and falls back upon traditional rule of thumb and operatic convention does Verdi show that he had not quite arrived.

Let us cite the three vocal touchstones of the opera, which—so vicious has the tradition become—are now almost the only reasons why *Rigoletto* is popular. *"Caro nome,"* meant to be a hushed, rapt, and exquisite meditation, comes off as a bravura piece for whatever lady is displaying her vocal athletics at the time. *"La donna è mobile,"* that perfect signature of the perfect libertine, establishes the Duke's character at once, and is used in the last scene to point the tragic irony of the entire opera. The tenor who plants himself downstage, and then sings it for applause, destroys Verdi's dramatic intentions. Finally, the great quartet, *"Bella figlia dell' amore,"* is a triumph of emotional counterpoint, with each character assigned an individually apt melodic line. Verdi's aim was to give each of them a spiritual separateness. As *"Bella figlia"* is usually rendered, it is made to sound as if (gestures apart) the four of them had decided to get together for a bout of part-singing. Is it any wonder that *Rigoletto* is dismissed by otherwise sensitive people as mere organ-grinder's music—a succession of tunes that you either do or do not like?

The tenseness of political conditions in 1850 was responsible for many changes in the book of *Rigoletto*. Founded on Hugo's *Le Roi s'amuse*, a ferocious drama built around the libertine Francis I, it came near to sharing the fortunes of its model. Hugo had dared to defy the government of Louis-Philippe, and the play had been banned after the first night. The Austrian censors objected violently, as much on moral as on political grounds, to *La Maledizione*—the original name of Piave's libretto. Verdi stood firm on essentials, but grudgingly agreed to change the French king into an unidentified duke of Mantua. He battled to the end against changing the hunchback Rigoletto into a normal human specimen, and for retaining the sack in which Rigoletto finds Gilda's body, disposing with withering logic of the objection that these elements were too repulsive. As Verdi wrote, "In my opinion, the presentation of this character, so deformed and ridiculous outside, so full of love and passion within, is a fine idea. Indeed, it was precisely on this account that I chose the subject." Things came to such a pass that the disputants—Verdi, Piave, and the secretary of the Teatro Fenice, at Venice, who naturally had to see eye to eye with the censor—signed an agreement that determined the final shape of the libretto. Incredibly, the result is one of the scant four or five good books Verdi ever managed to get at, and Hugo, who began by detesting *Rigoletto* as much as he had *Ernani*, ended up as its unstinting admirer.

From its first performance, on March 11, 1851, *Rigoletto* was a hit. Before that, Verdi had been a well-known composer, but *Rigoletto* immediately carried him to pre-eminence. After running like wildfire the entire length of the peninsula, where censorship trouble caused it to assume fabulously absurd *noms de guerre* such as *Viscardello* and *Clara di Perth*, within four years it was heard in Austria, Hungary, Bohemia, Germany, England, France, and the United States. In Paris, the soprano Erminia Frezzolini, whom Verdi had vainly tried to secure for the Fenice *première*, sang Gilda; the Maddalena was Alboni, and the Duke was Mario, who quickly made this one of his finest roles. *Rigoletto* came to the New York Academy of Music, then under lease to the violinist Ole Bull, on February 19, 1855, and was rarely out of its repertoire, Ronconi being a superb Rigoletto of this early period. On February 27, 1861, Clara Louise Kellogg, singing Gilda, made her world debut at the Academy, Adelaide Phillipps being the Maddalena. Fifteen years later, at Venice, the Hungarian Etelka Gerster, a future Academy of Music idol, entered opera as Gilda.

The Metropolitan, on November 17, 1883, staged *Rigoletto* as the ninth opera of its first season, with Sembrich as Gilda. Twenty years later, on November 23, when the Metropolitan used *Rigoletto* to initiate the season of 1903-04, she was again the Gilda, Scotti the Rigoletto, and Homer the Maddalena at the New York debut of Enrico Caruso (the Duke). Thus astutely did Heinrich Conried inaugurate his regime, and start Caruso on his unparalleled series of 607 Metropolitan appearances. Caruso had as signally captured London the year before, when he had used the same role for his first appearance there, playing opposite Melba (Gilda) and Renaud, possibly the greatest impersonator of the hunchback jester. Renaud, in turn, used Rigoletto as his New York debut role, at the Manhattan Opera House, on December 5, 1906, with Regina Pinkert as Gilda and Bonci as the Duke. Frances Alda made her Metropolitan bow as Gilda, on December 7, 1908, and, on November 4, 1912, Ruffo, as Rigoletto, made his American debut at Philadelphia.

Since 1915, *Rigoletto* has been a staple of the Metropolitan, where it has reached 165 performances. To name those who have interpreted the principal parts in this opera would be to call the roll of most of the great Italian-singing stars, but Amelita Galli-Curci must be specially mentioned: it was as Gilda that she made her world debut at the Costanzi, in Rome, in 1909, and as Gilda, too, that she provoked riotous demonstrations at her North American debut, at the Auditorium, Chicago, on November 18, 1916.* The most popular of recent Metropolitan Rigolettos has been Tibbett.

After finishing *Rigoletto*, Verdi returned to an old love of most horrifying aspect—a gory and wonderfully labyrinthine Spanish tragedy called *El Trovador*. Salvatore Cammarano and,

* In 1914, the Auditorium had been the scene of a quite different demonstration as the crisis of a quarrel between Cleofonte Campanini, generalissimo of the Chicago Opera Company, and his sister-in-law, Luisa Tetrazzini. Edward Moore, in his *Forty Years of Opera in Chicago*, thus recounts the incident that followed close on Tetrazzini's indiscreetly referring to Director Campanini as "merely a conductor": "She was singing Gilda in *Rigoletto* and he was conducting. She had reached '*Caro nome,*' and had skyrocketed into the cadenza with which she ended the aria when somehow or other she lost her place and her pitch, ending on a note which was high enough but many degrees away from the true one. Campanini's quick ear caught the mistake. Now a kindhearted conductor, even Campanini, if he had not had the previous row in his mind, would have allowed her note to die away, and while applause was raging, brought the orchestra in gently and softly, and probably no one in the audience would have detected the mistake. Instead, he sensed a devastating revenge. He took a firm grip of the baton, signaled the orchestra, and produced a crashing chord that jarred the roof and showed every one in the opera house the discordant spine-chilling distance that she had removed herself from the correct pitch. This is what 'merely a conductor' can do when unamiable. The two never appeared in the same performance again, never spoke again, in fact Mme. Tetrazzini never sang in Chicago again until after Campanini's death. And when she came to get out her autobiography, she made no mention of ever having sung in Chicago, and of Campanini only the fact that he had married her sister."

after his death, Emmanuele del Bardare achieved a libretto
with all essential situations intact, but all explanatory con-
nectives omitted, the result being an ellipsis undecipherable
without reference to the original play. With mounting doubts,
Verdi nevertheless set the book in either four or six weeks—in
either case, a wonder of speed. When the day of the *première*
of *Il Trovatore* came around, the Tiber had turned much of
Rome into a shallow lake. Yet the queue at the Teatro Apollo
began gathering early in the morning, despite weather and
advanced prices. The performance, by no means perfect, was a
triumph commensurate with that of *Rigoletto*, like which *Il
Trovatore* circumnavigated the globe in a few years. Many critics, however, refused to ride with the audience: calling upon
the names of Rossini, Bellini, and Donizetti, they pronounced
Il Trovatore the death of *bel canto*.

The critics were exaggerating: *bel canto* is a style of singing,
not a mode of composition, and it cannot be said to have
vanished completely even today. They meant, of course, that
Verdi was writing music that required dramatic interpretation,
both physical and vocal, sometimes at the expense of flawless
voice production. And *Il Trovatore* must have sounded to those
nostalgic lovers of the old times as though Verdi had composed
it to annoy. At forty, in his hale prime, after the artistic restraint of *Rigoletto*, he let himself go with hearty abandon. *Il
Trovatore* is strident, muscular—and spontaneous. Artistically
not half the opera *Rigoletto* is, it bursts with tunes of frank
and healthy vulgarity. Sensitive and critical lovers of music can
be forgiven for shuddering at what is most barefacedly noisy in
the opera—the "Anvil Chorus" is not music—but not for dismissing the entire opera with a sneer. In addition to the purely
musical charm of *"Il balen,"* a love lyric Verdi did not surpass,
and much of the last act, with its mingled wistfulness and
human tragedy, in *Il Trovatore* Verdi created, a full thirty-five
years before *Otello*, one of his most profoundly affecting characters. In the best sense, Azucena, the gypsy mother, is the
moving force of the opera, its *raison d'être*, even. She is no
lopsided abstraction of undiluted mother love, but a many-
sided woman of recognizable humanness. She is the descendant

of Eléazar in *La Juive*, and of Fidès, in *Le Prophète*—but the descent is purely chronological. *"Stride la vampa!"* and *"Ai nostri monti,"* her duet with Manrico, are revelations of character antithesis, not the irrelevant barrel-organ tunes they have been made to become.

The singers at the original *Il Trovatore*, on January 19, 1853, were of local importance, but the Leonora and Manrico of the Paris, London, and St. Petersburg *premières* were respectively Frezzolini and Mario, Viardot-García and Tamberlik, and Bosio and Tamberlik, proving that the opera was quickly taken up by stars of international reputation. In 1861, Colonel Mapleson inaugurated his management of the Lyceum Theater, London, with a brilliant performance that brought forward, under Arditi's baton, Tietjens (Leonora), Alboni (Azucena), Antonio Giuglini (Manrico), and Enrico delle Sedie (Di Luna), the last making his English debut.

Little more than two years after its Roman birth, *Il Trovatore* was staged by Maretzek at the New York Academy of Music, with Pasquale Brignoli, a luscious Italian tenor who was for many years a favorite on Fourteenth Street, as the Manrico. Annie Louise Cary, whose rich, pure contralto Anton Rubinstein had called the most beautiful in the world, made her debut, at Copenhagen, in 1867, as Azucena, and this became a popular fixture of her repertoire. In the heyday of the Academy she often sang it, in a galaxy that included Nilsson (Leonora), Italo Campanini (Manrico), and Del Puente (Di Luna). The third Metropolitan offering of the first season was *Il Trovatore*, the cast on that November 26, 1883, including Valleria, Trebelli, Roberto Stagno, and Kaschmann. Although popular, *Il Trovatore* has been allowed to degenerate, at the Metropolitan as elsewhere, into a mere routine penny-catcher. On February 20, 1915, it was completely restaged at the Metropolitan under Toscanini's supervision. The result was worth the trouble: Destinn, Margarete Ober, Martinelli, and Amato gave magnificent performances, and the audience was allowed to get a rare glimpse of what Verdi was trying for. By the season of 1940-41, it had slipped back so far that—at Toscanini's suggestion, it was rumored—it was again restudied, and once more with impressive results. The chief roles were taken by Norina Greco, a Metropolitan debutante, Castagna, Jussi Björling, and the Bronx-born Francesco Valentino.

After two huge successes, Verdi came up with a failure. Going against all operatic conventions, he selected a libretto laid in his own time. The characters wore costumes that his Venetian audience could have seen daily on the streets of Paris, and as opera was still largely a show, this was indeed radical. His heroine was a courtesan and a consumptive, and there were plenty of objections to her on both counts: it was not nice to show such laxity in a heroine, and for a singer to die of consumption was obviously ridiculous. Dumas' *La Dame aux camélias*,* from which Piave had expertly drawn the libretto, might have been convincing, but as an opera, with a stout and healthy heroine, *La Traviata* was too much for the first-night audience at the Fenice, on March 6, 1853. Worse than hissing, they burst into uproarious laughter at the most pathetic moments and left no doubt in Verdi's mind that his labors had been for nothing. "Is it my fault or the singers'?" he asked. "Time will show." Fourteen months later, *La Traviata* was revived with a credibly slender soprano and with costuming of the Louis XIII period. Venice revised its verdict, and at once *La Traviata* joined its two predecessors in public favor. These absurd costumes were adhered to until 1904, when Gemma Bellincioni, Stagno's wife, whom Verdi considered the best of Violettas, reverted to the crinolines of Dumas, which by that time had taken on a charming period character of their own.

Primarily a vehicle for the heroine, *La Traviata* has enlisted the interest of many of the most notable sopranos of the last ninety years, beginning with the delightful Marietta Piccolomini, who made her English debut in its London *première*, on May 24, 1856, at Her Majesty's, while, at Covent Garden, the equally charming Bosio was soon rivaling her in the same role. Before that year was out, New York had heard *La Traviata*, with Anna Caroline de La Grange and Brignoli, at the Academy of Music, on December 3, 1856. Violetta soon became, both here and abroad, a favorite debut role. Nilsson began her operatic career with it, at Paris in 1864, and used it for her first appearance in London. Lilli Lehmann, who could sing anything from the First Boy in *Die Zauberflöte* to

---

* On December 10, 1930, at the Chicago Civic Opera House, Mary Garden created her last role, that of Camille in another version of Dumas' play with music by Hamilton Forrest, a young American. *Camille* was coldly received.

Brünnhilde, and who is erroneously limited, in popular memory, to Wagnerian roles, burst on London as Violetta, on June 3, 1880.

Sembrich, the first Metropolitan Violetta, when *La Traviata* was given as the sixth offering of the first season, was most attractive, vocally and dramatically, in the role, which she chose, too, for her Metropolitan farewell, on January 23, 1909, when her Alfredo was Caruso. Among the three excerpts selected for her official farewell, two weeks later, was Act I of *La Traviata*, with the remarkable supporting cast of Caruso, Scotti, Didur, and Amato. Playing as a compliment to her elder colleague the small part of Flora Bervoise, Violetta's confidante, was Geraldine Farrar, herself a famous Violetta. Tetrazzini made her London and New York debuts, the latter at the Manhattan Opera House on January 15, 1908, as Violetta, and in that role Galli-Curci, on the opening night of the Metropolitan season of 1921-22, brought to their feet thousands of cheering New Yorkers as she concluded her debut there. Violetta has been a popular role with such artists as Patti, Melba, Bori, Ponselle, Helen Jepson, and Bidu Sayao. Even Máry Garden tried to sing it, but with more dramatic than vocal success.

Next to Violetta's, the baritone role of the elder Germont has been most popular with aspiring stars, chiefly because he has an opportunity to sing an unforgettably banal tune—*"Di Provenza il mar."* Renaud was perhaps the best of old-time Germonts, Tibbett the best of recent. Finally, it was in the bit part of the Doctor that a young Englishman by the name of Charles Santley began, at Pavia in 1857, his phenomenal fifty-eight-year career. As Alfredo, John McCormack made his New York debut, at the Manhattan Opera House, on November 10, 1909.

Historically speaking, *La Traviata* marks the first successful attempt to tap a vein that Verdi himself had found, some years before, in *Luisa Miller*, and, even more, in the poorly received *Stiffelio* (1850). This was realistic treatment, in opera, of scenes and situations from contemporary life, involving characters whose sole importance is their own personal drama. In turning to them, Verdi tacitly abandons—temporarily—the world of *la haute politique*, of monarchs and courtiers, of great wars, involved plots, ceremony, and ritual. He recognizes, in this bold departure, the triumph of the bourgeoisie: previously, the bourgeois had been admitted into comic opera, but Verdi was the first to make his tragedies the stuff of serious operas.

Luisa Miller had been an intuitive step in this direction: the characters were ordinary enough, but the scene was conventionally located two centuries back. *Stiffelio* tactlessly went the whole way in dealing with a domestic tragedy of nineteenth-century Germany, in itself palatable, but confusing to Verdi's Catholic audiences because its chief character was a married clergyman. *Stiffelio* did not please, and Verdi's remedy seems to prove that he was not ready for his own audacities. In *Aroldo*, the revision of 1857, he moved the locale to Scotland and England in the time of the Crusades and turned the characters into knights and ladies, but left the central psychological conflict as it was, not realizing that its implications were essentially modern. It is significant that he thus bungled this job after seeing *La Traviata* changed from failure into success by a mere recostuming. He saw, when *Aroldo* did not find a public, that there was no infallible way of salvaging these domestic pieces, and so never returned to them. They were taken up again, as the world well knows, by his successors, the verists.

La Traviata is almost a chamber opera. Sensitive to the kind of treatment demanded by the book, Verdi wrote the entire score on a smaller scale than was his wont. It is one of his few essays in sheer charm—the very antithesis of the fustian of *Il Trovatore*. *La Traviata* is quiet, almost monochromatic in spots, and would doubtless gain in effect if presented in theaters smaller than the average opera house. It calls for intimacy, and in a large hall much of its pathos is dissipated between stage and audience. It is not only a heroine's opera, it is also the vehicle of a frail and exquisite personality—a fact that Verdi did not forget, even though most producers do. His lovely preludes to Acts I and III, so different from his noisy overtures, are the signatures of certain aspects of Violetta's character and condition. The wonderful *scena* at the end of Act I is an abundant proof of Verdi's ability to take old, seemingly outworn forms and make them the unerring instruments of psychological verisimilitude. *"Ah! fors' è lui,"* followed by *"Sempre libera,"* is actually an old-fashioned slow cavatina developing into a rapid, pyrotechnical cabaletta. Earlier composers—and Verdi himself—had used this formula for any type of character, but here it is related, shaped with loving care, to the clearly conceived personality of Violetta, and to her situation at this stage of the narrative. It is creative dramatic music, and carries the story forward in a way only music can. And so, often by the use of this same sort of threadbare device handled with uncanny freshness and creative imagination, Verdi eloquently brings the moving story to its inevitable tragic finale.

During the eighteen years between *La Traviata* and *Aïda*, Verdi wrote five completely new operas, four of which have retained a precarious hold on the stage. Verdi, at forty successful and rich, could afford the luxury of meditating on his ideas before putting pen to paper and of working with care and deliberation after he got started. Besides, he was the squire of a large estate, with a gentleman farmer's interest in his land, and was for a time involved in politics at the insistence of his friend Cavour. The gaps between operas became wider: *La Traviata* is 1853, *Les Vêpres siciliennes* 1855, *Simon Boccanegra* 1857, *Un Ballo in maschera* 1859, *La Forza del destino* 1862, *Don Carlos* 1867, and *Aïda* 1871. However, longer time taken did not always mean better results. Of them all, only *Aïda* is, as a totality, equal to *La Traviata*, but almost all of them show progress in Verdi's command of musicodramatic techniques. Only one of the group, and that the earliest, is wholly poor stuff.

Les Vêpres siciliennes was Verdi's first order from the Paris Opéra, and he executed it with a timidity generally foreign to his nature, though he did flare up at the makeshift historical canvas that Scribe, in a tactless and unconciliatory mood, painted with his most careless brush. Faced with the need of setting a libretto in French, the already vexed composer did the natural thing: he left his own style in Italy and wrote imitation Meyerbeer. The results could have been expected. In the interminable five-act score, only the overture—which freakishly happens to be the best Verdi ever produced—is first-rate. The bastard French ballet music is frightful trash. The poorness of the vocal music might charitably be ascribed to Verdi's difficulties with French declamation, but when he recast the opera for Italy as *I Vespri siciliani* (its final title there), it was not noticeably ameliorated.

Ill duck dogged *Les Vêpres'* fortunes. Cruvelli, the diva chosen to create Elena, disappeared a few days before the *première*, giving rise to a scandal that the cynical Parisian newspapers delightedly played up under the caption, "Where is Cruvelli?" Although she turned up in time to fulfill her obligations in a composed manner, *Les Vêpres siciliennes* failed, on June 13, 1855, to please its first-night audience. Poor Verdi was in a dilemma with the libretto, which pleased neither the Italians, whom it represented as murderous desperados, nor the French, whom—greater insult!—it showed as the Italians' stupid victims. Nor has the opera caught on elsewhere.

Simon Boccanegra, a work that New York has come to know well since 1932 because of Lawrence Tibbett's interest in the title role, is another matter. Like *Macbeth*, it was revised many years after its *première*, and therefore includes elements from different periods of Verdi's development. First produced in 1857, in its final version (1881) it belongs to the long inter-regnum between *Aïda* and *Otello*. Piave had no forthright *Dame aux camélias* to work on, but one of those lengthy and intricately involved dramas by the same Spaniard—Antonio Gutiérrez García—who had written *El Trovador*. And just as Cammarano had miffed the job of abridging *El Trovador*, and so produced a puzzle to which only readers of Gutiérrez García have the key, Piave got out of his difficulty only by reducing *Simon Boccanegra* to nonsense. Arrigo Boïto, called in to doctor the libretto for the 1881 revision, was almost equally floored, and left the job little improved. Ironically, in providing a new scene for which Verdi wrote the most moving music of the later version, Boïto slowed up the action to the point of immobility. *Simon Boccanegra* is an opera of almost unrelieved gloom both atmospherically and spiritually. The chief character is tediously, inhumanly noble, and there simply is not enough drama to go around, during a prologue and three acts, for the large cast of characters. Yet, Verdi never worked more strenuously, and he ended by composing for *Simon Boccanegra* some of his richest pages. The music should keep it in the repertoire; the libretto has threatened, from the days of both *premières*, to relegate it to oblivion.

Only the fact that for the version of 1881 La Scala had secured the services of three of the greatest singers then alive—Maurel as Boccanegra, Tamagno as Gabriele Adorno, and Édouard de Reszke as Jacopo Fiesco—sufficed to make *Simon Boccanegra* more than a *succès d'estime*. It was not heard in America until the Metropolitan produced it on January 28, 1932, with Tibbett (Boccanegra), Martinelli (Adorno), Pinza (Fiesco), and Maria Müller as the Doge's daughter Amelia—one of the few contrasting notes in a somber score. Pinza gave a magnificent account of the best-known excerpt from the opera, the dramatic apostrophe, *"Il lacerato spirito,"* and Tibbett was altogether admirable as Boccanegra.

After leaving it in silence for a quarter of a century, the Metropolitan, on December 2, 1940, revived *Un Ballo in maschera* for the opening of the 1940-41 season, the first opera put forward after the purchase of the house by the resident company. Sumptuously mounted, and with an aggregation of singers headed by Zinka Milanov (Amelia), Thorborg (Ulrica), Stella Andreva (Oscar), Björling (Riccardo), and, in his Metropolitan debut, Alexander Sved (Renato), it was well received by the first nighters. It was, nevertheless, in many respects an absurd performance. The scenes were laid in Stockholm, but we were asked to believe in two Swedish characters called Sam (Norman Cordon) and Tom (Nicola Moscona). In a laudable attempt to return to the Sweden of Gustav III, which the librettist naturally had in mind for a story dealing with that monarch's assassination, Director Johnson had contented himself, unfortunately, with a half measure.

Antonio Somma, Verdi's librettist, had been forced by the censors, overjittery because of a recent attempt on Napoleon III's life, to move the scene to Boston (possibly because of the relaxed political conditions, no one had objected to Auber's *Gustave III, ou Le Bal masqué,* in 1833) and to change King Gustav into a titled colonial governor. The Metropolitan restored the original locale, but not the identities of the King—who remained "Riccardo, conte di Warwick"—or the other personages of the drama. This shilly-shallying did, and does, no

good for the cause of opera, and there were plenty to criticize ·
uncharitably this well-meant evasion of the whole problem.

It is fair to say, however, that *Un Ballo in maschera*, even if
restored completely to the conditions Verdi had in mind, would
never be a popular opera. The plot is unwieldy, unintegrated,
and the music not often ravishing to the ear. It is another milestone on Verdi's route between one period of mastery and
another. As such, it is interesting. For instance, Riccardo, a
later edition of the Duke in *Rigoletto*, has the variety of a fully
realized human being. More important is the introduction into
a tragic opera of an elegant, witty, foppish, and featherbrained
creature who might have stepped out of the pages of *Le Nozze
di Figaro*, so much does the Oscar of *Un Ballo* resemble Cherubino. This shows that Verdi, taking full advantages of the
opportunities his librettist had given him, was ready to project
a whole world, which, however predominantly tragic, had its
interludes of something else. Even the conspirators, Sam and
Tom, are not without their moments of lightness, while the
wronged and vengeful Renato is much redeemed by the beauty
of his great aria, *"Eri tu."*

The Teatro Apollo at Rome was the scene of the first performance, on February 17, 1859, of *Un Ballo in maschera*. Although
Paris had the first important performance outside Italy, real drama
surrounded the London *première*, on June 15, 1861, five months
later. Colonel Mapleson already had Arditi rehearsing it at Her
Majesty's when Frederick Gye, his rival at Covent Garden, decided
to race for the honor. Casts were well matched: Mapleson had,
among other notables, Tietjens, Giuglini, and Delle Sedie; Gye had
Miolan-Carvalho, already famous as the first Marguerite in *Faust*,
Nantier-Didiée, a popular but short-lived mezzo-soprano born in
the African island of Réunion, and Mario. Mapleson won by a
single week.

New York heard *Un Ballo* before London did, when it was presented at the Academy of Music on February 11, 1861. Lilli Lehmann, who, some years before, had sung Oscar, in Italian, at Berlin,
in a company headed by Désirée Artôt, a onetime flame of Tchaikovsky's, was the first Metropolitan Amelia when, on December
11, 1889, this Italian opera about the murder of a Swedish king
metamorphosed into a Cavalier governor of a Puritan settlement

in the wilds of North America was sung in German. After four performances that season, *Ein Maskenball* disappeared forever from the Metropolitan. The Italian version was first sung there on February 23, 1903, by a stupendous cast, including Gadski, Homer, Fritzi Scheff, Emilio de Marchi, Campanari, Édouard de Reszke, and Journet. This galaxy failed to put over *Un Ballo*, which was withdrawn after a single performance, to make its reappearance on February 6, 1905, when an even more imposing collection of artists sang it—Eames, Homer, Bella Alten, Caruso, Scotti, Plançon, and Journet. These held for two performances, and then another eight years went by before, on November 22, 1913, Gatti-Casazza tried it, again with an all-star cast—Destinn, Matzenauer, Hempel, Caruso, Amato, De Segurola, and Rothier. This time, it lasted ten performances scattered over three seasons. Then the long break until 1940. In view of those magnificent casts who valorously failed to establish *Un Ballo* in the past, its permanence in the repertoire does not seem likely now.

Fortunate circumstances rather than any popularity of the score itself seem to have kept Verdi's next opera—*La Forza del destino*—from *Un Ballo*'s fate at the Metropolitan. In the first place, one of the most wide-selling of the old Red Seal records (Victor 89001) had made Caruso and Scotti's dramatic singing of the third-act duet—*"Solenne in quest' ora"*—as much a household god as an oleograph of *The Sistine Madonna* or the Purple Seal record of Lucy Isabelle Marsh singing the "Italian Street Song" from Victor Herbert's *Naughty Marietta*. Therefore, thousands who would never have heard of *La Forza del destino* had been prepared, over ten years, to flock to the first performances. In the second place, when the Metropolitan got around to producing it, on November 15, 1918, it happened that Rosa Ponselle, an ambitious refugee from vaudeville, where with her sister Carmela, she had made up the "Ponzillo Sisters" act, was making her operatic debut opposite Caruso.* Oddly, not Scotti but De Luca, was chosen as the Don Carlo for Caruso's Don Alvaro. New York liked *La Forza del destino*, and before Caruso died, he had sung in it nineteen times at the

---

* In fact, it was a night of debuts, for Alice Gentle, a Manhattan Opera House recruit, and the tenor Giordano Paltrinieri made their Metropolitan bows in minor roles.

Metropolitan. The retirement of Ponselle has banished *La Forza* temporarily, and a revival does not seem likely until a dramatic soprano able to do comparable wonders with the difficult music assigned to Leonora comes forward.

La Forza del destino was composed to order for the Imperial Opera, St. Petersburg, and its reception there, on November 10, 1862, won Verdi a decoration from Alexander II and frigid attention from an audience half hostile because of the national composers' cabal against the Latin invader. He took his new opera to Madrid, where it was much more warmly received, due partly to the fact that the Spaniards were already familiar with the minutiae of the very detailed drama, by the liberal Duke of Rivas, on which it was based. Yet, *La Forza* was by no means the kind of hit Verdi had by this time become accustomed to, and in 1869 he tried for a larger public by shortening it somewhat. This helped measurably, and though the original version had been heard in New York as early as 1865, the revised was used in 1881, when a notable cast, including Annie Louise Cary, Italo Campanini, Galassi, and Del Puente, sang it at the Academy of Music. It was with the revision, too, that the Metropolitan chalked up thirty-seven performances during sixteen seasons.

La Forza del destino carried Verdi a step farther toward his artistic maturity. The ever-increasing attention to the shaping of the characters is apparent throughout, though it is unfortunate that, in the cases of Leonora and, to a lesser extent, some of the other personages, much of the music, in itself moving, is attached to beings whose lack of free will invests them with the nature of puppets. The roster of characters shows another interesting recruit: just as Verdi had introduced, in *Un Ballo in maschera*, the comic-opera figure of Oscar, so, in *La Forza del destino*, he imported from *opera buffa* the bluff, roistering friar, Melitone—a character whose presence speaks volumes for Verdi's broadened understanding of life's diversity. Melody pours forth unstintedly, but modeled with a growing attention to total effect, and along more spacious, longer-breathed lines. The accompaniment has abandoned the tedious naïveté of the earlier operas, and is at once subtler, more integral, and more solid. The orchestra, without ever dominating the singers, claims attention for itself as a necessary dramatic ingredient.

Although Verdi was moving relentlessly and utterly in his own way toward a conception of opera that can as legitimately be called music drama as anything of Wagner's, *La Forza* still has easily detachable set numbers, not a few of which are known in concert performance. Apart from *"Solenne in quest' ora,"* that splendidly dramatic tenor-baritone duet, the type of which had been adumbrated eloquently in *Les Vêpres siciliennes*, they range from the elaborately worked-out overture through Leonora's piteous prayer, *"Madre, pietosa vergine,"* and her tragic last-act outburst, *"Pace, pace, mio dio,"* through Don Alvaro's lamenting *"O tu che in seno agli angeli,"* to *"Non imprecare,"* the fine trio for the Abbot and two of the chief victims of fate —Leonora and her brother.

The difference between *La Forza del destino* and *Don Carlos*, its successor after five years, is, except for subject matter, purely formal. In the first, the tendency to repudiate the set-number formula was becoming obvious; in the second, it was accomplished. *Don Carlos* is, however imperfectly, a music drama. But it was, unhappily for Verdi, made for the Opéra, which meant a libretto in French—a language for which he composed insensitively. In 1867, it also meant a libretto in the style preferred by Meyerbeer, whose long dictatorship had been cut short by death only three years before. It meant, also, ballet music, the composition of which, then and always, invited Verdi to banality. It meant, finally, working with collaborators who were imperfectly acquainted with the processes of Verdi's thoroughly Italian mind. In the course of the collaboration, many misunderstandings arose, and it is no wonder that the product of this *mésalliance* was a hybrid of unstable character, sometimes musically equal to Verdi's best previous work—even hinting at what was to come in the masterpieces of his last years—and sometimes of an abysmal banality.

The librettists, Joseph Méry and Camille du Locle, took Schiller's *Don Carlos* and painstakingly robbed it of everything except the circumstances of exterior drama and encompassing gloom. Verdi, unable to cast off the heavy traditions of the

Opéra, set it in a style formally all his own, but texturally part himself, part Meyerbeer. And, in general effect, *Don Carlos* was comparable to those vast historical pageants to which the composer of *Les Huguenots* and *Le Prophète* was partial. Neither the public nor Verdi was ever satisfied with it, in either French or Italian, and though it was twice revised, the scattered modern performances show that nothing, not even collecting the cream of the three versions (as the Metropolitan did), can make *Don Carlos* convincing or popular.

The unhappy career of *Don Carlos* began with the *première*, at the Opéra, on March 11, 1867, at the height of the Exposition Universelle. The two leading stars of the cast—Sax and Faure— did not perform as brilliantly as usual, and when the Empress Eugénie, offended by heretical opinions expressed by one of the characters, ostentatiously turned her back to the stage, it was Paris' equivalent of thumbs down for *Don Carlos*. America first heard the opera about Philip II and his luckless son on April 12, 1877, at the Academy of Music, New York. More than forty-three years later, on December 23, 1920, the Metropolitan Opera Company presented the eclectic version edited by Gennaro Papi, one of its conductors, with staging and costumes by the lavish Joseph Urban. Ponselle had the nominal heroine's role of Elisabetta, but to Matzenauer, as the Princess Eboli, fell the task of singing the somberly tragic *"O don fatale,"* the one sure-fire number in the score. Sundelius, Martinelli, De Luca, and Didur rounded out the cast. In 1922, Chaliapin, assuming Didur's role of Philip II, acquitted himself so eloquently that he took the unusual liberty of repeating a part of the king's soliloquy in Act I. This performance was also notable for the restoration of the super-Meyerbeerian Inquisition scene, in which Rothier, as the Grand Inquisitor, showed himself a great singing actor. Yet, such productions failed to establish *Don Carlos* in America, and it has not been heard within the last twenty years. In England, in 1938, it was revived with some success, in an English translation, at Sadler's Wells.

The many grand pages in *Don Carlos* indicated that Verdi had been defeated only by the inadequacies of the libretto. His mature style was shaped: it only waited on a congruous and dramatic book for its effective display. It may be asked what this mature style was. It was, simply, Verdi's first and only style, subjected to refining, polishing, observation from a hundred different angles, meditation, so changing the original that it seemed to be something quite new. The trial-and-error method instinctively followed by this practical worker for the operatic stage had ended in the sloughing off of everything that was uncongenial to the perfect projection of dramatic values. In 1869, when Verdi was fifty-six years old, and already the composer of twenty-three operas, he had only just achieved this ideal instrument. Possessing it, he was not inclined to labor on a book unworthy of his genius.

Therefore, when Ismail Pasha, Khedive of Egypt, invited him to compose an opera on an Egyptian theme for the opening of the Suez Canal, Verdi had to be wooed. After two flat refusals, he finally consented to examine a scenario—the barest skeleton of an outline—by the French archeologist, Mariette Bey. He liked it and authorized Du Locle, one of the librettists of *Don Carlos*, to write a French book based on it. This was translated into Italian by Antonio Ghislanzoni,* for whom Verdi had the highest regard because of his revision of the text of *La Forza del destino*. Closely consulting on every phase of the script not only with Verdi but also with his wife, the erstwhile singer Giuseppina Strepponi, a remarkable woman of acute intelligence who had sung in her husband's first operas, Ghislanzoni produced a conventional but thoroughly dramatic libretto, full from start to finish of those strong situations which delight the heart of a born theatrical composer.

Aïda missed the opening of the Suez Canal, the Franco-Prussian War doing its best to hinder the plans of the various personages involved. However, Cairo did get the *première*, two years later, on December 24, 1871, with Verdi, irritated by all the fanfare, conspicuously absent. But he was as conspicuously present at *Aïda's* Italian *première*, at La Scala, on February 8, 1872, when Teresa Stolz, a German soprano he intensely admired, sang the name role, with another of his

---

* Not Ghislandoni, as the official Metropolitan Opera House libretto continues to spell it.

A Metropolitan Performance of Verdi's *Otello*, with Frances Alda (Desdemona), Florence Wickham (Emilia), Leo Slezak (Otello), and Antonio Scotti (Iago)

favorites, Maria Waldmann, as Amneris. The acclamations
that rang through the huge opera house that night foretold the
unique career in store for *Aïda*. Soon Verdi was deluged with
pleas to lend his presence to firsts of his new opera, but in
almost every case he refused. For instance, though he was in
London in 1876 to hear the Requiem he had completed in
1874 to honor the memory of Italy's most famous novelist,
Alessandro Manzoni, he refused to be present, on June 22, at
the Covent Garden *première* of *Aïda*, partly because he was
piqued that, for the heroine, Patti had been preferred to Stolz.
Patti's future husband, the tenor Nicolini, was the Rhadames,
and Scalchi the Amneris.

In Paris, where the early coldness toward Verdi had been tempered by his generosity to the French cause in the Franco-Prussian
War, complete reconciliation came on April 22, 1876, when the
Théâtre Italien (Verdi's long-standing unfriendly relations with
the Opéra were unchanged) produced *Aïda*, with Stolz, Waldmann,
Angelo Masini (Rhadames), and Édouard de Reszke (the King), the
last making his operatic debut. Although the Italian version was
very successful—there were sixty-seven repetitions at the Italien in
less than four years—apotheosis came four years later, on March
22, 1880, when the Opéra and Verdi made it up. At that French
Aïda, President Grévy made a speech and created Verdi a grand
officer of the Legion of Honor.

Before either London or Paris had heard *Aïda*, it had begun its
career as the most popular of all operas in America. First heard at
the Academy of Music, New York, on November 26, 1873, it starred
Ottavia Torriani (Aïda), Annie Louise Cary (Amneris), Italo Campanini (Rhadames), and Maurel (Amonasro), the last making his
American bow. It became a staple of the Academy, and was soon
being sung everywhere by traveling companies. Oddly, it did not
appear promptly at the Metropolitan; it was not until the fourth
season—1887-88—that *Aïda*, sung in German, ticked off, on November 12, the first performance of its amazing record in that house.*
Anton Seidl conducted. The Aïda was the wife of his first cellist, Victor Herbert. The Amneris was Brandt; Adolf Robinson was
Amonasro, and the Ramfis was Emil Fischer. After the downfall of

* The exact number, as this book goes to press, just before the inauguration of
the 1941-42 season, is 301.

the German regime, *Aïda* reverted to its original language, and is now always sung in Italian.*

More often than any other opera, *Aïda* has opened Metropolitan seasons. It was the first presentation of the Metropolitan group when it visited Paris in 1910, Destinn and Caruso being the lovers, Toscanini the conductor. *Aïda* had served, twenty-four years earlier, to speed this most famous of conductors on his career, for when, at Rio de Janeiro, on June 25, 1886, a staff conductor was hissed from the podium, his place was taken by Toscanini, then a nineteen-year-old cellist in the theater band; he brought *Aïda* to a triumphant conclusion. On November 16, 1908, Giulio Gatti-Casazza began his twenty-six years at the Metropolitan helm with a performance of *Aïda*,† presenting both Toscanini and Destinn to American audiences for the first time. It is one of the very few operas to be given at the Metropolitan twice in a single week. It was during a Saturday matinee broadcast of *Aïda*, on February 26, 1938, that Martinelli, seized with illness in the first act, tottered off the stage. The curtain was rung down, and stayed down while the audience waited and the station orchestra filled in with dreary salon music until the hastily summoned Jagel assumed his Italian confrere's role. This was an unprecedented action: had there been no radio audience, it is possible that the opera might have been called off and money refunded.

On November 3, 1910, the first resident company to try success at the twenty-year-old Auditorium, in Chicago, shrewdly chose *Aïda* for its opening gambit. Amneris was an Eleanor Broadfoot who, years before, had, by a fortunate marriage, been enabled to abandon

---

* A telling indication of the perennial appeal of *Aïda* to New York audiences is afforded by a mere listing of the most important singers who have sung its most important roles at the Metropolitan. (A *d* after a name indicates Metropolitan debut.) The Aïdas have included Lilli Lehmann, Nordica, Félia Litvinne, Eames, Melba, Celestina Boninsegna, Destinn (*d*), Mazarin (*d*), Muzio, Rosa Ponselle, Rethberg (*d*), Nanette Guilford, Maria Müller, Dusolina Giannini (*d*), Gina Cigna (*d*), and Stella Roman (*d*). Amneris has been sung there by Mantelli, Brema, Homer (*d*), Edyth Walker (*d*), Matzenauer, Ober, Onegin (*d*), Karin Branzell, Viola Philo (*d*), Carmela Ponselle (*d*), Maria Olszewska, Cyrena Van Gordon (*d*), Kathryn Meisle (*d*), Wettergren (*d*), Castagna (*d*), and Thorborg. Rhadames has brought forward Jean de Reszke, Tamagno, Saléza, Caruso, Riccardo Martin, Martinelli, Johnson, Lauri-Volpi, and Jagel (*d*). The Amonasros have included Maurel, Ancona, Campanari, Scotti, Amato, Danise (*d*), Fritz Feinhals, Michael Bohnen, Schorr, John Charles Thomas, Tibbett, Bonelli, and Leonard Warren. As Ramfis have been heard Édouard de Reszke, Plançon, Journet (*d*), Rothier, Mardones (*d*), Pinza, Chase Baromeo (*d*), and Nicola Moscona (*d*).

† His regime had tried its wings in Brooklyn two days earlier with a splendidly cast *Faust* (see p. 309).

that uncouth name for the more euphonious Eleanora de Cisneros. Mario Sammarco, a great baritone who later was on the managing board of La Scala, was the Amonasro. Cleofonte Campanini conducted. Hammerstein's New York debacle had been Chicago's gain, for the resident Chicago aggregation was substantially the same as the one with which the Manhattan Opera House had been making musical history.

What has made *Aïda* unquestionably the most popular opera of all time? The answer is not to be found in any one element, but in the combination of many masterfully controlled elements. In exactly right proportions, *Aïda* has the lure of pageantry and ceremonial, of exotic coloring and locale, of moving dramatic climaxes and lyric interludes—all against a background of beautiful melody treated with harmonic richness and orchestrated with a pertinence toward which Verdi had been striving, not always successfully, for years. *Aïda* is a gallery of clearly defined characters, their traits set forth with a sweeping sureness of touch that carries its own conviction. Their emotions are easy to understand, and the situations are richly varied without being complicated.

Aïda has everything—even that bit of cheapness which makes the whole world kin. In this score, which in performance gushes forth with untrammeled spontaneity, everything is so nicely calculated that it is impossible not to believe that Verdi measured out the right proportion of cheapness, too. The proportion in the score is small—and right—but in performance it is often so overemphasized as to appear predominant. Verdi could not know, for instance, of productions such as that which Mapleson sponsored in Chicago in 1886, when six hundred state militiamen and an extra chorus of three hundred and fifty swelled the triumphal march in Act II to Barnumidian proportions.

Strangely, the very effective opening scene begins with the, at first, banal *"Celeste Aïda,"* which Jean de Reszke could stomach so little that he generally omitted it, and which is, anyhow, rarely heard by late diners. The chief glories of the opera—the "Nile scene" in Act III and the entire last act—fortunately come late enough for even the most fashionable society to hear them. These are exquisitely beautiful, poignantly affecting tableaus, each dynamic and integrated. Although, in *Otello* and *Falstaff*, Verdi moved on to a more subtle musical speech, *Aïda* is a perfect thing of its kind. With it, after eighteen years of patient experimentation, often with disappointing results, Verdi had arrived, for the second time in his still-eventful career, at mastery.

There were sixteen years between *Aïda* and *Otello*, the first of the two masterpieces of Verdi's old age. During this long period, he composed only the deftly constructed if not very profound String Quartet (1873) and, in the following year, the "Manzoni" Requiem, but he was by no means in retirement. He traveled extensively, particularly when the overwhelming success of the Requiem brought constant demands for his presence as its conductor—demands he was loath to refuse, as he felt the obligation to be a patriotic one. Precisely halfway between *Aïda* and *Otello*, Boïto, whom Verdi had regarded coldly for many years because of Boïto's youthful criticism of his music, was reconciled to him. In 1879, Boïto, besides having written the libretto for Ponchielli's *La Gioconda*, was himself the composer of *Mefistofele*, an opera which, after a bad start, had gained popular suffrage. But Boïto, despite his own considerable fame, had so changed his estimate of Verdi that he was more than willing to put aside his own musical ambitions and become Verdi's Da Ponte.

Someone—probably Tito Ricordi, Verdi's publisher—therefore suggested that Boïto construct a book after Shakespeare's *Othello*. Verdi, approached in the matter, held back for numerous reasons: in addition to a natural suspicion of the converted Boïto, he did not care to shelve either his old idea of an opera based on *King Lear*, or of one on a comic subject. Finally, as Rossini's *Otello* still held the stage, Verdi was not eager to challenge comparison with the dead master. However, he was soon won over, and Boïto entrenched himself in Verdi's esteem by undertaking the thankless job of revising the text of *Simon Boccanegra* for the La Scala revival of 1881. By 1885, Verdi had begun actually to clothe Boïto's *Otello* with music, and the opera was completed the following year, though the meticulous production plans delayed the *première*, at La Scala, until February 5, 1887.

Supplied with a libretto that was not merely adequate as a theatrical vehicle, but was in itself a work of literary distinction, Verdi, at seventy-three more than ever hypersensitive to the demands of his text, rose to the perfect opportunity and wrote the most magnificent of his tragic operas. Its long period of gestation bore fruit new to Verdi's orchard, yet indubitably his own. He had always been supremely a melodist: in *Otello* he remained one. But his use of melody had changed: in *Aïda* he invokes a sweeping lyrical sentence to proclaim, there and forever, a certain character; in *Otello*, melodies much less broad and, in most cases, less lyrical, reveal, seriatim, the facets that make up character. The method does not, at first hearing, have as much attractiveness as that which Verdi discarded, but the man who composed *Otello* was even more interested in the subtleties of psychological verity than the man who had composed *Aïda*. In *Otello*, the principal characters reveal themselves until the moment of their usually violent end: it is literally true, for example, that Otello discloses the last fact about himself only with his death rattle.

When opera becomes the dramatic thing *Otello* is, it takes over some of the attributes of the legitimate theater and heightens them by its own magic. In *Otello*, that magic relies chiefly on the sensitive eloquence of the music itself, reflecting every mood, illuminating every situation. The music is, therefore, of an infinite variety. The pure, untroubled love scene in Act I has, as its musical expression, a shimmering, ecstasy-filled, and tenderly lyrical flood of song; the "Oath" duet in Act II contrasts malign craft with agonized doubt shading into blind jealousy not only by the type of music allotted respectively to Iago and Otello, but also by the shrewd exploitation of the psychological qualities of baritone and tenor; in Act III, when Otello and Desdemona sing their duet, for Otello purity is sullied and tenderness soured, and his scornful, raging spasms of sound spew out against her confused innocence. While the beauty of the score is sometimes forgotten in the intensity of the crowding drama, it has, nevertheless, not a few pages of intense loveliness. The last scene is as nearly perfect as anything Verdi ever did. It is all the more moving because the gross violence of the climax is preceded by Desdemona's exquisite "Willow Song" (*"Salce, salce"*) and poignant *"Ave Maria,"* and followed by Otello's quiet suicide soliloquy, which, by quoting the kiss motive from Act I, at once intensifies the tragedy, rounds out the character of the Moor, and clarfies the aesthetic problem.

Romilda Pantaleoni, the first Desdemona, was of local celebrity, and so remained, but Tamagno and Maurel, respectively the Otello and Iago of that La Scala *première*, were destined to become world famous in the parts they created. The very next year—1888— Italo Campanini attempted to establish Verdi's tragic masterpiece in New York. As lessee of the Academy of Music, he produced it on April 16, with his sister-in-law, Luisa Tetrazzini's sister Eva, as Desdemona, and his brother Cleofonte, Eva's husband, as the conductor. Galassi (Iago) and Scalchi (Emilia) acquitted themselves with distinction, but the cast had an unsatisfactory tenor, one Marconi, as the Otello. The reception was not reassuring, and Campanini, dismissing Marconi, tried the name role himself—in vain.

After seven repetitions of *Otello*, the Academy temporarily closed its doors, and the opera was not again heard in New York until Abbey and Grau presented it, during a spring season at the Metropolitan, on March 24, 1890. Tamagno, making his American debut, sang his old role, Del Puente being the Iago, and Scalchi the Emilia. Albani (Desdemona) was, though already well known in New York, a Metropolitan debutante. The resident troupe, with Jean de Reszke associated with Albani and Scalchi, gave *Otello* on January 11, 1892. At various times the opera has enlisted magnificent casts here, one of the most remarkable being that of December 3, 1894, when leading roles were assumed by Eames (Desdemona), Mantelli (Emilia), Tamagno and Maurel, the last in his Metropolitan debut. Opening the 1902-03 season, *Otello* had Eames, Homer (Emilia), Albert Alvarez (Otello), and Scotti (Iago).

A tenor who rivaled Tamagno in his interpretation of the Moor was Leo Slezak, who made his Metropolitan bow in the first Toscanini *Otello*, on November 17, 1909; Florence Wickham, the Emilia, was also making her Metropolitan debut that evening. Six performances were attained that season, equaling the number reached, the season before, at Hammerstein's Manhattan, where Melba, Zenatello, and Sammarco made an unforgettable impression. The opera remained in the Metropolitan repertoire until Slezak's departure, after which it was dropped until December 22, 1937, on which date Martinelli, though vocally past his prime, had, as the Moor, perhaps the greatest triumph of his career, sharing honors with Rethberg, Thelma Votipka, and Tibbett. A record of eight performances was established that season, the opera was used to open the following, and *Otello* is at last solidly fixed in public favor.

As Verdi was seventy-three years old when *Otello* was produced, it was reasonable to think, as he himself did, that it was his last major effort and that he would enter upon a well-earned retirement. But 1887 was not yet over when there were rumors of another work from his pen—this time a comic opera, probably based on *Don Quixote*. The rumors were only half right: in 1890, at a dinner party, Boïto proposed a toast to "Potbelly," which mystified the company until Giulio Ricordi blurted out "Falstaff!" After much hesitation, chiefly because of his advanced age, Verdi had given in to the persuasive arguments of Boïto, reinforced by those of Giuseppina, and consented to set a book based on *The Merry Wives of Windsor*, with touches lifted from *Henry IV*. Almost until the score was finished, Verdi pretended that he was writing only for his own amusement and might either never complete the work or give it only privately at Sant' Agata, his country villa near Busseto. Boïto provided a libretto so superior that Verdi, usually overzealous in finding ineptitudes in detail, asked for not a single change. Despite the fact that he gave only two hours a day to its composition (he had read somewhere that working longer was dangerous for old men), *Falstaff* was finished in less than two years.

Before *Falstaff* reached its *première* at La Scala on February 9, 1893, two dangers threatened its production. The first was Verdi's probably justifiable apprehension lest a house so large impair the effect of what was essentially a chamber opera. The other was his near-quarrel with Maurel, when the great baritone fruitlessly insisted that he be given exclusive rights to the role of Sir John. Both obstacles were overcome, and, fifty-three years after his only other comic opera, his second was heard by an audience that equaled the Bayreuth pilgrims in social and intellectual brilliance. For two of the three acts, enthusiasm was at a peak, and though acclaim was less warm in Act III, there was no doubt that *Falstaff* looked like a success. The critics were, with few exceptions, in raptures. But the presages were not wholly to be trusted. In Italy, the octogenarian composer's personal popularity was reflected in homage paid to this last of his masterpieces. But *Falstaff* waned after his death. It has never been, except recently in England, a truly popular opera.

In the United States, where *Falstaff* was first produced at the Metropolitan on February 4, 1895,* a splendid cast was assembled around the epic figure of the original Falstaff, Maurel, including Eames (Mistress Ford), De Lussan (Nannetta), Scalchi (Dame Quickly), and Campanari (Ford). But Maurel could not sell *Falstaff* to New York: two repetitions that season and three the next preceded a banishment of thirteen years. Revival came under Toscanini during his first season at the Metropolitan, when, on March 20, 1909, Scotti, playing Falstaff, rallied around him Destinn (Mistress Ford), Alda (Nannetta), Maria Gay (Dame Quickly), and Campanari. This time five performances in two seasons† sufficed. Except for a single performance by the Chicago company at the Lexington Theater in 1920, with Giacomo Rimini as Sir John, Raïsa as Mistress Ford, Defrere as Ford, and Schipa as Fenton, New York did not hear *Falstaff* for fifteen years. Then, on January 2, 1925, Lawrence Tibbett, as Ford, received a clamorous ovation that did much to win *Falstaff* the unprecedented total of six performances that season. Tibbett's chief associates were Scotti, Gigli (Fenton), Bori (Mistress Ford), Kathleen Howard (Mistress Page), Alda, and Telva (Dame Quickly). During the season of 1938-39, memorable because both operas of Verdi's old age were given, *Falstaff*, revived once more after thirteen years, with Tibbett this time as the fat knight, achieved four performances. Since then,

---

* South America stole a march on North: the Teatro Colón, Buenos Aires, performance, on July 9, 1893, was only five months later than the world *première*.

† For the repetitions of the 1909-10 season, there were the following interesting changes in cast: Jeanne Maubourg (Mistress Ford), Homer (Dame Quickly), and Pini-Corsi, resuming the role of Ford, which he had sung at the world *première*. Clément sang Fenton.

except for performances in English by the Juilliard School, it has not been heard in New York.

Yet, there is no doubt that this *Falstaff*, which, in the course forty-six seasons has had but twenty-one performances at the Metropolitan, is one of the very greatest of comic operas—the worthy pendent to the tragic *Otello*. It belongs to the select company of *Le Nozze di Figaro, Il Barbiere di Siviglia,* and *Die Meistersinger.* Musically, it employs the same idiom Verdi used for the most tragic purposes in *Otello*, with certain well-defined adjustments. First, the pace is breathless to the point of temerity—possibly the opera's lack of recognizable points of repose is partly responsible for the public's coolness toward it. It is literally too fast for the average auditor, who, however, would find many of his difficulties evaporating after a second or third hearing. The melodies have their lives rounded in a singer's breath, and naturally the set-number scheme has vanished utterly—*Falstaff* is no more like old-fashioned Italian *opera buffa* than is *Tristan und Isolde.* The melody is so abundant and ever-changing that it loses its identity as melody and becomes an excessively beautiful dramatic speech. Characterization reaches a new high: traits are ticked off at trigger speed, often in a single gnomic bar. In his late seventies, Verdi emerges as a master orchestrator of so refined and sensitive a touch that each syllable seems to get its own peculiar treatment. Yet, there is no feeling of excess.

Although the score of *Falstaff* can be read as a textbook of what instrumentation can be made to do in wit and brilliance, it is not closet writing. From an orchestral crescendo trill that is a favorite of admiring theorists to the eight-voice fugue that spins this genial burlesque to its close, there is no cessation of tactfully applied musical erudition. All this, spooling from the creative fancy of a mellowed genius, serves the comic spirit, serves it poetically, luminously—in the way Shakespeare would have liked. Ranging from the robust good humor and rollicking obscenity of Sir John to the dewy, tremulous love of Fenton and Nannetta, *Falstaff* has the variety demanded by its characters, by this particular little world of Shakespeare. For, by some extreme artistic miracle, it is even English.

Chapter XX

The Italians Slice Up Life

THE achievement of Arrigo Boïto in providing Verdi with
two librettos of surpassing excellence would be enough to
keep his name fresh in any history of the opera. His selflessness
in turning aside from the composition of his own *Nerone* to
serve another man has often been pointed out. Yet, an examination of his operas shows that Boïto's choice was a proof of his
critical acumen: his literary gifts surpassed his musical. An
intellectual of volatile character, sensitive, refined, squeamish,
and a touch feminine, Boïto, who had devoured libraries of
theory by his early twenties, was wont to ponder and polish a
musical phrase until it had lost not only its bloom but also its
connection with neighboring phrases on either side. Yet, he
managed to write one opera—*Mefistofele*—not too sicklied over
with the pale cast of thought. After that, he labored over
Nerone, his second and last completed opera, for fifty-four years.
He did not live to see this unwieldy epic performed: six years
after his death, Toscanini conducted its *première* at La Scala on
May 1, 1924. Received with riotous enthusiasm by a distinguished audience, *Nerone* nevertheless has not emigrated. The
character of the music may be deduced from a single suggestive
incident: in 1902, after permitting *Nerone* to be announced for
La Scala, this most encyclopedic of closet musicians withdrew
it, saying that he did not "know" harmony, and was going to
study it in some mountain retreat.

Mefistofele was merely a more youthful example of the
hesitant processes of this exacerbated mentality. It was first
produced at La Scala on March 5, 1868, and ran six hours, its
unqualified failure retiring it for seven years, during which
Boïto subjected it to a major overhauling. Faust was changed
from a baritone to a tenor, and the opera, much shortened, was
presented again at Bologna on October 4, 1875. This time it was
successful: it has remained popular in Italy and has had fitful
spells of popularity elsewhere. Examination of this version

shows that Boïto had studied the techniques of many masters—
Beethoven, Berlioz, Verdi, possibly Wagner. It shows him, more
ambitious than Messrs. Barbier, Carré, and Gounod, attempting
to compass the whole of Goethe's history of man. But it shows
him, unfortunately, less musically vital than Gounod, to whom
he might well have given some of his sheer power of intellection
in exchange for some of the Frenchman's sensuality. The music
is clever, but parched and thin. Life of its own it has but little—
certain performers, notably Chaliapin, the most famed of its
Devils, have been able to galvanize it with their own vitality.
That the score of *Mefistofele* was ransacked for ideas by many of
Boïto's younger contemporaries, even possibly by Verdi himself,
is unquestionable, and Huneker's summing up of the situation
is essentially true: "Boïto seems to have been the pivotal point
of the neo-Italian school—himself remaining in the background
—while the youngsters profited by his many experimentings."

One of the most interesting of the early *Mefistofeles* outside Italy
was the London *première*, on July 6, 1880, when the apparently
unrivaled quartet of Nilsson (Margherita and Elena), Trebelli
(Marta and Pantalis), Italo Campanini (Faust), and Nannetti
(Mefistofele) sang it at Her Majesty's. The Academy of Music
staged the first American *Mefistofele*, with Valleria, Annie Louise
Cary, Campanini, and Novara, on November 24, 1880. Excepting
Nannetti, the Her Majesty's group appeared in the first Metropolitan performance, on December 5, 1883, with Mirabella as the Devil.
Plançon and Renaud, both singing actors in the best French tradition, also interpreted Mefistofele in New York, but the role is most
intimately connected with the name of Fyodor Chaliapin, who
used it for his Metropolitan debut, on November 20, 1907. Farrar
was the Margherita, Rappold the Elena,* and Riccardo Martin,
also making his Metropolitan debut, the Faust, in which role
Beniamino Gigli also made his bow there, on November 26, 1920.
Although the Devil remained one of Chaliapin's most admired
roles, *Mefistofele* disappeared from the Metropolitan long before
he did and has not been heard there since the season of 1925-26.

Less interesting than Boïto as a personality and musical

* Those who know their Goethe will understand why Marguerite and Helen
of Troy are often sung by the same prima donna.

thinker, but quite as influential in the course of Italian opera because he taught Mascagni, Puccini, and Franco Leoni, was Amilcare Ponchielli, the composer of *La Gioconda* and several other works whose popularity was confined to Italy. Although Ponchielli began composing operas in his early twenties, he did not achieve a success until he was almost forty. This was a revision of an early effort—*I Promessi sposi,* which was based on Manzoni's famous novel, and which doubtless drew a large measure of its popularity from that fact. Coming in 1872, when Verdi, with the completion of *Aïda,* might have been expected to retire permanently, *I Promessi sposi* indicated Ponchielli as Verdi's successor, and indeed, during the rest of his comparatively brief career—he died in 1886, one year before the production of *Otello*—he enjoyed that position. *La Gioconda* was the first of his four tremendous successes at La Scala. Of the remaining three, *Il Figliuol prodigo* (1880), a Biblical opera of spectacular character, has been called his finest work—an opinion to be taken on trust by Americans, as the opera has never been performed here.

For all practical purposes, *La Gioconda* is Ponchielli. Its impressive career astoundingly exceeds its merits, though the reasons for its popularity are apparent. It began triumphantly at La Scala on April 8, 1876, with Gayarré in the important role of Enzo. The opera swept through Italy, but did not reach London until 1883. Seven months later, on December 20, New York heard it as the only novelty in the first Metropolitan season. The cast of the American *première* had six full-fledged stars: Nilsson (La Gioconda), Fursch-Madi (Laura), Scalchi (La Cieca), Stagno (Enzo), Del Puente (Barnaba), and Novara (Alvise). Malvina Cavallazzi, a favorite danseuse of the period, led in the Dance of the Hours. Fursch-Madi, with her powerful voice and dramatic temperament, not the static Nilsson, was the real heroine of this not quite first-rate performance. After three repetitions that season, *La Gioconda,* like many other Italian operas, fell victim to the limiting German regime, and was not heard again until November 28, 1904, when Nordica, Homer, Walker, Caruso, Eugenio Giraldoni, and Plançon were the six principals.

Hammerstein liked *La Gioconda* so much that he used it to open the second season of the Manhattan Opera House, on November 4,

1907, with Nordica, De Cisneros, Gerville-Réache, Zenatello, Ancona, and Didur. Two years later, on November 9, 1909, Henry Russell, impresario of the newly formed Boston Opera Company, selected *La Gioconda* for the inaugural performance of the Boston Opera House, with Nordica and Florencio Constantino heading the cast. One week later, the Metropolitan revived *La Gioconda* under Toscanini to open its season, with Destinn, Homer, Anna Meitschik, Caruso, Amato, and De Segurola, the last in his Metropolitan debut. The opera, which up to that time had accumulated only twelve Metropolitan performances, gathered thirty more in the next six seasons. Dropped for ten years, it was revived on November 8, 1924, with Easton and Gigli, the latter resuming the role of Enzo, in which he had made his world debut, at Rovigo, near Venice, ten years before. Later that season, Rosa Ponselle took over the name part and became perhaps the greatest of Giocondas. On December 21, 1932, the Ponselle sisters appeared in the same Metropolitan performance, Rosa as La Gioconda, Carmela as Laura. Since Rosa's retirement, the popularity of *La Gioconda* has waned, but not disappeared. Gina Cigna was a recent Gioconda, Rose Bampton a recent Laura.

La Gioconda is based on a second-rate blood-and-thunder historical melodrama by Victor Hugo. Ponchielli called in Boïto to make a credible libretto from this *Angelo, tyran de Padoue,* but he failed.* The libretto, unusual in that each act has its own title, is not credible. But it is violent and melodramatic, and the music is just like it. Krehbiel spoke happily of the "hot vigor" of the work—a phrase that can refer to both the music and the libretto. It abounds in glaring contrasts, robust declamation, bravura finales, and—what has probably contributed most to its popularity—unmistakable if sometimes banal lyric sweep. Musically, Ponchielli is more compelling than Boïto, though less an innovator and less careful in producing effects. The point is, he does produce them—by wrapping up his own free-flowing melody in packages collected from such international entrepreneurs as Meyerbeer, Halévy, Verdi, even Wagner.

La Gioconda has been called one of the ancestors of *verismo* —that realistic way of treating the violent, the sordid, and the

* The libretto was given out to be the work of Tobia Gorrio (an anagram of Arrigo Boïto), but there is no evidence that Boïto used this subterfuge to hide any shame he may have felt about his handiwork.

everyday which became endemic in Italy during the 1890's and which gradually spread to other countries. Yet, the well-known excerpts from *La Gioconda* are mostly not typical of a veristic opera: the Dance of the Hours is timeless salon music of not the highest order; *"Cielo e mar," "Voce di donna,"* and *"Pescator, affonda l'esca"* are lyrical numbers whose honesty of conviction alone saves them from banality; *"Suicidio!"* alone carries into the concert hall the predominant violence of the score, but even that is less veristic than Verdian.

Verismo may be said to have burst into full bloom as the result of a prize contest for one-act operas sponsored by the Milan music-publishing house of Edoardo Sonzogno. Second prize went to *Labilia*, by Niccola Spinelli, a twenty-five-year-old Turinese whose later *A Basso porto* has been heard in New York. First money plucked from obscurity a wan-faced starveling of twenty-seven, Pietro Mascagni, whose entry was entitled *Cavalleria rusticana*. When it was first produced at the Teatro Costanzi, Rome, on May 17, 1890, with Bellincioni and Stagno as Santuzza and Turiddu, the acclamations were such that there could be no reasonable doubt that a new popular favorite had arrived. It was soon resounding throughout Italy, and within two years had been heard in Berlin, New York, London, and Paris. Its success was everywhere immediate, and has endured.

Mascagni has composed more than a dozen operas since *Cavalleria*, and not one of them has had, at best, more than a passing *succès d'estime*. His career, by and large, has been that of an impertinent coxcomb. Not discouraged by several flat failures and the merely tepid interest in *L'Amico Fritz* (1891) and *Iris* (1898), Mascagni arranged to have the *première* of his *Le Maschere* take place simultaneously in seven of Italy's most important cities. This arrogant action was greeted with the sharp rebuff merited by the poor quality and imitative character of the music, Rome alone giving it a slight suffrage. In Milan, a knowing audience signified by catcalls of *"Ah! Puccini, viva Puccini!"* that one source of Mascagni's borrowings was only too obvious. At Genoa, *Le Maschere* was not allowed to proceed to the end. Since this fiasco, Mascagni's operations have been on a more modest scale, though there is no evidence of deflated ego.

In 1917, *Lodoletta,* based on a Ouida story Puccini had experimented with, achieved a mild world fame, and in 1918 even secured performance from a by then skeptical Metropolitan management, the cast being headed by Farrar and Caruso. *Lodoletta* failed to establish itself in New York, as did *L'Amico Fritz* despite Calvé, and *Iris* despite a *première* with Eames, Caruso, and Scotti (1907), a revival with Bori, under Toscanini (1915), and a try with Rethberg, Gigli, De Luca, and Pinza (1931). Next to the nearly two hundred Metropolitan *Cavallerias,* the total of twenty-six performances achieved by *L'Amico Fritz, Iris,* and *Lodoletta* makes a telling commentary on Mascagni's consistent lack, after a single youthful spurt, of inspiration.

Mascagni put everything he had into *Cavalleria*—like the familiar author of one successful autobiographical novel, he could not repeat. Before putting a note on paper, he had been possessed by the raw strength of Giovanni Verga's crude Sicilian tale, and when the strident chords of the finale flashed across his mind, he started, beginning with the end, to whelm down the music. All his impetuosity and young passion went into it, and it all but flames with conviction. He was desperately poor, and *Cavalleria* was written literally out of his need. Melodies flooded his imagination, and he let them gush forth without criticism. Had Mascagni been able to continue tapping this source, he might easily have secured for himself a place comparable to that Verdi would have if he had stayed at the *Il Trovatore* level. Unfortunately, Mascagni could neither do that nor go on to an *Aïda* or a *Falstaff*: for his immortality he must depend on *Cavalleria rusticana.* Its fiery lyricism, its black-and-white contrasts, its sultry Southern passions, its all-over catchiness—these are small change for the ferryman of the Styx, but the Intermezzo alone would assure passage. *Cavalleria* is the apotheosis of hurdy-gurdy and is occasionally somewhat better.

In the United States, there was a race for the honor of first producing *Cavalleria,* whose fame had been catapulted across the Atlantic. The enterprising Gustav Hinrichs, lessee of the Philadelphia Grand Opera House, won, and there, on September 9, 1891, conducted it, with a cast headed by the pious Polish soprano Selma Kronold, who was also to be the first American Nedda in *Pagliacci* before ending her career as a nun. Nineteen days later, on September 28, Minnie Hauk sang the role of Santuzza at the first Chicago *Cavalleria*. In both the Philadelphia and Chicago *premières*, Del Puente was the Alfio, and his future wife, Helen Dudley Campbell, the Lola. Three days after the Chicago performance, New York heard *Cavalleria* twice in one day: in the afternoon, Rudolph Aronson presented it at the Casino; that evening, Hammerstein staged it at the Lenox Lyceum. These early New York casts were mediocre.

Finally, the Metropolitan succumbed to Mascagnitis, and on December 30, 1891, after *Orfeo ed Euridice*, with the sisters Ravogli, had been sung as a curtain raiser, Eames gave a cold interpretation of the sultry Santuzza, a role she dropped after one season. The next Metropolitan Santuzza was Calvé, who used the role for her American debut there, on November 29, 1893, when the evening's bill was filled out with Gounod's *Philémon et Baucis*. Apparently the first Metropolitan doubling of the "heavenly twins," *Cavalleria* and *Pagliacci*—"Cav" and "Pag"—occurred on January 20, 1900, when the former featured Calvé and Andreas Dippel, the latter De Lussan, Thomas Salignac, and Scotti. Since the Toscanini revival of December 17, 1908, when Destinn (Santuzza), Gay (Lola), Marie Mattfeld (Mama Lucia), Caruso (Turiddu), and Amato (Alfio) made *Cavalleria* a memorable experience, and it was doubled with the American *première* of Puccini's first opera, *Le Villi,* it has never been out of the Metropolitan repertoire.

The career of *Pagliacci*, the other foundation stone of *verismo*, has been at least as spectacular as that of *Cavalleria*. This two-acter, composed, like the earlier work, for the publishing house of Sonzogno, was first given at the Teatro dal Verme, Milan, on May 21, 1892, with Toscanini conducting. Besides Ancona (Silvio), the cast was given éclat by its Tonio, Maurel, who had been instrumental in getting the opera produced. Its success showed that *Cavalleria* had a rival, but how serious a one was not immediately revealed.

Hinrichs secured the American *première*, with Kronold (Nedda) and Campanari (Tonio), at the Grand Opera House, Eighth Avenue and Twenty-third Street, New York, on June 15, 1893. The same year, on December 11, Melba (Nedda), Fernando de Lucia (Canio), and Ancona (Tonio) led the principals at the Metropolitan first. This, like the earliest Metropolitan *Cavalleria*, was on a double bill with Gluck's *Orfeo*, but unlike that *Cavalleria*, it was just short of a failure. Not until Caruso's assumption, on December 9, 1903, of the role of Canio, which he sang seventy-six times, could the opera be said really to have won New York. Since that notable performance, when Sembrich was the Nedda and Scotti the Tonio, *Pagliacci* has made up for lost time, and now stands fifth (tied with *Die Walküre*) in popularity in the Metropolitan roster, with a total of 223 performances. Jean de Reszke, singing in *Pagliacci* for the first and only time, at the Opéra in the fall of 1902, portrayed Canio in what proved to be his farewell to the stage.*

Leoncavallo wrote his own librettos, sometimes from episodes known to him personally. Such was *Pagliacci*, which was based on a murder committed by a member of a company of strolling players at a Calabrian village. As Leoncavallo's father had been the presiding judge at the actor's trial, the incident was indelibly graved on the composer's mind. This did not save him from being sued unsuccessfully for plagiarism by Catulle Mendès, who claimed that the central situation was stolen from his *La Femme de tabarin*. The libretto of *Pagliacci* is an excellent frame for the broad melodies, flavorsome declamation, and crashing volumes that Leoncavallo devoted to it. It is rank melodrama, but most theatrically believable and simple to follow. Like *Cavalleria*, *Pagliacci* was exciting stuff in the nineties, and it still is, though to a lesser degree. For one thing, we are so inured to the raw speech of *verismo* that its novelty is gone: today the power of these brief operas—a typical performance of the two-act *Pagliacci* is four minutes shorter than one of the single act of *Cavalleria*, which requires seventy-three minutes— is their pace, their terse, unpadded drama, and their melodic largess. *Pagliacci* contains some of the most familiar music ever composed: the Prologue, a curious bit of theatrical formalism whose roots go back to the infant beginnings of opera, to Peri's

---

* On January 13, 1910, Lee De Forest, from the stage of the Metropolitan, broadcast to his co-workers in New Jersey a portion of a Caruso *Pagliacci*. This is one of the earliest opera broadcasts on record.

Dafne, is one of these; the other is *"Vesti la giubba,"* the big sob song that has become the *locus classicus* of the clown with the broken heart. But these are only high spots in a score that is melodically attractive throughout.

Mascagni had composed *Cavalleria rusticana* out of an urgent need to keep himself and his family alive; Leoncavallo had composed *Pagliacci* out of an equally urgent need to make good. He was thirty-four, and his life had been full of failure. *Chatterton,* his first opera, had been on the verge of production when the impressario absconded; his second, *I Medici,* composed in one year, languished in the Ricordi files until Leoncavallo, impatient to hear himself performed, began dickering with the rival house of Sonzogno. Then came his one great success, and thereafter the parallel with Mascagni again became only too bitterly apparent. The yellowing scores of *Chatterton* and *I Medici* were dusted off and offered to the public without success.

Then Leoncavallo composed *Zaza,* hoping with it to equal the success of the play, which was familiar to multitudes of Englishmen and Americans because of Mrs. Leslie Carter's portrayal of the heroine. Despite the undoubted merits of his score, he achieved nothing remotely like that, and today *Zaza* is rarely heard. During Geraldine Farrar's last years at the Metropolitan, it had something of a vogue there because of her vivid interpretation. Indeed, so much was she admired in the part, that it was chosen for her operatic farewell, on April 22, 1922. Since that afternoon, *Zaza,* which had been heard at the Tivoli Opera House, San Francisco, as early as 1903, has not been sung in this country. Leoncavallo, without encouragement except from the unabating popularity of *Pagliacci,* went on grinding out operas up to his death in 1919. One of them, *Der Roland von Berlin,* was composed to order for Wilhelm II, whose favorite composer Leoncavallo was, and devotes itself earnestly to the business of glorifying early Hohenzollerns. Even the Prussian capital, where it had its *première* on December 13, 1904, could not stomach *Der Roland.*

Giacomo Puccini, most fortunately endowed of the verists,

early or late, was the last of the early group to arrive.* There is a marked resemblance between the beginnings of his career and those of Mascagni and Leoncavallo, though each worked out differently in detail. All, however, suffered from penury and despair. Puccini, whose musical ancestors were almost as numerous as Bach's, failed to win even honorable mention in a competition for a one-act opera sponsored by a newspaper. But he had friends—Boïto among them—who believed in *Le Villi*, the loser, and through their efforts it came to production at the Teatro dal Verme, Milan, on May 31, 1884. The forlorn hope was a huge success, and thus, under the rosiest auspices, was launched one of the most successful musical careers of modern times. Made over into a two-acter, *Le Villi* became the rage in Turin, and finally attained La Scala. It was the sole success Puccini was to experience for almost ten years. This young man, whose flair for the stage was to become a by-word, next accepted an impossible libretto based on one of De Musset's wildest melodramas, set it earnestly and capably, and had it produced at La Scala on April 21, 1889. The book had defeated him: *Edgar* was a fiasco, and it took courage for the house of Ricordi, which by this time had a vested interest in Puccini's career, not to falter in their support. They had not too long to wait: the promising score of *Manon Lescaut* was completed in 1892, and its promise redeemed early the next year.

The agony of work that went into the book of *Manon Lescaut* was symptomatic of the trouble Puccini never ceased having with his librettos. Had he had Leoncavallo's ability to write his own, he might have been saved years of painful search for suitable material, and we might have double the output of nine full-length and three one-act operas that he left, after an active career of forty years, at his death in 1924. In the case of *Manon Lescaut*, the very fact that he selected a version of the

---

* Except the talented Franco Leoni, another Ponchielli pupil, who, though a tireless composer of operas, is known in America only by *L'Oracolo* (1905), based on a Chinese horror story, which offered Scotti the chance for one of his best and most popular portrayals. The great baritone played the role of Chim-fen no less than forty-four times at the Metropolitan, and bade farewell to that house, as well as to opera, as the evil Chinese, on January 20, 1933, after a New York career of thirty-four years.

same Abbé Prévost story that had already been set with con-
spicuous success by Massenet showed that he was desperate for
opera-worthy material to which he could respond with warmth.
Before the libretto satisfied him, five men, including Giulio
Ricordi and the two playwrights who were eventually to provide his most viable books—Giuseppe Giacosa and Luigi Illica,
had tampered with it, and Puccini himself had added the finishing touches. It was well worth the effort, for when *Manon
Lescaut* finally reached its *première* at the Teatro Regio, Turin,
on February 1, 1893, it was immediately realized, in native musical circles, that Mascagni and Leoncavallo were in danger of
being eclipsed, though this opinion was not immediately echoed
abroad. At the London *première*, for instance, Bernard Shaw
was the lone critic who realized that Puccini, not Mascagni or
Leoncavallo, was the step after Verdi in Italian opera.

Like Verdi, Puccini reached his first maturity in his middle
thirties: *Manon Lescaut* was his *Rigoletto*. In it are, though
not frequently in final form, the elements of his musical individuality. Sweet, pungent, and diverse harmonies, lush romantic melodies, calculated contrasts, schooled effects carried
out with pared means—such are the qualities of *Manon Lescaut*, and such, often in more exaggerated guises, are those of
La Bohème, La Tosca, and *Madama Butterfly*, and, to a somewhat lesser extent, of the later operas. From Des Grieux' aria,
"Donna non vida mai," in Act I, descended the many throbbing love songs that can be depended upon to stop the show.
Even the Intermezzo, *"La Prigionia,"* which is a small tone
poem, has the harmonic tang, feminine charm, and intimate
flavor that were to remain the characteristics of Puccini's
instrumental interludes. Thus he early established the hall-
marks of his manner and told his admirers what to look for. He
did not often disappoint them thereafter by departing fla-
grantly from these stylistic norms. This is not to say that he had
a static talent: he improved upon what he had, without adding
much that was new. The point is that, except for one period of
fumbling, he did improve, and consistently. *Manon Lescaut*
set the pattern, too, by having a thoroughly credible libretto,
but it was far more disjointed than an experienced and self-

confident Puccini would ever again allow collaborators to devise for him.

Although *Manon Lescaut* had been presented at the Grand Opera
House, Philadelphia, as early as 1894, and in New York, at Wallack's Theater, in 1898, it had to wait for Metropolitan performance
until two of its successors, *La Bohème* and *La Tosca*, had been established in the repertoire of that house. The first cast there included,
on January 18, 1907, Lina Cavalieri (Manon), Caruso (Des Grieux),
and Scotti (Lescaut). After two seasons, *Manon Lescaut* was dropped
until November 12, 1912, when it opened the season. Giorgio
Polacco, the conductor, and Lucrezia Bori, the triumphant Manon,
were making Metropolitan debuts that night; Caruso and Scotti
resumed their former roles. Seventeen seasons later, on October
28, 1929, another Bori *Manon Lescaut* was the inaugural offering,
with Gigli as Des Grieux and De Luca as Lescaut. On December
28, 1929, Alda, who had recently been divorced from Manager
Gatti-Casazza, made her farewell, after twenty-one years at the
Metropolitan, in the role of Manon. The opera has not been heard
there since that season.

On February 1, 1896, at the Teatro Regio, Turin, Toscanini
conducted the *première* of Puccini's fourth opera, *La Bohème*,
three years to a day after that of *Manon Lescaut*. The facts of
its composition uncover one of the few discreditable episodes
in the life of a generally amiable, charming, and honorable
man. Before *Manon Lescaut* was completed, Puccini was already toying vaguely with a new idea—an opera about Buddha.
His friend Leoncavallo sent him a libretto of his own devising,
based on episodes from Henri Murger's *Scènes de la vie de
Bohème*. Puccini rejected it without much thought. Some time
after the launching of *Manon Lescaut*, he infuriated Leoncavallo by announcing calmly that Giacosa and Illica had given
him an excellent libretto based on the Murger novel. Leoncavallo, who meanwhile had decided to set his own libretto, pro-
tested that the idea belonged to him, only to be told that there
would be two *Bohème*s. Leoncavallo's opera came out first, and
failed. Puccini's, though at the beginning only modestly acclaimed, was such a success at Palermo that, even after most of
the orchestra had left the theater, the audience demanded, and

got, a repetition of the finale, with the principals in their street clothes. Had Puccini's opera failed too, instead of becoming one of the most popular operas in the world (it ranks fourth in total number of performances at the Metropolitan), Leoncavallo might have forgotten the episode. As it was, he never forgave Puccini.

Not until he developed a passionate interest in his material could Puccini begin to translate a libretto into music. He set this new opera *con amore*, for not only did the incidents in the book Giacosa and Illica had prepared remind him of his own student days in Milan, but he had fallen in love with the pathetic little heroine, Mimi. The score is Puccini at his best and worst. At his worst, he is mawkish, cloying, and sticky with adolescent sentimentality. At his best, he is eloquently dramatic, psychologically sound, and adroit in carrying passionate rapture along on a crest of swelling melody. In *La Bohème*, he is not only all these things, but most of them *in excelsis*.

A testimonial to the power of *La Bohème* is the fact that it provokes definite reactions: one either surrenders wholeheartedly to it or one rejects it completely. But no one, not even those most put off by its sentimental excesses, will deny that *La Bohème* is a credible story turned into an effective stage piece by music that provides a throbbing flesh for the story's skeleton. It is possible to dislike Mimi and Rodolfo, but it is the healthy dislike one feels for some real people, not for vague abstractions such as crowd most of the operas of Donizetti or Gounod. The music makes them real, gives them personality. And some of that music is so familiar that the gramophonic history of *La Bohème* would make a small volume in itself. Complete and slightly abridged recordings have been numerous and multilingual, while such excerpts as *"Che gelida manina," "Si mi chiamano Mimi,"* Musetta's Waltz Song, and Mimi's Farewell have been recorded scores of times each.

Mexico City and Buenos Aires heard *La Bohème* before New York, and both Los Angeles and San Francisco heard it more than six months earlier than its production at Wallack's, on May 16, 1898. It began its amazing Metropolitan career on December 26,

1900, that being the first of the 764 performances of Puccini's operas thus far (1941) given in that house. The cast, with the exception of Signora Occhiolini, the Musetta, was one of luminaries: Melba was the Mimi, Saléza the Rodolfo, Campanari the Marcello, Gilibert the Schaunard, and Journet the Colline. Melba had sung the role in England in 1899, and she continued to sing it throughout the world for a quarter of a century, toward the end much to Puccini's disgust, as he had not written the role for an old lady. On November 20, 1913, Martinelli sang Rodolfo in his Metropolitan debut, with Bori, Bella Alten, Scotti, De Segurola, and Didur. *La Bohème*'s popularity shows not the smallest sign of abating, and in Germany it has been the sole foreign runner-up to Wagner.

The history of the libretto of Puccini's next opera is quite as unsavory a morsel as that of the libretto of *La Bohème*. Some time in the late eighties, Puccini had seen Sarah Bernhardt in Sardou's *La Tosca* and seemingly had not been attracted to the drama. A good decade later, Verdi was quoted as having said that only his age kept him from setting Sardou's play. Then Puccini remembered that when he had heard Bernhardt, he had been able perfectly to follow the argument of the play without understanding the language in which it was written. This was ample evidence to the theatrically minded composer that *La Tosca* contained the elements of a good libretto. But he found that Illica had already sketched a libretto of *La Tosca* for Alberto Franchetti, a wealthy composer of the Meyerbeerian school. That the idea was ethically Franchetti's was but a slight barrier to Illica and Ricordi, who, as soon as they learned that Puccini was interested, bamboozled poor Franchetti into releasing the sketch. They argued that the material was too vile for operatic treatment and immediately presented the skeleton libretto to Puccini. Then Illica and Giacosa, with suggestions from Ricordi and Puccini himself, not to mention a plethora of useless comment from the doddering Sardou, finally got together a satisfactory book.

The Puccini score got its first hearing at the Costanzi, at Rome, on January 14, 1900, and barely escaped being a fiasco: rumors were rife that enemies of Puccini's success were out to "get" him, and when some latecomers caused muttering in the audience, the management, fearing the worst, rang down the curtain. As nothing dangerous developed, they raised it again, and the first *Tosca* proceeded eventlessly to its conclusion. The next morning, vicious newspaper criticisms echoed the arguments Illica and Ricordi had used dishonestly to Franchetti. But despite the fact that they called the story noisome, and charged that the torture scene by its very nature debased the art of music, *La Tosca* soon established itself as Puccini's third big success.

Like *Bohème*, *La Tosca* was introduced to Latin America before it reached New York, the New World *première* being at the Teatro Colón, Buenos Aires, on June 16, 1900. Almost eight months later, Ternina (Tosca) and Scotti (Scarpia), who had already sung the roles at Covent Garden, headed the first Metropolitan cast, on February 4, 1901; Cremonini was the Cavaradossi, Dufriche the Angelotti, and Gilibert the Sacristan. The popularity of the opera was immediate and lasting, and in thirty-six seasons it rolled up a total of 174 performances. As Tosca, Eames made her farewell to the Metropolitan on February 15, 1909, and the same role introduced Muzio to that house on December 4, 1916, with Caruso and Scotti. Tosca was one of Farrar's most admired roles, and even after Jeritza's spectacular interpretation of the tragic Roman singer had become a Metropolitan drawing card, Farrar was urged, when she announced her forthcoming retirement, to sing *Tosca* at her farewell. But the management chose *Zaza* for her valedictory.

Jeritza's first Metropolitan Tosca occurred on December 1, 1921, opposite Scotti and a most unobtrusive Cavaradossi, Aureliano Pertile. She wore no wig to cover her luxuriant blonde hair, though the text explicitly mentions her as brunette—and she sang *"Vissi d'arte"* face downward on the floor: these innovations upped *Tosca's* popularity to fantastic heights. Scotti's Scarpia was rivaled, perhaps excelled, by that of Renaud, who, however, did not sing the role at the Metropolitan. But even he never received the access of adulation that greeted the production of *Tosca* to mark Scotti's twenty-fifth anniversay at the Metropolitan. Opposite him was Jeritza, his thirteenth Metropolitan Tosca. The role of Cavaradossi, obviously so much less dramatic than Scarpia's, nevertheless has attracted many famous tenors. Caruso, to Ternina's Tosca, made his first big Metropolitan hit in this role, and it was one of the three McCormack sang as a regular member of the Metropolitan company—the other two were Rodolfo (*La Bohème*) and Pinkerton (*Madama Butterfly*). It was also chosen by Richard Crooks for his operatic debut, which occurred at Hamburg in 1927.

La Tosca is the most thrilling of Puccini's operas—heart-in-the-mouth entertainment from the three rasping chords that open it with the villainous Scarpia's signature to Tosca's suicide scream. The libretto is an unrelieved horror story, made up of such elements as attempted rape, torture, murder, execution, and suicide. The villain is black and sardonic, the hero white and angelic; only Tosca herself is human—in the libretto. By his music, however, Puccini managed to make the whole gory affair acceptable as a story. Much of the stage business could not be set to music, and for long stretches, therefore, the composer contented himself with writing clever illustrative music. But where passions, whether black or white, fused, Puccini provided lyricodramatic floods of song and heightened declamation, often a telling coalescence of the two. In song, he frequently retained some of the quality of speech, as can be seen in such climaxes as *"Recondita armonia," "Vissi d'arte,"* and *"E lucevan le stelle."*

All his life an aesthetic blotter, Puccini, during the *Tosca* period, was absorbing late Verdi, him of *Otello*, in every receptive fiber. And he was also beginning to point like a vane to each new wind in the musical sky—to profit by what his contemporaries outside Italy were doing. He was becoming an internationalist (without ever relinquishing his claims to his share in the heritage of Italian melody), and even in 1900 his harmonies were diverging sharply from tradition. He reacted like an intellectual. For instance, in *Tosca* he experimented with the whole-tone scale, with classical modes, and with outright harmonic heresies.

How international Puccini was becoming could more easily be told after examining the score of his next opera, *Madama Butterfly*. It is not merely that this is an American's story of a fictional Japan, limned with a realistic intent that never quite succeeds. It also makes use of authentic Japanese tunes—during the period of *Butterfly*'s composition, Puccini conscientiously imported hundreds of records from Japan—and quotes *The Star-Spangled Banner*. Moreover, it meets the issue of harmonic modernity even more bravely than *Tosca* did. Puccini did not quite achieve homogeneity of style with these disparate and perhaps immiscible elements, though Dyneley Hussey has perhaps overstated the case when he speaks of *Butterfly*'s "impure style . . . in which the Japanese and American tunes were never completely absorbed into the texture of the music but stick out of it like so many almonds on top of a trifle." In short, Puccini's music is finally as artistically incredible as the milieu he had to illustrate—a half-real, half-Gilbert-and-Sullivan Japan. When it is not being picture-postcard Japanesey, when it is at its best, that is, it is the good old Italian sweeping lyricism with which Puccini had seduced the world in *Bohème* and *Tosca*. And in *"Un bel di, vedremo,"* Cio-Cio-San's rapturous paean of hope, he composed what has become the best known of all his arias.

The history of the composition of *Madama Butterfly* parallels in some details that of *Tosca*. When Puccini was in London in 1900, he saw the play that David Belasco and John Luther Long had made from the latter's magazine story, *Madam Butterfly*. Although he understood little English, he was as gripped as he had been by Sardou's drama. In short, he fell in love with Cio-Cio-San, and soon secured rights to the use of the play as the basis of a libretto. Giacosa and Illica, turned loose on the tale, did their best—and last—job. Puccini set to work with feverish eagerness and, despite a serious motor accident, completed it in, for him, record time. It received its *première* at La Scala on February 17, 1904, and failed miserably. The fact that it was in two very long acts did not help it, but more serious was the flouting of tradition, both musical and theatrical. The harmonies, though still transitional, were strange, and the costuming did not square with romantic notions. Probably none of these considerations would have been decisive against the immediate success of the opera had not the temper of the Milanese audience been raised to choler by echoes, real or fancied, of *Bohème*. Characteristically, they felt that they were being cheated—having paid to hear a new opera, they de-

manded that all of it be new. Another, less exacting audience
might at once have declared for *Madama Butterfly*. As it was,
after a few revisions, the most important of which was making
a new division into three acts, it was staged at Brescia on May
28, 1904, and was acclaimed.

Butterfly soon took its place among the three most popular of
Puccini's operas. After its Covent Garden *première* on July 10,
1905, with Destinn, Caruso, and Scotti, it rapidly developed into
the smash hit of the London season. Performances in Paris, Vienna,
Prague, Berlin, and Brussels were followed by the North American
première,* in English, at the Belasco Theater, Washington, D. C.,
on October 15, 1906, with Florence Easton as Cio-Cio-San. It was
this same Savage English Grand Opera Company that gave the
first New York *Butterfly* on the following November 12, at the
Garden Theater. When the Metropolitan produced it, in Italian,
on February 11, 1907, Puccini was present to hear the superb
performance by Farrar (Cio-Cio-San), Homer (Suzuki), Caruso
(Pinkerton), and Scotti (Sharpless). Easton, who had come to the
Metropolitan in 1916, did not sing Cio-Cio-San there until March
13, 1920,† when Martinelli was the Pinkerton and De Luca the
Sharpless. The original Cio-Cio-San of the unfortunate Scala *première*, Rosina Storchio, sang the role with the Chicago Opera
Association in 1921, but in New York, at least, this prima donna
was not admired by audiences who had heard Destinn, Easton,
and, above all, Farrar. Recent Cio-Cio-Sans at the Metropolitan
have included Suzanne Fisher, Rethberg, and Licia Albanese.

It was just before the Metropolitan *première* of *Madama
Butterfly* that Puccini announced to the press that he was going
to collaborate on an opera with David Belasco, with whom he
had struck up a friendship during the negotiations over the
Long-Belasco play. He was exaggerating: Belasco was not a
librettist and wrote only in English. What Puccini had in
mind was something based on Belasco's hit melodrama, *The
Girl of the Golden West*. But Giacosa had died, and Illica by
himself was unsatisfactory to Puccini. Returned to Italy, the

---

* Both Buenos Aires and Montevideo had heard *Madama Butterfly* in 1904.
† According to Julius Mattfeld, quoting *The Radio Digest*, a Berlin Staatsoper
performance of *Madama Butterfly*, on June 19, 1920, was the first complete opera
to be broadcast publicly.

composer entered upon an unhappy period, both professionally and personally. For many months he looked vainly for a likely librettist and finally found one who could block out the general lineaments of the story and another who could help to give them life.

The book was finished, and Puccini had just begun to compose *La Fanciulla del West* (for such is its hybrid title), when his violently jealous wife disrupted his existence by driving to suicide a housemaid whom she had accused publicly of being the composer's mistress. Signora Puccini was tried, and convicted, for criminal slander after a post-mortem examination had proved baseless her charges of sexual intimacy. Puccini paid heavily to keep his wife out of prison, and for a time left her, though he eventually again lived with her, and happily. After almost a year's interruption, he returned to *La Fanciulla del West*, and finished it in October, 1910.

The *première* of the new opera had been promised to the Metropolitan, and there it occurred, on December 10, 1910. Belasco had painstakingly supervised the production, and Puccini was again on hand to answer to the calls of "Composer! Composer!" Thanks to the careful rehearsals, thanks to the conducting of Toscanini, and thanks, finally, to the performances of Destinn (Minnie), Caruso (Dick Johnson), and Amato (Jack Rance), with an overcrowded outfield including such celebrities as Didur, Pini-Corsi, De Segurola, Dinh Gilly, Albert Reiss, Angelo Bada, and Marie Mattfeld, there were many such calls. The New York public, if not enthusiastic, was at least cordial to its own Puccini opera,* and *La Fanciulla* lasted through four seasons of diminishing returns. After that it vanished—there was no Toscanini to put dynamics into its lifeless score, and it was only the phenomenal personal popularity of Maria Jeritza, who had already played Minnie in Vienna with great success, that angled *La Fanciulla* back into the repertoire for three seasons. Supporting Jeritza's first Minnie, on November 2, 1929, were Martinelli (Johnson) and Tibbett (Rance). Since the season of 1931-32, *La Fanciulla del West* has not been heard in New York.

* Seventeen days after the world *première*, Chicago heard *La Fanciulla* in a production supervised by Tito Ricordi. Carolina White, Bressler-Gianoli, Renaud, Dufranne, and Defrère were in the cast. Edward Moore has recorded that the audience laughed loudly at such Italianisms as *"Allo"* and *"Eep, eep, urra."*

Its fate elsewhere has been harsher, and even in Italy, where Puccini occupies a twin throne with Verdi, the work is not tolerated.

Even if the music of *La Fanciulla* were good (which it is not), the libretto would prove an all but insuperable bar to sincere appreciation. Singers dressed up as frontiersmen and shouting Italian in a Wild West saloon (the Polkadot) cannot be regarded, particularly by Americans, as the vessels of serious opera. If this obstacle deprived us of the ability to listen properly to some of Puccini's best music, rewriting the book might be worth the trouble. But *La Fanciulla* is as hopeless musically as it is theatrically. The shadows on Puccini's life do not show in it, but the lack of inspiration that visited him because of them is only too evident. Technical care is in the score, the attempt to capture the American flavor by use of native tunes, the gestures of a master craftsman—all are there, and yet fail utterly to animate this musical cadaver. In fact, *La Fanciulla* must have made some of Puccini's warmest admirers fear that the comet-like ascent had ended. *La Rondine,* which issued stillborn from his pen in 1917, after seven long years of waiting, was a poor Viennese-waltz operetta—which, nevertheless, Bori used, on March 21, 1936, as her farewell to opera. It must have made them shudder for his future. At fifty-nine, it is not easy to make a comeback.

The facts are that before *La Rondine* was begun, Puccini had composed part of a most spectacular comeback—a "triptych" of three contrasting one-act operas. As early as 1914, he had all but finished the first, *Il Tabarro,* a brutal lens focused on a Parisian slum tragedy. While completing it, after delays caused by the war and *La Rondine,* he was still searching for two more short librettos to fill out his scheme. Then Giovacchino Forzano, who had already provided Mascagni with the book of *Lodoletta,* came forward with two ideas, the first the story of a nun with an unhappy past, the second the droll story of a hoax perpetrated in Dante's Florence.

Early in 1918, all three sections of *Il Trittico* were ready— *Il Tabarro, Suor Angelica,* and *Gianni Schicchi.* Tito Ricordi closed with the Metropolitan for the world *première,* and there, accordingly, on December 14, 1918, it was given. Puccini was not present (it was only a month after the Armistice), and the operas were received with an indifference his presence might have prevented. Muzio and Farrar created the chief female roles in *Il Tabarro* and *Suor Angelica* respectively, but despite the popularity of these dramatic singing actresses, neither opera succeeded at the Metropolitan, where both disappeared after two seasons. Although the Italian *première* of *Il Trittico*, at the Costanzi, Rome, on January 11, 1919, with Toscanini conducting, and the King and Queen present, was an unparalleled personal triumph for Puccini, this brilliant send-off was not effective in establishing Parts I and II in the affections of the people. Throughout the rest of Europe, their fate was almost as dismal.

Gianni Schicchi's destiny was quite different. Easton, De Luca, and Didur covered themselves with glory at the world *première*, and slowly, definitely, the opera made its way. An unhappy experiment marked the revival of January 27, 1936, when an English version brought forward Tibbett as Gianni Schicchi. The dictional standard achieved may be judged from Irving Kolodin's complaint, in *The Metropolitan Opera: 1883-1939*, that of the large cast, "only Tibbett, Bentonelli, and Baromeo demonstrated a reasonable command of English enunciation." To quote Mr. Kolodin further: "As a final embarrassment, the production was directed and coached by Gennaro Papi, whose English is somewhat less than Oxonian."

Il Trittico shows Puccini gaining stature as a serious musician. In conception, design, and execution, it seems beyond the potentialities of the callow young melodist of *Le Villi*, and not to have been expected of the adroit romanticist who contrived *La Bohème*. *Il Tabarro* does not deserve its present obscurity. Plotted along simple, direct lines, it is a small masterpiece of uncompromising realism and musically works out the psychological problem with inexorable logic. It is a thriller, but not of the garish Mascagni-Leoncavallo school, for the music starkly, honestly hews to the action. *Suor Angelica* is impressionistic, almost Debussyan in its subtle evocation of atmosphere. Like so many neglected works, this was, of *Il Trittico*, the composer's favorite, but, by providing too many audience hurdles, he had made himself responsible for its failure. There are too many incidents too loosely integrated for the one-act frame, and the fact that all the voices in a largely feminine score are female tends to produce a soporific tedium.

Gianni Schicchi is a masterpiece of a quite un-Puccinian sort. While his in technique, spiritually it is the child of *Falstaff*. The libretto, though actually based by Forzano on a casual hint in *La Divina Commedia*, bears a curious resemblance to Ben Jonson's *Volpone*. It is good malicious fun all through and has just enough going on to make the one act perfect entertainment. The music is fast, witty, brilliantly apt, and overflowing —particularly when Gianni holds the center of the stage—with a kind of benevolent malice. It is a flawless score, with one exception, and that its best-known fragment—the lushly Italian *"O mio babbino caro,"* psychologically apt but, in its context, musically unsound.

Before his death on November 29, 1924, Puccini had completed all but the last scene of one of the most interesting operatic scores of the century. This was *Turandot*, with a libretto by Giuseppe Adami, who had written the book of *Il Tabarro*, and Renato Simoni, a poet who was something of a Sinologue. As Puccini's admiring biographer, Vincent Seligman, says, in *Puccini Among Friends*, "A Persian legend from the *Thousand and One Nights*; a Chinese fairy tale of a cruel Princess, whose hatred at last turned to love; a Venetian Masque; a play of Gozzi, a poem of Schiller, an overture of Weber—from such discordant elements was Puccini's masterpiece born." He worked on the score of *Turandot* for four years, and when he went to the Brussels hospital in which he died, he took thirty-six manuscript pages of sketch material and notes for the finale with him.

After Puccini's death, these pages were handed over to Franco Alfano, a harmless second-rater whose name is slightly green in the United States because of Mary Garden's revival, in French, of his elderly *La Risurrezione*. Alfano, consulting Toscanini, who had discussed *Turandot* in detail with Puccini, completed it in a workmanlike manner, and it was presented

A Metropolitan Performance of Montemezzi's *L'Amore dei tre re*, with Lucrezia Bori (Fiora) and Adamo Didur (Archibaldo)

at La Scala on April 25, 1926, with Raïsa (Turandot), Maria Zamboni (Liù), Miguel Fleta (Calaf), and Rimini (Ping). Toscanini conducted.

At the Metropolitan *première* on the following November 16, Jeritza, whom Puccini admired intensely, and for whom he is said to have designed the role, sang Turandot, with Martha Attwood, Lauri-Volpi, and De Luca in other leading roles. Performed eight times that season, used to make the opening of the following one an unforgettable spectacle, sung twenty-one times in all, *Turandot* has not been heard in New York since January 8, 1930.

Turandot is interesting chiefly because in it post-Verdian Italian operatic music, veristic and romantic, meets, and momentarily merges with, the surge of influences from northern and eastern Europe—the post-Wagnerism of Strauss, the atonality of Schönberg, and the polyrhythms and savage colors of Stravinsky. Whereas in *Madama Butterfly* Puccini had imported Japanese gramophone records for his exotic *appliqué* work, in *Turandot* he made a profound study of Chinese music and emerged with results reminiscent of Debussy's dilettante reactions to Javanese and Annamese music. In this complex score, Puccini never forgets that he is creating a musicodramatic work, and is almost always master of his materials. Yet it is Puccini all the way through, with a new genius for tragic utterance that reaches its height in the music he gave to the pitiable Liù. At its worst, where the ultramodern elements do not mix with the indigenous musical speech, *Turandot* may sound like *Butterfly* with wrong notes. Flawed though it is, and lacking the final polish that Puccini might have given it, *Turandot* is a worthy crown to his career of ever-increasing knowledge. With something slightly less than genius to work with, he might have gone on because of his insatiable intellect, his unimpaired melodic gift, and his technical mastery, to produce works in his old age as far ahead of *Manon Lescaut* as *Falstaff* was of *Ernani*. At sixty-six, he died too young.

In Puccini, Verdi had found a not unworthy successor, while in their early *Cavalleria rusticana* and *Pagliacci*, Mascagni and Leoncavallo had at least contributed novelty to the musical scene. But their contemporaries and followers in Italy, especially Mascagni's, were largely a sorry lot, constantly finding cruder, more blatant ways of repeating the same old shockers. They were, with few exceptions, pattern workers, and the exceptions rarely had sufficient creative strength to give enduring life to their feeble brain children. Among the lesser verists, Umberto Giordano is typical, except in his extraordinary success. No less than four of his dozen operas were considered sufficiently stageworthy to be produced at the Metropolitan, while a fifth—*Siberia*—was a little-liked novelty of Hammerstein's second season at the Manhattan. *Andrea Chénier,* with a libretto by Illica, is easily the most popular of his operas and is in some ways his most nearly engaging. Full of obvious melodies, bold declamation and effective stage tricks, it is, despite its title, a good vehicle opera for a dramatic soprano of large voice and a taste for heroics. It is exactly contemporary with *La Bohème,* having been first given at La Scala in 1896.

Andrea Chénier reached America before the year was out, in a tawdry production at Boston during Mapleson's forlorn attempt to make a comeback. On March 27, 1908, Hammerstein staged *Andrea Chénier* as a gala benefit for Cleofonte Campanini, at which the conductor's wife, Eva Tetrazzini, came from retirement to sing the role of young Maddalena di Coigny. The third Giordano work to reach the Metropolitan, its production, on March 7, 1921, brought forward Gigli in the title role, and, as Maddalena, Muzio, who was superbly cast. When *Andrea Chénier* left the Metropolitan repertoire with Ponselle, it had been given forty-four times in thirteen seasons.*

---

* *Fedora,* after Sardou's famous play, served to introduce Lina Cavalieri—and Giordano—to the Metropolitan. Caruso, who had sung with Gemma Bellincioni at the world *première* in Milan, Scotti, and Alten were other principals of this December 5, 1906, performance. *Fedora* lasted only two seasons, while the revival of 1923 for Jeritza and Martinelli, still with Scotti, lasted three. *Madame Sans-Gêne* had its world *première* at the Metropolitan on January 25, 1915, Farrar, a captivating and saucy Caterina, making the most of a primarily acting role. With her were Martinelli, Althouse, De Segurola, and Amato, the last singing Napoleon, who in real life could not sing at all. In 1924, Giordano set Sem Benelli's internationally known play, *La Cena delle beffe,* called *The Jest* in the United States, where John and Lionel Barrymore had acted it. This was the last Giordano opera to be staged at the Metropolitan—on January 2, 1926, the cast including Alda, Gigli, and Ruffo. *La Cena delle beffe* was not well received, and died unmourned in its second season.

Another disciple of Mascagni was Riccardo Zandonai, who as a student received from Mascagni's lips the gospel of verism. He followed his master, at some distance. Several of his operas have had continuing success in Italy, where he was eulogized by both Boïto and Puccini, but he has had little success in establishing himself elsewhere. In the United States, for example, only two of his operas are known, and those not well. The first, *Conchita*, with a sadistic Spanish libretto after Pierre Louÿs, was heard in San Francisco in 1912 and came East the next year with Tarquinia Tarquini, the original Conchita and Zandonai's future wife. The second, *Francesca da Rimini*, with a libretto by Tito Ricordi from the D'Annunzio play, had an all-star cast when it was first produced at the Metropolitan on December 22, 1916, among the players being Alda, Edith Mason, Garrison, Braslau, Martinelli, Amato, and Bada. Orchestral sophistication, a limited flair for the theater, and almost nothing original to say characterize Zandonai's scores. Like Giordano, he provides some of his few memorable moments when he allows the orchestra to have its say while the action is suspended temporarily.

No mere imitators, yet measurably removed from the experimental modernist school, are such men as Ferruccio Busoni, Ottorino Respighi, Italo Montemezzi, and Ermanno Wolf-Ferrari. An American will find difficulty in assessing Busoni as an operatic composer, for none of the operas of the great pianist,* teacher, theorist, and musical philosopher has been performed here. Busoni was, in musical preferences, rather more German than Italian, and his ardent, almost mystical preaching of Liszt and Wagner was scarcely preparation for a truly modern idiom. Those who have heard his four stage works recognize in them the utterance of a lofty and original, but not lyrically gifted, man. Busoni took his operatic compositions most seriously and wrote them to his own librettos. His most considerable opera, *Doktor Faust*, was completed after his death by his pupil, the

* Another famous pianist with almost as tireless a pen was Eugen d'Albert, whose *Tiefland* has been described as a "German *Carmen*." Although immensely popular in Germany, his adopted land, *Tiefland* survived only four performances at the Metropolitan, though Destinn was entrusted with the chief role. The *première* there occurred on November 23, 1908.

erudite Philipp Jarnach, and was presented at Dresden in 1925. Of it, Edward J. Dent has said, "Busoni's real masterpiece is *Doktor Faust*, a work in which he sums up the experiences of a lifetime; it is a drama on a spiritual plane far removed from the normal operatic level, and it will remain one of those operas, like *Les Troyens* of Berlioz, which are revived and presented only at rare and solemn intervals."

The popular composer of *Le Fontane di Roma, I Pini di Roma*, and other sumptuously accoutered orchestral works of derivative nature was persistent in his attentions to the theater. But though he experimented with numerous types, from comic opera to lyric tragedy, not to mention several of his own devising, Respighi suceeded signally, to the detriment of his stage pieces, in remaining a symphonic composer. He became, after Puccini's death, Italy's outstanding composer, and everything he wrote was eagerly performed, often with a success that ignored his failure to use pertinently the form he had selected. His operas (some of which he evasively labeled "a story," or "a mystery," or anything he chose) revealed his lack of understanding of the interrelation of orchestra and singers in a musicodramatic whole. They are episodic tone poems with words added. *La Fiamma,* about a witch, was the most acclaimed of his operas, only one of which, *La Campana sommersa,* after Hauptmann's play, *Die versunkene Glocke,* has been heard in the United States. The Metropolitan, on November 24, 1928, produced it with Rethberg, Martinelli, De Luca, and Pinza in the chief roles, Serafin conducting. Respighi, on hand for this *première,* said fulsomely, "In heaven itself I could not wish for such a production!"

Busoni died in 1924, full of honors and of exasperation at a world that did not understand him, at the age of fifty-eight. Respighi was not quite fifty-seven when death cut short his prolific activity in 1936. Montemezzi and Wolf-Ferrari, both living (1941), were born five months apart, in 1875 and 1876 respectively. The elder is also the less gifted. Like Mascagni and Leoncavallo, he is primarily a one-opera man, though three of his five operas have been produced at the Metropolitan. *Giovanni Gallurese* and *La Notte di Zoraïma* were undoubtedly staged in the hope of cashing in on the prestige of the composer of *L'Amore dei tre re*. They failed utterly.

The very successful *L'Amore dei tre re* is happy in an original libretto by Sem Benelli, somber, powerful, and direct. Fortunately, Montemezzi did not overreach his talents in setting the Benelli book, but was content to provide a musical atmosphere for the action. The result is very satisfactory: without being great music, *L'Amore dei tre re* is an artistic unit executed with taste and restraint. The music responds admirably to the situations and shouts only when they do. This is primarily an absorbing stage play with excellent background music. Philip Hale succinctly described its achievement: "Montemezzi has done in an Italian way for an Italian drama what Debussy in an ultra-modern French way did for the Belgian Maeterlinck."

Tullio Serafin conducted the world *première* of *L'Amore dei tre re* at La Scala on April 11, 1913, with the San Francisco-born Luisa Villani as Fiora and Edoardo Ferrari-Fontana as Avito. It failed there, and critics were not prepared for its success at the Metropolitan on January 2 following. It is believed in some quarters that Toscanini's conducting turned the trick, though when Montemezzi had Toscanini's interpretation described to him in detail, he was shocked. Evidently, the conductor had sacrificed fidelity to dynamics. The Metropolitan *première* had, besides Ferrari-Fontana, making his American debut in the role he had created, Bori (Fiora), Amato (Manfredo), and Didur (Archibaldo). On January 26, 1920, the Chicago Opera Company staged *L'Amore dei tre re* at the Lexington Theater, New York, with Garden a spectacular Fiora. Her Avito was Edward Johnson, who was making his New York operatic debut. In 1941, Montemezzi conducted several performances at the Metropolitan, with Grace Moore (Fiora), Charles Kullman (Avito), Richard Bonelli (Manfredo), and Pinza (Archibaldo). For an institution that had already presented *L'Amore dei tre re* forty-four times in fifteen seasons, Montemezzi provided some special between-acts music. Generally, the composer's reading of the score was as much praised as Moore's acting was derided.

All four of Wolf-Ferrari's best-known operas were composed to Italian texts, but produced first in Germany to German ver-

sions of the librettos. As his name suggests, the composer himself is half German, half Italian. He is similarly divided in artistic loyalties: roughly, his heart is with the Italians, his head
with the Germans—Italian melody and sparkle, German sound-
ness and technique. At his best, in three *opere buffe*, he is a
diminutive modern Mozart. These have been consistently successful in Europe, but in America they have been all but cold-
shouldered and still await their due.

The second of these *opere buffe*, the delicious one-act *Il Segreto di Susanna*, was the first to be introduced in New York,
where the Philadelphia-Chicago Opera Company, at the Metropolitan, presented Carolina White and Sammarco in the singing roles of the Countess and the Count, with Francesco Daddi
in the only other role, that of the mute servant, Sante. The resident company gave their first performance of *Il Segreto* on December 13, 1912, with Farrar, Scotti, and Bada. Bori, however,
rather than Farrar, became associated with the role of the
Countess, and the revival of 1920-21 was staged in her honor.
White and Bori, the latter at Ravinia Park, really popularized
Il Segreto in Chicago, but in New York it has not been heard
for twenty years.

Even less enduring was Manhattan's response to *Le Donne
curiose*, which was a Toscanini triumph at its Metropolitan
première, on January 3, 1912, while *L'Amore medico*, also with
Toscanini, having been brought forward unstrategically near
the end of the season, on March 25, 1914, suffered almost immediately an undeserved eclipse. Who was to blame? Surely not
Gatti-Casazza, who had given to his best conductor Farrar,
Jadlowker, and Scotti in *Le Donne curiose*, Bori, Pini-Corsi,
and Rothier in *L'Amore medico*. Not the critics, most surely,
who were enthusiastic to a man. Nor can the audience be fairly
blamed. The truth is that Wolf-Ferrari's brittle evocations of
the past—seventeenth-century France, eighteenth-century Venice, and mid-Victorian Piedmont—are too delicate for a vast
house like the Metropolitan, where fragile shafts of wit, subtle
raillery, and pervasive intimacy are crushed by vast, gilt-sur-
rounded open spaces.

Wolf-Ferrari's best-known, and in America—especially in

Chicago—most popular opera, *I Gioielli della Madonna,* a gory Neapolitan melodrama, is the most flagrant latter-day example of Mascagnitis. It can and should be dismissed with the descriptive word that headed Huneker's review of it—"Paste!" Pitts Sanborn has called it a Neapolitan *Louise,* which may be precisely true. It is hard to believe that *I Gioielli* is not the calculated—and very successful—potboiler of a most accomplished craftsman, so far is it, in style and quality, from his best work. It is so brash, so catchily tuneful, so thoroughly vulgar, that it reads like a parody of *Cavalleria rusticana.*

Chicago had the American first of *I Gioielli,* at the Auditorium on January 16, 1912, with White (Maliella), Louise Bérat (Carmela), Amadeo Bassi (Gennaro), and Sammarco (Rafaele), with Campanini conducting. The same group introduced it to New York during a Metropolitan visit, on March 5, of the same year. Rosa Raïsa and her husband, Giacomo Rimini, made their New York debuts as Maliella and Rafaele at the Lexington Theater on January 24, 1918. The first performance by the resident Metropolitan company, on December 13, 1925, included Jeritza, Telva, Martinelli, and Danise in the leading roles. Jeritza overacted and received twenty curtain calls. Despite this propitious beginning, *I Gioielli della Madonna* did not last more than two seasons at the Metropolitan. Until the Second World War, it is probable that London, where it was first sung on May 30, 1912, at Covent Garden, was, outside Italy, the chief center of the *Gioielli* cult.

At first blush, it had seemed as if the post-Verdian descendants of Ponchielli—the verists, that is—had enlarged the scope of opera, but as the newness of their works dulled, it became evident that they had contributed next to nothing* to its development, though they had enlarged its effective repertoire very considerably. They are important in the history of the opera house as a going concern, not of the art form allegedly fostered therein. Nor can all their gifts to the effective repertoire be put down to the credit of *verismo,* for the pure verist strain began

---

* Is this too summary a way to dismiss the final elimination of recitative from Italian opera? We think not, for Verdi had made that elimination inevitable. The substitution of continuous arioso, that flowing style of vocal speech, which compromises between pure aria and pure recitative, was seized upon as a veristic *sine qua non,* and has held its ground.

to peter out in multiple trickles almost as soon as it appeared. Puccini was never completely a convinced verist, and in *La Bohème*, for instance, he often gets swept away into purely romantic utterance. Wolf-Ferrari, except in the egregious *Gioielli*, exploited a tradition antedating romanticism, stemming from Mozart, Cimarosa, and Pergolesi.

Verismo, which was inclined to set itself up as realism, just as Zola had come to think of his *naturalisme* as a faithful mirror held up to reality, defeated its professed purpose by its over-emphasis on certain aspects of life to the almost total exclusion of others. As it approached the condition of Grand Guignol puppetry, the broader and more sensitive talents began to drift away from *verismo*, realizing that it was but one of several methods of treating dramatic material, however contemporary and "true to life." The result, until experimental modernism set in, was a growing eclecticism, chiefly along veristic lines. *Turandot,* produced in 1926, was at once the last, most sumptuous, and, in its very outlandishness, most typical result of this eclecticism, and a presage, significant as coming from one nurtured on the early promises of *verismo*, of Italy's final plunge into the vortex of the modern schools.

Chapter XXI

Strauss and Latter-Day Wagnerism

URING the two decades following the death of Wagner, the most important music composed in Germany was a series of big orchestral works by Richard Strauss. They began with *Aus Italien* in 1887, and ended with the *Sinfonia domestica* in 1903. Every one of them, without exception, was a *succès de scandale*, though not all of them won the public they had shocked. They established the right of a young man who had begun as a classicizing, textbook composer to assume the leadership of the *Zukunftsmusiker*, those Musicians of the Future parented by Liszt and Wagner. Also, by their overt theatricalism and programmatic drama, even the first of them hinted that it would not be long before their composer began writing opera. Were not his tone poems themselves substantially operas without stage action and words—Wagnerian music drama grafted onto the symphonic poem of Liszt? Strauss' choice was wise: in his reaction from academic classicism, it was less risk to carry the symphonic poem a step farther than to try, at the high noon of Wagner's apotheosis, the same with opera. But in 1893, Wagner was ten years dead, and Strauss, on the basis of *Don Juan* and *Tod und Verklärung*, was himself a *Meister*. And so, he wrote *Guntram*, his first opera. A really popular opera did not come from him for a dozen years: when *Salome* was produced in 1905, Strauss had completed all his tone poems.

In the tone poems, Strauss had perfected a manner of his own—an unmistakable way of arranging ideas of any provenance whatever. But when it came to composing *Guntram*, this most assured of eclectics turned his back on this manner, and borrowed everything—type of subject matter and musical style —from Wagner. Like Wagner, too, he even wrote the libretto, which was based upon those ideas of redemption through love which had haunted Wagner's mind through his long series of

419

stage works. The very names of the principal characters—Guntram, Freihild, and Friedhold—might have come from the *Ring*. The music, even to the turn of melody and closely imitative way of using leitmotivs, led straight back to Bayreuth. *Guntram* can be interpreted in two ways: it was either public proclamation that Strauss believed himself equipped to vie with Wagner, using the *Meister's* own tools, or it was a confession that Strauss had not yet devised his own style for the opera house. Most critics voted *Guntram* tiresome when it was staged on May 12, 1894, at Weimar, but Ernest Newman, in his minority report, later (1908) wrote: "Altogether *Guntram* is a great work, the many merits of which will perhaps some day restore it to the stage from which it is now most unjustly banished." Strauss himself got two things from the Weimar production: first, a realization that the public, having begun to tire somewhat of Wagner, would not stomach imitation Wagner, and second, a wife, Pauline de Ahna, who had sung Freihild.

In his second try for operatic acclaim, Strauss took a seven-mile leap by securing a libretto that was as shocking to some as his tone poems had been. Shock was a *sine qua non* of Strauss' technique—he simply had to have it to work successfully either in the concert hall or in the opera house. The libretto of his second opera, *Feuersnot* (besides containing attacks on Strauss' critics), is not only shocking, it is obscene, being a mixture of Rabelais and the German idea of the comic—not a bland mixture. For this farce, Strauss amended his Wagnerism in two directions. He allowed simple tunes, naïve, folksy, banal, to contaminate the Wagnerian stream, and from his tone poems he brought over a connoisseur's understanding, and use, of harmonic *Schrecklichkeit*. This tempered use of unresolved discords, unprepared modulations, and warring contrapuntal streams meant that Strauss was all but ready to project into opera his own carefully manufactured dual personality. *Feuersnot* found him arrived, but without all his baggage unpacked. It had the meager success that its trial-flight character deserved: outside Germany, it is hardly known at all. Its single American production at Philadelphia, on December 1, 1927, is notable

chiefly because Nelson Eddy played the minor role of Häm-
merlein.

In *Salome*, Strauss let himself go, arriving in one bound at
an operatic position as advanced as that which he had attained,
years earlier, in his purely instrumental work. Rather as a *coup*,
he had managed to secure Oscar Wilde's notorious play, which
in the Germany of that day was considered only less lofty than
Shakespeare or Goethe. Except for a few brief excisions, Strauss
accepted the play, in Hedwig Lachmann's faithful German
version, just as it was—a self-contained work of art, and a work
of art so jeweled, so static, so immalleable, that it did not require music, and would not have mixed well with it.

Strauss did not attempt to mix the two: he wrote a tone poem
with human voices as added instruments in the orchestra, the
whole designed to be accompanied by a stage spectacle of an
aggressively sense-stimulating nature. For the suggestive,
heavily perfumed, and rigidly mannered text, he wrote music
that exaggerated each of its qualities. The music tells more
than it has to say, is downright aphrodisiac, and ends in tetanic
catalepsy. Throughout, the music so overshadows the stage
action as to reduce it to mime, and even the greatest of dramatic
singers cannot utterly overcome the posed, almost hieratic
quality of the drama. Strauss' *Salome* is more decadent than
Wilde's play simply because it takes itself more seriously. Or,
perhaps, only seems to—with Strauss one is never sure, though
now that its magnificent tissue has begun to wear thin and reveal the cotton body to which the brocade is stitched, it is tempt-
ing to write *Salome* off as the cold-blooded fabrication of a
supercraftsman. And even in the tissue, which used to look so
golden and cunningly patterned, it now seems that there are
patches of the carelessly commonplace. But what remains of
Salome is enough, when a powerful singing actress is found for
the title role, to provide a good evening in the opera house.

Dresden, at whose Königliches Opernhaus *Salome* was first produced on December 9, 1905, accepted it enthusiastically and without
hesitation. Soon, despite the ban laid upon it in Berlin by Wilhelm
II, patron of Leoncavallo, it was given in many German cities.
It was shocking, but the audiences that thronged to see it in Ger-

many left their hypocrisy at home. *Salome*'s troubles with Anglo-Saxon morality began in New York, at the Metropolitan, on January 22, 1907.* Conried staged it, at doubled prices, as his annual benefit. Olive Fremstad was the Salome, Marion Weed the Herodias, Karl Burrian (as at Dresden) the Herod, and Karl Perron the Jokanaan. The next morning, a journalistic tempest broke over the heads of the Metropolitan management: the newspapers' morals had been outraged, and they demanded that the opera be dropped. The management could have weathered that, especially as audiences would no doubt have been capacity, but when the directors of the Metropolitan Opera and Real Estate Company threatened to cancel his lease, Conried withdrew the opera. It was seven years before any Strauss opera was heard at the Metropolitan, and twenty-seven years before *Salome* attained another performance there.

Meanwhile, Hammerstein had taken up arms against the freedom of the press to stifle progress in America, and, on January 28, 1909, produced *Salome* in French, at the Manhattan Opera House, with Garden rivaling Fremstad's realistic portrayal, yet failing to get Hammerstein into trouble. The following year, however, when she sang it first in Chicago, with De Cisneros (Herodias), Dalmorès (Herod), and Dufranne (Jokanaan), the most flattering vituperation came her way, and the opera was withdrawn after a single repetition. That same year, after the censor had been placated by changing the names of the Biblical characters, Aïno Ackté, the Finnish soprano, sang the title role at Sir Thomas Beecham's Covent Garden staging of the first *Salome* in England. *Salome* returned to the Metropolitan on January 13, 1924, when Göta Ljungberg was totally inadequate in the name role. In the most recent Metropolitan revival, Marjorie Lawrence was an unabandoned Salome.†

Salome dazzled the world with its piled-up brilliance, its quenchless energy, its battery of shattering effects. It was a magnificent envelope containing little, and musically it was bound to fade. It was a symptom of the bustling imperial Germany of

* A Tuesday, this performance followed the semipublic dress rehearsal of the preceding Sunday morning, when one thousand guests had a first clandestine glance. Although a Sabbath, the day brought no outbreaks.

† Erica Darbo, the best New York Salome since Garden, sang the role once at the Lewisohn Stadium in 1937. Rose Pauly, famed in Europe for her interpretation of Salome, has not been heard in the role in New York, though she has been a member of the Metropolitan company for several seasons.

the early twentieth century, with its boasts, its strutting muscu-
larity, its sumptuary excesses, and its glee in the superficials of
progress. *Salome* was another course in the continuous champagne banquet of expanding Germany, and it was, though not
in the old sense, a national opera. Those who were able to see
through the dazzle, being neither too shocked nor too carried
away, saw through to the synthetic core and said that Strauss
lacked conviction. They said that *Salome* had no inwardness,
and it was even whispered that Strauss' creative peak was
passed. In 1908, Ernest Newman ended his monograph on
Strauss, one of the first in English, on an ominous note: "His
new opera, which is to be produced early next year, will probably show whether he is going to realize our best hopes or our
worst fears."

The next opera was *Elektra*. For many, it confirmed their
worst fears. It was louder, more cacophonous, more unrelievedly psychopathic. *Salome* had emitted a mingled odor of
perfume and decay; *Elektra* omitted the perfume, and the decay
had become decomposition. Here was stench in terms of music.
Hugo von Hofmannsthal, they said, had distorted Sophocles
and made him hideous, and Strauss had further uglified the
result. It was the end, they said, and Strauss, besides being degenerate, was certainly insane. There could be no doubt that
so foul a betrayal of art would soon shrivel up and disappear.

But *Elektra* has done nothing of the sort: recent performances have tended to confirm the opinion, at first expressed
cautiously, and then with ever-growing conviction, that *Elektra*
is a tragic masterpiece of the very first order. It has not faded:
it is as shattering, as moving, as profound in terror, as on the
night of its *première*. What we can now hear that many of its
first baffled listeners could not, because of their consuming interest in its more obvious, less significant aspects, is the abiding
conviction that holds *Elektra* together. The noise, the cacoph-
ony, even the reek of twisted neuroses and unleashed passion—
all have integral functions. In short, *Elektra* is not a deliberate
shocker—it merely, since it deals with the naked psyche, has no
reticences. Within the limits imposed by the climactic character of the situations, the characters achieve a wholeness that

is the best proof of Strauss' searching care in projecting personalities. So intense was that care that the tender lyricism of certain scenes escapes that banality which is all too often Strauss'
only counterpoise to the horrible and the grotesque.

Elektra is formally and technically more satisfactory than
Salome. Little in the libretto or the music is extraneous to the
establishment of the atmosphere of tragedy and, in the largest
sense, the display of Electra's struggle with fate. To these great
issues Strauss' sure-fire theatrical devices—his pictorialism, his
automatic program-making, his underlining of each situation—
are tributary. In *Elektra*, he kept his unstanchable cleverness
in its place. The extreme chromaticism and discord, which
sometimes seem willful in *Salome*, are always relevant in
Elektra, in which they are much more abundantly used.
Elektra, too, is more singable than *Salome*. The voice parts, instead of doubling instruments in the orchestra, are throughout
the note of color that sustains the balance of the palette. In
Salome, the tone-poem base and the stage action practically
dispossess the voice; in *Elektra*, Strauss, become a master of
vocal declamation, establishes the parity of the vocal line without sacrificing the equilibrium of the whole structure. He did
not damp down the orchestra, the result being that the singers
have to work hard. But they work to effect.

At the world *première* of *Elektra* in Dresden, on January 25,
1909, Anna Krull (Electra), Margarete Siems (Chrysothemis), and
Perron (Orestes) were less famous than the Clytemnestra—Ernestine
Schumann-Heink, who never sang this role after the first performance. "It was frightful," she said. "We were a set of mad women.
There is nothing beyond *Elektra*. We have lived to reach the farth-
est boundary in dramatic writing for the voice with Wagner. But
Strauss goes beyond him. His singing voices are lost. We have come
to a full stop. I believe Strauss himself sees it."

A year and a week after the *première*, Hammerstein, using a
French version, by Henri Gauthier-Villars, of Hofmannsthal's text,
presented *Elektra* at the Manhattan Opera House, with Mariette
Mazarin (Electra), Gerville-Réache (Clytemnestra), and Gustave
Huberdeau (Orestes). Again the Clytemnestra renounced the role
as too taxing. Mazarin, though she fainted after the performance,

was evidently made of sterner stuff, for she recovered to sing it again six days later, while five days after that she sang Electra in the afternoon and Salomé, in Massenet's *Hérodiade*, in the evening. The holy band of Manhattan critics were almost unanimous in denigrating *Elektra*, but the public hurried to see Mazarin's surpassing interpretation, which was along truly Sophoclean lines.

The first Metropolitan *Elektra* did not occur until December 3, 1932, when Bodanzky conducted a beautifully integrated performance, with Gertrude Kappel (Electra), Ljungberg (Chrysothemis), Branzell (Clytemnestra), and Schorr (Orestes). Ljungberg was later promoted to the name role, while Branzell vacated that of Clytemnestra for Maria Olszewska. An Electra comparable to Mazarin reached the Metropolitan in 1938: Rose Pauly, a Hungarian soprano of marked dramatic gifts, who had previously astounded New York in a concert version of the opera. At the Metropolitan, Thorborg's Clytemnestra was scarcely less remarkable than the Electra.

Schumann-Heink's feeling that Strauss would, in some measure, recant was justified by his next stage work, which was quite different from anything he had done before. "This time I shall write a Mozart opera," he said—and *Der Rosenkavalier* was the result. Hofmannsthal supplied the libretto, this time a farce satire laid in the Vienna of the mid-eighteenth century, and written in a broad Viennese dialect that shocked its first Vienna hearers, though they used the same idiom themselves. Hofmannsthal's book is a masterly mélange of the ridiculous, the coarse, and the pathetic, to all of which Strauss gave due consideration when he set it. This time, he disappointed the expectations of those in his audience who had come to regard him as a provider of clinical studies, pathological thrillers. *Der Rosenkavalier* is shocking, but it is not psychotic: the affair between the mature Marschallin and the seventeen-year-old Octavian is only mildly perverse, while Baron Ochs is merely a lecherous country squire. Of course, the version given in Germany is far more outspoken than that used at the Metropolitan, where, for example, the Marschallin is discovered on a sofa in Act I, and not in bed, and where some lines have been excised. But the libretto is no more suggestive than that of *Le Nozze di Figaro* or *Così fan tutte*, while compared to *Salome* or *Elektra*, *Der Rosenkavalier* is healthy, bawdy fun—with just a tinge of Hofmannsthal's overripeness.

Response to Strauss' pleasant change of period, locale, and atmosphere was immediate and warm. After the Dresden *première* of January 26, 1911, *Der Rosenkavalier* was soon heard outside Germany, reaching London on New Year's, 1913. The following December 9, Frieda Hempel was the peerless Marschallin of the first Metropolitan cast, her chief colleagues being Margarete Ober (Octavian), Anna Case (Sophie), Otto Goritz (Baron Ochs), and Hermann Weil (Faninal). Alfred Hertz, who conducted, later (April 24, 1915) bade farewell to the Metropolitan with the same opera. As Sophie, Elisabeth Schumann first appeared at the Metropolitan, on November 20, 1914, while, at the first Bodanzky *Rosenkavalier* there, Edith Mason, also as Sophie, made her Metropolitan debut exactly one year later.

When the United States entered the First World War, and almost the entire German repertoire was dropped from the Metropolitan, *Der Rosenkavalier,* which in four seasons had attained twenty-two performances, vanished until November 17, 1922, when the following cast revived it: Easton (the Marschallin), Jeritza (Octavian), Sundelius (Sophie), Paul Bender, in his debut (Baron Ochs), and Gustav Schützendorf, also in his debut (Faninal). Later that season, Rethberg sang Sophie. Lotte Lehmann, most admired of Marschallins since Hempel, gave her first Metropolitan characterization on January 4, 1935, when her associates were Olszewska, Fleischer, Emanuel List, and Schützendorf. In recent years, Thorborg and Risë Stevens have made Octavian challenge parity with the Marschallin. Stevens, though still in her early twenties, has exhibited her splendid impersonation more than fifty times in various parts of the world.

Der Rosenkavalier has become a popular fixture at the Metropolitan—sixty-two performances by the end of the 1940-41 season—and several other great opera houses. It is probably the most popular opera composed since *Madama Butterfly*, and the chief reason is its uncommon allure. Not only is *Der Rosenkavalier* the most digestible of Strauss' three major operas, but one of the most digestible of modern stage works making use of an advanced harmonic technique. It is his most lush and entrancing work, like a single lyric outpouring. It is somewhat

Kerstin Thorborg as Clytemnestra, in *Elektra*

Rose Pauly as Electra, in Richard Strauss' *Elektra*

odd that Strauss, in his "Mozart" opera, cast his spells in the form of Viennese waltzes, but the answer to those who would have preferred him to use gavottes and minuets is that his anachronism comes off, for Strauss orchestrates a waltz as brilliantly as did Ravel. (Imagine a gavotte scored for full Straussian orchestra!)

It would have been better if Strauss had never brought up Mozart, for then *Der Rosenkavalier* could have been judged on its own merits, which are great.* The man who could create the sheer delight of the senses that is the scene of the presentation of the Silver Rose need not call falsely on the name of Mozart. But Strauss as much lacks proportion about himself as about the volume and complexity of his orchestration—*Der Rosenkavalier*, for all its charm, is overfreighted, too noisy, too elaborate. A smaller orchestra would have helped. As scored, the emotions of the characters are larger than life, and the orchestral riot that breaks forth when the Marschallin's lover leaves her, for the first time, without a kiss, is but one sample of a grave disproportion. These are major lapses in taste, but they do not prevent *Der Rosenkavalier* from brimming over with beauty. Nor is that all. It is peopled with convincing characters, two of whom—the Marschallin and Baron Ochs—are unforgettable full-lengths.

Der Rosenkavalier was a work of Strauss' high prime—he was not yet forty-seven when it had its *première*. Since then, he has written eight operas, two ballets, many songs, a symphony, a piano concerto for the left hand alone, a hymn for the opening of the Olympic Games, and a considerable miscellany of other music, his most recent effusion being an apparently Axis-inspired *Festmusik* to mark the twenty-six hundredth anniver-

* By coupling his name with Mozart's, Strauss invited attack from his ill-wishers, among whom is Cecil Gray, who for years has pursued the G.O.M. of German music with unmitigated scorn. Writing in *A Survey of Contemporary Music*, he lashed out: "The divinely innocent and virginal Mozartean muse cannot be wooed and won like an Elektra or a Salome; all we find in *Der Rosenkavalier* is a worn-out, dissipated *demi-mondaine*, with powdered face, rouged lips, false hair, and a hideous leer. Strauss' muse has lost her chastity. Does he himself actually believe that *Der Rosenkavalier* is like *Figaro*? Are we to regard this declaration as a pathetic self-deception, or as the last crowning perversity? It would be difficult to say, and it is perhaps more charitable to infer the former."

sary of the accession to the throne of Japan of the Emperor Jimmu. All of the operas have had titanically publicized *premières*, all have solved separate technical problems, and all have pages that do not shame the creator of *Salome, Elektra,* and *Der Rosenkavalier*. But, alas! only pages. Strauss seems to have fallen victim to something closely akin to premature senility. None of his later stage works has the cohesiveness, the vigor, or the over-all imagination that unified each of his three great operas. Technical victories are won, often of dazzling brilliance, but ever with material awkwardly, or not at all, related to its surroundings, or with material either appallingly banal or shoddily imitative of his own past inspirations.

In these later works, too, Strauss' indulgences in other people's styles break all restraint, and are substituted shockingly for his own lack of style. Cecil Gray was not too harsh when he complained: "The impurity of style and juxtaposition of dissimilar idioms which was always one of his outstanding faults is carried to a disconcerting extreme in *Ariadne auf Naxos* and *Die Frau ohne Schatten*. In the first, Mozart dances a minuet with Mascagni, and Handel with Offenbach; in the second, Wagner is reconciled to Brahms, and Mendelssohn to Meyerbeer. Needless to say, this admixture of styles is not effected with any deliberate satirical intention, but from sheer lack of taste and cynical indifference."

Of these later operas, the one that aroused the most hope was *Ariadne auf Naxos*, principally because it followed on the heels of *Der Rosenkavalier*. It was the main feature of a Strauss festival at Stuttgart, and the composer himself conducted its *première*, on October 25, 1912, with Jeritza as Ariadne, Jadlowker as Bacchus, and Sigrid Onegin in a minor role. It turned out to be a divertissement tacked on to a performance of Molière's *Le Bourgeois Gentilhomme* (itself with Strauss' vivacious incidental music—modern treatment of Lully). Its idea is good: a farce handling of the old *opera seria*, the tragic action being interrupted by five traditional masks from the *commedia dell'arte*, one of whom (Zerbinetta) sings a complex burlesque coloratura aria that is supposed to give the final *coup de grâce* to the traditional "mad scene." In this most trivial of his operas,

Strauss overreached himself by emphasizing too much the total inconsequentiality of the proceedings. He used an orchestra of only thirty-seven players, which helped along its unquestioned intimacy, but made it hopeless for a large house even after he had given it a prologue and detached it from *Le Bourgeois Gentilhomme*. For this reason, the Metropolitan has never attempted it, though it has been given both in Philadelphia (November 1, 1928) and at the Juilliard School, New York (1934). At the Philadelphia performance, Helen Jepson, as Echo, made her operatic debut.

Die Frau ohne Schatten came in 1919. This elaborate moral allegory—an attempt to give *Die Zauberflöte* a sequel—was followed, in 1925, by *Intermezzo*, to Strauss' own book. Based on a little incident in his own life, *Intermezzo* is interesting only because of Strauss' attempt to provide set numbers suitable for true *bel canto* singing, the connecting tissue being a free, light type of declamation that has some of the naturalness of ordinary speech. Three years later, Strauss composed the last of his operas that have been heard at the Metropolitan—the ponderous, complicated, and apathetic *Die aegyptische Helena*, whose dreariness is a libel on the vivacious Helen of Troy. On that November 8, 1928, five months after the world *première* at Dresden, the sumptuous Urban settings, the choice of the beauteous and popular Jeritza for the name role, and the scholarly conducting of Bodanzky could not hide the fact that neither Hofmannsthal nor Strauss was any longer anything more than mediocre. It disappeared after one season.

The following year, Hofmannsthal died, leaving Strauss the libretto of a Viennese musical comedy, *Arabella*. In it, Strauss is remembering, but not always vividly, *Der Rosenkavalier,* and its several lyrically charming pages are not enough to carry a three-act opera. *Die schweigsame Frau* (1935), an extraordinarily raucous affair based on Ben Jonson's *Epicœne, or The Silent Woman,* had a Stefan Zweig libretto, and it was this collaboration with a Jew that temporarily made Strauss *persona non grata* with the Führer, who, moreover, resented his past collaboration with another "non-Aryan," Hofmannsthal. *Der Friedenstag* (1938), a political morality play along lines acceptable to the Nazi regime (even though it celebrates peace), restored the old gentleman to favor, and when *Dafne* was produced later the same year, high Nazi officials were in the audience, and Strauss had to respond to twenty curtain calls. The final kiss of peace came in 1939, when Hitler journeyed to Vienna expressly to hear *Der Friedenstag* and congratulate Strauss on his seventy-fifth birthday. Since then, his elderly muse has confined himself to official pronunciamentos.

It is a long, sad story—these last thirty years. It is the story of one of the foremost masters of every kind of musical technique sinking to complete spiritual incompetence. At seventy-eight, Strauss is not likely to redeem himself, even if the ambience were suitable to the process of redemption. He occupies much the same position in the history of German opera that Puccini occupies in Italian: just as the latter came after Verdi, and developed certain new ideas in the musical atmosphere without himself becoming an evolutive force, so Strauss followed Liszt and Wagner, carrying their methods to extremes, and leaving them there without any tentacles waving to the future. What Paul Rosenfeld said of Strauss in general almost a quarter of a century ago applies peculiarly to his operas: "To us, who once thought to see in him the man of the new time, he seems only the brave, sonorous trumpet-call that heralded a king who never put in his appearance, the glare that in the East lights the sky for an instant and seems to promise a new day, but extinguishes again. He is indeed the false dawn of modern music."

Chapter XXII

Massenet, and Wagner in France

WITH the death of Gounod in 1893, no realist could feel that French opera had sustained an irreparable loss. The man who, thirty-four years earlier, had created a sentimental masterpiece in *Faust* had long since ceased, after numerous fiascos, to be an active worker in the field. From his foremost colleague, the octogenarian Thomas, nothing new could be expected after the silence of a decade. But Saint-Saëns was at the height of his stanchless, if not overvigorous, fecundity, and, moreover, Gounod's true successor had already declared himself. *Manon,* in some respects Massenet's most satisfactory opera, was already eight years old, and showed that the disciple was in no way inferior to the master—he was just more of the same thing. While there is a distinct sense of anticlimax in Italian opera after Verdi, there is none in French opera after Gounod. Verdi was an irreplaceable genius, Gounod a typical *chef d'école.* Thus, the composer of *Otello* and *Falstaff* set standards beyond the capability of even so outstandingly gifted a man as Puccini, whereas the composer of *Faust* and *Roméo et Juliette* established nothing more than a fashion. After accepting that fashion uncritically, to be his successor—and Thomas'—required a flair for the theater and a store of sentimental emotionalism. These Massenet had in abundance; besides, he was a wily craftsman. His success was inevitable: he found French opera mediocre, and tirelessly, in an interminable series of stage pieces with music, he did nothing to change it.

Massenet, for all his complaisant mediocrity, is less pompously banal than Gounod. He had surer taste, which kept him from taking on subjects too large for his limited palette, and which kept within decent limits the intensity of his discipleship. Certain elements of Gounod's pattern for success he never borrowed, probably for reasons of temperament: he has no bumptiousness, no knack of contriving thumping tunes, no Soldiers' Chorus. Gounod and Massenet were both unctious, but nothing in the latter, not even Thaïs' death in an incredible odor of sanctity, approaches the holy bilge of the *Faust* finale. What restrains Massenet is a pervasive sense of proportion, a latent wit that does not allow stage sanctity to be anything more than stage sanctity. But he and his audiences pay for his taste: he lacks energy, his scores are hyperfeminine, and, in avoiding overseriousness, he often sacrifices conviction. His best, most believing pages are devoted to love, deliciously on—but hardly ever over—the precipice of sexual delight. There is an excess of sugar in his musical stream, and yet, except in two or three instances (notably the *Méditation* from Act II of *Thaïs*), he never cloys as Gounod does.

As musicodramatic works of art, the operas of Massenet are not to be taken seriously. In his long career as a working composer, he was first and last a purveyor of entertainment. As such, he was enormously successful, and as such he should be judged. His operas, with few exceptions, are, in effect, plays with music—alternatives for theatergoers, not musts for operagoers. They require for effective projection, not singers, but actors and actresses who can sing. Many of them were composed with specific actors and actresses in mind, and this conception of opera as entertainment is a cornerstone of Massenet's art. While his way of working achieved its purpose at the time, it has proved a long-range loss. Some of Massenet's scores, successful when first produced, waned with the passing of the singers for whom they were written, and soon expired. In the United States, the retirement of Mary Garden and Geraldine Farrar shelved several of Massenet's most entertaining works, and in France itself only a small proportion of his twenty-five publicly performed operas holds the stage. Even more than with most operas, to hear a well-sung, but poorly acted and staged, performance of a Massenet score is not to have heard it at all. The same has been peculiarly true of the large majority of French operas ever since, and contributes saliently to their early disappearance from the repertoire.

Not until his fifth performed opera—*Manon*—did Massenet find a subject that brought out in happiest proportion his most reliable assets. A precocious Prix de Rome, he had begun his operatic career in a comic mood, but unsuccessfully. Two tries with serious material followed, the second of which, *Le Roi de Lahore,* on a subject from Hindu mythology, brought him ponderable success, including praise from Tchaikovsky. In it, his characteristic idiom is already uncovered: the famous arioso from Act IV, *"Promesse de mon avenir,"* is a full-blown example of Massenet's sensual-ecstatic love music.

Hérodiade was even more successful. Its *première,* at the Théâtre de la Monnaie, Brussels, on December 17, 1881, won the composer a personal ovation. Its Paris first (oddly, in Italian), three years later, with Maurel and the De Reszkes, confirmed his growing reputation. It is curious that this typical French grand opera, with, in this case, as much Meyerbeer as Gounod, did not reach the Opéra until forty years after its composition. By November 8, 1909, when *Hérodiade* was first sung in New York—seventeen years later than in New Orleans —Massenet had become so popular in the United States that *Manon* was being used, the same evening, to open the Metropolitan's Brooklyn season. *Hérodiade,* opening Hammerstein's fourth, and final, season at the Manhattan, had Gerville-Réache as Herodias, Cavalieri as Salomé, Dalmorès as Jean, and Renaud as Herod. It has much perfumed, voluptuous music, including the sung-to-death *"Vision fugitive,"* but it has not reached the Metropolitan, and for obvious reasons. It is not the competent evening's pastime Massenet guarantees at his best, and, moreover, Strauss' version of much the same events, in *Salome,* has made Massenet's seem, by comparison, suitable for student performance at a female academy.

For his next opera, Massenet went to a touching love story that had already attracted such diverse talents as Halévy, Balfe, and Auber, the last of whom turned out a score that was a favorite of Charles Dickens. This was the eighteenth-century *L'Histoire de Manon Lescaut et du chevalier des Grieux,* by the Abbé Prévost, which Henri Meilhac and Philippe Gille adapted for Massenet. First produced at the Opéra-Comique, on January 19, 1884, *Manon* was an instantaneous and enduring success. By October 16, 1893, it had chalked up two hundred performances at the Comique, and had brought more than a

million francs into the box office. With it, Massenet assumed
the leadership of French opera, and thereafter everything from
his pen was awaited breathlessly. He soon saw *Manon* coursing
through the civilized world, with Liverpool leading the way,
with an English version, in 1885.

The New York Academy of Music, in its dying days, introduced
Manon to America, in Italian, with Hauk as Manon; also in the cast
was Ferruccio Giannini, father of Dusolina Giannini. Sybil Sanderson, who had made her debut in this role at The Hague in 1888,
was chosen for the Metropolitan *première*, when, on January 16,
1895, New York first heard the French text. Her chief associates
were Jean de Reszke (Des Grieux), Ancona (Lescaut), and Plançon
(Comte des Grieux). It has been given an average of four times
every season since then. Farrar, most pathetic of Manons, first
interpreted the role on February 3, 1909, opposite Caruso, whose
Des Grieux, though untouchable vocally, did not come up dramatically to that of Clément, who used the role for his Metropolitan
debut early the next season. Farrar alternated with Alda, whose
world debut, at the Comique in 1904, had been as Manon. After
six years' absence, the opera was revived for Bori in 1929, and she
rapidly became the most admired of latter-day Manons. The most
recent lovers at the Metropolitan were Jarmila Novotna, the Czech
soprano, and Crooks, who, in 1935, had made his Metropolitan
debut in the same role.

When Puccini set the same subject matter almost ten years
after the *première* of the Massenet *Manon*, many wondered at
the boldness of the junior who had dared invite comparison
with a work to which a large section of the European public
was almost idolatrously attached. But it is now plain that Puccini had only its popularity to fear. His *Manon Lescaut* is, in
most musical respects, a far more interesting score than *Manon*,
which is its superior only in dramatic unity and impact. When
he composed *Manon Lescaut*, Puccini was not yet the master of
dramatic craft he grew into only a few years later, and he was
not equipped to set his libretto with the theatrical sophistication that Massenet had acquired in large measure. A few years
later, Puccini might have insisted on changes in the libretto
that would have made it as good a thing as Meilhac and Gille's

—the anticlimactic fourth act, with Manon's by that time un-affecting death outside New Orleans, would have been junked, and Act III capped as neatly as the last act of *Madama Butterfly*. Even as it is, the atmosphere of *Manon Lescaut* is boldly close to that of Prévost's tale, and so has a more astringent quality than that of *Manon*, where the amoral baggage has been lady-fied into an erring frail, and the rather shady Chevalier des Grieux robbed of his vices. Not all of this was accomplished by the librettists; a large part must be credited to Massenet's talent for the charming and the idyllic, and much of *Manon*'s popu-larity—it has been given over 1700 times at the Opéra-Comique —depends on the concentration of those qualities.*

Manon is the best representative of the type of opera Mas-senet made peculiarly his own, a type so beloved by the public that, even during his lifetime, there was much more or less expert poaching on his preserve. Short, voluptuously sweet mel-ody, entrancing but unambitious harmonies, and pervading feminine charm are at the tip of Massenet's wand always. These operas throb throughout with a somniferous lack of energy, and lull the listener by their genteel lack of originality. Depending on Gounod and Thomas for the *tournure* of his melodic ideas, Massenet cribbed devotedly certain structural devices, notably the use of leitmotivs (which he interpreted with academic smoothness and lack of imagination), from Wagner. In *Esclar-monde* (1889), he simply rewrote Wagner for the French market, and emasculated him in the process. The official French Wagnerian, Reyer, said enigmatically that *Esclarmonde* had many *"délicieuses surprises."* Generally, Massenet was content to keep his Wagnerism as a spicing and leave the rest to his native ancestors.

Every year or so, a new opera—and sometimes two or three—made its way from Massenet's atelier to the stage. Usually they

---

* In a one-act "epilogue" to *Manon*, presented at the Comique in 1894, Mas-senet showed a moralizing Des Grieux playing the strict uncle to his youthful nephew, and forbidding him to marry the girl of his choice because she is poor and a commoner. He relents when the girl, dressing up to look like a portrait of Manon that Des Grieux always has by him, turns out to be Manon's niece. Hence the title, *Le Portrait de Manon*.

were successes, but with such a strong family likeness that what is true of one is true of most of them.

More than a dozen of Massenet's operas have reached New York and—during Mary Garden's active career there—Chicago, and there is no doubt that they have been as well represented in some European capitals. But outside France, few have managed to maintain themselves on the boards, and in the United States, only *Manon* and *Thaïs*, the latter precariously, can be said to be in the repertoire. Besides these, several—*Werther, La Navarraise, Sapho, Le Jongleur de Notre Dame,* and *Don Quichotte*—invite comment because of variation from the mold or because of unusual historic interest.

Thaïs is merely a pattern opera of high quality. It has the *Méditation*, and it has a title role that, having been written for Sibyl Sanderson, a dazzling young American singer whom Massenet intensely admired, not unnaturally has continued to captivate ambitious young sopranos, from Mary Garden to Marjorie Lawrence. It has, also, a smoldering book based on Anatole France's suave and superficial re-creation of early Christian Alexandria, and therefore calls for the most sumptuous efforts of a Joseph Urban. It is high entertainment of a kind that demands no collaboration on the part of the audience. The shifting between murky, sensual religiosity and elegant Eastern pornography affords a contrast that is extraordinarily piquant. Thaïs and the easily tempted Athanaël are roles of juicy possibility, and when, on November 25, 1907, *Thaïs* had its first American showing, at the Manhattan Opera House, Garden, most unforgettable of Thaïses, played opposite the equally superb Renaud. It was the propitious beginning of her operatic career in America. Geraldine Farrar was the first Metropolitan Thaïs, on February 16, 1917, Amato being the Athanaël.

Werther is an opera of the *Manon* type, with strong infusions of weak verism. The undramatic libretto is derived from Goethe's *Die Leiden des jungen Werther,* and Massenet, who was not at his best in portraying virtuous women, set it without conviction. It has, therefore, some of the pensive charm of that generally dull book which was influential in starting a Continental suicide wave. Even though its hero (like Goethe's) shoots

himself on Christmas Eve, Massenet's *Werther* can be depended
upon to produce no such violent reaction. It is, in fact, something of a bore, though the music is skillfully contrived. Vienna
had the *première* in 1892, and Van Dyck created the title role.
It was Jean de Reszke's affection for *Werther* that gave it a first
spurt of popularity. He and Eames (Charlotte) were in the
first Metropolitan performance, on April 19, 1894. Primarily a
tenor's opera*—*"Pourquoi moi reveiller?"* is almost as popular
as *"Le Rêve"* from *Manon*—nevertheless, it owed its few later
American resuscitations to Farrar's and Garden's interest in
Charlotte as a good acting role. When, on November 16, 1909,
the Metropolitan began its experiment of supplementary performances at the New Theater, on Central Park West between
Sixty-third and Sixty-fourth Streets, *Werther* was the first opera
given there, with Farrar, Alma Gluck in her operatic debut
(Sophie), Clément in his American debut (Werther), and Dinh
Gilly (Albert), but even this strong cast won it only two performances, and it has not since been revived at the Metropolitan.

The next evening, at the Manhattan, Hammerstein, at the
height of his Massenetis, gave New York a more piquant sample
of his idol's unconvincing flirtation with verism. This was *Sapho*
(1897), a setting of Daudet's "shocking" novel of the Paris demi-
monde. Massenet had composed it for Calvé, but Garden sang
it for Hammerstein. Long after New York had forgotten
Werther and *Sapho*, Garden was interpreting with unaltered
verve both Charlotte and Fanny Legrand for enthusiastic Chicagoans. But *Sapho* was the waning of a flirtation which had had
its moment of real passion in 1894, when Massenet, taking the
measure of *Cavalleria rusticana*, turned out, in *La Navarraise*, a
perfect imitation of *verismo*, changing it subtly into *verisme*.

Massenet had composed *La Navarraise* with Calvé in mind,
and for Covent Garden, where it was heard on June 20, 1894,
with Alvarez, Gilibert, Plançon, and Dufriche supporting her.
Neither Calvé nor Sir Augustus Harris, manager of the theater,
failed Massenet. The performance was worthy of Belasco in its

* Yet Massenet rewrote Werther's part for the silver-voiced Italian baritone,
Mattia Battistini.

violent verisimilitude, and Calvé was daemonic. Bernard Shaw, giving that *première* his rare stamp of approval, reported that "she was a living volcano, wild with anxiety, to be presently mad with joy, ecstatic with love, desperate with disappointment, and so on in ever culminating transitions through mortification, despair, fury, terror, and finally—the mainspring breaking at the worst of the strain—silly maniacal laughter." In short, this violent, swift, and noisy opera runs the gamut of *Cavalleria* with letters to spare. Calvé was the Anita of the first Paris and Metropolitan (December 11, 1895) productions. *La Navarraise* fitted her so well that no one since has been able to do Anita justice. Gerville-Réache came closest to it, but two such gifted singing actresses as Farrar and Garden all but failed in their interpretations of the Navarraise.

Just as Massenet rewrote the title role of *Werther* for Battistini, he remodeled, at Garden's request, the tenor role in *Le Jongleur de Notre Dame* for soprano. Never was a remodeling more fortunate. Jean, the hero of Anatole France's little story, *L'Étui de nacre,* on which the opera is based, is a rather feminine adolescent more suitable for female than male impersonation, and Garden played Jean with the tenderness of real inspiration. She first sang the role at the Manhattan, on November 27, 1908, with Renaud as Boniface, a part he had created at the Monte Carlo *première,* and Dufranne. So identified did the opera become with her characterization that when Hammerstein attempted to please a small group of traditionalists (*Le Jongleur* was less than eight years old at the time) by reverting to a male Jean, he had to add *Cavalleria* to the bill in order to fill a house that would have been all but empty for a Gardenless *Jongleur.* With Garden's retirement, *Le Jongleur* vanished from American opera houses, and it is unlikely that it will reappear unless another singer of her stamp comes to the fore—a tenor could scarcely undertake a role still so inextricably connected with her name. Musically, the loss is negligible. *Le Jongleur* is Massenet at his least original and most eclectic, with such diverse sources as plainchant, Gounod, and Debussy contributing to a background of vague charm and suave religiosity. Garden transcended it: her moving and pathetic performance lent the opera a factitious importance.

Le Jongleur dates from 1902. During the next eight years, Massenet composed, among other things, three ponderous operas on classical themes, in which he tried to be profound, marmoreal, and Gluckian. But the capabilities were not there, and all three, despite epic performances by the contralto Lucy Arbell, failed to attract audiences. In 1910, however, at Monte Carlo, Raoul Gunsbourg produced *Don Quichotte,* and Massenet had his last success—due, once again, to a single performer. Chaliapin interpreted the Don with such sympathy and pathos that the opera was in demand for twenty-five years if he could be secured for the role. The libretto is a marvelously silly concoction, the music workmanlike but devoid of melodic inspiration. With these tawdry materials, Chaliapin, by *force majeure* and sheer personal magnetism, worked wonders. Vanni Marcoux, the first New York Don Quixote, when the Philadelphia-Chicago Opera Company presented *Don Quichotte* at the Metropolitan on February 3, 1914, had Garden as his Dulcinea and Dufranne as his Sancho Panza. At the first performance by the resident Metropolitan company, on April 3, 1926, Chaliapin's colleagues were Easton and De Luca.

Massenet was the last French operatic composer to combine fecundity with success. He continued the Gounod-Thomas tradition into the twentieth century, making it palatable by spicing it heavily (the French have ever been masterful with sauces) with Wagnerian harmonies, Debussyan atmosphere, any number of veristic tricks, and his own lack of originality. He added nothing, but his obvious interest in stepping up the histrionic side of the singers' function and the entertainment side of the opera as a whole (though in the latter his activities often misfired) influenced a whole generation of composers, most of them thoroughly second-rate. A tireless pedagogue, he taught many of his later competitors, though the best of them—Alfred Bruneau and Gustave Charpentier—owed, in their most vital aspects, little to him. Bruneau, for instance, most of whose operas were settings of Zola stories, used Wagnerian means to produce veristic results. Charpentier, as eclectic as his master, but apparently more sincere, and with more individuality of approach, was as meager in output as Bruneau was fertile. Yet, in some respects, *Louise,* the first of his two operas, was epoch-making.

The story of Charpentier as a composer is that of a man obsessed with his own struggles and dreams and with the city in which he struggled and dreamed. In a very real sense, most of his music is autobiographical, that for *Louise* and its much later sequel *Julien* being more obviously so only because they are attached to Charpentier's own librettos about an unhappy Parisian artist. *Louise* is a paean to the multifaceted Paris of the artist's imagining—a prolongation, in rhapsodic strophes, of Murger's *vie de Bohème.* His lifelong interest in stimulating the mental and artistic life of the poor working girls of Paris, especially sempstresses like his Louise, and his perpetual Bohemianism of garb and manner have their roots in a preoccupation with his own Montmartre past. To the first of his essentially vulgar operas, this gave conviction, vigor, and a kind of mesmeric force. Charpentier's weakness—failure to grow up, flight into an idealized past—is *Louise*'s strength, contributing to its best pages a brimming youthfulness and to its worst a tasteless mooncalfishness. When it was first produced, *Louise* was attacked as a glorification of vice: in fact, it has the total amorality of a man drugged by the vision of a certain kind of existence. Musically, the vision is scored to Wagner, Puccini, and Massenet. For many of his leitmotivs, Charpentier took the street cries of Paris. He accepted Puccini's romantic reading of verism, and enlisted Massenet's voluptuous melodic line for his sentimental and erotic crises, notably in the overlush *"Depuis le jour."* The result was sure-fire, and *Louise* was hailed—and reviled—in a way that made it seem rather more important than it was.

Louise opened at the Opéra-Comique on February 2, 1900, and conquered at once. From being just another Prix de Rome, Charpentier was catapulted to international fame, and he was fortunate in finding, though not immediately, a singing actress who for more than thirty years put Louise among the first, if it was not indeed the very first, of an impressive series of musical portraits. This was Mary Garden, who was in Paris awaiting her opportunity when the Charpentier opera burst upon the scene. She did not create the name role, but understudied Mlle Rioton, the first Louise, who was in ill health. Garden's chance came two months after the *première*, when Rioton was unable to go on for the third and fourth acts, and she found herself, after this world debut, catapulted much as Charpentier had been.*

It was Garden who introduced *Louise* to America, at the Manhattan Opera House, on January 3, 1908, with Bressler-Gianoli (the Mother), Dalmorès (Julien), and Gilibert (the Father). Farrar was the first Metropolitan Louise (January 15, 1921), and the role has been sung there since by Bori and Grace Moore, it being the latter's happiest operatic role. In six scattered seasons, the opera has attained little more than two dozen Metropolitan performances, while Garden, besides her stupendous record at the Comique, has sung it many times elsewhere, particularly in Chicago. In Paris, where the octogenarian Charpentier still lives as this chapter is written, the popularity of *Louise* has continued unabated, measured by the fact that its thousandth performance at the Comique is approaching.

In the sequel to *Louise*, the curious, pathological, thoroughly anticlimactic *Julien* (1913), Charpentier confessed his inability to do more than walk around the old battlefield, pointing out the landmarks. It is *Louise* over again—without the drama, the novelty, the passionate youthful charm. At the Metropolitan, in 1914, despite Farrar and Caruso in the leading roles, *Julien* could not get beyond a fifth performance. To keep the record of Charpentier's Louiseolatry straight, it should be added that he provided a special bit of music for Grace Moore's motion picture based on the opera, which was made in Paris in the late 1930's.

One person who was not impressed by *Louise* was Claude Debussy, the outstanding genius of modern French music. A

* Telling Carl Van Vechten of her debut, Garden said: "The audience, you may be sure, was none too pleased at the prospect of having to listen to a Mlle Garden of whom they had never heard. Will you believe me when I tell you that I was never less nervous? . . . I must have succeeded, for I sang *Louise* over two hundred times at the Opéra-Comique after that. The year was 1900, and I had made my debut on Friday, April 13."

onetime Wagnerite, Debussy was, by the time *Louise* began to carry everything before it, in full flight from the spells and sensual enchantments of Bayreuth. Even as Charpentier was celebrating his first triumphs, Debussy was compounding a counterirritant. In 1892, he had seen a performance of Maeterlinck's mystical, complexly symbolic *Pelléas et Mélisande*, and had been much attracted to this offshoot of *imagisme*, the French variety of which, bodied forth in the poetry of Mallarmé and Verlaine, had already inspired some of his loveliest songs, as well as the *Prélude à l'Après-midi d'un faune*. He started to write incidental music for the Maeterlinck play, changed his mind at mid-career, and then decided to use portions of the play, slightly altered, as the libretto of a full-length opera that would be a Gallic defi to Wagnerism.

Just as Debussy's earlier operatic efforts had proved abortive, it seemed as if he might never finish this one: one version he carried to its end, but it did not pass his exquisite critical eye. It may have been, despite him, too Wagnerian. A new version was begun in 1895, and finished seven years later. Its production was the culmination of a newspaper scandal: Maeterlinck had insisted vainly that the role of Mélisande be given to his common-law wife, Georgette Leblanc, who had played it in the speaking version. But Albert Carré, the manager of the Comique, had already promised the role to Garden, and despite threats of a duel, legal action, and all types of other nuisances, he stuck to his promise. The performance, on April 30, 1902, suffered from factional fighting within the theater. Debussy was too independent a spirit to be discomfited by the scorn and abuse of the French music critics, among whom Romain Rolland was a notable exception. Rolland called *Pelléas et Mélisande* "one of the three or four outstanding achievements in French musical history."

But the music critics and artistic diehards from all camps were quickly overruled by the persistent enthusiasm of a discriminating and influential wing of the Paris public. To this, at first, slightly cultish popularity the excellence of the Comique cast contributed largely. Garden turned in a well-nigh perfect performance, which she continued to polish until it became

Salome

Louise

Mélisande

Thaïs

Mary Garden in Four of Her Great Roles

one of the superlative experiences provided by the singing stage. Her piquant French, always with a delicious alien note, served her particularly well as Mélisande, "a princess from a far land." Jean Périer, her vis-à-vis, was a singer of exquisite refinement, and besides—what is of urgent importance in this opera—as poetically personable as Garden herself. Their colleagues were also first-rate artists: Gerville-Réache was Geneviève, Dufranne was Golaud, and Felix Vieuille was Arkel. André Messager, a second-rate composer but a conductor of genius, led the orchestra.

The same cast, except that Vittorio Arimondi was the Arkel, brought *Pelléas* to the Manhattan Opera House on February 19, 1908. The public was far more acclamatory than the press, which, by that time Wagnerian to a man, regarded Debussy as a heretic. Garden used Mélisande for her Chicago debut, on November 5, 1910, when her associates were Edmond Warnery (Pelléas), Bressler-Gianoli (Geneviève), Dufranne (Golaud), and Huberdeau (Arkel). The Metropolitan did not get around to staging this significant opera until March 21, 1925, with Bori and Johnson as the hapless lovers, assisted by Howard, Whitehill, and Rothier. Bori could not, except vocally, vie with Garden, but the ensemble was excellent. On March 7, 1940, Georges Cathelat, who had received special leave from the French army, was the Pelléas of a Metropolitan revival of the opera. He turned in a superb performance, despite the wooden inadequacy of Helen Jepson, his Mélisande.

Debussy's artistic conscience, working against a Wagnerism he had come to loathe, failed him, for *Pelléas* is, in one sense, more Wagnerian than Wagner. In it, the ideal of Peri and Caccini, of Gluck, of Wagner—that the music of an opera should obsequiously serve the text—found so comprehensive an embodiment that its music is all but without significance if separated from text and action. In fact, had the critics been somewhat more perceptive, they might have attacked Debussy, not as a Wagnerian heretic, but as one who had carried Wagner's professed ideals to the point of *reductio ad absurdum*.

But all that the critics could see were the superficials, which were remote from anything in Wagner's practice: the orchestra, reduced rather than expanded, until it is scarcely more than a chamber ensemble; the vocal line a susurrus of muffled half-voices conversing to music, moving up and down in languid intervals (*Pelléas* is, quite as much as Wilde's *Salomé*, Whistler's *Nocturnes*, and Conder's fans, self-consciously *fin-de-siècle*), the absence of the slightest hint of lyric separateness, and the nervous insistence on muffled volume. Moreover, while Debussy created a music drama that, as such, Wagner could not have criticized, in every other way he diverged from the *Meister*, most glaringly when ringing the changes on Wagnerian devices. For example, instead of using the sacrosanct Wagnerian leitmotiv, he evolved what Vincent d'Indy called "pivot themes," which "send out harmonic rays in all directions, rays that serve to present the musical speech in the ambience suited to it." Also, Debussy's use of separate timbres—and combinations of timbres—to hallmark certain situations and symbolic ideas had been hinted at only in the most rudimentary manner by Wagner.

On the basis of superficials, the challenge was taken up, and awkwardly, by traditionalists, in 1902. Now, when *Pelléas* is no longer a shocking work—gone are the days when it was possible to refer, as one New York critic did in 1908, to its "combinations of tones that sting and blister and pain and outrage the ear"—these same superficials may baffle those who approach the opera for the first time. *Pelléas et Mélisande* did not establish an easily imitated pattern, and operas that have followed it do not prepare us for listening to it.* There are those to whom *Pelléas*, symbol-freighted, twilit, exhaling alternately *tedium vitae* and passionate frustration, will always be a trying experience. The point is, any open ears, however prejudiced, however conditioned, will find experience in *Pelléas*. For those most susceptible to it, it has the compelling intensity of a dream, beautiful, piteous, evanescent, and, above all, true to its own poetic reality.

* Frederick Delius' *A Village Romeo and Juliet* might, if we had opportunities to hear it. Originally produced at Berlin in 1907 as *Romeo und Julia auf dem Dorfe*, it later received performance in England through the enthusiasm of Sir Thomas Beecham. The frequently played intermezzo, "The Walk to the Paradise Gardens," is typical of the music in the opera. An English-born German, who spent most of his life in France and Florida, Delius was at his best a second-rate Debussy. His only other opera of interest, *Koanga*, is a setting of George W. Cable's *The Grandissimes*, a famous American novel of the vanished South.

Chapter XXIII

Folk Notes From Many Lands

WHEN Glinka and his nationalist followers lavishly used folk tunes and color in their operas, they gave an imitable technique to composers in other countries possessing a clearly differentiated national style that had not been absorbed into the international currents of Western music. Glinka was not the first to compose an opera shot through with the national idiom of his country, but he was the first to depend for much of his effect upon the untamed strangeness of this national idiom. In Italy, France, and Germany, the separate national idioms had been largely dissolved in the changing stream of the classic and romantic schools. In Russia, the folk opera, which was in part a revolt against imported—in particular, Italian—elegancies, happened to beget a succession of geniuses whose national color was caught up in the magnificence of larger issues, and so transcended the circumscribed condition of folk art. It was precisely in those countries (including Russia, of course) which had a spiritual need of asserting their national selfhood that the folk opera came into being. Before passing on to these, in many cases, oppressed minorities, it is worth noting that *Der Freischütz* was, besides being a romantic protest against the influence of the hated foreigners, a voice of resurgent, post-Napoleonic Germany.

The folk opera struck roots early in Poland, in which a movement to keep the national culture alive and to win back political independence from the three countries that had gobbled her up had won the support of many artists and intellectuals. Among them was Stanislaw Moniuszko, ten years Chopin's junior, who, in 1858, at Warsaw, saw produced his *Halka*, which has become a touchstone of Polish culture. Too reminiscent of Glinka's methods of construction to attain complete individuality, this tragic opera of peasant life nevertheless has scenes of dramatic forcefulness, and throughout the folk element is asserted vigorously, particularly in scenes where actual dancing is itself the stage action. *Halka's* chief weakness is the conventionality of its transition passages. In America, it has never been presented at a major opera house, but the large, self-expressive Polish group in New York has supported two separate productions. The first, in 1903, was in Russian; the second, in 1930, in the original Polish.*

The Czechs, another racial group held in subjection, produced a more vigorous school of nationalist music. Its leader was, without question, Bedřich Smetana, a composer of definite if limited genius. Smetana wrote many operas, almost all of which contain numbers that could be salvaged separately for concert performance. Several of his operas were—before the German occupation, at least—still popular in Czechoslovakia. One of them—*Prodaná nevěstá* (*The Bartered Bride*)—is the most widely popular of all folk operas. Originally produced at the National Theater, Prague, on May 30, 1866, as a two-act Singspiel, it is now always given in three acts, with recitative supplanting the original spoken dialogue. It is a lighthearted, swiftly paced, vividly colored, and rhythmically vigorous panel out of Bohemian peasant life, in effect for all the world like a very superior operetta. Its original libretto, by Karel Sabina, is said to be riotously funny, and much of this broad humor fails to be dissipated in either the German or English versions heard in New York—a good proof of an inspired original. The energetic, boldly scored overture, the first-act polka, the "Stuttering Song" and furiant in Act II, and the lyrical "Alone at last" in Act III are universal favorites. There is a hint of Mozart in this graceful and apposite music, and the booby Wenzel is blood cousin to Papageno. The delights of *The Bartered Bride* are such that we feel indeed deprived when we read—in unimpeachable authorities—that others of Smetana's operas are as worthy of production and, in some respects, more original.

It was as *Prodaná nevěstá* that, at the Haymarket Theater, Chicago, on August 20, 1893, Smetana's most famous opera reached America. But sixteen years later, on February 19, 1909, at the first

* The *reductio ad absurdum* of the folk opera was early attained in Moniuszko's *Paria*, a story of India. In this odd concoction, a Hindu widow, with a not unnatural aversion to suttee passes the time singing Lithuanian folk songs.

Metropolitan showing, it had become *Die verkaufte Braut,* even though Emmy Destinn (Marie) and Gustav Mahler, the conductor, were Czechs. The superb 1926 revival of the German version enlisted, among others, Maria Müller (Marie), Laubenthal (Hans), Bohnen (Kezal), and George Meader (Wenzel), with Bodanzky conducting. Rethberg was a later Marie. The first English version at the Metropolitan occurred on May 15, 1936, during a special spring season. Again revived in English on February 28, 1941, *The Bartered Bride* brought forward the Czech soprano Jarmila Novotna in an overly aristocratic portrayal of the lusty peasant heroine, and supplied Charles Kullman, as Jenik, with perhaps his happiest role.

Antonín Dvořák, Smetana's successor as the dean of Czech music, achieved his most striking results in purely instrumental music. As a composer of operas, he was prolific, but not, by and large, fruitful. *Russalka,* on the same theme as Dargomizhsky's *Russalka,* Adam's *Giselle,* and Puccini's *Le Villi,* is a work of considerable fancy and charm; it has held the stage in Czechoslovakia. Among the many scores of Leoš Janáček, *Jeji Pastorkyna (Her Foster Daughter),* better known as *Jenufa,* stands out. Janáček was not so much a Czech composer as a locally Moravian one, and therefore his music shows more strongly Polish and Russian influences than does that of the true Bohemians. Janáček had a very individual style, terse, ejaculatory, and, because he was a lifelong propagandist of Moravian culture and artistic nationalism, dyed with the raw primes of local folk music. *Jenufa,* though it does not quote a single authentic folk tune, has the quality of folk opera projected by veristic means.

After its *première,* at Brünn on January 21, 1904, it gradually attained world fame. On December 6, 1924, this "dynamically prosodic Moussorgskyan" score, as Nicolas Slonimsky has called it, reached the Metropolitan, in German, as a vehicle for Jeritza, who won honors as Jenufa, while Matzenauer was excellent as the wicked foster mother. After five performances that season, this interesting work was dropped from the Metropolitan repertoire.

For a while, the bizarre folklore opera of the modern Czech composer Jaromir Weinberger, seemed as though it might establish permanent hold on the repertoire, but *Svanda Dudák*

(*Schwanda the Bagpiper*) is now known only through excerpts. Popular in Prague until the Nazi invasion, it has lost out even there because Weinberger neglected to have himself born an "Aryan." *Schwanda,* like *The Bartered Bride,* came to the Metropolitan, on November 7, 1931, in German, with Schorr in the name part, Branzell as the Queen, and Müller as Dorota. It was very popular, five performances being given that season. It was then unaccountably dropped, and has not been revived. Fortunately, the vivacious, ingratiating polka and fugue are concert perennials, and as long as they are played, chances for revival are good, especially since Weinberger now lives in the United States.

In neighboring Hungary, folk tunes did not assume a vital place in opera until comparatively recent times, though the country is rich in various sorts of folk music, notably that of the Magyar peasants, the gypsies, and the Rumanians of Transylvania. Hungarian music first became familiar to the outside world through Liszt, whose rhapsodies were based rather on the café music of gypsy orchestras than on either true Magyar or rural-gypsy tunes. The influential Karl Goldmark trailed after Wagner in his scores and showed little interest in the indigenous music of his country: by contrast, his famous opera, *Die Königin von Saba,* is full of pseudo-Oriental coloring and theme.* Jenö Hubay, famous for a vast miscellany of mediocre violin pieces, used Lisztian folk music in his wooden *A Falu Rossza (The Village Wastrel).*

A better era for true Magyar music dawned when two of the most distinguished of Hungarian composers, Béla Bartók and Zoltán Kodály, began to study and collect the native peasant tunes and dances in a collaborative effort to isolate the various ethnic strains. Much of Bartók's music has been influenced by these studies, but he has also evolved a personalized idiom of his

* For a while, this opera was tremendously popular at the Metropolitan. After its costly *première* there on December 2, 1885, with Lilli Lehmann as Sulamith, it had fourteen repetitions that season—a record at the house, its nearest rival being *Carmen,* which had twelve performances during the season of 1893-94. It was used to open the season of 1886-87, but after that of 1889-90, completely lost favor, and was dropped for sixteen years. On November 22, 1905, again most elaborately staged, *Die Königin von Saba* served to introduce the American soprano, Marie Rappold (Sulamith), to opera.

own, which is evident in so early a work as his single opera, *Duke Bluebeard's Castle* (1911). On the other hand, Kodály, in his lusty Singspiel *Háry János*, based on the exploits of a Hungarian Paul Bunyan, has created a genuine folk opera of great distinction. Its episodic construction, strong rhythms, resplendent, gaudy orchestration, and coarse humor are finely apposite. Unfortunately, the Second World War has held up the staging of *Háry János* in New York, originally announced as a feature of the New York World's Fair. But while Kodály, who was scheduled to conduct, is detained in Hungary, we are at least allowed to hear the well-chosen orchestral suite of excerpts from his opera. In the suite, the vocal parts are assigned to various instruments.

Turning from the lands of oppressed minorities to one of an oppressed majority—Spain—we find flourishing a long and persistent folk-music tradition. Just as Russian music gets much of its distinctive tang from Oriental sources, Spanish music is set off from other European streams by the racial contacts of the Spanish people—gypsy, Moorish, Arabian. As long ago as 1774, a Spanish Jesuit by the name of Antonio Eximeno promulgated the idea that the music of each nation should reflect the character of its folk music. Never was a doctrine adopted more eagerly. Spanish folk music has not only been taken up by native Spanish composers, but has become a kind of international style, frequently debased and watered down, and particularly favored by salon composers of little or no originality.

The first modern Spanish composer of any importance was Felipe Pedrell, a native of Catalonia. Scholarly, meticulous in his craft, and conscientiously a disciple of Eximeno, Pedrell left many operas, none of which ever had more than passing success. He lacked completely the element of popular appeal, and his importance resides chiefly in his influence as the teacher of Isaac Albéniz, Enrique Granados, and Manuel De Falla, as well as other noteworthy Spanish musicians. *Los Pirinéos*, a trilogy that is itself part of a larger trilogy drawing its subject matter from Spanish history, has been called the most important stage work created in Spain, but unfortunately not even Spaniards have a chance nowadays to verify this dictum. This, as well as *La Celestina,* the second part of the larger trilogy, is treated in a style compounded almost equally of Wagner and mysticism, with some hints of Slavic influence, and making use of old liturgical chants and Moorish, Catalan, and Spanish folk tunes. The third part, *El Comte Arnau,* is not strictly an opera, but a lyric poem for outdoor performance, recalling, but scarcely approximating, a performance of an ancient Greek drama. As is appropriate, this section is written in a lofty and archaic style. When the embittered Pedrell died in 1922, at the age of eighty-one, three of his pupils were world-famous, and he had outlived two of them—Albéniz for thirteen years, Granados for six.

Albéniz, whose piano pieces—the *Iberia* suites, in particular —are in the permanent repertoire, was a prolific composer of *zarzuelas,* one-act operettas with spoken dialogue and dancing, closely akin to the French *vaudeville,* and richly topical in material, literally tens of thousands of which have been written and performed since the early seventeenth century.* As an operatic composer, Albéniz may have suffered from a curious contract he made with Francis Money-Coutts (later Baron Latymer), a wealthy English banker with literary aspirations, who for seventeen years paid Albéniz a pension on condition that the composer set his librettos to music. At any rate, only *Pepita Jiménez* has penetrated successfully beyond Spain. It makes extensive use of folk melodies and is delightfully tuneful.

Unique among operas is Granados' *Goyescas,* which was built up (some critics think thinned out) from two piano suites by the same name. The first Spanish opera ever to be produced at the Metropolitan, and in Spanish, too, this tragic work, based on the composer's meditations on Goya's paintings of early nineteenth-century life, lacks, because of inept orchestration, some of the piquancy and insinuating appeal of the piano pieces. But at least the coloring is authentically Spanish, as Granados himself was at pains to point out in contrasting *Goyescas* and *Carmen.* In defense of the orchestration, it might be said that its

---

* Foreign operas were given in Spain from the very earliest days, but *zarzuelas* monopolized the stage insofar as native composers were concerned. True Spanish opera by Spaniards is a comparatively recent institution in Spain.

noise and blatancy are characteristic of the *zarzuela,* to which genre *Goyescas* would belong if it had spoken dialogue. The most effective part of the opera as music is an intermezzo Granados wrote specifically for the Metropolitan world *première* of January 28, 1916, when Anna Fitziu made her New York operatic debut in a cast that included Martinelli and De Luca. Granados was in the audience. On his way back to Europe on the *Sussex,* he died when the ship was torpedoed by a German submarine. He was not yet forty-nine years old.

The best known of Pedrell's pupils still lives, though at the time of this writing, his exact whereabouts and fortunes are impossible to determine. This is, of course, Falla, whose music, with that of Albéniz, has done most to popularize the true Spanish idiom. Of his two performed operas (a third, *Fuego Fatuo,* a comic piece that makes use of Chopin themes, has never been printed or produced), the first—*La Vida Breve*—was composed when he was not yet thirty. It shows a personality steeped in folklore and murky old wives' tales—a personality, moreover, profoundly pessimistic in cast. The musical idiom he chose, and which he preferred for years, came from Andalusia, where Moorish and gypsy influences are strongest, and where *cante flamenco* and *cante hondo,* those sinuous, melismatic types of semi-Oriental chanting, still flourish. Much of *La Vida Breve* sounds like folk music, but it is not. It is only Falla's spontaneous use of a musical language he had known from childhood. However spontaneous, it is none the less subtle, and Falla has not hesitated to add to it new sophistications found beyond the borders of Spain. His work evidences not only the influence of foreign composers who had written "Spanish" music, but also the technical results of an elegant borrowing, especially from Debussy and Stravinsky.

La Vida Breve, based on a tragic story of love between social unequals, is in reality a ballet-opera, with the dance used much more vitally, integrally, than is, unfortunately, the custom in opera. It contains many haunting passages for the voice, but even more memorable are the popular dances, composed with exquisite care and lovingness. *El Retablo de Maese Pedro,* the setting of an episode from *Don Quixote,* is a lyric scene for puppets and marionettes. The musical style is Falla's free adaptation of Spanish popular music at the time of Cervantes, but unhappily for the longevity of the score, the adaptation was not sufficiently free. It is late Falla (1922) and clearly shows a narrowly classicizing, antiquarian tendency.

La Vida Breve, less cerebral and more passionate than El Retablo, has had an international career. Although it had won an important local award in 1905, it was disdained by Spanish impresarios until its success at Nice and Paris in 1913 made it a desirable importation. Madrid heard it in 1914. Twelve years later, on March 7, 1926, it became the second Spanish opera to be sung in the original language at the Metropolitan, with Bori (Salud), and Tokatyan (Paco). It shared a double bill, the other feature being Stravinsky's Le Rossignol, also in its American première. After three repetitions, La Vida Breve was dropped from the Metropolitan repertoire, despite the admirable performance of the Spanish-born and popular Bori.

Taken all in all, Spanish nationalist opera—Spanish nationalist music in general—has not lived up to hope. Its great composers, one and all, have had a habit of receding into the distance, just when they might have been expected to rise above the surface allure they all, in company with second- and third-rate Spanish composers, have at their finger tips. Cecil Gray has summed up the case against them: "It is always pleasant to listen to, but reveals no distinctive personality. Spanish national music has so far produced no Borodin or Moussorgsky, but only three Rimsky-Korsakovs—which is three too many. To English ears, their work all sounds like endless variations on one Spanish folk-song, provided with an elaborate accompaniment of castanets and similar exotic percussion instruments."

Nor has Spanish America, despite its richness in the crossed breeds of Spanish and Indian music, provided more meritorious examples of folk opera. Even in Brazil, where the imported musical idiom loses its edges as the Spanish language does where Spain shades into Portugal, and where, to the Iberian and Indian is added a large infusion of African, the folk opera has shown persistency without—so far as it is possible to deter-

Lucrezia Bori as Salud, in Falla's *La Vida Breve*

mine—distinction. Beginning with Antonio Carlos Gomes, who mingled Amazon Indian themes with a hurdy-gurdy conception of Verdi in his once-famous *Il Guarany* (1870), the roster of Brazilian operatic composers has been voluminous. Its most noted contributor is Heitor Villa-Lobos, whose four operas may be expected to show the same mixture of sheer genius and tasteless mediocrity that characterizes his enormous instrumental output.

Finally, even England has a long folk-opera tradition. In some respects, Purcell's *Dido and Aeneas*, on the one hand, and the ballad operas, beginning with Pepusch and Gay's *Beggar's Opera*, on the other, may be considered folk operas, though the classical subject of Purcell's masterpiece removes it, strictly speaking, from that class. Thomas Augustine Arne wrote folk operas, some of them with airs of exquisite tenderness and delightful fancy.

The vigorous-minded Ethel Smyth, still (1941) very much alive in her early eighties, wrote many operas, of which the most popular is *The Boatswain's Mate* (1916), based on a comic tale by W. W. Jacobs. It mingles English folk tunes, sea chanteys, and popular songs with academic writing traceable to her thorough German training. Another opera, *Der Wald,* first performed in Dresden in 1901, has the distinction of being the only opera by a woman to receive production at the Metropolitan, its *première* there occurring on March 11, 1903, with Gadski, Blass, and Bispham. This, however, was not a folk opera.

Of the modern Englishmen who have consciously followed the folk ideal, the scholarly, serious, and archaicizing Ralph Vaughan Williams stands first. He is ever, no matter what the circumstances, English through and through, despite his chameleonlike changes of style. His first opera, *Hugh the Drover,* is almost parochial in its assimilation of crossroads lore and oldest-inhabitant wisdom. It has had some success in England, but its dependence on wholly English associations is likely to restrict its audience to the island. His latest opera, a setting of Synge's *Riders to the Sea*, marries ultramodernism to Irish folk tunes, and is, from all reports, of high interest.

This completes a confessedly cursory survey of a musical cul-
de-sac. It would be pointless to list the folk operas of the Bal-
kans, Scandinavia, or Switzerland. Nothing about folk opera
elsewhere gives any reason for believing that they would be a
whit more interesting than those passingly discussed. They
would be picturesque, tuneful, brightly colored, and obvious
members of the same far-flung family. The Russian nationalists
constitute an exception only in their genius, and their few
lasting achievements—*Boris Godunov, Prince Igor, Le Coq
d'or* even—attain greatness when they transcend the self-imposed limitations of folk art.

Chapter XXIV

A Modern Galaxy

THE twentieth century has not been a predominantly operatic period. With the notable exceptions of a few men who had already established themselves in the last years of the nineteenth century—Puccini, Debussy, and Strauss, most particularly—the energies of many of the best were consumed, when they turned to the stage, by the ballet. Part of this diversion from the more traditional interest was the old business of following the leader, and much of it can be laid at the door of the famous balletomane, connoisseur of the arts, and impresario, Serge Diaghilev, who began collecting his extraordinary group of staff composers before the close of the first decade of the century. For his sumptuous and fashionable Ballet Russe, some of the finest music of modern times was written: for instance, Stravinsky provided *Petrouchka* and *Le Sacre du printemps*, Ravel *Daphnis et Chloé*, and Falla *El Sombrero de Tres Picos*. Many of the works commissioned by Diaghilev are permanent additions to ballet, and, in many cases, suites arranged from them have become concert fixtures. The exciting theatricality, in the most complimentary sense of the word, of much modern ballet music suggests how much opera might have gained if it had had a Diaghilev of its own to draw these great talents to the more democratic art and to guide them in making it as glamorous and attractive as the Ballet Russe.

This does not mean that no interesting opera has been written, for absence from the repertoire—in practice, a collection of fortuitous choices—does not argue lack of merit. There is every likelihood that a few modern operas will, sooner or later, get their chances of immortality, though it will entail a mild revolution in the opera house. It will be a revolution that turns round to the past (the conventional kind, in short): it will get back to those not so distant days when impresarios and audiences were alike eager for novelties. It should be realized that the standard repertoire, as now interpreted, is a modern invention of which the old fogies of Mozart's, Beethoven's, Weber's, and Meyerbeer's times would have been heartily ashamed. Healthier times for opera in general, and happier times for composers and audiences, will have come when the enduring classics of whatever period, provenance, and category are considered merely the nucleus of a season's entertainment.

It would be possible to divide modern opera—as one department of modern music—into a hundred or more divisions on the basis of style alone. It is simpler, and certainly more illuminating, to consider it a three-ring circus, with a few delightful side shows. By and large, the first ring is filled with descendants of the Russian nationalists; the second is given over to those who acknowledge Wagner, Strauss, and certain of the German romantics, notably Schumann, as their ancestors, while in the last a smaller group, some of whom ape the tricks of those in the first ring, remain Parisians, compatriots of Debussy, despite their foreign dominos. Those in the first two rings make the most noise.

Igor Stravinsky, a pupil of Rimsky-Korsakov, began by producing brilliant imitations of his master. His first opera, *Le Rossignol*, begun when he was twenty-five, and completed six years later, shows the conflicting interests of a then extraordinarily vital artist who was developing at tremendous speed. The first act of *Le Rossignol* is reminiscent of *Le Coq d'or* not only in musical style, but in atmosphere; the second and third acts are asserted in the polyrhythmic, discordant idiom, not yet carried to extremes, that was to make Stravinsky one of the central revolutionaries of modern music. After its Metropolitan *première*, on March 7, 1926, with Talley as the Nightingale, Didur as the Emperor of China, and Ralph Errolle as the Fisherman, *Le Rossignol* was given there six times more in two seasons. Irving Kolodin has commented amusingly on this *première*: "The use of a French text for *Le Rossignol* lent an almost League of Nations internationalism to this production— the settings were by Serge Soudeikine, a Russian; the conductor was Italian; the leading singer an American; and the Oriental background originated in a story by Hans Christian Andersen!"

A second opera, *Mavra,* was composed at the height of Stravinsky's enthusiasm for Tchaikovsky. He was already turning his back on the style that had brought him world renown, and his growing neoclassicism was as apparent in *Mavra* as his love of Tchaikovsky. This brittle one-act *opéra bouffe,* after a story by Pushkin, had its *première* in Paris on June 3, 1922.* It has also been heard in the United States: it was performed at the Philadelphia Academy of Music on December 28, 1934, with Maria Kurenko as Parasha. Examination of Stravinsky's operas and pseudo operas leads inevitably to the conclusion that he is important in the history of opera not because of his works in that form, but because of his vast influence on music in general.

Altogether, the less influential Prokofiev has been more fruitful as an operatic composer. He has had a persistent interest in the stage from a very tender age—his first opera, *The Giant,* was composed to his own libretto when he was nine years old. He has written nine operas to date, including one based on Dostoyevsky's *The Gambler.* The best known of them all, outside Russia (where Prokofiev now shares with the considerably younger Shostakovich the leadership of Soviet music), is the delightful fairy opera, *L'Amour des trois oranges,* the world *première* of which took place at the Chicago Auditorium, during Mary Garden's directaship,† on December 30, 1921, with Nina Koshetz as Fata Morgana and José Mojica as the Prince. It was sumptuously staged, with *décors* by Boris Anisfeld. Yet, it failed to win popular enthusiasm.

L'Amour des trois oranges, however, is one of the most deserving of modern operas—concise, witty, vivid, and thoroughly entertaining, it catches perfectly the insouciant spirit of the Venetian fairy tale around which it is written. Some of the rhythmic exuberance of the music derives from Stravinsky, but

---

* It was on a double bill with the *première* of a curious little entertainment —"a burlesque chamber opera"—called *Le Renard.* Stravinsky's fondness for hybrid musicodramatic forms was further evinced in *Les Noces villageoises* (1923), "choreographic Russian scenes with song and music," as he himself labeled it, and in *Oedipus Rex* (1927, concert form; 1928, stage version), an opera-oratorio completely without dramatic impact, but impressive because of its superb choruses.

† This is not a misprint: Miss Garden insisted that she was the "directa," not the director, of the Chicago Opera Association.

it is far from being a musical shocker. Prokofiev's marked talent
for sarcasm and satire gets full play in this epigrammatic and
vigorously tuneful score. Its immediate resurrection is much to
be desired. Meanwhile, interest in *L'Amour des trois oranges*
is kept alive by the excerpts that appear frequently on concert
programs and in recordings—the march and the scherzo.

Neither Stravinsky nor Prokofiev has written an opera that
has caused as much controversy as Dmitri Shostakovich's *Lady
Macbeth of Mzensk*. Completed in 1932, and produced at the
Little Theater, Leningrad, on January 22, 1924, it is the story
of a bourgeois woman—a kind of Russian Emma Bovary—who
out of boredom takes a lover, murders her husband, and, exiled
to Siberia, commits suicide. Shostakovich comments with drastic, outspoken naturalism on this sordid material, interspersing
it with pertinent lyrical banalities of piercing saccharinity. It
presents, in short, the same mixture of brash vitality and long-
drawn-out sentimentality that his much-played symphonies do,
but in *Lady Macbeth of Mzensk* the mixture has authentic rea-
sonableness. Some of the entr'acte music is among the most
satisfactory pages Shostakovich has composed.

Lady Macbeth of Mzensk had great success in Russia, where
it was at first accepted as a crushing satire on bourgeois manners. Then it was performed in America, first, on January 31,
1935, at Severance Hall, Cleveland, and, five days later, at the
Metropolitan Opera House, New York, both times by The Art
of Musical Russia and the Cleveland Symphony Orchestra, conducted by Arthur Rodzinski. It was received with a deafening
applause that matched the extreme noise of the score, though
at first there was some inclination to boggle at orchestration
that in one scene unmistakably mimicked the sounds of sexual
intercourse. Finally, on December 26, 1935, it was produced in
Moscow, and little more than a month later, as if to censure
the naughty Muscovites for flocking to it, the awful voice of
Pravda, chief newspaper of the Communist Party in Russia,
thundered. *Lady Macbeth of Mzensk* was declared, in an article
notable for its muddy thinking, a decadent, bourgeois-catering
work, especially wicked for its antimelodic snobbishness. The
acclaim of fashionable foreign audiences had provoked *Pravda*'s

attack, and for a moment it appeared as if Shostakovich, until then a prize exhibit of Soviet culture, might be forced into has-beenism. But common sense gradually asserted itself: *Lady Macbeth of Mzensk* was suffered to go on portraying sordid bourgeois society, and Shostakovich once more instated himself in the good graces of the authorities by writing the excellent Fifth Symphony, which was construed as containing an acceptable ideology.

The Russians have, by and large, subsisted on their own musical past, with the addition of some borrowing from western Europe—from Wagner and Debussy, in particular. The Italians, on the contrary, except for those who have followed, more or less blindly, *verismo*, the *buffa* tradition, or Verdi, are frantic experimentalists—tasters of bewildering eclecticism, connoisseurs of ultimate shudders. With all their unquestioned ingenuity and eagerness, they are without first-rate significance.

Take Ildebrando Pizzetti, for instance, a seasoned composer of staggering technical competence who has been at his workbench for nearly half a century. He has composed in almost every musical form, and in many of them voluminously, but no definite musical personality has evolved. As a composer for the stage, he does not seem destined to survive, though he has written half a dozen operas and incidental music for numerous plays. Only one of his operas, but that the carefully constructed *Fra Gherardo* (the second part of an unrelated trilogy), has been heard in America, first in Buenos Aires, and then, on March 20, 1929, at the Metropolitan Opera House, with Maria Müller, Johnson, Pinza, and Mario Basiola. The work was given respectful attention, but neither the composer's own libretto about a medieval religious fanatic nor his finical delving into modal harmonies mingled with nonstructural, exterior modernistic touches could endear *Fra Gherardo* to the public. Four performances sufficed. Pizzetti has garnered many honors in his native land, but nowhere else has this official recognition been echoed. He is one of those unfortunate, perfectly respectable men of music whose destiny it is to have each successive work greeted with the exclamation "Interesting!" and then promptly forgotten.

Nor does that more truly gifted man, G. Francesco Malipiero, the hermit of beautiful Asolo in the Venetian hinterland, add up to much more than Pizzetti, despite his violent gyrations. Malipiero is another self-librettist, and his operatic books have a certain jangled and disjunctive poetry. So, too, have his scores. Malipiero believes, and justly, that Italian music has fallen on evil days, and his remedies—for he has several—are drastic, ranging from a complete rejection of the whole development of Italian music since Monteverdi (for example, he has relentlessly attacked Verdi) to the importation of the new harmonic system of Schönberg and Hindemith. Further to complicate the picture, *Petrouchka* and *Le Sacre du printemps* echo through some of his scores, as do Gregorian chant and the polyphonic patterns of Palestrina. Malipiero is not even averse —for he has none of the consistency of the small mind—to using a scandalously ripe Neapolitan melody. And so on. Among his many operatic works, the best known is a titanic trilogy called *L'Orfeide* which on a vast scale makes mock of civilization. No part of it is what we are accustomed to think of, even in the broadest sense, as opera. Not only are his dramatic sequences lacking in continuity for all except scholars, but his musical style is too consistently discordant ever to find large numbers of affectionate listeners.

If the number of operas written and produced were the sole criterion, Italy would still be the home *par excellence* of opera. Among the numerous Italians actively enlarging operatic dictionaries is Alfredo Casella, who came late to opera, and so, though almost sixty, has made only two operas, both aloofly neoclassical in form and intent, but modernistic in harmonic and rhythmic idiom. Casella has borrowed extensively from the Teutonic atonalists, but has stamped his work with his own dandified and elegant personality, indulging, besides, a Latin lyricism that is not without an acrid and sardonic note. *La Donna serpente* (1932), his first opera, was received with loud fanfares, possibly because Casella is the unofficial composer extraordinary to the Fascist regime, one of his most recent effusions being a lay oratorio on the Italian conquest of Ethiopia.

The slightly older Francesco Balilla Pratella, a voluminous

manufacturer of opera, has proclaimed himself attached to the allegedly violent futurist group headed by the poet and general jackanapes, Filippo Tommaso Marinetti. But his operas, despite their hysterical programs, are almost laughably innocuous. Basically Mascagnian, his most fearsome gesture is timorously skirting the Debussyan. One of his scores, *L'Aviatore Dro* (1920), is an early attempt to make use of aviation as operatic material. Far more interesting is said to be *Vola di notte* (1940), a one-act setting of Antoine de Saint-Exupéry's novel, *Vol de nuit*, by the most promising of the younger Italians, Luigi Dallapiccola, an atonalist who has recanted in favor of more indigenous inspirations. Far quieter in musical idiom than the deliberately frightening Dallapiccola is Mario Castelnuovo-Tedesco, now in exile from Italy for not being an "Aryan," whose *La Mandragola* (1926) deserves mention chiefly because it is founded on Machiavelli's Plautine comedy of the same name. Like most of Castelnuovo-Tedesco's work, it is tasteful, derivative, and forceless.

In France, the operatic scene is less cluttered. Neither Debussy nor the French Wagnerians established enduring schools, and the men who succeeded in making an impression in opera after *Pelléas et Mélisande* had only Gallicism in common— otherwise, they stubbornly, successfully took the roads they wanted. Paul Dukas, whose *L'Apprenti-sorcier* is among the best known of modern orchestral works (its modernism, however, is of the year 1897), composed one opera, *Ariane et Barbe-bleue*, to a Maeterlinck play. It dates from 1907, when the beautiful Lucienne Bréval was a superb Ariane, and mingles Debussyan and Wagnerian influences without sacrificing a highly individual orchestration and a sparkling wit as foreign to *Tristan* as to *Pelléas*, both of which are consciously quoted in the score by the sardonic composer. This delightful opera, which gave a refreshing precision to the muzzily created *théâtre* of Maeterlinck, has been heard at the Metropolitan less often than it should be. There, Toscanini conducted its first American performance on March 29, 1911, with Farrar as Ariane and Rothier as Bluebeard.

Another one-opera* man was Maurice Ravel, next to Debussy the outstanding musical genius produced by modern France. Unfortunately, *L'Heure espagnole* is not representative of Ravel at his best, though the qualities that made him the compeer of the greatest composers of his age—wit, satire, alluring rhythm, and utter mastery of the orchestra—are here, not, however, in prime strength. Ravel is often tagged as an impressionist, which he scarcely ever was, and in *L'Heure espagnole* he was reacting against both romanticism and impressionism in the direction of classical *bouffe*. Ravel's general popularity has served to win his opera numerous productions that it might not have gained on its own merits. In Paris, it has been heard both at the Opéra and the Comique. In the United States, it was first given at Chicago, on January 5, 1920, with Yvonne Gall (Concepcion) and Alfred Maguenat (Ramiro). At the Metropolitan, where it was sung first on November 7, 1925, Bori and Tibbett had the chief roles.

Still another one-opera man was the incredible Erik Satie, a *petit-maître* of so signal an originality as almost to be great. Satie, partly Scotch, brought to his lifelong, consuming interest in music a devastating logic and an ebullient flair for nonsense. Yet, his one opera, *Socrate*, was gravely conceived and more gravely executed. A setting of three incidents from the Dialogues of Plato, it represents the ultimate application of Satie's profoundly meditated theories of art. It goes more than a step beyond Debussy in never interfering with the flawless integrity of the text. In doing this, Satie never underlines or comments upon specific actions or words—he merely reacts to the whole atmosphere of the Dialogues. His music is never pictorial, never descriptive: *Socrate* is mood music, idea music, of the most rarefied sort, and comes nearer to the classical concepts of Peri and Caccini than their own music did. Of everything that the theater and the opera house have taught us to consider dramatic, *Socrate* is scrupulously free.

Satie, besides his effect on extramusical art, strongly influ-

---

* *L'Enfant et les sortilèges* (1925), to Colette's story of abused toys, is an opera-ballet. It makes use of an adapted jazz idiom, the orchestra including whistles, wood blocks, and cheese graters.

enced one so-called school of composers—*les six*—and was hailed as the father of another. The latter—the *école d'Arcueil* —fizzled out in a blaze of mediocrity, but several members of the now disintegrated *six*, sponsored in a series of brilliant manifestos by Jean Cocteau, are composers of true distinction. Only two of them, the Provençal Darius Milhaud and the Swiss Arthur Honegger, have worked significantly in the field of opera. Milhaud has responded like a healthy reed to a variety of influences ranging from Stravinsky to Brazilian folk music, which he absorbed while working in the French legation in Rio de Janeiro. His many operas are much diversified in subject matter, size, and treatment. Milhaud is as capable of doing a trilogy on the *Oresteia* of Aeschylus as he is of tossing off a piece of musical nut brittle like *Les Malheurs d'Orphée*, in which that time-honored *chanteur* is treated with supreme indignity. In 1927, he wrote three "minute" operas, each of which can be fitted onto the two sides of a twelve-inch record. All set to subjects from tragic Greek myth, these ultramodern, rigidly compressed musical crises are among the most moving manifestations of operatic neoclassicism.

Milhaud's most sensational opera, and one which urgently demands performance in the United States (not, be it said, for patriotic reasons), is *Christophe Colomb*, to a libretto by Paul Claudel. This two-part opera in twenty-seven scenes has been succinctly described by Nicolas Slonimsky as "containing elements of Greek drama (the use of suasive chorus), mystery play (allegory), music drama (use of musical mottoes), expressionist technique (Columbus conversing with his second self), symbolism and modern newsreel methods (the use of motion pictures). . . ." *Christophe Colomb*, which obviously has an affinity to German expressionist drama, was produced, not in Paris, but at the Berlin Staatsoper, on May 6, 1930, under the direction of Erich Kleiber.*

Honegger is by no means a tireless experimenter of Milhaud's stamp. His early tone poem, *Pacific 231*, with its vio-

* Milhaud, now a refugee in the United States, has asserted that certain materials essential to the production of *Christophe Colomb* have been detained in Germany.

lently realistic imitation of railroad sounds, was indicative of a passing phase. Honegger is not exclusively a "frightful modernist": in his stage works, he almost never uses an abnormally unfamiliar idiom. Like many of his contemporaries, he tends to create dramatic stage works that cannot readily be classified —dramatic psalms, mimed symphonies, lyric tragedies without action, and so on. So far, he has composed one opera alone, one in collaboration with Jacques Ibert, and an operetta, the last, based on Louÿs' *Le Roi Pausole*, humorously obscene in tone. With Ibert, he set Paul Claudel's mystery play, *Jeanne d'Arc au bûcher*. This score was first performed, at the folk theater in Mezières, as incidental music to the play.

It was for the same theater that Honegger was commissioned to provide incidental music for its director's Biblical drama, *Judith*, this later being turned into a three-act opera which vies with the dramatic psalm, *Le Roi David*, as his most impressive accomplishment. As produced at the Auditorium, on January 27, 1926, by the Chicago Opera Association, with Mary Garden, *Judith* was acclaimed as a work of genius—and lasted two performances. Its most striking feature is the grandeur of its choral masses and its bloodcurdling finale, with its strident, chaotic pyramid of noises as the Jewish heroine rushes from the Assyrian general's tent with his severed head in a basket. The simplicity of line and dramatic definition of this richly colored work constitute a refreshing contrast to the sometimes trackless mazes of run-of-the-mill modern operatic scores.

Among the Teutonic composers, Arnold Schönberg, a Viennese academe of vast erudition, stands, because of his audacious experiments and far-flung influence in many fields of composition, first. Although even today—over thirty years after the epochal *Erwartung* (1909)—the music of Schönberg can be known to but a small handful of concertgoers and closet musicians, his position as a force in modern music is second only to that of Stravinsky. Schönberg began as a sentimentally lush romanticist, influenced without noticeable violence by both Wagner and Brahms, but by the time he began to compose for the stage, he had quite got over that early foolishness and had begun to develop those complex mathematical formulas which have made him an Einstein of music.

All of Schönberg's operas are brief—the longest, the comic *Von Heute auf Morgen*, plays only fifty minutes. Such brevity betokens no poverty of idea. Rather, it is a considered reaction against the gaseous diffuseness of such late romantics as Bruckner and Mahler. Also, it is the simplest sign of a guiding compression, forcing the musical sentence into compact, explosive size. In *Erwartung*, Schönberg had begun to experiment with operatic form: a monodrama, it is an attempt to make a single character bear not only the action, but also its environing implications. It is asserted by Schönberg's disciples that here he has made a new musical dimension come into being—a rather grandiose way of saying that he had tried certain harmonic neoterisms and introduced novelties of declamation that were later developed further in the tremulously beautiful and eloquent *Pierrot Lunaire*, a dramatic song cycle dating from 1911, and in his two other operas, *Die glückliche Hand* (1913) and the above-mentioned *Von Heute auf Morgen* (1929), the latter Schönberg's attempt to show that his usually austere art could be made the expression of comic mood. *Die glückliche Hand*, produced in the United States in 1930 by the League of Composers with the assistance of the Philadelphia Orchestra, was heard in Philadelphia and New York a total of five times. In it, a baritone voice carries the commentary, while dancers mime the action and a chorus speaking on musical notes provides a mystical overtone. Here is Schönberg's favorite *Expresionismus*, and *in excelsis*.

Alban Berg, Schönberg's most gifted pupil, subscribed largely to the tenets of his master, but added many elements, most of which were drawn from a profound study of the musical past. In the first place, Berg was a belated romantic who naturally could not apply Schönberg's most relentless theories without qualification. Compared to Schönberg's, Berg's style is positively expansive: he is compact not from inner compulsion, but only when the urgent necessities of a given situation demand it. Mingled with the starkly modern harmonist is a broad lyricist of rather Schumannesque cast, who serves to make more palatable the rigid patterns of his musical thought.

In *Wozzeck* (1914-21), a three-act opera in fifteen scenes, Berg had already a thoroughly new, very complicated, and enormously effective method of characterization through assigning special harmonic sequences, capable of infinite variation and development, to each of the protagonists. Although this method is clearly a revolutionary adaptation of the theory behind the Wagnerian leitmotiv and its use, Berg cast aside Wagner's ideal of an endless musical web. He chose, instead, a series of set musical forms—fugue, sarabande, gigue, gavotte, and so on— each related with poetic illumination to the situation and characters involved. In *Lulu* (1928-34), a second opera, these ideas were developed and refined, always with such unerring intelligence and true musicianship that Berg's death, before the orchestration of the last act of *Lulu* was completed, may be regarded as an artistic catastrophe.

Wozzeck has had a career unique among modernist operas, for in the eleven years following its *première* at the Berlin Staatsoper, on December 14, 1925, it had 166 performances in twenty-nine separate cities. This furore would not have been a too extraordinary greeting to a ripe veristic work like *I Gioielli della Madonna*, for instance, but *Wozzeck*, written in difficult Schönbergian idiom, would not have seemed an easy work to produce or to take—the Berlin *première* required 137 rehearsals, and the score calls for four separate orchestras of widely varying make-up, one of them including the instruments of a military band. Finally, the composer, his own librettist, had, if anything, overemphasized the psychosexual sordidness of the drama on which it was based, a work of the symbolic naturalist Georg Büchner, who had lived almost a century before Hofmannsthal.

The early performances of *Wozzeck* created such violent partisanship pro and con that the topical literature about it was collected in a sizable volume. Little more than five years after the Berlin *première*, *Wozzeck* was staged by the Philadelphia Grand Opera Association, at Philadelphia (March 19, 1931), with Stokowski conducting. Anne Roselle was the Marie, Ivan

The Metropolitan Opera House, Philadelphia, Performance of Berg's *Wozzeck*, with Anne Roselle (Marie) and Ivan Ivantzoff (Wozzeck)

Ivantzoff the Wozzeck. Both this performance and its repetition in New York with the same forces, on November 24, brought most enthusiastic acclaim from music lovers of every stripe. Yet, the opera has not since been repeated in the United States. *Lulu,* based on a two-part "tragedy of sex" by Frank Wedekind, has never been heard in its entirety, only the first two acts, with completely orchestrated fragments of the third. having been given at the Zurich *première* (June 2, 1937). Fortunately, Berg had made a suite for orchestra from various numbers in the opera, and this very interesting music is occasionally heard.

Utterly antithetical to Berg, the romantic recluse, is Paul Hindemith, the prosaic, workaday craftsman who had made a profession of being a practical musician, able to turn out under contract any kind of work. Hindemith's once tenaciously held point of view, from which he has now somewhat receded, was the precise opposite of art for art's sake. In his mind, there was every reason a work of art should have a specific utilitarian purpose. He was an exponent, that is, of *Gebrauchsmusik.* As he is a master of several styles, not all of his operas conform to this fetish. An amusing *Gebrauchsoper* is his *Neues vom Tage* (1929), one of the episodes of which makes use of the universal habit of singing in the bathtub,* while another includes a business letter set for chorus.

Hindemith began as a romanticist, making use of classical forms in a way suggested by the once highly regarded Max Reger. Native inclinations quickly drew him toward a more incisive, impersonalized style. *Cardillac* (1929), his first full-length opera, set to one of E. T. A. Hoffmann's macabre stories, is a clever modern adaptation of the manner of Handel's chamber music. In it, Hindemith uses classical forms much as Berg does in his operas. Although *Cardillac* was eagerly awaited, and

---

* In his useful booklet *Opera*, published in England during the Second World War, Professor Dent says of *Neues vom Tage*: "The libretto was amusingly modern, and the sensation of the opera was a scene in which the heroine, lying in a bath at a hotel, sang the praises of electric heating—'constant hot water, no horrid smell, or danger of explosion,' etc. When the work was announced for performance at Breslau the local gas company applied for and obtained an injunction, as this song was considered damaging to their trade. Opera is taken seriously in Germany."

had a considerable measure of success after its *première* at Dresden, its neoclassical dryness has not helped its chances of survival.

Much better known because of the popularity of the symphony arranged from it, *Mathis der Maler* has more vital stuff in it. It was inspired by recently authenticated incidents in the life of Matthias Grünewald, painter of the Eisenheim Altar, from which the stage settings and costumes were derived. This opera would undoubtedly have been produced successfully in Germany had not Hindemith's style, or styles, of music been interdicted as *Kulturbolshevismus*, and the composer himself, though an "Aryan," eventually driven into exile. For these reasons, it first reached the stage at Zurich in May, 1938. The exciting quality of the symphonic *Mathis der Maler* makes the production of the opera in the United States an urgent desideratum.

Gebrauchsmusik has had, besides Hindemith, two important exponents in Kurt Weill and Ernest Křenek. Weill, a composer of uneven inspiration, who lets down his audiences with apparent *sang-froid*, has nevertheless written several important scores. In his two most interesting operas, he collaborated with Bert Brecht, a poet and stagecraftsman who is regarded as the originator of the *Gebrauchsmusik* movement. The earlier, *Mahagonny* (1929), satirizes something like a decadent New York in music that is hectic, obscene, and nerve-fraying. A series of set numbers, it rises to something like lyrical greatness in the sizzlingly ecstatic "Alabama Song." Jazz is used with greater plasticity and intelligence in *Die Dreigroschenoper* (see page 42). In recent years, Weill, who now resides in the United States, has frittered away his talents in a series of musical comedies of small distinction and incidental music of even less.

Most famous of all jazz operas, *Jonny spielt auf* is by the innately serious Křenek, whose most recent opera is *Karl V*, written in his own fearsome interpretation of Schönberg's most advanced harmonic technique. *Jonny* may be considered the successful aberration of a solemn experimentalist. It is the typical work of a period when Europe was discovering American jazz and almost completely distorting it, sometimes with satiri-

cal intent, sometimes out of sheer ineptitude and misunderstanding. *Jonny* was an explosive product: noisy, hilarious,
riotous with undirected energy, it captured the imagination of
Europe. Soon after its *première* at Leipzig, on February 11,
1927, it had been translated into eighteen languages and given
in more than one hundred cities. Somewhat bowdlerized, it was
a novelty—or perhaps a curiosity—of the 1928-29 Metropolitan
season. It entirely failed to convince Americans that European
music, in the person of Křenek, had the slightest understanding of what the jazz spirit was. At the *première*, on January 19,
1929, Bohnen was a superb Jonny and Fleischer a fine Yvonne,
but others in the cast, among them Easton and Schorr, could
not easily shed their grand-opera manners. Later, Tibbett undertook the role of Jonny. After seven performances that season,
Jonny spielt auf was dropped, unquestionably forever, from the
Metropolitan repertoire.

Chapter XXV

Opera in the United States

T HE history of American opera is a long, sad story—in contrast to that of its richly bedizened sister, opera in America. In its early phases, it is peopled by solitary lost souls
valiantly, sedulously, and vainly trying to ape foreign graces,
and those not always of the most unimpeachable sort. Going irrelevantly hand in hand with their frequently slavish subservi-
ence to foreign styles was, from the very beginning, a militant
profession of faith in American music. As was natural, when
musical stage works first came to be composed in the Colonies,
they were on the pattern of *The Beggar's Opera* and its progeny—ballad operas and *pasticci*. The librettos of these early
efforts have survived in many cases, but almost invariably the
music has vanished.

One of the most ambitious of these early stage works, however, was an oratorio opera by Francis Hopkinson, a signer of
the Declaration of Independence. *The Temple of Minerva*, set
to Hopkinson's own semihistorical allegory in honor of the alliance with France, was performed in 1781, in the presence of
George and Martha Washington and the French minister. The
music is lost, but the book shows that it was made up of solos,
choruses, and ensemble numbers, preceded by an overture.
Hopkinson was born in Philadelphia in 1737, and claimed, in
a letter to Washington that accompanied a gift of some of his
compositions, to be the first native of the United States to have
"produced a musical composition." Washington, in reply, said,
"I can neither sing one of the songs, nor raise a single note on
any instrument to convince the unbelieving. But I have, however, one argument which will prevail with persons of true
estate (at least in America)—I can tell them that *it is the production of Mr. Hopkinson*."

Mrs. Siddons' sister, Anne Julia Hatton, wrote the book for
a ballad opera by the already unsavory name of *Tammany*,
which dealt with a Cherokee chief of that name and his un-

fortunate encounters with Spanish explorers. Its composer, James Hewitt, an exact contemporary of Beethoven, conducted its first performance at the John Street Theater, New York, on March 5, 1794. Most of the airs were given to the heroine, Manana, which suggests that the piece was probably commissioned by John Hodgkinson, an English singing actor of the time, for his wife, also a singer. Benjamin Carr, also English-born, pioneered with Hewitt in music publishing, and composed the popular *The Archers or Mountaineers of Switzerland*, to an adaptation of Schiller's *Wilhelm Tell* by the painter William Dunlap, a founder of the National Academy of Design. A third composer of ballad operas was Victor Pelissier, a French French-hornplayer, who, using a libretto extracted from a poem in *The Vicar of Wakefield*, wrote *Edwin and Angelina*, which was given in New York on December 19, 1796, with the Hodgkinsons in the cast.

Shortly after this period, foreign grand-opera companies began to arrive in America: the Garcías came in 1825, the Montressor troupe in 1832, and finally, in 1838, Arthur and Ann Seguin, an energetic English couple who toured the United States and Canada extensively. Lorenzo da Ponte, Mozart's librettist, was an indefatigable propagandist for Italian opera in New York and Philadelphia. In New Orleans, opera had been an established institution from 1810, when it was inaugurated by a performance of Paisiello's *Il Barbiere di Siviglia*.

American composers responded timidly, slowly, to these stimuli, and it was not until 1845 that a true American grand opera reached the stage. This was William Henry Fry's *Leonora*, based on Bulwer-Lytton's popular play, *The Lady of Lyons*. Generally liked, *Leonora* had its *première* at the Chestnut Street Theater, Philadelphia, on June 4, 1845, by the Seguin company, and ran for twelve nights. Although Edward R. Fry, the composer's brother, was manager of the Astor Place Opera House in 1848 and 1849, *Leonora* was not heard in New York until 1858, at the Academy of Music. More than seventy years later, in May, 1929, excerpts from it, arranged for concert performance by Dr. Otto Kinkeldey, were presented in New York under the auspices of Pro Musica. The audience found it excruciatingly funny, much to the annoyance of certain critics with a sense of history. W. J. Henderson asked whether, "properly mounted and sung, Fry's ambitious opus would not, in its archaic way, furnish better diversion than [Strauss'] 'Egyptian Helen'?"

As evidence of the qualms and uncertainty with which American operatic composers were working, it is significant that Fry, who was ever belligerent about opera in English, not only allowed *Leonora* to be translated into Italian for the Academy of Music performance, but chose foreign subject matter for it and his other opera, *Notre Dame de Paris,** after Victor Hugo. A refreshing exception was George Frederick Bristow, a very influential musician who both preached and composed wholly American opera. His *Rip Van Winkle,* brought out at Niblo's Garden, New York, on September 27, 1855, ran for a solid month, and temporarily threatened to become an American *Bohemian Girl.* When Bristow died in 1898 at the age of seventy-three, he was engaged on his second opera, *Columbus.* John Knowles Paine, the long-time dean of American professors of music, and teacher of half the composers and critics of yesterday, died without hearing a performance of his only opera, *Azara,* though concert excerpts from it are interesting enough to suggest that Conried may have been wrong in changing his mind about producing it at the Metropolitan.

During the fifty-two years that elapsed between the Academy of Music performance of Fry's *Leonora* in 1858 and the Metropolitan *première* of Frederick Shepherd Converse's *The Pipe of Desire*—the first opera by an American composer to be given in that house by the resident company—countless operas by Americans had been composed, but not always performed. Amid the welter of dust-laden, mediocre scores and names of scores (for many of them have vanished), we come upon the eccentric Louis Moreau Gottschalk writing unwieldy historical tragedies, young Walter Damrosch and Victor Herbert penning their first operas, and several earnest females contriving such dramatic inanities as *Narcissus, Priscilla,* and *Last Summer.*

---

* Produced in Philadelphia in 1864, the year of Fry's death, *Notre Dame de Paris* was later heard in New York under Theodore Thomas.

But neither the Academy of Music nor the Metropolitan, its even more dominating successor, paid much attention to these desperate efforts.

It was not until the unhappy joint management of Gatti-Casazza and Dippel that the gates of New York's sacred temple of music swung reluctantly ajar, and then only to a one-acter that had already been presented at Boston four years earlier. *The Pipe of Desire* had received a medal offered by David Bispham, an untiring propagandist for opera in English. But, as matters turned out, this was insufficient reason for performing it at the Metropolitan, where it lasted but two performances. Besides the imitative music, which was inept Wagnerism, the libretto was rambling, insipid, and, moreover, poorly adapted to singing. The all-American cast thoughtfully provided by the management—Homer, Martin, Whitehill, and Witherspoon—was, except for Whitehill, unintelligible. To audiences unused to understanding German, French, and Italian texts, this would not, perhaps, have mattered if only the music itself had said anything.*

Victor Herbert, the melodious Irishman and eminent cellist, had already composed the majority of his famous operettas before the first of his serious operas reached the Metropolitan. This was *Natoma*, based on a story of early California, which reached New York three days after its *première* at Philadelphia on February 25, 1911. The cast, drawn from the roster of the Philadelphia-Chicago Opera Company, included Garden (Natoma), Lillian Grenville (Barbara), McCormack (Merrill), Sammarco (Alvarado), Huberdeau (Don Francisco), and Dufranne (Father Peralta). H. T. Parker described *Natoma* succinctly as "a dull text set to mediocre music," but praised the staging and Garden's vivid performance of the Indian heroine. But Krehbiel reported stage business that reduced the action to nonsense. The opera, scantily provided with the unforgettable tunes that had made Herbert's fortune, has van-

---

* Converse did not remain a passive Wagnerian. In 1927, his *Flivver 10,000,000*, a symphonic fantasy about the ten-millionth Ford, showed him to be critically and humorously *au courant* with twentieth-century life and twentieth-century harmony.

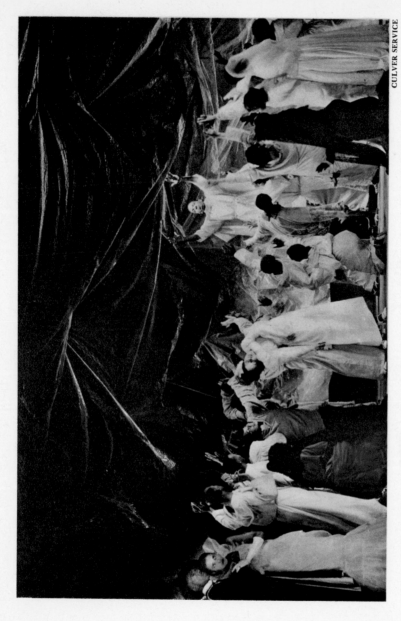

A Scene from Virgil Thomson's *Four Saints in Three Acts*, with Edward Matthews (St. Ignatius)

ished irretrievably, though a few excerpts, notably the Dagger Dance and Natoma's Spring Song, are heard occasionally. *Natoma* was never given by the resident Metropolitan company, but Herbert's second opera, *Madeleine*, was. It did not, however, long survive its *première* on January 24, 1914, when the leading roles went to Alda, Sparkes, Althouse, Pini-Corsi, and De Segurola. For this one-acter Herbert abandoned the American scene for an eighteenth-century French setting, with a star of the Opéra as the heroine. The undramatic story was matched by generally wooden music.

In the early days of their joint management, Gatti-Casazza and Dippel, stifling their native conservatism, offered a $10,000 prize for the best opera by an American composer, the text to be in English. Horatio W. Parker, a very respected professor of music at Yale, and already the composer of *Hora Novissima*, the best-turned-out oratorio to be written in America, won it with a gloomy work about the ancient Britons. The librettist of *Mona*, Brian Hooker, who achieved some fame as the translator of Rostand's *Cyrano de Bergerac*, conceived his listless lyrics as a protest against women's suffragism: Mona, a British princess, brings about her lover's death and her own by insisting on playing a man's part in the world. Parker was unfortunate in his libretto, which was dramatic only in spots, and also in the cast assigned to *Mona*. At the Metropolitan *première*, on March 14, 1912, Homer had the name role, her associates being Rita Fornia (Enya), Witherspoon (Arth), William Wade Hinshaw (Gloom), and Albert Reiss (Nial). Alfred Hertz conducted. Reiss alone of the principals seemed to have a grasp of his role. Yet, despite obstacles to success, *Mona* was successful, both critics and public expressing generous admiration and lively interest. No American opera had received comparable praise from competent judges, and the action of Gatti-Casazza in withdrawing it from the repertoire after four performances tends to cast suspicion on his many professions of interest in American music. The failure of later managers to revive it extends that suspicion to them.

For *Mona* is, despite certain unquestionable blemishes like occasional tediousness and a churchiness not always confined to the devotional scenes in the opera (and which, moreover, is Anglican rather than druid), a good opera. It shows an intelligent grasp of the musical resources of the period and a real talent for using them dramatically. The text is expertly set for singability. The declamation has eloquence, the instrumentation has aptness and distinction, and through the entire score there are moments of great individuality. *Mona* is frequently both beautiful and persuasive, and is remarkably free from the unctiousness that mars the work of so many oratorio and cantata composers—in fact, one of Parker's most individual touches is a biting, astringent note. Nor is he, in *Mona*, structurally uninteresting: twenty years before Alban Berg, he was assigning characteristic keys to various personages of the drama. Yet, there is little of the closet work about *Mona*—it is an opera realistically created for life on the stage.

Walter Damrosch has been writing opera since 1894. His first effort, *The Scarlet Letter*, showed that he had inherited from his father a devotion to Wagner that expressed itself, in his case, in extended imitation. A libretto in English by Hawthorne's son-in-law, George Parsons Lathrop, gave *The Scarlet Letter* a certain stamp of authenticity, but a largely German cast, headed by Gadski, murdered the language and completely destroyed any semblance of illusion. The *première* took place in Boston on February 10, 1896, and production at the Metropolitan followed, though not by the resident company. Soon *The Scarlet Letter* was known, and justly, as "the *Nibelungen* of New England."*

Damrosch's *Cyrano*, produced at the Metropolitan on February 27, 1913, put the New York critics at a disadvantage. The libretto was by one of their most distinguished confreres, W. J. Henderson, of *The Sun*, and the composer was conductor of the Symphony Society of New York. Henderson was treated somewhat better than Damrosch, whose musical borrowings were laughingly noted. After five performances that season, the first

* The young Italo-American composer Vittorio Giannini (brother of Dusolina Giannini) wrote his own English libretto for his version of *The Scarlet Letter*. This was rejected by the Metropolitan as being musically too Italian, but was produced in Germany, at Hamburg, on June 2, 1938, as *Das Brandmal*.

with Alda, Martin, and Amato, *Cyrano* was dropped.* Its reception apparently discouraged Damrosch for almost a quarter of a century, for he did not again dare the critical thunders with a new opera until May 12, 1937, when *The Man Without a Country* was graduated from McGuffey's readers, via a text by Arthur Guiterman, to the stage of the Metropolitan, with the composer conducting, and the magnificently voiced Helen Traubel in her first important role. Irving Kolodin said witheringly of the opera: "This was a score utterly without distinction. . . . The music was thoroughly derivative, competently put together, orchestrated with a heavy, inelastic hand."

Only one of the several operas and operettas of Charles Wakefield Cadman, composer of *At Dawning, I Hear a Thrush at Eve,* and other gems of the semipopular repertoire, has reached the Metropolitan. This was *Shanewis,* a tragic tale of a white man infatuated with an Indian girl. Cadman has always been interested in American Indian music, which he presents in a limp and treacly version, and the salient lyrical moments in *Shanewis* have much the quality of certain of his concert ballads —*From the Land of the Sky-blue Water,* for example. Sophie Braslau was the Shanewis, Althouse the Lionel, of the *première,* on March 23, 1918. Another Cadman opera, *A Witch of Salem,* lasted through three performances in Chicago and is said to be more dramatic than *Shanewis.*

Quite as insignificant as Cadman as a writer for the musical stage, and as mysteriously favored by important opera houses, was Henry Hadley, whose first opera, *Azora,* attained three performances by the Chicago Opera Association. The somewhat later *Cleopatra's Night,* to Alice Leal Pollock's adaptation of Théophile Gautier's story, is full of pseudo-Oriental sinuosities (especially prevalent during a protracted bacchanale) and ambitious orchestration, but neither element rescues the score from creeping dullness. Alda, Orville Harrold, and Jeanne Gordon were the principals at the Metropolitan *première* of

* Twenty years later, the all but octogenarian composer conducted a concert performance in Carnegie Hall, New York, of a revised version of *Cyrano.* Scandal was caused when Novotna and Pinza, who had been scheduled to appear as soloists with the Philharmonic Symphony Society in this performance, withdrew shortly before the concert. Various explanations were advanced at the time.

Cleopatra's Night—January 31, 1920. It was given there seven times, one less than *Shanewis*.

Far more fortunate has been the versatile and generally more gifted Deems Taylor, whose first opera, *The King's Henchman*, established a record for longevity among American operas at the Metropolitan,* only to have that record broken by his second opera, *Peter Ibbetson*. The first reached fourteen performances in three seasons; the second, sixteen in four. Taylor was also fortunate in his librettists: Edna St. Vincent Millay, at that time a writer of real distinction, provided the book for *The King's Henchman*, while Constance Collier helped the composer with her many years of theatrical experience when he decided himself to adapt her dramatic version of George Du Maurier's *Peter Ibbetson*.

When the Metropolitan commissioned *The King's Henchman*, Taylor was known chiefly as a witty journalist and as a composer of light orchestral works. The success of the *Henchman*, after its *première* on February 17, 1927, made him one of the most envied of American composers. Commentators blinded neither by the magnificence of the production—Urban settings, etc.—nor by spleen hailed Taylor as the clever eclectic he is. Pitts Sanborn, tracing the musical genealogy of the *Henchman*, had to mention the names and works of Puccini, Debussy, Massenet, Mussorgsky, Charpentier, Rimsky-Korsakov, and Grieg. But, he concluded grimly, "For the most part, *The King's Henchman* is based firmly upon Wagner." Easton, Johnson, and Tibbett, all equipped to sing understandable English, shared honors at the *première*, and helped to make the opera front-page news—quite a feat for an American music drama of tenth-century England.

New York heard Taylor's second opera almost four years later—February 7, 1931. *Peter Ibbetson* had been completed by means of a $5000 grant from the Juilliard Foundation, and it was awaited with taut interest. The ovation at the *première* bordered on the hysterical: thirty-six curtain calls, the tears of

* It was also the first full-length American work to be presented there since 1917, when Reginald De Koven's tuneful but completely unimportant *The Canterbury Pilgrims*—an operetta rather than an opera—was given there on March 8.

many listeners, and a public embrace from Walter Damrosch were among the composer's rewards for a score as little original as *The King's Henchman*, but quite as superb a job of joinery. Johnson and Tibbett again starred as interpreters of Taylor-made music, and Bori, in superb voice and beautiful in the period costumes assigned to the Duchess of Towers, was Easton's peer in intelligibility. This time, in addition to reminiscences of other composers, Taylor introduced French folk songs for sentimental effect. *Peter Ibbetson* established another precedent: on December 26, 1933, it was the first American opera ever chosen to open a Metropolitan season. Despite their popularity, neither *The King's Henchman* nor *Peter Ibbetson* has been revived after being dropped from the Metropolitan repertoire, and as these lines are written, it is announced that Taylor's third opera, *Ramuntcho*, based on a Basque novel by Pierre Loti, will have its *première* in Philadelphia during the 1941-42 season.

Aside from its burgeoning effect on Taylor's own career, the success of his two operas would seem to have made the Metropolitan management temporarily more hospitable to American works. The middle thirties would have been a notable era in the history of American music if only the operas chosen by the Metropolitan had been as worthy of the implied honor as the press agents claimed. The Russian-born Louis Gruenberg's *The Emperor Jones* was the first, and in many ways the best, of the three new American works the Metropolitan adopted. The setting of an O'Neill melodrama was in itself a bold and admirable departure, though the composer's failure to capitalize upon certain effectively theatrical portions of the play was widely and justifiably criticized. Yet, many pages of the score, particularly the choral passages, show a dramatic talent at work, and the use of a half-sung, half-spoken vocal style was frequently most happy. Tibbett, as Jones, made the most of this device in his intelligent characterization. Altogether, the effect produced by *The Emperor Jones* at its *première*, on January 7, 1933, was of frustrated excellence.*

---

* On September 7, 1937, the Columbia Broadcasting System, over a nation-wide hookup, presented Gruenberg's setting of W. H. Hudson's *Green Mansions*. Commissioned by CBS, and designed specifically to be broadcast, it proved amorphous, exotic, and completely lacking in dramatic impact.

Certainly, *The Emperor Jones* was in all ways superior to Howard Hanson's flaccid *Merrymount*, a tale of New England witchcraft, which reached Thirty-ninth Street and Broadway on February 10, 1934. This effort, by a scholarly but uninspired musician, had a pinched Nordic air that deceived no one. Again Tibbett covered himself with glory, this time as Wrestling Bradford; the Swedish Göta Ljungberg reached unprecedented heights of unintelligibility as Lady Marigold Sandys. It were completely irrelevant to compare *The Emperor Jones* with the last American novelty of Gatti-Casazza's regime, and the retirement of the veteran *régisseur* after flinging John Laurence Seymour's *In the Pasha's Garden* to the howling critics was not unfitting. It had literally nothing but Tibbett, who by this time had become the strong man of the American wing.

It was not surprising, therefore, when Tibbett was requisitioned to sing the villainous cuckold Guido in the Dutch-born Richard Hageman's *Caponsacchi*, based on episodes from Browning's *The Ring and the Book*. Its qualities were undistinguished: workmanlike, melodious, superficially and timidly modern, and without originality, *Caponsacchi* recalled Hageman's impressive academic background and the fact that he had composed several ingratiating songs. Its reception was not calculated to encourage Manager Johnson in investigating enthusiastically the box-office possibilities of American opera.

The production of *Amelia Goes to the Ball* may be construed as a cautious feeler from the Johnson office. Its composer, the youthful Gian-Carlo Menotti, was born in Italy, and his delightful little opera—modified Wolf-Ferrari in spirit—had a triumphant career before it reached the Metropolitan, from a *première* at the Curtis Institute of Music, Philadelphia, on April 1, 1937, to a repetition under the auspices of the Henry Street Settlement, in New York a few days later. Muriel Dickson, Chamlee, and Brownlee were the intelligently chosen principals of the first Metropolitan performance, on March 3, 1938. Given six times within two seasons, *Amelia Goes to the Ball* was unaccountably dropped. However, talk of reviving this sprightly if not very original *apéritif* persists, as does that of mounting *The Old Maid and the Thief*, a sardonically bright piece Menotti composed expressly for the National Broadcasting Company in 1939.

In his varied and busy career, George Gershwin, to a text based on Du Bose Heyward's *Porgy*, turned out an opera that was heard by more people than ever heard any other American opera. For *Porgy and Bess*, which opened at the Colonial Theater, Boston, on September 30, 1935, was, whatever its quality, unmistakably an opera, not a musical comedy or an operetta. Its excellence was flawed by some of that pretentiousness which invariably marred Gershwin's work when he deserted musical comedy, and the opera was at its best precisely at those spots where it came nearest to musical comedy. Numbers like "It ain't necessarily so" and "I got plenty o' nuttin' " might have come unchanged straight out of one of Gershwin's later musical shows. On the other hand, the lovely "Summertime" has a certain elegiac quality at which Gershwin previously had only hinted. Its predominantly Negro cast performed *Porgy and Bess* with gusto, giving all they had—and more—but utterly failing to project the less "popular" elements of the score. There can be no doubt that several numbers from this opera will outlast anything by many more solemn, more academic composers. Tibbett and Jepson, under Gershwin's supervision, recorded extensive portions of *Porgy and Bess*, and performance at the Metropolitan is not beyond the realm of possibility.

George Antheil, a one-time *enfant terrible* of American music, now tamed by Hollywood, has written several operas, none of them significant except as indicating trends. His first, *Transatlantic*, which was staged at Frankfort on the Main on May 25, 1930, was a typical product of the American *émigré* of the boom days (it was composed in 1927). Antheil described it as "the first modern political opera": it satirized capitalist corruption in the United States. It shows the influence of Křenek and Weill, and makes lavish use of early hot jazz. In it, too, Antheil showed a marked if intermittent dramatic grasp. Unfortunately, in his later operatic ventures, he did not progress. His *Helen Retires*, to a libretto by John Erskine, exhibited only a fractional appreciation of the rich comic possibilities of the *déclassé* days of Helen of Troy, and was musically insipid.

It came to judgment at the Juilliard School on February 28, 1934. For some years Antheil has been most occupied in turning out deft scores for the movies.

Far more gentle, and positively reticent as a musical modernist, is Virgil Thomson, the acidulous critic of the *New York Herald Tribune*. His operatic fame rests on a single work, *Four Saints in Three Acts*—"an opera to be sung"—to an apparently nonsensical, but always singable and amusing, libretto by Gertrude Stein. Produced with imagination and exquisite taste, and played with verve, knowingness, and delight by an all-Negro cast, this modest opera was one of the most attractive entertainments of the last theatrical decade in New York. After a *première*, on February 8, 1934, in Hartford, Connecticut, under the auspices of the Society of Friends and Enemies of Modern Music, it upset predictions by becoming a smash hit on Broadway. It is anything but a complicated score: it perfectly sets the satirically surrealist text and always suggests more than it says. The chief assets of this delicious music are aptness, simplicity, transparency—and unabashed triviality. It is the opposite of epochal.

After several trials, Marc Blitzstein came through with *The Cradle Will Rock*. Originally intended as a regularly staged production of Orson Welles' Mercury Theater, this violently Leftist tract ran into trouble with the stage union, and therefore had its first public performance, on June 16, 1937, under macabre conditions. There was no scenery; the actors, wearing street clothes, evaded union regulations by remaining in the audience, and the composer, seated at an upright piano (from which he gave a tendentious explanation of the action),* was the only orchestra. Perhaps as a reaction against the dull-conventional of the ordinary production, the public, whether Right, Left, or Liberal, came to love *The Cradle Will Rock*, and it ran its radical course for several months.

Blitzstein's flair for the stage is undeniable, and the Weill-like music that he used for this and succeeding political satires is lent bite, incisiveness, and point by his passionate sincerity. His radio opera, *I've Got the Tune*, a savage anti-Nazi pamph-

* Blitzstein writes his own librettos.

let, was effective, while his most recent stage work, *No For an Answer*, which also achieved notoriety when the New York civic authorities tried to close the theater where it was scheduled to play, was merely more of *The Cradle Will Rock*. Despite this apparent failure to develop, there is no doubt that Blitzstein is a forceful personality with a biting musical tongue. He is one of the few American composers who seem equipped to write a musicodramatic work of more than ephemeral significance.

Finally, there is Aaron Copland, a musician of vast cleverness, erudition, and vitality. He is conceded by all but the most conservative to be one of the two or three most gifted American composers. He has written only one opera, *The Second Hurricane*, and that of a very specialized nature. It was composed to be sung by young people from eight to eighteen. It was first produced, under Orson Welles' direction, and with A. Lehman Engel conducting, at the Grand Street Theater, New York, on April 21, 1937. A credible, simple story of modern American life by Edwin Denby, it is couched in a musical language utterly uncomplicated, direct, and briskly melodious. It seems, withal, a singularly classical work—in the dignity of its proportions, the studied balance of its elements, and its cool texture. It serves its purpose admirably. There is nothing condescending about the way the story is told, and it retains childlike freshness without strain. Much of Copland's instrumental music, including his inspired scores for the cinema versions of *Of Mice and Men* and *Our Town*, indicates a dramatic talent of impressive quality. No greater boost for the lagging cause of opera in America could be imagined than a full-length opera from Copland.

Thus far, the history of opera in America has been almost exclusively the history of the foreign repertoire that has been given in the principal cities of the United States—in all grades of performance—by a handful of opera companies. Today, most of the provincial companies have vanished, though a barnstorming troupe or two survive. In effect, the Metropolitan Opera Company has, for better or worse, spread-eagled the nation. It fans out from New York on periodical tours, and

the superficially independent Chicago and San Francisco companies are, particularly in the matter of singers, branches of it.
Most of its presentations are still the classics of the foreign
repertoire, with some second-raters of the same repertoire
thrown in for bad measure. Nor is this miscellany usually presented with anything approaching flawless taste, or with advantage taken of modern advances in stagecraft. Yet, under the
new dispensation of a company that has legal title to its own
theater,* certain advances have been noted. For instance, the
chorus has improved, guest conductors of distinction have been
salvaged from a Europe in chaos, popular operas have been
restudied and restaged, and there are some signs of a healthy
spirit of experimentation. The omens are good. Manager Johnson wields a power greater than any other Metropolitan manager has ever wielded. In short, the whole future of opera in
America—and opera by Americans—is in his hands. He is beginning to deal skillfully with the problem of his foreign
legacy, but there are no indications that he is ready to give
American composers the only kind of encouragement that
matters—performance.

* Tears and angry repinings over the indefinite perpetuation of the utterly
unsuitable building that the Metropolitan Opera Association has purchased—for
reasons not clear to the public that helped to purchase it—are now idle.

List of Recommended Recordings

The choice of a list of the best recorded performances to accompany *The Opera* has been a formidable but pleasant task. What to include has been simplified, to a certain extent, by closely following the authors' text. Certain omissions, therefore, were necessary, and only recordings made by the artists mentioned in the book (or, in some cases, by their contemporaries) are listed. Many recordings of historical value as to material illustrated or notability of performance, but which have been withdrawn (cut out) from the current lists, have had to be included. It has been advisable further to limit the choice by not drawing indiscriminately upon European sources from which, at the time of going to press, records are unobtainable. Only European recordings of exceptional merit, or those which are the only recorded examples of music discussed are included. Also, it has been necessary to exclude a large group of notable recordings because of the inability of the so-called modern reproducing instrument to play the hill-and-dale type of recording which was issued by Edison and Pathé.

All of the records listed are, at the time of going to press, obtainable, except the European ones mentioned in the above paragraph and those whose numbers are enclosed in parentheses and marked *co* (for example, V-542 co) and the special Odéon recordings made by the late Lilli Lehmann. These turn up from time to time in secondhand shops and other places frequented by inveterate record collectors.

As far as possible, I have tried to list the best performances first—regardless of the age of the recording.

GEORGE CLARK LESLIE

August 20, 1941

RECORD SYMBOLS

Domestic

V & VM	RCA-Victor
C & CM	Columbia
D	Decca
AS	L'Anthologie Sonore
MC	Musicraft
TC	Technichord
KN	Keynote
HRS	Historical Record Society
IRCC	International Record Collectors' Club

European

G & GM	HMV (England and Continental Europe)
C	Columbia (England, France and Italy)
D	Decca (England)
P	Parlophone (England)
T	Telefunken (Germany)
O	Odeon (Continental Europe)
PD	Polydor (Germany and France)
PAT	Pathé (France)
CET	Cetra (Italy)
MIA	Musiche Italiane Antiche (Italy)

CHAPTER I

JACOPO PERI

EURIDICE

"Funeste piaggie"
Ralph Crane (b)   V-21752 [10"]
Reinald Werrenrath (b)   (V-55051 co) [12"]
"Gioite al canto mio"
Salvatore Salvati (t), with harpsichord   MIA-1 [12"]

GIULIO CACCINI

EURIDICE

"Non piango e non sospiro"
Ralph Crane (b)   V-21752 [10"]

CLAUDIO MONTEVERDI

ARIANNA

"Lasciatemi morire"
Ezio Pinza (bs), with piano   V-17914 [12"]
Maria Peschken (c), with harpsichord and cello D-20164 [10"]

L'INCORONAZIONE DI POPPEA
"Oblivion soave"
Ezio Pinza (bs), with piano   V-17915 [12″]
Doris Owens (s, in English), with harpsichord   C-DB500 [10″]
"Sento un certo so che"
Isabel French (s), with harpsichord   TC-13B [10″]

ORFEO
Complete recording. Soloists, chorus, and orchestra,
with harpsichord and organ, conducted by Ferruccio
Calusio. Twelve 12″ records.   MIA-14/25
"Ecco purch' a voi ritorno"
Ralph Crane (b)   V-21747 [10″]
"Plaintes d'Orphée" (recitative, Act II), *"Ah! sven-
turato amante"* (recitative, Act III), *"Quel honor"*
(aria, Act IV)
Yvon Le Marc' Hadour (b), with strings, organ,
and harpsichord, conducted by Ruggero Gerlin
PAT-PAT76 [12″]

PIETRO FRANCESCO CAVALLI
SERSE
"Beato chi puo"
Giuseppe Flamini (bs), with harpsichord and *basso
continuo*   MIA-4 [12″]

CHAPTER II

GIOVANNI BATTISTA PERGOLESI
LA SERVA PADRONA
Excerpts (arranged by Berel, in French)
Jane Gatineau (s), Georges Serrano (t), André
Fijan (narrator), with orchestra, conducted by Al-
fred Henry   D-LY6014 [12″]
"Stizzoso, mio stizzoso"
Lucy Isabelle Marsh (s)   (V-55051 co) [12″]

DOMENICO CIMAROSA
IL MATRIMONIO SEGRETO
Overture
Milan Symphony Orchestra, conducted by Lorenzo
Molajoli   C-7194M [12″]

CHAPTER III

GEORGE FRIDERIC HANDEL
ALESSANDRO
"Lusinghe più care"
Lily Pons (s), with Renaissance Quintet   V-2151 [10″]

FLORIDANTE

"Alma mia"

Ezio Pinza (bs), with piano	V-17914 [12″]
Lily Pons (s), with Renaissance Quintet	V-2151 [10″]

"Caro amore"

John McCormack (t)	V-14305 [12″]

RADAMISTO

"Ombra cara"

Andrée Mirilliet (s, in French)	C-RF25 [10″]

RINALDO

"Lascia ch'io pianga"

Maria Olszewska (c)	G-DB1465 [12″]
Gladys Swarthout (c), with piano	V-16678 [12″]

SERSE

"Ombra mai fu" ("Largo")

Enrico Caruso (t)	V-8806 [12″]
Charles Kullman (t, in English)	C-9143M [12″]

SIROË

"Ch'io mai vi possa lasciar d'amare"

Marian Anderson (c), with piano	V-1787 [10″]

HENRY PURCELL

DIDO AND AENEAS

Complete recording. Soloists, chorus, and orchestra, conducted by Clarence Raybould. Seven 12″ records.   D-25573/9

Orchestral Suite (arranged by Lucien Cailliet)
Philadelphia Orchestra, conducted by Eugene Ormandy. Two 12″ records.   VM-647

"When I am laid in earth"

Marian Anderson (c), with piano	V-17257 [12″]
Olga Haley (s)	D-25258 [12″]

JOHANN CHRISTOPH PEPUSCH

THE BEGGAR'S OPERA (new version, by Frederic Austin)

Selections
Glyndebourne Opera Company: Audrey Mildmay (s), Constance Willis (c), Roy Henderson (b), Michael Redgrave (b), and others, with orchestra, conducted by Michael Mundie. Six 12″ records.   VM-772

Polly's Songs

Audrey Mildmay (s)	G-C3166 [12″]

CHAPTER IV

JEAN-BAPTISTE LULLY

CADMUS ET HERMIONE

"Il faut passer dans ma barque"
Charles Panzéra (b), with Mme Panzéra-Ballot
(piano)   G-DA4924 [10"]

LE BOURGEOIS GENTILHOMME (incidental music)

Cérémonie turque
Denis d'Inès (narrator), with chorus and orchestra
G-DB4855 [12"]

Exemples de danses, Act I
Comédie-Française Orchestra, with announcements
G-P809 [10"]

JEAN-PHILIPPE RAMEAU

CASTOR ET POLLUX

Ballet Music
Lamoureux Orchestra, conducted by Albert Wolff
D-CA8153 [12"]

"Tristes apprêts"
Jane Laval (s)   C-LF18 [10"]

JEAN-JACQUES ROUSSEAU

LE DEVIN DU VILLAGE

Arias
Martha Angelici (s)   AS-54 [12"]

CHAPTER V

CHRISTOPH WILLIBALD VON GLUCK

ALCESTE

Overture
BBC Symphony Orchestra, conducted by Sir
Adrian Boult   V-12041 [12"]
Concertgebouw Orchestra, conducted by Willem
Mengelberg   D-25571 [12"]
"Non, ce n'est point un sacrifice"
Rose Bampton (s)   V-18218 [12"]
"Divinités du Styx"
Suzanne Balguérie (s)   D-LY6065 [12"]
Helen Traubel (s)   V-17268 [12"]
"Ah, malgré moi"
Rose Bampton (s)   V-18218 [12"]

ARMIDE

"Ah! si la liberté"
Frida Leider (s)　　　　　　　　　　　G-DB1547 [12″]
"Plus j'observe ces lieux"
Joseph Rogatchewsky (t)　　　　　　　C-4127M [10″]

DON JUAN (ballet)

Excerpts
Chamber Orchestra, conducted by Hans von
Brenda　　　　　　　　　　　　　　V-13648 [12″]

IPHIGÉNIE EN AULIDE

Overture (Wagner edition)
CB Symphony Orchestra, conducted by Howard
Barlow. Two 12″ records (3 sides).　　CM-X138
"Diane impitoyable!"
Emil Schipper (b, in German)　　　　G-EJ490 [12″]
"O toi, l'objet le plus aimable"
Emil Schipper (b, in German)　　　　G-EJ490 [12″]

IPHIGÉNIE EN TAURIDE

"Unis dès la plus tendre enfance"
Georges Thill (t)　　　　　　　　　C-9116M [12″]
"O malheureuse Iphigénie"
Suzanne Balguérie (s)　　　　　　　D-LY6065 [12″]

ORFEO ED EURIDICE

Dance of the Happy Shades
Paris Symphony Orchestra, conducted by Henri
Tomasi　　　　　　　　　　　　　C-69250D [12″]
"Che faro senza Euridice"
Maria Olszewska (c)　　　　　　　　G-D1490 [12″]
Tito Schipa (t)　　　　　　　　　　G-DB1723 [12″]
Kerstin Thorborg (c, in German)　　D-23029 [10″]

ORPHÉE ET EURYDICE

Complete recording. Soloists, chorus, and orchestra,
conducted by Henri Tomasi. Eight 12″ records.　CM-Op.15

CHAPTER VI

Wolfgang Amadeus Mozart

LA CLEMENZA DI TITO

Overture
Vienna Philharmonic Orchestra, conducted by
Bruno Walter　　　　　　　　　　V-12526 [12″]
"Parto, parto, ma tu ben mio"
Ernestine Schumann-Heink (c)　　　IRCC-31 [12″]

COSÌ FAN TUTTE

Complete recording. Glyndebourne Festival Opera
Company, conducted by Fritz Busch. Twenty 12"
records   VM-812/14
Overture
  BBC Symphony Orchestra, conducted by Sir
    Adrian Boult   V-11714 [12"]
  Berlin Philharmonic Orchestra, conducted by
    Hans Schmidt-Isserstedt   T-E2522 [12"]
"In uomini, in soldati"
  Lucrezia Bori (s)   (V-545 co) [10"]
"Come scoglio in moto resta"
  Ina Souez (s)   C-9104M [12"]
"Un aura amorosa"
  Julius Patzak (t, in German)   D-CA8196 [12"]
"Ei parte, senti" (recitative) and *"Per pietà, ben
mio"* (aria)
  Felicie Hüni-Mihacsek (s, in German)   D-CA8202 [12"]

DON GIOVANNI

Complete recording. Glyndebourne Festival Opera
Company, conducted by Fritz Busch. Twenty-three
12" records.   VM-423/5
Overture
  London Philharmonic Orchestra, conducted by
    Sir Thomas Beecham   C-70365D [12"]
"Madamina, il catalogo"
  Salvatore Baccaloni (bs)   C-71048D [12"]
  Gerhard Hüsch (b, in German)   D-20022 [10"]
  Fyodor Chaliapin (bs)   G-DA994 [10"]
"Là ci darem la mano"
  Margherita Perras (s) and Gerhard Hüsch (b) (in
    German)   V-4374 [10"]
  Erna Berger (s) and Heinrich Schlusnus (b) (in
    German)   D-DE7070 [10"]
  Emmy Bettendorf (s) and Gerhard Hüsch (b) (in
    German)   D-20010 [10"]
"Or, sai chi l'onore"
  Frida Leider (s)   G-DB1547 [12"]
  Margarete Baumer (s) and Walter Schupp (t) (in
    German)   D-20069 [10"]
  Lilli Lehmann (s)   (Odeon-50398/9 co)
"Dalla sua pace"
  Richard Tauber (t)   P-R20444 [12"]
  Tito Schipa (t)   V-1308 [10"]
  Beniamino Gigli (t)   V-15601 [12"]
"Finch 'han del vino"
  Ezio Pinza (bs)   V-1467 [10"]

"Batti, batti, o bel Masetto"
Elisabeth Schumann (s)   V-7076 [12″]
Lucrezia Bori (s)   V-14612 [12″]
Elisabeth Rethberg (s)   V-7472 [12″]
Minuet
Wanda Landowska (harpsichord)   V-1199 [10″]
"Deh, vieni alla finestra"
Ezio Pinza (bs)   V-1467 [10″]
"Vedrai, carino"
Lucrezia Bori (s)   V-1846 [10″]
Elisabeth Schumann (s)   G-DA845 [10″]
"Il mio tesoro"
John McCormack (t)   G-DB324 [12″]
Richard Tauber (t)   P-R20444 [12″]
Tito Schipa (t)   V-1308 [10″]
Beniamino Gigli (t)   V-15601 [12″]
"Mi tradi quell' alma ingrata"
Felicie Hüni-Mihacsek (s, in German)   D-CA8194 [12″]
"Non mi dir bell' idol mio"
Felicie Hüni-Mihacsek (s, in German)   D-CA8194 [12″]
Eidé Noréna (s, in French)   G-DB4959 [12″]
Lilli Lehmann (s), with piano (recorded in Berlin, 1905)   (Odeon-50098/9 co)

DIE ENTFÜHRUNG AUS DEM SERAIL

Overture
Berlin Philharmonic Orchestra, conducted by
Hans Schmidt-Isserstedt   T-E2522 [12″]
Dresden State Opera Orchestra, conducted by
Karl Böhm   G-DB4692 [12″]
"Hier soll ich dich denn sehen"
Peter Anders (t)   T-A1874 [10″]
"Wer ein Liebchen hat gefunden"
Alexander Kipnis (bs)   V-1738 [10″]
"Ach, ich liebte"
Margherita Perras (s)   G-DB4439 [12″]
Lilli Lehmann (s)   (Odeon-80008 co)
"Durch Zärtlichkeit"
Adele Kern (s)   D-CA8117 [12″]
"Welcher Kummer"
Margherita Perras (s)   V-12328 [12″]
"Martern aller Arten"
Lilli Lehmann (s) (recorded in Berlin, 1907) (Odeon-80005 co)
Margherita Perras (s)   G-DB4439 [12″]
Ria Ginster (s), with piano   G-DB1832 [12″]
Frieda Hempel (s, in Italian)   G-DB331 [12″]
"Vivat Bacchus"
Wilhelm Strienz (bs) and Walther Ludwig (t) G-EG6347 [10″]

"In Morgenland gefangen"
    Peter Anders (t)   T-A1874 [10″]
"Nie werd' ich dein Huld verkannen"
    Erna Berger (s), Adele Kern (s), Max Hirzel (t),
    Carl Jöken (t), and Edward Kandl (bs)   D-CA8169 [12″]

IDOMENEO, RÈ DI CRETA

"Zeffiretti lusinghieri"
    Vera Schwartz (s, in German)   D-20361 [10″]

LE NOZZE DI FIGARO

Complete recording. Glyndebourne Festival Opera
Company. Soloists, chorus, and orchestra, conducted
by Fritz Busch. Sixteen 12″ records (31 sides).   VM-313/5
Overture
    London Philharmonic Orchestra, conducted by
        Sir Thomas Beecham   C-69058D [12″]
    Saxon State Orchestra, conducted by Karl Böhm
                                        G-DB4692 [12″]
    Berlin Philharmonic Orchestra, conducted by
        Wilhelm Furtwängler   D-CA8187 [12″]
"Se vuol ballare"
    Gerhard Hüsch (b, in German)   D-20009 [10″]
    Giuseppe de Luca (b)   (V-596 co)
"La vendetta"
    Alexander Kipnis (bs) and Else Ruziczka (ms)
        (in German)   G-DB1551 [12″]
    Salvatore Baccaloni (bs)   C-71193D [12″]
"Non so più cosa son"
    Elisabeth Schumann (s)   V-1431 [10″]
"Non so più andrai"
    Gerhard Hüsch (b, in German)   D-20009 [10″]
    Ezio Pinza (bs)   V-18008 [12″]
"Porgi amor"
    Lilli Lehmann (s, in German)   P-P063 [10¾″]
    Elisabeth Rethberg (s, in German)   D-20047 [10″]
    Lotte Lehmann (s, in German)   D-25817 [12″]
    Tiana Lemnitz (s)   V-15178 [12″]
"Voi che sapete"
    Elisabeth Schumann (s)   V-7076 [12″]
    Ria Ginster (s)   V-7822 [12″]
"Crudel! perchè finora"
    Felicie Hüni-Mihacsek (s) and Willi Domgraf-
        Fassbaender (b) (in German)   D-CA8198 [12″]
    Geraldine Farrar (s) and Antonio Scotti (b)   G-DK118 [12″]
"Dove sono"
    Meta Seinemeyer (s, in German)   D-25071 [12″]
    Tiana Lemnitz (s)   V-15178 [12″]

"Sull' aria! Che soave zefiretto"
Erna Berger (s) and Viorica Ursuleac (s) (in German)   D-DE7070 [10"]
Emma Eames (s) and Marcella Sembrich (s)   G-DK121 [12"]
Lilli Lehmann (s) and Hedwig Helbig (s)   (Odeon-50357 co)
"Deh vieni, non tardar"
Lucrezia Bori (s)   V-14614 [12"]
Elisabeth Schumann (s)   G-DB1011 [12"]
Margherita Perras (s, in German)   G-DB4484 [12"]
Lotte Lehmann (s, in German)   D-20279 [10"]

IL RÈ PASTORE

"L'amerò, sarò costante"
Elisabeth Rethberg (s)   V-7472 [12"]
Elisabeth Schumann (s)   G-DB1011 [12"]
Gabrielle Ritter-Ciampi (s)   D-CA8092 [12"]
Nellie Melba (s) and Jan Kubelik (violin)   G-DK112 [12"]

DER SCHAUSPIELDIREKTOR

Overture
BBC Symphony Orchestra, conducted by Sir
Adrian Boult   G-DB1969 [12"]

DIE ZAUBERFLÖTE

Complete recording (except dialogue). Mozart Opera
Society. Soloists, chorus, and Berlin Philharmonic
Orchestra, conducted by Sir Thomas Beecham.
Nineteen 12" records (37 sides).   VM-541/2
Overture
BBC Symphony Orchestra, conducted by Arturo
Toscanini   V-15190 [12"]
Berlin Philharmonic Orchestra, conducted by
Hans Schmidt-Isserstedt   T-E2627 [12"]
Berlin State Opera House Orchestra, conducted
by Herbert von Karajan   D-LY6145 [12"]
"Zum Leiden bin ich auserkoren"
Frieda Hempel (s, in Italian)   G-DB331 [12"]
"Bei Männern"
Margherita Perras (s) and Gerhard Hüsch (b)   V-4374 [10"]
Emmy Bettendorf (s) and Gerhard Hüsch (b)   D-20010 [10"]
"O Isis und Osiris"
Alexander Kipnis (bs), with chorus and orchestra V-1738 [10"]
Ezio Pinza (bs, in Italian)   V-6642 [12"]
Oscar Natzke (bs)   P-E11423 [12"]
"Der hölle Rache"
Miliza Korjus (s)   V-11921 [12"]
Frieda Hempel (s)   G-DB365 [12"]
"In diesen heil'gen Hallen"
Alexander Kipnis (bs), with chorus and orchestra V-8684 [12"]

"Ach, ich fühls"
  Dorothy Maynor (s), with Boston Symphony Or-
    chestra, conducted by Serge Koussevitzky   V-15826 [12"]
  Lotte Lehmann (s)   D-20279 [10"]
  Lily Pons (s, in French)   V-8733 [12"]
                                            also D-29004 [12"]
  Emmy Destinn (s)   (V-88510 co) [12"]

CHAPTER VII

LUDWIG VAN BEETHOVEN
  FIDELIO
    Overture
      BBC Symphony Orchestra, conducted by Bruno
        Walter   V-11809 [12"]
      London Philharmonic Orchestra, conducted by
        Felix Weingartner   C-69545D [12"]
    "Mir ist wunderbar"
      Erna Berger (s), Henrietta Gottlieb (s), Marcel
        Wittrisch (t), and Willi Domgraf-Fassbaender
        (b)   G-DB4417 [12"]
    *"Abscheulicher, wo eilst du hin?" and "Komm,
      O Hoffnung"*
      Elisabeth Ohms (s)   D-CA8086 [12"]
      Frida Leider (s)   (V-7118 co) [12"]
      Kirsten Flagstad, with Philadelphia Orchestra,
        conducted by Eugene Ormandy   V-14972 [12"]
      Lotte Lehmann (s)   D-25803 [12"]
      Lilli Lehmann (s) (1-10" and 2-12").
                                    (Odeon 50356, 80006/7 co)
    "O welche Lust"
      Metropolitan Opera Chorus, conducted by Giulio
        Setti   V-11249 [12"]
    *"Gott! welch' Dunkel hier" and "In des Früh-
      lingstagen"*
      Franz Voelker (t)   D-LY6113 [12"]
      Helge Roswaenge (t)   G-DB4522 [12"]
      Eyvind Laholm (t)   D-20452 [10"]
    "Er sterbe, doch er soll erst wissen"
      Henrietta Gottlieb (s), Walther Ludwig (t), Willi
        Domgraf-Fassbaender (b), and Walther Gross-
        mann (bs)   G-DB4417 [12"]
    "Leonore" Overture No. 1
      BBC Symphony Orchestra, conducted by Arturo
        Toscanini   V-15945 [12"]
    "Leonore" Overture No. 2
      London Symphony Orchestra, conducted by Felix
        Weingartner. Two 12" records.   In CM-X96

NBC Symphony Orchestra, conducted by Arturo
Toscanini. Two 10″ records.   G-DA1753/4
"Leonore" Overture No. 3
Vienna Philharmonic Orchestra, conducted by
Bruno Walter. Two 12″ records.   In VM-359
NBC Symphony Orchestra, conducted by Arturo
Toscanini. Two 12″ records.   G-DB5703/4
Minneapolis Symphony Orchestra, conducted by
Dmitri Mitropoulos. Two 12″ records.   In CM-X173

CHAPTER VIII

Carl Maria von Weber

ABU HASSAN

Overture
Symphony Orchestra, conducted by Max von
Schillings   D-25099 [12″]

EURYANTHE

Overture
BBC Symphony Orchestra, conducted by Sir
Adrian Boult   V-12037 [12″]
Chicago Symphony Orchestra, conducted by Fred-
erick Stock   C-11179D [12″]

DER FREISCHÜTZ

Abridged recording. Soloists, with Berlin State Opera
Chorus and Orchestra, conducted by Hermann Wei-
gert. Four 12″ records.   D-CA8132/5
Overture
London Philharmonic Orchestra, conducted by Sir
Thomas Beecham   C-68986D [12″]
Boston "Pops" Orchestra, conducted by Arthur
Fiedler   V-12040 [12″]
Berlin Philharmonic Orchestra, conducted by
Wilhelm Furtwängler. Two 12″ records (3
sides).   D-CA8262/3
"Leise, leise, fromme Weise"
Tiana Lemnitz (s)   D-CA8233 [12″]
Lotte Lehmann (s)   D-29007 [12″]
Emmy Destinn (s)   (C-A5605 co) [12″]

OBERON

Overture
London Philharmonic Orchestra, conducted by
Sir Thomas Beecham   C-69410D [12″]
Boston "Pops" Orchestra, conducted by Arthur
Fiedler   V-12043 [12″]

"Ocean, thou mighty monster"
Kirsten Flagstad (s, in German), with Philadelphia
Orchestra, conducted by Eugene Ormandy V-15244 [12"]
Lotte Lehmann (s, in German) D-29014 [12"]
Gertrud Bindernagel (s, in German) T-SK1144 [12"]

PETER SCHMOLL UND SEIN NACHBARN

Overture
Vienna Philharmonic Orchestra, conducted by
Clemens Krauss V-11429 [12"]

HEINRICH MARSCHNER

HANS HEILING

"An jenem Tag"
Heinrich Schlusnus (b) PD-67191 [12"]

KARL OTTO NICOLAI

DIE LUSTIGEN WEIBER VON WINDSOR

Overture
London Philharmonic Orchestra, conducted by
Sir Thomas Beecham C-68938D [12"]
Boston "Pops" Orchestra, conducted by Arthur
Fiedler V-12533 [12"]
"Als Büblein klein"
Alexander Kipnis (bs) G-D2018 [12"]
Duo (sung by Frau Reich and Frau Fluth)
Erna Berger (s) and Charlotte Müller (s) G-EG2857 [10"]
"Horch, die Lerche"
Julius Patzak (t) PD-30014 [10"]
Walther Ludwig (t) G-EH1020 [12"]
"Nun eilt herbei"
Lotte Schöne (s) G-DB1562 [12"]
Felicie Hüni-Mihacsek (s) PD-66586 [12"]

GUSTAV ALBERT LORTZING

CZAR UND ZIMMERMANN

Overture
Berlin Philharmonic Orchestra, conducted by
Hans Schmidt-Isserstedt T-A2270 [10"]
"Sonst spielt' ich mit Szepter"
Karl Schmitt-Walter (b) T-E2465 [12"]

FRIEDRICH, FREIHERR VON FLOTOW

MARTHA (known chiefly, in Italian, as *Marta*)

Overture
Victor Symphony Orchestra, conducted by Rosario
Bourdon V-35916 [12"]

"Siam giunte, o giovanette" and *"Che vuol dir"*
Frances Alda (s), Enrico Caruso (t), Josephine
Jacoby (c), and Marcel Journet (bs)   G-DM100 [12″]
"Presto, presto! andiam" and *"Dormi pur"*
Frances Alda (s), Enrico Caruso (t), Josephine
Jacoby (c), and Marcel Journet (bs)   G-DM101 [12″]
"M'appari"
Jussi Bjoerling (t)   V-13790 [12″]
Enrico Caruso (t)   V-7720 [12″]
Beniamino Gigli (t)   V-7109 [12″]

CHAPTER IX

GIOACCHINO ANTONIO ROSSINI
IL BARBIERE DI SIVIGLIA
Complete recording. Soloists, chorus, and orchestra
of La Scala, conducted by Lorenzo Molajoli. Six-
teen 12″ records (31 sides).   CM-op8
Overture
New York Philharmonic-Symphony Orchestra,
conducted by Arturo Toscanini   V-7255 [12″]
Berlin Philharmonic Orchestra, conducted by
Wilhelm Furtwängler   D-CA8218 [12″]
"Ecco ridente in cielo"
Tito Schipa (t)   V-1180 [10″]
"Largo al factotum"
Lawrence Tibbett (b)   V-7353 [12″]
John Charles Thomas (b)   V-15860 [12″]
Giuseppe de Luca (b, recorded in 1907)   P-P0141 [10¾″]
"Se il mio nome saper"
Tito Schipa (t)   V-1180 [10″]
"Numero quindici a mano manca"
John McCormack (t) and Mario Sammarco (b) IRCC-96 [12″]
Bruno Landi (t) and Benvenuto Franci (b)   G-DB1433 [12″]
"Una voce poco fa" (2 sides)
Lily Pons (s)   V-8870 [12″]
Conchita Supervia (ms)   D-25833 [12″]
Frieda Hempel (s, in German)   G-DB455 [12″]
. . . Abbreviated versions
Luisa Tetrazzini (s)   V-7883 [12″]
Amelita Galli-Curci (s)   V-7110 [12″]
"La calunnia e un venticello" ("Calumny Song")
Fyodor Chaliapin (bs)   V-6783 [12″]
Oscar Natzke (bs)   P-E11423 [12″]
"Dunque io son"
Lily Pons (s) and Giuseppe de Luca (b)   V-17233 [12″]
"Un dottor' della mia sorte"
Salvatore Baccaloni (bs)   C-71193D [12″]

LA CENERENTOLA

Overture
Milan Symphony Orchestra, conducted by Lorenzo
    Molajoli   C-68729D [12″]
"*Signore, una parola*"
Conchita Supervia (ms) and V. Bettoni (bs)   D-25836 [12″]
"*Nacqui all' affano*" and "*Non più mesta*"
Conchita Supervia (ms)   D-25835 [12″]
"*Nacqui all'affano*" (only)
Rose Bampton (s)   V-18217 [12″]

LA GAZZA LADRA

Overture
London Philharmonic Orchestra, conducted by Sir
    Thomas Beecham   C-68301D [12″]
"*Di piacer me balza il cor*" and "*Deh! tu reggi
in tal momento*"
Lina Pagliughi (s)   P-E11267 [12″]

GUILLAUME TELL

Overture
London Philharmonic Orchestra, conducted by
    Sir Thomas Beecham. Two 12″ records (3 sides).   CM-X60
"*Ah! Mathilde, idole de mon âme*"
Giovanni Martinelli (t) and Marcel Journet (bs)
    (in Italian)   G-DK120 [12″]
"*Sombre forêt*"
Eidé Noréna (s)   D-20115 [10″]
Lina Pagliughi (s, in Italian)   P-E11406 [12″]
"*Quand l'Helvétie est un champ*"
Giovanni Martinelli (t), Giuseppe de Luca (b),
    and José Mardones (bs, in Italian)   G-DK120 [12″]
"*Asile héréditaire*"
Francesco Tamagno (t, in Italian), with piano (re-
    corded in 1903)   G-DR103 [10″]

L'ITALIANA IN ALGERI

Overture
New York Philharmonic-Symphony Orchestra, con-
    ducted by Arturo Toscanini   V-14161 [12″]
"*Al capriccio della sorte*"
Conchita Supervia (ms) and Scatolla (bs)   D-25838 [12″]
"*Oh, che muso*"
Conchita Supervia (ms) and Scatolla (bs)   D-25837 [12″]
"*Per lui che adoro*"
Conchita Supervia (ms), Nino Ederle (t), Scat-
    tola (bs), and Bettoni (bs)   D-25836 [12″]
"*Amici, in ogni evento*"
Conchita Supervia (ms)   D-20398 [10″]

MOSÈ IN EGITTO

"Dal tuo stellato soglio" (Prayer)
Ezio Pinza (bs) and Turchetti (s), with chorus   G-DB698 [12″]

LA SCALA DI SETA

Overture
London Philharmonic Orchestra, conducted by Sir
Thomas Beecham   C-9077M [12″]
BBC Symphony Orchestra, conducted by Arturo
Toscanini   V-15191 [12″]

SEMIRAMIDE

Overture
New York Philharmonic-Symphony Orchestra,
conducted by Arturo Toscanini. Two 12″ records.   VM-408
London Philharmonic Orchestra, conducted by
Sir Thomas Beecham. Two 12″ records (3 sides). C-LX884/5
"Ah! quel giorno"
Eleonora de Cisneros   IRCC-189 [12″]
"Bel raggio lusinghier"
Rose Bampton (s)   V-18217 [12″]
Marcella Sembrich (s)   (V-88141 co) [12″]
Luisa Tetrazzini (s)   (G-DB537 co) [12″]
Irene Abendroth (s)   IRCC-189 [12″]

LE SIÈGE DE CORINTHE

Overture
Milan Symphony Orchestra, conducted by Alber-
goni   D-25163 [12″]

IL SIGNOR BRUSCHINO

Overture
La Scala Orchestra, conducted by Gino Marinuzzi
                                           G-DB3209 [12″]

TANCREDI

Overture
Milan Symphony Orchestra, conducted by Alber-
goni   D-25087 [12″]

GIOVANNI PAISIELLO

IL BARBIERE DI SIVIGLIA

Overture
Boston "Pops" Orchestra, conducted by Arthur
Fiedler   V-12519 [12″]

CHAPTER X

Vincenzo Bellini

NORMA

Complete recording. Gina Cigna (s), Ebe Stignani
(ms), Tancredi Pasero (bs), and others, with EIAR
Chorus and Orchestra, conducted by Vittorio Gui.
Eighteen 12″ records.   Đ-25900/17

"Ite sul colle, o Druidi"
  Ezio Pinza (bs), with Metropolitan Chorus and
    Orchestra   G-DB2396 [12″]
"Casta diva"
  Dusolina Giannini (s), with La Scala Chorus and
    Orchestra   V-17503 [12″]
  Rosa Ponselle (s), with Metropolitan Chorus and
    Orchestra   V-8125 [12″]
  Celestina Boninsegna (s)   (C-A5197 co) [12″]
  Lilli Lehmann (s)   (Odeon-52698 co) [10½″]
"Mira, o Norma!"
  Rosa Ponselle (s) and Marion Telva (ms)   V-8110 [12″]
  Alma Gluck (s) and Louise Homer (c)   (V-89101 co) [12″]
"Ah! del Tebro al giogo indegno"
  Ezio Pinza (bs), with Metropolitan Chorus and
    Orchestra   (G-DA1108 or DA1412) [10″]

I PURITANI DI SCOZIA
"A te, o cara"
  Giacomo Lauri-Volpi (t)   (G-DB2396 or DB1438) [12″]
  Miguel Fleta (t)   (V-948 co) [12″]
"Son vergin vezzosa"
  Lina Pagliughi (s)   P-E11335 [12″]
  Amelita Galli-Curci (s)   (V-6432 co) [12″]
"Qui la voce sua soave"
  Lina Pagliughi (s)   P-E11335 [12″]
  Amelita Galli-Curci (s)   (V-6128 co) [12″]
  María Barrientos (s)   (C-49370 co) [12″]
"Vien diletto"
  Luisa Tetrazzini (s)   IRCC-116 [12″]
  María Barrientos (s)   (C-49371 co) [12″]
"Suoni la tromba"
  Pasquale Amato (b) and Marcel Journet (bs) G-DK110 [12″]
  Mario Ancona (b) and Marcel Journet (bs) (V-88500 co) [12″]

LA SONNAMBULA
"Come per me sereno" and *"Sovra il sen la man
mi posa"*

María Barrientos (s), with piano (recorded in
1906)   P-P076 [10½″]
. . . *"Come per me sereno"* only
Lina Pagliughi (s)   P-E11277 [12″]
"Prendi: l'anel ti dono"
Toti dal Monte (s) and Tito Schipa (t)   G-DA1351 [10″]
Maria Galvany (s) and Fernando de Lucia (t) IRCC-64 [12″]
"Vi ravviso, o luoghi ameni" and *"Tu non sai"*
Tancredi Pasero (bs)   P-E11357 [12″]
Pol Plançon (bs)   IRCC-49 [12½″]
Fyodor Chaliapin (bs)   G-DA962 [10″]
"Son geloso del zefiro"
Maria Galvany (s) and Fernando de Lucia (t) IRCC-104 [12″]
"Ah! non credea"
Toti dal Monte (s)   G-DB1317 [12″]
Lina Pagliughi (s)   P-E11328 [12″]
Claudia Muzio (s)   C-9105M [12″]
Amelita Galli-Curci (s)   (V-6125 co) [12″]
"Ah! non giunge"
Luisa Tetrazzini (s)   G-DB533 [12″]

GAËTANO DONIZETTI

DON PASQUALE

Complete recording. Ernesto Badini (bs), Tito Schipa
(t), Afro Poli (b), and Adelaide Saraceni (s), with La
Scala Chorus and Orchestra, conducted by Carlo
Sabajno. Fifteen 12″ records.   VM-187
"Sogno soave e casto"
Tito Schipa (t)   V-1282 [10″]
Giuseppe Anselmi (t)   P-P061 [10½″]
"Quel guardo il Cavaliere" and *"So anch' io la virtù"*
Amelita Galli-Curci (s)   (V-6128 co)
Lina Pagliughi (s)   P-E11303 [12″]
Rosina Storchio (s), with piano (recorded in 1906)
                                             P-P0121 [10½″]
"Pronto io son" and *"Vado corro"*
Lotte Schöne (s) and Willi Domgraf-Fassbaender
(b)   G-DB1546 [12″]
Lucrezia Bori (s) and Giuseppe de Luca (b)   G-DK102 [12″]
"Cheti, cheti"
Gaëtano Azzoloni (bs) and Guilio Fregosi (b) D-29019 [12″]
"Com'e gentil"
Luigi Fort (t)   C-4157M [10″]
Enrico Caruso (t), with piano   G-DB159 [12″]
"Tornami a dir che m'ami"
Amelita Galli-Curci (s) and Tito Schipa (t) V-1755 [10″]
Toti dal Monte (s) and Tito Schipa (t)   G-DA1351 [10″]

L'ELISIR D'AMORE

Abridged recording. Soloists, La Scala Chorus and
Orchestra, conducted by Lorenzo Molajoli. Six 12″
records.   C-GQX10093/8
"Quanto e bella!"
  Beniamino Gigli (t)   G-DA797 [10″]
"Adina, credimi"
  Tito Schipa (t)   G-DA1016 [10″]
"Venti scudi!"
  Enrico Caruso (t) and Giuseppe de Luca (b) G-DM107 [12″]
"Una furtiva lagrima"
  Tito Schipa (t)   V-6570 [12″]
  Beniamino Gigli (t)   V-7194 [12″]
"Prendi: per me sei libero"
  Lina Pagliughi (s)   P-E11395 [12″]

LA FAVORITE (known chiefly, in Italian, as *La Favorita*)

Abridged recording. Soloists, La Scala Chorus and
Orchestra, conducted by Lorenzo Molajoli. Five 12″
records.   C-GQX10064/8
"Una vergine, un angel di Dio"
  Tito Schipa (t)   G-DA1016 [10″]
  Antonio Cortis (t)   G-DA757 [10″]
"Vien Leonora"
  Mattia Battistini (b)   (V-6044 co) [12″]
"Ah! l'alto ardor"
  Margarete Matzenauer (ms) and Pasquale Amato
  (b)   G-DK101 [12″]
"A tanto amor"
  Giuseppe de Luca (b)   (V-6080 co) [12″]
  Mario Ancona (b)   IRCC-108 [12″]
"O mio Fernando"
  Sigrid Onegin (c)   V-7191 [12″]
  Ebe Stignani (c)   P-E11344 [12″]
  Margarete Matzenauer (c)   (V-88363 co) [12″]
"Splendon più belle in ciel"
  Ezio Pinza (bs), with Metropolitan Chorus and Or-
  chestra   V-7552 [12″]
"Spirto gentil"
  Enrico Caruso (t)   G-DB129 [12″]
  Giovanni Malipiero (t)   P-E11384 [12″]

LA FILLE DU RÉGIMENT

Overture
  Milan Symphony Orchestra   D-25082 [12″]
"Chacun le sait"
  Toti dal Monte (s, in Italian), with La Scala
  Chorus and Orchestra   G-DB1152 [12″]
  Lily Pons (s), with Metropolitan Opera Orchestra
                                             C-71248D [12″]

"Il faut partir"
Toti dal Monte (s, in Italian)   G-DB1040 [12"]
Lina Pagliughi (s, in Italian)   P-E11328 [12"]
Lily Pons (s), with Metropolitan Opera Orchestra
    C-71248D [12"]
"Par le rang et par l'opulence"
Ninon Vallin (s)   PAT-PG36 [10"]
Toti dal Monte (s, in Italian)   G-DB1152 [12"]
Tyrolienne
Erna Berger (s, in German)   PD-10329 [10"]
"Pour me rapprocher de Marie"
John McCormack (t, in Italian)   (V-74221 co) [12"]
"Et mon coeur va changer"
Lily Pons (s), with Metropolitan Opera Orchestra
    C-71249D [12"]
"Salut à France"
Ninon Vallin (s)   PAT-PG36 [10"]
Clara Clairbert (s)   PD-66921 [12"]
Lily Pons (s), with Metropolitan Opera Orchestra
    C-71249D [12"]

LINDA DI CHAMOUNIX

"Ambo nati ni questa valle"
Mattia Battistini (b)   G-DB204 [12"]
"O luce di quest' anima"
Toti dal Monte (s)   G-DB1318 [12"]
Amelita Galli-Curci (s)   (V-6357 co) [12"]
Romanza di Pierotto
Ebe Stignani (ms)   P-E11371 [12"]

LUCIA DI LAMMERMOOR

Complete recordings.
Lina Pagliughi (s), Giovanni Malipiero (t), Giuseppe Manacchini (b), and others, with EIAR Chorus and Symphony Orchestra, conducted by Ugo Tansini. Thirteen 12" records.   P-31

Mercedes Capsir (s), Enzo de Muro Lomanto (t), Enrico Molinari (b), and others, with La Scala Chorus and Orchestra, conducted by Lorenzo Molajoli. Thirteen 12" records.   C-Op. 20

"Regnava nel silenzio"
Toti dal Monte (s)   G-DB1040 [12"]
"Quando rapita in estasi"
Maria Gentile (s)   PD-10330 [10"]
Graziella Pareto (s)   (V-76009 co) [12"]
"Verranno a te sull-aure"
Amelita Galli-Curci (s)   G-DB811 [12"]

"Che mi frena in tal momento" (Sextet)

Mercedes Capsir (s), Giovanni Molinari (b), Ida Mannarini (s), Enzo de Muro Lomanto (t), Salvatore Baccaloni (bs), and Emilio Venturini (t), with La Scala Chorus and Orchestra — C-9145M [12"]

Amelita Galli-Curci (s), Louise Homer (c), Beniamino Gigli (t), Giuseppe de Luca (b), Ezio Pinza (bs), and Angelo Bada (t) — V-10012 [12"]

Marcella Sembrich (s), Gina Severina (c), Enrico Caruso (t), Antonio Scotti (b), Marcel Journet (bs), and Francesco Daddi (t) — G-DQ101 [12"]

Luisa Tetrazzini (s), Josephine Jacoby (ms), Enrico Caruso (t), Pasquale Amato (b), Marcel Journet (bs), and Angelo Bada (t) — G-2-054034 [12"]

Amelita Galli-Curci (s), Minnie Egener (c), Enrico Caruso (t), Giuseppe de Luca (b), Marcel Journet (bs), and Angelo Bada (t) — V-10000 [12"]

"Il dolce suono mi colpi," "Ardon gl'incensi," and *"Spargi d'amaro pianto"* (Mad Scene)

Toti dal Monte (s) — V-36285 [12"]
Lily Pons (s) — V-7369 [12"]
Lina Pagliughi (s) — D-25823 [12"]

. . . abridged versions

Nellie Melba (s) — V-18143 [12"]
Luisa Tetrazzini (s) — G-DB535 [12"]

"Fra poco a me ricovero"

Galliano Massini (t) — C-17159D [10"]
John McCormack (t) — (V-6196 co) [12"]

"Giusto cielo! rispondete" and *"Tu che a Dio spiegasti l'ali"*

Beniamino Gigli (t) and Ezio Pinza (bs), with Metropolitan Chorus and Orchestra — V-8096 [12"]

. . . part II only

John McCormack (t) — (V-6196 co) [12"]

LUCREZIA BORGIA

Brindisi: "Il segreto per essere felice"

Sigrid Onegin (c) — V-1367 [10"]
Margarete Matzenauer (c) — (V-999 co) [10"]
Ernestine Schumann-Heink (c) — (V-6278 co) [12"]

"Come e bello quale incanto"

Giannina Arangi-Lombardi (s) — C-9129M [12"]

"M'odi, ah! m'odi"

Giannina Arangi-Lombardi (s) — C-9129M [12"]

"Vieni la mia vendetta"

José Mardones (bs) — (V-6456 co) [12"]
Fyodor Chaliapin (bs) — (G-DB403 co) [12"]

MARIA DI ROHAN

"Bella e di sol vestita" and *"Voce fatal di morte"*

Mattia Battistini (b)   (G-DB147 co) [12″]

POLIUTO

"Di quai soavi lagrime"

Maria de Macchi (ms)   IRCC [10″] Special

CHAPTER XI

ANDRÉ-ERNESTE-MODESTE GRÉTRY

CÉPHALE ET PROCRIS

Ballet Suite (arranged by Felix Mottl)

Brussels Conservatory Orchestra, conducted by
Désiré Defauw   C-69002D [12″]

LA ROSIÈRE REPUBLICAINE

Ballet Suite

Paris Philharmonic Orchestra, conducted by Selmar
Meyrowitz. Two 10″ records.   C-17067/8D

ZÉMIRE ET AZOR

"La Fauvette"

Amelita Galli-Curci (s)   (V-6784 co) [12″]
Lily Pons (s)   V-2149 [10″]

ÉTIENNE-NICOLAS MÉHUL

ARIODANT

"Femme sensible"

André Bauge (b), with orchestra, conducted by
Godfrey Andolfi   C-P9155M [12″]

LE JEUNE HENRI

"La Chasse du jeune Henri" (entr'acte)

Lamoureux Orchestra, conducted by Albert Wolff
D-CA8146 [12″]

JOSEPH

"Vainement Pharaon"

Georges Thill (t)   C-4126M [10″]

"Champs paternels"

John McCormack (t)   G-DB634 [12″]

FRANÇOIS-ADRIEN BOÏELDIEU

LE CALIFE DE BAGDAD

Overture

Vienna Philharmonic Orchestra, conducted by
Paul Kerby   C-69056D [12″]

LA DAME BLANCHE

Overture
Paris Symphony Orchestra, conducted by François
Ruhlmann   C-P69599D [12″]
"Ah! quel plaisir d'être soldat"
André d'Arkor (t)   C-RFX26 [12″]
"Viens, gentille dame"
André d'Arkor (t)   C-RFX26 [12″]

Louis-Joseph-Ferdinand Hérold

LE PRÉ AUX CLERCS

"Jours de mon enfance"
Eva Gauthier (ms)   IRCC-105 [10″]

ZAMPA

Overture
Symphony Orchestra, conducted by Georg Szell D-25172 [12″]

Daniel-François-Esprit Auber

LE CHEVAL DE BRONZE

Overture
London Philharmonic Orchestra, conducted by
Constant Lambert   V-12511 [12″]

LES DIAMANTS DE LA COURONNE

Overture
London Philharmonic Orchestra, conducted by
Constant Lambert   V-12806 [12″]

FRA DIAVOLO

Overture
London Philharmonic Orchestra, conducted by
Constant Lambert   G-C3084 [12″]
Victor Symphony Orchestra, conducted by Rosario
Bourdon   V-22008 [10″]
"Quel bonheur"
Margherita Salvi (s, in Italian)   P-E10817 [12″]
Lina Pagliughi (s, in Italian)   P-E11277 [12″]
Erna Berger (s, in German)   PD-10285 [10″]
"Pour toujours disait-elle je suis à toi"
Helge Roswaenge (t, in German)   G-DA4414 [10″]

LA MUETTE DE PORTICI (MASANIELLO)

Overture
BBC Symphony Orchestra, conducted by Sir
Adrian Boult   V-11838 [12″]
Paris Symphony Orchestra, conducted by Victor
Alex   D-25127 [12″]
Barcarolle
Wilhelm Strienz (bs, in German)   G-EH1093 [12″]

Jacques-François-Fromental-Élie Halévy
L'ÉCLAIR
"Call me thine own"
    Mabel Garrison (s, in English)   (V-74612 co) [12″]

Adolphe Adam
LE POSTILLON DE LONGJUMEAU
"Mes amis, écoutez l'histoire"
    Herbert Ernst Groh (t, in German)   D-20001 [10″]
    Peter Anders (t, in German)   T-A1901 [10″]
    Miguel Villabella (t)   PAT-PG27 [10″]
    Kolomon von Pataky (t, in German) ·   PD-66648 [12″]
"Je vais le revoir"
    Felicie Hüni-Mihacsek (s, in German)   PD-66616[12″]
Romance du Postillon
    Miguel Villabella (t)   PAT-PG27 [10″]

Jacques Offenbach
LES CONTES DE HOFFMANN
Legende de Kleinzach: "Il etait une fois"
    Richard Tauber (t, in German)   D-25758 [12″]
"Les oiseaux dans la charmille"
    Mabel Garrison (s)   (V-6135 co) [12″]
    Lily Pons (s)   D-23016 [10″]
    Miliza Korjus (s, in German)   V-11921 [12″]
"Belle nuit, o nuit d'amour" (Barcarolle)
    Ninon Vallin (s) and Madeleine Sibille (s)   PAT-X90058 [10″]
    Emmy Bettendorf (s) and Karin Branzell (c) (in
       German)   D-25115 [12″]
    Elisabeth Schumann (s, duet with self, in English)
                                  G-DB3641 [12″]
    Felicie Hüni-Mihacsek (s) and Willi Domgraf-
       Fassbaender (b) (in German)   D-CA8057 [12″]
    Alma Gluck (s) and Louise Homer (c)   (V-3010 co) [10″]
    Lucrezia Bori (s) and Lawrence Tibbett (b) (in
       English)   V-1747 [10″]
"O Dieux, de quelle ivresse"
    Miguel Villabella (t)   O-188598 [10″]
    Richard Tauber (t, in German)   D-25758 [12″]
"Elle a fui, la tourterelle"
    Lucrezia Bori (s)   (V-6049 co) [12″]
    Germaine Feraldy (s)   C-LF122 [10″]
    Ninon Vallin (s)   PAT-X90082 [12″]
"C'est une chanson d'amour" and *"J'ai le bon-*
    heur dans l'ame"
    Hedwig von Debicka (s) and Helge Roswaenge
       (t) (in German)   D-CA8057 [12″]

Emmy Bettendorf (s) and Herbert Ernst Groh (t)
(in German)   D-20000 [10″]

GAÎTÉ PARISIENNE (arranged by Manuel Rosenthal)

London Philharmonic Orchestra, conducted by
Efrem Kurtz. Two 12″ records.   CM-X115

CHAPTER XII

MARIA LUIGI CARLO ZENOBIO SALVATORE CHERUBINI

LES ABENCÉRAGES

"Suspendez à ces murs"
Georges Thill (t)   C-LFX274 [12″]

ANACREON

Overture
Concertgebouw Orchestra, conducted by Willem
Mengelberg. Two 12″ records.   D-25234/5

MÉDÉE

Overture
Milan Symphony Orchestra, conducted by Lorenzo
Molajoli   C-68779D [12″]

GASPARO LUIGI PACIFICO SPONTINI

LA VESTALE

"Tu che invoco" and *"O nume tutelar"*
Rosa Ponselle (s)   G-DB1274 [12″]

CHAPTER XIII

HECTOR BERLIOZ

BÉATRICE ET BÉNÉDICT

Overture
London Philharmonic Orchestra, conducted by
Sir Hamilton Harty   C-68342D [12″]

BENVENUTO CELLINI

Overture
Berlin Philharmonic Orchestra, conducted by
Artur Bodanzky   D-25355/6 [12″]
Paris Symphony Orchestra, conducted by Pierre
Monteux   V-11140/1 [12″]

Carnaval Romain
London Philharmonic Orchestra, conducted by Sir
Thomas Beecham   C-68921D [12″]

Boston "Pops" Orchestra, conducted by Arthur
Fiedler   V-12135 [12"]

LA DAMNATION DE FAUST

Complete recording. Mireille Berthon (s), José de
Trevi (t), Charles Panzéra (b), Louis Morturier
(bs), with chorus and orchestra, conducted by Piero
Coppola. Ten 12" records.   (GM-154)

Ballet Music: *Rakóczy March; Danse des sylphes;
Menuet des feux-follets;* Presto. London Philhar-
monic Orchestra, conducted by Sir Thomas
Beecham. Two 12" records.   CM-X94
"D'amour l'ardente flamme"
Yvonne Gall (s)   C-9117M [12"]

LES FRANCS-JUGES

Overture
BBC Symphony Orchestra, conducted by Sir
Adrian Boult. Two 12" records (3 sides).
                              V-13674/5 in VM-803

LES TROYENS À CARTHAGE

Overture
Paris Symphony Orchestra, conducted by Pierre
Monteux   V-11141 [12"]
"Chasse royale et orage"
Hallé Orchestra, conducted by Sir Hamilton Harty
                                            C-68043D [12"]
"Inutiles regrets"
Georges Thill (t), with chorus and orchestra C-9098M [12"]

CHAPTER XIV.

GIACOMO MEYERBEER
L'AFRICAINE

"Adieu, mon doux rivage"
Elisabeth Rethberg (s, in German)   D-20200 [10"]
"Sur mes genoux"
Margarete Matzenauer (ms, in Italian)   IRCC-120 [12"]
"Hola! matelots"
Titta Ruffo (b, in Italian)   (V-817 co) [10"]
"Adamastor, roi des vagues"
Titta Ruffo (b, in Italian)   V-7153 [12"]
"O Paradis"
Jussi Bjoerling (t, in Italian)   V-12150 [12"]
Enrico Caruso (t, in Italian)   V-14234 [12"]
Beniamino Gigli (t, in Italian)   V-7109 [12"]

"Conduisez-moi"
    Enrico Caruso (t, in Italian)   G-DB1386 [12″]

L'ÉTOILE DU NORD

"Je veux veiller sur vous"
    Amelita Galli-Curci (s)   (V-74748 co) [12″]
"O jours heureux"
    Pol Plançon (bs)   IRCC-81 [12″]
"Là, là, là, air chéri"
    Amelita Galli-Curci (s)   V-7655 [12″]
    Selma Kurz (s)   G-DB684 [12″]

LES HUGUENOTS

"Plus blanche que la blanche hermine"
    André d'Arkor (t)   C-RFX22 [12″]
    Enrico Caruso (t, in Italian)   G-DB115 [12″]
"Piff, paff"
    Louis Morturier (bs)   G-P733 [10″]
    Marcel Journet (bs)   G-DB307 [12″]
"Nobles seigneurs, salut!" and *"Une Dame noble et sage"*
    Sigrid Onegin (c)   V-7146 [12″]
    Margarete Matzenauer (c)   (V-6471 co) [12″]
"O beau pays de la Touraine"
    Clara Clairbert (s)   PD-66920 [12″]
    Frieda Hempel (s)   G-DB276 [12″]
    Eidé Noréna (s)   (C-7302M co) [12″]
    Lilli Lehmann (s, in German)   IRCC-37 [10″]
Conjuration: "Des troubles renaissants" and *"Bénédiction des poignards"*
    André Pernet (b), Doniau-Blanc (s), Deleu, and Bussonet, with chorus and orchestra, conducted by Bigot   G-DB5044 [12″]
    Marcel Journet (bs), with chorus   (V-6173 co) [12″]

LE PARDON DE PLOËRMEL (DINORAH)

"Dors, petites, dors tranquille"
    Amelita Galli-Curci (s)   (G-6469 co) [12″]
"Ombre légère"
    Vina Bovy (s)   G-DB4997 [12″]
    Amelita Galli-Curci (s, in Italian)   V-1174 [10″]
"Ah! mon remords te venge"
    Mario Ancona (b, in Italian)   IRCC-108 [12″]

LE PROPHÈTE

"Pour Berthe moi je soupir"
    Francesco Tamagno (t, in Italian), with piano   G-DR104 [10″]
"Ah! mon fils"
    Sigrid Onegin (c)   V-6803 [12″]

Margarete Matzenauer (c)   V-36287 [12"]
Ernestine Schumann-Heink (c)   (V-6279 co) [12"]
Prelude: Quadrille (Skating Scene), Act III
    Sadler's Wells Orchestra, conducted by Constant
        Lambert   V-36238 [12"]
Marche du couronnement
    New York Philharmonic-Symphony Orchestra, con-
        ducted by Willem Mengelberg   V-7104 [12"]
    London Philharmonic Orchestra, conducted by
        Constant Lambert   G-C3112 [12"]
"Roi du ciel"
    Charles Dalmorès (t)   IRCC-131 [10"]
    Francesco Tamagno (t, in Italian), with piano G-DR104 [10"]
"O prêtres de Baal"
    Sigrid Onegin (c)   V-7146 [12"]
    Ernestine Schumann-Heink (c)   IRCC-93 [12"]
. . . *"O toi qui m'abandonnes"* (Part II)
    Louise Homer (c), with piano   IRCC-103 [12"]
    Ernestine Schumann-Heink (c)   (V-6279 co) [12"]

ROBERT LE DIABLE
"Valse infernale"
    Marcel Journet (bs), with chorus   (V-6176 co) [12"]
Romance of Alice
    Emmy Destinn (s, in German)   IRCC (Odeon Special) [10½"]
"Nonnes, qui reposez"
    Ezio Pinza (bs, in Italian)   G-DB1088 [12"]
    Fyodor Chaliapin (bs, in Italian)   G-DB106 [12"]
    Pol Plançon (bs)   (V-6371 co) [12"]
"Ah l'honnête homme" and *"Le bonheur est
    dans l'inconstance"*
    Edmond Clément (t) and Marcel Journet (bs) IRCC-138 [12"]
"Robert, toi que j'aime"
    Frieda Hempel (s)   (G-DB297 co) [12"]
    Carolina White (s, in Italian)   (C-A5353 co) [12"]
    Margarete Matzenauer (ms, in Italian)   (V-88365 co) [12"]
Gnadenarie
    Lilli Lehmann (s, in German)   (Odeon 80009 co) [12"]

JACQUES-FROMENTAL-ÉLIE HALÉVY
LA JUIVE
"Si la rigueur et la vengeance"
    Ezio Pinza (bs)   (V-1246 co) [10"]
    Michael Bohnen (bs, in German)   D-25810 [12"]
"O Dieu, Dieu de nos pères"
    Giovanni Martinelli (t), with Metropolitan Chorus
        and Orchestra   (V-8165 co) [12"]

"Dieu que ma voix tremblante"
    Giovanni Martinelli (t)   (V-6545 co) [12″]
"Vous qui du Dieu vivant"
    Ezio Pinza (bs)   (V-1246 co) [10″]
"Rachel! quand du Seigneur"
    José de Trevi (t)   PAT-X90044 [12″]
    Giovanni Martinelli (t)   (V-6545 co) [12″]
    Enrico Caruso (t)   G-DB123 [12″]

CHAPTER XV

RICHARD WAGNER

DIE FEEN

Overture
    London Symphony Orchestra, conducted by Albert Coates   V-36321 [12″]

DAS LIEBESVERBOT

Overture
    Berlin State Opera Orchestra, conducted by Alois Melichar   PD-27296 [12″]

DER FLIEGENDE HOLLÄNDER

Overture
    London Philharmonic Orchestra, conducted by Sir Thomas Beecham. Two 12″ records (3 sides). CM-X-107
Steuermannslied: "Mit Gewitter und Sturm"
    Lauritz Melchior (t), with chorus and orchestra, conducted by Edwin McArthur   V-17725 [12″]
"Die Frist ist um" (Recitative) and *"Wie oft in Meers tiefsten Schlund"*
    Friedrich Schorr (b) with Berlin State Opera Orchestra, conducted by Leo Blech   G-DB1813 [12″]
Spinning Chorus
    Nellie Walker (c) and Royal (Covent Garden) Opera Chorus and Orchestra, conducted by John Barbirolli   V-7117 [12″]
"Jo-ho-hoe! Traft ihr das Schiff"
    Emmy Bettendorf (s) with chorus and orchestra, conducted by Edouard Mörike   D-25075 [12″]
    Elisabeth Rethberg (s)   G-DA1115 [10″]
    Florence Austral (s) with Royal (Covent Garden) Opera Orchestra and Chorus, conducted by John Barbirolli   V-7117 [12″]
"Wie aus der Ferne"
    Friedrich Schorr (b)   G-DB1355 [12″]
"Versank ich jetzt in wunderbares Träumen"
    Elisabeth Ohms (s) and Theodor Scheidl (b)   D-CA8150 [12″]

LOHENGRIN

Prelude to Act I

New York Philharmonic-Symphony Orchestra, conducted by Arturo Toscanini   V-14006 [12"]

"Einsam in trüben Tagen"

Tiana Lemnitz (s)   D-LY6144 [12"]
Kirsten Flagstad (s)   V-14181 [12"]
Helen Traubel (s)   V-16345 [12"]
Elisabeth Rethberg (s)   V-6831 [12"]

"Mein Herr und Gott"

Josef Manowarda (bs), J. Prohaska (b), F. Voelker
(t), Maria Müller (s) and M. Klose (c) with Bayreuth Festival Chorus and Orchestra, conducted
by Heinz Tietjen   T-SKB2050 [12"]

"Euch lüften, die mein Klagen"

Tiana Lemnitz (s)   D-LY6144 [12"]
Kirsten Flagstad (s) with Philadelphia Orchestra,
conducted by Eugene Ormandy   V-1901 [10"]

"Ortrud, wo bist du?"

Emmy Bettendorf (s) and Karin Branzell (c)   D-25051 [12"]

Bridal Chamber Scene

Kirsten Flagstad (s) and Lauritz Melchior (t),
with Philadelphia Orchestra, conducted by
Edwin McArthur

. . . Abridged version

Tiana Lemnitz (s) and Torsten Ralf (t), with
Berlin State Opera Orchestra, conducted by
Bruno Seidler-Winkler   G-DB4667 [12"]

"In fernem Land"

Lauritz Melchior (t) with Philadelphia Orchestra,
conducted by Eugene Ormandy   V-17726 [12"]

"Mein lieber Schwan"

Lauritz Melchior (t) with Philadelphia Orchestra,
conducted by Eugene Ormandy   V-15213 [12"]

DIE MEISTERSINGER

Act III—Complete Recording. Hans Hermann Nissen
(Hans Sachs); Sven Nilsson (Pogner); Eugen Fuchs
(Beckmesser); Torsten Ralf (Walter); Martin Kremer
(David); Margaret Teschemacher (Eva); Lene Jung
(Magdelena), with Chorus of the Dresden State Opera
and the Saxon State Orchestra, conducted by Karl
Böhm. Fifteen 12" records.   VM-537/8

Overture

London Philharmonic Orchestra, conducted by Sir
Thomas Beecham   C-68854D [12"]
Berlin State Opera Orchestra, conducted by Karl
Muck. Two 12" records (3 sides).   V-6858/9

Pittsburgh Symphony Orchestra, conducted by
Fritz Reiner   C-11580D [12″]
*Kirchenchor: "Da zu dir Heiland kamm"; "Wach'
auf!"; Preislied.*
Torsten Ralf (t), Rudolf Bockelmann (b), Tiana
Lemnitz (s), with Messrs. Jones, Worthington,
Devereux, Sale, Lloyd, Hitchin, Horsman and
Woodhouse, with Royal (Covent Garden) Opera
Chorus and Orchestra, conducted by Sir Thomas
Beecham. Two 12″ records (Recorded at actual
performance in 1936).   CM-X87
"Das schöne Fest, Johannistag"
Alexander Kipnis (bs)   V-7894 [12″]
"Am stillen Herd"
Lauritz Melchior (t) with Philadelphia Orchestra,
conducted by Eugene Ormandy   V-17728 [12″]
"Gut'n abend, Meister"
Göta Ljungberg (s) and Friedrich Schorr (b)   V-7680 [12″]
"Jerum! Jerum!"
Friedrich Schorr (b)   V-7426 [12″]
"Wahn! Wahn! überall Wahn"
Friedrich Schorr (b)   V-7319 [12″]
"Sieh' Ev'chen! Dächt' ich doch"
Elisabeth Rethberg (s) and Friedrich Schorr (b)   V-8195 [12″]
Quintet: *"Selig, wie die Sonne"*
Elisabeth Schumann (s), Gladys Parr (c); Friedrich
Schorr (b); Lauritz Melchior (t) and Ben Wil-
liams (t)   V-7682 [12″]
"Euch macht ihr's leicht"
Friedrich Schorr (b)   V-7682 [12″]
Preislied: "Morgenlich leuchtend im rosigen Schein"
Torsten Ralf (t) (see excerpts conducted by Sir
Thomas Beecham)
Lauritz Melchior (t), with Philadelphia Orchestra,
conducted by Eugene Ormandy   V-17728 [12″]
Charles Kullman (t)   C-9146M [12″]
"Verachtet mir die Meister nicht"
Friedrich Schorr (b)   V-9285 [12″]

PARSIFAL

Excerpts: Flower Maidens' Scene; Good Friday
Music; Grail Scene; Transformation Scene, and
Prelude to Act III. Fritz Wolff (t), Alexander Kipnis
(bs), with Bayreuth Festival Orchestra, conducted by
Karl Muck. Eight 12″ records.   CM-337

Act III—Complete recording except for scene be-
tween Kundry and Gurnemanz. Gotthelf Pistor
(Parsifal); Ludwig Hoffmann (Gurnemanz); and
Cornelius Bronsgeest (Amfortas) with chorus and

orchestra of the Berlin State Opera, conducted by
Karl Muck. Eight 12″ records.   VM-67

Prelude to Act I and Good Friday Music
  Berlin Philharmonic Orchestra, conducted by Wil-
  helm Furtwängler. Three 12″ records.   VM-514
  Philadelphia Orchestra, conducted by Leopold
  Stokowski. Four 12″ records.   VM-421

Scene between Kundry and Parsifal, Act II
  Kirsten Flagstad (s), Lauritz Melchior (t) and
  Gordon Dillworth (b), with Victor Symphony
  Orchestra, conducted by Edwin McArthur. Four
  12″ records (7 sides)   VM-756

. . . *"Ich sah' das Kind"* (only)
  Frida Leider (s), with orchestra, conducted by Al-
  bert Coates   V-7523 [12″]
  Kerstin Thorborg (c), with Victor Symphony Or-
  chestra, conducted by Bruno Reibold   V-17223 [12″]
  Margarete Matzenauer (ms)   (V-6327 co) [12″]
. . . *"Amfortas! die Wunde!"* (only)
  Lauritz Melchior (t), with Philadelphia Orchestra,
  conducted by Eugene Ormandy   V-15212 [12″]
. . . *"Nur eine Waffe taugt"*
  Lauritz Melchior (t), with Philadelphia Orchestra,
  conducted by Eugene Ormandy   V-17213 [12″]

RIENZI

Overture
  Paris Conservatory Orchestra, conducted by Felix
  Weingartner. Two 12″ records (3 sides).   CM-X169
  Boston "Pops" Orchestra, conducted by Arthur
  Fiedler. Two 12″ records (3 sides).   VM-569
"Gerechter Gott!"
  Ernestine Schumann-Heink (c)   IRCC-31 [12″]
"Allmacht'ger Vater, blich' herab"
  Lauritz Melchior (t)   G-D2057 [12″]

DER RING DES NIBELUNGEN
DAS RHEINGOLD

Excerpts (arranged by Leopold Stokowski)
  Philadelphia Orchestra, conducted by Leopold
  Stokowski. Three 12″ records.   VM-179
Prelude
  London Symphony Orchestra, conducted by Al-
  bert Coates   V-9163 [12″]
Alberich steals the gold
  Arthur Fear, Edna Trenton, Elsie Suddaby, Nellie
  Walker and London Symphony Orchestra, con-
  ducted by Albert Coates   G-DB1546 [12″]

Wotan and Loge descend into Nibelheim
Walter Widdop, Arthur Fry, Howard Fear, with
London Symphony Orchestra, conducted by Al-
bert Coates   G-DB1546 [12"]
Erdas Warnung: "Weiche, Wotan, weiche!"
Kerstin Thorborg (c) and orchestra, conducted by
Bruno Reibold   V-17221 [12"]
Ernestine Schumann-Heink (c)   V-7107 [12"]
"Abendlich strahlt der Sonne Auge"
Freidrich Schorr (b), with soloists and Berlin State
Opera Orchestra, conducted by Leo Blech   V-6788 [12"]
Hans Hermann Nissen (b), with German Opera
House Orchestra, conducted by Bruno Seidler-
Winkler   G-DA4460 [10"]
. . . Orchestra (only)
Berlin Philharmonic Orchestra, conducted by Hans
Schmidt-Isserstedt   T-E2783 [12"]
London Symphony Orchestra, conducted by Al-
bert Coates   V-9109 [12"]

DIE WALKÜRE

Act I—Complete Recording: Lotte Lehmann (Sieglinde), Lauritz Melchior (Siegmund), Emanuel List
(Hunding), with Vienna Philharmonic Orchestra,
conducted by Bruno Walter. Eight 12" records.   VM-298

Act II—Complete Recording: Lotte Lehmann (Sieg-
linde), Marta Fuchs (Brünnhilde), Margarete Klose
(Fricka), Lauritz Melchior (Siegmund), Hans Hotter
(Wotan), Ela Flesch (Brünnhilde), Alfred Jerger
(Wotan), Emanuel List (Hunding), with Berlin State
Opera Orchestra, conducted by Bruno Seidler-
Winkler, and Vienna Philharmonic Orchestra, con-
ducted by Bruno Walter. Ten 12" records.   VM-582

"Winterstürme wichen"
Lauritz Melchior (t), with Philadelphia Orchestra,
conducted by Eugene Ormandy   V-2035 [10"]
"Ho-jo-to-ho"
Kirsten Flagstad (s)   V-1726 [10"]
"Der alte sturm, die alte Müh!"
Emmi Leisner (c) and Friedrich Schorr (b). Two
12" records.   V-7742/3

Ride of the Walküre
Berlin Philharmonic Orchestra, conducted by Hans
Schmidt-Isserstedt   T-E2746 [12"]
Brünnhildes Bitte: "War es so schmälich?"
Marta Fuchs (s), with Berlin State Opera Orches-
tra, conducted by Bruno Seidler-Winkler   G-DB4555 [12"]

Wotans Abschied and *Feuerzauber*
Wilhelm Rode (b). Two 12" records.   D-LY6169/70
. . . *Abschied* (only)
Friedrich Schorr (b), with London Symphony Or-
chestra   V-9177 [12"]
Rudolph Böckelmann (b), with Berlin State Opera
Orchestra   G-C2179 [12"]
. . . *Magic Fire Music* (only)
Philadelphia Orchestra, conducted by Leopold
Stokowski   V-15800 [12"]
London Symphony Orchestra, conducted by Al-
bert Coates   G-DB1797 [12"]

SIEGFRIED

Excerpts: Lauritz Melchior, and Rudolf Laubenthal
(Siegfried), Albert Reiss (Mime), Emil Schipper and
Rudolph Böckelmann (The Wanderer), Maria Ol-
szewska (Erda), Frida Leider (Brünnhilde), Nora
Grünebaum (Wood-Bird), with London Symphony
Orchestra, conducted by Albert Coates; Vienna State
Opera Orchestra, conducted by Robert Heger and
Karl Alwin, and Berlin State Opera Orchestra, con-
ducted by Leo Blech. Ten 12" records.   VM-83

Acts I & II—Excerpts: Lauritz Melchior, Friedrich
Schorr, Eduard Habich and Heinrich Tessmer, with
London Symphony Orchestra, conducted by Robert
Heger. Six 12" records.   VM-161

Act III—Final Scene: Florence Easton (Brünnhilde),
Lauritz Melchior (Siegfried), with London Symphony Orchestra, conducted by Robert Heger. Four
12" records (7 sides) (Includes Prelude to Act I).   VM-167

Waldweben—Concert Version
New York Philharmonic-Symphony Orchestra, con-
ducted by Willem Mengelberg   V-7192 [12"]

DIE GÖTTERDÄMMERUNG

Excerpts
Famous artists, with the London Symphony and
Berlin State Opera Orchestras, conducted by Al-
bert Coates, Lawrence Collingwood, and Leo
Blech. Sixteen 12" records.   VM-60

"Zu neuen Thaten"
Kirsten Flagstad (s) and Lauritz Melchior (t), with
San Francisco Opera Orchestra, conducted by
Edwin McArthur   V-17729 [12"]
Waltraute's Narrative
Kerstin Thorborg (c), with Victory Symphony Or-
chestra, conducted by Karl Reidel   V-17222 [12"]
Ernestine Schumann-Heink (c)   V-7107 [12"]

Hagen's Watch
Ludwig Weber (bs), with London Philharmonic
Orchestra, conducted by Sir Thomas Beecham C-69048 [12″]
Hagens Ruf: "Hoi-ho!"
Ludwig Weber (bs), Herbert Janssen (b), with
Royal Opera (Covent Garden) Chorus and Lon-
don Philharmonic Orchestra, conducted by Sir
Thomas Beecham. Two 12″ records (3 sides).   CM-X83
Siegfrieds Tod
Berlin Philharmonic Orchestra, conducted by Wil-
helm Furtwängler   D-CA8173 [12″]
Berlin State Opera Orchestra, conducted by Karl
Muck   V-6860 [12″]
Brünnhilde's Immolation Scene
Frida Leider (s), with Berlin State Opera Orches-
tra, conducted by Leo Blech. Two 12″ records
(3 sides).   G-D2025/6
Kirsten Flagstad (s), with San Francisco Opera Or-
chestra, conducted by Edwin McArthur. Two
12″ records.   V-15841/2

TANNHÄUSER

Slightly abridged recording, made during Bay-
reuth Festival of 1930.
S. Pilinsky (Tannhäuser), Maria Müller (Elisa-
beth), Ivar Andresen (Landgrave), Herbert Jans-
sen (Wolfram), R. Jost-Arden (Venus), and others,
with chorus and orchestra, conducted by Carl
Elmendorff. Eighteen 12″ records.   CM-154
Overture and Venusberg Music (Paris version)
and Prelude to Act III.
Philadelphia Orchestra, conducted by Leopold
Stokowski. Five 12″ records (9 sides).   VM-530
Overture
London Philharmonic Orchestra, conducted by Sir
Thomas Beecham. Two 12″ records.   CM-X123
Bacchanale
London Symphony Orchestra, conducted by Al-
bert Coates. Two 12″ records (3 sides).   V-36345/6
"Dir töne Lob!"
Lauritz Melchior (t), with Victor Symphony Or-
chestra, conducted by Edwin McArthur   V-17726 [12″]
"Dich, teure Halle"
Helen Traubel (s), with Victor Symphony Orches-
tra, conducted by Charles O'Connell   V-17268 [12″]
Kirsten Flagstad (s), with orchestra, conducted by
Hans Lange   V-14181 [12″]

Johanna Gadski (s)   V-18142 [12″]
Olive Fremstad (s)   IRCC-12 [12″]
Prelude to Act III
Paris Conservatory Orchestra, conducted by Felix
    Weingartner   C-69793 [12″]
Elisabeths Gebet: "Allmächt'ger Jungfrau"
Kirsten Flagstad (s), with orchestra, conducted by
    Hans Lange   V-8920 [12″]
Tiana Lemnitz (s)   D-CA8243 [12″]
Geraldine Farrar (s)   (V-88053 co) [12″]
"O du mein holder Abendstern"
Lawrence Tibbett (b)   V-8452 [12″]
Gerhard Hüsch (b)   G-DB4049 [12″]
Friedrich Schorr (b)   G-D1355 [12″]
Rome Narration: *"Inbrunst in Herzen"*
Lauritz Melchior (t), with Victor Symphony Or-
    chestra   V-17727 [12″]

TRISTAN UND ISOLDE

Abridged recording, made during Bayreuth Festival of 1928.

> Nanny Larsen-Todsen (Isolde), G. Graarud (Tris-
> tan), Anny Helm (Brangäne), R. Bockelmann
> (Kurwenal), Ivar Andresen (King Mark), and
> others, with Bayreuth Festival Chorus and Or-
> chestra, conducted by Carl Elmendorff. Nineteen
> 12″ records.   CM-101

Act III. Abridged recording

> Göta Ljungberg, Widdop, Guszalewicz, Fry,
> Habich, with orchestras conducted by Albert
> Coates, Lawrence Collingwood, and Leo Blech.
> Five 12″ records.   VM-41

Prelude and *Liebestod*

> Berlin Philharmonic Orchestra, conducted by Wil-
> helm Furtwängler. Two 12″ records.   VM-653

Love Duet: *"Isolde! Tristan! Geliebter"*

> Frida Leider (s) and Lauritz Melchior (t). Two 12″
> records.   V-7223/4
> Kirsten Flagstad (s) and Lauritz Melchior (t), with
> San Francisco Opera Orchestra, conducted by
> Edwin McArthur. Two 12″ records.   V-16238/9

"Einsam wachend"

> Kerstin Thorborg (c), with Victor Symphony Or-
> chestra, conducted by Karl Reidel   V-17223 [12″]

Prelude to Act III

Paris Conservatory Orchestra, conducted by Felix
    Weingartner   C-68905D [12″]

Liebestod

Kirsten Flagstad (s), with orchestra, conducted by
Hans Lange   V-8859 [12″]
Kirsten Flagstad (s), with San Francisco Opera
Orchestra, conducted by Edwin McArthur   V-15840 [12″]
Frida Leider (s)   V-7523 [12″]
Gertrud Bindernagel (s)   T-SK1162 [12″]
Lillian Nordica (s)   C-74025 [12″]
Emmy Destinn (s)   P-PX084 [12″]
Johanna Gadski (s)   (V-88058 co) [12″]
Olive Fremstad (s)   (C-A5521 co) [12″]

ENGELBERT HUMPERDINCK

HÄNSEL UND GRETEL

Abridged recording (arranged by Weigert and
Maeder). Soloists, with Berlin State Opera Chorus
and Orchestra, conducted by Weigert. Four 12″
records.   D-CA8000/3

Die Duoptisten. Three 10″ records.   V-J7
Suite
CB Symphony Orchestra, conducted by Howard
Barlow. Two 12″ records.   CM-424
"Ein mänlein steht im Walde," "Der kleine Sand-
mann bin ich," and *Abendsegen*
Elisabeth Schumann (s), with E. Lush (piano)   V-1948 [10″]
"Suse, liebe Suse" and *"Der kleine Sandmann"*
Alma Gluck (s) and Louise Homer (c)   (V-8030 co) [12″]

VINCENT D'INDY

FERVAAL

Introduction to Act I
Lamoureux Orchestra, conducted by Albert Wolff
PD-67003 [12″]

ERNEST REYER

SALAMMBÔ

Air des Colombes
Germaine Martinelli (s)   PD-66991 [12″]

SIGURD

Overture
Paris Conservatory Orchestra, conducted by Piero
Coppola   G-DB4947 [12″]
"Je savais tout" (Air d'Uta)
Jeanne Manceau (c)   PD-62698 [10″]
"Et toi, Freia"
Arthur Endrèze (b)   PAT-X90035 [12″]

"J'ai garde mon ame ingenue"
César Vezzani (t)   G-P753 [10"]
Esprits gardiens: "Le bruit des chants"
César Vezzani (t)   G-P753 [10"]
Georges Thill (t)   C-9147M [12"]
"Salut splendeur du jour"
Marjorie Lawrence (s)   V-15892 [12"]
"Ô palais radieux"
Marjorie Lawrence (s)   V-15892 [12"]

CHAPTER XVI

GEORGES BIZET

L'ARLÉSIENNE SUITE, NO. 2

Boston "Pops" Orchestra, conducted by Arthur
Fiedler. Two 12" records.   VM-683

CARMEN

Complete Recording: Visconti, Marthe Nespoulous
(s), Georges Thill (t), Guenot, and others, with
chorus and orchestra, conducted by Élie Cohen. Fifteen 12" records.   CM-Op. 1

Habanera. "L'amour est un oiseau rebelle"
Ninon Vallin (s), with chorus and orchestra   C-P9152M [12"]
Maria Jeritza (s)   V-8091 [12"]
Marguerite D'Alvarez (c)   V-1145 [10"]
Kerstin Thorborg (c, in German)   D-23038 [10"]
Dusolina Giannini (s)   G-DB1792 [12"]
Gladys Swarthout (ms)   V-14419 [12"]
Geraldine Farrar (s)   (V-621 co) [10"]
Zélie de Lussan (s)   IRCC-22 [10"]
Emma Calvé (s)   V-18144 [12"]
Maria Gay (c)   (C-A5279 co) [12"]
Risë Stevens (ms)   C-71192D [12"]
"Parle-moi de ma mère"
Fanny Heldy (s) and Fernand Ansseau (t)   G-DB1115 [12"]
Lucrezia Bori (s) and Miguel Fleta (t)   HRS-1039 [12"]
Seguidilla: "Pres des ramparts de Seville"
Gladys Swarthout (ms)   V-14419 [12"]
Conchita Supervia (ms)   D-25894 [12"]
Marguerite D'Alvarez (c)   V-1145 [10"]
Geraldine Farrar (s)   (V-6108 co) [12"]
Bruna Castagna (c)   V-1936 [10"]
Chanson bohème: "Les tringles des sistres tintaient"
Ninon Vallin (s)   C-P9152M [12"]
Maria Jeritza (s)   V-8091 [12"]
Geraldine Farrar (s)   (V-6109 co) [12"]

Emma Calvé (s)   G-DB638 [12"]
Bruna Castagna (c)   V-2161 [10"]
Clotilde Bressler-Gianoli (c)   IRCC-5009 [10"]
Chanson du Toreador: "Votre toast"
Lawrence Tibbett (b), with Metropolitan Opera
    Chorus and Orchestra   V-8124 [12"]
Pasquale Amato (b), with chorus and orchestra
                                                 (V-6040 co) [12"]
Giuseppe Campanari (b, in Italian)   (V-85073 co) [12"]
George Baklanoff (b, in Italian)   (C-A5272 co) [12"]
Air de la fleur: "La fleur que tu m'avais jetée"
Jussi Bjoerling (t)   V-12635 [12"]
Edward Johnson (t)   V-9293 [12"]
Enrico Caruso (t, in Italian)   V-14234 [12"]
Beniamino Gigli (t, in Italian)   V-14030 [12"]
Giacomo Lauri-Volpi (t)   V-7389 [12"]
Charles Dalmorès (t)   V-18141 [12"]
Giovanni Martinelli (t)   (V-6191 co) [12"]
"Halte la!"
Geraldine Farrar (s) and Giovanni Martinelli (t)
                                             G-DK108 [12"]
"La bas de la montagne"
Emma Calvé (s) and Charles Dalmorès (t)   G-DB638 [12"]
Geraldine Farrar (s)   (V-6108 co) [12"]
"Voyons que j'essaie"
Dusolina Giannini (s)   G-DB1792 [12"]
Bruna Castagna (c)   V-1936 [10"]
Jeanne Gerville-Réache (c)   IRCC-5 [10"]
Maria Gay (c, in Italian)   (C-A5279 co) [12"]
Geraldine Farrar (s)   (V-6109 co) [12"]
Clotilde Bressler-Gianoli (c)   IRCC-5009 [10"]
"Je dis que rien ne m'epouvante"
Eidé Noréna (s)   V-14742 [12"]
Elisabeth Rethberg (s, in German)   D-25285 [12"]
Emma Eames (s)   IRCC-32 [12"]
Geraldine Farrar (s)   (V-6113 co) [12"]
Alma Gluck (s)   (V-6145 co) [12"]
"Si tu m'aimes, Carmen"
Geraldine Farrar (s) and Pasquale Amato (b)   G-DK107 [12"]
"C'est toi"
Geraldine Farrar (s) and Giovanni Martinelli (t)
                                             G-DK108 [12"]
"Je t'aime encore"
Geraldine Farrar (s) and Giovanni Martinelli (t)
                                             G-DK107 [12"]
Suite: Preludes, Act I; Act IV; Act II; Act III;
    Changing of the Guard; *Danse bohème.*

London Philharmonic Orchestra, conducted by Sir
Thomas Beecham CM-X144

LA JOLIE FILLE DE PERTH
Suite
London Philharmonic Orchestra, conducted by Sir
Thomas Beecham. Two 12″ records. CM-X28
"A la voix d'un amant fidele"
Jean Planel (t) PAT-X90046 [10″]
"Quand la flamme d'amour"
Marcel Journet (bs) G-DA759 [10″]
André Balbon (bs) PAT-X90075 [10″]
Charles Gilibert (b) (V-6140 co) [12″]

LES PECHEURS DE PERLES
"Au fond du temple"
Jose Luccioni (t) and Pierre Deldi (b) C-9133M [12″]
Beniamino Gigli (t) and Giuseppe de Luca (b)
(in Italian) V-8084 [12″]
Edmond Clément (t) and Marcel Journet (bs)
(V-8017 co) [12″]
"Je crois entendre encore"
Enrico Caruso (t) V-7770 [12″]
Tino Rossi (t) C-4212M [10″]
"Comme autrefois dans la nuit"
Amelita Galli-Curci (s) G-DB255 [12″]
Lina Pagliughi (s, in Italian) P-E11406 [12″]
Toti dal Monte (s, in Italian) G-DB1316 [12″]
Luisa Tetrazzini (s, in Italian) G-DB544 [12″]
"O Dieu Brahma!"
Toti dal Monte (s, in Italian) G-DB1316 [12″]
Luisa Tetrazzini (s, in Italian) G-DB544 [12″]

ALEXANDRE-CHARLES LECOCQ

LA FILLE DE MME ANGOT
"Certainement j'amais Clairette"
André Bauge (b) PAT-PG59 [10″]
"Pour être fort on se rassemble"
André Bauge (b) PAT-X91035 [10″]
Duo politique
Ninon Vallin (s) and André Bauge (b) PAT-PD4 [10″]
"De la mère Angot, je suis la fille" and *"Ah!*
c'est donc toi madam' Barras"
Edmée Favart (s) PAT-X91032 [10″]
"Jours fortunes de notre enfance"
Ninon Vallin (s) and Madeleine Sibille (s) PAT-X90058 [10″]
Légende de la Mère Angot: "Marchande de
marée" and "Tournez, tournez"

Mireille Berthon (s) with Chorus of the Opéra-
Comique   G-P769 [10"]

CHAPTER XVII

CHARLES-FRANÇOIS GOUNOD

FAUST

Complete recording. Mireille Berthon (s), César Vezzani (t), Marcel Journet (bs), Marthe Coiffier, Louis
Mussy, and others, with chorus and orchestra, conducted by Henri Büsser. Twenty 12" records.   VM-105

"Mais ce Dieu, que peut-il pour moi?" and
    "O Merveille!"
    Fernand Ansseau (t) and Marcel Journet (bs)   (V-8185 co) [12"]
    René Maison (t) and Julien Lafont (bs)   D-25858 [12"]
. . . *"O Merveille"* (only)
    Enrico Caruso (t) and Marcel Journet (bs)   G-DM115 [12"]
Kermesse: "Vin ou bière"
    Metropolitan Opera Chorus   V-9697 [12"]
"Avant de quitter ces lieux"
    Lawrence Tibbett (b)   V-8452 [12"]
    Giuseppe de Luca (b, in Italian)   V-7086 [12"]
    Antonio Scotti (b, in Italian)   (V-6284 co) [12"]
"Veau d'or"
    Fyodor Chaliapin (bs)   V-7600 [12"]
    Ezio Pinza (bs), with Metropolitan Opera Chorus V-1753 [10"]
    Pol Plançon (bs)   (V-81038 co) [10"]
Scene des Epées: "A votre santé"
    Pasquale Amato (b) and Marcel Journet (bs), with
        Metropolitan Opera Chorus   G-DK101 [12"]
"Ainsi que la brise legère"
    Metropolitan Opera Chorus   V-9697 [12"]
"Faites-lui mes aveux"
    Margarete Matzenauer (c)   (V6618 co) [12"]
    Marthe Nespoulous (s)   C-RF61 [10"]
"Salut, demeure"
    Jussi Bjoerling (t)   V-13790 [12"]
    Giacomo Lauri-Volpi (t)   V-7389 [12"]
Ballade: "Il etait un roi de Thulé" and *Air des bijoux*
    Eidé Noréna (s)   V-14725 [12"]
    Elisabeth Rethberg (s)   V-7179 [12"]
    Geraldine Farrar (s)   (V-6107 co) [12"]
. . . *Air des bijoux* (only)
    Marcella Sembrich (s)   G-DB429 [12"]
    Nellie Melba (s)   G-DB361 [12"]
    Emma Eames (s)   (V-88006 co) [12"]

"Seigneur Dieu" and *"Eh quoi toujours seule?"*
　Geraldine Farrar (s), Mme Gilibert (s), Enrico
　　Caruso (t), and Marcel Journet (bs)　　　　G-DM102 [12″]
"Il se fait tard" and *"O nuit d'amour"*
　Geraldine Farrar (s) and Enrico Caruso (t)　　G-DM108 [12″]
"Elle s'ouvre sa fenêtre"
　Geraldine Farrar (s) and Marcel Journet (bs)　G-DK106 [12″]
"Vous que faites l'endormie"
　Fyodor Chaliapin (bs)　　　　　　　　　　　V-7600 [12″]
　David Bispham (b)　　　　　　　　　　(C-A5010 co) [12″]
　Marcel Journet (bs)　　　　　　　　　(V-6174 co) [12″]
"Que voulez-vous messieurs?"
　Enrico Caruso (t), Antonio Scotti (b), and Marcel
　　Journet (bs)　　　　　　　　　　　　　G-DO100 [12″]
.Mort de Valentine
　Antonio Scotti (b)　　　　　　　　　　(V-88282 co) [12″]
"Seigneur daignez permettre"
　Geraldine Farrar (s) and Marcel Journet (bs) (V-8021 co) [12″]
Walpurgis Night Scene
　Royal Opera Orchestra. Two 12″ records.　　　V-9646/7
"Mon coeur est penetré" and *"Attends voici la rue"*
　Geraldine Farrar (s) and Enrico Caruso (t)　　G-DM109 [12″]
. . . *"Alerte!"*
　Geraldine Farrar (s), Enrico Caruso (t) and Mar-
　　cel Journet (bs)　　　　　　　　　　　　G-DK106 [12″]

MIREILLE

Overture
　Grand Symphony Orchestra, conducted by Cloëz D-20093 [10″]
Valse: "O légère hirondelle"
　Yvonne Brothier (s)　　　　　　　　　　　G-P689 [10″]
　Lily Pons (s)　　　　　　　　　　　　　　D-23016 [10″]
　Clara Clairbert (s)　　　　　　　　　　　PD-66794 [12″]
　María Barrientos (s)　　　　　　　　(C-7338M co) [12″]
"La brise est douce"
　Germaine Feraldy (s) and Edmond Rambaud (b)
　　　　　　　　　　　　　　　　　　　　C-LFX99 [12″]
　Yvonne Brothier (s) and Marcelin (b)　　　G-W684 [12″]
"Trahir Vincent"
　Clara Clairbert (s)　　　　　　　　　　　PD-66793 [12″]
"Si les filles d'Arles"
　Louis Guenot (b)　　　　　　　　　　　　C-D14211 [12″]
"Le jour se lève"
　Germaine Feraldy (s)　　　　　　　　　　PAT-PG63 [10″]
"Heureux petit berger"
　Germaine Feraldy (s)　　　　　　　　　　C-D13055 [12″]
"Anges du paradis"
　Georges Thill (t)　　　　　　　　　　　　C-9147M [12″]
　Miguel Villabella (t)　　　　　　　　　PAT-X90059 [10″]

"Foi de son flambeau"
Germaine Feraldy (s) and Edmond Rambaud (b)
C-LFX99 [12″]
Yvonne Brothier (s) and Marcelin (t)   G-W684 [12″]

PHILÉMON ET BAUCIS

"Au bruit des lourds marteaux"
Pol Plançon (bs)   IRCC-25 [10″]
"O riante nature"
Amelita Galli-Curci (s)   (V-7658 co) [12″]

LA REINE DE SABA

"Inspirez-moi, race divine"
Enrico Caruso (t)   V-15732 [12″]
"Plus grand dans son obscurité"
Jeanne Gerville-Réache (c)   IRCC-73 [12″]
"Sous le pieds"
Marcel Journet (bs)   (V-74269 co) [12″]

ROMÉO ET JULIETTE

"Allons jeunes gens"
Pol Plançon (bs)   (V-81035 co) [10″]
Ballade de la Reine Mab
Arthur Endrèze (b)   D-25892 [12″]
Valse: "Je veux vivre dans ce rêve"
Eidé Noréna (s)   V-14742 [12″]
Lucrezia Bori (s)   (V-542 co) [10″]
Emma Eames (s)   IRCC-43 [12″]
Geraldine Farrar (s) (recorded in 1906)   IRCC-29 [10″]
Geraldine Farrar (s) (recorded in 1911)   IRCC-114 [12″]
Amelita Galli-Curci (s)   (V-6133 co) [12″]
Luisa Tetrazzini (s, in Italian)   (V-6345 co) [12″]
Suzanne Adams (s)   IRCC-98 [10″]
"Ange adorable"
Eidé Noréna (s) and Gaston Micheletti (t)   D-25889 [12″]
Geraldine Farrar (s) and Edmond Clément (t) G-DB172 [12″]
"Ah! lève-toi soleil"
Fernand Ansseau (t)   (V-6880 co) [12″]
César Vezzani (t)   G-DB4931 [12″]
Charles Dalmorès (t)   (V-85121 co) [12″]
Richard Crooks (t)   V-15542 [12″]
"Oh nuit divine" and *"Ah! ne fuis pas encore"*
Eidé Noréna (s) and Gaston Micheletti (t)   D-25890 [12″]
. . . *"Ah! ne fuis pas encore"* (only)
Lucrezia Bori (s) and Beniamino Gigli (t)   (V-3027 co) [10″]
"Va, je t'ai pardonné" and *"Non, ce n'est pas le jour"*
Eidé Noréna (s) and Gaston Micheletti (t)   D-25891 [12″]

Germaine Feraldy (s) and Miguel Villabella (t)
                                              PAT-PGT8 [12″]
Scène du Tombeau
  Germaine Feraldy (s) and Georges Thill (t). Two
    12″ records.   C-LFX1/2
  . . . *"Salut, tombeau"* (only)
  Fernand Ansseau (t)   (V-6880 co) [12″]
  César Vezzani (t)   G-DB4931 [12″]

SAPHO

"O ma lyre immortelle"
  Ernestine Schumann-Heink (c)   IRCC-93 [12″]
  Jeanne Gerville-Réache (c)   (V-88166 co) [12″]

Charles-Louis-Ambroïse Thomas

HAMLET

"Doute de la lumière"
  Marcella Sembrich (s) and Emilio de Gogorza (b)
                                              IRCC-148 [12″]
  Maria Galvany (s) and Titta Ruffo (b)   (V-92500 co) [12″]
Chanson Bachique: "O vin dissipe la tristesse"
  John Charles Thomas (b)   V-1639 [10″]
  Armand Crabbé (b)   G-DB1043 [12″]
  Titta Ruffo (b, in Italian)   V-18140 [12″]
  Mattia Battistini (b, in Italian)   (G-DB202 co) [12″]
Scène de Folie
  Eidé Noréna (s)   D-25932 [12″]
  Amelita Galli-Curci (s)   G-DB927 [12″]
  Nellie Melba (s)   G-DB364 [12″]
"Comme une pale fleur"
  Titta Ruffo (b, in Italian)   G-DB569 [12″]
  Mattia Battistini (b, in Italian)   (G-DB202 co) [12″]

MIGNON

Abridged Recording. Mme. Germaine Cernay (Mig-
non); Lucienne Tragin (Philine); André d'Arkor
(Wilhelm); M. Demoulin (Lothario); Valére Mayer
(Laerte), with Chorus and Orchestra of Théâtre de
la Monnaie (Brussels), conducted by Maurice Bastin.
Five 12″ records.   CM-Op. 19

"Connais-tu le pays"
  Lucrezia Bori (s)   V-1361 [10″]
  Zélie de Lussan (s)   IRCC-22 [10″]
  Marcella Sembrich (s)   (G-DB429 co) [12″]
  Geraldine Farrar (s)   (V-6113 co) [12″]
  Bruna Castagna (c)   V-2161 [10″]
  Risë Stevens (ms)   C-71192D [12″]

"Légères hirondelles"
  Ninon Vallin (s) and Julien Lafont (bs)   D-20509 [10"]
  Geraldine Farrar (s) and Marcel Journet (bs)   D-DO101 [12"]
Styrienne: "Je connais un pauvre enfant"
  Geraldine Farrar (s)   (V-6394 co) [12"]
  Ebe Stignani (ms)   P-E11344 [12"]
"Adieu Mignon, courage"
  Beniamino Gigli (t, in Italian)   V-6905 [12"]
  Tito Schipa (t, in Italian)   G-DB843 [12"]
Polonaise: "Je suis Titania"
  Lily Pons (s)   V-17232 [12"]
  Amelita Galli-Curci (s, in Italian)   V-7110 [12"]
  Luisa Tetrazzini (s, in Italian)   G-DB540 [12"]
  Lillian Nordica (s, in Italian)   C-74028 [12"]
  Bessie Abott (s, in Italian)   IRCC-78 [12"]
Berceuse: "De son coeur j'ai calmé la fièvre"
  Ezio Pinza (bs)   V-6642 [12"]
  Pol Plançon (bs)   IRCC-94 [12"]
"Elle ne croyait pas"
  Beniamino Gigli (t, in Italian)   V-6905 [12"]
  Tito Schipa (t, in Italian)   G-DB843 [12"]

Léo Délibes

LAKMÉ

Blanche Dourga
  Miliza Korjus (s, in Italian)   V-12136 [12"]
  Luisa Tetrazzini (s, in Italian)   IRCC-27 [12"]
"Viens, Mallaika, les lianes en fleurs" and *"Sous
  le dôme épais"*
  Germaine Feraldy (s) and Andrée Berdadet (s)   C-9133M [12"]
  Emma Eames (s) and Louise Homer (c)   IRCC-44 [12"]
"Fantasie aux divins ménsonges"
  Tito Schipa (t)   G-DA870 [10"]
"Pourquoi dans les grands bois"
  Lily Pons (s)   D-23014 [10"]
  Lucrezia Bori (s)   (V-1009 co) [10"]
Air des clochettes: "Où va la jeune Hindoue"
  Lily Pons (s)   V-1502 [10"]
  Amelita Galli-Curci (s, in Italian)   G-DB263 [12"]
  Luisa Tetrazzini (s, in Italian)   (V-88297 co) [12"]
  María Barrientos (s, in Italian)   (C-49151 co) [12"]
"Ah! viens dans la forêt profonde"
  André d'Arkor (t)   C-RF62 [10"]
  John McCormack (t, in Italian)   (V-3029 co) [10"]

SYLVIA

Excerpts: *Prélude; Valse Lente; Pizzicato.*
  London Philharmonic Orchestra, conducted by
    Efrem Kurtz   C-69323D [12"]

COPPÉLIA

Excerpts: *Prélude; Mazurka; Andante; Valse lente; Ballade de l'épi; Scène et valse de la poupée.*
Paris Symphony Orchestra, conducted by François Ruhlmann. Two 10″ records.   C-P17128/9
Excerpts: *Danse des automates; Valse lente; Czardas*
Boston "Pops" Orchestra, conducted by Arthur Fiedler   V-12527 [12″]

ÉDOUARD LALO

LE ROI D'YS

"De tous côtes j'aperçois" (Air de Margared)
Odette Ricquier (s)   (G-DA4875 co) [10″]
"La salut nous est promis"
Miguel Villabella (t)   PAT-X90064 [10″]
Aubade: "Vainement, ma bien aimée"
Edmond Clément (t)   V-6062 [12″]
Tino Rossi (t)   C-4185M [10″]
Jean Planel (t)   PAT-X90036 [10″]
César Vezzani (t)   G-DB4845 [12″]
"A l'autel j'allais rayonnant"
Jany Delille (s) and Jean Planel (t)   PAT-PG40 [10″]
Yvonne Brothier (s) and César Vezzani (t)   G-DB4854 [12″]

CHAPTER XVII

CAMILLE SAINT-SAËNS

HENRI VIII

Ballet Music
National Symphony Orchestra, conducted by Walter Damrosch. Two 12″ records.   V-7292/3

SAMSON ET DALILA

"Arretez, o mes frères"
Giovanni Martinelli (t), with Metropolitan Chorus and Orchestra   (V-8159 co) [12″]
Francesco Tamagno (t, in Italian), with piano   G-DR101 [10″]
"Je viens célèbrer la victoire"
Enrico Caruso (t), Louise Homer (c), and Marcel Journet (bs)   G-DM126 [12″]
"Printemps qui commence"
Sigrid Onegin (c)   V-7320 [12″]
Marguerite D'Alvarez (c)   (V-6590 co) [12″]
Karin Branzell (c)   (B-50158 co) [12″]
"Amour! viens aider ma faiblesse"
Gladys Swarthout (ms)   V-14143 [12″]
Louise Homer (c)   (V-6165 co) [12″]

"Mon coeur s'ouvre à ta voix"
  Germaine Cernay (c) and Georges Thill (t)   C-9109M [12"]
  Maria Olszewska (c)   G-DB1465 [12"]
  Margarete Matzenauer (ms)   V-36287 [12"]
  Louise Homer (c)   (V-6164 co) [12"]
"Vois ma misère, hélàs!"
  Georges Thill (t), with chorus and orchestra   C-9121M [12"]
  Enrico Caruso (t), with chorus and orchestra   G-DB136 [12"]
Bacchanale
  Boston "Pops" Orchestra, conducted by Arthur
    Fiedler   V-12318 [12"]

CHAPTER XVIII

MIKHAIL IVANOVICH GLINKA
A LIFE FOR THE TSAR
  Sussannin's aria: "They guess the truth"
    Fyodor Chaliapin (bs) (recorded in 1908)   (G-DB629 co) [12"]
    Fyodor Chaliapin (bs)   (V-6534 co) [12"]

RUSLAN AND LYUDMILLA
  Overture
    Boston "Pops" Orchestra, conducted by Arthur
      Fiedler   V-4427 [10"]
  Farlaf's Rondo
    Fyodor Chaliapin (bs)   V-7704 [12"]
  Gorislava's aria: "Oh! my Ratmir!"
    S. A. Barurina (s)   (V-4108 co) [10"]

ALEXANDER SERGEIVICH DARGOMIZHSKY
RUSALKA
  Ballet Music
    London Philharmonic Orchestra, conducted by
      Antal Dorati. Two 12" records.   C-DX804
  Miller's Aria
    Fyodor Chaliapin (bs)   V-7704 [12"]
  Olga's Aria
    A. Zelinskaya (s)   (V-4066 co)[12"]
  Mad Scene and Death of the Miller
    Fyodor Chaliapin (bs) and Pozemkovsky   G-DB1531 [12"]

ALEXANDER NIKOLAEIVICH SEROV
HOSTILE POWER
  Merry Butterweek
    Fyodor Chaliapin (bs)   (G-DB1511 co) [12"]

ALEXANDER PORFIRIEVICH BORODIN
PRINCE IGOR
Overture
  Symphony Orchestra, conducted by Albert Coates V-9123 [12″]
"I hate a dreary life"
  Fyodor Chaliapin (bs)   V-1237 [10″]
Arioso of Jaroslavna
  Nina Koshetz (s)   V-9233 [12″]
"Daylight is fading away"
  Charles Kullman (tenor, in German)   C-9099M [12″]
  Vladimir Rosing (tenor, in Russian), with piano D-25188 [12″]
"No sleep, no rest"
  George Baklanoff (b)   D-25122 [12″]
"How goes it, Prince?"
  Fyodor Chaliapin (bs)   V-6867 [12″]
Polovtsian Dances
  London Philharmonic Orchestra, conducted by Sir
    Thomas Beecham. Two 12″ records (3 sides).   CM-X54

MODEST PETROVICH MUSSORGSKY
BORIS GODUNOV
Opening Chorus: "Why hast thou abandoned
  us?" and Pilgrim's Chorus
  Riga Opera Chorus (in Russian)   D-25402 [12″]
Coronation Scene
  Fyodor Chaliapin (bs), with Royal (Covent Gar-
    den) Opera Chorus and Orchestra, conducted
    by Albert Coates   V-11485 [12″]
Varlam's Song: "In the town of Kazan"
  Fyodor Chaliapin (bs)   V-1237 [10″]
Monologue: "I have attained the highest power"
  Fyodor Chaliapin (bs)   V-14517 [12″]
  Vanni-Marcoux (b, in French)   G-DB1112 [12″]
Clock Scene: "Ah! I am suffocating"
  Fyodor Chaliapin (bs)   V-14517 [12″]
Garden Scene
  Margarete Ober (c) and Paul Althouse (t) (in
    Italian)   (V-76031 co) [12″]
Maidens' Chorus: "In the shade of the willow"
  and Polonaise
  Riga Opera Chorus   D-25403 [12″]
"Farewell, my son; I am dying" and Death of
  Boris
  Fyodor Chaliapin (bs) (recorded Covent Garden,
    July 4, 1928)   V-15177 [12″]
  Fyodor Chaliapin (bs)   V-6724 [12″]
  Georges Baklanoff (b)   D-25813 [12″]

KHOVANTCHINA

Prelude
    Boston Symphony Orchestra, conducted by Serge
        Koussevitzky   V-14415 [12″]
"The time of darkness came"
    V. Shushlin (bs)   (V-4099 co) [10″]
Martha's Divination
    A. Zelinskaya (s)   (V-4090 co) [10″]
Shaklovitov's aria: "The Streltsys are sleeping"
    K. L. Knijnikov (b)   (V-4091 co) [10″]
Dances of the Persian Slaves
    London Symphony Orchestra, conducted by Al-
        bert Coates   V-11135 [12″]
    CB Symphony Orchestra, conducted by Howard
        Barlow   C-17286D [10″]
Entr'acte
    EIAR Symphony Orchestra, conducted by Willy
        Ferrero   D-25948 [12″]

THE FAIR AT SOROCHINTZY

Introduction: "A hot day in little Russia"
    Symphony Orchestra, conducted by Clöez   D-20116 [10″]
"Why my sad heart"
    Dmitri Smirnov (t)   (G-DB753) [12″]
Gopak
    London Philharmonic Orchestra, conducted by
        Walter Goehr   C-69154D [12″]

Nikolai Andreivich Rimsky-Korsakov

LE COQ D'OR

Suite
    London Symphony Orchestra, conducted by
        Eugene Goossens. Three 12″ records.   VM-504
Hymne au Soleil
    Eidé Noréna (s)   D-20115 [10″]
    Lina Pagliughi (s, in Italian)   D-29018 [12″]
    Miliza Korjus (s, in German)   V-12021 [12″]
    Lily Pons (s)   V-17232 [12″]
    Mabel Garrison (s)   (V-638 co) [10″]
    María Barrientos (s)   (C-7069M co) [12″]
Cortége des Noces
    Boston "Pops" Orchestra, conducted by Arthur
        Fiedler   V-4526 [12″]

PSKOVITYANKA

Hunt and Storm Music, Act III
    London Symphony Orchestra, conducted by Al-
        bert Coates   V-11454 [12″]

MAY NIGHT

Overture
London Symphony Orchestra, **conducted** by Al-
bert Coates   V-11424 [12"]
"Sleep, my beauty"
Leonid Sobinov (t)   (G-DB890 co) [12"]
Song of the Village Mayor
Joseph Laoute (t), with Choir of Red Army of
U.S.S.R.   C-4215M [10"]
Slumber Song
Irene Jessner (s, in French)   V-17559 [12"]

MLADA

Cortége des nobles
London Symphony Orchestra, conducted by Al-
bert Coates   V-11443 [12"]

SADKO

"O yon dark forest"
S. J. Lemeshov (t)   (V-4092 co) [10"]
"By Lake Ilmen"
A. Zelinskaya (s)   (V-4067 co) [10"]
Song of the Viking Guest
Fyodor Chaliapin (bs)   V-6867 [12"]
Song of the Hindu Guest ("Song of India")
Beniamino Gigli (t)   V-1570 [10"]
Berceuse
Nina Koshetz (s)   V-9233 [12"]

SNEGUROCHKA

"To go berrying"
D. T. Sprishevskaya (s)   (V-4093 co) [10"]
"Je connais, je connais ma mère"
Lucrezia Bori (s, in French)   (V-542 co) [10"]
Carnival
Russian Opera Chorus and **Orchestra**   (V-4122 co) [10"]
Shepherd Lehl's Song
A. Zelinskaya (s)   (V-4096 co) [12"]
Alma Gluck (s)   (V-647 co) [10"]
"How painful"
D. T. Sprishevskaya (s)   (V-4093 co) [10"]
"Full of wonders"
José Mojica (t)   (V-6892 co) [12"]
"Joyous day departs"
Leonid Sobinoff (t)   (G-DB890 co) [12"]
Dance of the Buffoons
London Symphony Orchestra, conducted by Al-
bert Coates   V-11454 [12"]

"Clouds plotted with thunder"
   A. Zelinskaya (s)   (V-4066 co) [10"]
Death of the Snow Maiden
   D. T. Sprishevska (s)   (V-4112 co) [10"]

THE TALE OF THE INVISIBLE CITY OF KITEZH

Fevrona's Aria: "My forest"
   S. A. Baturina (s)   (V-4108 co) [10"]

THE TSAR'S BRIDE

Lubasha's aria: "It cannot be"
   A. Zelinskaya (s)   (V-4109 co) [10"]
Martha's Aria: "In Novgorod"
   D. T. Sprishevska (s)   (V-4070 co) [10"]
   Miliza Korjus (s, in German)   V-12021 [12"]
"You will pay"
   A. Zelinskaya (s)   (V-4109 co) [10"]
Sobakin's Aria
   V. Shushlin (bs)   (V-4099 co) [10"]
Martha's Mad Scene
   D. Sprishevskaya (s)   (V-4070 co) [10"]

PIOTR ILYICH TCHAIKOVSKY

EUGEN ONEGIN

"I love you Olga"
   L. Sobinoff (t)   G-DB889 [12"]
Letter Scene
   Beata Malkin (s, in German)   D-25840 [12"]
"Written words"
   Georges Baklanoff (b)   D-20423 [10"]
"Faint echo of youth"
   Charles Kullman (t, in German)   C-9099M [12"]
   Dimitri Smirnov (t)   G-DB581 [12"]
   Enrico Caruso (t, in French)   G-DB127 [12"]
Polonaise
   Boston "Pops" Orchestra, conducted by Arthur
     Fiedler   V-12429 [12"]
"Alas, there is no doubt"
   Georges Baklanoff (b)   D-20423 [10"]

PIQUE-DAME

"Forgive me, bright celestial visions"
   A. M. Davidov (t)   G-EK45 [10"]
"Once in Versailles"
   K. Knijinkov (b)   (V-4072 co) [10"]
"It is night"
   Thalia Sabanieva (s) and Anna Criona (s)   (V-9303 co) [12"]

"Dear friends"
    A. A. Zelinskaya (s)   (V-4117 co) [10″]
"From whence these tears"
    S. Baturina (s)   (V-4065 co) [10″]
"When you choose me for your husband"
    Heinrich Schlusnus (b, in German)   PD-35003 [12″]
"My darling friend"
    S. A. Baturina (s) and A. A. Zelinskaya (s)   (V-4123 co) [10″]
    Thalia Sabanieva (s) and Anna Criona (s)   (V-9294 co) [12″]
    Emmy Destinn (s) and Maria Duchène
        (s, in French)   G-DK105 [12″]
"It is near to midnight"
    Xenia Delmas (s)   PD-66883 [12″]
    Emmy Destinn (s, in German)   (V-88518 co) [12″]
    Irene Jessner (s, in Italian)   V-17559 [12″]

CHAPTER XIX

GIUSEPPE VERDI

AÏDA

Complete Recording. Dusolina Giannini (Aïda); Irene Menguhini-Cattaneo (Amneris); Aureliano Pertile (Rhadames); Giovanni Inghilleri (Amonasro); Guglielmo Masini (The King) and Luigi Manfrini (Ramfis), with La Scala Chorus and Orchestra, conducted by Carlo Sabajno. Nineteen 12″ records.   VM-54

"*Celeste Aïda*"
    Enrico Caruso (t)   V-7770 [12″]
    Jussi Bjoerling (t)   V-12039 [12″]
    Giovanni Martinelli (t)   V-6595 [12″]
    Ellison Van Hoose (t) (recorded in 1907)   IRCC-117 [12″]
"*Ritorna vincitor*" and "*I sacri nomi di padre*"
    Rosa Ponselle (s)   V-7438 [12″]
    Elisabeth Rethberg (s)   V-7106 [12″]
    Eva Turner (s)   C-L2150 [12″]
    Emmy Destinn (s)   G-DB646 [12″]
    Giannina Russ (s) (recorded in 1905)   P-PO108 [10½″]
    Félia Litvinne (s)   IRCC-Spl.
    Johanna Gadski (s)   (V-6122 co) [12″]
Temple Scene: "*Immenso Ftha*"
    Ezio Pinza (bs) and Giovanni Martinelli (t), with
        Metropolitan Chorus and Orchestra   V-8111 [12″]
"*O cieli azzuri*" ("*O Patria mia*")
    Elisabeth Rethberg (s)   V-7106 [12″]
    Emmy Destinn (s)   (V-6084 co) [12″]

*"Ciel mio padre!"; "Rivedrai le foreste imbalsamate";
"Su, dunque"*
Elisabeth Rethberg (s) and Giuseppe de Luca (b)
G-DB1455 [12"]

*"Pur ti reveggo"; "Fuggiam gli ardori"; "La, tra for-
este vergine"; "Sovra una terra estrania"*
Elisabeth Rethberg (s) and Giacomo Lauri-Volpi
(t)   G-DB1341 [12"]

"Ah, no! fuggiamo!"; "Ma dimmi"
Elisabeth Rethberg (s), Giacomo Lauri-Volpi (t)
and Giuseppe de Luca (b)   G-DB1458 [12"]

*"Gia i sacerdoti adunansi"; "Morire! ah! tu dei
vivere"; "Aïda a me togliesti"*
Louise Homer (c) and Enrico Caruso (t)   G-DM111 [12"]

*"La fatal pietra"; "Presago il core"; "Morire! si pura
e bella"; "O terra, addio"*
Rosa Ponselle (s) and Giovanni Martinelli (t)   V-1744/5 [10"]
Johanna Gadski (s) and Enrico Caruso (t)   G-DM114 [12"]

ATTILA

"Te sol quest' anima"
Elisabeth Rethberg (s), Beniamino Gigli (t), and
Ezio Pinza (bs)   V-8194 [12"]

UN BALLO IN MASCHERA

"La rivedrà nell'estasi"
Enrico Caruso (t), Frieda Hempel (s), Leon Rothier (bs), Andrés de Segurola (bs), with Metropolitan Chorus and Orchestra   G-DM103 [12"]

"Volta la terra"
Frieda Hempel (s)   (V-87235 co) [10"]

"All vita che t'arride"
Antonio Scotti (b)   IRCC-75 [10"]

"Re dell' abisso, affrettati"
Margarete Klose (c, in German) with chorus   V-17560 [12"]

"Di tu se fedele" (Barcarolla)
Helge Roswaenge (t, in German), with chorus   V-17560 [12"]
Enrico Caruso (t), with Metropolitan Chorus   G-DA102 [10"]
Alessandro Bonci (t), with chorus
C-GQX10148 [12"] or (C-A1277 co) [10"]

"E scherzo od è follio"
Enrico Caruso (t), Frieda Hempel (s), Duchène
(ms), Leon Rothier (bs), Andrés de Segurola
(bs), with Metropolitan Chorus and Orchestra
G-DM103 [12"]

"Ma dall' arido stelo divulsa"
Elisabeth Rethberg (s)   (V-7582 co) [12"]
Gina Cigna (s)   C-9122M [12"]
Johanna Gadski (s)   G-DB661 [12"]

"Morrò, ma prima in grazia"

Elisabeth Rethberg (s)	(V-7582 co) [12″]
Gina Cigna (s)	C-9122M [12″]
Johanna Gadski (s)	G-DB661 [12″]
Emmy Destinn (s)	(V-6084 co) [12″]

"Eri tu, che macchiavi"

Lawrence Tibbett (b)	V-7353 [12″]
Alexander Sved (b, in German)	D-CA8265 [12″]
Pasquale Amato (b)	(V-6040 co) [12″]
Titta Ruffo (b)	G-DB398 [12″]

"Ah, l'ho segnato"

Enrico Caruso (t)	G-DB137 [12″]

"Saper vorreste"

Luisa Tetrazzini (s)	G-DB539 [12″]
Selma Kurz (s)	G-DB398 [12″]
Adelaide Saraceni (s)	G-DA1340 [10″]

DON CARLOS

"Dio, che nell'alma infondere"

Enrico Caruso (t) and Antonio Scotti (b)	G-DM111 [12″]
Giovanni Martinelli (t) and Giuseppe de Luca (b)	(V-8047 co) [12″]

"O don fatale"

Sigrid Onegin (c)	V-7191 [12″]
Gertrude Rünger (s, in German)	D-LY6114 [12″]
Margaret Matzenauer (c)	(V-6618 co) [12″]

"Ella giammai m'amo"; "Domiro sol nel manto mio regal"

Tancredi Pasero (bs)	P-E11367 [12″]
Fyodor Chaliapin (bs)	(V-88665 co) [12″]
Leon Rothier (bs)	(C-A5812 co) [12″]
Ezio Pinza (bs)	(V-6709 co) [12″]

"Per me giunto"

Giuseppe de Luca (b)	(V-6078 co) [12″]

"O Carlo, ascolta"

Giuseppe de Luca (b)	(V-1591 co) [10″]

ERNANI

Abridged version. Iva Pacetti (Elvira); Antonio Melandri (Ernani); Gino Vanelli (Don Carlo); Corrado Zambelli (Don Ruy); Ida Mannarini (Giovanna); Giuseppe Nessi (Don Riccardo); Aristide Baracchi (Jago), with La Scala Chorus and Orchestra, conducted by Lorenzo Molajoli. Five 12″ records. G-GQX10069/73

"Ernani, involami"

Ina Souez (s)	V-14493 [12″]
Rosa Ponselle (s)	V-6875 [12″]
Frieda Hempel (s)	(G-DB294 co) [12″]
Marcella Sembrich (s)	(V-88022 co) [12″]

"Infelice, è tuo credevi"
Ezio Pinza (bs)   V-7552 [12"]
Fyodor Chaliapin (bs)   G-DB403 [12"]
Édouard de Reszke (bs)   IRCC-28 [10"]
José Mardones (bs)   (C-5058M co) [12"]
"O dei verd' anni miei"
Titta Ruffo (b)   G-DB398 [12"]
Mario Ancona (b)   (V-88062 co) [12"]
"O sommo Carlo"
Giuseppe de Luca (b), Alfio Tedesco (t) and Grace
    Anthony (s), with Metropolitan Chorus and
    Orchestra   G-DB1436 [12"]
Mattia Battistini (b), and others, with La Scala
    Chorus and Orchestra   V-18144 [12"]

FALSTAFF

Complete recording. Giacomo Rimini (Falstaff),
Tassinari (Alice), Tellini (Nannetta), Buades (Dame
Quickley), D'Alessio (Fenton), Ghirardini (Ford),
Mme Monticone, Messrs Venturini and Nessi, with
Chorus and Orchestra of La Scala, conducted by
Lorenzo Molajoli. Fourteen 12" records.   CM-Op. 16

"Quand' ero paggio"
Victor Maurel (b), with piano   IRCC-4 [10¾"]
Antonio Scotti (b)   (V-6283 co) [12"]
"Sul fil d'un soffio etesio"
Toti dal Monte (s) with La Scala Chorus and Or-
    chestra   (G-DB1317) [12"]
Frances Alda (s)   IRCC-111 [12"]

LA FORZA DEL DESTINO

"Madre, pietosa Vergine"
Dusolina Giannini (s)   G-DB1217 [12"]
"Il santo nome di Dio"
Ezio Pinza (bs) with Metropolitan Opera Chorus
    and Orchestra   G-DB1203 [12"]
"La Vergine degli angeli"
Rosa Ponselle (s) and Ezio Pinza (bs) with Metro-
    politan Chorus and Orchestra   V-8097 [12"]
"O tu che in seno agli angeli"
Enrico Caruso (t)   V-6000 [12"]
Giovanni Martinelli (t)   (V-6637 co) [12"]
"Solenne in quest' ora"
Enrico Caruso (t) and Antonio Scotti (b)   V-8000 [12"]
Beniamino Gigli (t) and Giuseppe de Luca (b)   V-8069 [12"]
"Sleale! il segreto"
Enrico Caruso (t) and Giuseppe de Luca (b)   G-DM107 [12"]

"Invano Alvaro ti celasti al mondo"
Giovanni Martinelli (t) and Giuseppe de Luca (b)

G-DB1172 [12″]

Enrico Caruso (t) and Pasquale Amato (b)   G-DM106 [12″]
"Pace, pace, mio Dio"
Rosa Ponselle (s)   V-6875 [12″]
Claudia Muzio (s)   C-9106M [12″]
Dusolina Giannini (s)   G-DB1228 [12″]
Luisa Tetrazzini (s)   G-DB538 [12″]
"Io muojo! Non imprecare"
Rosa Ponselle (s), Giovanni Martinelli (t) and Ezio
Pinza (bs)   G-DB1202 [12″]

I LOMBARDI ALLA PRIMA CROCIATA

"Qual volutta trascorrere"
Elisabeth Rethberg (s), Beniamino Gigli (t) and
Ezio Pinza (bs)   V-8194 [12″]
Frances Alda (s), Enrico Caruso (t) and Marcel
Journet (bs)   · (G-DM126) [12″]
Polonesa: "Qual prodigio"
Blanche Arral (s) with orchestra   IRCC-19 [12″]

LUISA MILLER

"Quando le sere al placido"
Tito Schipa (t)   (G-DB1372) [12″]

MACBETH

Chorus of Refugees
Berlin State Opera Chorus   T-E1656 [12″]
"Ah! la paterna mano"
Enrico Caruso (t)   (G-DB118) [12″]
Sleep Walking Scene: *"Una macchia é qui
tuttora"*
Gertrud Rünger (s, in German)   D-LY6114 [12″]

NABUCODONOSOR (NABUCCO)

Overture
Milan Symphony Orchestra, conducted by Alber-
goni   D-25096 [12″]
"Tu sul labbro de' veggenti"
José Mardones (bs)   (V-6434 co) [12″]

OTELLO

Complete recording. Fusati (Otello); Granforte
(Iago); Carbone (Desdemona); with Girardi, Balai,
Zambelli, Spada and La Scala Chorus and Orchestra, conducted by Carlo Sabajno. Sixteen 12″
records.   VM-152

Abridged recording. Giovanni Martinelli (Otello);
Lawrence Tibbett (Iago); Helen Jepson (Desdemona), and others, with Metropolitan Opera House
Chorus and Orchestra, conducted by Wilfred Pelletier. Six 12″ records.   VM-620

Brindisi: "Inaggia l'ugola"
    Antonio Scotti (b)   (V-6283 co) [12″]
"Già nella notte densa" and *"Venga la morte"*
    Claudia Muzio (s) with Francesco Merli (t)   C-9100M [12″]
"Credo in un Dio crudel"
    Titta Ruffo (b)   V-8045 [12″]
    John Charles Thomas (b)   V-17639 [12″]
"Ora e per sempre addio"
    Albert Alvarez (t)   IRCC-178 [10″]
    Francesco Tamagno (t), with piano   (G-DS100) [12″]
    Leo Slezak (t)   (C-A5385 co) [12″]
    Giovanni Zenatello (t)   P-PO107 [10½″]
"Era la notte"
    Victor Maurel (b), with piano   IRCC-4 [10¾″]
"Si, pel ciel"
    Enrico Caruso (t) and Titta Ruffo (b)   V-8045 [12″]
    Giovanni Zenatello (t) and Pasquale Amato (b) P-PO107 [10″]
"Dio ti giocondi" and *"Esterrefatta fisso"*
    Claudia Muzio (s) and Francesco Merli (t)   C-9102M [12″]
Canzone del Salce (Willow Song)
    Elisabeth Rethberg (s)   V-7393 [12″]
    Tiana Lemnitz (s, in German)   G-DB4595 [12″]
    Nellie Melba (s)   G-DB366 [12″]
    Frances Alda (s)   (V-88214 co) [12″]
"Ave Maria"
    Elisabeth Rethberg (s)   V-7393 [12″]
    Tiana Lemnitz (s, in German)   G-DB4595 [12″]
    Nellie Melba (s)   G-DM118 [12″]
    Emma Eames (s)   IRCC-125 [12″]
    Frances Alda (s)   (V-88213 co) [12″]
"Niun mi tema"
    Francesco Tamagno (t), with piano   G-DS100 [12″]
    Giovanni Zenatello (t)   P-PXO129 [12″]

RIGOLETTO

Complete recording. Lina Pagliughi (Gilda); Piazza
(Rigoletto); Folgar (Duke); Salvatore Baccaloni
(Sparafucile), and others, with La Scala Chorus and
Orchestra, conducted by Carlo Sabajno. Fifteen 12″
records.   VM-32

Complete recording. Mercedes Capsir (Gilda); Riccardo Stracciari (Rigoletto); Dino Borgioli (Duke)
and others, with La Scala Chorus and Orchestra, conducted by Lorenzo Molajoli. Fifteen 12″ records.   CM-Op.18

"Questa o quella"
Tito Schipa (t)   V-1282 [10″]

"Veglia o donna"
Lily Pons (s) and Giuseppe de Luca (b)   V-17233 [12″]

"Caro nome"
Luisa Tetrazzini (s)   V-7883 [12″]
Lily Pons (s)   V-7383 [12″]
Amelita Galli-Curci (s)   V-7655 [12″]
Nellie Melba (s)   G-DB346 [12″]
Marcella Sembrich (s)   G-DB431 [12″]

"Cortigiani, vil razza dannata"
Robert Weede (b)   C-71261D [12″]

"La donna è mobile"
Jussi Bjoerling (t)   V-4372 [10″]
Enrico Caruso (t)   V-1616 [10″]
Alessandro Bonci (t)   (C-A1286 co) [10″]

Quartet: *"Bella figlia dell' amore"*
Amelita Galli-Curci (s), Louise Homer (c), Beniamino Gigli (t), and Giuseppe de Luca (b)   V-10012 [12″]
Lucrezia Bori (s), Josephine Jacoby (c), John Mc
Cormack (t), and Reinald Werrenrath (b)   G-DM104 [12″]
Marcella Sembrich (s), Gina Severina (c), Enrico
Caruso (t), and Antonio Scotti (b)   G-DQ101 [12″]
Bessie Abott (s), Louise Homer (c), Enrico Caruso (t), and Antonio Scotti (b)   G-DO100 [12″]
Nellie Melba (s), Josephine Thornton (c), John
McCormack (t), and Mario Sammarco (b)   G-DM118 [12″]
Luisa Tetrazzini (s), Josephine Jacoby (c), Enrico
Caruso (t), and Pasquale Amato (b)   IRCC-36 [12″]

SIMON BOCCANEGRA

"Il lacerato spirito"
Alexander Kipnis (bs), with chorus   V-8684 [12″]

"Figlia tal nome palpita" and *"Piangi su voi"*
Rose Bampton (s), Lawrence Tibbett (b), Leonard
Warren (b), Giovanni Martinelli (t), and Nicholson (b), with Metropolitan Opera House Chorus and Orchestra, conducted by Wilfred Pelletier
       V-15642 [12″]

LA TRAVIATA

Complete recording. Mercedes Capsir (Violetta),
Cecil (Alfredo), Galeffi (Germont), and others, with
La Scala Chorus and Orchestra, conducted by
Lorenzo Molajoli. Fifteen 12″ records.   CM-Op.2

Complete recording. Rosza (Violetta), Ziliani (Alfredo), Borgonovo (Germont), and others, with La
Scala Chorus and Orchestra, conducted by Carlo
Sabajno. Fourteen 12″ records.   VM-112

Prelude to Act I
New York Philharmonic-Symphony Orchestra, con-
    ducted by Arturo Toscanini   V-18080 [12"]
Brindisi: "Libiam nei licti calici"
Alma Gluck (s) and Enrico Caruso (t), with Metro-
    politan Opera House Chorus and Orchestra G-DJ100 [10"]
"Ah! fors è lui" and "Sempre libera"
Mary Garden (s, in French)   (C-A5824 co) [12"]
Eidé Noréna (s, in French)   (G-DB4870 co) [12"]
Luisa Tetrazzini (s)   G-DB531 [12"]
. . . both arias, but cut
Lilli Lehmann (s)   (Odéon-50353/4 co)
Marcella Sembrich (s)   V-18140 [12"]
Nellie Melba (s)   G-DB346 [12"]
Luisa Tetrazzini (s)   (V-6344 co) [12"]
Helen Jepson (s)   V-14184 [12"]
Amelita Galli-Curci (s)   G-DB257 [12"]
. . . *"Ah! fors è lui"* only
Lucrezia Bori (s)   V-7438 [12"]
. . . *"Sempre libera"* only
Geraldine Farrar (s)   IRCC-45 [10"]
Amelita Galli-Curci (s)   G-DA216 [10"]
"Di Provenza il mar"
Giuseppe de Luca (b)   V-7036 [12"]
Pasquale Amato (b, recorded in 1909)   P-PXO81 [12"]
Prelude to Act III
New York Philharmonic-Symphony Orchestra, con-
    ducted by Arturo Toscanini   V-18080 [12"]
"Addio del passato"
Claudia Muzio (s)   C-9106M [12"]
Luisa Tetrazzini (s)   IRCC-116 [12"]
Lucrezia Bori (s)   (V-543 co) [10"]
"Parigi, o cara"
Maria Caniglia (s) and Beniamino Gigli (t)   V-15602 [12"]
Lucrezia Bori (s) and John McCormack (t)   G-DM104 [12"]

IL TROVATORE

Complete recording. Carena (Leonora); Minghini-
Cattaneo (Azucena); Aureliano Pertile (Manrico);
Granforte (di Luna), and others, with La Scala
Chorus and Orchestra, conducted by Carlo Sabajno.
Fifteen 12" records.   VM-106

"Tacea la notte"
Amelita Galli-Curci (s)   V-7652 [12"]
"Stride la vampa"
Louise Homer (c)   V-1422 [10"]
Margarete Ober (c)   (V-64506 co) [10"]

"Mal reggendo all' aspro assalto"
Louise Homer (c) and Giovanni Martinelli (t)　　　V-8105 [12″]
Louise Homer (c) and Enrico Caruso (t)　　　G-DM112 [12″]
"Il balen"
Giuseppe de Luca (b)　　　(V-1591 co) [10″]
Miserere: "Ah! che la morta ognora"
Rosa Ponselle (s) and Giovanni Martinelli (t), with
　Metropolitan Opera Chorus and Orchestra　　　V-8097 [12″]
Emmy Destinn (s) and Giovanni Martinelli (t),
　and Metropolitan Chorus　　　G-DB333 [12″]
Frances Alda (s) and Enrico Caruso (t), and Metro-
　politan Chorus and Orchestra　　　(V-8042 co) [12″]
"Ai nostri monti"
Louise Homer (c) and Giovanni Martinelli (t)　　　V-8105 [12″]
Louise Homer (c) and Enrico Caruso (t)　　　(G-DM112) [12″]
Ernestine Schumann-Heink (c) and Enrico Caruso
　(t)　　　V-8042 [12″]
"D'Amor sull' ali rosee"
Amelita Galli-Curci (s)　　　V-7652 [12″]
Emmy Destinn (s)　　　G-DB646 [12″]
Luisa Tetrazzini (s)　　　G-DB536 [12″]
"Ah si ben mio"
Jussi Bjoerling (t)　　　V-2136 [10″]
Giovanni Martinelli (t)　　　G-DB333 [12″]
Enrico Caruso (t)　　　G-DB112 [12″]
"Di quella pira"
Giovanni Martinelli (t), with Metropolitan Chorus
　and Orchestra　　　V-8109 [12″]
Jussi Bjoerling (t)　　　V-2136 [10″]
Francesco Tamagno (t), with piano (recorded in
　1903)　　　G-DR102 [10″]
Enrico Caruso (t)　　　G-DA113 [10″]

I VESPRI SICILIANI

"O tu, Palermo"
Ezio Pinza (bs)　　　G-DB1087 [12″]
Bolero: "Mercè, dilette amiche"
Miliza Korjus (s)　　　V-12603 [12″]

CHAPTER XX

ARRIGO BOÏTO

MEFISTOFELE

Complete recording. Mafalda Favero, Giannina
Arangi-Lombardi, Melandri, De Angelis, and others,
with La Scala Chorus and Orchestra, conducted by
Lorenzo Molajoli. Seventeen 12″ records.　　　CM-Op. 17

"L'Altra notte in fondo al mare"
Claudia Muzio (s)   C-9108M [12″]
"La Notte del Sabba Classico"
Maria Castagna, Augusta Concato, Righetti,
Nessi, and Ciniselli, with La Scala Chorus and
Orchestra, conducted by Ettore Panizza. Three
12″ records (5 sides).   D-25177/9

NERONE

A series of recordings by members of the original
cast was issued by HMV (G-DB732/4 & D939). Artists represented were Marcel Journet, Carlo Galeffi,
Luisa Bertana. These disks have long been unobtainable.

AMILCARE PONCHIELLI

LA GIOCONDA

Complete recording. Giannina Arangi-Lombardi
(Gioconda); Ebe Stignani (Laura); Rota (La Cieca);
Granda (Enzo); Vivani (Barnaba); Zambelli (Alvise),
and others, with Chorus and Orchestra of La Scala,
conducted by Lorenzo Molajoli. Nineteen 12″
records.   C-GQX10600/18

"Voce di donna o d'angelo"
Margarete Matzenauer (c)   (V-6471 co) [12″]
"Pescator, affonda l'esca"
Giuseppe de Luca (b), with Metropolitan Opera
House Chorus and Orchestra   V-8174 [12″]
"Cielo e mar"
Jussi Bjoerling (t)   V-12150 [12″]
Beniamino Gigli (t)   V-7194 [12″]
Dance of the Hours
Boston "Pops" Orchestra, conducted by Arthur
Fiedler   V-11833 [12″]
Chicago Symphony Orchestra, conducted by Fred-
erick Stock   C-11621D [12″]
"Suicidio!"
Eva Turner (s)   C-L1976 [12″]
Lillian Nordica (s)   C-74021 [12″]
Gina Cigna (s)   C-9127M [12″]

IL FIGLIUOL PRODIGO

"Raccogli e calma"
Mario Basiola (b)   C-69602D [12″]

PIETRO MASCAGNI

L'AMICO FRITZ

"Son pochi fiori"
Lucrezia Bori (s)   (V-967 co) [10″]

Duetto dell ciliege: "Suzel, buon di"
    Mafalda Favero (s) and Beniamino Gigli (t)   V-15837 [12″]
"Non mi resta che il pianto"
    Lucrezia Bori (s)   (V-967 co) [10″]

CAVALLERIA RUSTICANA

Complete Recording: Giannina Arangi-Lombardi (Santuzza); Maria Castagna (Lola); Antonio Melandri (Turiddu); Gino Lulli (Alfio), and Ida Mannarini (Lucia), with La Scala Chorus and Orchestra, conducted by Lorenzo Molajoli. Ten 12″ records.   CM-Op.7

Prelude and *Siciliana*
    Giovanni Martinelli (t), with Metropolitan Opera
    Chorus and Orchestra, conducted by Guilio Setti
    V-8109 [12″]

"Voi lo sapete"
    Dusolina Giannini (s)   G-DA892 [10″]
    Claudia Muzio (s)   C-9084M [12″]
    Elisabeth Rethberg (s, in German)   D-20200 [10″]
    Emma Calvé (s)   G-DB160 [12″]
"Tu qui Santuzza"
    Dusolina Giannini (s) and Beniamino Gigli (t),
    with Orchestra of La Scala, conducted by Carlo
    Sabajno   V-17697 [12″]
Intermezzo
    Boston "Pops" Orchestra, conducted by Arthur
    Fiedler   V-4303 [10″]
"Addio alla madre"
    Enrico Caruso (t)   V-15732 [12″]

IRIS

"In pure stille"
    Lucrezia Bori (s)   (V-545 co) [10″]
"Un di al tempio"
    Lucrezia Bori (s)   IRCC-70 [12″]

LODOLETTA

"Se Franz dicesse il vero"
    Galliano Massini (t)   C-9151M [12″]

RUGGIERO LEONCAVALLO

LA BOHÈME

"Io non he che una povera stanzetta" and
"Testa adorata"
    Enrico Caruso (t)   G-DB122 [12″]

PAGLIACCI

Complete Recording: Beniamino Gigli (Canio); Iva Pacetti (Nedda); Mario Basiola (Tonio), with Giu-

seppe Nessi, Leone Paci, and La Scala Chorus and
Orchestra, conducted by Franco Ghione. Nine 12"
records.   In VM-249

Prologue: *"Si puo"*
   Lawrence Tibbett (b)   V-6587 [12"]
. . . Abridged version
   Robert Weede (b), with orchestra, conducted by
     Erich Leinsdorf   C-71261D [12"]
"Quae fiamma avea nel guardo!"
   Mary Lewis (s)   V-6578 [12"]
"Vesti la giubba"
   Enrico Caruso (t)   V-7720 [12"]
   Giovanni Martinelli (t)   V-6754 [12"]

DER ROLAND VON BERLIN
Elisabeths gesang
   Geraldine Farrar (s) (Recorded in Berlin in 1905)
                           IRCC-132 [10"]

ZAZA
"Il bacio"
   Geraldine Farrar (s) and Giuseppe de Luca (b) (V-625 co) [10"]
"E un riso gentil"
   Giovanni Martinelli (t)   (V-736 co) [10"]
"O mio piccolo tavolo ingombrato"
   Giovanni Martinelli (t)   (V-6194 co) [12"]
"Mama usciva di casa"
   Geraldine Farrar (s)   (V-625 co) [10"]
"Buona Zaza" and *"Zaza piccola zingara"*
   Titta Ruffo (b)   (V-824 co) [10"]
. . . *"Zaza piccola zingara"* only
   John Charles Thomas (b)   V-15859 [12"]

GIACOMO PUCCINI

LA BOHÈME
Complete recording: Rosetta Pampanini (Mimi);
Luba Mirella (Musetta); Luigi Marini (Rodolfo);
Gino Vanelli (Marcello); Tancredi Pasero (Colline),
with Salvatore Baccaloni, Baracchi, Nessi, and La
Scala Chorus and Orchestra, conducted by Lorenzo
Molajoli. Thirteen 12" records.   CM-Op.5

Act IV—Complete recording: Lisa Perli (Mimi);
Stella Andreva (Musetta); Heddle Nash (Rodolfo);
John Brownlee (Marcello), with Robert Alva and
Robert Easton, and London Philharmonic Orches-
tra, conducted by Sir Thomas Beecham. Four 12"
records (7 sides; last side "Addio"—Perli).   CM-274

"Che gelida manina"
Jussi Bjoerling (t)   V-12039 [12"]
Giovanni Martinelli (t)   V-6595 [12"]
Orville Harrold (t)   (V-6151 co) [12"]
"Si, mi chiamano Mimi"
Lucrezia Bori (s)   V-6790 [12"]
Geraldine Farrar (s)   (V-6106 co) [12"]
"Quando me'n vo soletta"
Lucrezia Bori (s)   V-1333 [12"]
Alma Gluck (s)   (V-649 co) [10"]
Addio di Mimi—"Donde lieta usci"
Lucrezia Bori (s)   V-6561 [12"]
Nellie Melba (s) (recorded at Melba's Farewell,
    Covent Garden, June, 1926)   G-DB943 [12"]
Lisa Perli (s) (included in Act IV—Complete
    recording)
Death Scene: *"Sono andati?"*
Lucrezia Bori (s) and Tito Schipa (t)   V-8068 [12"]

LA FANCIULLA DEL WEST

"Ch'ella mi credo libero"
Jussi Bjoerling (t)   V-4408 [10"]
Edward Johnson (t)   (V-689 co) [10"]

GIANNI SCHICCHI

"Firenze e come un albero fiorito"
Piero Pauli (t)   G-DA1204 [10"]
"O mio babbino caro"
Frances Alda (s)   (V-528 co) [10"]

MADAMA BUTTERFLY

Complete Recording: Toti dal Monte (Butterfly);
Beniamino Gigli (Pinkerton); Vittoria Palombini
(Suzuki); Mario Basiola (Sharpless), with Maria
Huder, Adelio Zagonara, Gion Conti, Ernesto
Dominici, and Chorus and Orchestra of Royal Opera
(Rome), conducted by Oliviero De Fabritiis. Six-
teen 12" records.   In Set VM-700/1

Complete Recording: Rosetta Pampanini (Butterfly);
Alessandro Granada (Pinkerton); Conchita Velas-
quez (Suzuki); Gino Vanelli (Sharpless), with Ferrai,
Nessi, Baracchi, Salvatore Baccaloni, Binardi, and
La Scala Chorus and Orchestra, conducted by
Lorenzo Molajoli. Fourteen 12" records.   In Set CM-Op.4

"Ancora un passo"
Geraldine Farrar (s)   (V-616 co) [10"]
Hilde Konetzni (s), with chorus (in German)   T-E2246 [12"]
Frances Alda (s)   (V-528 co) [10"]

Love Duet: *"Viene la sera"*
 Dusolina Giannini (s) and Marcel Wittrisch (t)   V-8921 [12″]
 Geraldine Farrar (s) and Enrico Caruso (t)   (V-8011 co) [12″]
"Un bel di vedremo"
 Lucrezia Bori (s)   V-6790 [12″]
 Geraldine Farrar (s)   V-18141 [12″]
Flower Duet: *"Tutti i fior?"*
 Meta Seinemeyer (s) and Helene Jung (c) in Ger-
  man   D-25193 [12″]
 Geraldine Farrar (s) and Louise Homer (c) (V-89008 co) [12″]
"Tu, tu piccolo iddio!" (Butterfly's Death Scene)
 Geraldine Farrar (s)   (V-617 co) [10″]

MANON LESCAUT

Complete recording: Zamboni, Bassi, Francesco
Merli, Conati, Bordinali, Nessi, Baracchi, and Villa,
with La Scala Chorus and Orchestra, conducted by
Lorenzo Molajoli. Thirteen 12″ records.   C-GQX10119/31

"Donna non vida mai"
 Alessandro Ziliani (t)   V-1735 [10″]
 Beniamino Gigli (t)   V-1213 [10″]
 Galliano Masini (t)   C-17159D [10″]
"In quelle trine morbide"
 Dusolina Giannini (s)   G-DB1264 [12″]
 Lucrezia Bori (s)   IRCC-101 [10″]
Intermezzo, Act III (*"La Prigionia"*)
 Grand Symphony Orchestra, conducted by Alber-
  goni   D-25185 [12″]
Prelude, Act IV
 Milan Symphony Orchestra, conducted by Tansini
                                                    D-25440 [12″]

LA RONDINE

"Ore dolci e divine"
 Lucrezia Bori (s)   V-14615 [12″]

SUOR ANGELICA

Intermezzo
 Royal Opera Orchestra, conducted by Vincenzo
  Bellezza   V-11417 [12″]
"Senza mamma"
 Augusta Oltrabella (s)   G-DB5350 [12″]

IL TABARRO

"Scorri fiume"
 Dinh Gilly   (G-DA559 co) [10″]

LA TOSCA

Complete recording: Maria Caniglia (Tosca), Beniamino Gigli (Cavaradossi), Dino Borgioli (Scarpia),

with Dominici, Tomei, Mazziotti, Conti, Marcangeli, and Chorus and Orchestra of Royal Opera (Rome), conducted by Fabritiis. Fourteen 12″ records.   VM-539/40

"Recondita armonia"
Jussi Bjoerling (t)   V-4372 [10″]
Giuseppe Lugo (t)   V-2143 [10″]
Enrico Caruso (t)   V-511 [10″]
Te Deum: "Tre sbirri"
Lawrence Tibbett (b)   V-8124 [12″]
"Mi dicon venal"
Antonio Scotti (b)   V-18142 [12″]
"Vissi d'arte"
Rosa Raisa (s)   V-14400 [12″]
Dusolina Giannini (s)   G-DA892 [10″]
Geraldine Farrar (s)   (V-6110 co) [12″]
Emmy Destinn (s)   G-DB223 [12″]
Nellie Melba (s)   (V-6220 co) [12″]
"E lucevan le stelle"
Jussi Bjoerling (t)   V-4408 [10″]
Giuseppe Lugo (t)   V-2143 [10″]
Enrico Caruso (t)   V-511 [10″]

TURANDOT

Complete recording: Gina Cigna (Turandot), Olivero (Liù), Francesco Merli (Principe), with Neroni, Giannotti, Bravura, Poli, Zangonara, Del Signore, and EIAR Chorus and Symphony Orchestra, conducted by Franco Ghione. Sixteen 12″ records.   P-R20410/25

Umberto Giordano
ANDREA CHÉNIER

Complete recording: Bruna Rasa, Conti, Bassi, Marini, Galeffi, Salvatore Baccaloni, Baracchi, Nessi, Villa, and La Scala Chorus and Orchestra, conducted by Lorenzo Molajoli. Thirteen 12″ records.   CM-Op.21

"Nemico della patria"
Titta Ruffo (b)   V-7153 [12″]
John Charles Thomas (b)   V-17639 [12″]
"La Mamma morta"
Claudia Muzio (s)   C-9107M [12″]
Rosa Raisa (s)   V-14400 [12″]
Irene Jessner (s)   V-17256 [12″]
"Un di all' azzurro" and *"Come un bel di di Maggio"*
Giovanni Martinelli (t)   V-6707 [12″]

LA CENA DELLE BEFFE

"Ahi che tormento," Act I, and *"Mi svesti,"*
Act II
Antonio Cortis (t)   (V-1240 co) [10″]

"Mi chiamo Lisabetta" and *"Sempre cosi"*
Frances Alda (s)   (V-1359 co) [10″]

FEDORA

Complete recording: Famous soloists, with La Scala
Chorus and Orchestra, conducted by Lorenzo Molajoli. Eleven 12″ records.   C-GQX10496/506

"Amor ti vieta," Act II
Richard Crooks (t)   V-2063 [10″]
Alessandro Ziliani (t)   V-1735 [10″]
Edward Johnson (t)   (V-689 co) [10″]

SIBERIA

"Qual vergogna tu porti," Act III
Maria Caniglia (s)   G-DA1563 [10″]
"La Pasqua"
La Scala Orchestra, conducted by Gino Mar-
inuzzi   G-DB3209 [12″]

Ermanno Wolf-Ferrari

LE DONNE CURIOSE

"Tutto per te, mio bene"
Geraldine Farrar (s)   IRCC-114 [12″]
"Il cor nel contento"
Geraldine Farrar (s) and Hermann Jadlowker
(t)   G-DK124 [12″]

I GIOIELLI DELLA MADONNA

Intermezzo, No. 1
Minneapolis Symphony Orchestra, conducted by
Eugene Ormandy   V-1742 [10″]
Serenata: "Aprila, o bella"
Giuseppe de Luca (b)   (V-3055 co) [10″]
Intermezzo, No. 2
Minneapolis Symphony Orchestra, conducted by
Eugene Ormandy   V-1743 [10″]

IL SEGRETO DI SUZANNA

Overture
Boston "Pops" Orchestra, conducted by Arthur
Fiedler   V-4412 [10″]
"Gioia, la nube leggera"
Lucrezia Bori (s)   V-14616 [12″]
Geraldine Farrar (s)   (V-88424 co) [12″]
"Il dolce idillio"
Geraldine Farrar (s) and Pasquale Amato (b)   G-DK124 [12″]

CHAPTER XXI

RICHARD STRAUSS

DIE ÄGYPTISCHE HELENA

Helen's Awakening and Funeral March
Berlin State Opera Orchestra, conducted by Fritz
Busch   D-25031 [12″]
"Bei jener Nacht," Act I, and *"Zweite Braut-
nacht! Zaubernacht!"* Act II
Rose Pauly (s)   D-25850 [12″]

ARABELLA

"Aber der Richtige"
Marta Fuchs (s) and Elsa Wieber (s)   T-SK1477 [12″]
Lotte Lehmann (s) and K. Heidersbach (s)   D-23048[10″]
Viorica Ursuleac (s) and Margit Bokor (s)   D-DE7025 [10″]
"Das war sehr gut, Mandryka"
Viorica Ursuleac (s) and Alfred Jerger (b)   D-DE7024 [10″]
"Und du wirst mein Gebieter sein"
Marta Fuchs (s) and Paul Schöffler (b)   T-SK1477 [12″]

ARIADNE AUF NAXOS

"Grossmächtigste Prinzessin"
Maria Ivogün (s)   (G-DB4405 co) [12″]
Adele Kern (s)   D-LY6181 [12″]
"Sie lebt hier ganz allein, Sie atmet leicht"
Lotte Lehmann (s)   D-25186 [12″]

LE BOURGEOIS GENTILHOMME

Incidental Music
Vienna Philharmonic Orchestra, conducted by
Clemens Krauss   VM-101

DAPHNE

*Verwandlung der Daphne; "O wie gerne blieb
ich bei dir"; "Götter Brüder im hohen"*
Margarete Teschemacher (s) and Torsten Ralf (t)
(original creators of the roles), with Dresden
State Opera Orchestra, conducted by Karl Böhm.
Two 12″ records.   VM-660

FEUERSNOT

Love Scene
Vienna Philharmonic Orchestra, conducted by
Clemens Krauss   G-C1841 [12″]

DER ROSENKAVALIER

Abridged recording: Lotte Lehmann (Marschallin),

Elisabeth Schumann (Sophie), Maria Olszewska
(Octavian), Richard Mayr (Ochs), with Michalsky,
Paalen, Madin, Gallos, Ettl, and Chorus, with Vienna
Philharmonic Orchestra, conducted by Robert Heger.
Thirteen 12″ records.   VM-196

Waltzes
  Saxon State Orchestra, conducted by Böhm   G-DB4557 [12″]
  Berlin Philharmonic Orchestra, conducted by Alois
    Melichar   D-CA8268 [12″]
  Royal Philharmonic Orchestra, conducted by
    Bruno Walter   C-67892D [12″]
Arie des Sängers: "Di rigori armato"
  Charles Kullman (t)   C-4153M [10″]
Monolog der Marschallin
  Frieda Hempel (s)   (G-DB373 co) [12″]
Finale Act II—*"Herr Kavalier!"*
  Alexander Kipnis (bs) and E. Ruziczka (c)   V-7894 [12″]
  Richard Mayr (bs) and Anni Andrassy (c)   C-9087M [12″]
Trio: *"Ich weiss auch nix"*
  Viorica Ursuleac (s), Erna Berger (s) and Tiana
    Lemnitz (s)   D-CA8238 [12″]
"Ist ein Traum"
  Erna Berger (s) and Tiana Lemnitz (s)   D-CA8238 [12″]

SALOME
Salomes Tanz
  Saxon State Orchestra, conducted by Karl Böhm
                             G-DB4639 [12″]
  Berlin Philharmonic Orchestra, conducted by
    Bruno Walter   C-67814D [12″]
Final Scene: *Salome und das Haupt des
    Jokanaan*
  Marjorie Lawrence (s, in French). Two 12″
    records.   V-8682/3

JULES MASSENET
DON QUICHOTTE
Death of Don Quichotte
  Fyodor Chaliapin (bs) and Olive Kline (s)   (V-6693 co) [12″]

HÉRODIADE
"Il est doux, il est bon"
  Ninon Vallin (s)   D-25847 [12″]
  Mary Garden (s)   (C-5289 co) [12″]
  Maria Jeritza (s)   V-6604 [12″]
  Emma Calvé (s)   G-DB162 [12″]
"Vision fugitive"
  John Charles Thomas (b)   V-1639 [10″]

Arthur Endréze (b)   D-25880 [12″]
Maurice Renaud (b)   IRCC-38 [12″]
"Salomé, Salomé!"
John Charles Thomas (b)   V-15859 [12″]

LE JONGLEUR DE NOTRE DAME

"O liberté ma mie"
Mary Garden (s)   (C-A5289 co) [12″]
Légende de la sauge: "La Vierge entend";
"Fleurissait une sauge"
Marcel Journet (bs)   V-6785 [12″]
Le Miracle
Friant (t), Roger Bourdin (b) and Dupré (bs).
Three 10″ records.   D-20585/7

MANON

Complete recording: Germaine Feraldy (Manon),
Joseph Rogatchewsky (Des Grieux), G. Villier (Lescaut), Louis Guenot (Comte des Grieux), and others,
with chorus and orchestra, conducted by Élie Cohen.
Eighteen 12″ records.   CM-Op.10

"Adieu, notre petite table"
Lucrezia Bori (s)   V-14616 [12″]
Geraldine Farrar (s)   (V-6111 co) [12″]
"On l'appelle Manon"
Geraldine Farrar (s) and Enrico Caruso (t)   G-DM110 [12″]
Le Rêve
Tino Rossi (t)   C-4185M [10″]
Jussi Bjoerling (t)   V-12635 [12″]
Edmond Clément (t)   V-6052 [12″]
Gavotte: "Obsessions quand leur voix appelle"
Lucrezia Bori (s)   V-1846 [10″]
"Ah, fuyez douce image!"
Jose Janson (t)   PAT-PAT153 [12″]
Richard Crooks (t)   V-15543 [12″]
Sydney Rayner (t)   D-29001 [12″]

LE ROI DE LAHORE

"Promesse de mon avenir"
Maurice Renaud (b)   IRCC-38 [12″]

SAPHO

"O Magali, ma tant amado"
Emma Calvé (s)   IRCC-134 [12″]

THAÏS

"Voilà donc, la terrible cité!"
Arthur Endréze (b)   D-25880 [12″]

"Dis-moi que je suis belle"
   Helen Jepson (s)   V-14153 [12″]
"L'Amour est une virtue rare"
   Mary Garden (s)   (C-A5440 co) [12″]
Prélude and Scène de l'Oasis
   Emma Luart (s) and Roger Bourdin (b). Two 12″
    records.   D-25878/9
Mort de Thaïs
   Mary Lewis (s)   V-6578 [12″]
   Geraldine Farrar (s)   (V-88594 co) [12″]

WERTHER

Complete recording: Ninon Vallin (s), Germaine
Feraldy (s), Georges Thill (t), Narcon, Rocque,
Guenot, and Niel, with chorus and orchestra, con-
ducted by Élie Cohen. Fifteen 12″ records.   C-LFX151/65

Air des lettres: "Werther! Qui m'aurait dit"
   Ninon Vallin (s)   D-25846 [12″]
Air des larmes: "Va! laisse couler mes larmes"
   Jeanne Gerville-Réache (c)   IRCC-109 [10″]
"Pourquoi me reveiller?"
   Tito Schipa (t)   G-DA870 [10″]
   Tito Schipa (t, in Italian)   V-8422 [12″]
   Mattia Battistini (b)   (G-DB149) [12″]
"J'aurais sur ma poitrine"
   Sydney Rayner (t)   D-29001 [12″]

GUSTAVE CHARPENTIER

LOUISE

Abridged recording: Ninon Vallin (Louise), Georges
Thill (Julien); Lecouvreur (La mère); Pernet (Le
père); Gaudel (Irma), with chorus and orchestra,
conducted by Eugène Bigot. Eight 12″ records.   CM-Op.12

"Depuis longtemps que j'habitais cette chambre"
   Edward Johnson (t)   V-9293 [12″]
   Orville Harold (t) and Eva Gauthier (c)   (V-6151 co) [12″]
"Depuis le jour"
   Lucrezia Bori (s)   V-6561 [12″]
   Dorothy Maynor (s)   V-17698 [12″]
   Mary Garden (s)   (V-6623 co) [12″]
   Mary Garden (s)   (C-A5440 co) [12″]
   Grace Moore (s)   V-17189 [12″]
   Nellie Melba (s)   G-DB354 [12″]
Couronnement de la Muse de Montmartre
   Chorus and symphony orchestra, conducted by
    Gustave Charpentier. Two 12″ records.   D-25929/30
Berceuse: "Reste, repose-toi"
   Marcel Journet (bs)   V-6785 [12″]

CLAUDE-ACHILLE DEBUSSY
PELLÉAS ET MÉLISANDE

Abridged recording: Marthe Nespoulous (Mélisande), Alfred Maguenat (Pelléas), Croiza (Genevieve), Hector Dufranne (Golaud), and Narcon (Arkel), with orchestra, conducted by Georges Truc. Six 12″ records. CM-Op. 13

Abridged recording: Yvonne Brothier (Mélisande), Charles Panzéra (Pelléas), Vanni Marcoux (Golaud), and Tubiana (Arkel), with orchestra conducted by Piero Coppola. Four 10″ and four 12″ records.   VM-68

"Mes longs cheveux"
Mary Garden (s) with Claude Debussy (piano) recorded Paris, 1904; re-recorded 1937   IRCC-106 [10″]

CHAPTER XXIII

STANISLAW MONIUSZKO
HALKA

Jontek's Arias: "Do You Still Believe Him?" Act II, and "The Wind Wails in the Hills," Act IV
Wladyslaw Ladis (t)   D-20450 [10″]
"O moj malenki"
Ewa Brandrowska (s)   O-Rxx217862 [12″]

BEDŘICH SMETANA
PRODANÁ NEVĚSTÁ (The Bartered Bride)

Complete recording: Prague National Opera Company, conducted by Otakar Ostrčil. Fifteen 12″ records.   VM-193

Overture
London Symphony Orchestra, conducted by Bruno Walter   G-DB3652 [12″]
Boston "Pops" Orchestra, conducted by Arthur Fiedler   V-4498 [10″]

DALIBOR
"War 'es wahr?"
Emmy Destinn (s)   IRCC-184 [12″]

ANTONÍN DVOŘÁK
RUSALKA

Orchestral Selections
Berlin State Opera Orchestra, conducted by Frieder Weissmann. Two 12″ records.   D-25292/3
"O lovely moon"
Emmy Destinn (s)   IRCC-65 [12″]

Jaromir Weinberger

SVANDA DUDÁK (SCHWANDA)

Orchestral Selections
Berlin State Opera Orchestra, conducted by Frieder
Weissmann   D-25306 [12″]
"Ich bin der Schwanda" and *"Wie kann ich
denn vervessen?"*
Theodor Scheidl (b)   D-CA8104 [12″]
Polka and Fugue
Minneapolis Symphony Orchestra, conducted by
Eugene Ormandy   V-7958 [12″]

Karl Goldmark

DIE KÖNIGIN VON SABA

"Lockruf"
Selma Kurz (s)   G-DB498 [12″]
"Magische Töne"
Leo Slezak (t)   IRCC-99 [10″]

Zoltán Kodály

HARY JANOS

Orchestral Suite
Minneapolis Symphony Orchestra, conducted by
Eugene Ormandy. Three 12″ records.   VM-197
Vocal excerpts
Izabella Nagy and Imre Pallo. Three 12″ and one
10″ record.   G-AM1687 and AN208,212/13

Isaac Albéniz

PEPITA JIMÉNEZ

Intermezzo
Madrid Symphony Orchestra, conducted by Enrique Fernández Arbós   C-67820D [12″]

Enrique Granados

GOYESCAS

Intermezzo
Madrid Symphony Orchestra, conducted by En-
rique Fernández Arbós   C-68923D [12″]
Boston "Pops" Orchestra, conducted by Arthur
Fiedler   V-12429 [12″]
Pablo Casals (cello)   V-6635 [12″]

"La maja y el ruiseñor"
José Iturbi (piano)   V-11562 [12″]

MANUEL DE FALLA

LA VIDA BREVE

Air de Salud: "Vivan los que rien"
Lucrezia Bori (s)   V-14615 [12″]
Danza No. 1 and No. 2 (with chorus)
    Orchestra of Théâtre de la Monnaie (Brussels) C-67818D [12″]
Introduction and Danza No. 1
    Paris Symphony Orchestra, conducted by Cloëz D-25299 [12″]

ANTONIO CARLOS GOMES

IL GUARANY

"Gentil di cuore"
Bidu Sayao (s)   V-11561 [12″]
Sophie del Campo (s)   V-4037 [10″]
"Sento una forza indomita"
Emmy Destinn (s) and Enrico Caruso (t)   V-6355 [12″]
Carmen Gomes (s) and R. de Silva (t)   V-91500 [12″]
"C'era un volta in principe"
Bidu Sayao (s)   V-11561 [12″]
Sophie del Campo (s)   V-9394 [12″]

RALPH VAUGHAN WILLIAMS

HUGH THE DROVER

Excerpts—Mary Lewis (s), Constance Willis, Nellie
Walker, Tudor Davies, and Peter Dawson, with
chorus and orchestra, conducted by Malcolm Sar-
gent. Five 12″ records.   (G-D922/6 co)

CHAPTER XXIV

IGOR STRAVINSKY

Le Chant du rossignol: Chinese March
    London Symphony Orchestra, conducted by Al-
        bert Coates   V-11160 [12″]

SERGE PROKOFIEFF

L'AMOUR DES TROIS ORANGES

Symphonic Suite—*Les ridicules; Scene infernale; Marche; Scherzo; Le prince et la prin-
cesse; La fuite*
    Orchestra of the Concerts Poulet, conducted by
        Gaston Poulet. Three 12″ records (5 sides). D-25123/5

ALFREDO CASELLA

LA DONNA SERPENTE

Selections
    EIAR Symphony Orchestra, conducted by Ar-
        mando la Rosa Parodi   CET-CC2186 [12″]

PAUL DUKAS

ARIANE ET BARBE-BLUE

"Oh! mes clairs diamants," Act I, and *"Ah! ce n'est pas encore la clarte veritable,"* Act II
Suzanne Balguérie (s)   C-LFX23 [12"]

MAURICE RAVEL

L'HEURE ESPAGNOLE

Complete recording: Jane Krieger (s), Louis Arnould (t), Raoul Gilles (t), I. Aubert (b), and Hector Dufranne (b), with orchestra, conducted by Georges Truc. Seven 12" records.   CM-Op. 14

DARIUS MILHAUD

Opéras-Minutes—L'Abandon d'Ariane; La Déliverance de Thésée; L'Enlèvement d'Europe
Pro Musica Ensemble, with orchestra and chorus, conducted by the composer. Three 12" records.   CM-309

ARTHUR HONEGGER

JUDITH

Cantique funèbre, Invocation, Act I, Fanfare (Prelude, Act II), Incantation Interlude, *Cantique des Vierves, Cantique de la victorie*
Claire Croiza (s) and J. van Hertbruggen (s), with Coecilia Chorus and orchestra, conducted by L. de Vocht. Two 12" records.   CM-X78

PAUL HINDEMITH

MATHIS DER MALER

Symphonic Suite—*Engel Konzert; Grablegung; Versuchung der heiligen Antonius*
Berlin Philharmonic Orchestra, conducted by Paul Hindemith. Three 12" records.   T-E1647/9

KURT WEILL

AUFSTIEG UND FALL DER STADT MAHAGONNY

Vocal and Orchestral Selections
Lotte Lenja (s) and Kurfürstendam Theatre Chorus and Orchestra, conducted by H. Somer
                                        G-AN764 [12"]

"Alabama Song" and *"Denn wie man sich bettet"*
Lotte Lenja (s) and Three Admirals, with Jazz Orchestra, conducted by Theodor Mackeben
                                        (T-A371 co) [10"]

DIE DREIGROSCHENOPER

Abridged recording. (Spoken narration by Kurt Gerron.) Lotte Lenja (s), Kurt Gerron, W. Trenk-Trebitsch, E. Helmke, E. Ponto, and Lewis Ruth Band, conducted by Theodor Mackeben. Four 10″ records.   T-A752/5

ERNEST KřENEK

JONNY SPIELT AUF

Orchestral Selections
Dajos Bela Orchestra   D-25785 [12″]
"Leb' wohl mein Schatz" and *"Nun ist die Geige mein"*
Ludwig Hofmann (bs)   D-25003 [12″]

CHAPTER XXV,

VICTOR HERBERT

NATOMA

"I list the trill of Golden Throat" (Spring Song)
Alma Gluck (s)   (V-6147 co) [12″]
"No country can my own outvie" (Paul's Address)
John McCormack (t)   (V-74295 co) [12″]
Orchestral Selections: Habanera, Vaquero's Song, Natoma Theme, Dagger Dance, and Finale
Victor Concert Orchestra, conducted by Nathaniel Shilkret   V-9907 [12″]
Dagger Dance (only)
Boston "Pops" Orchestra, conducted by Arthur Fiedler   V-11932 [12″]

MADELEINE

"A Perfect Day"
Frances Alda (s)   (V-6370 co) [12″]

CHARLES WAKEFIELD CADMAN

SHANEWIS

Spring Song of the Robin Woman
Elsie Baker (c)   (V-45495 co) [10″]

DEEMS TAYLOR

THE KING'S HENCHMAN

"Oh! Caesar, great were thou!" Act I; "Nay, Marcus, lay him down," Act III

Lawrence Tibbett (b), with Metropolitan Opera
Chorus and Orchestra, conducted by Giulio Setti

V-8103 [12″]

PETER IBBETSON

Orchestral Suite: Waltzes, Act I; Inn Music,
Act II, and Dream Music, Act III
C B Symphony Orchestra, conducted by Howard
Barlow. Two 12″ records.   CM-X204

LOUIS GRUENBERG

THE EMPEROR JONES

"Standin' in the need of prayer"
Lawrence Tibbett (b)   V-7959 [12″]

HOWARD HANSON

MERRYMOUNT

" 'Tis an earth defiled"
Lawrence Tibbett (b)   V-7959 [12″]
Symphonic Suite: Overture; Children's Dance;
Love Duet; Prelude to Act II, and Maypole
Dances
Eastman-Rochester Symphony Orchestra, con-
ducted by the composer. Two 12″ records.   VM-781

RICHARD HAGEMAN

CAPONSACCHI

"This very vivid morn," and "Lullaby"
Helen Jepson (s)   V-14183 [12″]

GIAN-CARLO MENOTTI

AMELIA GOES TO THE BALL

Overture
Philadelphia Symphony Orchestra, conducted by
Eugene Ormandy   V-15377 [12″]

GEORGE GERSHWIN

PORGY AND BESS

Selections: Overture; "Summertime"; "My
man's gone now"; "I got plenty o' nuttin' ";
Buzzard Song; "Bess, you is my woman"; "It
ain't necessarily so"; The Requiem; Porgy's
Lament, and Finale
Anne Brown (s) and Todd Duncan (b), with Eva
Jessye Choir and orchestra. Four 12″ records.   D-145

Selections
>Helen Jepson (s) and Lawrence Tibbett (b), with
chorus and orchestra, conducted by Alexander
Smallens. Four 12″ records.   VM-C25

MARC BLITZSTEIN

THE CRADLE WILL ROCK
>Original cast, with narration and piano accom-
paniment by the composer. Seven 12″ records.   MC-18

NO FOR AN ANSWER
>Original company, with the composer at the
piano. Three 10″ and two 12″ records.   KN-105

Index

NEW YORK HERALD TRIBUNE SUNDAY, FEBRUARY 1, 1942

Of M-

Giuseppe Verdi, after a portrait by Giovanni Boldini